To my dear ones,
Jim, Megan, and Kristy,
whose well-being is my concern
and in whose sustaining love I am fulfilled.

CONTENTS

1

A Path to Healthy Living   **1**

4   Death & Loss   119

7   Work   226

8   Stress & Coping   277

9   Love   327

10 Intimate Relationships   363

11 Sexuality   400

12 Loneliness and Solitude   433

13   Antipathy, Anger & Aggression   461

14 Happiness   **505**

15 Meaning and Values   **539**

PREFACE

It is a great joy to come to understand oneself. Psychology has much to offer students in terms of making sense of themselves and their relationships with friends and family. This book is intended to help students apply to their everyday experience what psychologists have learned about people. It is written for college students of any age and for anyone who wishes to increase self-awareness. Readers are encouraged to examine the direction they are taking in their lives and see their role in the unfolding quality of their experience.

This book explores the process of personal growth and translates this process into strategies that can help students in their own self-exploration. Hopefully, this exploration will give readers more security and understanding in making and following their personal choices as they move toward becoming the people they would like to be. The ideas discussed in this text should encourage students to think about and more fully enjoy their lives.

For many years, psychologists have embraced the concept of "giving psychology away" by sharing their findings with the public. Over decades of research, psychologists have learned a great deal about what makes people happy, as well as what are the characteristics of those who are particularly adept at coping with the strains of everyday life, and with catastrophic occurrences. The ability to cope with adversity comes from developing a set of skills. One aim of this text is to help students see how to use psychology to cope with life's challenges such as dealing with death and loss, anger management, relationship issues, and loneliness.

Themes explored in this text are identity, self-awareness, human communication, effective negotiation of social relationships, gender roles and sexuality; personal and social development, career exploration, social responsibility, coming to grips with mortality, loneliness and shyness; and the value of articulating a philosophy of life. Also discussed are personality development during the childhood years as well as the effects of early learning on a person's current behavior and outlook. The text presents these themes in a personal manner to encourage individual reflection and group discussion.

A conceptual framework has been provided that should help students understand and apply psychological concepts to their own lives. Research evidence is blended with classic theory. This text draws its ideas from four theoretical perspectives: Inherited characteristics (dispositional theory), learned behaviors (behavioral theory), unconscious drives (psychoanalytic theory), and the desire to reach full personal potential (humanistic theory) are all factors

Hi! You may recognize me as Miss Liberty. I'll be your guide on this tour. Come along...

working within a person. These and other concepts are developed within their theoretical framework for better understanding rather than presenting isolated psychological terms out of context. Fundamental principles underlying the major theories of psychology are presented in a personally relevant and useful manner. A strong academic approach presents multiple perspectives in psychology, developing a meaningful context for practical self help strategies. Abstract ideas are translated into concrete examples and exercises so that students can work with them.

Throughout these pages are gathered together ideas from philosophy and psychology that have relevance for everyday living in this exciting and rapidly evolving world. This text embraces Abraham Maslow's focus on human possibility and human growth. Maslow wished to fuse spiritual considerations, psychology, and philosophy into a science of values. His contemplation "of the basic human predicament, that we are simultaneously worms and gods" touches on the existential concerns that provide structure for this text.

Fundamentally the approach of this text is humanistic and existential, with an emphasis on exploring how individuals create meaning in their lives. From Baby Boomers to the so-called Generations X and Y, people are searching for meaning in the complex and sometimes overwhelming human community. The events of World War II, and more recently those in Bosnia and Kosovo show us that everything can be taken away from us: our loved ones, our health, our social status, our material possessions, and our physical freedom. What always remains, however, is our existential freedom. This is our liberty to decide how we will respond to the events of our lives. Ultimately, what happens to us does not dictate the attitude we take toward our predicament. We are capable of making ourselves unhappy in the midst of great blessings, as well as of finding peace in the face of adversity.

Personal meaning is important for health and well-being. A necessary first step toward enjoying a meaning-filled life is finding an answer to the question, "Who am I? What makes this search so difficult is that we both want to know ourselves and yet fiercely defend ourselves against self-awareness. What if we are shocked and ashamed upon discovering something unpleasant about ourselves? The discovery gives us the opportunity to change that something. If that something is unchangeable, we at least have the benefit of knowing about it. The value of this knowledge lies in our demonstration of courage in being willing to look at ourselves, as well as in the ability to be non-defensive when with others who are free at any time to make observations about us. No one can shock us with the truth about ourselves if we already know it. That truth is the beginning of our freedom and power. The purpose of this book is to provide opportunities for increased self-awareness and to present some new ideas that might enable readers to identify and construct their own personal life philosophy.

Chapter 1 introduces the metaphor for this book that life is a journey, and our personal philosophy, that is, our beliefs, values, and assumptions about reality, provides the map we use to get to our desired destination. Also introduced in the first chapter are the existential concerns that will be considered throughout the text.

In Chapter 2, three key psychological theorists are introduced: Abraham Maslow, Carl Rogers, and Viktor Frankl. Maslow's model of the self-actualized person and Rogers' of the fully functioning person are presented to give readers some background as to how humanistic psychologists describe the healthy person. Also considered is Frankl's proposal that self-transcendence is key to fulfillment.

The subject of Chapter 3 is the manner in which our attitudes and sense of self are shaped by early life experiences and decisions. Personality is influenced by the quality and nature of social relationships in childhood. The developmental theories of Sigmund Freud and Erik Erikson are presented.

Chapter 4 looks at death from an existential point of view. Even the least inclined among us to philosophize about life must develop a philosophy of death. Otherwise we would not be able to endure awareness of our mortality. Fear of dying and of an early end can be overwhelming, and in extreme cases may lead to a folding of one's cards; a failure to play the hand that has been dealt.

Chapter 5 covers how we come to have a moral sense. In developing a philosophy of life, we must look at our own ethical principles, how we formed them, and what we would be willing to sacrifice to remain true to them. Most psychologists tend to believe that people acquire moral values from what their particular culture deems to be right or wrong. Many claim that there are some universal moral principles that will be embraced by any individual with a developed ethical stance. The humanistic perspective presupposes an innate capacity to develop values that are prosocial and cooperative.

Chapter 6 concerns itself with some of the rules human beings make to regulate social behavior, among which are rules about appropriate behavior for men and women. Our identity stems perhaps more from our gender than from any other single aspect of us. Whereas, what it means to be a woman or a man has been changing in the past generation, even in these times of unprecedented freedom, our gender dramatically influences our answer to the questions, Who am I? and Where do I fit in?

Chapter 7 explains that work is more likely to be gratifying if it meshes well with who we are. Our choice of occupation becomes a part of our personal identity. The relationship between identity and career choice is reciprocal: The career we select will influence our subsequent personal development. Likewise, our existing personality and abilities can guide us as to appropriate career options to consider.

Chapter 8 offers strategies for coping with stress. Living in today's world requires that we manage a great many activities and concerns. Our emotional responses to these internal and external experiences affect our physical health. Stress and other psychological factors influence the immune system's ability to do its job of keeping the body well. We need to understand just how this process works, since safeguarding our immune system can be a matter of life and death. Freedom from troublesome anxiety should allow us to feel more at home in our world than would be the case if we were overwhelmed. Thus, effective coping strategies benefit us by addressing our ultimate concerns. Strategies from cognitive therapy that are useful in alleviating stress are explained.

Chapter 9 explores love. Throughout the world today, people report that one of their lifetime ambitions is to find a romantic partner and to form a committed, secure relationship. The accomplishment of this task is one of the greatest challenges in life, requiring both skill and effort. Psychologists and philosophers alike proclaim that loving relationships make life meaningful and thus worthwhile. In a sense, our relationships help us address the existential question, What is the purpose of my life?

Chapter 10 examines emotional intimacy. According to psychologist Robert Sternberg, intimacy is one of three components that make up complete love. When we achieve intimacy with another person, we feel known and understood. Closeness does not come about automatically. We earn it by letting others know us, rather than keeping our thoughts, feelings, and reactions to ourselves. Unsatisfied hunger for contact leads to feelings of alienation and loneliness. The need for a feeling of fellowship with others is a component to a meaningful life for most people.

Chapter 11 considers sexual intimacy. Sexual expression is a valued aspect of life for almost everyone, providing a source of pleasure and joy through physical intimacy. In those cultures that embrace the romantic ideal, sexual attraction supplies the basis for forming an intimate relationship. Yet, in spite of the fact that we live in an age of greater sexual liberation than in the past, many people do not experience genuine satisfaction in their sexual relationships. Inhibitions surrounding sex hamper our ability to establish a sexual identity, which forms a significant portion of our answer to the question, Who am I?

Chapter 12 discusses loneliness. In a sense, *all* of us are alone in life, or so say the existentialists. Being alone, we may feel lonely, but this result is not a given, just as the presence of others will not necessarily alleviate our loneliness. No one else can completely share our unique world of feelings, thoughts, hopes, and memories. Occasional awareness of our aloneness can be expected, no matter how much we seem to have satisfactorily formed relationships. If we accept that no one can take away *all* our loneliness, we can deal more effectively with the times when we long for human companionship. This acceptance enables us to be productively engrossed in our projects and relationships rather than using them to escape the dread of sensing our isolation from others.

Chapter 13 considers anger and aggression. We cannot avoid experiencing anger at times, so it behooves us to learn skills to negotiate through the inevitable tensions that crop up in our relationships. Angry feelings are neither right nor wrong, neither legitimate nor illegitimate. What is often problematic, however, is the behavior motivated by anger. Anger is considered one of the most negative forces on the planet, because its expression oftentimes takes a destructive form. The issue of how to deal with anger touches on a basic tension between self-expression and being socially agreeable. Learning too well to control anger can damage our relationships and so can indiscriminate venting of anger.

Chapter 14 covers emotional well-being. Theories about the secrets of happiness have developed throughout human history. It appears that our psychological well-being, happiness, and success in life are determined as much or more from within us as from without. With an investigation into the nature and the causes of happiness, we may be approaching an answer to the questions, Where am I going? and, Why am I here?

Chapter 15 delves into meaning and values. By being aware of our values and living in accordance with them, we can find meaning in our lives. We may not have a clear idea as to what we hold most dear and as to what is guiding our behavior unless we spend time thinking about the matter. Since values can be embraced at an unconscious level, it is possible for people to deceive themselves about their real values, or simply to be oblivious to them. Yet, if we look within ourselves and observe our own behavior, we can become aware of that which we deem to be truly worthwhile. It is up to us to engage in a search for our values in order to construct a purpose in life. Each of us also needs to answer the question, What is the value of my life? and, What is my contribution to the world?

The style of this text is personal and conversational, yet in-depth so that academic grounding is provided without losing student interest. Each chapter presents vocabulary within the context of the theories relevant to the topic. Applied activities at the end of each chapter offer readers the opportunity to integrate the main ideas of each chapter's topic into their lives. Students can look at themselves as they absorb the book's content, so that they may engage in self-discovery. Issues of cultural diversity have been addressed as they crop up, so that they are integrated into the book's central themes.

The instructor's manual accompanying this text includes 20 multiple choice test items for each chapter, questions for thought and discussion (which may also be used as essay test questions), suggested activities and exercises for classroom participation, suggested readings, and a course evaluation instrument to assess the impact of this course on students.

ACKNOWLEDGMENTS

Friends, colleagues, reviewers and students have generously provided feedback that has enabled me to make substantial improvements in this book. I have a special debt to those colleagues who reviewed and commented on entire chapters of this manuscript: Dr. Julian Delgadio, Dr. Adrian Novotny, Dr. Heinz Fischer, Lyle Speegle, and Donette Steele. I would especially like to thank my colleague, Dr. Aaron Cohen, for his patient and detailed critique of several manuscript chapters.

I also want to thank Todd Wohlfarth for his collaboration with the section on homosexual relationships. He supplied some of the resources and a rough draft of that section.

I appreciate the contribution of Richard Wormstahl, who, while a student of mine wrote the description of his meditation experience as a part of his philosophy of life paper assignment for my class.

The text I used for my course when I first started teaching was Gerald Corey's *I Never Knew I Had A Choice.* This text inspired me and provided me with an appealing model. I have felt complimented whenever an occasional reviewer mentioned that my manuscript was reminiscent of the Corey text.

I have been thoroughly impressed by the kindness, patience, and professionalism of my editors at Prentice Hall. Bill Webber and Jennifer Cohen have been exceedingly good to me. I especially appreciate Bruce Hobart, the book's production editor, and his staff at Pine Tree Composition, Inc. of Maine. We collaborated innumerable times to sort out the structure of this book, and the contact was always a pleasure. Throughout the production experience, I felt that I was in very capable hands. Carolyn Ingalls did a wonderful job as copy editor. She'd be rich is she had earned a dollar for every time I wrote "which" when "that" was called for. She'll be happy to learn that I am cured of the habit. Jill Dougan was very helpful in obtaining the needed permissions. I'd like to thank Sherri Dietrich for preparing the index.

Finally, I'd like to thank three important people in my life for their suggestions, enthusiasm and encouragement—my fiancé Dr. James Brock, and my daughters Megan and Kristy.

Tricia Alexander
Long Beach City College

1

A Path to Healthy Living

Happiness lies not in satisfying all of our desires but in separating the chaff from the wheat, winnowing destructive from wholesome desires, and practicing voluntary simplicity.
—Sam Keen

➤ *PREVIEW QUESTIONS:* In what way is a journey a good metaphor for a person's life? Once people encounter adversity in their lives, what are the advantages and disadvantages of occupying the victim role? What are the benefits of being proactive, making tough decisions and accepting responsibility for those decisions? In what way is making a mistake a good thing?

➤ *INTRODUCTION: YOUR LIFE IS A JOURNEY;*
DO YOU KNOW WHERE YOU ARE GOING?

Do you look forward each day to doing your normal activities? If you could fashion a life that you would live with great enthusiasm, what would it be like? You are invited to take an overview of your life so far, past and present, and to project yourself into the future—to imagine where you might like to end up, say five years from now, and even fifty years from now. There is no universal path to finding a meaning in life. Your life path has been and will continue to be unique. This book is intended to provide some light along the way.

What gives your life purpose? The quest for purpose or meaning is considered by philosophers and psychologists to be a universal human motive, as fundamental as our need for food and water. Empirical research has demonstrated that a strong sense of personal meaning is associated with life satisfaction (Myers, 1992; Seligman, 1988). Personal meaning is derived from having goals as well as from a coherent philosophy of life (Maslow, 1971). In order to have goals, you must be able to envision what you wish for yourself in the future. A philosophy of life comes from deliberating on what is important to you, what is worth doing and being. It includes answering the question, "What do I believe in?"

Our lives are ours to construct as we wish. It's up to us to determine what constitutes a satisfying life and to move in the direction of creating it. We may use the metaphor of going on a journey. Each one of us has the opportunity to consult a map, settle upon a destination, and chart a course. Along the way, we can anticipate breathtaking scenery, as well as flat tires and even ditches that could lead to fatal crashes. The latter we want to avoid. When we know where we want to end up, we'll probably be able to figure out how to get there. We are not born with a map giving our destination or the preferred route. We must create the map ourselves. Once made, the map may have to be revised repeatedly. Even so, having one is invaluable.

You are going to have fun on this trip, because we are going to talk about you. Just as a successful trip needs to be planned, so does an effective life. The better the vehicle you have as transportation, the more easily you can cruise along. Consider this your owner's manual, in case your vehicle could use a tune-up.

You will find that this book advocates that you adopt certain attitudes on your journey, which should make your trip more enjoyable. Although philosophers and psychologists cannot say with certainty what would make your life worth living, they are able to suggest possibilities that can enlarge your view of what you might like to do with your life. You will be invited to get to know yourself, to consider being genuinely yourself. Hopefully, you'll be induced to be responsible and focused on your desired destination. You will be encouraged to strive for excellence in whatever you do, as well as to extend yourself to others. To help you on your way, this text introduces a variety of tools, some to assist you in making decisions and solving problems, others to help you get organized. Certain ones should enable you to feel comfortable with yourself, and some will facilitate your getting along with other people. Theories and research on problems in coping with the stresses of life will be examined, such as the end of a love relationship, difficulties at work, managing anger, and helping a friend who is suicidal. Let's get started.

➤ ON THE ROAD TO PERSONAL GROWTH

Personal growth is a psychological process that can be a lifelong adventure. We do not arrive at a level where no more growth is possible; we proceed ever further along a continuum towards greater awareness and fulfillment of our life's purpose. At some point, we find ourselves feeling good much of the time—integrated and authentically ourselves. Psychological development improves our relationship with ourselves, which in turn enhances our relationships with other people, our community, and the rest of the world. We grow by getting to know ourselves through spending time alone and having a "dialogue" within. We also mature through our engagement with other people, by trying to understand them and in being understood by them.

Growth in the sense used here refers to personal development in a desired direction. Of course, people's values differ, so we may not agree as to what constitutes desirable change. What we consider to be growth for one person may not be the same as progress for another. For example, we may feel that a particular individual shows growth when he settles down and becomes more conscientious in his undertakings. We may conclude that another person has improved when she loosens up, becomes more spontaneous, and stops worrying so much. Regardless of the direction we choose, having one seems to be important to human beings. These are our goals and dreams, our vision of the future. Having a purpose in life gives us a reason to go on. It is understood that our purpose may evolve over the years, and thus our objectives will change somewhat. Even so, having goals at any given time enables us to focus and build momentum. Generally, an individual is said to show growth when he or she becomes more capable and competent, more productive and creative, more perceptive, insightful, and understanding, or more knowledgeable, prudent, and discerning. Personal growth will enable us to achieve our goals in life, whether they be to get better grades, to have more interesting careers,

to obtain a comfortable financial status, or to enjoy a satisfying love relationship.

With this in mind, it should be clear that we do not have to be maladjusted to seek personal growth. Many relatively well-functioning people seek more from life by removing blocks to their personal creativity and freedom. If the humanistic psychologists are correct, we have an inborn urge towards personal growth and the maximizing of our potential. If we are stuck, it is because something is thwarting this inner momentum. We may have tremendous potential for further development and an inborn impulse toward self-expression, but there are also obstacles that can keep us from becoming all we could be. We can get stuck because we fear losing what we have or because we tell ourselves "I've always been that way." We may have concerns that if we strive and fail, we shall think less highly of ourselves.

Many people find it difficult to get going and start working towards their goals. They may prefer to consider themselves "lazy" rather than "a failure" or "dumb" or "incompetent." There are payoffs for self-immobilization, but with them may come a lower quality of life or even self-destruction. It is preferable that we dare to want something and to risk going after it. On this journey, we shall examine the principles by which we are currently guiding our lives and shall determine whether we wish to alter them. We'll talk about what causes procrastination and how to overcome it.

➤ THE ROAD AHEAD: ABOUT THIS TEXT

The premise of this textbook is that knowledge of psychology can help you in your life. Psychology involves the scientific study of the human mind and human behavior. Although psychologists also study animals, they do so only as a means for understanding human beings and for promoting their welfare. It is our spectacular minds that set us apart from other species. As far as we know, only human beings can plan their future and celebrate . . . or regret their past. A major goal of psychology is to explain all that human beings are and do.

Although originating as a branch of philosophy, psychology has been around for only a little more than a century (Wertheimer, 1970). During this time, three major approaches have emerged for helping people with their problems in living: **psychoanalysis, behaviorism,** and **humanism.** An additional theory, the **dispositional** approach to understanding personality development, will help us gain an understanding of how we came to be the persons we are today. Psychoanalysis views human beings as motivated by biological forces that are rooted in the unconscious mind and are closely tied to our animal nature. In order to become truly well-adjusted, we must be socialized by our parents or other responsible adults, as representatives of the culture in which we live. Behaviorism proposes that human behavior is influenced by external forces (Watson, 1913) and that we have learned to be the way we are. If we are currently having problems, we can learn new, more adaptive ways of being. It was the principles of behaviorism that helped make psychology a science, rather than a branch of philosophy (Richelle, 1995). Humanists suggest that people are born with an urge to fulfill their inborn potential, which is viewed as inherently positive. When reared in a benevolent environment, people will essentially unfold much as a seed germinates, using the energy and nutrients stored within itself to produce leaves and blossoms. People unfold into sociable and self-fulfilling organisms. Those with a dispositional orientation emphasize the role of inherited predispositions in shaping their actions. This last approach implies that there are potentials and limitations that form a framework within which each person has to operate.

During the past several decades, these original and rather disparate theories have been researched and to some extent integrated. Each orientation is as yet incomplete in its substantiation and provision of explanations for the broad array of human thoughts, feelings, and behaviors. These theories will be referenced throughout this text, as a way of helping us understand everyday experiences. We'll see that although some strategies give considerable weight to the role played by the environment and our genetic inheritance in shaping behavior, each viewpoint provides avenues by which we can shape our own lives. We shall look at psychological research on self-efficacy, optimism, goal-setting, overcoming depression and anxiety, learning social skills, happiness, and more.

So, which theory is correct?

The theories that are outlined in this text have distinctly different views about what is human nature, what shapes individual personalities, and how people can be helped when they develop personality or other problems. You might well have asked yourself, "But which theory is right?" Psychologists cannot yet answer this question. To date, no theory adequately accounts for all of the complexities of human personality and behavior. Some theories are constructed in ways that defy empirical tests of their validity, yet scientific investigation of each theory has been under way for decades. Already clinicians trained under the disparate disciplines behave more similarly in face-to-face interactions with their clients than was the case forty years ago. There is overlap in these theories, of course. In the field of psychology, one must "stay tuned" for new revelations. New research-based insights pour forth in the profession's journals each month. In the meantime, there are aspects of each theory that you should find useful in your quest for personal development.

Moral and Social Codes

The "rules of the road" in life can be said to be our moral and social codes, as well as the physical laws of nature. That is, there are behavioral expectations and constraints placed on us by our society. Eventually these teachings tend to become a part of our own internal ethical principles. In addition, we live within physical bodies and in a physical world. These realities affect our experience.

There have been many views of human nature, including disputes over whether human beings are inherently good or evil, or perhaps have the potential for both types of deeds. One of the basic controversies has been to what extent we are programmed by our genetic heritage at conception to be the persons we are today, and conversely, to what extent we are shaped by our experience. Psychologist Carl Rogers (1961) proposed that human nature is basically constructive, trustworthy, and social, whereas B. F. Skinner (1953) believed that ethical behavior must be taught like any other behavior. Sigmund Freud (1930) viewed human nature as largely ruled by the irrational, unruly impulses of the id (Liebert & Spiegler 1994). The views of Jean Piaget (1928), Lawrence Kohlberg (1969), Carol Gilligan (1982), and William Perry (1970) on ethical development will also be discussed.

Virtually all moral teachings promote prosocial behavior, which are actions that foster friendly interpersonal relationships. Prosocial behaviors include altruism, cooperation, generosity, caring, empathy, respect, and civility. Accepting the value of a moral code and developing consensus with others as to how we ought to behave are analogous to developing rules of the road, so that we know which side of the highway on which to drive and can have some confidence that others are aware of and will abide by the same laws.

The terms "norm" and "role" refer to social rules that govern accepted and expected behavior. These rules exert a powerful influence on our actions. In order to achieve comfort in social settings, individuals must be sensitive to the social rules, or norms, that attach to a particular situation. Norms benefit us by allowing us to predict the behavior of others, including strangers. Roles are made up of norms that attach to a given social position. Each of us has several roles to play, with different expectations attached to each. Roles are reciprocal in nature, meaning that they are acted out in the context of relationships with others.

Over the centuries of our existence, we humans have developed social roles based on gender. Within the past several years, both men and women have increasingly experimented with nontraditional attitudes, behavior, and adornment. Although they have become less pronounced during the past few decades, gender roles still exist in our culture. Thus, we can meaningfully refer to a traditional masculine role and a traditional feminine role, by which is meant those tasks and attributes that have typically been assigned to men or to women. However, at times we may feel we have no guidelines for how to behave as a "modern man" or a "progressive woman." There are many situations today in which we experience role confusion and "normlessness."

Love and Work

Sigmund Freud once said that "love and work" are the two activities that occupy the well-adjusted adult's life. Today, when asked, most people say they want to find a romantic partner and to form a committed, secure relationship. We'll explore why a successful love relationship involves both skill and effort, as well as why psychologists and philosophers alike proclaim that loving relationships are among the handful of ways to make life meaningful. Robert Sternberg's (1988) model of love should provide a useful way of distinguishing among three components of love: intimacy, passion, and commitment. We'll look at how people develop and maintain love relationships.

Finding a career to fit our personality is crucially important and takes planning. It is the dispositional approach to understanding human beings that places the greatest emphasis on this idea. Whereas the psychoanalytic, behavioral, and humanistic approaches promote ways to help people adjust to the situations in which they find themselves, the dispositional theorists emphasize selection of environments that fit one's stable personality characteristics (Liebert & Spiegler, 1994). Taking into account our motivation, inborn potential, interests, and values can help us get started in thinking about appropriate career choices. Gratification of an individual's psychological needs through work and leisure activities has a beneficial effect on physical and mental health, as well as overall life satisfaction.

A follower of Freud's, Alfred Adler, added societal tasks to the love and work tasks outlined by Freud. This addition acknowledges that people do not accomplish their goals in life in a vacuum but instead that they do so with the help of other people. Human beings are social by nature and thus must develop positive relationships with others in order to be fulfilled.

The Mental-Physical Health Link

Psychological and medical research has made increasingly clear the relationship between mental and physical health. We experience stress when there are a great many things occurring around us that are relevant to our well-being and thus must be responded to. Our reactions to external and internal stimuli prompt us to engage in various adaptive and maladaptive behaviors. External stimuli include situations surrounding us at work, at school, and at home, whereas internal stimuli are typically the thoughts and feelings that we have about what is going on around us. This text will offer suggestions for increasing healthy responses and decreasing self-destructive ones.

All reactions to life events can be handled through healthy coping mechanisms. We actually have a surprising ability to inoculate ourselves against stress, either with the help of others or alone. A combination of lifestyle factors contributes to our sense of well-being. These factors include how we think and feel, how we work and play, how we handle our relationships with others, how we keep physically fit, how and what we eat, how we relax, and how we maintain our spiritual well-being.

The Dark Side of the Road

No matter how much we look at the events of our lives with optimism or perhaps equanimity, we all find that troubles will at times dim our path. Part of life involves dealing with disheartening events from loneliness, depression, or unfair treatment at the hands of others, to the loss of a loved one. It is to our advantage to learn how to face these troublesome times in our lives. Most important is for us to get past them and not to let their pain hinder us in such a way that we are too discouraged to go on. A successfully navigated life can even be enriched by these adversities, difficult as they are to get through.

Everyone experiences anger. Each of us finds management of this emotion a task essential for getting along with others. Our culture does not deal particularly effectively with this emotion, as evidenced by the greater incidence of violent acts in this country as compared with any other industrialized nation. We will pay particular attention to anger and aggression later (Chapter 13).

The Lighter Side

From the time of the ancient Greeks, people have been speculating on the roots of happiness. The Greeks concluded that pursuit of excellence was the road to happiness, and a similar finding has emerged from current research (Myers, 1991). This aspect of happiness has been termed **flow** (Csikszentmihalyi, 1990) and involves having the competence successfully to handle challenging tasks.

A surprise discovery by psychologists has been that happiness functions something like a personality trait (Myers, 1991). That is, it seems to have more to do with an individual's attitude than what is happening around him or her. Because of its relationship to one's attitude or outlook, our level of happiness also tends to be fairly stable over time.

Self-esteem, another predictor of a person's level of happiness with life in general, has been described as a sense of personal competence and worth (Myers, 1991). It reflects the judgment we make about our ability to cope with the challenges of life and our right to be happy (Branden, 1986). One of the characteristics of self-esteem is that we are at peace with ourselves and with others.

► THE NEED FOR A MEANINGFUL LIFE AND OTHER EXISTENTIAL CONCERNS

One of the discoveries you are likely to make in your self-exploration throughout these pages is that you have some anxieties and aspirations that stem from your particular life experiences and are thus not shared by people whom you know. Perhaps you have a younger sibling who is autistic, a relative who suffered a disability in an automobile accident, or a friend who has diabetes. These life events would be likely to prompt you to think about the blessings of being able-bodied, more so than would a peer who had not known someone coping with a disability. On the other hand, if your sister had just won the lottery, you might be preoccupied with thoughts of how you too could enjoy early retirement. Thus, your unique life experiences shape your values; what you think is important to pay attention to and work towards.

You may be surprised to realize that on a more basic level, you very much want the same things out of life that everyone else wants. Abraham Maslow, the founder of the humanistic movement in psychology, believed that we all want to belong among our fellow human beings and to have self-esteem. The humanist existentialists, such as Viktor Frankl, Eric Fromm, and Irvin Yalom, have suggested that being intelligent creatures, human beings wonder about the purpose of their existence. **Existentialism** is a branch of humanistic psychology formed around the idea that human beings are set apart as a species by their awareness of certain predicaments brought about by simply being alive. There are some basic existential concerns that address each person's "situation" in the world and that cut beneath any individual's personal life history. Erich Fromm (1963) listed *the need for a sense of identity* as one existential concern. Our search for identity involves asking the following questions: (1) Who am I? (this is never settled for good because we are changing as we go); (2) Where do I fit in? (this relates to our need for belongingness); (3) Where am I going? (these are our goals for a lifetime); and (4) Why am I here? (this addresses our purpose in life and is something we must decide for ourselves).

Here are four additional existential concerns delineated by Irvin Yalom (1980):

1. *We must face the prospect of our own death and confront our fear of it.* Each person faces the prospect of his or her mortality, of being torn from life through death. The confrontation of this fact of existence is painful but ultimately strengthening. Our attitude toward death affects the way we live, in that our fear of death can seriously curtail our purposefulness, autonomy, spontaneity, and engagement in life. Encountering the time-limited nature of our existence can give us the motivation to make the most of the time we have. Embracing the naturalness of death may enable us to enjoy life without fear.

2. *We must find or create our own meaning in life.* According to the existentialists, it is up to us to engage actively in a search for meaning in life because it is not automatically bestowed on us. To ask, What is the meaning of my life? is to inquire about the purpose to be fulfilled, some overriding goal or goals to which to apply ourselves. People strive for more than mere survival. We are curious creatures, who have a need for stimulation or excitement, and a great distaste for boredom. We also want to understand our place and function in the world. Existentialism holds that human beings define themselves in the course of the life they choose to lead.

To look for "cosmic meaning" implies that human life fits into some overall coherent pattern and that it infers a design existing outside of and superior to the individual. It invariably refers to some spiritual ordering of the universe. The "personal meaning" of one's own life can have foundations that are entirely secular, since a personal sense of meaning can exist without cosmic meaning. Although many of us may embrace a cosmic meaning that is experienced as highly relevant to our lives, we shall limit ourselves in this text to addressing the personal meaning of our lives. This latter form of meaning can be addressed as a purpose in life, from which goals for the future can be derived.

Human beings live life by symbolizing their experiences. We seek understanding of what is happening to us. We want to know the plot of our own life story, the destination of our journey. We sense that we are forward moving, but to what purpose?

Many college students today are loath to project themselves into the future and imagine what might be in store. This trend is disturbing, as there is ample evidence (Bandura, 1986) that the most reliable route to success, however the individual defines it, is through coming to terms with what one wants and becoming committed to objectives toward that end. Setting realistic goals and accomplishing them is perhaps the most dependable road to healthy self-esteem.

3. *We must face the fact that we are ultimately alone inside our skin*, so that even though we may be among people, no one else knows us as we know ourselves.

Human beings have a need for relatedness and unity with others, and experience isolation as loneliness. "To overcome their feelings of aloneness and isolation from nature and from themselves, humans need to love, to care for others. Love is a union with somebody or something outside of self" (Fromm, 1955, p. 37; 1973, p. 233).

Although a sense of connection with others can make life meaningful, existential isolation exists regardless of how gratifying are one's personal relationships or how integrated is one's personality. Every self-reflective person experiences moments when that which ordinarily seems so meaningful fails to seem so. At such times, one's relationship with the world is so profoundly shaken that the world loses its familiarity. "Though interpersonal encounter may temper **existential isolation,** it cannot eliminate it" (Yalom, 1980, p. 397). Intimacy can be highly rewarding, but there are things it cannot give us. We must learn what we cannot get from others, and recognize that no matter how close we feel to others, we must face life alone.

4. *We must understand that we have freedom of choice but that exercising this freedom requires us to take responsibility for the consequences of our choices.* This fourth existential concern links freedom and responsibility. Freedom has many connotations. For our purpose, freedom will be defined as the individual's ability to make choices in creating his or her own life, and to desire, to act, and to change (Yalom, 1980). Responsibility will be used to refer to accountability for and authorship of one's thoughts, feelings, actions, and destiny. Those who blame others or outside forces for the predicaments they face in life will be ineffective in handling those predicaments.

Responsible action begins with a wish or desire for something. We can take action on behalf of our desires only if we are aware of them. We may have difficulty either with knowing what we want or with deciding how to get what we want. Many individuals under psychological distress are not able to get much done in their lives. They are unable to develop a clear intention to make a specific thing happen. What psychotherapists generally do is liberate the motivation of their clients by removing encumbrances that bind it. Accordingly, self-awareness is typically the first step in making our lives more satisfying. Once we know why we don't want to do our homework, go to work, or attend parties, we'll find it easier to modify our own behavior to steer towards having the experiences we want in life. If we decide we want a college degree, a career, and/or a romantic relationship, we next need to know how to go about getting these things. Perhaps the most liberating thing we can do in life is to learn to speak our honest convictions and feelings, and then live with the consequences.

➤ ARE YOU IN THE DRIVER'S SEAT?

You may be skeptical about the notion that your life is yours to construct as you wish. You may feel powerless, in the grip of external circumstances. It is true that each person has limitations to cope with and thus may be thrown by unexpected life events. For instance, we do not determine our race, gender, or most aspects of our physical appearance. At this point in our lives, our genetic inheritance is blended with a fair amount of social conditioning, which we also did not control. We will always be subject to fortuitous life events. A car driven by a drunk driver may smash into our car as we drive the freeway, causing us permanent bodily damage, or we might inherit money from a relative. Although most of us would like the opportunity to adjust to the unexpected blessing of coming into a small fortune, we are tempted to get discouraged about limitations and unexpected tragedies.

Even in the most fortunate lives there are times when things go wrong. We must have a philosophy of life that enables us to go on when adversity hits. Sometimes accepting a victim stance has the appeal of making us feel in control of others, as they attempt to comfort us. A closer look would seem to suggest that as victims, we give up a great deal of our freedom to explore more constructive possibilities for our lives. Most psychologists have concluded that being proactive leads to more effective adjustment and greater life satisfaction (Yalom, 1980). Making decisions is one of the ways in which we take a proactive stance in life. No one can take action or make decisions without the risk of making a mistake, so cultivating a benevolent attitude towards mistakes is one of the secrets of having the courage to act. Such a kindly attitude toward screwups will help us resist the urge to disclaim responsibility for our behavior when it doesn't lead to desirable consequences.

Being a Victim: Advice to the Traveler

What's coming next is a very sensitive area for discussion. It is an area that most people have strong feelings about: the topic of victimization.

Recovering from a negative life experience is one of the great challenges of life. Those who have not experienced a particular tragic event may instead have had to cope with an underdog status. Understandably, some of us make the mistake of accepting a victim role in life and getting by on the offerings of others who feel sorry for us. It is not a good idea to go that route. One way to resist such a temptation is to latch onto some examples of people who have suffered worse setbacks than the ones with which we are dealing and who have achieved something worthwhile in spite of serious limitations. Here are some examples of such people, of whom you may have heard: Helen Keller (a deaf and blind writer), Ray Charles, Stevie Wonder, Jose Felliciano, Doc Watson (all four are musicians who are blind), Itzhak Perlman (a polio victim, who is one of the most famous violinists in the world), and U.S. President Franklin D. Roosevelt (another polio victim). Perhaps the most recent heroic figure we could keep in mind is Christopher Reeve, the actor known best for his role as Superman, who became a quadriplegic as the result of a horseback riding accident. He has not taken on a victim role, although he may be entitled to, but rather has taken control of his life and disability. He remained in the driver's seat by drawing his power to do so from inner resources.

QUESTIONS: *Who else belongs on this list? Can you name some athletes, politicians, or people in your own life who have excelled in spite of limitations? Do you have someone you keep in mind as a model of courage, for occasions when you may feel discouraged or hopeless?*

We do not have to be passive victims in life. Our parents (or someone else) may have mistreated us or misunderstood us in the past, and that harshness is unfortunate. Still, we can change our lives today rather than live by past conditioning. We have the ability to find love now if we were formerly denied it. We can learn how to be loving, even if perhaps we did not see love modeled for us in our family of origin. There is nothing that has happened to any of us that someone else hasn't overcome, to go on to be successful.

It must be acknowledged that there are forces operating in our lives that are truly external to us and thus uncontrollable. To ignore this would be to "**blame the victim**" for invariably causing his or her own suffering. Still, a theme of this text is that we generally lean in the other direction and fail to take responsibility for our active or passive contribution to the predicaments of our lives. To make this mistake is as grave a matter as discarding one's compass when lost at sea after a storm has thrown us off course, because our personal power to affect outcomes in our lives is tied to our willingness to accept responsibility for our actions. Within the limitations of our physical constitution and past conditioning, we have the flexibility to choose our actions and chart our course for the future.

When suffering is unavoidable, we can still choose our attitude about it. Christopher Reeve had broken his neck but decided not to be broken by what had happened to him. His attitude is heroic; his mastery of his situation is admirable. He has become a role model for how to retain dignity in the face of tragedy.

Sometimes the victim stance isn't realistic. When we view ourselves only as having been acted upon, rather than as participants in the events of our lives, we discount our influence over the results we get. If we walk into class after missing the previous class meeting, only to find out that the exam date was moved up to today, we may feel mistreated. Although we might argue about whether the instructor has done something inappropriate, the point here is that we could have attended class last time or called the instructor to find out what we missed. Even a burglary victim may play some part in "arranging for" the burglary. Windows or drapes are left open, no dead bolts have been installed, newspapers are allowed to pile up while the residents are on vacation. These are examples of inaction that aids burglars. We may also decide not to buy a Doberman pinscher to protect our property; we leave the house or apartment, rather than stay home to protect our property. We simply estimate the probability that we will regret these choices, and then we act. So, in a sense, we nearly always bear some measure of responsibility for what happens to us, though we are not used to thinking in these terms. There will be many occasions when we will find virtually nothing (and rare occasions when there actually is nothing) we did to contribute to an unfortunate occurrence. The point here is that it is a good practice to look for our own participation in the outcomes of our lives. This frame of mind will better enable us to achieve our goals.

QUESTIONS: *Do you agree that we nearly always bear some measure of responsibility for what happens to us? How do you explain negative events to yourself?*

There are some advantages to being perceived by ourselves and/or others as a victim. We may enjoy righteous indignation and a feeling of moral superiority. Another potential benefit, perhaps, is control of others through guilt that we induce in them. Yet these advantages are short-term, whereas the drawbacks are long-term.

What are the disadvantages of adopting the victim stance? Projecting blame can lead to paranoia. If we habitually fault others for our mistakes and misfortunes, we may begin to suspect them of being untrustworthy or even "out to get" us. We may also convince ourselves that we are helpless and thus gradually give up our ability to make changes that would improve our lives.

However, we have the option to make a different choice: We can actively seek to avoid becoming a victim.

Are there payoffs for staying out of the victim role? Yes, there are. We can feel empowered and encouraged about making changes for the better in our lives. We are able to foster honest, straightforward dealings with others. What are the disadvantages of foregoing a victim stance? We must accept responsibility for our mistakes and often some culpability for the unfortunate things that happen to us. This acceptance may cause us to blame ourselves, and if we do, our self-esteem could suffer. We'll say more about this problem when we cover making mistakes later in this chapter.

Being Proactive: Blazing a Trail

Do you wonder why some people succeed while others fail? One answer seems to be that successful people are proactive. They are motivated by internal desires and goals. Being **proactive** means deciding ahead of time what they want and taking action to make it happen, rather than reacting to events as they occur.

Instead of being passive bystanders in life, we might actively set goals and priorities for ourselves and chart our progress towards attainment of those objectives. In addition, we can determine to make the most of our resources and decide to become as accomplished as our inborn potential will allow. Generally, psychologists agree that "taking charge" of one's own life insures more effective adjustment and greater life satisfaction (e.g., Miller et al., 1986; Parkes, 1984). If you refer to the box entitled "Profile of 'Super Performers,'" you should find this quality among those attributed to successful people.

Effective living requires being proactive in one's own life. It calls for us to accept the weight of responsibility for our action, a burden we might prefer to escape. Abraham Maslow (Chapter 2) proposed that having goals is a necessary component of being a "self-actualized" person. A self-actualizer is one who fulfills his or her life potential and enjoys what life has to offer. This text promotes the notion that both having goals and making active coping efforts are generally superior strategies to being passive, complacent, and directionless.

Making Decisions

Making decisions is one of the ways we take a proactive stance in life. We are constantly presented with choices, which determine the course of our lives. Even failing to decide constitutes selecting an option and can be considered a style of decision making, but not a proactive one. Opportunities have deadlines. An example would be waiting until it's too late to have children, without having first decided to be childless.

PROFILE OF "SUPER PERFORMERS"
Charles A. Garfield, Peak Performance Center, Berkeley, California

High performers spend more than two-thirds of their time doing things they want to do. They accomplish this goal through effective time management, saying yes to "A" tasks, getting through "B" tasks rapidly and efficiently, and saying no to "C" tasks.

High performers are healthier than average because they make time for relaxation and exercise. They realize that good health contributes significantly to high performance.

High performers do what they do for the art of it and are motivated by internal goals. By contrast, workaholics work to compensate for some inadequacy or need in their lives that is not being met.

High performers define success internally, and progress is measured against what has been accomplished in the past. They care about outcomes but also enjoy the process of reaching goals.

High performers solve problems rather than place blame. Others tend to ask who or what caused a problem. High performers ask, "What is the situation now, where do we want to be, and how do we get there?"

High performers confidently take risks after laying out the worst possible consequences. Most people look at benefits and liabilities and then go back and forth, and they may never make a final decision. High performers ask, "What is the worst that can happen?" and "Can I live with it?" If the answer is yes, the risk is worth taking, and they proceed. If the answer is no, they don't take the risk.

High performers have a positive self-image and self-esteem, which come from knowing who they are and valuing that. Individuals begin to improve their self-image when they think about their positive qualities, consider their potential for improvement, and practice mental rehearsal.

High performers are able to rehearse coming events or actions mentally. They imagine themselves performing at desired levels or in desired situations. They practice over and over like a tennis player mentally rehearsing the perfect serve, thereby leading to increased performance and a positive self-image.

High performers have a sense of their own commitment, mission, and purpose in life. When they can't identify a commitment, they make finding a commitment their immediate purpose.

QUESTION: *What are some of the reasons why people put off making decisions?*

Effective decision making is an important skill to learn if we want to be the ones to map a route to our desired destination. Sometimes it is better to make a marginal decision than none at all (Halpern, 1989). It keeps us from getting a backlog of unmade decisions, which we ponder while other dilemmas pile up. Often the situation gets much worse when an unpleasant decision is put off. Most decisions aren't so important that they'll have a major effect on our lives. A good example of an occasion for minor decision making is sorting through the mail. An efficient way to do this is to start with a trash container nearby. Many productive people have advised throwing away any items of mail that are not going to be acted upon immediately and taking action on the rest. Although doing this isn't always practical, it is a good rule-of-thumb procedure.

One reason we may put off making decisions is that we tend to be overly harsh in blaming ourselves for our "obvious" bad decisions, a phenomenon known as hindsight bias (Hawkins & Hastie, 1990). Hindsight bias refers to the finding that people overestimate their ability to have foreseen an outcome when encountering it after the fact. Learning that something has happened makes it seem more inevitable, as though we should have known all along that this event would happen.

We are tempted to be hard on ourselves for not foreseeing a negative outcome in our lives. Many nationally known Democrats who were presumed to have presidential ambitions declined to enter the race against Republican President George Bush in his 1992 bid for reelection, because President Bush's popularity ratings were sky-high after the Persian Gulf War. He was considered unbeatable at the point in the election cycle when candidates typically announce their intentions. This situation paved the way for an almost unknown presidential hopeful, Governor Bill Clinton from Arkansas, to become president. As the governor of a small state, Bill Clinton's chances to win the nomination would have presumably been slight against nationally recognized figures such as Representative Richard Gebhardt. In hindsight, Gebhardt and others in his position might well have regretted staying out of the race.

The hindsight bias phenomenon also says that we are prone to credit ourselves for our "obvious" good choices or decisions. This fallacy in thinking, combined with the fact that decisions inevitably have to be made on the basis of incomplete information, explains in part why we are often so reluctant to make decisions when they are before us. Most poor decisions aren't fatal, however. The mistake of making a poor decision can be an essential part of growing, because it provides feedback that allows us to take corrective action. In Chapter 7, we'll learn how use a decision making worksheet. This is only one of many good strategies for selecting a course of action.

Although the problems we have today probably stem from the decisions we have made in the past, our feelings about those decisions stem from our understanding about making mistakes. In order to make future decisions without undue procrastination, we need to understand the value of making mistakes. By understanding the context of a past decision along with its consequences, we set the stage for considering an alternate, and perhaps better, choice in the future. Thus, the feedback helps us improve our judgment.

Making Mistakes

Of course, in order to be able to tolerate making mistakes, we'll need to cultivate an attitude that doing so is normal, natural, and completely okay. It is not that we want to knock around recklessly, but rather that we accept goof ups and setbacks as esential to the learning process and a part of life. We must dare to fail, since occasional failure is unavoidable. As Ben Franklin put it, "The man who does things makes many mistakes, but he never makes the biggest mistake of all—doing nothing."

For instance, learning to ice-skate requires the feedback from the inevitable falls through which we must suffer. Have you ever watched the Olympic skaters practice their moves? They fall on their duffs *constantly!* Everybody has seen a baby learn to walk, going through the same falling process. Another example of the importance of feedback is that if we were to throw darts at a dartboard 1,000 times but received no feedback, we wouldn't be any better on the one-thousandth throw than on the first. So, in a certain light, mistakes can be considered valuable, since they give us the information we need to correct our course. When during an interview about his invention of the lightbulb, Thomas Edison was asked how he could tolerate so few results, he quipped, "Results? Why, man, I have gotten lots of results! If I find 10,000 ways something won't work, I haven't failed. I am not discouraged, because every wrong attempt discarded is another step forward. Just because something doesn't do what you planned it to do doesn't mean it's useless."

An important skill to develop is the ability to detach ourselves from our mistakes and to view them objectively. In the long run, we are the people we are as a result of both our successes and our failures. Whether or not we succeed on any given occasion, we can keep the courage or our convictions and our belief in ourselves. If we do not have confidence in ourselves, we cannot expect anyone else to. Viewing mistakes and failings as "just part of the deal" and as good information will enable us to overcome discouragement and keep faith in ourselves.

Taking Responsibility

It is a common admonition that we must take responsibility for our actions. Yet many of us are reluctant to do this, because it suggests blame, shame, and self-condemnation. Further, we may not notice the ways in which we disclaim responsibility for our actions, nor understand our motivation for doing so.

Viktor Frankl (1963) viewed responsibility for one's own life as the very essence of human existence. He once proposed that the citizens of the United States consider erecting a Statue of Responsibility on the West Coast, since

A Statue of Responsibility?

we already have a Statue of Liberty on our Eastern shore, and he urged that we must not forget that these two qualities work together.

Remember that freedom refers to our ability to choose our own direction in life. Frankl said that freedom is not a condition of the environment; but that it is a condition of the person. Each person has many choices from among the options presented by the environment. Freedom means that we have the internal power to exercise those options. Responsibility will be used to refer to accountability for and authorship of our thoughts, feelings, actions, and destiny. Those who blame others or outside forces for their life predicament can do nothing about it. Those who look for their participation in the event can intentionally influence the outcome for the better.

At first glance, freedom might seem to be in conflict with commitment. Some of us avoid obligations because we fear that through them, we'll lose the liberty that we prize. If we make a commitment, then we are not as free as before. When we marry, we agree to forego other romantic relationships. Yet, part of freedom is the ability to choose and decide. What good is this freedom if it is never exercised?

Taking responsibility for the direction of our own lives is daunting and is likely to make us feel anxious. To avoid this anxiety, we may refuse to examine our choices and their consequences. We designate other people or outside institutions as accountable for the direction of our lives. This passivity allows us to avoid experiencing the weight of responsibility for deciding what to do. Yet, it is the very act of deciding through which we define ourselves.

As individuals, we are free to imbue the events which happen to us with significance. In fact, we cannot help doing this, and in the process, we are answerable for the "spin" we put on things. We are also liable for our actions and our failures to act. There is no avoiding this accountability, either. The acceptance of responsibility for ourselves is a precondition of personal growth. These existential themes will be revisited in subsequent chapters throughout this text.

➤ *Adjustment to Society versus Individual Self-Expression*

One of the questions embedded in human social organization is to what extent individual citizens should be allowed freedom to pursue their own dreams and wishes and to be as eccentric as they like. On the other hand, to what extent do we expect people to conform to the standards of society?

The term "adjustment" implies that some ideal or norm exists by which people should be measured. The problem with the concept of measuring up to a standard lies in the question, Who determines the standards of "good" adjustment? Consider this: Surgery is sometimes performed on cojoined twins (formerly referred to as Siamese twins) that sacrifices one infant so that the other of the pair might have a chance to lead a "normal" life. This behavior suggests that a society can come to some degree of consensus as to what constitutes a normal or "good" life. However, it is possible that the twins might be considered poorly adjusted in our culture and well-adjusted in another culture. There may be societies in which cojoined twins are considered special or even divine beings. After all, some ancient deities had extra hands and other extra body parts. Another example might be that the personality that is adaptive in a juvenile gang is maladaptive in society as a whole. Also, the U.S. culture values a "competitive spirit" in its citizens, so that many behaviors that are considered acceptable to gain a competitive edge would be considered uncooperative or surly in other cultures, such as Japan and China.

Clearly, the concept of individual adjustment seems to be partially tied to the culture in which the person participates. Still, a student of history or philosophy could muster a great body of ideas to demonstrate that there does seem to have been some agreement throughout the ages as to how to be a happy, purposeful, and moral person. This text makes use of some of these time-honored principles.

Sigmund Freud (1930), the founder of psychoanalysis, believed that human beings are by nature irrational and destructive unless socialized, that is, taught to be civilized, ethical citizens. He suggested that individuals must learn to *adjust to* their lot in life, to accept responsibility for themselves, and to go to work to earn a living. He believed that human beings would rather regress to a point where they are completely taken care of than grow into responsible, independent persons. The reward for all of this adjustment is that such persons "fit in" to society and can enjoy loving relationships. Implicit in Freudian theory is the contention of a necessary, intrinsic opposition between the desires of the individual and the needs of society.

Behaviorists describe actions as either adaptive or **maladaptive.** They view people as being controlled by their environment (Skinner, 1953). Specifically, they believe that the rewards and punishments that are the consequence of a person's behavior, shape that person's future activities. Rewarded behaviors will be performed more frequently in the future, whereas punished actions should diminish in frequency. For this reason, a person would be expected to be well-adjusted to society because he or she is continuously responding to external cues with changes in behavior. In other words, society has the power to control the rewards offered individuals. A problem might arise, however, whenever behavior is reinforced in the short run but maladaptive in the long run. A good example would be alcohol abuse, which in the short run serves to help people forget their problems but in the long run makes them worse.

Humanistic psychologists believe that behavior is primarily organized around the positive motive of self-fulfillment. Human beings are thought to be born basically good, moral, and prosocial. Individuals become misdirected when societal values and constraints have caused them to veer from their inner knowing, which provides an innately sound sense of self-direction. There is, however, no intrinsic opposition between the individual and society (Maslow, 1971). In general, individuals can be trusted to be both self-fulfilling and interested in promoting the well-being of others. Psychological adjustment is a social phenomenon and thus requires dealing successfully with an environment that includes other people.

However, humanist Abraham Maslow (1971), who investigated highly functioning people noted that they were not well adjusted in sense of being excessively conforming to societal norms. Whereas these self-actualizing people got along with their culture in various ways, they maintained a certain inner detachment from the society in which they were immersed. In some ways the individuals studied by Maslow seemed to be more healthy than their American culture.

A final viewpoint is sometimes termed the dispositional, or genetic, approach, which is a biological view that human dispositions are at least in part transmitted genetically. For this reason, personality characteristics, inclinations, attitudes, and abilities are relatively stable and enduring within the individual. Even from birth, infants differ in the vigor and style of their responses to frustration and reward (Buss & Plomin, 1984). Dispositional psychologists attempt to explain the individual differences and similarities of adults by looking at inherited tendencies. This approach suggests that individuals attain fulfillment by finding environments suitable to their personalities.

QUESTIONS: *What do you think? Should we seek to be well-adjusted in society or to "do our own thing" and follow our personal bliss?*

Most likely *both* adjustment and development of one's own individuality are desirable and feasible. Each society has slowly evolving standards for its citizenry as to what constitutes good behavior and, conversely, what behavior will not be tolerated. Sanctions against unacceptable behavior are necessary for human civilization to prosper.

In the United States, where individual liberty is arguably more protected than anywhere else in the world, societal norms are more flexible and transitory than in other cultures, where order is held in higher esteem than is personal freedom. In such a climate as exists in the U.S., we enjoy unprecedented freedom to create our own definitions of ourselves as persons. This freedom doesn't mean that we should "do our own thing" without considering the rights of others. We can consider other people and still retain our integrity, by making our own choices in life. No one can be considered healthy who completely ignores the norms of the culture in which he or she is imbedded. We do need to fit in somehow. One aspect of being a well-developed person, then, is the ability to get along with others and to find a place for oneself in one's world. We must seek a balance between practicing independent self-expression and accommodating the wishes of our fellow citizens.

➤ GETTING TO KNOW YOURSELF

In achieving any worthwhile goal, we can expect some tough going, and gaining self-awareness is no exception. There is some discomfort associated with discovering more about ourselves. Out of fear, we may prefer to remain unaware of our inner lives. We dread taking an honest look at the unknown within us. What if we discover terrible things about ourselves, things of which we are ashamed? Humanistic psychologist Abraham Maslow (1966) recognized this concern:

> More than any other kind of knowledge we fear knowledge of ourselves, knowledge that might transform our self-esteem and our self-image . . . While human beings love knowledge and seek it—they are curious—they also fear it. The closer to the personal it is, the more they fear it. (p. 16)

Perhaps at this point an offer to guide you toward personal growth doesn't sound all that appealing. What's all this talk about "discomfort?" you may want to ask. Here is something else to think about as you decide whether you want to venture along this path. Whenever you are willing to tolerate thinking about something that brings you mental anguish, you build inner strength and enable yourself to begin a growth process. You are recovering from being afraid and are gaining courage. When you deny your fears and problems, they have the potential to plague you for a lifetime. Only when you confront them, do you have an opportunity to defeat them. Thus, while becoming self-aware, you are likely to discover some unpleasant truths about yourself. You are a fallible human being and yet essentially lovable.

Since we want to be able to experience self-acceptance, becoming aware of faults we possess should motivate us to reconsider some of our habitual behavior and thought patterns. Once we make such changes, we shall like ourselves better and shall experience greater contentment. This is the natural result of personal growth. Self-improvement generally brings about euphoria in the long run.

In gaining self-awareness, we shall have an opportunity to examine our assumptions, inferences, opinions, prejudices, and skills. We'll be on intimate terms with ourselves and in this way will be prepared to comfortably interact with others. The first part of the journey involves self-awareness, and the rest consist of the passage from awareness to action. Self-knowledge is a prerequisite to forming plans for the future. We may be going on a journey in life, but our destination is in many ways internal. The securing of a lasting happiness is an inside job.

You may be heartened to know that it is natural to experience some fear about actively participating in class, especially since it involves taking risks

"Who am I? And what am I doing here?"

©Jim Unger/distributed by United Media, 1998.

you don't usually take in your college courses. Be prepared for some sense of being unsettled in your life. If you find yourself feeling, thinking, or acting differently, you may be surprised to discover that those who are close to you do not want you to change. Because they have some investment in the "old" you, you may unexpectedly encounter their resistance rather than their support.

Sometimes emotional or practical obstacles get in the way of our goals. Typical impediments to wishing for something are fear of failure and reluctance to give up alternate choices. Practical stumbling blocks are insufficient skill or experience, or lack of the physical attributes required for the job. Depending on the type of impediment, we can apply various strategies, such as verbal affirmations or specific skills training to overcome these hurdles.

Trust: The Only Way to Get from Here to There

Establishing trust is the first step toward having meaningful relationships with others. You may discuss your feelings of mistrust toward the group or individuals in the class. By doing this, you actually help to establish a higher level of trust, because expressed negative feelings tend to dissipate. Your willingness to risk saying something about lack of trust, and then to have nothing terrible happen to you as a consequence of expressing negative feelings, helps everyone feel more trusting. Mutual trust tends to increase awareness, mostly because it leads to self-disclosure. Without trust, relationships cannot develop, because intimacy is established through allowing ourselves to be open and thus vulnerable.

In general, the healthier the personality, the more there is willingness to share about oneself, and the less felt need to keep secrets. In support of this idea, research has shown that extroverts are happier than are introverts (Myers, 1991). Extroverts are people who are outgoing, whereas introverts are more reserved. Analyst Carl Jung expressed this concept when he said, "I am only as sick as my secrets" (in Campbell, 1987). While Jung was the first to recognize that each person is born with an inclination toward either introversion or extroversion, he admonished his patients to seek balance in their personalities by exercising potentialities within themselves that run counter to their preferred modes of behavior.

Forced exposure is undesirable and usually ineffective, since the experience of threat tends to decrease perception. Awareness is a basis for new action and new ways of interacting with people. When we initially meet strangers, we'll probably want to go slowly in offering to trust, to see whether the stranger's behavior matches his or her words. This is one way we learn to disclose in an emotionally safe way.

Self-Disclosure: The "Royal Road" to Intimacy

Self-disclosure refers to the sharing of our inner thoughts and feelings with another person. Talking to others is one way we come to know ourselves more fully. We can retain our need for privacy by deciding how much we will disclose and when it is appropriate to do so.

Some of us may believe that if people knew our "true self," they would not find us likable. To some extent, we all wear public masks that allow us to present our most acceptable selves to the world. Choosing to trust another person enough to allow him or her to see beyond the mask takes courage, since we risk the possibility that our "true selves" will be rejected. Unless we are willing to drop our masks as we form relationships, we may find ourselves caught up in a charade from which we cannot extract ourselves. Indeed, the worst outcome of all would be that we might be fooled by the charade ourselves and thus fail to know our true selves. We may dare to be authentic with others only when we have taken the trouble to know ourselves.

We fear that which we don't understand. To the extent that we live among strangers whom we do not understand, we remain on guard. We may erroneously assume that we know the motives, thoughts, and reactions of another person. Even if people tell us what they are thinking and feeling, many of us wonder whether that individual is actually the way he or she seems (Jourard, 1971). When a person fully, spontaneously, and honestly discloses his or her experience to another, then the mystery that this person was decreases enormously. We learn the extent to which we are similar and the degree to which we differ from one another in thoughts, feelings, hopes, and dreams. For instance, we may think a friend looks sad, but when asked, the friend indicates she is content yet tired. Another person may seem aloof, but is in fact merely shy.

One of the most common sources of misunderstanding in intimate relationships is the assumption we make that others know what we are thinking and feeling. Most of the time, others do not know what is going on with us unless we tell them. Even when we explain how we think or feel, we might want to ask for feedback to make certain we have been understood. The best we can hope for is to have companions who care about us and who want to comprehend what we are experiencing. When this is so, much of the time we'll feel understood.

However, no one can know and accept us at all times. We must get comfortable with the reality that this understanding will break down periodically. No other person has had precisely our set of experiences in life, nor does anyone else (with the exception of an identical twin) have our same genetic inheritance. Thus, no one else can completely understand us. The best we can hope for is to be fairly articulate in sharing with others what is going on within us and then to have those others be interested enough in us to try and comprehend who we are and how we view things. When others fail in their attempts to have empathy for us, we realize that we are ultimately alone in life. Ironically, acceptance of this idea allows us to treasure our relationships with others without having undue expectations of them (Yalom, 1980). We'll no longer demand that they always know what we need or how we feel.

We can voluntarily share only those thoughts and feelings of which we are aware. At times we may discover within ourselves motives, thoughts, and underlying reactions to events going on around us of which we were previously unaware. We can truly be a mystery to ourselves! Self-disclosure, then, helps make us known to others, and also to ourselves.

Introspection

As we have observed, we are able to share with others only those things we know about ourselves; however, there are many things about ourselves of which we remain unaware. This concept is at the core of Freudian psychology. Have you ever been unable to answer the question, How do you feel? Many of us do not know how we feel. Years of suppressing our feelings and hiding them from others may result in being cut off from our own internal dialogue and emotional responses. We may have to learn to hear our inner thought process. When we do get in touch with how we feel, initially these emotions may be so unfamiliar that we tend to discount them as irrelevant. If this is so, we may actually have to catch ourselves having a feeling. It helps to practice asking ourselves what we are feeling several times a day, until we can name our emotional state with relative ease.

QUESTION: *How do you feel right now?*

There are several levels at which we can experience ourselves and the world (McGill, 1985). There is the external world, which we come to know largely by observing events and the behavior of others. There are our own behaviors, where the focus of our attention is on our own actions—what we are doing. Finally, there are our own internal thoughts and feelings. Most people experience the world at the first level, as observers of others. Some are also skilled at self-observation. An awareness of how we think and feel requires **introspection,** which involves observation or examination of one's own mental and emotional state. It is the act of looking within oneself.

Much of what we know about ourselves, we share with our intimates, so that these things are known to ourselves and to others. In Jungian terms, these aspects that are known to self and to others make up our **persona,** our public selves. However, some known aspects of ourselves we keep to ourselves. In addition, we have attitudes and characteristics of which we remain unaware. Certain of these attitudes and characteristics are also hidden from outside observers, though others are not. This arrangement leaves us with the eerie consideration that there are things about us that are known to others, yet unknown to ourselves! The accompanying table depicts how self-disclosure and introspection affect what is known to oneself and others.

THE JOHARI WINDOW

	Known to Self	Not Known to Self
Known to Others	1 (open)	2 (blind)
Not Known to Others	3 (hidden)	4 (unknown)

Quadrant 1 is the area of free activity, or open area. It represents behaviors, feelings, and motivations known to ourselves and to other people.

Quadrant 2 is the blind area. It represents a situation in which other people can see things in us of which we are unaware.

Quadrant 3 is the avoided, or hidden, area. It represents things that we know but that we do not reveal to other people (e.g., hidden agendas or strategies, or matters about which we have sensitive feelings).

Quadrant 4 is the area of unknown activity. It represents an area where neither we nor other people are aware of certain motives or feelings that are in us. Yet we can assume that they exist because eventually some of these things become known, and we then realize that these unknown motives or feelings were influencing our relationships all the time.

Principles of Change:

1. A change in any one quadrant will affect all other quadrants.

2. Introspection tends to increase Quadrants 1 and 3.

3. Interpersonal learning means a change has taken place so that Quadrant 1 is larger and one or more of the other quadrants has grown smaller.

4. The smaller Quadrant 1 is, the poorer the communication.

5. There is a universal curiosity about the area unknown to either self or others (Quadrant 4), but this is usually held in check by custom, social training, and/or fear.

6. Sensitivity means appreciating the covert aspect of behavior in Quadrants 2, 3, and 4, and respecting the desire of others to keep them so.

7. When the hidden or avoided area (Quadrant 3) is reduced, usually through self-disclosure, less energy is tied up in defending this area.

8. A key assumption is that as Quadrant 1 increases, a person will experience greater satisfaction with his or her work and social interactions. (Luft, 1970).

The Johari Window

The Johari Window is a simple model of the levels of awareness between and within human beings. In the table, notice that there are four boxes. Taken altogether, the four boxes represent everything there is to know about you, which would include such things as your values, your interests, and your likes and dislikes.

Since we are not actually aware of everything about ourselves, the area represented by the four boxes could be partitioned into parts of ourselves that we are aware of and aspects that we are not. All there is to know about us could be divided another way, to show things about us that others know and parts of us that others do not know. These divisions yield the four boxes of the Johari window.

➤ PERSONAL GROWTH STRATEGIES FOR AN ACADEMIC JOURNEY

We have discussed the value of taking charge of our life experience rather than being passive in life. The benefit of taking an active role in constructing our experience applies to our academic career as well. A large body of research confirms that those students who actively participate in their own learning get more out of every learning opportunity (e.g., Bransford, 1979). To be an active learner means thinking about the material presented in class and asking questions that come to mind. It also means questioning whether what goes on in school has value to us in our lives. Educator Terry O'Bannion (1997, p. 91) wrote that "the ultimate goal of education is to help the student develop satisfactory answers to the questions: Who am I? Where am I going? What difference does it make?" Time and effort must be invested to make college learning experiences meaningful.

An essential part of education is learning our identity. At its best, education helps us to grow and to learn what we want to grow into, as well as what is good and bad, what is desirable and undesirable, and what to choose and what not to choose. Sometimes we'll see that such dichotomies are inappropriate. The guideposts for making these selections are not necessarily to be found in the external environment. Making decisions about our lives requires the clarification of our values and purpose, so that we develop a sense of direction from within.

You will get the most benefit from this course if you decide what you want for yourself from this experience. Think about what problems and personal concerns you are willing to explore. Set goals for yourself, which you intend to accomplish by the end of this course. Give yourself specific assignments relating to changes you want to make. Think of ways to apply what you learn in class to everyday life. It is vital that you think and decide things for yourself. It's your road map and your journey!

➤ *SUMMARY*

YOUR LIFE AS A JOURNEY   The premise of this textbook is that psychology can be used as a source of illumination for you as you forge your way through life. Your life is yours to construct as you wish. Inherent in this freedom is the responsibility to determine what constitutes a satisfying life and to move in the direction of creating it. This text promotes the notions that both having goals and making active efforts towards them are generally superior strategies to remaining passive and directionless. There is no universal path to creating a meaningful life. Yours has been and will continue to be unique. Even so, psychology may be able to help.

ON THE ROAD TO PERSONAL GROWTH   A good understanding of yourself, a measure of self-acceptance, effective coping skills, and a healthy life philosophy should equip you for a happy life. This text aims to help you gain self-awareness. A wish for self-acceptance supplies the motivation to make changes, once we become aware of aspects of ourselves of which we disapprove. In addition to self-understanding and good coping skills, a moral foundation and a sense of purpose in life seem to be essential to enjoying a good life. Developing a philosophy of life requires us to define our purpose so that we may make changes within the framework of an overall life plan.

THE ROAD AHEAD: ABOUT THIS TEXT   The field of psychology has developed three major approaches to helping human beings with their problems in living: Psychoanalysis, behaviorism, and humanism. A fourth approach, the dispositional, explains much of human behavior as genetically based and therefore quite stable. This text uses a theoretically eclectic approach, as each viewpoint provides avenues by which individuals can shape their own lives. Psychoanalysis views human beings as motivated by unconscious biological forces that are closely tied to our animal nature. In order to become truly human, we must be socialized by our parents or other responsible adults. Behaviorism emphasizes the influence of external forces on human behavior. Humanists suggest that people are born with an urge to fulfill their inborn potential, which is viewed as inherently positive. The psychoanalytic, behavioral, humanistic, and dispositional approaches will all be employed in the service of helping you use psychology to enhance your enjoyment and sense of purpose in life.

THE NEED FOR A MEANINGFUL LIFE AND OTHER EXISTENTIAL CONCERNS   Viktor Frankl, a humanistic existential therapist, viewed responsibility for one's own life as the very essence of human existence. Freedom to make decisions is inextricably linked to responsibility for the consequences. Taking responsibility for the direction of our own lives is daunting and is likely to make us feel anxious. To avoid this anxiety, we may refuse to examine our choices and their consequences.

We may feel ourselves to be in the grip of external circumstances and thus powerless to shape our lives as we wish. It is tempting to get discouraged over unexpected tragedies or during recovery from a negative life experience. Some of us accept a victim role in life and get by on the offerings of others who feel sorry for us. There are advantages to avoiding this approach and, instead, focusing on our own participation in the outcomes of our lives. Most psychologists agree that "taking charge" of one's own life insures more effective adjustment and greater satisfaction in life.

Effective decision making is an important skill to learn if we want to map out a route to our destination. One reason we may put off making decisions is that we tend to be overly harsh in blaming ourselves for our "obvious" bad decisions, a phenomenon known as hindsight bias. In order to be able to tolerate making mistakes, we need to cultivate an attitude that doing so is normal. We may dare to fail, after realizing that occasional failure is unavoidable and potentially valuable. Yet many of us are reluctant to take responsibility for our actions, to make a decision, fearing that these actions may bring blame and self-condemnation.

SOCIAL ADJUSTMENT VERSUS PERSONAL FREEDOM   Every society sets standards for its citizens as to the extent that persons will be allowed freedom to pursue their own interests and desires, as well as to what degree they must conform to societal standards. Sigmund Freud, the founder of psychoanalysis, suggested that individuals must learn to adjust to society and to their lot in life. Behaviorists view people as being controlled by their environment, so that society curbs most antisocial behavior by punishing it. The humanists believe that each individual is born with a moral sense and an inclination to be prosocial. Thus, we need not fear allowing people a great deal of freedom to pursue their own ends. The dispositional approach is a biological view that human dispositions are largely transmitted genetically. Therefore, it is easier to shape the environment to suit the person and to get the person to adjust to his or her situation.

Most likely both adjustment and development of one's own individuality are desirable and feasible. Every society has slowly evolving standards for its citizenry as to what constitutes good behavior and, conversely, what behavior will not be tolerated. Sanctions against unacceptable behavior are a necessary aspect of civilization. The U.S. culture highly regards individualism. Yet, no one can be considered healthy who completely ignores the norms of the culture in which he or she is imbedded. One aspect of being a well-developed person, then, is the ability to get along with others and to find a place for oneself in one's world. Psychological development improves our relationship with ourselves, an outcome that in turn enhances our relationships with other people, with our community, and with the rest of the world.

GETTING TO KNOW YOURSELF.   Without the ability to trust others, we cannot develop intimate relationships, because intimacy is established through *self-disclosure*. Self-disclosure refers to the sharing of our inner thoughts and feelings with another person. Disclosing ourselves to others is one way in which we come to know ourselves more fully. Self-disclosure takes courage, since we risk rejection. In general, the healthier the personality is, the more willingness there is to share about oneself and the less felt need to keep secrets. However, forced awareness is undesirable, since the experience of threat tends to decrease awareness. We can retain our need for privacy by deciding how much we will disclose and when it is appropriate to do so. If we find that we don't trust people in general, we might want to gain an understanding of our fear of others.

We are able to share with others only those things of which we are aware about ourselves. At times, we may discover within ourselves motives, thoughts, and underlying reactions to events going on around us of which we were previously unaware. The Johari Window is a simple model of the levels of awareness between and within human beings.

Learning the Language of Psychologists

psychoanalysis	blame the victim
behaviorism	proactive
humanism	maladaptive
dispositional	self-disclosure
flow	introspection
existentialism	persona
existential isolation	

Chapter Review Questions

1. What is the view of personal growth expressed in Chapter 1?
2. What are existential concerns in general, and which five will be the focus of this text?
3. What is the major advantage of steering clear of the victim role?
4. Why is it often advisable to make a marginal decision rather than none at all?
5. How does hindsight bias affect our feelings about our decisions, once we know their outcome?
6. What did Freud think about the need for individuals to adjust to the demands of society? What would a behaviorist say about this belief? What would be the position of a humanist?
7. Why would a dispositional theorist advise us to find an environment that suits us as we are?
8. What are some benefits that derive from being an active learner?

9. What is the relationship between self-disclosure and intimacy?
10. How can self-disclosure help us know *ourselves* more fully?

ACTIVITIES

1. *LARGE GROUP EXERCISE:* **Getting Acquainted.** Move around the class and try to find students who have had the experiences indicated on your list on pages 42–44.
2. *COMPLETE INDIVIDUALLY:* **Am I Proactive in My Student Role?**
3. *SMALL GROUP EXERCISE:* **Personal Reflections on My Style of Life.**
4. *DYADS EXERCISE:* **Who Am I?** Working in pairs, stick with answering as fully as you can this one question: "Who am I?" In describing yourself to your partner, list as many adjectives as you can to show who you are. (The easiest way most of us describe ourselves is with nouns, such as I am a *husband, father, bookkeeper, golfer, fisherman,* and so on. Try to use adjectives instead, such as *considerate, funny,* etc.) Reveal as many dimensions of your various selves as possible. After each of you has had a turn to describe yourself, write down the answers to the question of who you are. Provide as many answers as possible. Next, eliminate all but five of the descriptions that you have listed. After you have finished, talk with your partner about how difficult or simple this exercise was for you to do. Finally, eliminate all but one of the descriptions. What have you kept, out of all the other possibilities?
5. *COMPLETE INDIVIDUALLY:* **The Psychological Viewpoint Questionnaire.**

Getting Acquainted

Directions: This exercise should help you get acquainted with your classmates. Circulate around the room and ask various persons whether they can sign off on any of the following statements as applying to them. Each class member may sign in the blank space on one or two of the statements, and then you must move on to a new person.

1. Someone who has questioned the grade given him/her by a teacher.   _____

2. An individual who likes to spend time alone on a regular basis.   _____

3. A classmate who regards himself/herself as a victim or an underdog.   _____

4. Someone who has a big decision to make. _____

5. A class member who is an only child. _____

6. A person who personally knows someone who has struggled with suicide. _____

7. Someone who thinks that the woman should offer to pay on the first date in a heterosexual relationship. _____

8. Someone who thinks that househusbands are as acceptable as housewives. _____

9. A class member who wants an equal partnership in marriage. _____

10. Someone who is in favor of euthanasia. _____

11. A person who would like his/her children to follow the same sexual behavior patterns as he/she is doing. _____

12. Someone who believes that divorce is an acceptable solution to an unhappy marriage relationship. _____

13. A classmate who feels that he/she doesn't have time for a romantic relationship right now. _____

14. A person who would speak up if a close friend were doing something illegal. _____

15. Someone who gets angry easily and often. _____

16. Someone who doesn't mind hearing about the successes of peers. _____

17. A class member who made New Year's resolutions this year. _____

18. Someone who avoids speaking up in class whenever possible. _____

19. A person who could describe his/her purpose in life. _____

20. Someone who has had the same career goal since middle school.

21. Someone who is currently in love.

22. A person who believes he/she is a very different person than he/she was five years ago.

23. A classmate who frequently visits professors in their offices.

24. Someone who fears dying more than death itself.

25. Someone who is satisfied with his or her weight.

26. A person who regularly uses a "To-do" list.

27. Someone who enjoys "nonpeople" work.

28. Someone who has spent a Christmas or other holiday alone.

29. A person who would like to become more assertive.

30. A classmate who would like to express feelings more easily.

31. Someone who has narrowly escaped dying.

32. A person who keeps a journal.

33. Someone who has a regular exercise program.

34. A person who thinks sex without love is dissatisfying.

35. Someone who feels he/she doesn't have enough time for relaxation.

36. Someone whose values are similar to those of his/her parents.

37. A person who thinks men should display more courage and strength than should women.

38. A person who frequently remembers his/her dreams. _____

39. A class member who wants to move to get away from local violence. _____

40. Someone who feels happy most of the time. _____

Am I Proactive in My Student Role?

Please indicate your responses to the following statements, by marking:

    1 = if you strongly disagree   3 = if you agree
    2 = if you disagree   4 = if you strongly agree

Leave an item blank if none of the statements is applicable.

1. Outside of class I think about the material presented in my classes. _____

2. I ask questions in class and make comments that come to mind. _____

3. I find it difficult to attend my classes on a regular basis. _____

4. I learn best from the lectures in my classes. _____

5. I learn better in classes that use learning activities (such as small group discussions, projects, and computer use) than in classes that use only lecture. _____

6. I wish there were a way to give my honest, anonymous opinion to my instructors about how the class is going or what I'm learning. _____

7. In most of my classes I am encouraged to think for myself and express my ideas openly. _____

8. Course material in my classes is related to real life situations. _____

9. I take notes during lectures and review them later. _____

10. I take responsibility for learning. _____

11. Take notes during lectures and review them later. _____

12. I can describe my plan for achieving my educational goals. _____

13. I contact the instructor outside of class when I don't understand something. _____

14. I have effective study skills and habits. _____

15. I complete classroom assignments even if I am not required to turn them in. _____

16. I value doing my own thinking instead of relying on what other people think. _____

17. I volunteer feedback to the instructor as to how the classroom experience can better meet my needs. _____

18. I ask around among other students to find instructors who are knowledgeable and enthusiastic, and whose class presentations are well planned. _____

Directions: Read each of the following questons, and then write your answers in the blanks.

19. Do you question the meaning of what you do in school, and what its value is to you in your life? Think about this issue now. What is the value of your school experience in your life?

_____

_____

_____

_____

20. After ideas are presented in class, do you think about them on your own and sometimes share interesting parts with others? If so, what was the last piece of information or classroom experience you shared with someone? If you did not do so, why not?

_____

_____

_____

_____

21. Are you able to disagree with the professor when you would like to? If so, describe the last occasion when you did this, and tell how it turned out. If not, why not?

_____

_____

_____

_____

Personal Reflections on My Style of Life

Directions: Read each of the following questions, and then write your answers in the blanks.

1. What are some of your thoughts and feelings about self-disclosure (opening up to others)? Would you describe yourself as a risk-taker? A trusting person? Do you share your inner self with others? To whom do you disclose your plans for and insecurities about the future? Under what circumstances would you trust others with information about yourself?

   _____

   _____

   _____

   _____

2. Have you ever "enjoyed" the role of the victim? Try to think of an instance when you have had the opportunity to make demands upon others because of your underdog status.

   _____

   _____

   _____

   _____

3. Who are your role models? Who is one person you could use as a model who has overcome an obstacle worse than any you have encountered so far in your life?

   _____

   _____

   _____

   _____

4. Do you have a backlog of unmade decisions? Think about one decision that you currently need to make. How much time do you have before a decision is needed? Are all of the alternatives clear? What will happen if you don't decide? Is there a "right decision"?

   _____

   _____

   _____

   _____

5. Describe your attitude toward making mistakes, both when you make them and when others do.

   _____

_____

_____

_____

6. Do you consider yourself responsible for how your life is going right now? If so, to what extent, and if not, who or what is more responsible than you are?

_____

_____

_____

_____

7. Do you seem to "fit in" to the society in which you live? In what ways is this the case, and to what extent is this not the case?

_____

_____

_____

_____

8. Do you have a philosophy about fortuitous disasters—bad things that simply happen to people? Write below your explanation of the causes of such unfortunate and apparently undeserved calamities.

_____

_____

_____

_____

9. What do you want for yourself from the experience of taking this course? Think about what problems and personal concerns you are willing to explore. Identify one goal for yourself that you intend to accomplish by the end of this course and state it below.

_____

_____

_____

_____

10. Are there some areas in your life where you feel in charge of things, while in other areas, you feel more-or-less swept along by outside forces? Try to think of an example of each.

_____

_____

_____

_____

11. Complete the following sentence: "In general, I view life as . . ."

_____

_____

_____

_____

12. Complete the following sentence: "I want to know . . ."

_____

_____

_____

_____

13. Complete the following sentence: "I usually feel awkward when . . ."

_____

_____

_____

_____

14. Complete the following sentence: "What I want most in life is . . ."

_____

_____

_____

_____

The Psychological Viewpoint Questionnaire

Psychologist William R. Miller of the University of New Mexico has constructed a Psychological Viewpoint Questionnaire that you can use to clarify some of your beliefs about human nature. It will also tell you with what major psychological theories you are likely to find yourself in sympathy as you read this chapter.

Directions: Read each of the following statements, and decide whether you agree more than you disagree or whether you disagree more than you agree with each one. Write an *A* next to those statements with which you agree more than disagree, and write *D* next to those statements with which you disagree more than agree. Express your opinion about every statement even though you may have some trouble deciding in some cases.

1. In attempting to understand human beings, one should stick to what can be directly observed and avoid theory or concepts that cannot be seen or observed. _____

2. Events taking place in the present are systematically linked to events that have occurred in one's past. _____

3. A specific piece of human behavior cannot be understood without considering the person and his or her life as a whole. _____

4. People are basically good (as opposed to neutral or evil). If left to a natural state without external controls, they seek health and personal growth while respecting the right of others to do the same. _____

5. A person's character is largely determined before he or she reaches adulthood. The only changes that one can expect from an adult are relatively small ones, and these occur slowly and over time. _____

6. General laws of behavior and experience that apply to all people are not very helpful if you want to understand a particular individual. _____

7. Much behavior, both normal and abnormal, is directed by unconscious impulses and motivations. _____

8. Aggression is an inherent and inescapable part of human nature. _____

9. People are capable of making major and lasting changes in themselves within a relatively brief period of time. _____

10. Human behavior can be understood as a continuous attempt to increase pleasure and to avoid pain and discomfort. _____

11. There are no values inherent in human nature or the human condition—only those that are discovered or learned through experience. _____

12. Learning processes play a major determining role in the formation of personality and human behavior. _____

13. Events that occur early in life are more important in determining one's adult personality and behavior than are similar events occurring after the person has reached adulthood. _____

14. Looking inside a person for the causes of behavior (for needs, impulses, and motivations) is probably more misleading than enlightening. _____

15. The use of scientific experiments is not an appropriate way to try to understand the psychology of human beings. _____

16. People are neither inherently good nor basically selfish. _____

17. In order to change a present pattern of behavior, it is important for the person to explore the past, particularly childhood, to find the causes of the behavior. _____

18. Little or none of what people do is the result of free will. Behavior is controlled by lawful principles, and free choice is an illusion. _____

19. The therapist who wants to help a person change should not give direct advice or suggestions. Rather, the best approach is for the therapist to allow the person to talk and explore his or her feelings without direction or evaluation. _____

20. A person is free to be what he or she wants to be. _____

Scoring the Psychological Viewpoint Questionnaire

Following are twenty lines of letters corresponding to the twenty items of the Psychological Viewpoint Questionnaire. For each item, circle all of the *A*s in that row if you agreed with the statement, or circle all of the *D*s in that row if you disagreed with the statement. (B = Behavioral, E = Existential, H = Humanistic, P = Psychoanalytic.)

Item	B	E	H	P
1.	A	A	D	D
2.	A	D	D	A
3.	D	A	A	A
4.	D	D	A	D
5.	D	D	D	A
6.	D	A	A	D
7.	D	D	D	A
8.	D	D	D	A
9.	A	A	A	D
10.	A	D	D	A
11.	A	A	D	D
12.	A	D	D	A
13.	D	D	D	A
14.	A	D	D	D
15.	D	A	D	D

16.	A	A	D	D
17.	D	D	D	A
18.	A	D	D	A
19.	D	A	A	A
20.	D	A	A	D
Totals:	—	—	—	—

Reprinted by permission from the author, William R. Miller.

2

Self

He who knows others is clever, he who knows himself is enlightened.
—Lao-tzu

➤ PREVIEW QUESTIONS: How does one develop a sense of self? What factors enhance and diminish self-esteem? What does it mean to be self-actualized? How did Carl Rogers describe the fully functioning person? How does physical appearance affect self-esteem?

➤ INTRODUCTION: WHAT IS SELF?

Who are you, *really?* In order to know and accept others, you must come to terms with yourself, an undertaking that is easier said than done. We begin with an exploration of the self.

In recent years, the self has become an area of focus in both theory and research in psychology. The self could be described as the awareness on the part of an individual of his or her identity. Before 1960, there were relatively few references to the self in psychology. Freud's theory of psychoanalysis did not specifically have a concept of self, although the ego is roughly equivalent. Until recently the behavioral theories also did not make use of such an idea. It was primarily the humanists who proposed to help people with their problems through use of the notion of self.

Self-concept refers to our view of ourselves. It is our perception of our own personality traits and consists of our ideas and feelings about who we are (Potkay & Allen, 1986). In terms of the Johari Window discussed earlier (Chapter 1), one's self-concept would include Quadrants 1 and 3, which encompass all things known about oneself, whether or not known to others. Self-concept includes both the way we would ideally like to be and the degree to which we accept ourselves as we are. Whatever our opinion of ourselves, we tend to behave in ways that persuade people to adopt our view of ourselves. Many psychologists, particularly those who are humanistic, believe that self-concept has a major impact on our behavior and our subjective sense of well-being.

We could say that any given individual has several facets of self-concept. We may be proud of our artistic talent, but feel woefully inadequate in keeping up with current events in the nation and the world.

Our self-concept has a measure of stability, because once we have a particular view of ourselves, we tend to selectively attend to feedback from the external world which confirms our self-concept, and ignore information we come across that contradicts our current beliefs about ourselves.

Self-esteem can be defined as a feeling of personal competence and an evaluation of our personal worth. It reflects the judgment we make of our ability to cope with the challenges of life, that is, our estimation as to whether we can handle the problems of day-to-day living and to stand up for our own interests and needs. Self-esteem can affect virtually every aspect of our lives. When we have high self-esteem, we feel competent and worthy of happiness. With low self-esteem, we feel somehow inappropriate and out of place (Branden, 1986). How we feel about ourselves plays a major part in determining our professional success, how comfortable we are in social situations, and how we interact in relationships.

Positive self-esteem has been compared with the immune system (Branden, 1984), in that a healthy sense of self-esteem provides resistance, resilience, and a capacity for psychological regeneration. When self-esteem is low, the person's ability to face life's adversities is diminished. Such a person cannot withstand the same vicissitudes as might a hardier person. He or she is oriented more toward avoiding pain than in seeking joy.

➤ HUMANISM AND THE SELF

Humanism developed during the 1950s. It was called the "third force" in psychology by its founder, Abraham Maslow, because humanistic psychology emphasizes the healthy side of personality and thus offered an alternative to the pessimistic **determinism** of Freudian psychoanalysis (Chapter 3), as well as to the mechanistic determinism of behaviorism (Chapter 8). Both psychoanalysis and behaviorism viewed a person's actions as controlled by forces outside his or her conscious choice. Psychoanalysts proposed that unconscious drives motivate much of what people do, whereas the behaviorists saw the environment as the major influence on human behavior. Humanists believe that human beings have **free will**, which is the opposite of determinism, and contend that behavior is primarily organized around the positive motive of self-fulfillment. They believe, furthermore, that behavior is directed by the volition of the individual regardless of external influences.

The theoretical views of Abraham Maslow and Carl Rogers lie at the center of the humanistic movement. Viktor Frankl, a psychotherapist with a humanistic existential orientation, will also be discussed in this chapter. In addition, the ideas of Nathaniel Branden, a humanistic psychotherapist who has specialized in the study of self-esteem, will be presented. The relevance of psychoanalysis and behaviorism to self-development will be explained in later chapters.

Maslow, Rogers, and Branden agreed that a healthy self-esteem is a necessary precondition for life satisfaction. All three men viewed the formation of a purpose in life as an important component of well-being, as did Frankl. Humanists agree that an accurate perception of reality is crucial to becoming one's best possible self. Of the three main schools of thought in clinical psychology, psychoanalysis, behaviorism, and humanism, the humanists have placed the greatest emphasis on the impact that one's self-evaluation has on all areas of one's life.

Abraham Maslow (1908–1970)

Maslow started his career as a psychoanalyst and then trained as a behaviorist. Upon the birth of his first child, Maslow rejected behaviorism as "foolish" (Maslow, 1976, p. 163), as it does not explain how a person learns to become a good human being, nor how one can go about becoming his or her best possible self.

Maslow criticized the psychologists who base their ideas about human nature on their clinical observations with their patients. Maslow studied healthy, creative, and productive people. He wondered how those who seemed to be using almost all of their talents and potentials were different from the average person. To answer this question, he began studying the lives of great men and women, such as Thomas Jefferson, Albert Einstein, William James, Benedict de Spinoza, Jane Addams, Eleanor Roosevelt, Abraham Lincoln, John Muir, Ludwig von Beethoven, Walt Whitman, Henry David Thoreau, Albert Schweitzer, Aldous Huxley, and so on. Maslow chose historical figures and contemporaries who met his conception of psychological health. In all, a total of thirty-seven people made up his list of "good specimens."

As a result of his investigation, Maslow developed the concept of **self-actualization.** When living a good life, human beings exhibit certain characteristic attitudes and behaviors, which Maslow described. This optimal level of functioning enabled Maslow's good specimens to make full use of their potential.

QUESTIONS: *Before you read further, what would you guess are the qualities of self-actualized people? Whom do you think of as living life to the fullest?*

HIERARCHY OF NEEDS   Maslow suggested that the needs that motivate human behavior are ordered in a hierarchy from basic needs that are required for mere survival to qualities that promote optimal levels of personality functioning. He proposed that two types of needs motivate us: deficiency needs and growth needs. There are three levels of deficiency needs. On the most basic level are physiological needs, such as the physical requirements of food, water, and air. On the second level of needs are those involving safety and security. These might be needs for shelter and protection against danger, threat, or deprivation. A final deficiency need, that for love and belongingness, refers to the need of human beings to affiliate with one another. We seek acceptance from friends, family, and other social groups.

Once these basic needs are met, we can go on to the growth needs, the expression of which makes us distinctly human. Higher needs cannot emerge until lower ones have first been satisfied. If satisfaction of a particular

SAFETY AND SECURITY NEEDS

Dear Megan,

I was hoping you'd be home, as I wanted to talk with you further about your fear of being hurt by someone who might attempt to rob your workplace. Your friends have told you some horror stories, and you seemed to be pretty worried.

One of the hard things about being human is that we are smart enough to realize that there are dangers all around us, and that we don't really know when someday we might be in the wrong place at the wrong time, through no fault of our own, and get hurt or killed. Even though this is unlikely to happen, the possibility of it still bothers us.

I think there are three things we need to do to cope with this reality: (1) be careful, (2) have courage, and (3) have faith.

First, we can cut down our chances of being harmed by not engaging in high-risk behaviors. For example, the fact that you don't drink means that you won't be driving around drunk (a high-risk behavior) and that you won't ever be too drunk to defend or protect yourself should you get into a pickle. Young people who get drunk or high are much more vulnerable to being taken advantage of. If you want some further examples of this, you can read the book *Go Ask Alice*, which is by an anonymous author.

Second, have courage. You can't really enjoy your life if you are continuously terrified that something might happen to you. Once you have done the first step, and decided to take good care of yourself, you have to realize that you don't really control everything going on around you. Living *always* involves risk. You can't get around it.

That's where the faith aspect comes in. You can have faith in God's protection, or you can have faith in your fellow human beings, because the vast majority of them wouldn't hurt you for anything. You can even have faith in the statistics which tell us how few murders there are, and how rare it is for robbers to enter an occupied store and hurt the employees.

I hope this helps. If not, we can talk more next time you and I are home together.

Love,
Mom

need is a chronic problem, then the next highest need in the hierarchy will fail to develop full potency. People whose biological needs are satisfied are likely to turn to poetry, photography, art, music, or some other meaningful way to spend their energies and occupy their time. The first growth need on the hierarchy is the need for self-esteem. We seek recognition and status; a feeling of being worthwhile.

After we have achieved a stable and positive sense of self-esteem, we are available to experience the pinnacle of being human; in other words, we become

self-actualized. When we reach this state, we emerge as the best person possible. With this motive comes understanding, creativity, aesthetic appreciation, and self-realization. In Maslow's words, self actualization

> . . . may be loosely described as the full use and exploitation of talents, capacities, potentialities, etc. Such people seem to be fulfilling themselves and to be doing the best that they are capable of doing, reminding us of Nietzsche's exhortation, "Become what thou art!" (Maslow, 1971, p. 150)

PEAK EXPERIENCES   The self-actualized person has "peak experiences." These are mystic states characterized by feelings of limitless horizons opening. There is often a loss of time sense. One who has undergone such moments comes away from them feeling that the world "looks different." As Maslow (in Gordon, 1968) put it,

> The lovers come closer to forming a unit rather than two people, the creator becomes one with his work being created, the mother feels one with her child, the appreciator becomes the music (and it becomes him) or the painting, or the dance, the astronomer is "out there" with the stars (rather than a separateness peering across an abyss at another separateness through a telescope-keyhole) (p. 276)

To explain peak experiences, Maslow referred to William James's (1902) description of religious experiences. According to James, there are four identifiable characteristics of religious or mystical states. The first characteristic is ineffability, which is something indescribable, so that it must be experienced individually and cannot easily be shared or explained to others. The second is a noetic quality; *noetic* comes from a Greek word meaning "intellect." According to James, a mystic experience has an intellectual quality, which seeks "truth." The third is transiency, so that the state does not last long before ordinary reality resumes. The fourth is passivity, in which the person has the experience that his or her own will is being suspended or that something else holds power over him or her.

According to Maslow's findings, the easiest and most common ways of getting peak experiences are through music, dancing, and sex. However, "there are many paths to heaven" (p. 169), including inspiration gained from a beautiful meadow or an intellectual insight. One typical "trigger" for peak experiences appears to be any encounter with excellence, goodness, truth, or perfection. The person has a vision of another level of living, which becomes a reference point, a place one wants to return to or build upon.

Another way to explain peak experiences is to say that they change one's frame of reference. The person comes away from a peak experience feeling more integrated, whole, and unified—more at one with the world, as if the person were at the peak of his or her power, more fully oneself. Such an individual may feel free of inhibitions, blocks, doubts, and self-criticisms. Studying history, anthropology, philosophy, or science gives one a new perspective on the human condition and of one's own place in the big picture, the landscape of human development. Such moments of revelation are gained either by being the discoverer of something new in one's field or by reading about such a discovery. Intellectual illumination, or understanding, is a reliable source of peak experiences. If we are conscious enough and philosophical enough about what we are doing to use those occasions that most easily produce rapture experiences, we should be able to enjoy peak experiences. Maslow took the existence of peak experiences as evidence that human beings have a higher and transcendent nature.

Maslow discovered that ordinary people, not exclusively self-actualized people, have peak experiences. However, some people resist them. They respond defensively, trying to escape or avoid such unusual happenings. Maslow believed that this tendency to stay clear of potential peak experiences cuts such persons off from an important spiritual aspect of life.

SELF-ACTUALIZATION   From his study of highly productive people, Maslow identified characteristics of the self-actualizing individual. Some of these qualities are listed below:

1. *Self-awareness.* Maslow's subjects generally had an accurate perception of reality. They displayed an ethical awareness and tended to be free of inhibitions, blocks, doubts, and self-criticisms. These subjects sought to express fully their personalities in any activity that they undertook. Also, they possessed an unusual ability to detect phony and dishonest behavior.

2. *A Freedom to be and to express one's potential.* Self-actualizers are inventive. They do not strive merely for survival but are motivated by a desire to know and to satisfy curiosity. The epitome of self-actualization is "the desire to become more and more what one idiosyncratically is, to become everything that one is capable of becoming (Maslow, 1970, p. 46). Maslow believed that everyone has potential for "greatness," but most people fear becoming all that they might be. Daring to try requires a willingness to shoulder the responsibility for failure.

3. *Basic honesty and caring.* Self-actualizers accept all kinds of information without distorting it to fit their desires and fears. They also display a sense of social interest, a concern for the welfare of others, as well as a capacity for love and fusion with another. Likewise, they have the ability to love and respect themselves.

4. *Detachment and individuality.* Maslow found that self-actualizing people have a need for privacy. Although they enjoy their relationships with significant others, they need time alone (Sumerlin & Bundrick, 1996).

Maslow's subjects exhibited a resistance to blind conformity. They were involved in a search for purpose and meaning, and had attained an acceptance of themselves and others. Overall, they felt a comfort with being in the world.

Creative, innocent, and healthy people are in the process of becoming completely themselves; they are more real, authentic, and less influenced by a need to placate others. Such people are able to free themselves from the distractions, fears, and petty influences imposed by other people and to devote themselves to whatever task is at hand.

5. *Innocence.* Maslow believed that people are inherently good and are capable of developing in healthy ways if given a benevolent environment in which their inborn potential can be expressed. He regarded the truly healthy personality as one that possesses sufficient personal fortitude and creativity to be "innocent." Innocence, in the sense that Maslow used the term, refers to the healthy personality's capacity to live without pretense, to be genuinely free of guilt in thought, word, and action. Self-actualizers have a freshness of appreciation when encountering new ideas or people, a spontaneity, and a childlike sense of wonder. This innocence is an expression of human nature. Maslow (1971) explained it thus:

> The great discoveries Freud made, we can now add to. His one big mistake, which we are correcting now, is that he thought of the unconscious merely as undesirable evil. But unconsciousness carries in it also the roots of creativeness, of joy, of happiness, of goodness, of its own human ethics and values. We know that there is such a thing as a healthy unconscious as well as an unhealthy one. (p. 167)

A general openness to new experiences, including peak experiences, is another aspect of the innocence described by Maslow. The most favorable frame of mind for preparing the way to bring about a peak experience is one of receptivity, which is a state something like passivity, or surrender, a willingness to let things happen without interfering.

6. *Commitment to a purpose.* Maslow found that those he identified as self-actualizers generally had a mission to fulfill in life, some project that made their lives rich with meaning. They tended to focus on problems external to themselves and to invest energy in "causes." They seemed to be in quest of truth, beauty, and other lofty purposes that gave their lives meaning. Maslow concluded that to be truly self-actualizing, one must be committed to long-term goals. On the other hand, some people suffer from the "existential" neuroses of being without direction.

7. *Absence of fear.* Maslow described his subjects as less afraid than most people of what others would want from them or think of them. The self-actualizers were more concerned about self-approval but also seemed to have crossed some threshold in that they *did* basically approve of themselves. Thus, they went through their lives with confidence. In comparison with average people, Maslow found his subjects to be less concerned about their own thoughts even when their ideas were "wild" or "crazy." Self-actualizers were also less afraid of being overwhelmed by emotion.

8. *A sense of humor.* Maslow (1987) described self-actualizers as "cheerful, humorous, and playful" (p. 154). His subjects tended to have a philosophical sense of humor, in that they could laugh at themselves as well as at the human condition. They gracefully accepted their own shortcomings and those of others. Because of his subjects' ability to gain perspective on things, their sense of humor was without hostile overtones.

Maslow did not make many recommendations on how to become self-actualized, but the following suggestions might be made in reference to his writings (Maslow, 1967, 1971, 1987):

1. Be flexible; willing to change: Ask yourself whether you are happy with yourself and your life.
2. Take responsibility for your life, and don't blame others for your shortcomings.
3. Discover who you are; know your strengths and weaknesses.
4. Learn to trust your own feelings rather than to judge yourself by other people's standards.
5. See things the way they really are and not the way you would like them to be.
6. Commit yourself to what you are doing and get involved with problems outside yourself.

Self-actualization is an ongoing process, not an end-point at which a person arrives once and for all. Yet, once a person achieves a stable sense of self-esteem, he or she is in a position to enjoy peak experiences as an ongoing pleasure in life.

Maslow acknowledged that his grand theory lacked sufficient data to verify its veracity. His view of human nature was subjective and optimistic rather than scientific. The support for his theory came from biographical studies. Even so, one criterion for a good theory is that it is fruitful. That is, good theories must generate a great deal of research. Maslow's research has certainly done that.

Viktor Frankl (1905–1997)

In Maslow's view, self-esteem must precede achievement and self-fulfillment. This self-fulfillment, or self-actualization, is the ultimate human experience. Humanistic existentialist psychiatrist Viktor Frankl disagreed, suggesting that **self-transcendence** is a higher goal than self-actualization. He proposed that the real aim of human existence cannot be found in self-actualization. Self-transcendence is the need to rise above narrow absorption with the self. One achieves self-transcendence by overlooking oneself and by giving of oneself to other people and good causes. Finding meaning involves, in part, transcending personal interests. A fulfilling life involves not only actualizing one's own potential but also focusing outward and making a difference in the lives of others. Careful consideration of our situation will often lead us to the conclusion that our personal interests are not separate from the interests of others.

Making self-actualization (or happiness) the direct object of our pursuit, in Frankl's view, is ultimately self-defeating. Such fulfillment can occur only as "the unintended effect of self-transcendence." The proper perspective on life, Frankl believed, is not what it can give us but what it expects *from* us. President John F. Kennedy's famous statement "Ask not what your country can do for you, but what you can do for your country" would seem to be expressing a similar sentiment (Ruggiero, 1995).

Daniel Yankelovich (1981) also critiqued Maslow's theory, and concluded that it contained two flaws. The first flaw is that self-fulfillment is of utmost importance and that individuals are encouraged to focus on their inner needs as the key to self-fulfillment. The second is that Maslow's hierarchy implies that economic security is a precondition to satisfying the human spirit. To the contrary, warm relations with others and doing good works on behalf of one's community are primary sources of meaning in one's life, according to Yankelovich, and do not require much in the way of financial resources.

To develop further our thoughts on self-actualization, let us consider Frankl's and Yankelovich's comments. It seems that there is room for Frankl's, Yankelovich's, and Maslow's perspectives. Recall that Maslow found self-actualized persons to be goal-directed and often dedicated to causes. We want to become self-aware, as well as to contribute to the well-being of others. Together these purposes could define a productive and satisfying life. Further, Maslow's hierarchy contemplates the need for love and belongingness as a basic human need. Close, loving relationships are also at the heart of both Frankl's and Yankelovich's philosophy as to what creates meaning and has value in life.

Carl Rogers (1902–1987)

Carl Rogers is second only to Abraham Maslow in being considered a founder of the humanistic movement. He assumed that basic human nature is positive and that there is nothing inherently negative or evil about humans. In Rogers's view, all human behavior has the underlying motive of actualizing and maintaining the individual. He suggested that if we are not forced into socially constructed molds but rather are accepted for what we are, we will live in ways that enhance both ourselves and society. According to Rogers, human beings basically need and want both personal fulfillment and close, intimate relationships with others. He believed that if people are freed from restricting, corrupting social influences, they can achieve a high level of personal and interpersonal functioning. With this freedom, people can avoid the distortions of reality that they employ to protect themselves but that also prevent their achievement of ever-greater growth and fulfillment.

UNCONDITIONAL POSITIVE REGARD VERSUS CONDITIONS OF WORTH   To attain a high level of adjustment, the individual needs to experience **unconditional positive regard,** a term Rogers used to express a sense of being valued for oneself regardless of the degree to which specific behaviors are approved or disapproved by parents or significant others. Positive regard means that we receive acceptance, respect, sympathy, warmth, and love from significant others. The love of a parent for a child often has this unconditional quality. For example, a mother may express verbal disapproval of her child's sloppy table manners, but she will nevertheless communicate her fundamental love and acceptance of the child, who is, after all, just learning how to eat properly. According to Rogers, one should criticize inappropriate action but not the person. His concept of unconditional positive regard is sometimes misunderstood to mean that parents should allow their children to do whatever they want. Rogers recognized that one of the functions of parents is to guide their children toward appropriate behavior. His intention was to have parents teach and discipline children without making them ashamed of themselves.

Conditional positive regard, the acceptance of a person that is dependent on the positive or negative evaluation of that person's actions, leads to the development of **conditions of worth.** Children quite often have conditions of worth placed upon them by parents and society. When this is the case, they feel appreciated and accepted only conditionally, when certain expected behaviors are performed. Actions and feelings are categorized by such children as either good or bad, depending on whether they bring approval or punishment coming from parents or significant others.

When we are preoccupied with conditions of worth, we tend to be defensive, as well as closed off from new experiences and inclined to ignore internal cues. We lose contact with real experiences, reporting what we "should" feel, rather than what we actually feel. It is quite normal to behave differently than we feel in order to avoid the disapproval of friends, parents, and other important figures. For instance, we may act as though we enjoy a particular movie or a rock group that we actually dislike because we fear that our friends would think less of us if we expressed our real feelings. The problem arises when we begin to deceive ourselves and dissociate from our true feelings. This behavior generates discrepancies between the objective world and our subjective world, producing anxiety, which in turn blocks self-actualization.

It is important for a person to replace learned conditions of worth with trust of his or her inner urges and intuitions. Rogers's fundamental faith in the goodness of human nature led him to believe that human beings can be trusted to behave well when following their inclinations.

QUESTION: *One of the ways in which you can understand condition of worth is to examine admonitions you heard when growing up. What are some of the "shoulds" or "don'ts" you heard as a child?*

CONGRUENCE VERSUS INCONGRUENCE Rogers viewed the self-concept as the integrating core of personality. All experiences are organized and interpreted around a person's self-concept, which tends to filter perceptions so that they confirm the person's view of himself or herself. When emotions and self-concept are "congruent," or integrated, the person can engage in self-actualization.

Rogers also believed that there needs to be **congruence** within the person. That is, there should be agreement or correspondence among our **ideal self,** which represents who we want to be; the **true self,** which is who we really are; and our **self-image,** which reflects whom we see ourselves as being. If these three aspects are not in congruence with one another, inner conflicts arise within a person. Personality is a result of the interaction of these three aspects of self and is affected by the degree of congruence among the three.

Rogers's different selves correspond to some extent to the quandrants of the Johari Window that was discussed in Chapter 1. The "self" or "true self" contains all four quadrants, all aspects of self, whether known or unknown to self or whether known or unknown to others. Self-image includes all of quadrants 1 and 3, all those aspects of ourselves of which we are aware. The ideal self might be a subset of quadrants 1 and 3, and may dwell to a greater extent in quadrant 3, if we are reluctant to share with others the way we would like to be.

According to Rogers, experiences that match the self-image are admitted to consciousness and contribute to gradual changes in the self. Psychologically well-adjusted people generally perceive themselves and their environment as other people do. This agreement between self-perception and the perception that others have of us allows us to be with others without feeling defensive. Information or feelings inconsistent with the self-image are said to be incongruent. Experiences that are seriously incongruent with the self-image can be threatening and are often denied conscious recognition. Blocking, denying, or distorting experiences prevents the self from changing and creates a gulf between the self-image and reality. As the self-image grows more unrealistic, the incongruent person becomes confused, vulnerable, dissatisfied, or seriously maladjusted.

Whereas Freud contended that human beings employ defense mechanisms to ward off threat and anxiety from sexual and aggressive impulses, Rogers thought that defensive processes were caused by experiences that are incompatible with one's self-concept. A defensive behavior indicates incongruence between the ideal self and the true self, which leads to a faulty self-image. To compensate for this fault, some aspects of the true self are denied. Because of these unhealthy adjustments, it is impossible for the person to see himself or herself as he or she truly is, a combination that ultimately forms a vicious cycle of perceptual distortion and denial. For example, if Bob gets feedback from his girlfriend that he is a bit too quick to lose his temper, he may rationalize that she is merely trying to interfere with his spontaneous self-expression. Further, he may fail to recall that he has received this feedback before from someone else.

If the three elements of self are out of sync, the person may be very defensive about his or her shortcomings and may project them onto other people. A great deal of human behavior can be understood as an attempt to maintain consistency between one's self-image and one's actions. The Rogersian view of personality might be summarized as a process of maximizing potential by accepting information about oneself as realistically and honestly as possible.

CLIENT-CENTERED THERAPY   Rogers built his entire theory and practice of psychotherapy on the concept of the "fully functioning person," a concept much like Maslow's self-actualizing person. The fully functioning person is one who has achieved an openness to feelings and experiences and who has learned to trust inner urges and intuitions. This person is sensitive and responsive to inner sensations, feelings, thoughts, and so on, as well as to the external environment.

Rogers developed **client-centered therapy,** basing his ideas on his work with clients. The goal of client-centered therapy is to release the inherent capacity in a potentially competent individual. Whereas psychoanalysis involves the exploration of long-forgotten or repressed childhood experiences, humanistic therapy emphasizes the client's current life circumstances and places less importance on the circumstances of the person's childhood. Unlike psychoanalysis, client-centered therapy does not address unconscious material, but instead focuses on the client's conscious thoughts and feelings.

A client-centered therapist's job is to create an "atmosphere of growth" and to help remove obstacles to full functioning. The client needs a source of unconditional positive regard, or complete acceptance. The therapist offers the client this unconditional positive regard by accepting the client for his or her true self, without criticisms or demands for change. This acceptance leads to a dissolving of conditions of worth. Total acceptance by the therapist is the first step toward self-acceptance by the client.

The therapist also responds empathically, that is, the therapist lets the client know that he or she is trying to comprehend how the client views the world. The goal of the counselor is to achieve the internal frame of reference of the client. In this way, the client feels understood, a necessary precondition for feeling accepted by the therapist.

When the client feels validated and experiences empathy from the therapist, the need to deny or distort the true self begins to diminish. The therapist serves as a psychological "mirror" in which the client learns to see himself or herself more clearly. The therapist not only paraphrases the content of what the client says but also reflects back to the client the feelings he or she is communicating. This process leads to the achievement of a self that is congruent with experience. Rogers was convinced that a person armed with a realistic self-image and a new level of self-acceptance would gradually discover solutions to his or her life problems.

A final goal of client-centered therapy is to help people use their insight to guide them rather than to be controlled by external demands. Rogers assumed that an individual can work through his or her own problems if there is enough freedom from self-deception and fear to recognize those problems for what they are. This recognition helps people become who they really are, enabling them to be free for normal growth and development. Their development is directed by an inborn actualizing tendency. Fully functioning people trust themselves. They are free to do what "feels right" at any given moment, fully expecting that they will prove competent to meet any challenge, judge accurately any obstacle, and regulate their behavior realistically as the situation demands.

Human beings do not know their full potential, according to Rogers. They are in a state of "being and becoming," which makes it inappropriate to establish absolute criteria about the level of actualization that can be achieved. Everything possible should be done to promote an atmosphere in which people can continue to develop themselves personally and socially.

QUESTION: *How did Freud and Rogers differ on their views of the purpose of defense mechanisms?*

➤ THE FEELING SELF AND THE THINKING SELF

Whereas Rogers's client-centered therapy and other humanistic therapies have as a goal getting their clients more in touch with their feelings, sometimes psychotherapy aims at the opposite effect. What is desirable for healthy functioning is a balance between feeling and thinking. Patients suffering from mental disorders such as schizoid personality disorder have unusually low levels of emotionality. However, other mental disorders, such as borderline personality disorder, major depression, bipolar disorder (alternating mania and depression), as well as the anxiety disorders, inhibit a person's daily life functioning because of excesses of emotionality. A psychotherapist makes an initial assessment as to whether the client needs to move in the direction of greater or lesser emotionally. A person with schizoid personality disorder may be encouraged to label his feelings in order to become more aware of them, whereas a person with borderline personality disorder may be taught anger management skills, in order to reign in her emotional excesses. The regulation of mood can be achieved through cognitive therapy as well as through medication.

➤ SELF-FULFILLING PROPHECY

The **self-fulfilling prophecy** is a powerful concept in psychology. It refers to a prediction that when made, influences the course of events toward fulfilling the prediction. Our expectation as to how others will behave toward us tends to elicit responses from others that confirm those expectations. This result occurs partly because our anticipation will subtly affect our behavior. For instance, if we believe that people will not like us when they first meet us, we will probably become nervous, shy away from them, not make eye contact, nor initiate conversation. On the other hand, if we believe that people tend to like us when we first meet them, we may greet them enthusiastically, with an expectant smile. Surely these two behaviors would be likely to yield different responses from other people.

The self-fulfilling prophecy works whether the anticipation is positive or negative, so that others tend to live up *or* down to our forecast. Allowing ourselves to believe that a particular change is possible can provide the momentum for effecting that change. Once we experience ourselves differently, others are likely to experience us in a new way.

Our beliefs about both ourselves and others can become self-fulfilling prophecies. Thus, a teacher's belief about his or her lecturing abilities may affect teaching performance, and also the teacher's expectations of the students will be likely to elicit responses in the students that will confirm the teacher's expectation (Rosenthal & Jacobson, 1968). Low expectations do not condemn a competent child to failure, nor do high expectations convert a slow learner into a valedictorian. Still, many studies of the phenomenon have shown that teacher expectations do matter (e.g., Rosenthal, 1991).

Researchers have reported that teachers look, smile, and nod more at students who the teachers have been made to believe have a "high potential" (Babad, Bernieri, & Rosenthal, 1991). Also, teachers may teach more to their "brighter" students, set higher goals for them, call on them, and give them more time to answer (Cooper, 1983; Harris & Rosenthal, 1985, 1986; Jussim, 1986; Jussim & Eccles, 1992).

Another example of the self-fulfilling prophecy comes from research conducted in Great Britain by Scanlon, Luben, Scanlon, & Singleton (1993). The study compared each Friday the thirteenth with each Friday the sixth for a couple of years starting in 1989, looking at the number of emergency room visits from automobile accidents. As many as 52 percent more accident victims were treated on Friday the thirteenth even though fewer cars were driven that day. According to the researchers, the higher accident rate for Friday the thirteenth was probably caused by increased anxiety about the date, which reduced attention to driving so that more accidents resulted.

Such evidence might seem to suggest that our best strategy would be to expect great things from ourselves and from others. However, expectations are something of a double-edged sword. When we have great expectations of others, we shall inevitably suffer disappointment, as other people do not always satisfy our fantasies about them. As with many aspects of human affairs, a balance is desirable here. As to our own behavior, formulating a strategy in keeping with how we would like to behave increases the likelihood that we will actually do it.

➤ SELF-BOUNDARIES

Some psychoanalysts think that the most basic part of the self-concept is a person's sense of an invisible **self-boundary** separating himself or herself from other people and the rest of the environment. The idea of boundaries is based on a definition of what is "self" and what is "not self." It is the region separating these two psychological constructs. Psychological boundaries of the self can be thought of as having properties similar to those of physical boundaries. Good self-boundaries are firm and distinctive, drawing a clear line between self and others, yet not so rigid or impermeable that they block connection with others.

In some close relationships, such as between parent and child or between spouses, the self-other boundary may be so weakened that the person may be unable to discriminate between his or her own feelings and ideas and those of the significant other. A psychological term for this condition is **enmeshment** (Minuchin, 1974). An individual such as this might take on the opinions and attitudes expressed by another, or might be unaware of differences in attitudes between self and a partner or other family member. A depressed mood in one family member would spread by contagion to the others, as would excitement or fear.

Extreme difficulties of this type may result in a dependent personality disorder. A person with this disorder tends to have difficulty making everyday decisions without an excessive amount of advice and reassurance from others. This individual needs others to assume responsibility for most major areas of his or her life, and may have difficulty initiating projects or doing things independently (DSM-IV, 1944).

This dependent way of relating to others seems to invite relationships with those who have an unhealthy desire to control the lives of other persons. In these relationships, the parties show a confusion over personal boundaries when they become unclear about the matter of individual responsibility. Each partner focuses on the other person's actions as prompting his or her own behavior, thus falling into the habit of blaming the other for causing him or her to react in a particular manner. Blaming of this sort blurs the boundaries between self and other in a close relationship. Instead, each partner must retain responsibility for his or her responses to the partner.

Another difficulty that comes about because of weak interpersonal boundaries is that individuals with "boundary issues" may inadvertently but inappropriately tread upon the territory of others. An extreme example of this behavior was portrayed by actor Bill Murray in the film *What About Bob?* Murray played a therapy client who invaded the private life of his newly acquired therapist by locating the therapist on vacation. As one thing led to another, Murray ingratiated himself to the therapist's family to such an extent that he practically became a member of the household, while the besieged therapist did everything he could think of to set limits with this client. In real life, relationships do not tend to get quite so much out of hand, but we may occasionally experience a new friendship or romantic relationship developing with more clinginess or invasiveness than is comfortable.

Loss of self-boundaries is not always a bad thing. To a certain extent, a mother who is attuned to her infant has the quality of merging two selves. During sexual union, lovers commonly experience a psychological oneness; and those having a spiritual communion with a group may feel "one" with the others participating in the ceremony. According to Maslow, the highest level of self-actualization is achieved in those moments when one is able to transcend the self and to merge with the rest of humanity. Maslow's conception is similar to that of Eastern religions, which also place the loss of self or ego at the pinnacle of human consciousness. These religions have developed systematic and lengthy training procedures that facilitate the attainment of this level of consciousness. The loss of boundaries is not maladaptive in these instances because it entails temporary psychological merging in the service of closeness or enlightenment.

Group Psychology and Loss of Personal Boundaries

Some temporary experiences of loss of self-consciousness are not so adaptive. Much aggression is committed by groups, because the group situation seems to amplify aggressive reactions of individual members. One reason offered to explain the violent behavior of group members is the loss of self-awareness, self-consciousness, and personal responsibility that results from an individual's being immersed in a group. This phenomenon, which is known by psychologists as **deindividuation,** tends to occur when people are emotionally aroused and their sense of responsibility is diminished.

QUESTION: *If you could do anything humanly possible with complete assurance that you would not be detected or held responsible, what would you do? Write your answer on a piece of paper. Then continue reading.*

When you have answered the preceding question, consider what you answered when asked what you would do if not pressured by social norms and sanctions. Were you motivated to do something socially positive? Something negative, or even illegal? Perhaps your choice of action would fit neither category. If you were to be your ideal self, the best possible person by all that you judge to fall under the concept of "goodness" in a person, how would you occupy your time if given the preceding opportunity?

David Dodd (1985) used the first question in a research study and reported that the data obtained from several classes fell into eleven content categories. People reported that they would engage in (1) aggression, (2) academic dishonesty, (3) crime, (4) sexual behavior, (5) political activities, (6) social disruption, (7) interpersonal spying, (8) eavesdropping, (9) charity, (10) escapism, (11) travel, and (12) miscellaneous other acts. The answers were also categorized as: 9 percent prosocial, 36 percent antisocial, 19 percent non-normative (counternormative, that is, violating social norms but without specifically helping or hurting others), and 36 percent neutral. The most frequent activities were criminal acts (26 percent), sexual acts (11 percent), and spying behavior (11 percent). The most common single activity was "rob a bank," which accounted for 15 percent of all responses. Apparently, anonymity gives us permission to act more impulsively, whether those impulses are for negative or for positive ends.

Sigmund Freud (1965) discussed this phenomenon, noting that individuals are transformed by group membership, so that they feel, think, and act in a manner quite different from the way they would in a state of isolation. He believed that the emotional ties found in groups stem from identification, which is the earliest expression of an emotional tie with another person.

Freud viewed group members as regressing, allowing themselves to be governed by the unconscious. Groups easily go to extremes. For instance, a trace of antipathy can be quickly transformed into furious hatred. A group cannot tolerate any delay between its desire and the fulfillment of that desire. It has a sense of omnipotence; an awareness of its own great strength. The improbable does not exist for the group that is "feeling its oats." It knows neither doubt nor uncertainty; its members are open to influence and seem to have no critical faculty. Anyone who wishes to stir up a group need not have a logical case to put before it but has only to stir it up with demagoguery. In the mental operations of a group, the function for testing the reality of things falls into the background in comparison with the strength of wishful impulses with the group's emotional charge.

Groups are likewise capable of exalted motives, such as unselfishness and devotion to an ideal. At times we intentionally seek deindividuating group experiences such as dances, worship experiences, and group encounters, where we can enjoy intense positive feelings and a sense of closeness with others. McDougall, in his book on *The Group Mind* (1920), contended that the most remarkable and also the most important result of the formation of a group is the "exaltation or intensification of emotion" produced in every member of it (p. 24). In McDougall's opinion, human emotions are stirred in a group to a pitch that they seldom attain under other conditions; and it is a pleasurable experience for those who are concerned, to surrender themselves so unreservedly to their passions.

In other instances, deindividuation is demoralizing. Studs Terkel (1997), author of the popular book *Working*, has recommended giving mass-production workers personal recognition in order to reduce deindividuation on the job. Philosopher Rick Roderick (1991) claims that Freud's goal for individual patients was to help them make the unreflected areas of their psyches known to them. The person becomes enlightened with self-knowledge. For Roderick, the goal of a mass telecommunications culture such as ours is psychoanalysis in reverse. In post-modern culture, the last remaining parts of the psyche become unconscious. Individuals give up privacy and autonomy to merge with the rest of the public. For instance, with telephone sex, one's deepest fantasies are made public. In either case, whether for better or for worse, and whether it produces pleasurable or unpleasant emotions, deindividuation goes along with diminished self-awareness.

Self-Boundaries and Culture

Culture has an important impact on the way we see ourselves and others (Markus & Kitayama, 1991). The emphasis on firm self-boundaries appears to be a distinctly Western phenomenon. Western societies, particularly the

United States, encourage independent attitudes and behaviors in its citizens. In contrast, there are other cultures, as well as Native Americans in the U.S. culture, that emphasize fluid self-boundaries. The Japanese emphasize the group rather than the individual, yet do not have mob violence, which was just discussed as a potential accompaniment of individuation.

Social ties influence our thoughts, feelings, and motivations. Western culture views the self as an inner entity, occupying an inner space, capable of controlling the body and of actualizing itself. In contrast, many other cultures see the self as more inclusively defined in terms of one's connections with others. In some cultures, there is no individual self; the self is largely a repository for spirits and ancestors. Even within Western culture, there are groups that exhibit a predominance of "we-ness" rather than an encouragement of individuality. The traditional culture of African Americans in the days of slavery provides one example. The sense of community among slaves was demonstrated in the communal nature of their music; there was almost no solo music among the slaves (Levine, 1996). "When Black Americans developed the blues in the late nineteenth and early twentieth centuries, it represented the first African American music in the United States to be dominated by the individual persona of the singer" (p. 153).

The flexibility of the self to perceive individuality or to experience merging is an achievement. Such a person is considered "well centered" and in control of his or her self-boundaries. What is accomplished is that this person can at will withdraw ego investment in things outside the self. As with so many other human characteristics, a balance is desirable between self-awareness and self-consciousness on the one hand, and a sense of connection with people on the other.

QUESTION: *What are some attributes of healthy versus unhealthy ego boundaries?*

➤ Body Image

Physical Attractiveness

One's own physical appearance has an impact on self-concept. As others gaze upon a child and respond to the child's physical appearance and demeanor, the reaction is registered by the child as information about self. These reactions are repeated thousands of times during the child's early development.

Physical attractiveness greatly influences early impressions that others form of us. Physically attractive people are viewed more positively than are less attractive people, a phenomenon referred to by psychologists as the **halo effect.** In a study by Bersheid and Walster (1972), subjects were shown pictures of men and women of varying degrees of physical attractiveness and were asked to rate their personality traits. The physically attractive people were viewed as more sensitive, kind, interesting, strong, poised, modest, sociable, intelligent, witty, honest, more sexually responsive, happy, successful, and less socially deviant than were the average-looking people. Although beauty is a factor in initial acquaintance, more substantial personal qualities become important later in the relationship. Still, as Aristotle is reputed to have said, "Beauty is a greater recommendation than any letter of introduction."

Physical attractiveness is to some extent under our control, as with our weight, physical fitness, facial expression, and care taken in grooming. Yet, there is much about our physical self that we cannot change, such as height and other aspects of our bone structure. A person's self-concept can be damaged as a result of physical deformity. In William Shakespeare's play *Richard III*, the main character provides an extreme example of an individual steeped in resentment over having been cursed with an ugly physical form:

> But I, that am not shaped for sportive tricks,
> Nor made to court an amorous looking-glass;
> I, that am rudely stamp'd, and want love's majesty
> I, that am curtail'd of this fair proportion,
> Cheated of feature by dissembling Nature,
> Deform'd, unfinish'd, sent before my time
> Into this breathing world, scarce half made up,
> And that so lamely and unfashionable,
> That dogs bark at me as I half by them;
>
> And therefore, since I cannot prove a lover,
> To entertain these fair well-spoken days,
> I am determined to prove a villain,
> And hate the idle pleasure of these days.

Richard III's soliloquy says, in essence, "Nature has done me a grievous wrong in denying me that beauty of form that wins human love. Life owes me reparation for this, and I will see that I get it. I have a right to be an exception, to overstep those rules for appropriate behavior set by my culture. I may do wrong myself, since wrong has been done to me." For another fictional example of coping with a physical disadvantage, see the box on facing page.

Weight and Physical Attractiveness

One aspect of physical attractiveness over which we do exert a measure of control is our weight. Dramatic overeating or self-starvation are signs of psychological disturbance. Parents often encourage overeating in their children, as they associate feeding their children with loving and providing for them. Cranky children, who have been appeased by the parents with food, may learn to regard unpleasant emotions as cues to eat and may continue overeating into adulthood. This association can create a vicious cycle of feeling down

THE DWARF
By Ray Bradbury

Ray Bradbury wrote a short story involving a circus, in which one of the attractions was a house of mirrors. Some of the mirrors were distorted so that they made people look short and fat, while other mirrors distorted the human body the other way to make it look tall and thin.

As the story opens, a male attendant who sells tickets to the house of mirrors is talking with a woman who also works for the circus, when a dwarf walks up to buy a ticket. After the dwarf begins his walk through the pathways of mirrors, the attendant remarks that this same dwarf visits the house of mirrors late every night, long after most people have gone home from the circus. The attendant then gets a mischievous, or perhaps malevolent, look on his face and motions for his female coworker to follow him as he quietly trails after the dwarf from the other side of the mirrored hallway.

The two circus workers catch up with the dwarf, who is now in a room completely lined with the distorted mirrors that would make a normal-size person tall and thin but that make the dwarf look to be of normal height. The dwarf is enjoying himself immensely, pirouetting in front of the mirrors, examining himself as he moves this way and that.

The female coworker is filled with compassion and tracks down the dwarf at his residence. She finds him to be an author, who spends most of his life cooped up in his room and who goes out only when necessary, or when he makes his nightly pilgrimage to the circus. The woman decides to try to arrange for the dwarf to have one of the extra circus mirrors at his home, much to the objection of her coworker, who wants the income from selling tickets to the dwarf.

How would you finish this story?

because one is unhappy with one's overweight appearance, and then being is prompted to eat as a method of self-soothing.

In contrast to the problem of obesity, some people respond to emotional distress by becoming chronically underweight. Not all cultures place so much emphasis on slenderness as an important component of physical beauty as does the U.S. culture. As a result, the eating disorder anorexia nervosa is found in the United States and other cultures that place a similar emphasis on slenderness as a measure of physical beauty of women, but is not found in societies that deemphasize the amount of body fat as a standard of attractiveness.

Anorexia is a nervous loss of appetite, or self-starvation, which is generally caused by an obsessive fear of gaining weight, usually in women or adolescent girls. This problem affects as many as one in one hundred females between ages 12 and 18. Only about 5 percent of anorexics are males. Typically, the problem starts with normal dieting that gradually begins to dominate the person's life. It may be caused by conflicts about maturing sexually. By starving themselves, adolescent girls can limit figure development and prevent menstruation. This behavior symbolically delays the time when they must face adult responsibilities.

Many anorexics continue to feel hunger and struggle to starve themselves. In time, anorexics suffer physical weakness and a dangerous risk of infection. From 5 to 18 percent die of malnutrition or related health problems. Although some victims realize the harm they are causing to themselves through excessive dieting, they feel powerless to stop. Turn to the end of this chapter for the Fear of Fat Scale, which can help you assess your level of concern about gaining weight.

A second destructive method of coping with unwanted weight gain is bulimia nervosa. Bulimics typically gorge on food and then induce vomiting or take laxatives to avoid gaining weight. Alternatively, they may attempt to control weight gain by compulsive exercise. Unlike those suffering from anorexia, bulimics are typically at around normal weight.

Binge eating may represent an attempt to escape from self-awareness by shifting attention from the self to food (Baumeister, 1989; Heatherton et al., 1992). Perhaps a better alternative would be to focus on the source of stress and take direct action to reduce or remove it (Cohen, 1979).

As with anorexia, bulimia is far more prevalent in women than in men. A recent study of college women found that 5 percent are bulimic (Hart & Ollendick, 1985). This disorder may cause numerous health problems, including sore throat, hair loss, muscle spasms, tooth decay, swelling of the salivary glands, menstrual irregularity, loss of sex drive, and even heart attack.

The Benefits of Regular Exercise

A healthy way to maintain one's desired weight is through regular exercise. Ornstein & Sobel (1993) claimed that physical activity is the key to successful weight maintenance. Following exercise, metabolic rate stays up for as long as twenty-four hours, with the result that extra calories are burned even after the exercise stops. In contrast, dieting lowers metabolism, so that the body uses calories in a more efficient manner. Finally, "exercise seems to readjust the body's set point for fat. Signals are sent to the brain to reduce the amount of fat stored in adipose tissue, so fat levels drop naturally" (p. 94).

Human beings need some daily exercise or physical activity, not just for weight control but for optimal health. The type and the amount of exercise that have been shown beneficial to health involve about half an hour a day of moderate exertion. Many pleasant activities such as walking, bicycling, dancing, tennis, gardening, and even lovemaking are sufficient to satisfy this daily requirement. According to Ornstein and Sobel (1993), "a mile and a half of walking is equivalent to jogging a mile, and for many walking is safer and more enjoyable" (p. 104). Thus, we do not need to push ourselves to the limit of endurance in order to benefit from exercise. Our bodies were not designed for 26-mile marathons or jogging for miles each day on pavement. Instead, we are physically suited for milder activities such as long-distance walking, quick bursts of energy such as when catching up with children, and the plodding movements involved in tending plants.

Throughout history, we have engaged in plenty of exercise each day, just going about the business of surviving. Unfortunately, many contemporary lifestyles are too sedentary. A regular exercise program that includes both aerobic exercise that strengthens the heart and muscle toning, will enhance our physical well-being and vitality. Throughout human history, attractiveness has been associated with physical health. Healthy people make good mates, who can assist with ensuring the survival of offspring. The awareness of having physical strength enhances self-esteem in both men and women. Not only does regular exercise help individuals keep weight off, but it also counteracts some effects of long-term degenerative diseases that lessen longevity (Chapter 8). "People who are physically inactive have roughly twice the rate of heart disease and heart attacks as do more active people" (Ornstein & Sobel, 1989, p. 107). Women who exercise have a lesser chance of developing osteoporosis. As an additional benefit, regular exercise reduces the tension produced by stressful life events. Physical activity may help boost immunity to infection and lower cancer rates (Ornstein & Sobel, 1993).

Body awareness and enjoyment of the body, which can be gained through athletics or dancing, were found by Maslow (1971) to be a good path to peak experiences. This, in turn, was likely to lead to an intellectual appreciation of "the ultimate values of being" (p. 170). Thus physical exercise tends to be therapeutic for the body, the mind, and, if you will, the spirit. Maslow explained the relationship this way:

> It happens that music and rhythm and dancing are excellent ways of moving toward the discovering of identity. We are built in such a fashion that this kind of trigger, this kind of stimulation, tends to do all kinds of things to our autonomic nervous systems, endocrine glands, to our feelings, and to our emotions." (p. 171).

The discovery of identity, then, is aided by tuning into one's intuition, as well as one's bodily sensations, both pleasant and unpleasant, and by cultivating the attitude that such sensations matter, that they are not entirely to be overruled by schedules, clocks, or other external cues as to what one should be doing.

Beauty from the Inside Out

Research on the benefits of physical attractiveness, has established that physical beauty is certainly an advantage in initial encounters, but eventually as people try to form lasting relationships, personality qualities and common interests become relatively more important. Those blessed with shining good looks become tarnished in our eyes if their pleasing appearance is not matched by a pleasant disposition. Likewise, an initial appraisal of someone as disagreeable in appearance tends to give way to a more kindly assessment of that person's physical attributes when they are accompanied by a charming or kindly personality.

➤ GAINING SELF-ESTEEM

Self-esteem develops over time and through successful life experiences. College students tend to have higher self-esteem than do adolescents, and middle-aged adults have more self-esteem than do college students (Thompson, 1972).

The original source of self-esteem is from others. To a large extent, our self-concept is formed by what others tell us about ourselves, especially during childhood. Children get to know themselves in part by observing their own behavior and also by listening to what others say about them (Ornstein, 1993). If in childhood we received positive feedback from our parents, we would probably be confident in our abilities and likely to achieve our goals. On the other hand, if as children, we were teased for being overweight, dumb, ugly, unathletic, or called unfriendly because of our quiet nature, we may have formed a negative self-image that carried over into the adult years, resulting in low self-esteem.

From ages 6 to 12, the view we have of ourselves is influenced greatly by the quality of our school experiences, by contact with our peer group and with teachers, and by our interactions with our family. Hopefully, our parents will cherish us and will pay attention to us when we are growing up, as we are learning about who we are. During our first few years of life, we look up into the eyes of adults countless times and watch their faces react to us. In this way, we learn who we are. Children who are largely ignored and thus do not receive this "mirroring" tend to have personality disturbances as adults that reflect this deficit. They may spend a lifetime trying to get others to look at them in a vain attempt to feel like somebody important.

To some extent, we all continue to seek from others the recognition of our value. We learn to be more subtle than children, so that we rarely ask, "Do you see how great I am, how important?" We may even cultivate a self-effacing demeanor. Even so, we still want to know whether others value us. Self-esteem is undoubtedly enhanced by the respect given a person who is considered wealthy or one who is particularly attractive. Although worldly success and/or an attractive physical appearance may be sources of self-esteem, they do not guarantee it.

Many of us may be unaware of our particular ways of seeking and earning self-esteem. Our mode of being in the world is formed in childhood, before we have much understanding of what we are trying to accomplish or what we are reacting to. Some of us achieve self-esteem by being physically or sexually alluring. Others make themselves attractive through the use of their intellect, by being highly skilled at something, by making money, or by being generous and helpful. Each of us has hit upon ways of deriving self-esteem.

Some of the individual differences in acquiring self-esteem may be inborn, in that differences in energy level, resilience, and disposition to enjoy life may be a part of our genetic inheritance (Ornstein, 1993). Although there is growing evidence of inherited aspects of self, the brain changes throughout life, so that by changing our behavior, we have an opportunity to reprogram ourselves (Ornstein, 1993). "The symbolizing self is *developmentally* sensitive to influences from early childhood but never entirely "determined" in outcome by any of them" (Lifton, 1993, p. 29). Within the limitation of basic human nature and our individual selves, there is room for change.

Although a damaged self-image may not be easy to repair, everyone has the potential to develop a healthier sense of self. Also, not everyone gains self-esteem—or loses it—in the same manner. Still, there are a limited number of ways that we obtain a sense of worth. Following are some general suggestions to help improve self-esteem:

1. Do something for yourself at least once a day. When we're feeling down, we tend to neglect ourselves. Even the simplest activity, like reading a book, working on the car, or puttering in the garden can make us feel better.

2. Do something for someone else. An act of kindness helps transcend one's immediate sorrows and concerns. Self-esteem depends on our social role.

3. Set a goal. Taking the risk of setting a goal helps build self-esteem because we grow through facing our fears. The feelings of success gained by even a small accomplishment can inspire optimism and a desire to move ahead. You might decide that you will read your textbook for thirty minutes each weekday evening or that you will get the laundry done.

Setting attainable goals that one ultimately accomplishes has been shown to be a reliable route to self-esteem. Many of us automatically think of wealth as a worthwhile goal in life, assuming that wealth is the primary route to happiness. As will be discussed in the chapter on happiness, earning enough money to keep a person from constantly worrying about it does indeed promote happiness (Chapter 14), although wealth beyond this point does not.

4. Maintain structure during difficult times. Keep up with your responsibilities. Maintaining even minimal structure in your daily tasks forces you into an action mode and may prevent you from getting too complacent. For instance, continuing to attend class and to go to work, even when you are feeling bad about yourself, will help distract you from such thoughts. A kindly remark or enthusiastic smile from someone you encounter may even provide you with something to counteract your glum thoughts.

5. Take care of your body. Don't use food, sex, drugs, cigarettes, or alcohol to deal with emotional pain. This behavior only distances you from your feelings and compounds the problem you're trying to avoid. Taking good physical care of yourself is both a reflection of and a source of self-esteem.

6. Ask for help. Whether it's just conversing with a friend or seeking the help of a professional, talking with someone else can help you gain a clearer, more clear and positive picture of yourself and your situation. Shyness, timidity, fear of self-assertion, and reticence about personal relationships are all direct expressions of poor self-esteem (Branden, 1994). A primary task of psychotherapy is to help strengthen self-esteem.

An Accurate Perception of Reality as a Route to Self-Esteem

According to humanistic psychologist Nathaniel Branden (1986), one of the most significant characteristics of healthy self-esteem is being at peace with oneself and with others. Healthy self-esteem is the basis of the ability to respond actively to the opportunities of life in work, love, and play. It is also the foundation of that serenity of spirit that makes the enjoyment of life possible.

As mentioned previously, our self-concept is who and what we think we are. Self-esteem is a part of self-concept, as are self-respect and self-confidence. Branden proposes that self-confidence and self-respect can be generated by "living consciously," that is, using our intelligence to reflect upon our behavior. Our ability to think affords us our basic means of survival and is also responsible for all of our distinctively human accomplishments. Success in life depends on how well we use our intelligence. Branden's principle of living consciously involves a commitment to awareness. He contends that the appropriate use of our consciousness is not automatic but instead is an active choice. We can choose to see reality or to deny it. Human beings have countless ways to distort reality. We can wish to know or can remain unaware. We can choose to live consciously, semi-consciously, or for all practical purposes, unconsciously. For Branden, this choice is the ultimate meaning of free will. Our self-respect and well-being depend upon the extent to which we value the clear perception of reality. We cannot feel good about ourselves if we wander about in a self-induced mental fog. If we exist unthinkingly, our sense of worthiness suffers regardless of anyone else's approval or disapproval. We know our own lapses, whether or not anyone else does.

Confronting previously avoided conflicts or challenges is a good general strategy for maintaining contact with reality. Branden (1994) likes to ask his clients two questions: "How do you feel about yourself when you avoid an issue you know, at some level, needs to be dealt with? And how do you feel about yourself when you master your avoidance impulses and confront the threatening issue?" (p. 75). Answering these questions allows clients to see the consequences that their actions have on their level of self-esteem.

We evaluate ourselves in a variety of ways. Over time, we gain a sense of the kind of person we are, by considering the kind of choices we make. Self-esteem is the reputation we acquire with ourselves. It is a function of the honesty of our relationship to reality. Hence, Branden echoes ideas of both Maslow and Rogers that an accurate perception of reality is an integral part of being a self-actualized person. We will not like what we see in all cases, but we recognize the need to face reality. Our wishes, fears, and denials do not alter facts.

QUESTIONS: *Nathaniel Branden asserts that self-esteem and self-respect come from a willingness to face reality and deal with the world as it is, rather than to deny reality or portions of it, and to live in our fantasy of how things could be. What do you think of his position? What do you think might be other sources of self-esteem?*

➤   ## OTHER PEOPLE AS A SOURCE OF SELF-ESTEEM

It is common in relationships for one person to try and change the other by the sheer force of his or her love. Attempting to love someone enough to "enable" him or her to change typically ends up feeling like a maneuver to control the partner. One partner feels resentful for being pressured to change, while the other feels resentful that no change is occurring, despite his or her hard work to be supportive and encouraging.

A person with low self-esteem is more likely to feel comfortable with a partner who reinforces his or her self-image than with someone who does not, even when the other has a more positive view of the person (Sternberg, 1991). Without being aware of it, individuals with low self-esteem prefer partners who view them in a similar fashion. Apparently we don't trust people who view us more highly than we view ourselves.

QUESTION: *Can other people give us self-esteem?*

The Authentic Self

Carl Rogers (1961) drew some conclusions about his clients as they progressed in therapy. First, he found that they moved away from the facades with which they typically faced the world. Even when they didn't as yet know who they really were, they grew willing to let go of who they were not. In addition, Rogers's clients began to worry less about pleasing others, about living up to the "shoulds" and "oughts" of their childhood, and about meeting the expectations of others. They did not want to be anything artificial or to mold themselves to conform to an external standard. "They realize that they do not value such purposes or goals, even though they may have lived by them all their lives up to this point" (p. 170).

Gradually Rogers's clients became autonomous enough to form goals of their own. They slowly found the courage to experiment with defining who they were and in what direction they wished to go. "Freedom to be oneself is a frighteningly responsible freedom, and an individual moves towards it cautiously, fearfully, and with almost no confidence at first" (p. 171).

➤ *SUMMARY*

The self, or self-concept, could be described as the awareness on the part of the individual of his or her identity. Freud's theory of psychoanalysis did not specifically have a concept of self, but the ego is roughly equivalent. Until recently, the behavioral theories did not have such an idea. It was primarily the humanists who made use of the notion of self, saying that one's entire experience of life is colored by one's self-concept.

HUMANISM AND THE SELF   Abraham Maslow was the founder of the humanistic orientation in psychology. He suggested that the needs that motivate human behavior are ordered in a hierarchy from basic needs to higher needs. The three levels of deficiency needs are physiological needs, safety and security, and love or belongingness needs.

The higher levels of human needs are for self-esteem and self-actualization. Self-esteem is achieved when the individual feels worthwhile and competent. Once a person achieves a stable sense of self-esteem, he or she is in a position to enjoy self-actualization, which is at the top of the hierarchy and includes strivings for understanding, creativity, aesthetic needs, self-realization, and the need to fully develop one's potential. The self-actualized person has "peak experiences," which Maslow took as evidence that human beings have a higher and transcendent nature.

Viktor Frankl proposed that "self-transcendence" is a higher goal than Maslow's self-actualization. Self-transcendence means going beyond one's self-interests and immediate life projects, to extend oneself by concern for others. A fulfilling life involves not only actualizing one's own potential but also making a difference in the lives of others.

Carl Roger's assumed that human beings are born naturally good, seeking both personal fulfillment and close relationships with others. If freed from corrupting social influences, humans can achieve high levels of personal and interpersonal functioning. In order to attain this level of adjustment, people need to experience *unconditional positive regard* to feel valued for themselves regardless of whether or not their behaviors do them credit. Instead, children sometimes have *conditions of worth* placed upon them by parents and society. Children then feel that they are valued only after they meet certain expectations that others have of them. Rogers believed that it was important for people to replace learned conditions of worth with trust in their inner urges and intuitions in order to lead authentic lives.

Rogers's fully functioning person is analogous to Maslow's self-actualizing person. Such a person is open and responsive to his or her inner feelings and thoughts as well as to the external environment. The fully functioning person has *congruence* between the true self, the ideal self, and the self-image. Client-centered therapy aims at helping the client gain congruence and self-acceptance. Total acceptance by the therapist (unconditional positive regard) paves the way for self-acceptance by the client. Rogers was convinced that a person armed with a realistic self-image and with a new level of self-acceptance will gradually discover solutions to life problems.

Although Rogers's client-centered therapy has as a goal getting clients more in touch with their feelings, sometimes psychotherapists encourage clients to pay *less* attention to their feelings or at least to act upon them less impulsively. What is desirable for healthy functioning is a balance between feeling and thinking. A psychotherapist makes an initial assessment as to whether the patient needs to move in the direction of greater or lesser emotionality.

Self-Fulfilling Prophecy The self-fulfilling prophecy refers to a prediction that when made, influences the course of events toward fulfilling the prediction. The self-fulfilling prophecy works whether the anticipation is positive or negative and whether it is in relation to oneself or others.

Self Boundaries Some psychoanalysts think that the most basic part of the self-concept is a person's sense of boundaries. The idea of boundaries is based on a definition of what is "self" and what is "not self." Psychological boundaries allow a person to draw a clear line between self and others, yet not one so rigid or impermeable that it blocks connection with others. Western cultures' view of the self stands in contrast to that of many other cultures that consider the self to be more inclusively defined in terms of one's connections with others.

Body Image One's own physical appearance has an impact on self-concept. Physical attractiveness greatly influences early impressions that others form of us. Physically attractive people are viewed more positively than are less attractive people, a phenomenon referred to by psychologists as the "halo effect." Conversely, a person's self-concept can be damaged as a result of physical deformity. Throughout human history, attractiveness has been associated with physical vitality. A regular exercise program that includes both aerobic exercise and muscle toning will enhance our sense of well-being and physical attractiveness.

One aspect of our physical attractiveness over which we do exert a measure of control is our weight. Significant overeating and undereating are signs of psychological disturbance. Whereas many suffer with the problem of obesity, others respond to distress about their physical appearance by becoming chronically underweight. Anorexia nervosa is a nervous loss of appetite, or self-starvation. Bulimia nervosa typically involves gorging on food, then inducing vomiting or taking laxatives to avoid gaining weight. Both are caused by an obsessive fear of gaining weight.

GAINING SELF-ESTEEM Self-esteem has been described as a sense of personal competence and worth. Self-esteem develops over time and through successful life experiences. We acquire self-esteem through positive feedback from others, first from our parents and later from peers. Such feedback enables us to experience self-acceptance. How we feel about ourselves plays a major part in determining how we succeed professionally, how comfortable we are in social situations, and how we interact in relationships.

Everyone has the potential to develop a healthier sense of self. Some suggestions for increasing self-esteem are as follows: (1) Do something enjoyable; (2) do something for someone else; (3) set a goal; (4) maintain a routine that prompts you to engage in regular activity; (5) take good physical care of yourself; and (6) ask for help from friends or a professional psychotherapist.

Psychotherapist Nathaniel Brandon links increased self-esteem to "living consciously," or maintaining an accurate perception of reality. Denial of reality will ultimately results in loss of self-respect and thus lowered self-esteem.

OTHER PEOPLE AS A SOURCE OF SELF-ESTEEM It is a common myth in relationships that one person can change the other by the sheer force of his or her love. For a variety of reasons, this approach is generally ineffective.

LEARNING THE LANGUAGE OF PSYCHOLOGISTS

self-concept	**ideal self**
self-esteem	**true self**
determinism	**self-image**
free will	**client-centered therapy**
self-actualization	**fully functioning person**
peak experience	**self-fulfilling prophecy**
self-transcendence	**self-boundary**
unconditional positive regard	**enmeshment**
conditions of worth	**deindividuation**
congruence	**halo effect**

CHAPTER REVIEW QUESTIONS

1. What is self-esteem?
2. How did Abraham Maslow's theory of human nature differ from that of Freud?
3. What was Frankl's objection to Maslow's concept of self-actualization?

4. How does acceptance of oneself lead to acceptance of others?
5. According to Rogers, how is one's self-concept formed?
6. What is the purpose of client-centered therapy, which was developed by Carl Rogers?
7. What is a self-fulfilling prophecy?
8. What is the "halo effect"?
9. Why are the disorders of anorexia nervosa and bulimia nervosa prevalent only in some cultures?
10. According to Brandon, how does living consciously lead to self-esteem?

ACTIVITIES

1. *COMPLETE INDIVIDUALLY:* **The Short Index of Self-Actualization.**
2. *COMPLETE INDIVIDUALLY:* **Self-Esteem Scale.**
3. *COMPLETE INDIVIDUALLY:* **Fear of Fat Scale.**
4. *COMPLETE AS A GROUP:* **Personal Reflections on My Level of Self-Esteem.**
5. *COMPLETE INDIVIDUALLY:* **Self-Portrait.** Find a box large enough to hold the objects that you feel represent you. Choose a variety of materials to attach to the inside and outside of the box, to express different aspects of yourself. The inside of the box should represent what you keep to yourself, your personality as you know it. The outside is what you show to other people, your "persona." Be prepared to give a short oral presentation to share your project.
6. *COMPLETE AT HOME:* Try this exercise when you can find some quiet time alone. Close your eyes and imagine yourself as a child. Picture this child looking at you. What is the expression on his or her face? Imagine taking your child self into your lap. Put your arms around your child self and comfort him or her. What would it be like for you to be in a nurturing relationship with your child self?
7. *SUGGESTED READING: Go Ask Alice,* by Anonymous. Englewood Cliffs, NJ: Prentice-Hall, 1998.

The Short Index of Self-Actualization

Directions: Indicate whether you agree or disagree with the following statements by circling the *A* or the *D*.

A   D   1. I do not feel ashamed of any of my emotions.
A   D   2. I feel that I must do what others expect me to do.
A   D   3. I believe that people are essentially good and can be trusted.

A   D   4. I feel free to be angry at those I love.

A   D   5. It is always necessary that others approve of what I do.

A   D   6. I don't accept my own weaknesses.

A   D   7. I can like people without having to approve of them.

A   D   8. I fear failure.

A   D   9. I avoid attempts to analyze and simplify complex domains.

A   D   10. It is better to be yourself than to be popular.

A   D   11. I have no mission in life to which I feel especially dedicated.

A   D   12. I can express my feelings even when they may result in undesirable consequences.

A   D   13. I do not feel responsible to help anybody.

A   D   14. I am bothered by fears of being inadequate.

A   D   15. I am loved because I give love.

Scoring: Agreeing with items 1, 3, 4, 7, 10, 12, and 15; and disagreeing with items 2, 5, 6, 8, 9, 11, 13, and 14 are scored as self-actualizing.

Source: Jones & Crandall, (1986).

Self-Esteem Scale

Directions: Circle *Yes* if each of the following statements applies to you, and circle *No* if it does not.

Yes   No   1. I usually feel sure of myself.

Yes   No   2. I often wish that I were someone else.

Yes   No   3. Most people like me.

Yes   No   4. I find it hard to make a presentation before a group.

Yes   No   5. I seldom worry.

Yes   No   6. I wish that I were younger.

Yes   No   7. I can make up my mind with ease.

Yes   No   8. There are many things I'd change about myself if I could.

Yes   No   9. I am lots of fun to be with.

Yes   No   10. I get upset easily at work.

Yes   No   11. I usually do the right thing.

Yes   No   12. I like others to give me directions.

Yes   No   13. I am proud of the things I do.

Yes   No   14. It takes me a long time to adjust to new situations.

Yes   No   15. I often meet persons who seem like old friends.

Yes   No   16. I'm often sorry for the things I do.

Yes   No   17. I adapt to strangers easily.

Yes	No	18. I give in easily when others seem displeased.
Yes	No	19. I am popular with the opposite sex.
Yes	No	20. My boss expects too much of me.
Yes	No	21. I usually am happy.
Yes	No	22. I often become aware of my shyness.
Yes	No	23. My working associates usually consider my feelings.
Yes	No	24. I often feel ashamed of my actions.
Yes	No	25. I find much in life to appreciate and enjoy.
Yes	No	26. I wish that I were more attractive.
Yes	No	27. I feel that I understand myself quite well.
Yes	No	28. I often feel that I don't care what happens to me.
Yes	No	29. If I have something to say, I usually say it.
Yes	No	30. I get upset easily when my ideas are not accepted.
Yes	No	31. I feel that my superiors respect me.
Yes	No	32. I wish that my ideas carried as much weight as the ideas of others.
Yes	No	33. It is easy for me to start a conversation even with strangers.
Yes	No	34. I often get depressed.
Yes	No.	35. I can usually take charge in an emergency.
Yes	No	36. Things disturb me and cause me to perform poorly at times.
Yes	No	37. I am proud of the place where I work.
Yes	No	38. I often get discouraged.
Yes	No	39. I seldom let things bother me.
Yes	No	40. It is easy to blame myself.
Yes	No	41. I can be depended on.
Yes	No	42. I find it difficult to express my opinions.
Yes	No	43. Things usually run smoothly in my life.
Yes	No	44. People tend to ignore me.
Yes	No	45. My ideas are accepted and often looked up to.
Yes	No	46. It's different to be me.
Yes	No	47. I find joy in my work.
Yes	No	48. Living in this changing time in history is frightening.
Yes	No	49. I can make up my own mind and stick to it.
Yes	No	50. I have a low opinion of myself.

Scoring: Count up the number of *yes* scores on the odd numbered items and multiply by four, which gives you the score: _____. A score of 80 and above indicates a healthy level of self-esteem. A score of below 80 indicates a lower level of self-esteem than is desirable.

Fear of Fat Scale

Directions: Read each of the following statements, and write in the number from the key that best represents your own feelings and beliefs.

1 = very untrue   2 = somewhat untrue   3 = somewhat true   4 = very true

1. My biggest fear is of becoming fat. _____

2. I am afraid even to gain a little weight. _____

3. I believe there is a real risk that I will become overweight some-day. _____

4. I don't understand how overweight people can live with them-selves. _____

5. Becoming fat would be the worst thing that could happen to me. _____

6. If I stopped concentrating on controlling my weight, chances are I would become very fat. _____

7. There is nothing that I can do to make the thought of gaining weight less painful and frightening. _____

8. I feel as if all my energy goes into controlling my weight. _____

9. If I eat even a little, I may lose control and not stop eating. _____

10. Staying hungry is the only way I can guard against losing control and becoming fat. _____

TOTAL: _____

Scoring: To determine your score, add up the numbers in the blanks. The mean score for nondieting college women was 17.9. The general female population sampled scored a mean of 18.3. Those college women who were dissatisfied with their weight and who have dieted more than three times in the past year scored a mean of 23.9 Bulimics scored 30 and anorexics in treatment scored a mean of 35.

Source: Goldfarb, Dyken, and Gerrard. 1985.

Personal Reflections on My Level of Self-Esteem

Directions: Read each of the following questions, and then write your answers in the blanks.

1. In your opinion, how prevalent is unconditional positive regard? In your own life, how often are you regarded positively by others regardless of how you act? From whom, if anyone, have you received unconditional positive regard?

_____

_____

_____

_____

2. How often do you give other people unconditional positive regard?

_____

_____

_____

_____

3. Did you experience "conditions of worth" as a child? That is, did you have fears that you would not be worthy of love if you didn't live up to certain standards of behavior?

_____

_____

_____

_____

4. Can you recall a time when you were given feedback about yourself (a possible reflection of your true self) that contrasted strikingly with the way you saw yourself (your self-image)? If so, what was the feedback?

_____

_____

_____

_____

5. Is there some way(s) in which you see yourself (self-image) as being substantially different from the way you would like to be (your ideal self)?

_____

_____

_____

_____

6. Check any of the following that apply to you:

a. _____ having feelings of loneliness, anger, or guilt

b. _____ overeating or drinking

c. _____ doubting your abilities

d. _____ engaging in self-criticism

e. _____ having difficulty handling praise from others

f. _____ having difficulty handling criticism from others

g. _____ being a "perfectionist"

h. _____ procrastinating

i. _____ having fear of taking risks

j. _____ blaming others for your problems

7. The preceding experiences are sometimes cited as symptoms of low self-esteem. Do you agree? Why, or why not?

_____

_____

_____

_____

8. What people have been important in your life in helping you feel good about yourself?

_____

_____

_____

_____

9. Have there been people in your life who have caused you to devalue yourself? If so, what happened?

_____

_____

_____

_____

10. What do you think of Maslow's concept of the self-actualized person? How do you think self-actualized people differ from the average person?

_____

_____

_____

_____

11. What was the single most joyous, happiest, most ecstatic, and most blissful moment of your whole life? How did you feel different about yourself at that time? How did the world look different? Did the experience change you in some way?

_____

_____

_____

_____

12. Have you ever had a pleasurable emotional experience from studying? Can you think of an occasion when you may have had a "peak experience" brought on by an intellectual activity?

_____

_____

_____

_____

13. How do you feel about your looks? What do you like and dislike?

_____

_____

_____

_____

14. Complete this sentence: "I like myself most when I . . ."

_____

_____

_____

_____

15. Now complete this sentence: "I like myself least when I . . ."

_____

_____

_____

_____

16. Three things about myself that I want to change are the following:

a. _____

b. _____

c. _____

17. Do you feel heroic in your life? That is, do you stand out in some positive way, in comparison with a sibling, your classmates, or other peers? Do you have a heroic quest around which to shape your life?

_____

_____

_____

_____

18. Both Maslow and Rogers agreed that self-confidence, in the sense of trusting oneself to find a good direction in life, is something that healthy people have. How would you rate your level of self-confidence, on a scale of 1 to 10, with 1 representing no self-confidence, and 10 designating complete confidence? Do you have more self-confidence than you did two years ago? Why, or why not?

_____

_____

_____

_____

19. Can you recall an experience in which your expectations influenced the outcome of an event in the manner described in this chapter as the self-fulfilling prophecy?

_____

_____

_____

_____

20. What gives you a sense of belongingness?

_____

_____

_____

_____

3

Psychosocial Development

Do not be too timid and squeamish about your actions.
All life is an experiment.
—Ralph Waldo Emerson

➤ PREVIEW QUESTIONS: At what age did Sigmund Freud say that personality development was complete? According to Freud, what can interrupt development and cause a fixation? How did Erik Erikson expand the Freudian theory of development? Does the type of emotional attachment that a toddler forms with his or her mother have lasting effects?

➤ INTRODUCTION: THE LIFELONG GROWTH PROCESS OF HUMAN BEINGS

Each stage of life has its own challenges. In general, we move from a state of dependence on others towards autonomy, although healthy maturation also means developing a comfortable interdependence with others. Our attitudes and sense of self are largely shaped by our experiences and decisions during our early years of life. This early influence affects later attitudes about our identity, gender-role, work, body, love, sexuality, intimacy, loneliness, death, and meaning . . . all topics that will be discussed throughout this text. Before going on to discuss the specific themes just mentioned, we shall look at the developmental stages that make up the human life cycle.

Although children do confront matters such as death and identity early in life, they are not equipped intellectually to contemplate the full weight of such existential issues as mortality or their place and purpose in life until they reach adolescence (Piaget, 1952). In adolescence, concerns arise such as What's going to happen to me?, Where am I going?, and Where do I fit in?

The first developmental theory was offered by Sigmund Freud, the founder of psychoanalysis. Freud's observations have had a tremendous influence on psychological theory, psychotherapy, and human culture in general. The terminology of psychoanalysis is present in our everyday conversation. For this reason, we need to discuss psychoanalytic theory to become aware of how it has shaped attitudes about human nature, child development, psychopathology, and psychological health. Freud's theory was later modified by his follower, Erik Erikson, and by many others.

➤ PSYCHOANALYSIS

Sigmund Freud (1856–1939)

Sigmund Freud is generally credited with the beginning of modern personality theory and psychotherapy. As the founder of psychoanalysis, he popularized the concept that much of what motivates our behavior comes from our unconscious mind. By the unconscious mind, Freud meant that we store in our brains memories and motivations of which we are unaware and that we cannot voluntarily access. Freud was convinced that people have very strong physical drives that reside in the unconscious, particularly the need for sexual expression. Later Freud added an aggressive drive, but he always considered the sexual drive as primary.

Also residing in the unconscious are thoughts, feelings, memories, and desires that are too anxiety-provoking to retain in conscious awareness. To protect the self, the mind represses upsetting material, in an automatic fashion, making it inaccessible. It is only those thoughts and memories connected to impulses that are unacceptable to the person's conscious ethical standards and that would cause intense psychological pain that are repressed. When an individual represses certain thoughts and motives, they remain active at an unconscious level and continue to influence behavior in important ways. Negative behavior and psychological symptoms represent conflict at an unconscious level, and have a definite meaning that is tied to a problem belonging to the person concerned. For example, a patient of Freud's, Fräulein Elisabeth, developed pains in her legs after an afternoon's walk with her ill sister's husband. During the walk Elisabeth had the thought that she wished she could possess a man like her brother-in-law. In order to reminisce about the pleasant afternoon, she later returned to the spot where the walk had taken them. When she arose, she had pains in her legs that persisted until she sought relief through psychoanalysis. Such pains could be expected to make future walks with her brother-in-law infeasible. Thus, the leg pain seemed to be self-inflicted, the result of guilt feelings.

A psychoanalyst who believes in the theories of Sigmund Freud views psychopathology as essentially caused by a repression of unconscious sexual and aggressive drives. This view is an aspect of Freudian theory that has only a small proportion of adherents among psychologists and psychiatrists today. Even so, many of the facets of Freudian theory have been incorporated into contemporary theory and practice.

Freud created a model of the mind with three structures: the id, the ego, and the superego. He conceived of these as three distinguishable agents within the organism. The **id** is the original source of personality, present at birth. The **ego** (which is the rational, problem-solving part of us) and the **superego** (which is the seat of our moral self) are personality structures that develop later from the id. This model was intended by Freud to be understood metaphorically rather than literally. Thus, we would not expect to dissect a human brain and locate an "ego" or an "id."

THE ID   The id consists of a collection of basic biological drives that provides the energy for the operation of the entire personality, for the id itself, and for both the ego and the superego. This psychic energy source is referred to as the **libido.** Freud hypothesized that two major instincts operate in all of us at an unconscious level: the life (or sexual) instinct and its opposite, the death (or aggressive) instinct. Freud referred to the id as "das es" (which is German for "the it"), signifying that the id and its motivations were unknown to the conscious self.

For Freud, the source of motivation for human behavior is psychic energy. People have a fixed amount of energy, so that if large amounts of psychic energy are being used for earning a living, for instance, relatively little will be available for social or family activities. The psychic energy can be refocused and can be freed from neurotic preoccupations, such as repression of childhood trauma, so that the individual can have energy to pursue productive activities.

The id is buried at the deepest level of the unconscious mind, far removed from conscious reality. It engages in **wish fulfillment,** where the id attempts to reduce tension by forming a mental image of its desires. For example, a starving person might form a mental image of a delicious meal. According to Freud, the objects and events conjured up in dreams represent attempts to fulfill some impulse of the id, usually in disguised ways. However, the id cannot fulfill its wishes and dreams and therefore needs the ego structure of the personality to negotiate with the real world in order to satisfy the id impulses.

The id is said to operate on the **pleasure principle:** It seeks to avoid pain and obtain pleasure, regardless of any external considerations. For example, a person who is overly impulsive without thinking through his or her actions would be said to have an overly strong id. Human beings, in general, have difficulty controlling id impulses. Freud used the analogy of a rider (the ego) struggling to stay on top of a wild horse (the id) to describe the human condition.

THE EGO   The ego is the part of us of which we are consciously aware. Freud called the ego "das Ich," which means "the I" in German. The ego is analogous to the humanistic concept of self. Although the ego operates for the most part on a conscious level, some unconscious processes are involved also.

The ego is said to operate on the **reality principle.** Its role is to test mental images for their reality. Such images (wishes) do not satisfy needs; reality must be considered. For example, because a starving person cannot eat mental images of food formed by the id, the ego must eventually find a way to satisfy the very real hunger.

The practical, logical ego plans how to achieve satisfaction of id drives. For example, it delays gratification of sexual impulses until conditions are appropriate. According to Freud, the ego's job is so difficult that at times a person unconsciously resorts to psychological defenses to ward off uncomfortable feelings. Individuals may achieve personality stability by investing energy in creating these defense mechanisms, but they do so at the cost of distorting reality. If a person cannot deal with reality as it actually is, he or she can try to alter it and make it appear to be in agreement with his or her wishes or ideals. Although these strategies on the part of the ego falsify reality, they are effective in affording protection from the disabling effects of anxiety and frustration. The most common of these ego defense mechanisms will be described shortly.

The ego is the "executive" of the personality. It decides what actions are appropriate and thus determines which id instincts will be satisfied and in what manner. The ego must counteract the wishful thinking of the id as well as the moralistic thinking of the superego, in order to avoid a distortion of reality (Hall, 1954).

THE SUPEREGO   The superego is the internalized representation of societal values, as taught to the child by parents and others. Initially, parents control children's behavior directly through rewards and punishments. Through the gradual incorporation of parental standards into the superego, behavior is brought under self-control. For example, as adults we don't need anyone to tell us that it's wrong to take another person's property without permission. The superego judges whether an action is right or wrong. It admonishes us with concepts such as "You should . . ." Freud called the superego "das uber Ich" (literally, "the over I"), by which he meant to describe the way the superego sits in judgment of the ego.

The superego is composed of the "conscience," which incorporates all the things the child is punished or reprimanded for doing, and the "ego ideal," which encompasses those actions for which the child is rewarded. The conscience punishes by making the person feel guilty, and the ego-ideal rewards by making the individual feel proud. The superego, which develops slowly and at an unconscious level, gradually gains the power to criticize and supervise the id and the ego. It inhibits id impulses that are unacceptable to the self or society, and strives for perfection. For the most part, the socialization process occurs without conscious perception: We may discriminate between right and wrong without being aware of how we do so. For instance, we may feel hostile toward punk rock types or conventional types, but not be able to explain why.

Freud developed the concepts of id, ego, and superego as a way of explaining inner conflict. In a normal person, these three aspects of the personality work as a team, producing integrated behavior. Sometimes, however, they can be at odds: the ego postpones the gratification that the id wants right away, and the superego battles with both the id and the ego because the behavior falls short of the moral code it represents. The ego is essentially pressured, or in Freud's words, "hemmed in on three sides" by the external world, the superego, and the id. All of these demands must be considered when the ego plans a course of action.

PSYCHOLOGICAL DEFENSE MECHANISMS   The ego has several **defense mechanisms** at its disposal to protect itself from being overwhelmed by anxiety. Anxiety arises when the ego tries to resolve the conflicting demands made by the id, the superego, and the reality of the external environment. A defense mechanism is a process used to avoid, deny, or distort sources of threat or anxiety.

Defense mechanisms are also used to maintain an idealized self-image so that we are able to live comfortably with ourselves.

Three characteristics of defense mechanisms to remember are that they (1) are ways of trying to reduce anxiety, (2) involve denial or distortion of reality, and (3) operate at an unconscious level. According to Freud, the use of defense mechanisms spawns unhealthy patterns of behavior. People who rely excessively on them become less adaptable, because defense mechanisms consume great amounts of emotional energy to control anxiety and to maintain an unrealistic self-image. A clear perception of reality is a hallmark of psychological health (Chapter 2).

Are there any really "healthy" defense mechanisms? In a sense, all defense mechanisms are useful in that they help the person to cope, but in another sense no defense is entirely healthy, since all defenses interfere with our understanding of what is really occurring from moment to moment. There are a couple of ways of coping with anxiety, **sublimation** and **compensation,** that are fairly benign in that they tend to have more positive than negative results. These will be described after the less healthy defense mechanisms of **denial, repression, rationalization, projection, reaction formation, regression,** and **displacement** are explained. All nine of these make up the most common defense mechanisms.

Denial.   This is the most primitive, infantile defense mechanism. When external reality is too unpleasant to face, we may simply deny that it exists. Denial often explains why a person may be the "last to know" when a marriage partner is having an affair. Even when signs of infidelity are clear, the person may fail to perceive them until long after they are obvious to others.

Elisabeth Kübler-Ross (1976) noted that people suffering from terminal illnesses typically go through a stage of denial before being able to come to grips with their situation. Denial is typically elicited by the death of a loved one, terminal illness, and similar painful or threatening experiences. For example, if you were informed that you have only three months to live, you might respond by saying, "Someone must have mixed up the X rays" or "The doctor must be mistaken!"

Repression.   This defense mechanism involves selective remembering. It is unconscious forgetting (not to be confused with suppression, which is intentional, conscious forgetting). Impulses, thoughts, or memories that are threatening are actively excluded from conscious awareness by some psychological force. The personality is thus protected from being overwhelmed by anxiety. A child may repress awareness of past sexual abuse or the memory of parental rejection.

Since the ego must expend energy to keep the material from entering consciousness, it may leak through in slips of the tongue and other accidents, or as symbols in dreams. The ego may also be so taxed by the expenditure of energy that the individual has relatively little psychic energy left over for productive work.

Good morning, beheaded—uh, I mean beloved"

Repression may seem similar to denial, but there is a difference. Repression is a rejection of internal perception, whereas denial involves external reality. For example, let's say that you are often criticized by others for being selfish. If you are aware of the criticism but refuse to believe that it is meant seriously, you are using denial as a defense. If, on the other hand, you selectively forget that your selfishness has been mentioned several times before by various friends, such repression would leave you totally unaware of your fault. In the first instance, you are aware of the criticism but deny its seriousness; in the second, you repress the criticisms entirely.

Rationalization. This defense mechanism involves thinking up logical, socially approved reasons for past, present, or future behaviors. Rationalization has two major defensive values: It helps justify specific behaviors, and it softens the disappointment connected with unattainable goals. Justifying one's own behavior by giving reasonable and "rational" but false reasons for it is typical. A case of justification would be when a student asserts that he or she had to cheat on an exam, because he or she really is a good student but did not have time to study for this particular exam. Rationalization is also used in an attempt to cover up one's failures or mistakes. With a little effort, people may be able to justify to themselves a great many things, such as ignoring their tight financial situation in order to spend money on lavish entertainment or neglecting work for more enjoyable pursuits.

A classic example of rationalization to soften disappointment is represented in the sour grapes fable. In this story, a fox spots some delicious-looking grapes high on the vine. He is eager to eat them, thinking that they appear juicy and sweet indeed. However, try as he might, he cannot reach them. Eventually, he gives up. As he walks away, he consoles himself with the thought that the grapes are probably sour anyway!

Projection. This defense mechanism involves the transfer of blame from oneself to others, who are seen as responsible for one's own mistakes or misdeeds. Others may also be perceived as harboring one's own unacceptable impulses, thoughts, and desires. For instance, on an unconscious level, a man wants to break off his relationship with his girlfriend, who is deeply in love with him. He may say to her, "I do not think you love me anymore." Even inanimate objects are not exempt from blame. For example, a three-year-old who falls off a rocking horse may attack it with blows and kicks, exclaiming that it is a naughty horsie.

Projection is one of the most powerful and dangerous defense mechanisms. It works very well to reduce anxiety, but it does so at the risk of completely distorting the truth about oneself and others. The negative traits of others are exaggerated in order to direct attention away from one's own failings. If others are to blame for our misfortunes, those others must be evil-intentioned. In its most exaggerated form, projection becomes a paranoid form of psychosis.

Reaction Formation. This defense mechanism involves the development of a personality trait that is the opposite of the original, unconscious trait. Sometimes people protect themselves from dangerous desires not only by repressing those desires so that they remain unaware of them but also by developing conscious attitudes and behavior patterns that are just the opposite. The more socially unacceptable a motive, the more likely it is to be expressed indirectly. The most indirect way to express a motive is as its opposite. Hostility may come out as friendly and loving acts. Indirect expression gives undesirable motives an outlet without the person's feeling the anxiety or guilt normally associated with socially objectionable motives.

Anxiety that is aroused by unacceptable impulses resulting from one instinct, such as a desire to hurt one's spouse (a form of the aggressive instinct), might be held in check through reaction formation, so that a wish to harm might instead be transformed into "overly loving" behavior. Similarly, a mother who resents her children may be overprotective of them (smother love). Other examples of this defense mechanism would be "replacing" cruelty with kindness; desires for sexual promiscuity with moralistic sexual attitudes and behavior; macho behavior to cover up fearfulness; and grandiose behavior intended to cover up feelings of inferiority. When someone "protests too much," a reaction formation may be operating. Reaction formation also can be detected when it leads to excessive harshness or severity in dealing with the lapses of others.

Regression. This defense mechanism refers to a reoccurrence of behavior or other response patterns long since outgrown. It involves a return to an earlier level of development, with less mature responses and typically a lower level of aspiration. For example, most parents who have a second child have had to put up with some infantile behavior from the older child. Frustrated by a new rival for attention, the older child may exhibit childish speech, bed-wetting, or a wish to return to drinking out of a bottle. An adult who throws a temper tantrum or a married adult who "goes home to mother" may be regressing in the face of an anxiety-producing situation.

One of the pessimistic aspects of Freudian theory relates to regression. Freud was convinced that human beings are regressive by nature. That is, we have an inborn inclination to revert to a less mature mode of coping, particularly in the face of challenging situations, and long to return to a period of development when we were taken care of and did not have to fend for ourselves.

Displacement. The transference of emotions produced in one situation to another is what characterizes displacement. What takes place is a redirection of an emotional attachment away from its original object and toward another, less threatening object. It can involve the expression, in a new situation, of feelings that one is afraid to show in the original situation. For example, kicking the cat when you are angry with your spouse is a form of displacement. Also, a child who is restricted at home may become belligerent at school. Displacement is related to sublimation, in that both involve a channeling of energy away from its proper object and toward a substitute. However, sublimation is a healthier defense, because the substitute behavior is more acceptable.

Sublimation. Considered to be one of the most mature defense mechanisms, sublimation involves channeling energy away from a motive that causes anxiety and into a more noble form in terms of the values of one's society. The primitive (id) impulses of love and hate are converted into activities that are socially acceptable. The Shakespeares and Michelangelos of the world may have channeled forbidden sexual urges into artistic creativity. A college student who has a strong need to fight and win may become captain of her college debating team. Likewise, athletes are sometimes urged by their coaches to avoid sexual activity the night before an important competition, to "save it for the game."

Compensation. Like sublimation, this defense mechanism is more positive than most others. Compensatory reactions are defenses against feelings of inferiority. A person who has a defect or weakness (real or imagined) may go to unusual lengths to overcome the weakness or to compensate for it by excelling in other areas. For example, U.S. President Theodore Roosevelt was a sickly child who later became an elephant hunter, cowboy, health enthusiast, and commander of the voluntary cavalry unit known as the rough riders. The perceived weakness may be compensated for in a different area. An unpopular person may try to get extraordinary grades, and a short or fragile man may seek a position of power and authority.

Biographers of great athletes sometimes note that as children, these athletes may not have been well endowed physically. They may have been relatively puny in stature and musculature, and relatively small for their age. Instead of submitting to their fate, they reacted against their limitations by developing a degree of physical prowess and endurance that no one expected them to attain. Once weak, they became strong; once apparently incapable, they became models of capability, demonstrating what people can do once they set their mind to the task.

FREUD'S FIVE STAGES OF PERSONALITY DEVELOPMENT   Freud based his theory of personality development on observations of himself and his patients. He noticed that his patients seemed to have gone through very similar developmental crises as children. At each stage of development, the child learns to tolerate frustration and delay gratification. Eventually, Freud decided that during childhood, each person (hopefully) passes through five stages of development that affect personality. During each stage, the pleasure-seeking impulses of the id focus on a particular area of the body and on activities connected with that area.

1. *Oral stage (birth to 1 year).* The focus of the infant is on oral activities such as sucking, swallowing, nursing, thumb sucking, biting, crying, tasting, and vocalization. All such oral stimulation produces sensual pleasure in the child. The crisis in the first year of life is weaning, which causes a period of frustration and conflict. This is the child's first experience of not getting what it wants. The more difficult it is for the child to leave the mother's breast or the bottle, the more libido is fixated at the oral stage.

Separation anxiety arises when the infant becomes aware that the mothering person is separate from itself and can thus leave the infant. The potential loss of the mother is a grave matter to the infant, as the child depends on the mother for survival. When left by its primary caretaker, the child suffers fear of abandonment, which is termed by psychoanalysts as fear of loss of the love object.

There are many adult behaviors thought to represent fixation at the oral stage. Oral characters are likely to engage in activities aimed at obtaining erotic pleasures through the mouth, such as talking too much, overeating, chain smoking (Freud himself was fond of cigars), or an exclusive focus on oral sex. The orally fixated person is still trying to release libidinal energy through oral activities. Since weaning is a prototype for dependency, those fixated in the oral stage are likely to be compliant. They may exhibit additional qualities, such as having a preoccupation with giving and taking; extremes of optimism and pessimism; and hastiness, restlessness, and impatience.

2. *Anal stage (ages 2 to 3).* When the child is weaned, libido shifts from the mouth to the anus. The anus is an erogenous zone, which along with the mouth and genitals, is especially sensitive to erotic stimulation. The expulsion of the feces is believed to bring relief from tension and pleasure in the stimulation of the mucous membranes in that region. The crisis for this stage is delayed gratification, as experienced through toilet training. During the first year of life, parents make few demands on children, but now the mother requires that her child retain his or her feces and exert bladder control until on the toilet. Thus the child must violate the pleasure principle and delay the pleasure of evacuation or be punished. The focus of toilet training is on withholding or producing feces at the appropriate times and on being clean. The toddler learns to fear being unclean and thus inappropriate.

Muscle control becomes the prototype for self-control in general. When children find their parents' demands for toilet training difficult, they will show resistance, which may be either active or passive. The child exhibiting active resistance effectively delivers the message, "You can't make me do that." The

"Hoarding is just as human as sharing."

child may defecate in inappropriate places. If the child adopts a strategy of direct opposition as a general coping strategy, he or she might become an anal expulsive character. Anal expulsive types may express anger by becoming promiscuous; having poor impulse control; being wasteful, disorderly, and messy; or by being a spendthrift. Passive resistance to toilet-training demands involves retaining feces. When this strategy is successful, it may be adopted by the child as a general coping strategy known as the anal retentive character. Adult behaviors indicating anal retentive fixation are excessive neatness, stubbornness, closed-mindedness, envy, and stinginess ("not letting go"). This type is also careful, systematic, and orderly.

3. *Phallic stage (ages 4 to 6).* The crisis of this stage is the awakening of sexual desire for the opposite-sex parent, which violates the incest taboo, and the rejection by that parent of the child's overtures. In the earlier stages of development, both boys and girls are focused on their mothers (as their usual caretaker), so that their emerging emotional attachment gets focused on her. During the phallic stage, the boy's ever-increasing interest in pleasurable sexual activity continues to be focused on his mother. His desire for exclusive possession of his mother is thwarted by the presence of the father as the mother's partner. The son experiences his father as a formidable rival for the attentions of the mother and has thoughts of how nice it would be if the father were out of the picture. Such thoughts frighten the boy, partly because of his conviction that his father can read his thoughts and is thus aware of this naughty idea. According to Freud, the boy fears that his father will retaliate for this naughtiness by castrating the son. This "castration anxiety" motivates the son to give up wooing of his mother and to identity with his father, hoping someday to woo a female just like his mother. The resolution of the Oedipus complex results in the identification of the boy with his father and in the establishment of a "superego," the aspect of the psyche representing the incorporation of moral strictures from the parents.

In the boy, the Oedipus complex is resolved by the real or fantasized threat of castration. Since the girl does not fear the loss of a penis, not being in possession of one, she assumes that its absence indicates that she has already been castrated. This "realization" initiates the girl's transfer of some of her earlier intimate attachment to her mother, who was her first love object, to her father, who is valued for his possession of a penis. With her discovery that she lacks what, in her view, is an essential anatomical feature, the girl develops "penis envy." This is the female version of the Oedipus complex. In light of her discovery that the lack of a penis is a universal attribute of females, devaluation of the mother and abandonment of her as the primary love object occurs. She wishes to symbolically obtain a penis by association with her father, since she cannot obtain one from her mother, who also lacks one. She desires a symbolic penis substitute, a baby. Whereas the boy's desire for possession of his mother is brought to an abrupt end by fear of castration, a girl's focus on her father was thought to fade slowly with time. The difference between boys' and girls' resolution of their complexes was thought by Freud to carry the implication that women do not develop as strong a conscience (superego) as men.

It should be noted that not all psychologists agree with the Freudian theory outlined here. Freud was apparently convinced that women are psychologically as well as physically inferior to men. Karen Horney (1939) was one psychoanalyst who took issue with Freud's contention that girls suffer from penis envy when they become aware of their natural inferiority. Horney suggested that girls do envy boys when they realize that in a patriarchal culture, males have more privileges than do girls. In response to Freud's contention that girls experience envy of boys' penises, contemporary psychologist, Carole Tavris (1996) remarked, "Freud was right about penis envy, just not which sex suffers from it." Horney, on the other hand, suggested that it would not be surprising if boys were to experience "womb envy," as they are unable to bear children, yet Freud didn't include such an idea in his theory.

Adult behaviors that signal a fixation (being stuck) at the phallic stage are delayed marriage due to an unresolved Oedipus complex and/or marrying someone much older than oneself and relating to that person as a father/ mother figure. Also, rage, abandonment, recklessness, jealousy, loneliness, assertiveness, love, and guilt are emotions associated with a fixation at this stage. According to Freud, if the phallic period is traversed with but little restraint or frustration, the child may not experience enough guilt to make him or her an endurable member of society.

4. *Latency period (ages 6 to puberty)* The crisis for this time of life is identification with persons of the same gender. Identification begins during this "natural homosexual period" when children develop heroes and heroines of the same sex to model themselves after. The wish to possess the opposite-sexed parent is repressed, and the focus on sexuality is reduced or sublimated, meaning that sexual impulses are redirected into learning tasks, as children turn their attention to developing skills needed for coping with the environment. Peer relationships become important. Children engage primarily in same-sex play and show disinterest in the other sex. The fear of the superego motivates a child at this age, as the child wishes to avoid feeling guilty or conscience-stricken.

5. *Genital stage (puberty to death).* Freud believed that personality was completely formed by adolescence. The crisis at this stage was thought to be identification with the parent of the same sex. The focus of the person is on

hunting for an ideal lifestyle in which his or her main means of discharging libido comes through heterosexual activities as well as productive work. The adolescent is biologically capable of procreating and likewise psychologically propelled by the adult sexual aim of consummating the sexual act to accomplish reproduction. Heterosexual intimacy is the desired goal of the adolescent. (The changed perspective on homosexuality among psychologists will be discussed in Chapter 11). The genital period is the culmination of the previous stages of development of the libido, begun in infancy and played out through the biological development of the mature human being. If all goes well through these stages, the person becomes a fully functioning adult. In Freud's view, the two basic qualities of the productive adult life are the ability to love well and the ability to work well.

FIXATION Freud developed the concept that many adult emotional problems can be traced to specific disturbances during the oral, anal, and phallic stages; wherein some crucial aspect of development in childhood was not mastered. The person is believed to be stuck, or fixated. He or she cannot continue to grow until he or she returns to this childhood predicament and conquers it. For instance, committing to marriage represents a momentous step in the lives of most people. Some people are unable to take this step because of debilitating fear. Freudians would say that such people are fixated in development. To protect their egos against what they perceive as the overwhelming anxiety that marriage will bring, they unconsciously remain at the stage of emotional development where they found themselves when contemplating this action.

As a result of fixation, the individual develops an adult character type, such as an oral character or an anal character, reflecting the poorly resolved conflict (Freud, 1908). Once formed, character types are believed to be quite stable and to influence greatly one's choice of mate and occupation (Baudry, 1988). Freud's discovery of the enduring influence of childhood experience led him to stress the relative fixedness of individual character (Lifton, 1993).

PSYCHOANALYTIC THERAPY Freud developed a form of therapy based on his theory that psychological disturbances arise from anxieties rooted in unconscious conflicts (between the id, ego, and superego). The goal of psychoanalysis is to bring unconscious conflicts into conscious awareness where they can be dealt with and to strengthen the ego, to enable the person to cope with life.

Psychoanalysts use the technique of **free association,** in which the patient verbalizes all thoughts and feelings that come to mind. The purpose of free association is to lower defenses so that unconscious material may emerge. Patients recline on a couch during therapy, to encourage relaxation and a free flow of ideas and images from the patient's unconscious. They must verbalize even painful and embarrassing thoughts that come to mind without censoring anything. Ideas are allowed to move freely from one association to the next. The psychoanalyst looks for symbolic content and the thread that connects the associations.

When appropriate, the psychoanalyst does an **analysis of transference,** based on the patient's free association material. Transference occurs when the patient relates to the psychoanalyst as though he or she were a significant person from the patient's past. For instance, the patient may view the analyst as a rejecting father or an overprotective mother. Thus, patients may view their psychoanalyst as a lover, confessor, friend, rival, villain, and hero, calling up changing perceptions of the therapist from previous relationships with important people in the patient's life. The role of the psychoanalyst is to be ambiguous or impersonal to allow the patient to transfer feelings to the analyst arising from these important past relationships. To the extent that the patient knows about the analyst as a person, the transference is made more difficult. When made aware of the transference, the patient is able to discontinue this automatic, unconscious way of relating. Through this reexperiencing of old relationship patterns in a safe environment, the patient learns better ways to relate to others. He or she is now an adult and doesn't need some of the old coping behaviors learned as a child.

During treatment, the patient may resist talking about certain topics. Such resistance is said to reveal important unconscious conflicts. It is a reaction to any attempt to bring repressed strivings and fantasies into awareness. Resistance to recalling significant emotional events is another form of defensive maneuver that the conscious mind employs to protect the person from threatening thoughts. Consider Freud's famous case study of Fraülein Elisabeth, wherein he discovered that she actively resisted becoming aware of her desire to possess her sister's husband, because such a betrayal of her sister was too disagreeable an idea for Freud's patient to admit to conscious awareness (Freud, in Breuer & Freud, 1893–1895). As the analyst becomes aware of resistance to awareness of something, he or she brings it to the patient's attention so it can be dealt with. This process is referred to as an **analysis of resistance.** Freud found that if the analyst touched on repressed material, the patient would "resist" the psychoanalyst's therapeutic approach. This resistance is not a matter of conscious unwillingness on the part of the patient or of dishonesty or of secretiveness; the patient is defending himself or herself against the discovery of the painful, unconscious material without being aware either of the material or of his or her resistance.

There are many reasons why a person may repress certain strivings, often throughout life. He or she might be afraid of being punished, of not being loved, or of being humiliated if the repressed impulses were known to others (or to the self, insofar as self-respect and self-love are concerned). Resistance can generate a variety of reactions: The patient can turn away from the sensitive topic and talk about something else, feel sleepy and tired, find a reason not to come to the therapy sessions, or become very angry with the psychoanalyst and find some reason to quit the analysis.

Freud's Approach to Dreams   **Dream analysis** is a fundamental tool used in psychoanalysis. Freud came to believe that dreams, neurotic symptoms, and slips of the tongue conceal ideas that are not acceptable to the conscious personality. Freud called dreams the "royal road to the unconscious" and used them as one of his primary ways to uncover the unconscious conflicts, which he believed caused mental illness in his patients. In fact, he considered dreams the single best source of information about a person's unconscious.

According to Freud, the objects and events that we conjure up in our dreams represent attempts to fulfill some impulse of the id, usually in disguised ways. Freud contended that dreams represent, in hidden or symbolic form, repressed desires, fears, conflicts, and wishes. Dreams are particularly likely to be expressions of repressed sexual wishes and fears, as well as aggressive impulses. Forbidden desires and unconscious feelings are more freely expressed in dreams than in a wakeful state.

The repressed material surfaces in disguised fashion in dreams because the brain's censor (the part of the brain believed by Freud to repress anxiety-provoking material) is less vigilant during sleep. Dreams are structured to conceal significant but unacceptable motives from consciousness. A special agency of the conscious mind, called the "censorship system," acts as a border guard between the unconscious and conscious systems of the mind. Wishes or urges that arise from the unconscious during sleep are heavily censored by this ethical arm of the mental apparatus.

Freud referred to the remembered version of the dream as the **manifest content.** It consists of all those recalled sights, images, ideas, sounds, and smells that compose the story of the dream. Although the manifest content may be easily recalled by the dreamer, the latent content can be arrived at only by careful interpretation of the manifest content.

The **latent content** of the dream is deciphered through dream analysis, which involves making associations to the content of the remembered dream. Whereas the manifest content is the obvious portion of the dream, the latent content is its hidden aspect. It contains the "perverse," unacceptable impulses that lie like "masked criminals" beneath the facade of recallable elements (Freud, 1925, p. 132). Accurate interpretation of the dream lifts the disguise, makes intelligible the distortions, and replaces absurdity with understanding. When correctly translated, a dream's latent content may contain a wish that dates from childhood: "... to our surprise, *we find the child and child's impulses still living on in the dream*" (Freud, 1900, p. 191). Dream processes are a *regression* to the earlier years of the dreamer's mental life.

Although few modern psychotherapists have subscribed wholeheartedly to all of Freud's ideas, they would not deny that his teachings have profoundly influenced the development of most modern theories and techniques of therapy. When a person seeks out a therapist because of some current life difficulty, in addition to inquiring about the symptomatic history, the clinician will typically elicit the person's recollections of what his or her childhood and adolescent development was like. The clinician is interested in what impressions the person has of his or her relationship to parents, siblings, and other important figures in his or her past. Eventually, the person's symptoms will be related to his or her psychological development, that is, to the disappointments, upsets, and injuries that the child suffered or believes he or she has suffered, by chance or design at the hands of the people who raised him or her. If this purpose is achieved, a meaningful explanation can be developed as to how the person's childhood experiences came to determine his or her character and to account for his or her behavior as an adult.

➤ ERIK ERIKSON'S RECONCEPTUALIZATION OF FREUD'S DEVELOPMENTAL STAGES

Erik Erikson was a follower of Sigmund Freud and is thus considered to be a neo-Freudian. He is best known for his reconceptualization of Freud's developmental stages. In contrast to Freud, who believed that personality was essentially completely formed by the end of childhood, Erikson (1950; 1968) proposed that personality development is a lifelong process.

In comparison with Freud, Erikson decreased emphasis on unconscious drives as shaping personality development, and instead focused on the influence of early social relationships on the unfolding personality. He examined central problems faced by people of the same age and sociocultural background over their life span. Eventually, he delineated eight major dilemmas, or crises, that he believed were experienced by each human being over the life course. Each dilemma has a positive (desirable) pole, which represents social maturity, and is opposed to a negative (undesirable) pole, which represents the fixated characteristic of that developmental crisis.

Each of Erikson's eight stages focuses on life tasks that must be resolved, and their resolution at each stage is the way a person acquires a healthy personality. With the tackling of each new life crisis, the ego incorporates a new quality into the global personality, so that the individual becomes a more complex person with a much wider range of interests. With each new resolution, there is a growing sense of personal achievement and an expanding sense of ego identity.

➤ ERIKSON'S EIGHT STAGES OF PSYCHOSOCIAL DEVELOPMENT

Early Infancy (Birth to 1 year) (Comparable to Freud's Oral Stage)

Erikson saw the crisis for the infant to be that of *trust versus mistrust*. The newborn is completely dependent on others. The infant learns trust by being held, caressed, and cared for. Mutual recognition between infant and caretaker is important, as through this care-taking, the infant learns to feel loved and accepted. Touch is the first form of love experienced by a human being. The result of successful negotiation of this crisis means that the child will grow into a human being who is able to give and receive love, master fears, and feel secure and adequate as a person. Erikson said that the first lesson in life is "You can trust your mother."

Mistrust is caused by inadequate or unpredictable care given by parents who are cold, indifferent, or rejecting. For example, if a mother is unkind or undependable in meeting the infant's needs, the infant would be expected to acquire a suspicious view of the world. The child will have a tendency to reject affection from others. He or she will fear loving or trusting enough to be intimate and thus will be unable to form close relationships. This inability will result in feelings of isolation.

The child may also become insecure. He or she will be likely to feel fearful in novel situations. As an adult, the person may exhibit greediness and acquisitiveness, if material things become a substitute for love and attention from parents. Since material goods are poor substitutes, the person never feels that he or she has enough possessions. The person may experience a failure to attain maturity both socially and emotionally (and be still yearning for what was missed during infancy).

Erikson attempted to sum up in a single term the strength a person gains from each stage. He called these strengths the "associated virtue" for each stage. The associated virtue to be gained in early infancy is *hope*. This is a very basic human strength, which we need to live. Hopelessness has a well-documented relationship with depression and the wish to end one's life. Hope is a basic human attitude that, if lost, must be restored.

QUESTIONS: *Do you know anyone who acts as though he or she cannot afford to trust others? Do you think that this type of orientation toward others comes from early in life or from disappointments in adulthood?*

Early Childhood (Ages 1 to 3) (Freud's Anal Stage)

The crisis at the second stage of life is *"autonomy versus shame and doubt."* The tasks for toddlers are to develop a sense of self and accept their personal power. They are beginning the journey toward autonomy. Children at this age develop the wish to make decisions by themselves. They learn independence by doing things for themselves, and there is much exploring by climbing and touching. Being able to care for some of their own physical needs is important to children at this age. A crucial determinant for success here is whether they experience primarily success or failure in learning to control their own bodily functions. Toilet training is thought to be a significant milestone on the road to autonomy. It can also become a source of shame and doubt.

Shame is necessary in human life, according to Erikson. This is the age when children begin to blush and show embarrassment. Both autonomy and shame must emerge, though the ratio should be in favor of autonomy. At this age, children should learn skills to cope with negative feelings such as anger and rage. The "negativism" characteristic of two-year-olds is renowned.

The result of successful negotiation of this crisis is that children can view themselves as persons apart from their parents but still dependent on them. Successful children develop confidence and feel proud of themselves in their efforts to do for themselves. They develop the ability to feel and express negative feelings without shame or doubt or without feeling evil for having such emotions. Children who have a favorable resolution of the crisis at this stage are able to make mistakes and still feel that they are basically worthwhile. The associated virtue for this stage is *will*.

If parents do not appreciate their children's efforts, the children may feel ashamed of themselves. Parents who ridicule their children or overprotect them may cause them to doubt their abilities. As a result of ridicule, children may feel inadequate, wanting to hide their inadequacies, and may curtail learning basic skills like walking and talking. Overprotection by parents may cause children to sense their parents' fearfulness, and thus conclude that the outside world is a dangerous place.

Preschool Age (Ages 3 to 6) (Freud's Phallic Stage)

The crisis for this stage is *initiative versus guilt*. Children at this age engage in planning and other proactive behavior. They seek to find out how much they can do. Children now begin to develop a sense of right and wrong. They also learn basic attitudes regarding sexuality and gender-role identity.

A successful negotiation of this crisis results in children who learn to move around in their world and to assert their own needs. They take initiative in expressing their own desires. Children of this age have lively imaginations, and they vigorously test reality. They establish a sense of competence; they imitate adults, anticipating future roles; and they learn to give and receive affection.

The associated virtue for this stage is *purpose*. This is the time for development of goal-directedness. Children at this age begin to think of being big and begin to have "projects."

Failure at this stage means inability to accomplish goals, which often leads to feelings of guilt. If parents criticize severely, prevent play or discourage questions, children may feel guilty about activities that they initiate. Such children lack spontaneity. They will tend to have a fear of questioning and thinking for themselves, and a blind acceptance of parental dictates.

These children suffer from role inhibition. They may experience gender-role confusion. Also, they may feel guilty about natural impulses and feelings. Unless these children can discover socially acceptable ways to express sexual needs, they will be obsessed with guilt throughout life. Rigidity, severe conflicts, guilt, remorse, and self-condemnation can result.

Middle Childhood (Ages 6 to 12) (Freud's Latency Period)

The crisis during this stage is *industry versus inferiority*. Children learn the basic commerce and technology of their culture. They are interested in learning. Erikson agreed with Piaget (another developmental psychologist, who will be discussed in Chapter 5) that learning has a drive of its own. This theory represents a departure from the Freudian view that learning represents sublimated sexual energy.

At this stage, children engage in social tasks. They develop new communication skills, learn to give and take, and develop peer relationships. Hopefully, they learn to tolerate people who are culturally different. Children broaden their concept of appropriate feminine or masculine roles. They develop heroes and heroines of the same sex to model themselves after. Children now also expand their understanding of the physical world, and they learn physical skills that enable them to cope with the environment. At this time, they learn to read and write and calculate. Children develop a sense of values, learn to tolerate ambiguity, and achieve a sense of productivity, learning to focus on goals.

The result of success at this stage is that children have a sense of duty and accomplishment. They develop scholastic and social competencies, undertake real tasks (e.g., scouting or athletics), and learn to use the world's tools. Children put fantasy and play into better perspective. Success during this period results in an industrious, hard-working adult. The associated virtue for this stage is *competence.*

Failure at this stage means that children may develop a **fixation,** which is an inhibition in learning and a wish to go back or regress. These children have poor work habits, avoid strong competition, and may conform in a slavish manner. They have a sense of futility and inadequacy, and a lowered sense of self-worth.

Children are influenced by school experiences and their contact with peer group and teachers. They are still influenced by interactions with the family, but for the first time, teachers, classmates, and adults outside the home become as important as parents in shaping attitudes toward self. At this time, children are in a lull before the potential storm of puberty.

Adolescence (Ages 12 to 18) (Freud's Genital Stage)

The crisis for this stage is *ego identity versus role confusion.* Erikson considered the main task of adolescence to be building a stable identity, and he considered adolescence the most important stage of development. Teens spend time wondering about who they are and where they're going. Adolescents ask, "Where do I fit in, in this culture?"

Tasks for this stage involve integrating the various dimensions of one's identity that have developed so far. For example, identification with the same-sex parent has generally occurred by this time. Children from single-parent homes might turn to same-sex models outside the home. Teens need to establish a separate identity from their family, a process that is called "individuation" by many psychologists (Chapter 6). They must find a meaning for living and must sometimes cope with a sense of uselessness. Adolescents also need to continue the process of preparing for the future.

Erikson suggested that adolescents often experience an **identity crisis** (a term he coined), worrying about who they are. This self-confrontation involves physical elements such as the awakening of sexual drives, cognitive developments associated with the attainment of logical thought, and social elements. The desire to feel unique and distinctive does battle with the wish to "fit in."

The identity crisis is often successfully resolved with the adoption of an ideology that gives personal and social meaning back to the person caught up in feelings of distress. Adolescents develop ideological commitments and are often quite idealistic in their devotion to a cause. When all goes well during this stage, teens develop and accept their personal identity with regard to sexuality, social interactions, and plans for the future. They experiment with different roles and have the self-confidence to take risks. Such young people understand leader-follower roles, so that they can learn from adults through an "apprenticeship" relationship. Also, they become prepared to experience a mature sexual relationship.

The associated virtue for this stage is *fidelity*. Teenagers must develop a capacity to perceive and abide by values. When and adolescent reaches a certain age, he or she has to learn to be faithful to something. To fail to do this is to develop a weak ego or become a delinquent.

The result of failure is that identity problems weaken a person, who becomes self-conscious. The teen suffers role-fixation and experiences work paralysis. Adolescents behave in disingenuous ways when the need to be liked and accepted is stronger than the need for self-respect. Teenagers may fail to achieve a sense of identity when feeling overwhelmed by the pressures placed on them. They remain confused about just who they are and what might be their role in life. The adolescent may experience bisexual confusion. (Note that Freud and the neo-Freudians held to the idea that a heterosexual orientation is the hallmark of a mature personality.) Authority confusion may result in rebellion against all authority figures. Those who go to the extreme of attempting to be totally different from their parents are still using their parents as the standard of behavior and are thus not free of parental values. Just the reverse may be the problem: Overidentification with some individual or clannish group may result from an inability to develop a consistent and satisfying sense of self.

Young Adulthood (Ages 18–35)

The crisis here is *intimacy versus isolation*. By "intimacy" Erikson meant an ability to care about others and to share experiences with them. Intimacy is the ability to fuse one's identity with someone else's without worrying about losing one's own selfhood. The ability to establish an intimate relationship depends in large part on whether people have achieved a stable sense of identity. After establishing a stable selfness, a person is prepared to share meaningful love and/or deep friendship with others. A "clinging" type of person isn't likely to be happy or productive, because he or she is preoccupied with fears of losing the strong, competent partner to whom he or she is attached.

Successful negotiation of this crisis involves the establishment of intimacy with another human being. The associated virtue for this stage is *love*.

Failure to establish intimacy with others leads to a sense of isolation. The person feels alone and uncared for in life. This circumstance often sets the stage for later difficulties. In some cases, the isolating patterns are disguised by a series of intense but brief affairs or by stable but distant relationships. Many adult relationships remain superficial and dissatisfying. The fact that an individual gets married is not necessarily an indication that this crisis has been resolved in favor of intimacy, since two individuals can spend a lifetime together and yet be psychologically isolated.

Middle Adulthood (Ages 35 to 60)

Generativity versus stagnation is the crisis for this time of life, according to Erikson. One learns to take responsibility for what one creates. The procreative drive in this sense is basic to human beings. Everything that is generated—children, works of art, infrastructure, production of ideas—contributes to an accomplishment of the middle-age task.

The task associated with middle adulthood is to develop an interest in guiding the next generation. People of this age need to broaden their concerns and energies to include the welfare of others and of society as a whole. They achieve **generativity** by (1) caring for their children; (2) helping other children or young adults, and looking to the future, for example, becoming teachers, coaches, scout leaders, mentors, members of the clergy, or activists in social issues; or (3) engaging in productive and creative work. The associated virtue for this stage is *care*. When we care for or take care of something, we are expressing generativity.

People who have a sense of generatively tend to focus more on what they can give to others than on what they can get (Hamacheck, 1990). They are absorbed in a variety of activities outside themselves, such as contributing to society or in other ways reflecting a concern for others.

Concern only for one's own needs and comforts leads to stagnation. Stagnating people display self-centered attitudes and values. They avoid risks and choose the security provided by a routine existence rather than showing an interest in making the world a better place. Stagnation also occurs when a person wants to hang onto the past. For example, a middle-aged woman who gets a face-lift and talks constantly about her youth would be displaying stagnation. People caught in this mode tend to have feelings of being trapped. They experience personal bitterness about the inevitability of aging.

Late Adulthood (Age 60+)

The crisis for this stage is *integrity versus despair.* On the basis of having lived a long life, a person may come to understand the wisdom of the ages. In part because of the inevitable infirmities of old age, the person withdraws from involvement in activities with which he or she had previously been occupied.

After about the age of 60, our central developmental tasks include the following: (1) accepting inevitable losses, such as adjusting to the death of spouse and friends, loss of the attractiveness and status of a young person, adjusting to decreased physical and sensory capacities, and adjusting to retirement; (2) being able to relate to the past without regrets; (3) finding a new meaning in life when former sources of meaning, such as parenting minor children, are gone; (4) maintaining outside interests; and (5) enjoying grandchildren.

By despair, Erikson meant that people may feel that they have a lot of unfinished business, that life has been a series of missed opportunities and bad decisions. Some might conclude that other people or they themselves spoiled their plans. They think that they have wasted their lives and let valuable time slip by. Perhaps they feel that they have failed and that it is too late to reverse what has been done. Consequently, these persons are filled with regret. They may long for a second chance at the life cycle with more advantages.

For such people, there is an inability to accept oneself and one's life. They may develop a sense of hopelessness and feelings of self-disgust. These individuals find no meaning in human existence and have no feeling of world order or spiritual sense. They fear death; the threat of death becomes a source of depression. These are people who die unhappy and unfulfilled.

People who succeed in achieving ego integrity feel that they have managed to cope with failures as well as successes, that they can look back over the events of a lifetime with a sense of acceptance and satisfaction. They experience self-acceptance, and are able to feel that their lives have been productive and worthwhile. When this outcome happens, "death loses its sting," according to Erikson. The associated virtue for this phase of life is *wisdom*.

LOOKING BACK OVER A LIFETIME

Eighty-five-year-old Nadine Stair reviewed her life and reflected on how she would live differently if she had her life to live over again:

"If I had my life to live over, I'd dare to make more mistakes next time. I'd relax. I would limber up. I would be sillier than I have been this trip. I would take fewer things seriously. I would take more chances. I would take more trips. I would climb more mountains and swim more rivers. I would eat more ice cream and less beans. I would perhaps have more actual troubles, but I'd have fewer imaginary ones.

"You see, I'm one of those people who live sensibly and sanely hour after hour, day after day. Oh, I've had my moments and if I had it to do over again, I'd have more of them. In fact, I'd try to have nothing else. Just moments, one after another, instead of living so many years ahead of each day. I've been one of those persons who never goes anywhere without a thermometer, a hot water bottle, a raincoat, and a parachute. If I had to do it again, I would travel lighter than I have.

"If I had my life to live over, I would start barefoot earlier in the spring and stay that way later in the fall. I would go to more dances. I would ride more merry-go-rounds. I would pick more daisies."

➤ CHILDHOOD REVISITED . . . BEYOND ERIKSON

Erikson's stage theory is a major one in the psychological literature explaining human development. His theory may not match your life experience. Don't worry about this. Additional theories and research have supplemented our understanding of the maturation of people throughout childhood and adulthood. Some have noted that events encountered in one's life have greater impact on personality development than does the aging process, per se. Others have observed that with better nutrition and healthcare, the adult life stages posited by Erikson have become longer, so that middle-age doesn't begin until age 40, nor late adulthood until a person reaches 65.

Psychologist Mary Ainsworth (1973; 1989; Ainsworth et al., 1978), a professor at the University of Virginia, did research to discover the nature of infants attachments to their mothers. During the first year of life, children form attachments to their caretakers, who are usually their mothers. By their first birthday, most babies demonstrate this attachment by displaying "separation anxiety." That is, when babies are left alone with a stranger, they cry and protest vigorously against having their mothers leave.

Ainsworth arranged to have mothers interact with their babies in a laboratory setting and then to have the mothers leave for a short period of time. She differentiated three types of infant-mother bonds, on the basis of how the infants responded to their mothers upon the mothers' return. The most desirable bond is a "secure attachment," because these babies have a stable and positive emotional bond with their mothers. Securely attached children show some distress when the mother leaves the room; they seek comfort and contact upon her return and then gradually continue their play. "Insecurely attached–avoidant" infants tend to turn away from the mother when she returns. Ainsworth inferred from this finding that these infants have an anxious emotional bond with their mothers, as do those babies with "insecure-ambivalent" attachments. This third group of children became quite upset and anxious when the mother left, and when she returned, they could not be comforted. Although they sought to be near the returning mother, they angrily resisted contact with her.

Mothers of securely attached infants tend to be responsive to their baby's cues (Isabella, 1993; Susman-Stillman et al., 1996). Anxious emotional connection is fostered by mothers who behave in an inappropriate, insufficient, intrusive, overstimulating, or rejecting manner (Isabella & Belsky, 1991).

Infants who are securely attached at the age of one year show more resiliency, curiosity, problem-solving ability, and social competence in preschool (Collins & Gunnar, 1990), suggesting that these early patterns have lasting effects. Likewise, there is research suggesting that we may maintain these attachment styles in adulthood (Chapter 9), repeating them in our romantic relationships (Shaver & Haven, 1993). Moreover, these attachment patterns have been found in several cultures (Sagi, 1990).

During their early years, children form life scripts or projects, which are shaped by the manner in which their parents relate to them and become a part of their self-definition. These early decisions about themselves are played out in adulthood.

Erikson's contention that adolescence is a period of turmoil has been challenged by research on adolescent rebelliousness, which suggests that only about 20 percent of adolescents go through a serious emotional disturbance in the teen years (Offer & Offer, 1975; Adelson, 1979; Dusek & Flaherty, 1981; Blyth & Traeger, 1983). Also, uncertainty about attitudes, values, ethics, career opportunities, and religious beliefs is not limited to the adolescent years, but is apparent in the adult stages, too (Cote & Levine, 1989). Even identity formation may be an ongoing process throughout the life span (Berzonsky, 1990).

➤ YOUNG ADULTHOOD REVISITED . . . BEYOND ERIKSON

In support of Erikson's view, 75 percent of college-age men and women rank a good marriage and family life as their primary adult goal (Bachman, O'Malley, & Johnston, 1978). More recently, psychologist John Harvey (1998) indicated that 83 percent of college students rated a close-knit family as their highest priority.

Another research-based perspective on adulthood suggests that what matters in adult development is not how old a person is but what that person is doing (Baum, 1988). For instance, having a child has stronger effects on an adult than at what age the person has the child (Helson, Mitchell, & Moane, 1984). Entering the workforce has powerful effects on a person's self-esteem and worldview regardless of *when* the individual starts working (Kohn & Schooler, 1983; Lykes & Stewart, 1982). Men and women facing retirement confront similar issues whether they are retiring at age 40, 50, or 60. Divorced people have similar problems whether they divorce at age 25 or 45.

QUESTION: *Think about Erikson's proposal that at each age, we must all encounter and resolve universal developmental issues, versus Baum's findings that life events create the crises in our lives rather than where we are in the life cycle. What is your thinking on this controversy?*

➤ MIDDLE AGE . . . BEYOND ERIKSON

Carl Jung (1935) believed that two major periods of self-development are "youth" (puberty to about age 35) and "adulthood" (ages 35 or 40 to old age). As with Erikson, Jung disagreed with Freud's view that personality development was completed in childhood. Instead, Jung concluded that the most significant phase of psychological growth occurs in adulthood, which is the time when the individual reaches his or her full potential. At around age 40, men and women develop more balanced personalities than was the case in early adulthood. They also develop a more refined sense of spirituality and commitment to loved ones. In contrast to the mythology surrounding an inevitable "midlife crisis," Jung held that this period of life is when an individual comes into his or her own. Research on the existence of a "midlife crisis" (Myers, 1992) has revealed that most people do not experience a major upset and rearranging of their lives.

Building on the work of Erikson, other studies of adulthood point to stable periods with a duration of five to seven years, during which energy is expended on career, family, and social relationships, punctuated by "transitional" periods lasting three to five years, during which assessment and reappraisal of major life areas occurs (Levinson, 1986). These transitional periods open the door for a new prioritizing of what activities are worth one's time and energy. Daniel Levinson has found five periods during adulthood when people tend to make life transitions. Such transitions are noticeable shifts in one's work arena, significant relationships, or self-concept. Levinson outlined a midlife transition, which takes place between the ages of 40 and 45.

Many men do apparently reevaluate their position in life between the ages of 37 and 41. Most men do not find this process overly stressful, but a minority go into a period of decline. On the other hand, some men decide to get out of some deadening patterns and spend the next decade building a new life in some significant way.

Levinson studied men first, but when he turned to women, he found that much of what he had discovered about men held true for women as well. However, women were less likely to enter adulthood with clearly formulated goals. When they neared age 40, women tended to focus on changes in personal identity, such as becoming more self-reliant, rather than on a reassessment of career-related goals (Levinson & Levinson, 1996).

➤ OLD AGE . . . BEYOND ERIKSON

The process by which elderly people tend to look back on their lives and to reflect and reminisce about what has transpired was termed **life review** by psychologist Robert Butler (1963). Such a review most frequently occurs at the time of retirement, at the death of a spouse, or at one's own imminent death. Seniors who engage in life review tend to weave their lives into a coherent picture in the telling. When individuals are satisfied with their lives, this process helps them to adjust to their impending death.

Writer Sven Birkerts (1994) is also interested in the value of creating a narrative for one's life, believing that this is how we make sense out of our lives and find them meaningful (Chapter 15). We gain wisdom by taking in the narratives offered by others, so that we can contemplate the truths about the human condition. Wisdom, according to Birkerts, is based on "the assumption that one person can somehow grasp a total picture of life and its laws, comprehending the whole and the relation of parts. To *comprehend:* to 'hold together.' We once presumed that those parts added up, that there was some purpose or explanation to our being here below." (p. 74).

In Rumer Godden's (1986) novel *The Peacock Spring*, an adolescent Indian describes his Hindu grandmother as being in the third stage of life, retirement. This is depicted as a highly desirable time of life, which involves a spiritual preparation for the end of this earthly esixtence. The grandmother was gradually withdrawing herself from emotional investment in everyday concerns. This undertaking seems to provide a positive connotation to the notion of retirement, in contrast to that of the Western value judgment placed on retirement as a process of being set aside in favor of fresh, young workers. By implication, such a philosophy as that reflected in Godden's work may lend some grace to the process of approaching the end of life.

Of course, such retirement as described in Hindu society is based on belief in reincarnation. The purpose of Evans-Wentz's (1960) *The Tibetan Book of the Dead* is to instruct believers on how to prepare for death. Since human beings know that they will die and that death is not an easy thing, they must learn how to do it.

In contrast, Westerners admire older adults who refuse to retire, but instead work and produce until they die. As Walt Disney lay dying in the hospital, he whispered in a reporter's ear for 30 minutes, describing his vision for various new attractions and buildings he had in mind for the new Walt Disney World that wouldn't be open to the public for another six years (Vance & Deacon, 1996).

➤ SUMMARY

Freudian Psychoanalysis

The first developmental theory in psychology was offered by Sigmund Freud, the founder of psychoanalysis. Freud developed the concepts of the id, the ego, and the superego as a way of explaining inner conflict and psychopathology. The id consists of two major instincts, the sexual instinct and the aggressive instinct. Both instincts are unconscious and motivate much of human behavior. The id operates on the pleasure principle, seeking to avoid pain and obtain pleasure. The id engages in wish fulfillment, attempting to reduce tension by forming a mental image of its desires. The conscious ego is the executive of the personality and is said to behave according to the reality principle. The ego decides how id instincts will be satisfied, as well as how superego demands will be met. The superego is composed of a "conscience," which incorporates all the things that the child is reprimanded for doing, and an "ego ideal," which encompasses those actions for which the child is rewarded.

The ego employs defense mechanisms to protect itself from being overwhelmed by anxiety, which arises when the ego tries to resolve the conflicting demands made by the id, the superego, and the reality of the external environment. Defense mechanisms protect the ego, but involve distortion of reality and operate at an unconscious level. Several of the most common defense mechanisms are denial, repression, rationalization, projection, reaction formation, regression, displacement, sublimation, and compensation.

Freud's theory of personality development is embedded in his five psychosexual stages of development. During each stage, the pleasure-seeking impulses of the id focus on a particular area of the body. In the first or oral stage, the focus of the infant is on activities such as sucking, swallowing, biting, crying, and tasting. After the child is weaned, libido shifts from the mouth to the anus, and the child thus enters the anal stage. The emphasis during this stage is delayed gratification, as experienced through toilet training. The toddler learns to fear being unclean, and thus inappropriate.

The crisis of the phallic stage comprises the awakening of sexual desire for the opposite-sex parent and the rejection by that parent of the child's overtures. The boy's desire for exclusive possession of his mother is thwarted by the presence of the father, who, the boy fears, will retaliate for the son's rivalry by castrating him. This "castration anxiety" motivates the son to give up pursuit of his mother and to identify with his father, hoping someday to woo a female of his own. Superego formation is accomplished through resolution of the Oedipus complex.

The female version of the Oedipus complex centers around her discovery that she lacks a penis. The girl assumes that she has already been castrated and thus develops "penis envy." This "realization" initiates the girl's transfer of some of her attachment from her mother to her father, who is valued for his possession of a penis.

During the latency period, sexual impulses are sublimated or redirected into learning tasks. Children turn their attention to developing skills needed for coping with the environment.

Freud believed that personality was completely formed by adolescence, which he referred to as the genital stage. The focus of the person is on contemplating a future lifestyle in which his or her main means of discharging libido comes through heterosexual activities.

Freud developed the theory that many adult emotional problems can be traced to specific disturbances during the oral, anal, and phallic stages. When a crucial aspect of development in childhood was not mastered, the person becomes stuck, or fixated. As a result of fixation, the individual develops an adult character type, which reflects the poorly resolved conflict.

Freud created a form of therapy, psychoanalysis, based on his theory that psychological disturbances arise from unconscious conflicts. Psychoanalysts use the technique of free association, in which the patient verbalizes all thoughts and feelings that come to mind. This process allows unconscious material to become conscious. The psychoanalyst does an analysis of transference, on the basis of the patient's free association material. Transference occurs when the patient relates to the psychoanalyst as though he or she were a significant person from the patient's past. During free association, the patient may also resist talking about certain topics. An analysis of the resistance is done by the therapist to discover its cause.

Dream analysis is used in psychoanalysis to uncover unconscious conflicts. Freud termed the remembered version of the dream the *manifest content*. The *latent content* of the dream is deciphered through dream analysis, which involves making associations between the remembered dream and the patient's unconscious wishes or conflicts.

Erikson's Eight Stages of Development

Erik Erikson reinterpreted Freud's five stages of personality development, shifting the emphasis from libidinal energy to the social interactions between a child and his or her caretakers. In contrast to Freud, who believed that personality was essentially formed by the end of childhood, Erikson proposed that personality development continues throughout life. He described eight major crises that he believed were experienced by each human being over the life course.

EARLY INFANCY (BIRTH TO 1 YEAR).   Erikson saw the crisis for the infant to be that of "trust versus mistrust." The newborn learns trust by being held and cared for. If all goes well, the child will feel secure as a person. Mistrust is caused by inadequate or unpredictable care. The mistrustful person will fear intimacy and thus will be unable to form close relationships.

EARLY CHILDHOOD (AGES 1 TO 3).   The crisis at the second stage of life is "autonomy versus shame and doubt." Children of this age learn independence by doing things for themselves. Toilet training takes place during this stage and can be a milestone on the road to autonomy or a source of shame and doubt. Children who have favorable resolution of the crisis at this stage are able to make mistakes and still feel that they are basically worthwhile. Parents who ridicule their children or overprotect them may cause them to doubt their abilities.

PRESCHOOL AGE (AGES 3 TO 6).   The crisis in this stage is "initiative versus guilt." Children at this age take the initiative in expressing their own desires. They establish a sense of competence. If parents criticize them severely, prevent play, or discourage questions, children may feel guilty about activities that they initiate.

MIDDLE CHILDHOOD (AGES 6 TO 12).   The crisis during this stage is "industry versus inferiority." Children learn physical skills, as well as scholastic and social competencies. Success during this period results in an industrious, hardworking adult. Failure means that children may develop an inhibition in learning and a wish to regress.

ADOLESCENCE (AGES 12 TO 18).   The crisis in this stage is "ego identity versus role confusion." Erikson considered the main task of adolescence to be the building of a stable identity. Teens may experience an identity crisis, worrying about who they are. The identity crisis is often resolved with the adoption of an ideology that gives personal and social meaning to the person. The result of failure is that identity problems weaken a person.

YOUNG ADULTHOOD.   The crisis here is "intimacy versus isolation." By intimacy, Erikson meant an ability to care about others and to share experiences with them. Failure to establish intimacy with others leads to a sense of isolation.

MIDDLE ADULTHOOD.   The crisis in this period is "generativity versus stagnation." Middle-aged adults achieve generativity by guiding the next generation or by productive and creative work. The concern only for one's own needs and comforts leads to stagnation.

LATE ADULTHOOD.   The dilemma here is "integrity versus despair." People who succeed in achieving ego integrity feel that they have managed to cope with failures and enjoy successes in life. Doing this brings self-acceptance. By despair, Erikson meant that people may feel they have a lot of unfinished business and missed opportunities. Consequently, they are filled with regret.

Erikson's stage theory can be contrasted with Baum's perspective on adulthood, which suggests that what matters in adult development is not how old a person is, but what that person is doing. Entering the workforce, marrying, having a baby, or retiring all have strong effects on a person regardless of when the individual has the experience.

Psychologist Mary Ainsworth did research to discover the nature of infants' attachments to their mothers. Ainsworth discovered that infants may have one of three types of infant-mother bond: secure attachment infants, who have a stable and positive emotional bond with their mothers; and either insecure-avoidant infants or insecure-ambivalent infants, who seem to have an anxious emotional bond with their mothers. These three types of attachment have been linked to maternal behaviors, as well as to the child's future well-being. During their early years, children form life scripts or projects, which are shaped by the manner in which their parents relate to them and become a part of their self-definition. These early decisions about themselves are played out in adulthood.

The process by which elderly people tend to look back on their lives and to reflect and reminisce about what has transpired was termed "life review" by psychologist Robert Butler, and is considered a route to gaining acceptance of the life that one has lived. For most people, late adulthood is a time of retirement from one's career, but attitudes about retirement among Westerners are ambivalent.

LEARNING THE LANGUAGE OF PSYCHOLOGISTS

id	compensation	analysis of transference
ego	denial	analysis of resistance
superego	repression	dream analysis
libido	rationalization	manifest content
wish fulfillment	projection	latent content
pleasure principle	reaction formation	fixation
reality principle	regression	identity crisis
defense mechanisms	displacement	generativity
sublimation	free association	life review

CHAPTER REVIEW QUESTIONS

1. What did Freud say caused mental disorder?
2. What is a defense mechanism, and what are the most common defense mechanisms?

3. When is a conscience formed, according to Freudian theory?
4. According to Freudian theory, at what point is personality development complete?
5. What is meant by a "fixation" at a given stage in life?
6. How does the defense mechanism of regression fit into Freud's view of human nature?
7. What are the eight stages of Erikson's theory of personality development?
8. How would Erikson explain the "terrible twos"?
9. What is meant by an "identity crisis," and at what age is it typically experienced?
10. What is the purpose of the "life review" process for senior citizens?

ACTIVITIES

1. *SMALL GROUP EXERCISE:* **Personal Reflections on My Own Personality Development.**
2. *SMALL GROUP EXERCISE:* **Ego Defense Mechanisms.**
3. *COMPLETE INDIVIDUALLY:* **Life Stage Interview.**
4. *SMALL GROUP EXERCISE:* **Life Inventory.**
5. *COMPLETE INDIVIDUALLY:* **Freudian Dream Analysis.**
6. *COMPLETE INDIVIDUALLY:* **How to Remember Your Dreams.**
7. *COMPLETE AT HOME:* **Lifeline.** Sketch your Life Line on a poster board (approximately 2' x 3'). Draw a horizontal line across the bottom of the longer side of your paper. Put a dot at each end of the line. Over the left dot, put the number zero. This dot represents your birth. Write your birth date under this dot. Over the right dot, put a number that indicates your best guess as to how many years you will live. Now place a dot that represents where you are right now on the line between birth and death. Write your current age under this dot. Make sure that your lifeline is drawn to scale.

   Sketch the events, places, people, experiences, etc. that have been influential in your life from birth until now. Draw your future, including your educational plans, career and family goals, and whatever else you want. Don't forget to include retirement and leisure if you have plans for these things. With the second dimension on your paper, you can draw your lifeline with "peaks" and "valleys," representing the "highs" and "lows" in your life so far, or the ones you anticipate in the future. Note: Be sure not to gloss over the section on your future. Give it considerable thought; plan out your life as you imagine it might unfold. Be prepared to discuss your project with the class.

Personal Reflections on My Personality Development

Directions: Read each of the following questions, and then write your answers in the blanks.

1. Try to think of an example in which you can identify a way that you have of interacting with a friend or romantic partner that seems to be a transference from the way that you related to family members as a child. Describe this way of relating that can be traced back to your childhood.

   _____

   _____

   _____

   _____

2. Is there a particular Eriksonian crisis that you have not managed smoothly or are not coping with well? For instance, did your social relationships go smoothly in grade school? Did you keep up with the other kids in school? Discuss an aspect of your development that corresponds to one of Erikson's stages.

   _____

   _____

   _____

   _____

3. Are you conscious of "trying on" or borrowing aspects of others that you admire? Whom do you remember looking to in order to establish your identity?

   _____

   _____

   _____

   _____

4. What are your lifetime goals? Do you have a "life plan"? If so, briefly describe your plan and goals. If not, do you have an intentional philosophy that avoids making such plans, or have you not thought much about it?

   _____

   _____

   _____

   _____

5. Give an example of a middle-aged person you know who might be said to have achieved generativity. Do you know of anyone in middle adulthood who appears to be stagnated?

_____

_____

_____

_____

6. Describe the similarities you see between your life and that of a character in a particular myth, legend, or folktale.

_____

_____

_____

_____

7. Complete this sentence: "My childhood was . . ."

_____

_____

_____

_____

8. Complete this sentence: "My main concern as a teenager was (or is) . . ."

_____

_____

_____

_____

9. Complete this sentence: "Mother gave me a view of myself as . . ."

_____

_____

_____

_____

10. Complete this sentence: "Father gave me a view of myself as . . ."

_____

_____

_____

_____

11. Complete this sentence: "My family gave me a view of myself as . . ."

_____

_____

_____

_____

12. Complete this sentence: "When I grow old . . ."

_____

_____

_____

_____

Ego Defense Mechanisms

Problem: Defense mechanisms work for us in helping us reduce stress and anxiety, but they also cause us problems by denying or distorting reality. Though we want to be neither "pathologically undefended" nor psychotic (out of touch with reality), we seem to be better off when we can recognize our own and others' use of defense mechanisms.

Directions: Divide into small groups (3 to 5 people). Discuss the examples that follow, and decide which defense mechanism is represented in each case.

1. Bob would like to break off with his girlfriend but feels guilty about it because they have gone together for four years. He justifies his behavior by telling her she'll be better off if she gets a little more experience dating other men. _____

2. The former neighborhood bully becomes a trophy-winning professional football player. _____

3. A baseball player who strikes out may carefully examine his bat. _____

4. Melissa has a fight with her husband and "goes home to mother." _____

5. Manuel disregards obvious signs that his wife is "cheating on him." _____

6. A man who is angry with his boss goes home and yells at his children. _____

7. A woman forgets a doctor's appointment to be tested for possible cancer. _____

8. A man rejected by a woman convinces himself that she was not nearly so attractive or interesting as he had supposed. _____

9. A middle-aged person characterizes all young people as "full of filthy thoughts about sex." _____

10. Sandy is so anxious about her impending divorce that she resorts to eating three hot fudge sundaes at a sitting, just as she did in early adolescence. _____

11. A parent ignores evidence that his child is involved with drugs and alcohol. _____

12. A man who unconsciously wishes to divorce his wife showers her with lavish gifts. _____

13. A woman witnesses a person beating someone to death. Later she cannot remember what she saw. _____

14. Mai, who has an ungratifying sexual relationship with her husband, lavishes attention and affection on her children. _____

15. Leroy can't match the grades of his older sister, so he works out in the gym every day, and he letters in three sports at school. _____

16. A young woman insists over and over that she loves the mother whose feigned ill health requires the young woman to give up an independent social life. _____

17. A thief takes money from a wealthy man, saying that the man will never miss it. _____

18. A man who is angry with his next-door neighbor goes hunting and kills a deer. _____

19. A greedy shop owner justifies his sharp and deceptive business practices by believing that his customers are greedy and dishonest. _____

20. Sarah, who is not nearly so attractive as her mother or sister, has gained a reputation for being nurturing and helpful to others. _____

*"And then I say to myself, 'If I really wanted to talk to her,
why do I keep forgetting to dial 1 first?'"*

21. A 42-year-old college student moves back
home and relies on his parents to make his car
payment.   _____

Life Stage Interview

Problem: Ageism refers to discrimination or prejudice on the basis of age. In
Western cultures, ageism has a negative impact on older individuals. It may
be expressed as an aversion, hatred, or rejection of the elderly, or as a refusal
to take them seriously. One of the best ways to combat ageism is to counter
stereotypes with facts. Thinking about how others are living during the life
stages beyond the one you are in could be instrumental in helping you make
choices now that will influence what you will someday say about your own
middle or late adulthood.

Directions: In accordance with Erikson's scheme, plan an interview with
someone who is not in your life stage. Develop five questions that would be
relevant to ask, given the crisis typical of that stage, and then find someone to
interview. For example, you might ask a person in middle adulthood to share
some of the issues he or she is facing that are different from those tackled in
young adulthood. Are there any things that stand out that the person wishes
he or she had done differently? Is the person more involved in altruistic activities than was the case in adolescence or early adulthood?

In forming your questions, be sure to make them open-ended rather than ones that can be answered with a simple yes or no. For instance, asking "These days, women have a broader range of career choices than when you were my age; how might the choices you made at my age be different if you were making them today?" will probably elicit a more extensive answer than "Do you wish you had gone to college?"

Person interviewed_____ Age_____

Relationship to you_____

Life Inventory

Directions: Form into pairs. One student will interview the other, and then they will switch roles. The interviewer will ask questions such as the ones that follow, in order to help the interviewee look at some of the major themes and events of his or her life. The interviewer should refrain from advising the interviewee about any aspect of his or her life.

1. What was the happiest year or period in your life?
2. What things do you do well?
3. Tell about a turning point in your life.
4. What has been the lowest point in your life?
5. Was there an event in which you demonstrated great courage?
6. Was there a time of heavy grief? More than one?
7. Tell about some things that you do poorly, which you have to continue doing anyway.
8. What are some things that you would like to stop doing?

ROBOTMAN reprinted by permission of Newspaper Enterprise Association.

9. What are some things that you would really like to get better at?
10. Tell about some peak experience that you have had.
11. Tell about some peak experiences that you would like to have.
12. Are there some values that you are struggling to establish?
13. Tell about one missed opportunity in your life.
14. What are some things that you want to start doing now, right at this point in your life?

Source: Adapted from Simon, Howe, & Kirschenbaum (1972).

Freudian Dream Analysis

Problem: Even in modern times, speculations about dreams have been long on theory and short on observation. McConnell (1983) suggested that dreams are products of the creative, emotional right side of the brain. Scientists from several laboratories have found that the right half of the brain is much more active electrically during dreaming than is the left. This view is in keeping with Freud's belief that different parts of the mind seem to perform quite different tasks, with logic and rational thought taking place in what he called "the conscious regions of the mind," whereas creative and artistic perceptions were products of what he called "the unconscious portions of the mind." Freud was also convinced that during dreaming, unconscious material is more available to a person than it is during normal waking consciousness.

Freud believed that dreams are mental states designed to bring about the fulfillment of wishes or desires. While dreaming, we structure events, not as they are in the external world, but as we would like them to be. Sometimes, however, unconscious desire clashes with conscious restraint, so that the dream processes pursue devious paths to wish fulfillment. Freud concluded that "the interpretation of dreams is the royal road to a knowledge of the unconscious mind" (1900, p. 608).

Freud was able to isolate four separate processes in the dream work that account for the form of the manifest content. An understanding of these is necessary for the unraveling of the manifest content to reveal the latent content (Monte, 1991).

Condensation. A remembered dream can be recounted in relatively few words. In contrast, the associations aimed at uncovering the latent content may produce as much as twelve times the amount of the manifest content. Each manifest element has varied and reciprocal relationships with every other element. The manifest dream content is said to be *overdetermined*. Several unconscious ideas cluster together to contribute as a group some energy to form one common manifest element.

Displacement. Here a latent dream element is replaced by a more obscure idea to achieve a shifting of the dream's remembered emphasis away from a central concept and toward a peripheral one. Whereas condensation is responsible for compressing the latent thoughts into the abbreviated form of the manifest content, displacement is responsible for choosing elements from which the manifest dream is constructed. The censorship system selectively distorts the wish, transforming it into an alternate form that does not clash with the conscious ethical standards of the personality. Conversely, the only way that the unconscious drives can achieve satisfaction for their pressing urges is to evade the censor by masquerading the unacceptability of its wishes behind a facade of related, but more neutral, ideas.

Visual representation. Abstract thoughts are converted into concrete visual images. This translation typically involves converting the symbolic labels representing the idea into an actual physical act. For example, the abstract concept of "possession" can be transformed into the visually concrete act of "sitting on the object." Children often use this strategy to protect a preferred toy from the clutches of an overbearing playmate. The images employed are likely to be a function of the dreamer's particular life experiences and imagination. The psychoanalyst must understand the personal symbols and meanings of the dreamer in order to proceed with a dream analysis.

Secondary revision. The first three mechanisms described result in a distorting and a breaking apart of the latent elements' form and organization, yielding a fragmented product. When a person tries to recall a dream, he or she must create a coherent and consistent narrative from the dream fragments. To organize what otherwise would be experienced as a jumble of images, the mind organizes and thus makes sense of the confused array of thoughts and images. In the moments just before waking from a dream, the preconscious system of the mind molds the dreamer's recollected fragments into a form understandable to waking intelligence.

Directions: Describe a dream or dream fragment that you have had recently. (If any of you have trouble remembering your dreams, consult "How to Remember Your Dreams," which follows.) Your written description of the details of the dream will be your manifest content. Next, write a section in which you report any associations you can make or meanings you attach to your dream segment. This will be your attempt to uncover the latent content of your dream. Finally, comment on whether you were able to identify any of Freud's four separate processes in dream work: *condensation, displacement, visual representation* (of course you will find this), and *secondary revision* (you probably won't be able to catch this).

How to Remember Your Dreams

Problem: A lot of people complain that they can't remember their dreams. Although each of us dreams several times a night, we are likely to be awakened abruptly in the morning by an alarm clock and to dash out of bed, propelled by thoughts of the busy day ahead. This type of lifestyle chases dreams out of awareness. The Senoi Indians of Malaysia have no trouble remembering their dreams because they see their dreams as part of their everyday lives. They get together every morning and discuss their dreams. In their culture, this is what they discuss at breakfast. And they all remember their dreams.

Directions: To assist yourself in dream recall, do the following:

1. Tell yourself before you go to sleep that you will remember all of your dreams from this night. Picture yourself remembering your dreams and writing them down in the morning.

2. Have paper and a pencil next to your bed so that you can easily record your dreams.

3. When you wake up, do not move. Instead, review your dreams while you remain in your drowsy state. After you have reviewed your dreams, write them down in as much detail as possible.

4. Alternatively, write out a quick outline as soon as you wake up. When you get time to come back to your dream later in the day, you'll remember the details, but if you don't make a few notes when you wake up, you probably won't recall much.

5. If it's dark when you wake and you don't want to turn on the light, keep a voice-activated tape recorder by your bed.

6. If you cannot remember your dreams, set your alarm clock to go off 90 minutes after you go to sleep, so that you will wake up during your first dream cycle.

7. You can also set your alarm clock a half hour earlier or for random times during the night, in hopes of capturing a dream.

8. An alternative strategy is to let yourself wake up naturally, whenever you are rested. If this is the case, you are likely to be waking from a REM (dreaming) state. *Note:* REM means "rapid eye movement."

9. Often you wake with just a fragment of a dream. Ask yourself, What does the fragment make me think of? Write down whatever floats up in your mind in response to that fragment, and think about the connection to other parts of the dream. You may start recalling other elements.

4

Death and Loss

He who pretends to look on death without fear lies. All men are afraid of dying, this is the great law of sentient beings, without which the entire human species would soon be destroyed.
—Jean-Jacques Rousseau

> ➤ PREVIEW QUESTIONS: How does facing our own mortality make life pre-
> cious to us? Does living in a society that avoids talking about death make facing
> our own inevitable end more difficult? What is a normal grief process? Why do
> people commit suicide? How does one avoid feeling "psychologically dead"?

➤ INTRODUCTION: FACING CRISIS

All of us face times of hardship in life. Tragic events befall us and make us
uncertain as to how we are going to manage to go on. Times of crisis, such as
losing our house in a flood or fire, or critical illness of a family member, jeop-
ardize everything we have worked hard to accomplish and to build in our
lives. We are driven to consider what means we have to escape the situation,
and may even think of committing suicide. The crisis may disrupt our belief
that life makes sense, leaving us confused and frightened.

We feel best when we are active and seem to be able to surmount the
small obstacles encountered while pursuing our goals. We go about our busy
lives making plans, organizing our lives, balancing endless tasks, and relating
to others in a variety of social contexts at home, at school, or at the office.
When an emergency hits, we feel a sudden disconnect from our day-to-day existence. We do not do as well in moments of crisis, in part due to their departure from the norm, but perhaps also because we have not developed a meaningful philosophy of life through which to view them.

There are philosophies within our culture that imply that we do not
have to experience adversity if we think right and live right. Some "new age"
philosophies and spiritual movements take a mind-over-matter approach, implying that adversity can be completely avoided. An unfortunate consequence
of this belief system is that when individuals encounter inevitable hardships,
they may feel guilty about having caused their own troubles. While it is true
that we sometimes need to take more responsibility for our problems than we
are sometimes inclined to do (Chapter 1), we also have to realize that no matter how conscientious we are about how we conduct our lives, we'll occasionally have to confront difficulties that are not of our making.

Another, more evidence-based philosophy suggests that the effect that
hardships have on our lives depends on the way we think about them. Norman Vincent Peale's (1952) "power of positive thinking" is one example of
this type of philosophy. Abraham Lincoln, perhaps our greatest American
President, said that people were just about as happy as they made up their
minds to be. These men suggested that we can triumph over adversity by
thinking about the events in our lives in a productive way. This train of
thought is highly useful and will be elaborated on later (Chapter 8).

Viktor Frankl (1963) suggested that suffering is inevitable, deeply
human, and even a grace. He believed that when a person must face inevitable

suffering, the attitude that he or she takes towards the adversity has the potential to provide meaning or purpose in the experience. Longitudinal research conducted by psychologists has documented that even the most resilient and most successful of us will have occasion for disillusionment (Vaillant, 1977). Studies of such persons have indicated that it is not the case that successful people are lucky enough to escape hard knocks in life, but rather that they have developed effective ways of looking at and otherwise handling whatever adversity turns up. These studies may help us come to understand that times of crisis are a part of the process of coming to terms with reality and of gaining an understanding of the meaning of life.

All other forms of adversity pale in comparison with facing terminal illness in a loved one or in oneself or the unexpected death of a significant other. Fear of death is one of the core existential concerns discussed previously (Chapter 1). It is difficult at best for people even to imagine nonbeing, let alone accept it. Our thoughts turn to questions such as, What happens when I die? and Will I be remembered and leave anything important behind? Frankl (1955) proposed that the meaning we assign to death affects the meaning we find in life.

Unless we pass away suddenly, we shall have the opportunity sooner or later to face such a realization. Even those of us who depart without warning must confront in the process of normal life anxiety due to awareness of our inevitable end. In a sense, we are all terminal cases.

➤ FINDING MEANING IN LIFE THROUGH FACING DEATH

Facing Our Mortality Can Enhance Zest for Living

All human beings suffer the uneasiness that accompanies the knowledge of our own mortality. This shared fate can provide a sense of a common predicament with our fellow beings. Awareness of our impermanence can make it easier to overlook the false distinctions, prejudices, and ideologies that often separate us. This capacity may explain why, throughout history, spiritual leaders, philosophers, and psychologists have urged us to contemplate our inevitable demise.

The humanistic existentialist philosophy views anxiety over one's mortality as a universal concern and encourages conscious awareness of the very natural dread of death. Although this topic might seem morbid or depressing, an honest understanding and acceptance of death and loss can lay the groundwork for a meaningful life. Promoting rather than denying our awareness of death compels us to see our lives as a whole, with a beginning and an end. This view prompts us to set goals with a time-limited life plan in mind and thus makes our every act and moment count.

The point of view that death makes a positive contribution to life is not one easily accepted. Generally, we view death as such an unmitigated evil that we dismiss any contrary view as an absurd proposal. If we view death as unreal, beyond the horizon, or as something we should not think about, we may allow our lives to be guided by an unconscious denial born of fear. When left unconscious, death anxiety tends to incapacitate us. We may develop, as a pervasive life theme, a style of avoiding what we fear. The act of making fear conscious tends to mobilize us (Brock, 1998).

A danger in dismissing death is that we will not confront ourselves with the need to develop a direction in life. The acceptance of our mortality can prompt us to make our lives purposeful. It stimulates us to look at our priorities, and to ask ourselves whether we are living the way we want to live. Elisabeth Kübler-Ross (1975) wrote, "It is the denial of death that is partially responsible for people living empty, purposeless lives; for when you live as if you would live forever, it becomes too easy to postpone the things that you must do" (p. 164). When we arrive at the end of life, we may be filled with remorse over wasted years and goals left unattained. This is what Erik Erikson referred to as a state of despair that is possible in the final stage of life (Chapter 3). Ironically, immortality could be viewed as "a fate worse than death," because it would destroy pleasure, creativity, and purpose (Arkoff, 1995).

Here is an example of how the act of confronting our own mortality can lead to a renewed enthusiasm for living. Psychologist Abraham Maslow, while recovering from a heart attack, expressed the enlightenment he gained from the experience:

> The confrontation with death—and the reprieve from it—makes everything look so precious, so sacred, so beautiful that I feel more strongly than ever the impulse to love it, to embrace it, and to let myself be overwhelmed by it. My river never looked so beautiful . . . Death and its ever present possibility makes love, passionate love, more possible. I wonder if we could love passionately, if ecstasy would be possible at all, if we knew we'd never die (in Arkoff, 1995, p. 212).

It is well documented that a near brush with physical death can bring about a reordering of priorities in one's life. Apparently this is the case whether or not the brush with death is intentional. A leisure-time activity called "bungee jumping" has gained popularity in recent years. The jumper dives off a precipice, with an elastic cord attached to his or her legs, which rescues the person at the last moment from being smashed against the ground. Many individuals who have ventured to engage in this activity report an exuberance over surviving the experience, which is similar to that reported by sky divers. These persons often reenter their daily lives with a sense of having been emboldened and invigorated.

An enhanced zest for living has also been noted in individuals who have been informed that they are terminally ill. Kübler-Ross (1975), a psychiatrist well-known for her work with the dying, reported that when she first began to work with terminally ill patients, she expected them to focus on thoughts of dying and death. Instead, she found them occupied with living. They may contact relatives while they have the chance. If well enough, they may take trips and do other activities that they have always wanted to do. Otherwise, they take in the ordinary activities of life: listening to birds chirp or watching a family member cook. These everyday occurrences represent living itself.

Physician Deepak Chopra (1991) reported that some of his terminally ill patients actually seem "relieved" (p. 6) upon hearing the news of their illness. According to Chopra, such news can open opportunities denied to us in ordinary life. Sickness can have an element of escapism in it, because children do not have to go to school when ill and adults can give themselves permission to stay home from work. Adults and children alike may be indulged while ill with gifts and attention. Beyond temporary illness, apparently terminal illness provides the ultimate in liberation for some.

The escape may not be from life so much as from the assumptions that we make about the burdens we must carry in life. If we have been driven with the need for achievement, we now have an excellent reason to give up that pursuit. Many of us live for the future. We sacrifice enjoyment today and look towards the day when our delayed gratification will pay off. Although the ability to delay gratification is the sign of a mature person in general, when carried to an extreme, this characteristic can be problematic. We may plan to enjoy ourselves in the future for a lifetime! This future-orientation is a core personality trait (Zimbardo, 1995), which means that it is difficult to change. With the news of a terminal illness, we discover the necessity of living for today and being fully present in the current moment.

This shift in perspective does not seem to be reserved for persons who have a close brush with death. An individual can contemplate his or her mortality and, as a result, experience a sense of rejuvenation *without* having to come close to death on a physical level. This strategy for gaining a new perspective is safer, and thus preferable to self inflicted, death-defying acts such as bungee jumping. The full realization that we are mortal, that not only must we die one day but indeed might die at any moment, makes life more precious. When compared with death, even the most tumultuous life crises begin to look manageable. In *Journey to Istlan*, Carlos Castenada (1972) describes a conversation concerning death with his mentor, don Juan, a Yaqui medicine man:

> "Death is our eternal companion," don Juan said with a most serious air. "It is always to our left, at an arm's length . . . It has always been watching you. It always will until the day it taps you . . . The thing to do when you're impatient," he proceeded, "is to ask advice from your death. An immense amount of pettiness is dropped if your death makes a gesture to you, or if you catch a glimpse of it, or if you just have the feeling that your companion is there watching you . . . Death is the only wise adviser that we have. Whenever you feel . . . that everything is going wrong and you're about to be annihilated, turn to death and ask if that is so. Your

Calvin and Hobbes
by Bill Watterson

death will tell you that you're wrong; that nothing matters outside its touch. Your death will tell you, 'I haven't touched you yet.'" (pp. 54–55).

The awareness of death prompts us to search for meaning in life and reminds us that we do not have forever to do so. The Stoics of ancient Greece had a saying: "Contemplate death if you would learn how to live." A good look at the worst thing that could happen to us puts the rest of life in perspective.

Means of Symbolically Conquering Death

We have good reason to avoid thinking about death. If we have to die, so that nothing might matter, why should anything matter now? As human beings, we are meaning-hungry creatures. We want our lives to have stood for something.

Psychiatrist and author Jay Lifton (1993) wrote, "Awareness of death becomes . . . central to human evolution because that knowledge could not be erased, only symbolized, and symbolizations stemming from it are powerful and ever present" (p. 30). The symbolizing function of the conscious mind strives to incorporate the awareness of its finite life span into some framework that will permit it to find meaning and transcend despair over the realization of one's mortality.

There is more than one way to come to terms with the finite nature of life. A person may imagine living on through his or her children. This view represents a biological form of immortality. On a molecular level, we shall all continue on as an eternal part of nature, although the molecules which make up our physical body will be rearranged. We can extend ourselves beyond death through a creative product left behind or through personal influence (Chapter 15). Our spiritual beliefs form a religious mode of transcending death. It is also possible, according to Lifton, to defeat death by achieving an experiential transcendence, ". . . a form of intense or quiet ecstasy within which time and death disappear" (p. 29). This concept may be comparable to Maslow's peak experiences (Chapter 2).

According to Lifton, the symbolizing self is always involved on both the level of immediate experiences and the ultimate level at which one is aware of one's existential predicament. "One seeks a sense of vitality generally associated with the proximate level (with connection, movement, and integrity), and a sense of larger human continuity or symbolic immortality associated with the ultimate one. But neither sense is significantly available in the absence of the other" (p. 29).

Cultural and religious beliefs affect the way in which people view death. Some belief systems emphasize making the most of this earthly life, for it is viewed as the *only* existence. Others are convinced of a natural continuity and progression of this temporal life into an afterlife. Just as our convictions and values affect our fear of death, so do they affect the meaning that we attribute to death (and life) and the level at which we acknowledge death. For example, whether or not we say to another who has lost a beloved mother, "You can take comfort in knowing she is better off where she is now," will depend on our spiritual beliefs, and hopefully, we would take into account the belief system of the grieving person. A strong, deeply felt religious commitment (regardless of denomination) is associated with lower anxiety about death. Ultimately, coming to terms with one's fear of death is an individual matter and is greatly influenced by personality and family background (Rosenheim & Muchnik, 1984/1985).

➤ THE DENIAL OF DEATH

In the United States, there is great variability among ethnic groups, churches, and socioeconomic status in how death is dealt with so that one must be careful with generalizations about American society. Even so, American culture is in general youth-oriented, energetic and forward-moving, so that illness and death are responded to as something of an embarrassment; it doesn't fit with the American way of life. The realities of old age, sickness, poverty, and death are something we cannot quite reconcile with upward mobility, and with things continuing to prosper and multiply. Death is an impolite subject in our society (Borkenau, 1965). We send the elderly and the sick to hospitals or convalescent homes.

It is as though two worlds exist side by side: one for the well, and one for the ill. While those who are able-bodied plan their weekends and their vacations, and check their retirement accounts, the dangerously ill must call upon whatever inner stamina they can muster, to cling to life and their dignity. Those who are well take a few moments from busy schedules to send cards and flowers to those who are suffering.

A recent episode in American cultural life is illustrative of how little pause is given to acknowledge death. Siskel and Ebert were a well-known team of movie critics. Among other means used by the pair for dispensing advice to movie-goers was a weekly television program that is aired on Sunday night in the author's local area. One Sunday night, Gene Siskel was absent, and Roger Ebert mentioned several times during the course of the program how he missed his sidekick who was undergoing surgery, and could hardly wait for Siskel to return. The following Sunday, Ebert was again solo, but this time he only mentioned Siskel once, reporting that Siskel would be out for the season. Siskel died from a brain tumor the following Saturday. The next day, a brief comment was made about Siskel's death at the beginning of the Sunday program, while a still photo of him was displayed on screen. Then, an announcement was made that the regular program, which has been recorded earlier in the week, would be shown. In a few minutes, there was Roger Ebert with another film critic, providing viewers with movie tips. The following Sunday brought a touching tribute, and an announcement that the show would go on.

In former days, less hurried times, a one year mourning period was customarily observed when a loved one passed away. This tradition allowed those grieving the time and space to do so, and announced to the community the state of things. Family members wore black and were responded to with due respect for their vulnerable condition. Black wreaths were placed upon the front doors or gates of the homes of those who were grieving. In this way, the loss was made a publicly acknowledged event.

The "American way of death" (Mitford, 1963) can be contrasted to the way that other cultures have integrated this aspect of human existence. Psychiatrist Elisabeth Kübler-Ross (1969) recalled an incident that took place in her native country, Switzerland, when a local farmer sustained a fatal injury:

> The old man had had a fall, and when it became evident that he would not survive, he finished his life in a most beautiful and graceful manner. He took care of the financial legalities of his small estate. He had long talks with various members of the family about the affairs of the farm and the house. His neighbors and friends visited him during his fairly long illness and made their farewells toward the end. His family was with him during his last moments. He received the last rites and died in dignity and peace. The funeral and burial were moving tributes to the man's life and achievements (p. 5).

In the United States, our old folks typically die in hospitals, with the result that we are seldom a witness to death. When patients are in the critical care unit, they are allowed few visitors, generally only adult family members. Children are often kept away from the uncomfortable reality of growing old and dying. It is also not practical to have children around the delicate hospital equipment in intensive care units. We send "get well" cards even when the terminal nature of the illness is known. Sometimes the inevitable decline of the patient is kept from family members, and the patient's own denial is encouraged. When the person ultimately dies, few people attend the funeral and burial. Families often make these ceremonies private. The original meaning of funeral was a torch-like procession, whereby the living ushered the dead on their solemn journey from this world to the next. This task involved the entire community. Although sometimes there is still a formal viewing of the body at funeral homes, such events are becoming less common. We have gone from trying to make the corpse look lifelike to removing it from view. Many families opt for cremation. After the burial, coworkers and friends may feel awkward in bringing up the death, out of concern that the grieving person will be reminded of their loss, and be overcome with emotion.

There is no doubt that modern medicine has done phenomenal strides in prolonging life. When we have a serious illness, most of us will gladly turn to the medical community for help. Much of the way we treat death and dying, although it undoubtedly prolongs life, may have the unintended consequence of causing us to dread the end of life throughout our lives. The end of life might be expensive and might involve a lowered quality of life by being impersonal, painful, and entailing a prolonged decline.

Regardless of our denial of death, we are fascinated by it (Gorer, 1967). We like murder mysteries and "action" movies (a euphemism for plenty of maiming and murder). Newspapers enable us to read the details of actual murders and accidental deaths. Finally, television provides all of the above; real death as well as pretend. Somehow gory depictions of death on the silver screen are entertaining, whereas a personal encounter with death of someone familiar is abhorrent. Freudian theory might explain the wish to see death enacted again and again as a **repetition compulsion;** that is, we go through the process over and over in an attempt to master it. It seems that although we consciously deny death, we cannot help but be preoccupied with it.

Facing the reality of old age and death would be likely to reduce our fear of it. An analogy might be the child's fear of a bee sting, which is greater if the experience remains a mystery, a menace of unknown dimensions. Likewise, young women seems to fear childbirth more so than young mothers who are considering a subsequent pregnancy. Knowledge of anything demystifies it.

QUESTION: *Might we be better off to face and respect death so that we would not fear it so much?*

> ## STAGES OF DYING: THE PATH AHEAD

Plato once wrote that "what we are afraid of is *not* death but dying—the phase that confronts us with the loss of our world and its familiar being—the only home we know." Also, many of us fear dying in a slow painful, torturous manner.

Elisabeth Kübler-Ross spent years working with dying patients. Eventually, she identified five stages that are typical of the dying process. The initial shock of the news begins the denial stage, which is followed by anger, bargaining, depression, and acceptance. The five stages of dying as outlined by Kübler-Ross (1969) are described in the following sections.

Denial

Denial is typically the first response to receiving news of one's own terminal illness or the death of a loved one. It is a defense mechanism (Chapter 3) that occurs when the truth is too painful to comprehend at first. The most common response given by people, which signals denial of reality, is that "it can't happen to me." The impending death is not talked about openly, nor even acknowledged. Denial can be a healthy form of protection that gives us time to adjust to the reality.

However, we cannot stay in denial forever. We must accept the loss before we can start the healing process. Dr. Bernie Siegel (1989) made a useful distinction between "healing" people with serious illnesses and "curing" them. Whereas a "cure" has to do with making the disease go away, healing involves enabling patients to recover psychologically from the traumatic realization of their illness. If our first reaction to catastrophic news is to think, "No, it's not true, it cannot be happening to me," this response has to give way to a new reaction, when it finally dawns on us, "Oh, yes, it is me, it was not a mistake." Not many individuals are able to maintain a make-believe world in which they are healthy and well until they die.

Anger

Anger is also a typical response to dying. When the first stage of denial cannot be maintained any longer, it is replaced by feelings of anger, rage, envy, and resentment. The next logical questions are these: "Why me?" and "Why couldn't this be happening to someone else?" Dying people may resent healthy people, who are going to be able to go on enjoying the experiences of which the dying person will soon be deprived. Anger may be displaced (that is, redirected onto safe but undeserving targets) in all directions. It is also projected onto the environment and the people in it, at times almost at random.

Dying people have reason to be enraged over having to suffer in this way when they have so much to live for. All of their life activities have been interrupted prematurely. The anger stage is likely to be more prominent if the death will be an untimely one.

Bargaining

Bargaining for more time may occur, usually with God. This stage is an attempt to postpone the inevitable end. The person may promise to be devout or to devote his or her time to others, if only allowed to continue living. The person may "just want to finish this one last thing."

The bargaining resembles a childlike stage of ethical development described by Lawrence Kohlberg (Chapter 5). "If God has decided to take us from this earth and He did not respond to my angry pleas, He may be more favorable if I ask nicely." The bargaining may also be with the doctor, as in "I'll eat right and exercise regularly, if I live." A bargain may also be struck with oneself. We are all familiar with this reaction when we observe a child first demanding and then asking for a favor. The child may volunteer to do some tasks around the house, which under normal circumstances the parents never succeeded in getting the child to do.

The opera star asks to "give one more performance" before she dies; the mother just wants to live long enough to attend her son's wedding. Kübler-Ross reported that if the terminally ill person succeeds in having the last request "granted," the person is still not content but thinks of another postponement she or he wishes to ask for. The individual responds as does a child who says, "I will never fight with my brother again if you let me go" or "I'll feed and walk the dog everyday if you let me have one."

Depression

Depression is typical when coping with death and dying. People mourn their own impending death. The feelings may be both of loss and a fear of the unknown.

The dying person has many losses to endure. For example, sometimes losing one's hair and beauty, or loss of a body part accompany the dying process. A parent would be likely to despair over loss of time with children. With medical treatment and hospitalization, financial burdens are added to those left behind, causing the dying person to feel some guilt, particularly if these burdens may deprive the nonterminal family members of planned-for dreams. Only by grieving over these losses will the terminally ill be able to find some peace and serenity, and an acceptance of death.

Another aspect of depression in dying people seems not to involve regret over past losses, so much as taking into account impending losses. When the depression is a tool to prepare for the anticipated loss of all the love objects in order to facilitate the state of acceptance, the sadness is appropriate and unavoidable. The dying person is in the process of losing everything and everybody he or she loves.

Acceptance

Acceptance of the inevitable is the final stage of the process. If people allow themselves to mourn their losses, the process of grieving usually leads to a stage of acceptance. At this point, the person is not happy but rather is more or less devoid of feelings. To get to this stage, it is crucial that we freely express and fully experience our feelings in the prior stages. The dying person will have broken through denial of the inevitable end; the person will have been able to express his or her envy of the living and the healthy, will have mourned the impending loss of so many meaningful people and places, and then will contemplate the coming end with a certain degree of quiet expectation. This process allows the person to reach the final stage of acceptance with peace and dignity.

➤ A Bleak-Looking Stretch of Road:
   Allowing Ourselves to Grieve the Loss of Another

No matter what the cause is or how prepared we are, the death of someone close to us is difficult to experience. The grief process can be ushered in by the news that someone close to us is seriously ill, or it can begin with an unexpected death. Whatever the circumstance, by letting ourselves grieve, we can deal with the loss in a healthy manner and grow stronger in the process.

Grief is necessary and natural after a significant loss. Sometimes people feel numb in response to the loss of a significant person, as though they are functioning on automatic pilot. Once the numbness wears off, they are likely to feel worse. Sometimes this reaction takes people by surprise, since they got through the funeral without much emotion. It can be months later when they begin grieving.

Some people are never able to accept the death of a child or a spouse. They may get stuck by denying their feelings and by not facing and working through their pain over the loss. When this situation occurs, they cannot heal psychologically. When people attempt to deny their pain, they inevitably wind up being stuck and are unable to express a range of feelings.

Each individual's grieving process is different. People experience a range of emotions and at varying times. Even so, there are some typical responses to dealing with an impending or actual loss of someone close. It is common to respond with disbelief, sadness, feelings of helplessness and hopelessness, fear, guilt, renewed sadness related to a past loss, lack of motivation and interest in usual activities, a need to talk and stay focused on recounting events that led up to the death, and a resurfacing of psychological problems. Special occasions such as holidays, birthdays, and anniversaries may bring back feelings of mourning. Grieving allows us to experience the pain and to begin to overcome it by crying, talking about it, or writing it down. Just as a physical wound needs time to heal, so does the emotional recovery from a death.

Here are some suggestions for coping with the news of a life-threatening illness or a death of someone close to you:

1. Expect a range of emotional responses; this is normal, and you are not going crazy.
2. Forgive yourself for what you did or did not do for the person in the past.
3. Be available to talk to others who share in your grief, since it can be mutually beneficial to do so.
4. Allow yourself opportunities to cry when you feel like crying and even to scream if you feel like screaming.
5. Seek help from friends or professionals; you do not have to go through the experience alone.

If a friend, family member, or coworker is diagnosed with a serious illness, try to be there for him or her to give strength, companionship, love, support, and encouragement. Even though you may feel uncomfortable and may not be sure what to say, do not avoid one who is bereaved, unless explicitly asked to do so. Offer help with chores or answering correspondence and phone calls. Talk about things of common interest, and give the person an opportunity to talk about his or her life and to share stories and dreams. Recall moments you have had together that have meant something to you. Doing these things can be helpful to both of you.

It is not unusual for the "normal" state of depression that we call grieving to last for a year or even longer. A person who is still grieving for a loved one three years after the loss may find it helpful to seek counseling in order to learn ways to cope with the loss and thus to bring the grieving to an end.

➤ CHOOSING DEATH

Although most of us do our best to avoid death, as well as sometimes even the thought of it, we all know that others among us choose death. This choice is one of the paradoxes of the human condition. Suicidal behaviors are generally preceded by a common mood state known as depression. (Depression is fully discussed in Chapter 12.) In the following sections, we shall discuss suicide, the most serious consequence of depression.

THE FAR SIDE   By GARY LARSON

:0-23 Larson

Suicide

Suicide ranks as the seventh most common cause of death in the United States. Approximately one person out of one hundred attempts suicide during his or her life. More women attempt suicide, though more men succeed. The ratio of attempted suicides for male to female is 1:4. The ratio of completed suicides for male to female is 4:1 (Davis, 1968; Mrela, 1995). This paradoxical situation occurs because men use more lethal means, typically guns. Women use poisons, especially barbiturates.

For young people, ages 15 to 24, suicide is the third most common cause of death. Research indicates that fantasies about suicide are common among adolescents. Still, most suicides occur among older people. The groups most likely to commit suicide are depressed men over forty; single, divorced, or widowed people; individuals who have experienced a recent bereavement; people who live alone; alcoholics (20 percent of alcoholic deaths are from suicide); and elderly people who are medically ill. Suicide sometimes occurs in cases of terminal illness, regardless of age.

There is a high frequency of suicidal behavior among elderly Asians living in the United States (approximately 27 in 100,000), which stands in contrast to the extremely low occurrence of this behavior among elderly Asians living in their countries of origin (Paniagua, 1994). Perhaps this finding says something about the relative status of the elderly in the United States versus Asian countries.

QUESTION: *Why do people commit suicide?*

The psychological factor most frequently associated with serious suicide intent is the individual's sense of hopelessness. Most people attempt suicide to escape a situation that they perceive as intolerable. These people may feel that their options are limited, that there is "no way out." In such cases, the act may be motivated by the belief that there are no other viable choices. Escape may be seen as the only way of dealing with a situation about which the person feels ashamed, guilty, or fearful. The terminally ill may feel guilty, a burden on their families.

Suicidal people may also be avoiding humiliation over past behavior or failure to achieve some desired goal. Many who elect suicide are seeking to escape unbearable psychological pain. Those who attempt suicide may not want to continue in such a deadening pattern, or they may see life as intolerable. Physician and author Deepak Chopra (1991) has stated that the number one cause of depression is lack of meaning or purpose in life. The person who is suffering may decide that being dead is better than enduring a futile struggle to find meaning in life. In reporting on recent research into the causes of suicidal behavior, Beth Azar (1997) wrote, "People who commit suicide almost always have some form of mental illness . . . But mental illness alone doesn't provoke people to kill themselves, and the severity of a person's illness does not increase the likelihood of an attempt" (p. 29). People who commit suicide tend to be impulsive and aggressive, as well as less able to cope with the pain of their mental illness, reported Azar. Contemplating suicide may give people a renewed sense of power over their own lives.

Not all people who consider and even attempt suicide want to die. Some potential symbolic meanings of suicide include the following:

1. A cry for help: "I cried out, but nobody heard me!"
2. A form of self-punishment: "I don't deserve to live."

3. An act of hostility: "I'll get even with you; see what you made me do."

4. An attempt to control and exert power over people: "I will make others suffer for the rest of their lives for having rejected me."

5. An attempt to be noticed: "Maybe now people will talk about me and feel sorry for the way they treated me."

6. A relief from a terrible state of mind: "Life is too stressful, and I'm fed up."

7. An escape from a difficult or an impossible situation: "I hate living in an alcoholic family, and death seems like one way to end this situation."

8. A relief from hopelessness: "I see no way out of the despair I feel. Ending my life will be better than hating to wake up each morning."

9. An end to pain: "I suffer extreme physical pain, which will not end. Suicide will put an end to this nightmare."

Helping a Suicidal Person: Streetlights for a Moonless Night

Although many of us think about committing suicide but never take action, suicide is a common enough occurrence to take seriously any disclosure that a person is considering suicide. It is important to establish rapport by offering emotional support, acceptance, and caring. Almost all clinicians agree that encouraging a patient to talk about his or her suicidal ideas can help the person to overcome them as well as to provide necessary information for therapeutic intervention.

There are behaviors that tend to help another person gain insight into a personal problem, as well as actions that are hindrances. Showing acceptance of the troubled person through supportive statements, patience, and respect is recommended. A respectful and accepting comment might sound like this: "From what you have told me, I think I can understand a little bit of why you are feeling pretty desperate." On the other hand, any judging or moralizing, and ridicule or sarcasm, are likely to be hurtful to the individual faced with an overwhelming predicament. At a time like this, saying "You've made a pretty mess of things in your life" is inappropriate. Active listening should also prove helpful. This involves reflecting feelings and paraphrasing your understanding of what the other person is saying. Open-ended questioning may also be useful, but probing painful topics, criticism, and opinionated statements should be avoided. An open-ended question would be something like this: "Why don't you tell me the things you think about that seem to make you feel overwhelmed and self-condemning?"

It may be necessary for you to assess for suicide potential in a friend or relative. To do this, you might ask the depressed person whether he or she has thoughts about taking his or her life. It is okay to ask about this. If you get an affirmative response, you would want to ask whether this person has developed a plan and whether he or she has the means to carry out the plan, if there is one. Also, information about prior suicide attempts presents an important warning signal, since approximately 75 percent of completed suicides have a history of a previous attempt or threat; knowing of such a prior attempt can be used as a gauge of the person's likelihood of taking action. Of every ten potential suicides, eight give warning beforehand (Leenaars, 1995; Rudestam, 1971; Shneidman & Farberow, 1957; Slaby, Garfinkel & Garfinkel, 1994). A person's familiarity with lethal dosages of drugs or other forms of self-destruction should be assessed. Other clues are secretiveness, a sudden decision to make a will, or verbal statements, such as, "I don't want to go on living."

It may be difficult to detect the suicidal intent of another person. Some systematic studies have shown that a period of calm may follow a decision to commit suicide (Keith-Spiegel & Spiegel, 1967). A sudden appearance of tranquillity in a previously agitated patient is a danger signal that is often misinterpreted as a sign of improvement. The improvement in mood may be coming from an anticipation that suffering is at an end. The person may express no concern about the usual deterrents to suicide such as hurting family, breaking religious rules, or the fact that suicide is an irreversible action. A person who has a concrete, workable plan, the means to carry it out, and voices the intention to do so, should be asked to accompany you to the emergency ward of a hospital or a local police station.

Ethical Considerations Surrounding Suicide

QUESTION: *If individuals wish to take their own lives, what right or obligation do others have to interfere?*

Many ethical considerations are imbedded in the topic of suicide. Most clinicians believe that their duty is to keep people from killing themselves. Their thinking is that along with depression goes a particularly pessimistic train of thought, which does not allow the depressed and suicidal person to objectively assess the situation and perhaps to see that it is temporary. In effect, the depressed person's negativistic thinking is a symptom of the depression and distorts the person's judgment about viable alternatives to suicide.

Suicide was considered an appropriate solution to stressful situations in ancient Greek society and has traditionally been deemed by the Japanese to be the only honorable thing to do in the face of shame. Most North Americans respect the preservation and fulfillment of human life as a worthwhile value, and therefore consider suicide not only tragic but also wrong. Thomas Szasz (1977) said that we have transformed Patrick Henry's "Give me liberty or give me death" into "Give him commitment, give him electroshock, give him lobotomy, give him life-long slavery, but do not let him choose death!"

However, this attitude toward suicide may be changing, at least under special conditions. With the medical establishment's ever-increasing ability to prolong bodily functioning, Americans have begun a national debate on doctor-assisted suicide in cases in which individuals are suffering from terminal illness and the quality of life of the patient has been irreparably damaged.

QUESTION: *Do you think that there are some situations under which choosing death is acceptable or even perhaps desirable?*

Assisted Suicide

Dr. Jack Kavorkian has been a crusader in championing the individual's right to die when his or her life has become unbearable and has no prospect of returning to a tolerable condition. When people reach this point in their lives, they are often unable to take their own lives if they so desire. Many people who are not in such a situation may nevertheless feel insecure about their ability to plan a painless, peaceful departure. For this reason, Dr. Kavorkian developed a procedure for assisting terminally ill patients to end their lives. Dr. Kavorkian has paid a price for his innovative and controversial practice of **assisted suicide.** He has been in and out of courtrooms and jail cells, defending himself against murder charges for the past several years. Each time Dr. Kavorkian was acquitted. This result may have been, in part, due to his carefully videotaped interviews with patients and close family members, which made the situation in each case clear that Dr. Kavorkian's patients had spent time considering the seriousness of the decision, and that they clearly wished assistance in ending their lives. This relatively new practice raises some intriguing issues. Recently, Dr. Kavorkian has moved the discussion further along the continuum by performing **active euthanasia.** This practice involves the doctor in administering the lethal injection, rather than having the patient self-administer the dose. Kavorkian's first case involving active euthanasia has resulted in his being prosecuted and sentenced to prison.

QUESTIONS: *To whom does the life of an individual person belong—to the state (as is the law in Great Britain), to God, to one's family, or to oneself? Does an individual have a duty to stay alive under certain conditions, or not?*

The majority of Americans feel that assisted suicide in the case of terminal illness is an act of mercy. This attitude represents a change in thinking; for many years, Americans, partially on religious grounds, were opposed to suicide for any reason and voted for laws to make suicide illegal. Many Americans still object to assisted suicide because it violates their religious teachings. Others worry that such a practice will cheapen human life by construing caretaking of the ill and the frail elderly to be an unreasonable burden. However, those who care for elderly parents or spouses often report deriving great satisfaction from it. Even so, this issue is likely to remain prominent, since among college students, the most common concern regarding death is anxiety over the way that they will die.

➤ THE UNLIT LAMP: PSYCHOLOGICAL
NUMBING AS A FORM OF DEATH

As yet, we have been considering only physical death. Our exploration of the psyche of the suicidal person provided a glimpse of the possibility that a person may experience a sort of "living death" brought on by a psychological numbing. When overwhelmed, our minds seek to block out much of the imagery and information available to us by building a protective wall against all that questions or threatens our **homeostasis.**

We can become fragmented, so that aspects of our self-concept are dissociated. The fragmentation may stem from severe trauma, which—if it occurs early in life—can either shape or misshape our self-concept and deny it adequate form virtually from its beginning. We may experience intense feelings of separation and disintegration.

One manifestation of this despair is a sense of having no future, a breakdown of connection to groups or principles larger than oneself. There is a loss of sufficient grounding or of a sense of being connected to one's own history. As a result, experience takes on a floating quality; actions and associations become isolated from one's own prior experience as well as from others around one, and nothing seems psychologically trustworthy.

As our self-concept fragments, our capacity for empathy is lost (Lifton, 1993). So absorbed in our own struggle to hold together, we are unable to be concerned with others and tend to be unable to mobilize the capacity to perform an empathic act.

From such misery arises the potential for change. Sometimes growth requires that we be willing to let go of old and familiar ways of being, particularly if they are deadening patterns that make life seem intolerable. If our current patterns are experienced as boring or stifling, a new route must be found. Sources of stimulation can be intellectual, emotional, social, or physical.

Intellectual and Emotional Change

Intellectual challenges may provide the needed spark to enliven daily existence. From the ancient Greeks to Abraham Maslow, the intellectual experience of seeing one's world in a new light has been equated with "peak experiences" and the greatest happiness human beings can know.

If we are generally comfortable in the intellectual realm, we might seek to enjoy life through living more emotionally. This process might begin by looking for the playful and curious side within each of us. All of us have these human potentials. It might help to observe children from one year to six years of age to gain a role model for this natural, spontaneous side, to learn how to bring this quality out in ourselves.

Many of us tend to submerge feelings and to *think* our way through life. This practice does enable us to avoid experiencing some pain, although closing off negative feelings dampens positive feelings as well. Those of us who are emotionally reserved are reticent in showing joyous effervescence as well as in expressing rage and grief. **Emotional insulation** functions as a blanket over all feelings. Sometimes we find it difficult to recognize our blunted emotional state. To begin assessing how alive we are emotionally, we might ask ourselves such questions as these: "What activities do I enjoy most?" "When was the last time I did this activity?" "Is there something in the next week that I am looking forward to with eager anticipation?"

Social Change

Some of our relationships can produce a form of psychological death. Human beings, by nature, seek out the company and acceptance of others. Yet, once we enjoy the security of ongoing relationship, we may stop investing in them. When both parties do this, the relationship becomes stagnant and begins to feel more like a constraint than a blessing. Adding new ideas and plans is each person's job, and yet doing so requires an adjustment to the changes. We may find that there is a trade-off between security and vitality in our relationships.

If Alfred Adler and other psychologists are correct, investing in the lives and welfare of others should contribute to our enthusiasm over daily activities. When our own lives seem bleak, we may find an anecdote to this bleakness by shifting our focus to some concrete good deed for a friend or an acquaintance. This behavior increases self-esteem by allowing us to view ourselves as kindly and by enabling us to make friends, who are among the true "riches" in life.

Physical Change

Many of us function as "talking heads," virtually disconnected from our physical selves. Particularly as college students, we may wish to ignore messages from our bodies. For example, if we are studying late at night and our body is sending signals that it is time for sleep, many of us have had occasion to pour ourselves another cup of coffee and to return to our textbook. This type of tuning out of our physical cues can become a lifelong habit. Taking good care of one's body is a way to feel vital, energetic, and happy. As noted earlier (Chapter 2), there is a well-documented relationship between physical and mental health.

Many writers and philosophers have observed that an enemy of enjoyment of life is the belief that one must hurry along through it (Hesse, 1905; Lindbergh, 1955). We do not have time for frivolity; we are busy earning a living, going to school, taking care of children or other loved ones, as well as doing errands. The increasing opportunities of modern life have necessitated increased haste to take advantage of them, and for many of us, this haste has done away with the concept of leisure time. We must do as much as possible, as fast as possible. Even children are tightly scheduled, so that they must hurry from one activity to the next. Such hot pursuit of entertainment may be counterproductive, in that it makes time go by quickly, but perhaps not

"He's like, 'To be or not to be,' and I'm like, 'Get a Life.'"

meaningfully. Leisure time means "not employed, occupied, or engaged; unhurried, freedom from time-consuming duties, responsibilities, or activities" (*American Heritage Dictionary*, 1978). Ironically, we may have more entertainment but less enjoyment than in the past. Our competitive spirit may not allow us the luxury of missing a movie premiere, a popular sporting event, or a friend's party. Perhaps we should reexamine our activities, with the value of leisure in mind. A balanced life might consist of valuable objectives and spontaneous enjoyment, with plenty of leisure for reflecting on one's life.

➤ ENLIVENING YOUR LIFE WITH CELEBRATIONS

One way to enjoy life is to celebrate our own successes and those of others. When dissatisfied with ourselves, we may feel irritated by the accomplishments of others and may even fail to notice our own triumphs. Consider, for instance, the reaction of a student of the authors, who left the classroom in a funk, having received a score of 98 out of 100 points on her exam. This behavior is an example of a pessimistic reaction to an occasion for celebration. Another student of the author was upset when her boyfriend received a better score on a paper than she did even though both papers earned As. These occurrences are opportunities for rejoicing, which were construed by the students involved as cause for gloom. There is some thought process that these students have that orients toward the negative aspects of the situation.

Celebrations are life-affirming. Even gatherings in recognition of a death have this effect, in that funerals imply that life goes on for those gathered to honor the end of one among them. Those attending the funeral acknowledge death as a significant event and commemorate the life that was. The need to celebrate life's big occasions should not be underestimated. We feel connected to the joy of living through our celebrations, ceremonies, and rituals. These feelings of observance give validity to the events of our lives.

"Observance has considerable power. If you observe Christmas, for instance, you'll be affected by that special season precisely because of your observance. The mood and spirit of the time will touch your heart. And, over time, regular observance may come to affect you deeply" (Moore, 1994). Even the timing of death indicates the deep significance of celebrations for human beings. Christians die in disproportionately greater numbers after Christmas, and the death rate drops prior to the holiday. On the other hand, for those of Jewish faith, death rates are affected by Yom Kippur and Hanukkah. Rituals and celebrations elevate occasions, solemnizing and making them meaningful. In this way, our lives gain meaning through purposeful preparation for engagement in and recollection of significant events.

Celebrations can be internal, a state of mind. Some people feel reticent about calling attention to their successes by sending out announcements or throwing a party. Instead, they are quietly jubilant. Celebrations do not have to be external. A quiet self-affirmation in which you feel good about what you have done or experienced would qualify as a legitimate celebration. What is missing is the sharing of your triumphs with others. For most people, some sort of public acknowledgment of the significant life events enhances the experience.

➤ *SUMMARY*

FACING CRISIS People may do quite well when they are busy with their lives and pursuing their goals. However, tragic events or other life crises seem to threaten everything they have worked so hard to achieve and to acquire. Many people may contemplate running away from it all or may even think of committing suicide. Their conviction that life is meaningful may be shattered.

Viktor Frankl suggested that suffering is inevitable, deeply human, and even a grace. He believed that when a person must face the inevitable suffering of a terminal illness or of the sudden loss of a loved one, the attitude one takes towards the adversity has the potential to provide meaning in the experience. Longitudinal research conducted by psychologists has documented that even the hardiest and most successful people have suffered setbacks. Such studies have revealed that successful people have developed effective ways of looking at and handling whatever adversity turns up.

FINDING MEANING IN LIFE THROUGH FACING DEATH All human beings suffer the uneasiness that accompanies awareness of their mortality. Although this topic might seem morbid or depressing, an honest understanding and acceptance of death can lay the foundation for a meaningful life This common fate can provide a sense of a shared predicament with other human beings.

Treating death as unreal or as something to avoid thinking about can lead to a pervasive life theme of avoidance or unconscious denial of what is feared. What is lost is the sense of urgency to get on with one's life pursuits. Failure to confront the need to develop a purpose in life may cause regret later in life over ambitions left unfulfilled.

The full realization that we are mortal, that not only must we die one day but indeed we might die at any moment, can give us the motivation to make the most of the time we have. A good look at the worst thing that could happen to us puts the rest of life in perspective. When compared with death, even the most serious life crisis looks manageable.

According to Jay Lifton, human beings overcome despair from knowledge of their mortality in a variety of ways, including continuing on through their children, or other lasting contributions, belief in an afterlife existence, or through transcendent experiences.

Cultural and religious beliefs affect the way in which people view death. Some belief systems emphasize making the most of this life, whereas other belief systems focus on the natural continuity and progression of this temporal life into an afterlife. A strong, deeply felt religious commitment is associated with lower anxiety about death.

ARE WE A DEATH-DENYING SOCIETY? Living in a society that avoids talking about death may make coping with thoughts about it more difficult. A more comfortable sense of death would lessen fear of it. Denial of death may be expressed in a preoccupation with viewing or reading about it in an attempt to master it.

For many, the fear of dying in pain is greater than dread of death itself. Elisabeth Kübler-Ross, who worked with terminally ill patients, identified five stages of dying: *denial, anger, bargaining, depression*, and *acceptance*. Denial is typically the first response to receiving news of one's own terminal illness or the death of a loved one. When the denial cannot be maintained any longer, it is replaced by feelings of anger over anticipated loss of possessions, loved ones, and life itself. Bargaining for more time may occur, usually with God. Depression is typical as people mourn their imminent death. The final stage of the dying process is acceptance, wherein the person is more or less devoid of feelings and contemplates the coming end with quiet expectation.

The loss of a loved one typically precipitates a normal state of depression that is called grieving. It is common to respond with disbelief, sadness, feelings of helplessness and hopelessness, fear, guilt, lack of motivation and of interest in usual activities, a need to talk and recount events that led up to the death, and a resurfacing of earlier psychological problems. Grieving allows those who have suffered the loss of a loved one to openly experience the pain and to begin to overcome it.

SUICIDE Contrary to the attitude about death that most people harbor, those who are in pain, whether physical or psychological, may choose death. These individuals are typically depressed and consider their situation hopeless. When depressed people are helped through the crisis of feeling suicidal, they are generally grateful. When the depression lifts, they can see opportunities that were not apparent to them earlier.

Suicide ranks as the seventh leading cause of death in the United States. Approximately one person out of one hundred attempts suicide during his or her life. More women attempt suicide, though more men succeed. The groups most likely to commit suicide are depressed men over forty; single, divorced, or widowed people; individuals who have experienced a recent bereavement; people who live alone; alcoholics; and elderly people who are medically ill.

It is wise to take seriously any disclosure that a person is considering suicide. Encouraging a person to talk about his or her suicidal ideas can help the individual to overcome them, as well as to provide information as to how seriously the person is thinking about suicide. Anyone who has a concrete, workable plan, the means to carry it out, and voices intention to do so should be taken to the emergency ward of a hospital or the police department.

EUTHANASIA Most Americans support the practice of doctor-assisted suicide in cases in which individuals are suffering from terminal illness and the quality of life of the patient has been irreparably damaged. Dr. Jack Kavorkian has been a crusader in championing the individual's right to die when life for that person has become unbearable and has no prospect of returning to a tolerable condition.

BEING PSYCHOLOGICALLY NUMB AS A FORM OF DEATH Living empty, joyless lives can be equated with being psychologically dead. New intellectual challenges may provide the needed spark to brighten daily existence. One might also seek to enliven daily life through living more emotionally.

By nature, humans seek out the company and acceptance of others. Feeling stuck in deadening roles or relationships can feel like a form of psychological death.

Many people function in a manner virtually disconnected from their physical selves. Taking good care of one's body is a way to feel vital, energetic, and happy.

Perhaps the best antidote to the routine of daily existence is to make the most of occasions for celebration. People feel connected to the joy of living through celebrating successes in life, those of others and their own.

One obstacle to the savoring of special moments in life is being too busy. The increasing opportunities of modern life have prompted increased haste to take advantage of them, and for many, this hurry has resulted in a reduction of leisure time. Such hot pursuit of entertainment may be counterproductive, in that it makes time go by quickly but perhaps not meaningfully.

LEARNING THE LANGUAGE OF PSYCHOLOGISTS

repetition compulsion   **homeostasis**
assisted suicide   **emotional insulation**
active euthanasia

CHAPTER REVIEW QUESTIONS

1. From the humanistic existential viewpoint, what is the benefit of acknowledging and thinking about our own death?
2. What are some of the appropriate responses to make when a person whom you know looks depressed or reveals that he or she is contemplating suicide?
3. According to Siegel, what is the distinction between healing and curing a person with a life-threatening physical illness?

4. In what way is the United States a "death-denying" society?
5. According to Kübler-Ross, what are the five stages we typically go through in processing the news of terminal illness (our own or that of a loved one)?
6. Can the grieving process be avoided? If so, how? If not, why not?
7. What do existential psychologists say about the fear of death?
8. How does assisted suicide differ from active euthanasia?
9. What are some means of symbolically comquering death?
10. What are the signs that a person is at serous risk for suicide?

ACTIVITIES

1. *COMPLETE INDIVIDUALLY:* **My Will.**
2. *COMPLETE INDIVIDUALLY:* **My Obituary.**
3. *COMPLETE INDIVIDUALLY:* **My Epitaph.**
4. *COMPLETE AS A GROUP:* **Personal Reflections on My Own Mortality.**
5. *SUGGESTED READING:* **The Notebook** by Nicholas Sparks, 1996. Warner Books.

My Will

Directions: One way to face the inevitability of your own death is to think about it and even to plan for it. This exercise is designed with that goal in mind.

1. Have you made known your choice between having or not having your life extended through artificial measures in the event that there is no reasonable expectation of your recovery from physical or mental disability? Use the following blanks to write out your thoughts on this matter, at this point in your life.

_____

_____

_____

_____

2. Have you either planned your own funeral or planned to dispense with a funeral, and have you made these plans known? Write down your current thinking on this matter.

_____

_____

_____

_____

_____

3. Have you selected and made known a plan for the disposal of your body after death? If you have, describe your plan here.

_____

_____

_____

_____

My Obituary

Directions: The purpose of this exercise is to help you see your life more clearly from the perspective of your imagined death. The exercise may raise specific issues about the quality of your life, and it can reinforce the fact that you still have a life ahead of you to do with whatever you want.

Think about what you would like your own obituary to say. Following is a sample format, although you are free to write your obituary in your own form. You can use as many of these suggestions as you wish, or you can add your own.

On a separate sheet of paper, write your obituary as you would like it to appear five years from now or at the end of your life, but first write it as it might appear this week.

Jack Bloomington, age 25, died yesterday from . . .
He was a member of . . .
He is survived by . . .
At the time of his death, he was working on becoming . . .
He will be remembered for . . .
He will be mourned by . . . because . . .
The world will suffer the loss of his contributions in the areas of . . .
He always wanted, but he never got to . . .
The body will be . . .
The funeral arrangements are as follows . . .
Flowers may be sent . . .
In lieu of flowers . . .

Source: Adapted from Simon, Howe, & Kirschenbaum (1972).

My Epitaph

Directions: Sometimes it helps to gain perspective on life by contemplating death. This strategy helps us look at the meaning of our lives in a simple but challenging way. Consider this: What would you want engraved on your tombstone? What would be an accurate description, in a few words, of you and your life?

Personal Reflections on My Own Mortality

Directions: Read each of the following questions, and then write your answers in the blanks.

1. What is the first word that comes to mind when you think of the word *death*? _____

   Does your response have a negative connotation? _____ yes _____ no
   Did you draw a mental blank, so that it took you a long time to think of a word that you associate with death? _____ yes_____ no

2. In thinking about your own death, what concerns do you have? Check any of the following statements that apply to you:

   a. _____ I worry about the way I will die.

   b. _____ I am anxious about my loved ones who will be left behind.

   c. _____ I regret that I won't be able to achieve all that I want to achieve before I die.

   d. _____ I dread not having control over how and when I will die.

   e. _____ I fear non-existence.

   f. _____ I am concerned about dying with dignity.

   g. _____ I dread dying in physical pain.

   h. _____ I care about being forgotten.

   i. _____ I anticipate the regret I'll feel over all the things I'll miss after I die.

   j. _____ I worry about dying young.

   k. _____ I fear being a burden to my family if I deteriorate slowly.

   l. _____ I wonder what will happen to me after death.

3. Do your fears primarily involve death itself or the experience of dying?

   _____

   _____

   _____

   _____

4. How might your fears about dying be affecting how you choose to live now?

   _____

   _____

_____

_____

5. Do you believe that anything awaits you after you die? Do not concern yourself with dying, but write down what, if anything, you imagine will follow when you are dead.

_____

_____

_____

_____

6. In this chapter (p. 124), the concept of symbolically conquering death was discussed. Were you able to relate to any of the routes that were mentioned? If so, which ones?

_____

_____

_____

_____

7. Discuss the way in which the subject of death was dealt with in the family you grew up in and how you would like to deal with it in the family you have or might establish yourself.

_____

_____

_____

_____

8. Denial is a common defense mechanism employed by people to help them deal with death. Discuss any examples from your own life in which you have been aware of denial being used in this manner.

_____

_____

_____

_____

9. Do you think that people have the right to take their own lives? If so, do people have this right carte blanche or only under certain circumstances? If not, why not?

_____

_____

_____

_____

10. What specific things would you most like to change about your life so that you could feel more alive? What can you do to make these changes?

_____

_____

_____

_____

11. Have you cleaned up past misunderstandings in your current relationships, so that if your life ended today, you would feel satisfied with the way you have left things? If not, list any "unfinished business" with others that you would like to clear up.

_____

_____

_____

_____

12. We may be able to learn from the occasions when we lose someone or something very important, such as a loved one, how to prepare for the loss of everything we enjoy in life. We may develop a permanent disability or may lose a relationship or position, or suffer a great financial reversal, or come to the realization that something we have dreamed of and hoped for will never come to pass. Think of losses you have experienced. Have you learned anything that might prepare you for the end of your life?

_____

_____

_____

_____

13. Do you make a point of enjoying the little joys of life? How might you do more of this?

_____

_____

_____

_____

14. Do you think you keep busy to avoid awareness of death, loneliness, or other painful experiences in life? If so, explain what you do.

_____

_____

_____

_____

15. Are there some conditions under which you would choose death? If so, what are they? If not, what is your rationale for wanting to stay alive at all costs?

_____

_____

_____

_____

16. How do you hope to leave your human community or "mother earth" a little bit better off when your life is over? If this is not one of your goals, explain your thinking.

_____

_____

_____

_____

17. Do you let yourself and others feel sadness and grief over a loss? Do you let yourself cry if you feel like crying? Do you try to cheer people up when they are sad or depressed, instead of allowing them to experience their feelings?

_____

_____

_____

_____

18. Are you in too much of a hurry to enjoy your life?

_____

_____

_____

19. What observances of occasions add flavor to your life on a regular basis?

_____

_____

_____

_____

20. Complete this sentence: "When it comes to celebrating, I . . ."

_____

_____

_____

_____

5

Moral/Ethical Development

Goodness is the only investment that never fails.
—Henry David Thoreau

Morals are an acquirement—like music, like a foreign language, like piety, poker, paralysis—no man is born with them.
—Mark Twain

> ➤ *PREVIEW QUESTIONS:* Are people born with a "moral sense," or do moral principles have to be taught to children? According to Lawrence Kohlberg, at what level of moral development is the person motivated by fear of disapproval by others? How did Carol Gilligan describe the ethical principles of females as differing from those of males? Is there such a thing as universal moral principles, or are such principles completely dictated by one's culture? What makes people engage in prosocial behaviors?

➤ INTRODUCTION: WHAT IS OUR NATURE?

Morality has to do with our standards for good behavior. Our moral principles are our rules of right and wrong conduct, and our concept as to what constitutes good and evil. Morality has to do with being virtuous or prone to vice. In developing a philosophy of life, we must look at our own ethical principles, how we came to have them, and what we would sacrifice to remain true to them.

Throughout history, there have been mutually contradictory views of human nature. Many of these views address the issue as to whether human nature is inherently good or whether human beings must be taught to be good. We have been discussing the question, Who am I? Now, in attempting to settle this matter of human nature, we also address the question, *What* am I? or What kind of creature is a human being?

Views about what constitutes human nature have implications for child-rearing practice. Some have urged parents to help their children develop pride and self-esteem by building them up. Others have felt that a child's natural pride and stubbornness should be broken. A child is seen as a little savage who is filled with selfish and greedy instincts, until civilized society teaches the child to be otherwise. Thomas Hobbes was a British philosopher in the seventeenth century who believed that aggressiveness was natural to human beings and that society must be organized to restrain people's most violent impulses. Sigmund Freud also adhered to this view of human nature, hypothesizing an id containing dark and unruly instincts.

Certain philosophers have proposed that a baby is born with all the personality it will ever have, including a moral sense that the child simply needs time to reveal. Descartes (1596–1605) wrote of the existence of innate ideas. Plato (427–347 B.C.) also believed that learning involved drawing out knowledge that already existed in the soul at birth. Plato did not, however, espouse the view of innate ideas (nativism), since he contended that knowledge is acquired through effort and hard work. In his *Republic*, Plato emphasized the importance of education and clearly acknowledged the impact of early experience on development. Charles Darwin, author of *Origin of Species*, in which he outlined his theory of evolution, proposed that the human species is an inherently moral

one—in fact, the only moral animal species. He wrote, "A moral being is one who is capable of comparing his past and future actions or motives, and of approving or disapproving of them" (Wright, 1994).

Theorists from the Greek philosopher Aristotle in 400 B.C. to American psychologist John B. Watson in the early twentieth century have proposed that a baby is born knowing nothing at all, that it is an empty package, waiting to be stuffed with experience (Watson, 1913). Watson founded the school of behaviorism, which is based on the idea that the environment shapes individuals, making them the persons they become. Swiss-French philosopher Jean-Jacques Rousseau (1712–1776) and British philosopher John Locke (1632–1704) believed that infants possess unformed minds and that early experience has significant consequences on later behavior. Both philosophers believed that the education of children was a serious issue, but beyond this, their ideas about human beings diverged.

Rousseau, in his book *Émile*, indicated that children possess an innate goodness that should not be spoiled by exposure to punitive teachers. A child is a little moralist, filled with noble and generous instincts, until uncivilized society teaches the child to be otherwise. Children, according to Rousseau, should be exposed to environments that will guide them in a natural progression through the stages of life. Nativists such as Rousseau, believed that humans are born with a form of built-in knowledge that must merely unfold and be accessed through life. Psychologist Carl Rogers expressed ideas very much in this vein.

In contrast, Locke, who was a member of the British school of empiricism and is most commonly associated with the concept of tabula rasa, or blank slate, proposed that the infant is naive at birth, like a slate that starts out clean and is gradually etched with information through interaction with the world. The child learns through repeated associations formed by practice and drill. This belief in the significance of association is characteristic of the empiricist point of view. Such a view emphasizes the role of experience on human development.

QUESTION: *Which view of human nature seems most accurate to you?*

➤ MORAL DEVELOPMENT FROM A PSYCHOLOGICAL VIEWPOINT

Most psychologists tend to believe that each individual acquires moral values from what his or her particular culture deems to be right or wrong. Both psychoanalysts and behaviorists define moral development as the direct internalization of external cultural norms. Psychoanalytic theory sees morality as tied to the development of the superego. This approach focuses on guilt as the basic motive for morality. The child behaves ethically in order to avoid guilt. Behavioral theory assumes that conditions of punishment and reward lead to the learning of society's standards.

In contrast to psychoanalysis and behaviorism, the humanistic perspective presupposes an innate capacity for valuing. By having caring parents who do not impose conditions of worth (Chapter 2), the child develops moral structure on his or her own. According to the humanists, the values developed are prosocial and cooperative.

Psychoanalytic Viewpoint

The psychoanalysts have been concerned with the emotional and motivational aspects of morality, particularly the acquisition of a conscience, which causes one to feel guilt when one violates one's own moral principles. The formation of the superego is the central feature of moral development in the psychoanalytic theory (Chapter 3). Superego development refers to the child's internalization of prohibitions and standards learned from his or her parents and society. The internalization of moral standards occurs around the age of four or five, during the phallic stage, with the resolution of the Oedipal conflict through **identification** with the same-sex parent.

Freud implied that identification plays a major role in the internalization of moral standards that constitute the superego. He considered defensive identification (identification out of fear) more central in superego formation than was anaclitic identification (identification out of affection). Freud also believed that boys develop stronger, more integrated superegos than girls do because the Oedipal conflict is more intense in boys. Since boys fear castration at the hands of their fathers, they fear their fathers more than girls fear their mothers. The child's conflict is resolved by trying to be like the same sex parent.

Although there is some empirical research support for the idea that identification facilitates the internalization of moral standards, the available evidence contradicts Freud's ideas that fear is the basis of superego formation, that boys develop stronger moral characters, and that there is a rapid consolidation of a moral sense around age 4. Neither defensive nor anaclitic identification has been shown to be linked directly to moral behavior. In contrast to the psychoanalytic expectation, defensive identification, which is associated with a more punitive home environment in which children fear physical punishment, tends to be related to weak moral development in the children. Those who are raised in affectionate, nurturant households tend to have greater internalization of moral standards (Hoffman, 1970).

Research evidence also contradicts Freud's notion that boys show more integrated standards of morality than do girls. Maccoby and Jacklin (1974) found that girls tend to be more consistent in their ethical attitudes and actions than do boys. Furthermore, contrary to the psychoanalytic tenant that superego formation does not begin until around the age of 4, there is evidence that children show signs of a conscience before that age. Children younger than 4 will monitor their own behavior to resist forbidden acts and often admit when their attempt at resistance was insufficient to inhibit the misbehavior (Sears, Rau, & Alpert, 1965).

Given the current research evidence, Freud's explanation of the development of moral principle in the form of a superego is flawed. Freud modified his original concept of the superego as an unconscious, relentless inner censor that hinders and punishes the expression of id impulses, by introducing the notion of an **ego ideal**, which consists of an idealized picture of the self, the self to which the person aspires, or a set of personal ambitions toward which the individual strives (Hall & Lindzey, 1970). Schafer (1960) proposed that the positive ideals and moral sense that make up the ego ideal derive from the child's identification with the loving qualities of the parents.

Psychoanalytic theory posits that the child becomes humanized and social when he or she is willing to punish himself or herself with guilt, so that the parent no longer needs to do so. The child becomes a social person by orienting towards what others wish of him or her, rather than basing his or her actions on what is personally pleasing.

Humanistic Theory

Maslow (1970) wrote that "it can certainly be granted by now that our knowledge is sufficient to reject any claim that human nature is, in its essence, *primarily, biological, fundamentally* evil, sinful, malicious, ferocious, cruel, or murderous. But we do not dare to say that there are *no* instinctlike tendencies at all to bad behavior" (p. 83). Maslow contended that antisocial emotions such as hostility and jealousy, result from frustration of more basic, positive impulses for love, security and belonging. He placed transcendent and moral values at the top of the ladder on his hierarchy of needs.

Carl Rogers (1961) was equally optimistic in his view of human nature. At their core, people are positive, "basically socialized, forward-moving, rational and realistic" (p. 91). He described the psychologically mature individual as relatively nondefensive, socialized, and accepting of reality. Rogers further concluded that such individuals give evidence of a socialized system of values. Antisocial feelings are not fundamental to human nature. People are essentially self-preserving and social.

Rogers wrote about the basic trustworthiness of human nature. When freed from defensiveness, people are constructive and forward-moving. Because of their desire for affiliation and communication with others, people do not need to be socialized. The inborn need to be liked by others, as well as the inclination to give affection, will check aggressive impulses. Whereas Freud proposed that children become socialized by growing concerned with what others think of them, Rogers warned that children must not become overly concerned with pleasing others, if doing so means disregarding their own inner sense of how they should conduct themselves.

Moral development is not automatic, however. Even those who suggest that human beings are born with a moral sense readily admit that any such inborn tendencies can be thwarted by environmental influences (Rogers, 1961; J. Q. Wilson, 1993). Thus, the quality of the social environment has a significant influence on the level of moral reasoning that a person attains. Antisocial behavior of individuals is viewed by the humanists as caused by corruptive societal influences.

Behavioral/Social Learning Theory Viewpoint

The behavioral perspective accounts for the acquisition of moral behavior by stating that children acquire all behaviors, moral or otherwise, by being rewarded after engaging in them. On the other hand, they inhibit behaviors for which they are punished.

Social learning theory, a derivative of behaviorism, has been concerned with mechanisms for the acquisition of the child's moral behaviors. As with any other social behavior, moral behavior is learned through the experience of being disciplined after engaging in unethical action, that is, by violating parental rules. The child is also rewarded for following parental standards. Eventually, the child becomes conditioned to feel fear even when thinking about breaking a rule. This discomfort inhibits the misdeed even in the absence of likely discovery and consequent punishment. In addition, the child comes to feel guilty following misbehavior and learns to reduce that guilt through self-punitive remarks and confession (Aronfreed, 1964). Finally, the child also learns to make self-directive statements that help control and inhibit socially disapproved actions. These statements, such as, "Don't hit Mommy" or "Don't take a cookie," are often initially spoken aloud by the child, but they eventually become internal thoughts that provide the basis for the voice of conscience.

Observational learning is also a key concept in social learning theory. Children learn moral behavior from role models (Bandura & McDonald, 1963). These models can be individuals in their lives, such as parents, siblings, and friends, or they can be people observed in the media. Youngsters tend to imitate the behavior of others that seems to pay off for those others. Likewise, children refrain from patterning their actions after others when the consequences of those others' behavior is negative.

Social learning theorists contend that deviant behaviors such as lying, cheating, and stealing depend on the situation (Harshorne & May, 1928). This view calls into question whether it is meaningful to label a typical person as moral or immoral, since the actions of individual persons have been found to vary considerably in different contexts.

QUESTION: Does it seem plausible that moral behavior is taught to us as children through rewards and punishments, just as is any other behavior?

Cognitive Viewpoint

JEAN PIAGET   Cognitive theorists have sought to understand the development of ethical conduct in children, as well as the changes in their perception of right and wrong. Jean Piaget, a Swiss developmental psychologist, was the first systematically to investigate the development of children's moral concepts. He studied the comprehension of moral principles rather than ethical behavior. To examine moral understanding, Piaget asked children of different ages questions about moral issues, such as, "Why shouldn't you cheat in a game?" and then elicited from them examples of unfair or bad behavior. In addition, Piaget (1928) wanted to understand the basis that children used for ethical judgments and the way that these criteria changed over time. In one type of judgment research, he created pairs of stories in which an intentional act that caused a small amount of property damage was compared with an unintentional act that resulted in a large amount of damage. The child was then asked to judge which of the acts was "naughtier." In one such story, a child is called to dinner and upon opening the dining room door, slams into a hidden tray, causing fifteen cups on the tray to break. In the comparison story, a boy wants to get some forbidden jam from a cupboard while his mother is away. To reach the jam, he has to climb onto a chair, and in the process, he reaches over a cup and breaks it. Piaget found that younger children tended to consider breaking the larger number of cups as naughtier, basing their judgments on the objective fact of amount of damage done. On the other hand, older children tended to see the intentional act in which only one cup was broken as naughtier, basing their judgments on the intent of the child.

The younger child is also more unqualified in his or her moral judgments. Younger children consider lying to be wrong, regardless of the situation, and without question, they adopt parental standards as their criteria for what is moral. Piaget refers to this period of rigid rules and unquestioning reliance on authority, lasting until the age of 7 or 8, as the stage of *moral realism*. A second moral stage, the *morality of cooperation*, from approximately 8 to 11, is distinguished by belief in equal treatment and reciprocity, or taking turns, as the basis for deciding what is fair. Finally, around the age of 11 or 12, children enter the third and final stage, in which judgments become more relativistic. This is the stage of *moral relativism*, in which the same behavior can be evaluated as good or bad depending on the particular circumstances and the events that led to the action.

Research has validated Piaget's idea that children's sense of justice and their ethical judgments do develop and change with age (Rest, 1983; Shultz, Wright, & Schliefer, 1986). There is also a correspondence between the child's mental development and moral judgments. For example, children between the ages of 7 and 13 whose thinking reflects the capacity to take on the viewpoint of another person are more likely to base their moral judgments on the principle of reciprocity, whereas children who have difficulty in perceiving the world from the perspective of others are more likely to apply inflexible standards of authority when making ethical judgments (Stuart, 1967).

Basic to Piaget's theory is the hypothesis that children's understanding of social rules progresses in phases from an egocentric stage to a stage of genuine cooperation around ages 11 to 12. However, the evidence does not support the idea of discrete steps that characterize the distinctive kinds of moral judgments that children make. For instance, the child's views about the inevitability of punishment for misbehavior (*immanent justice*) and the child's greater use of outcome than intention information are only weakly related. If both were expressions of the same stage of cognitive development, as Piaget assumed, this finding would be unexpected. Furthermore, whether a child or an adult bases his or her judgment of an act on the actor's intention or on the consequence of the act depends on the situation. For example, when the outcome of an unintentional act is particularly damaging, such as when a loaded gun accidentally goes off and kills someone, both adults and children are in favor of punishment for the act (Weiner, Kun, & Benesh-Weiner, 1980). Finally, both adults and children evaluate behavior by looking at both intent and consequence, although they may "weight" or use the information differently.

QUESTION: *What are some examples, other than an accidental death, of seriously harmful consequences that would be punishable, even when the perpetrator had no intention of causing harm?*

LAWRENCE KOHLBERG   Piaget's approach was extended by Lawrence Kohlberg, an American psychologist at Harvard University. He reaffirmed Piaget's contention that moral reasoning progressed in stages. Kohlberg expanded the number of stages to six and extended the time period over which moral development takes place into adolescence and adulthood (Kohlberg, 1969b).

Piaget's and Kohlberg's models of moral development assume that the child's reaction to rules and to rule breaking depends on the child's moral stage, which in turn is related to the child's general level of cognitive development. Kohlberg agreed with Piaget that moral principles are learned, in part, as children develop the ability to think and reason.

As children move through Kohlberg's six stages, they express an increased valuing of human life. This moral imperative to value life becomes increasingly independent of the factual properties of the life in question. Kohlberg's theory stressed the universal nature of adequate moral judgments. Although not all values are universal, basic moral values are. His theory is based on the formalist school of ethics, which has a long tradition in philosophy, from the classics of Immanuel Kant to the more recent papers of R. M. Hare.

QUESTIONS: *Do you think Kohlberg is accurate about there being some basic ethical principles that are universal across all cultures? If so, what are some of these universal moral standards?*

In extending Piaget's description of children's moral judgment to the moral judgment of adolescents and adults, Kohlberg (1976) distinguished three perspectives on moral conflict and choice. Tying moral development in adolescence to the growth of reflective thought at that time, Kohlberg termed these three views of morality *preconventional*, *conventional*, and *postconventional*, to reflect the expansion of moral understanding from an individual to a societal and, finally, to a universal point of view.

At the preconventional level, moral thinking is determined by the consequences of one's actions. Examples of possible consequences would be punishment, reward, or an exchange of favors. Children functioning at the preconventional level have an orientation toward satisfying their own needs with little regard for others. Their viewpoint is egoistic and hedonistic. Such children will have little interest in conventional standards of conduct and will act impulsively whenever there is little chance of being punished. They are capable of tracking the personal consequences of their actions and will engage in disruptive behaviors or display conduct problems whenever they perceive a personal advantage in doing so.

The preconventional level is subdivided into two stages. In Stage 1, moral thought equates "good" with behaviors that are rewarded and "bad" with behaviors that are punished. Moral judgments are based on conformity to authority figures. Since preconventional reasoning is based on deference to a superior power, youngsters at this level are likely to be more variable in their conduct than their conventional counterparts who are more autonomous in their functioning. The less mature preconventional reasoners will respond more to environmental events than will those at the conventional level. In Stage 2, children do not have a clear understanding of right and wrong but are aware of desirable and undesirable consequences of their actions. Ethical judgments are based on concrete reciprocal hedonism. Kohlberg gives the example of a 10-year-old boy who was asked about "being a good son." His response was "be good to your father and he will be good to you." Possible guilt reactions are ignored, and punishment is viewed in a pragmatic manner. The child differentiates his or her own fear, pleasure, or pain from punishment or from other consequences. In the preconventional level, the child cannot yet form moral judgments based on a shared, societal viewpoint. The ability to do so signals that the conventional level has been attained.

In the conventional level, actions are directed by a desire to conform to the expectations of others or to socially accepted rules and values. Conventional morality equates the right or good with the maintenance of existing social norms. Children who reason at the conventional level believe that group interests and expectations are often more important than the desires of the individual. They are oriented toward pleasing and helping others and toward maintaining the social order. Stage 3 joins the need for approval with the wish to care for and help others. Moral judgments are based on the desire for social approval. The person can differentiate disapproval from punishment, fear, and pain. In Stage 4, a "law and order" orientation characterizes moral judgments. Action is motivated by anticipation of dishonor, such as institutionalized blame for failure of duty, and by guilt over concrete harm done to others.

At the postconventional level, behavior is directed by self-accepted moral principles. Postconventional judgment transcends the shared societal viewpoint and adopts a reflective perspective on societal values and moral principles that are universal in application. In Stage 5, there is concern about maintaining the respect of equals and of the community (assuming their respect is based on reason rather than emotions). One has concern about one's own self-respect, for instance, to avoid judging oneself as irrational or inconsistent. Moral thought has a social contract, legalistic orientation. Aside from what is democratically agreed on by the society, what is right is a matter of personal values. Stage 6 is called the stage of "individual principles of conscience." Moral thought is based on self-chosen ethical principles that are universal and consistent, such as justice and the equality of human rights, and the dignity of human beings as individual persons. In other words, moral judgments are based on the development of one's own set of ethical principles. The person distinguishes between institutionalized blame, community respect, and self-respect, and distinguishes between self-respect for achieving rationality and self-respect for maintaining moral principles.

QUESTION: *Does everyone eventually reach the last level of Kohlberg's development process?*

Kohlberg found that people advance through the stages at different rates and that many people fail to reach the postconventional level. The preconventional level is most characteristic of young children and delinquents. The group-oriented morals of the conventional level are characteristic of older children, beginning at approximately age 9, and most of the adult population. The minority of persons who reach the postconventional level do so in late adolescence, around the age of 20. Kohlberg estimated that postconventional morality, representing self-direction and universally acceptable moral principles, is achieved by only about 20 percent of the adult population. Researchers other than Kohlberg have found that complexity of moral reasoning increases with age roughly along the line suggested by Kohlberg's theory (Rest, 1983).

These stages emerged from an analysis done by Kohlberg of responses by children and adults to a series of stories that presented ethical dilemmas. On the basis of the story content, subjects of different ages and cultures reported their moral judgments, saying what they think that the actors in the story should do and why. Here is a sample dilemma used by Kohlberg:

In Europe, a woman was near death from cancer. One drug might save her, a form of radium that a druggist in the same town had recently discovered. The druggist was charging $2,000, which is ten times what the drug cost him to make. The sick woman's husband, Heinz, went to everyone he knew to borrow the money, but he could only get together about half of what it cost. He told the druggist that his wife was dying and asked him to sell it cheaper or let him pay later. But the druggist said, "No." The husband got desperate and broke into the man's store to steal the drug for his wife.

Subjects were asked, "Should Heinz have done that? Was it actually wrong or right? Why?" The answers were ranked in stages based on the reasons given for the decision rather than on whether the action was judged right or wrong. Following are the responses given by children to the Heinz dilemma, which depict each stage in Kohlberg's hierarchy (Kohlberg, 1981, p. 121–122).

Preconventional Level

Stage 1: Action is motivated by avoidance of punishment, and the child's "conscience" consists of an irrational fear of punishment. Moral thought is based largely on being good to avoid punishment.

Yes: "If you let your wife die, you will get in trouble. You'll be blamed for not spending the money to save her and there'll be an investigation of you and the druggist for you wife's death."

No: "You shouldn't steal the drug because you'll be caught and sent to jail if you do. If you do get away, your conscience would bother you thinking how the police would catch up with you at any minute."

Stage 2: Action is motivated by desire for reward or benefit. Moral thought is like that of the market place. "You scratch my back, and I'll scratch yours."

Yes: "If you do happen to get caught you could give the drug back and you wouldn't get much of a sentence. It wouldn't bother you much to serve a little jail term, if you have your wife when you get out."

No: "He may not get much of a jail term if he steals the drug, but his wife will probably die before he gets out so it won't do him much good. If his wife dies, he shouldn't blame himself, it wasn't his fault she has cancer."

Conventional Level

Stage 3: Action is motivated by anticipation of disapproval of others, actual or imagined. Moral behavior is that which is approved by others.

Yes: "No one will think you're bad if you steal the drug but your family will think you're an inhuman husband if you don't. If you let your wife die, you'll never be able to look anybody in the face again."

No: "It isn't just the druggist who will think you're a criminal, everyone else will, too. After you steal it, you'll feel bad thinking how you've brought dishonor on your family and yourself; you won't be able to face anyone again."

Stage 4: The person has a "law and order" orientation; a respect for authority, a wish to be honorable and do one's duty.

Yes: "If you have any sense of honor, you won't let your wife die because you're afraid to do the only thing that will save her. You'll always feel guilty that you caused her death if you don't do your duty to her."

No: "You're desperate and you may not know you're doing wrong when you steal the drug, but you'll know you did wrong after you're punished and sent to jail. You'll always feel guilty for your dishonesty and law-breaking."

Postconventional Level

Stage 5: Moral thought is centered on the social contract; what is democratically agreed on by the society. Moral judgments are based on achieving the good of all.

Yes: "You'd lose other people's respect, not gain it, if you don't steal. If you let your wife die, it would be out of fear, not out of reasoning it out. So you'd just lose self-respect and probably the respect of others, too."

No: "You would lose your standing and respect in the community and violate the law. You'd lose respect for yourself if you're carried away by emotion and forget the long-range point of view."

Stage 6: Concern about self-condemnation for violating one's own principles.

Yes: "If you don't steal the drug and let your wife die, you'd always condemn yourself for it afterward. You wouldn't be blamed and you would have lived up to the outside rule of the law but you wouldn't have lived up to your own standards of conscience."

No: "If you stole the drug, you wouldn't be blamed by other people, but you'd condemn yourself because you wouldn't have lived up to your own conscience and standards of honesty."

Kohlberg discovered that the emergence of moral understanding of children of other cultures, including Mexico and Taiwan (Kohlberg, 1968), Israel (Snarey, Reimer, & Kohlberg, 1985a, 1985b), and Turkey (Nisan & Kohlberg, 1982) was similar to that of American children. Research also supports Kohlberg's conclusion that the order of stages does not vary and that most of a child's ethical judgments invariably reflect a particular stage (Kohlberg, 1976; Turiel, 1966). For instance, in a longitudinal follow-up of a sample of Turkish children and adolescents, the progression of developmental changes took place in agreement

"This conversation's going nowhere if you keep injecting the human factor."

with the order outlined in Kohlberg's theory. This order was shown by both village and city subjects, but the village sample lagged behind the city group in rate of development. John Snarey (1985) reviewed more than 45 cross-cultural studies and generally found support for Kohlberg's theory.

In spite of considerable supportive evidence, Kohlberg's theory has been controversial. Some critics of Kohlberg's theory have claimed that moral *reasoning* that is judged by people's verbal responses to moral dilemmas may not be closely related to moral *behavior* (Kurtines & Greif, 1974). To reach the highest levels of moral development, a child needs to be able to see the situation from the viewpoint of another person. However, this understanding is no guarantee that the child will respect the rights of others. There is more to morality than simple understanding. Kohlberg's evidence supports the contention that moral thought and moral action are closely related. In general, research has supported the contention that moral reasoning stage predicts behavior, but not perfectly (Blasi, 1980; Rest, 1983).

CAROL GILLIGAN   The moral judgment systems of Kohlberg (1981) and both Piaget (1928) and Freud (1927) focus on the morality of rights, justice, autonomy, and critical thought. When compared with men on these criteria, women appear developmentally delayed. For example, a woman who is concerned about what pleases or helps others would be placed at stage 3 in Kohlberg's system. Fewer females than males will move on to the "higher" stages, where concern for others is not so preeminent. However, Carol Gilligan (1982) maintained that caring is an important aspect of moral development and suggested that males may lag behind females in this area (Gilligan & Attanucci, 1988).

Gilligan, a student of Kohlberg's had been working with him classifying the interview responses on moral dilemmas when she noticed that many of the female's responses did not fit neatly into Kohlberg's categories. She gradually concluded that the responses of girls reflected an altogether different approach to moral dilemmas. Gilligan contended that relatively little study has been devoted to interdependence, intimacy, nurturance, care, concern, responsibility, and contextual thought as values within a system of moral development. She proposed such a system, labeling what she believed to be a woman's way of valuing as the "ethic of care," and the traditional or masculine system articulated by Kohlberg as the "ethic of justice." For instance, women are concerned with the greatest good for everyone involved. Women socialized in traditional roles were expected to think of others first. When ethical development is equated with personal autonomy (having the right or power of self-government), concern with relationships appears as a weakness in women rather than as a human strength.

Women's construction of the moral problem as a problem of *care and responsibility* in relationships rather than as one of *rights and rules,* ties the development of their moral thinking to changes in their understanding of responsibility and relationships. The conception of morality as justice ties men's development to the logic of equality and reciprocity. Thus, the logic underlying an ethic of care is a psychological logic of relationship, which contrasts with the formal logic of fairness that underlies the justice approach (Gilligan, 1982).

Gilligan did research presenting moral dilemmas to girls, including the Heinz dilemma used by Kohlberg, and provided support for her three-stage theory of moral development in girls. However, other researchers have not found much evidence for gender differences in ethical development (Mednick, 1989; Walker, 1984, 1989; F. L. Wilson, 1995). So far, Kohlberg's cognitive stage theory of moral development does not appear to be gender biased. However, Kohlberg (1983) acknowledged that his emphasis on the virtue of justice does not fully reflect all that is recognized as being a part of the moral domain. In addition to justice, there are the virtues of charity, love, caring, community that are emphasized by Christian ethical teaching. These virtues are referred to in American psychological research as prosocial behaviors (Rushton, 1982; Mussen & Eisenberg-Berg, 1977). Furthermore, Kohlberg admits that these aspects of morality have not been adequately represented in his work.

QUESTION: *Does it seem to you that boys and girls are raised with different sets of ethical principles?*

WILLIAM PERRY   William Perry (1970) and his associates at Harvard University derived a cognitive stage framework focusing on intellectual and ethical development, which describes how college students approach learning. Nine positions or stages, each representing a qualitatively different mode of thinking about the nature of knowledge, make up the Perry model. The nine positions are grouped into four categories: dualism, multiplicity, relativism, and commitment within relativism.

Perry's theory of intellectual and ethical development has traced the typical journey of college students as they look for answers about life's problems during their college years. In the beginning, many are caught up in a black-white thinking that he refers to as "dualism," which divides knowledge, people, and everything else into two realms: good-bad, right-wrong, success-failure, or we-they. Students who are dualistic thinkers believe that experts have an answer for every problem. The viewpoint of such students might be expressed this way: "Authorities know the right answers, and if we work hard, read every word, and learn the right answers, all will be well."

These unqualified beliefs are challenged by the diversity of ideas found in college, so that students come to see that there are areas without right answers or in which answers depend on contexts. Ultimately, as they mature, students accept the task of constructing sets of answers that are right for themselves. They can then seek answers that will serve to guide their lives but not to shut off future modifications or preclude respect for the differing answers of others. Students who evolve into a relativistic viewpoint might express themselves like this: "I must be wholehearted while tentative, fight for my values yet respect others', believe my deepest values right yet be ready to learn. I see I shall be retracing this whole journey over and over—but, I hope, more wisely" (Perry, 1970, p. 79).

> **Dualism:** The first two positions represent a view of knowledge as dualistic. All knowledge is assumed either known or knowable, and the learner views himself or herself as a receptacle ready to receive truth from the person in authority.
>
> *Position 1:* The student sees the world in polar terms of "we," "right," "good" versus "they," "wrong," "bad." Right answers for everything exist in the absolute, known to the authority whose role it is to teach them. Knowledge and goodness are perceived as quantitative results of discrete rightness to be collected by hard work and obedience.
>
> *Position 2:* The student perceives diversity of opinion and uncertainty, and views both as unwarranted confusion in poorly qualified authorities or as mere exercises set by authority figures "so we can learn to find the right answer for ourselves."
>
> **Multiplicity:** Positions 3 and 4 represent the broadening of the student's view. More diversity of opinion is grasped by the student and now must be accounted for.
>
> *Position 3:* The student accepts diversity and uncertainty as legitimate but still temporary in areas where the authority "hasn't found the right answers yet." She or he supposes that the authority grades in those areas on "good expression" but remains puzzled as to the standards.
>
> *Position 4:* (a) The student perceives legitimate uncertainty (and therefore diversity of opinion) to be extensive and raises it to the status of an unstructured realm of knowledge in which "anyone has a right to his or her own opinion," a realm that she or he sets over against the authority's realm where right-wrong still prevails, or (b) the student discovers qualitative, contextual, relativistic reasoning as a special case of "what they want" within the authority's realm: "They want us to think in relativistic terms, with judgments based on the situation."

Relativism: Contextual relativism is marked by what Perry refers to as a "revolution" in the thought structure of the student. The student has now begun to master the tasks of analysis and synthesis and can use them to work with academic and nonacademic material. The student is comfortable with differing perspectives and has the tools (or the means of acquiring the tools) with which to make judgments about the viewpoints.

Position 5: The student perceives all knowledge and values (including those of authorities) as contextual and relativistic, and subordinates dualistic right-wrong functions to the status of a special case.

Position 6: The student understands the necessity of orienting herself or himself in a relativistic world through some form of personal commitment (as distinct from unquestioned or unconsidered commitment to simple belief in certainty).

Commitment in Relativism: During positions 7, 8, and 9, the student gradually accepts the responsibility of the pluralistic world and acts by commitment to establish and affirm his or her identity. Commitment requires that there are legitimate alternatives to be considered, that the individual goes through doubt, and that the act of committing is a statement of identity.

Position 7: The student makes an initial commitment in some area.

Position 8: The student experiences the implications of commitment.

Position 9: The student experiences affirmation of identity among multiple responsibilities and realizes commitment as an ongoing, unfolding activity through which she or he expresses her or his lifestyle.

Perry found that college students may delay (temporize), deflect (escape), or regress (retreat) in the face of the developmental task at hand. When *temporizing,* the student delays in the same position for years, exploring its implication or explicitly hesitating to take the next step. By *escape,* Perry meant that the student exploits the opportunity for detachment offered by the structures of positions 4 and 5 to deny responsibility through passive or opportunistic alienation. In *retreat,* the student becomes entrenched in the dualistic, unqualified structures of positions 2 or 3.

To the extent that moral development is contingent upon the maturation of cognitive structures, it will be a gradual process. Moral development involves the transforming of one's way of reasoning, expanding one's perspective to include criteria for judging that were not previously considered.

QUESTION: *Do you agree that commitment and taking responsibility for your decision to commit to something are an integral part of development as a moral person?*

ARE THERE UNIVERSAL ETHICAL PRINCIPLES?

Nihilism refers to the philosophical doctrine that all values and beliefs are unknowable and worthless, and that therefore existence is meaningless.

Ethical nihilism refers to the denial of the existence of any possible bases for the establishment of an ethical or moral philosophy. Whereas Lawrence Kohlberg proposed that there are some basic universal moral principles that all ethical persons would come to embrace, psychologist and philosopher Friedrich Nietzsche's position was that the highest values held by human beings throughout the ages have lost their value. In his famous pronouncement that "God is dead," Nietzsche is thought to have meant that Christian doctrine and faith have given way in contemporary (nineteenth-century) culture to a seeking of power. If we have no answer to the "What for?" of our behavior, we are very close to nihilism (Barrett, 1958). A related concept, **ethical relativism** is the view that moral standards and principles are relative to the nature of the particular society in which they exist and admit of no outside criticism or evaluation.

➤ RELIGION AS A SOURCE OF MORAL STANDARDS

Some Functions of Religion

It is a common belief that morality springs from religious convictions, so that only religion provides a rationale for doing the right thing, for being good. According to Ernest Becker (1971), religious principles serve the purpose of guiding a society towards realizing its fuller humanity. To achieve this purpose, most religious leaders admonish followers to turn away from worshiping the material pleasures in life and to strive to be good. Overly loved material objects must be put back into their relative positions in the finite world. These objects include not only money but also country and loved ones. According to Becker, excessive loyalty to loved ones or to the nation works to the detriment of the stranger, the fellowman, and thus the whole of humanity.

Anthropologist Adrian Novotny (1995) proposed that religion is directly related to the development of the human brain and that one of the functions of religion is to explain the unknown. Every religion answers these questions: Why am I here? Where do I go when I die? What is my purpose? What is the soul? Why am I deprived of loved ones? Why are some babies born with handicaps? Religion undertakes to provide human beings with an explanation about the origin of the universe. "If you are not religious, you will need to find a way to get the job done," said Novotny, "perhaps through employment or through therapy." People need answers to these questions, because such answers help people create meaning in their lives. According to an authority on religious behavior, Dean Kelley (1972), the basic business of religion is to explain the ultimate meaning of life.

A second function of religion according to Novotny, is to reduce anxiety. Religion also assures human beings of protection and of ultimate happiness in the ups and downs of life. Prayer is an attempt to influence spirits and thus gives human beings some sense of power over their experience. A third function of religion is to promote social solidarity, by providing a bonding experience, as well as a losing of anonymity. An individual becomes a "sister" or "brother" to other members of the congregation. This bonding takes the place of the breakdown of the extended family. Primates need ongoing, positive interaction, support, and reinforcement. To be completely independent and free is to be lonely.

A fourth function of religion is to sanction human conduct. A religious organization influences the behavior of others by rewarding goodness and by punishing bad behavior. Morality is taught. The individual church members agree to adhere to a specific doctrine, which defines what is "good" and what constitutes "bad" conduct. Each religion directs the thoughts and actions of its adherents by precepts that it lays down with its whole authority (Freud, 1933). A passage from Plato's *Apologia* describes Socrates going to his death saying that whether or not there is an afterlife one must act on the basis of conscience (Thorndike, 1901b). For those not prepared to adhere to the teachings of Socrates, one's potential experience in the afterlife looms as the ultimate reward or punishment proffered by many organized religions.

A drawback to tying ethical behavior to a spiritual commitment is that "moral certitude" often comes with the territory. Moral certitude can be defined as a belief that it is possible to have divine knowledge of good and evil as opposed to taking a position that such behaviors are defined by the consensus of a social group. This position is akin to the unquestioning commitment to proscribed truths that characterized William Perry's dualistic stage of ethical and intellectual development. With God on our side, we consider our principles to be good, right, and even holy. However, other people who do not adhere to our dogma are bad, evil, sinful, and despicable. In the name of moral superiority, thousands of murders were committed during the Crusades. In recent times, the war in Bosnia has had aspects that can be likened to a holy war. Here is an observation by Jay Lifton (1993):

> Holy terror, as linked to messianism, has important historical model in the Islamic Assassins of the eleventh to thirteenth centuries, the Jewish zealots of the first century, and the Christian crusades of the eleventh to thirteenth centuries . . . more recently, following the breakup first of the Soviet empire and then of the Soviet Union itself, there have been intense, frequently violent expressions of ethnic nationalism throughout Central and Eastern Europe. Immediate antagonisms (as in, for instance, the Serbs' attack on Bosnian Muslims) have become totalized and genocidal in their visions of purification, or "ethnic cleansing." (p. 163)

Yet another function of religion is to maintain cultural literacy; for instance, through keeping traditions. In ancient times when few citizens could read, churches depicted biblical stories through frescoes and statues on both the inside and the outside of church walls. Such depictions enabled illiterate individuals to learn history, morality, and religious doctrine.

Kohlberg (1981) found no important differences in the development of moral reasoning among Catholics, Protestants, Jews, Buddhists, Moslems, and atheists. This research suggests that the threat of eternal damnation is not a universal underpinning of moral behavior.

QUESTIONS: Do you think religious instruction is necessary for the development of a moral sense? How do you think human beings develop moral principles? Did a particular viewpoint make more sense to you than the others?

Religion from the Viewpoint of Psychological Theorists

Sigmund Freud (1933) used the German concept of **Weltanschauung** to describe a worldview that "solves all the problems of our existence uniformly on the basis of one overriding hypothesis, which, accordingly, leaves no question unanswered and in which everything that interests us finds its fixed place. It will easily be understood that the possession of a Weltanschauung of this kind is among the ideal wishes of human beings. Believing in it one can feel secure in life, one can know what to strive for, and how one can deal most expediently with one's emotions and interests" (p. 39). One's worldview is one's basic outlook on the meaning and possibilities of one's life. The total tapestry of one's beliefs and assumptions about society and life may lie outside of awareness. Alternatively, such a worldview may consist of ideas by which one consciously guides one's daily activities.

Do psychologists subscribe to a particular Weltanschauung? To a certain extent this is so, in that as a science, psychology accepts a scientific perspective to explain the various phenomena under investigation. Although science has a standard methodology for gaining knowledge, that which can be investigated scientifically is limited to observable phenomena. This limitation makes the study of conscious and unconscious experience difficult, if not impossible. Even so, psychologists have worked around the problem of needing observables, first by asking research subjects to report on their thoughts and feelings, and currently with neuroimaging techniques such as positron emission tomography (PET), which allow researchers to watch the brain activity of a living person.

To the extent that psychology is founded in the realm of science, it does not attempt to answer the "ultimate questions," such as, What is the point of living? (Gould, 1987; Medawar, 1984). The strength of the scientific method is that it provides a way of eliminating the errors that are part of our knowledge base, not that it can answer all questions. Questions addressed by science must be stated in a testable form, so that observable evidence can be collected to support or reject that testable statement. Scientist Stephen J. Gould (1987) explained that "we acknowledge limits in order to proceed with power and confidence" (p. 16). Scientists are forever open to having current theories revised in light of new information and are thus skeptical about any source that claims to have the ultimate answer to any question.

Although the science of psychology does not attempt to answer the ultimate existential questions, such as What is the meaning of my life?, psychologists do recognize that these questions occur to almost everyone, and are thus important psychological issues in people's lives. There are psychotherapists who integrate spiritual concerns, as well as the need for a sense of meaning and purpose, into the traditional approaches to psychotherapy. This sensitivity to psychospiritual strategies has historical roots. Even though Sigmund Freud viewed religion as the antithesis of healing and the embodiment of regressive pathology (O'Connor, 1996), Carl Jung challenged Freud's pathologizing of the spiritual by offering a rich and often mystical psychology of the human spirit.

Jung characterized psychotherapy as a spiritual or ministerial occupation. He believed that human beings need religion and the concept of God as a way of being for people to aspire to. Such strivings allow us to transcend our animal existence. The Jungian concept of self is the totality of opposites, a unique combination of perfection and baseness, which is represented in much of the mythology and religion of human culture as the God-man. The animal side of human beings is joined with the perfection of the immortals. For Jung, the question of God's existence cannot be answered. At any rate, it is important that humans believe in God's existence, according to Jung, because this belief allows an inherent drive toward self-fulfillment and wholeness to come to fruition.

Viktor Frankl also took issue with Freud's position, saying, "No one will be able to make us believe that man is merely a sublimated animal once we can show that within him there is a repressed angel." Frankl was concerned with the spiritual needs of his patients. He considered moral conflicts to be spiritual problems, and developed logotherapy to assist patients in finding meaning in their lives. Later, Abraham Maslow placed transcendent and moral values at the top of the ladder on his hierarchy of needs. In the United States during the 1940s and 1950s, the alcoholism recovery movement known as Alcoholics Anonymous was formed and was based on an integration of spirituality and psychological processes. Today this program is acknowledged by psychiatrists, psychologists, and the rest of the helping community as highly effective in promoting a lifestyle free of alcohol abuse.

Some psychologists (Thorndike, 1940; Myers, 1992) have taken the tact of researching whether people are benefited by holding religious beliefs. Although science may not provide information about the existence or nature of an afterlife, scientific methods can assess the value of having faith in an existence beyond death. If people are better off, that is happier or less anxious, when embracing a spiritual belief, this is worth knowing.

➤ PROSOCIAL BEHAVIOR

Ethical principles are concerned with good and bad behavior. Rules governing appropriate interpersonal behavior form the basis for human culture. According to Mussen and Eisenberg-Berg (1977), "Pro-social behaviors refer to actions that are intended to aid or benefit another person or group of people without the actor's anticipation of external rewards." Other sources would apply this definition to describe the concept of **altruism,** and use the term prosocial to define *any* helping behaviors, of which altruism is only one subcategory. Staub (1978) regards prosocial behavior as action that benefits others or has positive social consequences. In any case, positive social behaviors are highly desirable, and psychologists have turned their attention to discovering what circumstances promote them. A sampling of such helping behaviors include altruism, cooperation, generosity, empathy, respect and civility.

Altruism

Altruism is a helping behavior that is voluntary, costly to the altruist, and motivated by a desire to improve another person's welfare rather than by the anticipation of a reward (Batson, 1987). One of the questions pondered by psychologists interested in altruistic behavior is that of whether human beings are truly capable of putting others' interests ahead of their own. Those who engage in altruistic acts may in fact be reinforced by means of an internal reward system, through a feeling of pride, a sense of obligation, or a reduction of guilt.

Many of the traditional psychological theories have a difficult time explaining altruism. Freudian psychoanalytic theory rests on the assumption that human nature is instinctively selfish and aggressive. Behaviorism claims that people repeat those behaviors that result in positive consequences for them. Altruism, on the other hand, has negative consequences for the altruistic person, in terms of expenditure of effort, perhaps in terms of loss of money, and in some cases even possible loss of life.

Batson (1987, 1990) has been able to provide research evidence that genuine altruism exists and is motivated by empathic concern that is stirred within the helper for the plight of the one who is helped. Empathically aroused people will help even when they could easily relieve their own distress by escaping the situation in which they were exposed to the suffering of others. In order to feel better, empathic individuals must do something to alleviate the distress of the sufferer.

There also seems to be some genetic basis for individuals with an altruistic personality, who help across a wide variety of situations (Matthews et al., 1981; Rushton et al., 1986; Rushton, 1989). J. Phillipe Rushston and his colleagues found that identical twins, who share the same genes, responded more similarly to questions intended to elicit altruistic and empathic responses than did fraternal twins, who share roughly half the same genes. The finding that identical twins did not respond in an identical fashion also reveals that learning has some influence on this behavior.

The evidence of a genetic basis to altruism is surprising, since Charles Darwin's evolutionary theory says the "survival of the fittest" is the ruling principle. To the extent the altruistic acts endanger survival, they should prevent passing on of the altruistic individual's genes, by preventing that organism from reproducing. Therefore, the genes of altruistic members of the species should die out, if such acts provide no survival advantage, whereas those of less self-sacrificing individuals should persevere. Sociobiologists have argued that it is the survival of genes, which are shared with relatives or kin rather than the survival of individuals, that matters in evolution. Therefore, if altruistic acts usually benefit blood relatives, those behaviors still make sense from an evolutionary perspective.

Empathy

Another reason that individuals engage in these helping behaviors is that they have **empathy** for others. The term empathy refers to a person's ability to understand the needs and feelings of other people because they share in those feelings. Those with good empathy are capable of accurately labeling feelings in others; of seeing the world from the perspective of another person; and of responding with feeling (N. Feshbach, 1978). For some time, empathy has been considered a significant factor in promoting positive behavior toward others (Aronfreed, 1970; Krebs, 1975; Stotland, 1969).

Studies of young children responding to the distress of other children have provided evidence of there being an emotional component to empathy (Sagi and Hoffman, 1976). Even before the age of twelve months, babies will display agitation in response to another infant's cries (Martin & Clark, 1982). This tendency of babies to cry at the sound of another infant's cries is referred to as "emotional contagion." It appears during the first weeks of life, and is considered in current theories on empathy development to be the first sign of empathy. By 24 months, babies can be observed patting and bringing objects to a distressed child (Zahn-Waxler & Radke-Yarrow, 1982). Children scoring high on a measure of empathy were rated by their teachers as high in cooperation, and they tend to be low in aggressiveness, whereas children scoring low in empathy tend to be high in competitiveness (Barnett, Matthews, & Howard, 1979; N. Feshbach, 1978; Feshbach & Feshbach, 1969; Marcus, Telleen, & Poke, 1979). On the other hand, the link between empathy and prosocial behavior appears to depend on a number of other factors (Radke-Yarrow, Zahn-Waxler, & Chapman, 1983). In studies with older children, using other measures of empathy, fairly consistent positive relationships have been found between empathy and prosocial behaviors, as well as inverse relationships between empathy and aggressiveness (Eisenberg & Miller, 1987; Miller & Eisenberg, 1988). In addition, empathy has been shown to be associated with higher levels of moral reasoning (Eisenberg et al., 1987). This finding is consistent with the view that empathy in older children and adults has an important cognitive component as well as an emotional component (N. Feshbach, 1978).

Whether or not an empathic response will be forthcoming depends in part on the situation. For example, research with children has shown that they are more likely to display an empathic response when the child needing help is similar to the child in terms of race and/or gender. That is, boys respond with more empathy to boys, and girls to girls. African American children respond more to other African Americans, and Caucasian white children to Caucasian (Feshbach & Roe, 1968; Klein, 1970). For a further discussion of empathy, see the discussion on reducing aggression (Chapter 13).

Moral conduct seems to depend on a number of factors. One is the ability to reason about moral dilemmas. Another is the ability to empathize with other people, that is, to put oneself in their place. Mischel and Mischel (1974) have pointed out that some people cheat in one situation, but not in another, indicating that the specific situation has a significant effect on moral behavior.

QUESTIONS: Psychologist James Brock (1996) suggested that morality arises out of empathy. That is, we seek to help others and avoid harming them to the extent that we can imagine being in their position. Do you agree? Why, or why not?

Cooperation

One type of prosocial behavior is cooperation, or collaboration. Cooperation refers to the tendency to work together for mutual benefit, and it is generally contrasted to competition, which is working against each other for a larger share of the benefits.

Many animal species display cooperative social patterns. Even instances of self-sacrifice are not uncommon. Chimpanzees display unusual cooperation and coordination when in pursuit of prey (Teleki, 1973), and when the food supply is limited, chimpanzees will beg from one another and share food (E. O. Wilson, 1975; Goodall, 1991). Positive social behaviors are common among African elephants. "Young calves of both sexes are treated equally and each is permitted to suckle from any nursing mother in the group. Adolescent cows serve as 'aunts,' restraining the calves from running about and nudging others awake from their naps" (Wilson, 1975, p. 494).

Human beings also display cooperative behavior, from the time that they are in preschool (Hay, 1979). By two years of age, children verbalize sympathy to individuals in distress and make efforts to assist them (Zahn-Waxler & Radke-Yarrow, 1982). These positive social behaviors are related to the child's general mental development (Emmerich, Cocking, & Sigel, 1979) and personal adjustment (Block and Block, 1980).

In adults, either cooperative or competitive attitudes displayed by one person in a social interaction have been found to elicit the corresponding attitudes in the responding person (Black & Higbee, 1973; Enzle et al., 1975; Kuhlman & Marshello, 1975; Rosenbaum, 1980). Such reciprocity is a fundamental rule of human social interaction and has a strong influence on whether cooperation or competition will occur.

Cooperation is not always desirable, nor is competition always to be deplored. When people are cooperative regardless of how the other person behaves, they may be exploited and taken advantage of (Shure et al., 1965; Solomon, 1960). Competition in business and science can lead to better services, products, inventions and discoveries. However, research has shown that competition can decrease work motivation and stifle achievement, as well as make people feel insecure, jealous, and hostile (Kohn, 1992). Conversely, when adults work together in a cooperative group, they often like one another better and are less hostile than when they are competing against each other (Deutsch, 1949; 1980). Under the right circumstances, teamwork produces higher motivation, better problem solving, greater satisfaction, and increased participation (Smither, 1994; Sundstrom, De Meuse, & Futrell, 1990).

Generosity and Helpfulness

Cultures that favor generous, supportive, and cooperative behavior promote these responses by reinforcing prosocial behavior. People who are cooperative are also more likely to come to the aid of people in distress. Several of the factors that promote cooperation, such as personal adjustment, cognitive level, imitation, and cultural background, also affect generosity and helpfulness.

The generosity of children is generally expressed in interactions with playmates and siblings. In research studies, the children's relatively brief observation of an adult who modeled generous behavior had a substantial positive effect on their generosity. This increase in generosity was in evidence even months after the exposure to the model (Midlarsky & Bryan, 1972; Rushton, 1976). Research has also shown that when parents place a high value on such behavior, their children are more generous (Feshbach, 1975; Hoffman, 1975). A very different source of data reflecting parental influence on prosocial behavior is provided by a study of Christians who rescued Jews from the Nazis (London, 1970; Oliner & Oliner, 1988). In their interviews, the rescuers conveyed a strong identification with their principled parents.

Adults are likewise influenced to behave generously after being the recipients of generosity. Male college students were offered a cookie by a stranger, who was a confederate in an experiment, while they were studying in the campus library. A few minutes later, another confederate made a request of each student that he participate in a psychology experiment. Half of the students were told that their participation would involve helping subjects, while the other half were told that they were needed to distract students who were preparing for exams. The same request for participation was made of students who had not been offered a cookie. Those students who had been offered a cookie were significantly more likely to agree to participate when it meant being helpful to other participants than were those students who had not been offered a cookie. However, the cookie recipients were *less* likely to volunteer to distract fellow students (Isen & Levin, 1972). Subsequent studies have confirmed that inducing a good mood in subjects increases helpfulness to others in need (Aderman, 1972; Rosenhan et al., 1981; D. O. Wilson, 1981).

Respect and Civility

There seems to be a national discussion about how our culture has been increasing in incivility during the past generation. Whereas showing respect for another, even when respect might be at times undeserved, was considered a sign of good breeding in times past, now in some circles, an individual can gain merit in the eyes of his or her peer group by thinking up a clever retort "dissing" (show disrespect for) another person. This behavior suggests a cultural shift from rewarding kindness and self-restraint to applauding a more open expression of hostility through rudeness. Perhaps there is a lessening of concern over being respectable, along with an increased vigilance to make sure one is respected.

Stephen Carter (1998), author of *Civility*, calls for restoring civility in our society. He believes that we are losing a sense of obligation to others. He defines civility as the sum of all the sacrifices we make for our common enterprise of living together.

George Washington used a set of fifty-four maxims to which he referred often, covering everything from not picking one's teeth in public to not opening other people's letters (Baldrige, 1978). Even so, Carter reported that in the early days of the United States, European visitors were frequently appalled by how ill-mannered they observed North Americans to be. The advent of the passenger train, however, prompted an interest in etiquette, as people found themselves crammed together in passenger cars. For the first time, travel was possible on a grand scale, and everyone who could manage it wanted to enjoy the experience. Several books on etiquette were published, which advised people not to spit or talk in loud voices while pushed together on the train seats. In contrast, these days people do most of their traveling in cars, where they have the illusion that they travel alone.

Although a society cannot legislate civility, parents can teach their children values that will enable them to get along with others. Carter recalled that the teaching of values used to be considered analogous to a three-legged stool: The legs were "the home," "the school," and "the church." If any source of training failed, the stool would have only two legs and would not be able to stand. According to Carter, today children learn their values from television. He particularly rued the decline in religious teachings. The obligation to love our neighbors as ourselves calls upon people to make sacrifices for others. Religion focuses people's attention on transcendent goals.

Carter concluded that civility must begin with the individual person making small sacrifices for others. Many small sacrifices can make a big difference. People in contemporary society are in a hurry and they find themselves deindividuated, or somewhat anonymous, particularly in large, metropolitan areas. Both factors may well contribute to our inclination to be abrupt and even rude with one another. Respect means "to look at" according to Erich Fromm (1963). Perhaps we need to slow down and look at one another.

Whereas there is some concern over a lessening of civility in contemporary U.S. culture, institutionalized forms of incivility have lessened. Today, mistreatment of African Americans, Latinos, Asians, Jews, and women is less acceptable than was the case earlier in the twentieth century and before. On the international scene, there also seems to be a new trend emerging over the past decade. The United Nations has taken an interventionist approach toward nations engaging in inhumane acts, even when such conduct could easily be construed as a civil war. Perhaps this trend has roots in the post World War II Marshall Plan, a novel approach to the aftermath of a war that involved the victorious countries in helping defeated nations regain their economic prosperity.

➤ *Summary*

Theories Explaining Moral Development

Throughout history, attempts have been made to address the question as to whether humans are born with a moral sense or whether ethical behavior must be taught. The humanistic perspective presupposes an innate capacity for moral reasoning, whereas both psychoanalysts and behaviorists define moral development as the direct internalization of external cultural norms. Cognitive theorists have proposed explanations of ethical development, among them are the theories of Piaget, Kohlberg, Gilligan, and Perry.

The psychoanalysts view morality as tied to the development of the superego, which consists of an internalized set of prohibitions and standards

acquired by the child in the resolution of the Oedipal conflict through identification with the same-sex parent.

The humanistic viewpoint suggests that by having caring parents who
do not impose conditions of worth, the child develops certain inborn cooperative and prosocial tendencies. Humanist Carl Rogers described the psychologically mature individual as relatively nondefensive and socialized, as well as
accepting of reality in himself or herself and in his or her social environment.

For behaviorists and social learning theorists, moral behavior is no different from any other social behavior. It is acquired through punishment for
deviation from social rules and through reinforcement for conforming to social standards.

Cognitive theorist Jean Piaget divided the moral development of children into three stages. He found younger children (up to age 8) in the stage of
moral realism, where they accept without question the standards of parental
authority as the criteria for what is moral. A second moral stage, the *morality
of cooperation,* from approximately 8 to 11, is characterized by belief in equal
treatment and reciprocity, or taking turns, as the basis for determining what
is fair. Finally, around the age of 11 or 12, children enter the third and highest
stage of *moral relativism,* where the same action can be judged as good or bad
depending on the particular circumstances and the events that led to the
action.

Piaget's approach was extended by Lawrence Kohlberg, who expanded
the number of stages to six and extended the time period over which moral
development takes place into adolescence and adulthood. Kohlberg distinguished three perspectives on moral conflict and choice, termed *preconventional, conventional,* and *postconventional,* to reflect the expansion of moral
understanding from an individual to a societal, and finally to a universal,
point of view. Kohlberg's theory stresses the universal nature of adequate
moral judgments, particularly the valuing of human life.

At the *preconventional* level, moral thinking is determined by the consequences of one's actions. In Stage 1, moral thought equates "good" with behaviors that are rewarded by authority figures and "bad" with behaviors that
are punished by authority figures. In Stage 2, moral judgments are based on
concrete reciprocal hedonism.

In the *conventional* level, actions are directed by a desire to conform to
the expectations of others or to socially accepted rules and values. Stage 3
joins the need for approval with the wish to care for and help others. In Stage
4, a "law and order" orientation characterizes moral judgments.

At the *postconventional* level, behavior is directed by self-accepted
moral principles. In Stage 5, moral judgments are based on achieving the good
of all. Stage 6, the highest level of moral thought, is based on self-chosen ethical principles that universally recognize the inherent value and equality of all
human life.

The moral judgment systems of both Kohlberg and Piaget focus on the
morality of rights, justice, logical thought, and independence. When compared with men on these criteria, women appear developmentally delayed,
and their concern with relationships looks like a weakness rather than a

strength. However, Carol Gilligan believes that caring about the greatest good for everyone is also a major element of moral development, and she suggests that males may lag in achieving it. She labeled what she believed to be a woman's way of valuing the "ethic of care," and what was the traditional or masculine system articulated by Kohlberg as the "ethic of justice." When ethical development is equated with personal autonomy, concern with relationships, appears as a weakness in women rather than a human strength.

William Perry derived a nine-stage model of intellectual and ethical development, which applies to college students. The nine positions are grouped into four categories: *dualism, multiplicity, relativism,* and *commitment within relativism*. Perry viewed the well-developed ethical person as one who commits himself or herself to a viewpoint, while respecting the rights of others to choose other points of view.

As they enter college, many students are caught up in the black-and-white thinking, which Perry refers to as "dualism," that divides knowledge, people, and everything else into good-bad, right-wrong, success-failure, or we-they. These dualistic beliefs are challenged by the diversity of ideas found in college, so that in the multiplicity stage, students come to see that there are areas without right answers or in which answers depend on the context. During the relativism stage, the student acquires analysis and synthesis skills, and can use them to make judgments about differing viewpoints. Ultimately, during the commitment within relativism stage, students accept the task of constructing sets of answers that are right for themselves—answers that will serve to guide their lives but not shut off future modifications or preclude respect for the differing answers of others.

RELIGION AND MORAL DEVELOPMENT   Religion is considered by many to be the primary source of moral teachings for humanity. Religion provides a rationale for doing the right thing, for being good, as well the consequences for failure to display appropriate conduct. Religious faith reduces anxiety by explaining the unknown and by providing a sense of having a powerful support system as a backup in one's life. Prayer represents a vehicle for influencing this powerful force outside of oneself. Another function of religion is to promote social solidarity.

Some psychotherapists integrate both spiritual concerns and the need for a sense of meaning and purpose into the traditional approaches to psychotherapy. Carl Jung offered a psychology of the human spirit and characterized psychotherapy as a spiritual occupation. Viktor Frankl was also concerned with the spiritual needs of his patients. Frankl noticed that people can develop debilitating anxieties due to moral conflicts. He considered these moral conflicts to be spiritual problems. Finally, Abraham Maslow placed transcendent and moral values at the top of the ladder of his hierarchy of needs.

PROSOCIAL BEHAVIOR   Prosocial behavior refers to actions that are intended to benefit another person, and it includes altruism, cooperation, generosity, caring, empathy, respect, and civility.

The term *empathy* refers to an understanding of other people's needs and feelings through identification with those needs and feelings. Studies of empathy in older children have shown that those high in empathy tend to be cooperative and that children scoring low in empathy tend to be high in competitiveness. Empathic children tend to be low in aggressiveness. In addition, empathy has been shown to be associated with higher levels of moral reasoning.

Cooperation refers to the tendency for people to work together for mutual benefit and is generally contrasted to competition, working against each other for a larger share of the benefits. In social interaction, cooperation tends to be matched by cooperation in return, whereas competition provokes competitive reactions.

People who are cooperative also tend to be more generous in their willingness to come to the aid of others in distress. In addition, many of the variables that influence cooperation, such as personal adjustment, cognitive level, imitation, and cultural background, also influence generosity and caring behavior. Research has found that when parents place a high value on prosocial behaviors, their children are more generous and caring.

Many would agree that U.S. culture has been increasing in incivility during the past generation. There seems to be a cultural shift from rewarding kindness and self-restraint to applauding a more open expression of hostility through rudeness. On a national and international policy level, however, a trend toward more humane treatment of individuals can be observed.

LEARNING THE LANGUAGE OF PSYCHOLOGISTS

identification	**ethical relativism**
ego ideal	**Weltanschauung**
nihilism	**altruism**
ethical nihilism	**empathy**

CHAPTER REVIEW QUESTIONS

1. In what way does identification play a role in moral development, according to Freud?
2. What do contemporary psychologists have to say about Freud's explanation of the development of a conscience?
3. What do the humanists say about the development of a moral sense?
4. How did Piaget view moral development as tied to cognitive development? What is the relationship between intellectual and moral/ethical development, according to later theorists?
5. What are Piaget's three stages of moral development, and what distinguishes each stage?

6. What are the major characteristics of each of Kohlberg's three levels of moral development?
7. How do social learning theorists explain the presence or absence of moral behavior in children and adults?
8. How does Lawrence Kohlberg's perspective on moral development differ from that of Carol Gilligan?
9. According to William Perry, how does a college student get beyond the belief that everyone is entitled to his or her opinion, and that there is no way to decide among different opinions on a given subject?
10. What is moral certitude? What is ethical relativism?
11. What is the function of religion, according to Novotny?
12. Is there such a thing as true altruism?
13. What is the relationship between empathy and ethical conduct?

ACTIVITIES

1. *SMALL GROUP EXERCISE*: **Personal Reflections on My Ethical Positions.**
2. *SMALL GROUP EXERCISE*: **Lifeboat Dilemma.**
3. *INDIVIDUAL EXERCISE*: **Are You Rude?**
4. *LARGE GROUP EXERCISE*: **Debate.** Form two groups and engage in a debate on the topic, Resolve: Religion forms the basis for all moral behavior.

Personal Reflections on My Ethical Position

Directions: Read each of the following questions, and then write your answers in the blanks.

1. What are some of your ethical principles? Name a couple of central moral guidelines that you embrace and try to live by.

_____

_____

_____

_____

2. How did you come by your ethical principles? What is the basis or foundation for your ethical principles?

_____

_____

_____

_____

3. What would you sacrifice to remain true to your ethical principles?

_____

_____

_____

_____

4. Who is the most ethical person you know? What are some of the qualities of that person that influenced you to select him or her?

_____

_____

_____

_____

5. Is it OK to use your company's computer to print some posters for the garage sale that you are going to have at your home next Saturday? Is it OK to use the office copier to make a copy of your personal tax return? Is it ethical to make personal calls to your friends from the office on company time? Give your reasons.

_____

_____

_____

_____

6. Does a retail store have the right to install TV cameras and special mirrors in dressing rooms in order to control shoplifting? Does an employer have the right to put TV cameras in offices, employee lounges, or bathrooms to monitor employee activities or to reduce employees' thievery? Is more consideration due to an employee than to a customer? Explain.

_____

_____

_____

_____

7. Is it OK for an American sales manager working abroad to offer a bribe to a foreign purchasing agent in order to obtain an order, when working in a country where bribes are customarily given? Give your reasoning.

_____

_____

8. Is it ethical to spend millions of dollars to advertise cigarettes and to-bacco products in third world countries? What about encouraging mothers in indigent countries to use Similac and other baby formula preparations in place of breast milk to feed their infants?

9. A domestic company has in storage a large quantity of products that it cannot sell in this country, because the product does not meet the safety standards required by our government. Should the company sell this product in foreign markets where there are no strict regulations, even if the product could be unsafe to buyers and consumers? Give your reasons for answering as you do.

10. Should an employer have the right to intervene in office romances? Why, or why not? If your response is that "it depends," upon what does it depend?

11. Why might we, at some point in life, subscribe to a dogmatic form of religion? Is acceptance of a religion that prescribes the "right way" to live a way to avoid accepting our own freedom and responsibility? Is the fear of responsibility so great that we seek comfort in having the "right way" shown to us?

12. Complete this sentence: "Religion for me . . ."

_____

_____

13. To enhance your self-awareness in terms of your spiritual beliefs, and in terms of what gives life meaning, check any of the following statements representing your beliefs.

a. _____ There is a God, a creator of earth and humanity.

b. _____ Evolution is a sufficient explanation for the existence of human beings.

c. _____ There is an afterlife, an existence beyond death.

d. _____ Death is the end of human existence.

e. _____ A human being's purpose in life is to glorify God by doing good works.

f. _____ A human being's purpose in life is to be happy.

g. _____ Financial security is among the most important goals in life.

h. _____ Caring for others and for oneself is the most important objective in life.

i. _____ A sense of belonging, of being loved and cared about is what really matters in life.

j. _____ Those who harm us should be forgiven.

k. _____ Those who harm us should expect retaliation.

l. _____ There must be suitable sanctions when people engage in bad behavior.

m. _____ Evil exists as a force in the world, promoted by Satan or a similar outside force.

n. _____ Pursuit of excellence in all things is the most noble aim of all.

o. _____ A caring God oversees all that is happening on earth, and can be petitioned to take action.

p. _____ Human beings have been given free will, and are thus on their own in conducting their affairs.

q. _____ True happiness in life comes from setting and accomplishing goals.

r. _____ Improvement of the human condition is the most worthy mission in life.

14. What are the sources of guilt in your life? When do you feel guilty? What feelings do you experience that produce guilt? What behavior produces guilt? Is this guilt realistic? How did you learn to feel guilty about these things?

_____

_____

_____

_____

Lifeboat Dilemma

Directions: The people listed in the numbered items were among the passengers on a luxury cruise aboard the *Titanic*. While in the North Sea, the ship rammed an iceberg and sank. Suppose only one lifeboat got free of the ship before it sank. This lifeboat contains enough space, food, and water for ten people to survive. You must decide who, of the people listed here, shall be the ten people to survive. Place a check mark in the blanks at the right for each of your ten choices.

1. a homosexual third-year medical student   _____
2. a police officer with a gun (the gun goes with the officer)   _____
3. a 24-year-old bookkeeper   _____
4. the bookkeeper's pregnant wife   _____
5. a 21-year-old nude dancer   _____
6. the President of the United States   _____
7. the wife of the President of the United States (the First Lady)   _____
8. a seven-year-old girl with Down's syndrome   _____
9. a Hispanic woman who is a dental hygienist   _____
10. a 68-year-old Vietnamese physician   _____
11. Oprah Winfrey   _____
12. Tom Cruise   _____
13. Michele Pheiffer   _____
14. "Magic" Johnson   _____
15. Pope John Paul II   _____
16. a college student   _____
17. the Reverand Jesse Jackson   _____
18. a famous historian-author and rabbi, 46 years old   _____
19. a 2-year-old boy   _____
20. General Colin Powell   _____

"It's probably all for the best. Those meals were awfully rich."

Are You Rude?

Directions: Answer each of the following questions by writing "yes," "sometimes" or "no" in the blanks.

1. Are you frequently late for appointments, meetings, or returning telephone calls? _____

2. Do you frequently promise to do something and then fail to do what you have promised? _____

3. Do you put down your fellow employees, mate, children or friends in public? _____

4. Do you consistently let others pick up the tab?   _____

5. Do you borrow money, books, or clothing and not return the item?   _____

6. Do you cancel appointments on the day they are scheduled? This includes social engagements.   _____

7. Do you talk during a movie or someone's presentation?   _____

8. Do you butt ahead in line or take someone else's parking space?   _____

9. Do you insist on smoking in nonsmoking areas or in the home of someone who doesn't smoke?   _____

10. Do you fail to send thank-you notes after receiving gifts or special consideration from others?   _____

11. Do you attend office parties or family gatherings without bringing your fair share of food, or sit while everyone else does the preparation and cleanup?   _____

12. Do you fail to pick up after yourself, whether it be dirty dishes or dirty clothes?   _____

13. Do you often interrupt in a conversation?   _____

14. Do you talk too much or too little at meetings and social gatherings?   _____

15. Do you tend to forget other people's birthdays, anniversaries, and special occasions?   _____

16. Do you simply hang up when you realize you've dialed the wrong number?   _____

17. Do you let your dog bark for hours, run loose, or do its business on someone else's lawn?   _____

18. Do you forget to give others their messages?   _____

19. Are you likely to take out your frustrations on a sales clerk, telephone operator, receptionist, or fellow employee? _____

20. Do you talk against your ex-spouse to your children or hold back child support payments? _____

21. Do you make noise around the house with no thought that others are sleeping? _____

22. Do you call someone on the telephone and then put the person on hold while you check an incoming call? _____

23. Do you fix yourself a cup of coffee or a snack without offering it to others in your presence? _____

24. Do you let your children run wild at the home of relatives or friends? _____

25. Do you drive in such a way that will cause another driver difficulty? _____

26. Do you ask those you live with to tell callers you are not at home? _____

Scoring: If you have four or more *yes* answers, you have too many rude behaviors.

Source: Adapted from *Helmering 1995.*

6

Gender Roles

Man is a creature who lives not upon bread alone, but principally by catchwords; and the little rift between the sexes is astonishingly widened by simply teaching one set of catchwords to the girls and another to the boys.
—Robert Louis Stevenson

> ➤ PREVIEW QUESTIONS: What are social roles, and how do they help predict individual behavior? In what ways might gender role be considered the most salient feature of a person's identity? In whom do men and women confide? On what personality dimension do men and women most consistently differ? What are the advantages and disadvantages of the blurring of gender roles?

➤ INTRODUCTION: DIVIDED HIGHWAY

This chapter concerns itself with some of the rules humans make to regulate social behavior. The concepts of "norms" and "roles" will be introduced. Finally, an important subcategory of role, that of gender roles, will be discussed. Current trends in redefining gender roles will also be taken up.

A partial answer to the question, Who am I? for each of us is that we are either males or females. Our identity stems perhaps more from our gender than any other single aspect of us. Yet, what it means to be a woman or a man has been changing in the past generation. With the blurring of gender roles comes greater freedom of choice as to what roles we might choose in life. Recall that with freedom of choice comes anxiety that is due to the weight of responsibility for the consequences of those choices (Chapter 1). Even in these times of unprecedented freedom, our gender to some extent determines our answer to the question, Where do I fit in?

➤ NORMS

Norms are defined as rules for accepted and expected behavior. They are culturally based rules concerning what is appropriate or inappropriate action. Norms are sometimes guidelines for behavior and at other times, demands for behavior. They are developed through consensus, meaning that people living within a culture typically set and enforce the norms because they agree with them. Norms serve the purpose of greasing the social machinery and reducing anxiety stemming from concern over what to expect from others. We feel uneasy when our social norms are violated. Even in a college classroom, we feel comfortable largely because each person is following the rules for normal behavior. If one person were to stand on a desk, as did both teacher and students in the movie *Dead Poet's Society*, we would be likely to become so uncomfortable that we would immediately leave the classroom!

Norms involve sanctions, which are rewards and punishments. Sociological literature refers to the social disapproval resulting from the violation of social norms as negative sanctions (or simply sanctions). For example, a parent allowing his or her children to jump on the beds at a furniture store would probably have to suffer disapproving frowns from other customers and perhaps some words of criticism from the store owner. Such negative sanctions help produce conformity to social norms (Pleck, 1981). Laws are specialized cases of norms, which have become formalized and given serious sanctions.

In unfamiliar situations, the norms may be unclear, so that we may carefully monitor the behavior of others and adjust our own accordingly. As cultures change over a period of time, new situations arise for which no norms have had a chance to develop. For example, the dependency of elderly parents is a relatively new cultural phenomenon that has created a pocket of "normlessness" in the social fabric. What should one do about caring for an aged, ailing mother or father? At the beginning of the twentieth century, parents typically lived only a couple of years beyond the time when their last child left home, so that there was no "empty nest" period. Another example of a new social phenomenon for which no norms existed until recently is that of "no fault divorce" and "joint custody" of children. Joint custody created the need for divorced spouses to cooperate in child-rearing. Through this cooperative effort, former spouses often develop a measure of respect and affection for one another, which had no chance to evolve when the norm in the United States was for divorced fathers to leave the children with their mothers and have relatively little to do with them. Since joint custody has become the norm, it's not unheard of for former spouses to get together for holidays in order to share the children. This new sort of cooperative arrangement has been termed the "binuclear family" (Ahrons, 1989). If each former spouse re-marries, two nuclear families are created, with shared children between them. The new partners may well be included in the holiday festivities.

A further example of norms in transition can be found in the area of marriage. When asked, the majority of young persons living in Western cultures say that they envision having an equal partnership with their mates when it comes time to marry. This ideal of the egalitarian marriage may have tremendous advantages for the partners who embrace it, yet without doubt it has stripped men and women of their traditional rules for relating to one another. The changing expectations for men and women, in terms of marriage and beyond, will be the focus of much of this chapter.

➤ ROLES

A **role** can be defined as a set of norms that describe how people in a given social position ought to behave. Roles are expected behavior patterns tied to various social positions and are analogous to a script in a play. There is consensus about what roles mean and what they are to be like. Roles allow some freedom of expression but also contain aspects that must be performed. For instance, students may typically chose whether or not to participate in classroom discussions, but they must complete and turn in the course products that are to be graded, such as exams or papers. As with norms, roles tend to be useful in that they organize our daily interactions with others. Roles allow us to anticipate the behaviors of others, thus reducing our anxiety in social settings.

QUESTION: Do you think that your individual personality causes you to behave in a given way when you enter a new environment, or do you think that the situation will have a greater influence on you?

Roles Exert a Powerful Influence on Behavior

The influence of roles on behavior was dramatically illustrated by the Stanford Prison Experiment, which was conducted by social psychologist Phil Zimbardo, a professor at Stanford University. Student volunteers at Stanford were given personality tests to screen them for psychological problems and then were randomly assigned to play the roles of "prisoners" or "guards." The experiment was arranged to go on for two weeks but had to be discontinued within six days of its start. After little more than a day of role-playing, the guards and prisoners had gotten caught up in the situation. The guards had become brutal, tormenting the prisoners with insults and demeaning tasks. The prisoners became traumatized, passive, and dehumanized.

Zimbardo's interpretation of what happened in the experiment was that the students' assigned roles became so powerful that these roles became reality for them. The demands for a particular set of behaviors attached to the assigned role essentially wiped out the effects of the students' individual personality traits. As a general rule, when the situational demands are great, personality does not predict behavior, because anyone in the situation will likely be pressured into conforming to the demands of the situation. This finding implies that if we step into a role that carries with it strong expectations, we tend to act in pretty much the same way that anybody else would. Most of us don't realize how much we are affected by role expectations and other types of social influence. We pride ourselves in being individuals, yet we are unaware of the extent to which we conform to the demands of our culture.

Another report of a personality transformation due to role change came from Frederick Douglass, a former slave and one of the most influential nineteenth-century American writers. Douglass was born into slavery in 1818. His owner's wife was a Northerner and did not know about the state law forbidding slaves to learn to read and write. This state of ignorance was a lucky accident, because the woman taught Douglass enough so that he could learn to read and eventually become educated. However, it did not take the new wife long to become much like the slave owners around her. Douglass recalled changes in his new slave mistress as she absorbed her role as the wife of a slave owner:

> My new mistress proved to be all she appeared when I first met her at the door—a woman of the kindest heart and finest feelings. She had never had a slave under her control previously to myself, and prior to her marriage she had been dependent upon her own industry for a living. She was by trade a weaver; and by con-

stant application to her business, she had been in a good degree preserved from the blighting and dehumanizing effects of slavery. I was utterly astonished at her goodness . . . the meanest slave was put fully at ease in her presence, and none left without feeling better for having seen her. Her face was made of heavenly smiles, and her voice of tranquil music.

But, alas! This kind heart had but a short time to remain such. The fatal poison of irresponsible power was already in her hands, and soon commenced its infernal work. That cheerful eye, under the influence of slavery, soon became red with rage; that voice, made all of sweet accord, changed to one of harsh and horrid discord; and that angelic face gave place to that of a demon. (Douglass, 1860, pp. 57–58)

Interrole Conflict

Each of us has several roles, with different expectations attached to each. Getting caught in a conflict between two different roles can be uncomfortable. An example would be that a teacher who must give a failing grade to a friend's son or daughter could be expected to experience interrole conflict. Students must often struggle to meet the conflicting demands from their student role and the roles of employee, family member, friend, romantic partner, and so on.

On the other hand, there are advantages to having multiple roles. If trouble is brewing at work, we may be able to take comfort in our student or family member role. Doing so preserves self-esteem. It also helps prevent burnout caused by an overly intense, exclusive involvement in a single life role.

QUESTION: *Do you have any roles that are in conflict?*

➤ GENDER ROLES

No other aspect of our identity is as central to how we see ourselves as is our gender. Typically, the first question asked about a new baby is whether it is a girl or a boy.

Over the centuries of their existence, human beings have developed social roles based on gender. Although there have been some changes in these roles, it is probably fair to say that there has been a great deal of consistency in gender roles. Thus we can refer to a *traditional* masculine role and a *traditional* feminine role, to designate those tasks and attributes that have generally been assigned to men or to women.

In a minority of the world's cultures, males and females divide the care of young children almost evenly. Among the Trobrianders of Melanesia, the father participates actively in the care, feeding, and transport of young children. Similarly, in a number of other cultures including the Taira of Okinawa and the Ilocos of the Philippines, father and mother share in infant and child care (Parke, 1981).

Margaret Mead's (1935) observations of the Tchambuli people of New Guinea revealed a reversal of traditional American gender roles. Tchambuli women do the fishing and manufacturing, and they are expected to control the power and economic life of the community. Women also take the initiative in courting and sexual relations. Tchambuli men are expected to be dependent, flirtatious, and concerned with their appearance. Art, games, and theatrics occupy most of the Tchambuli males' time, and males are particularly fond of adorning themselves with flowers and jewelry.

Albert (1963) identified cultures in which women do the heavy work because men are considered too weak for it. In Russia, roughly 75 percent of all medical doctors are women, and women make up a large portion of the workforce. These examples suggest that the roles played by men and women are not biologically predetermined. Instead, the definition of gender roles can vary considerably depending on the social, ideological, and physical conditions in different cultures.

➤ THE TRADITIONAL AMERICAN MALE

There are a number of themes that describe the traditional male gender role in our culture. According to Brannon (1988), these could be described as (a) a denial of traditional feminine characteristics, including openness and vulnerability; (b) a striving for status; (c) the display of hardiness, confidence, and self-reliance; and (d) the projection of an image of daring and aggression. Psychologist Aaron Cohen (1996) notes that this is *not* the picture of mental health, even if (or especially if) these norms are perfectly adhered to.

The Denial of Traditional Feminine Characteristics

A man may find it difficult to express warmth, tenderness, and compassion, because he identifies these characteristics as feminine. This denial of the feminine attributes within himself can make it difficult for a man to relate comfortably to and experience empathy with women.

Mothers participate in encouraging their sons to eschew feminine qualities. As toddlers, boys are naturally curious about the activities of their mothers and may wish to wear make-up, nail polish, and so on. More traditional mothers let their sons know that they may not imitate mother in this way but must be manly instead.

Early in life, children of both genders identify most powerfully with their mothers, the parent typically in charge of child-rearing (Chodorow, 1978). Boys and girls gradually become aware that they will grow up to be either a man or a woman. Children are uncertain about gender permanence, believing that a boy can change into a girl if he puts on a dress.

A girl child has her mother to imitate and thus has an easier time learning the details of her gender role. Boys, on the other hand, cannot use their mothers as role models. They must give up the imitation of mother and must model themselves after their fathers or other males. This task is thought to be made more difficult by the absence of the father during daytime hours, or by the father's absence on a more permanent basis. An added pressure on boys is that parents, particularly fathers, are more upset when a son violates appropriate gender role norms than when a daughter does so. It is tolerable for a girl to be a "tomboy," but a boy must never be girlish in any way. This is the case because it is more permissible to imitate a higher status group than a lower status group and because the norms of acceptable behavior in boys and girls are not symmetrical (Cohen, 1996).

According to Brannon, boys lucky enough to grow into big, hairy, and deep-voiced men enjoy an edge over other men, because they are automatically considered more masculine, aside from their behavior. Since women are thought to be clean and orderly, a man should not be overly concerned about these qualities. Women wear perfume, make-up, jewelry such as earrings, and they dye their hair or wear it long, or in curlers. Until recently, men would not seriously consider engaging in any of these behaviors. In the late 1960s, when adolescents first began to wear their hair longer, most older men observed them in shocked disbelief. For the traditional man, there is a stigma attached to feminine verbal expressions, food, hobbies, mannerisms, style of dress, and choice of profession.

AVOIDANCE OF PHYSICAL CONTACT   A traditional man has a difficult time expressing affection by touching others. He may believe that he should touch a woman only when he is intending sexual intimacy. He may fear touching or expressing affection for other men because he doesn't want to be considered homosexual. The male role totally prohibits displays of tenderness toward members of the same sex except, perhaps at a sporting event. Few men can live a normal lifetime without experiencing these supposedly forbidden feelings, so that fear of being a latent homosexual is common among men.

EMOTIONAL UNAVAILABILITY   Traditional men are not encouraged to be open. They cannot disclose much of their inner experience, because it would make them feel vulnerable. Keeping feelings under wraps is good training for much of the work world, where most of the activity is competitive in nature. In the business arena or in the military service, socializing men to be stoic is adaptive.

Men are prohibited from expressing those emotions that would make them appear weak, such as anxiety, depression, fear, affection, and tenderness. They also avoid feeling and expressing sadness. In particular, a man does not cry. A traditional man hides his fears from himself and others. He equates feeling afraid with lacking courage, and lack of courage is unmanly. To protect himself, this man may become emotionally insulated and may project an aura of toughness, competence, and decisiveness. Men may channel less acceptable feelings into more manly displays of anger, contempt, impatience, hostility or cynicism.

Jourard (1971) found that men make themselves known substantially less than do women, no matter who the audience is, and that both sexes disclose less to men than to women. The avoidance of self-revelations serves as a protection of a man's inner self. He may be unaware of his own feelings and thus unable to disclose them to others. Besides this tendency, he may not consider it to be in his best interest to disclose his feelings to others. With other men he keeps himself hidden, because they are competitors and thus potential enemies. Although he may have numerous companions, he is likely to lack trusted male friends in whom he can confide. It isn't uncommon for men to state that they don't have a single male friend in whom they can confide.

QUESTION: *Do you share more with a person of the same gender as yourself or with a person not of the same gender?*

Even with women, a man may not disclose himself because he is afraid that they will think of him as unmanly if they see his vulnerability. With his female romantic partner, a man shows his caring by providing material comforts, and in marriage by being a good provider. While happy to receive gifts and the promise of economic security, a woman generally wants more. She wants her mate to share his thoughts and feelings, dreams and frailties, as she does with him. He often does not know how to respond to her expression of feelings, because he denies his own emotions. As a consequence, he may try to quickly fix her problem so that she will stop feeling so strongly. When he is not emotionally forthcoming, his female partner complains that she feels shut out by him.

A Striving for Status

THE PROVIDER ROLE   In the traditional nuclear family, the male was the sole breadwinner. Even if his job was dull, he left home, dutifully labored, and "brought home the bacon." To the extent that a male is a good provider, he is successful and masculine.

In early human history, when people lived in hunter-gatherer societies, the men who were probably judged competent were those who had good hunting skills. In such societies, the women were the "gatherers" and supplied the largest proportion of the food needed to sustain the group. With the rise in agriculture, men who were good farmers were considered successful. The industrial revolution brought about a change in the relationship between the sexes. Prior to this time, men and women had lived and worked together. As men left home to work in factories, the work environments of men and women became divided. For the first time, men became the sole providers for their families. According to sociologist Jessie Bernard (1981), "families became display cases for the success of the good provider" (p. 2).

Being a good provider came to be synonymous with manliness. Men began to equate their financial success and possession of goods with virility. Thus, whenever unemployment occurred on a large scale, the adverse consequences to men were psychological as well as economic.

During the last thirty years, a large proportion of women have reentered the labor force. In 1952, approximately 25 percent of all married women worked outside the home, whereas by 1978, that figure reached 55 percent. In 1998, 75 percent of women between the ages of 20 and 54 were employed (U.S. Department of Labor, 1999).

DRIVE TO SUCCEED   The belief that success at work is the measure of a man's value, is a part of the socialization of traditional men. Men feel that they are expected to accomplish and produce, to be "the best," to get ahead and stay ahead. One of the basic routes to manhood in our society is for the man to be looked up to for what he has achieved.

Success is usually defined in terms of occupational prestige and achievement, wealth, fame, power, and visible positions of leadership. According to Brannon (1988), being highly successful at almost *anything* seems inherently manly, even in less masculine fields, such as hairdressing or culinary arts. Intellectual prominence is also a worthwhile accomplishment, but for most people, earning a large amount of money is the ultimate standard of success.

A man who is successful enjoys the admiration of all who know of his accomplishments, but when he is among strangers, he needs outward signs that signal his status. If he invests in fine clothes, an expensive car, and other status symbols, he can convey to strangers that he is a man of some importance.

COMPETITIVENESS   Men often attempt to outdo one another, so that much of their conversation may be permeated with touting their strengths and prowess, with the goal being to impress other males. This behavior is an aspect of being achievement oriented, which is a characteristic of traditional men.

When a man puts most of his energy into being successful at work, he leaves little time and energy for his family. This type of man is at his best when he has a challenging task to perform, a problem to be solved, or some opposition to wage battle against. This pattern fits the concept of pursuing a female until she is "won" but then having less ability to engage her when it comes to all of the intricate negotiations involved in having a relationship.

The Display of Hardiness, Confidence, and Self-Reliance

Traditional men may feel that they should be self-reliant in all things. Such men feel a strong need to seem knowledgeable, on top of things, and generally equal to any situation that arises. This kind of need may lead some men to make up something as an answer to a factual question rather to than admit they don't know. In addition to attempting to do physical and mental work on their own, some men may find it hard to ask for emotional support or nurturing.

There is a distinct sense of manliness cultivated by some men, which is not a belligerent attitude, but rather a tough and self-possessed demeanor. This aura emerges from a combination of independence, determination, indifference to opposition, courage, and seriousness. This kind of man is a force to be reckoned with, not a straw that blows with the changing wind. He has backbone, and he thinks for himself. The traditional man's quiet confidence is expressed in a stoic exterior.

In his demonstration of hardiness, a traditional man is likely to ignore physical symptoms that may signal a problem. He relies on his body to steadfastly respond with strength and endurance, as a tool that won't break down or wear out. He may not attend to his physical symptoms until his body collapses from exhaustion.

The Projection of an Image of Daring and Aggression

Although it would be burdensome to feel *obliged* to be successful, to earn respect, or to have confidence and determination, there is nonetheless nothing inherently bad about these qualities. However, there are attributes of the male gender role that are *not* basically constructive or benign. Masculinity may be seen as synonymous with aggressive striving. Research on gender differences in aggression typically find that men and boys behave more aggressively than women and girls (Eagly, 1987; Frodi et al., 1977; Maccoby, 1990). This aggression or toughness may take the form of a wish to hurt, conquer, embarrass, humble, outwit, punish, or defeat others. When a man does not want to be viewed as soft or weak, he may turn sadness and other more "passive" emotions into rage.

AGGRESSIVENESS   There is considerable ambiguity about just what constitutes aggressiveness and where the line is drawn between approved and frowned-on behavior. A positive meaning of the word *aggressiveness* connotes vigor and energy. When used in a negative sense, it means an attack with the intention to do harm.

Our society has a deeply ambivalent attitude toward aggression, showing both fascination for and abhorrence of it. The seemingly insatiable interest in violence is shown by its prevalence in our movies, novels, and television programs. Most fathers convey the message to their sons that it's a tough world out there, so that a male has to be prepared to defend himself or others if the need arises. The line between self-defense and seeking trouble for its entertainment value may be blurred among adolescent boys who are out of the sight of adults, where the adage that "might makes right" usually rules supreme (Brannon, 1988).

For adult men, the attraction to violence may take a more disguised form, such as an avid interest in football, hockey, and boxing or other contact sports. Men may also express their aggressiveness as a defiance toward life in general. The result can be a seeking out of reckless adventure and daring exploits of all kinds. Examples would be the survival games played out in the wilderness, where men set up harrowing experiences from which they must extricate themselves with the use of only a few tools and their cunning; rock climbing expeditions; and an avid interest in television programs such as *McGiver.*

AGGRESSIVENESS AND SEX   We are raised on media depictions of male aggressiveness and female submissiveness. By adulthood, both men and women grow up in our culture thinking that it is natural and normal for men to be the sexual aggressors. Even among contemporary men and women, erotic fantasies often involve the man as the determined aggressor and the woman as the helpless, passive one who submits. Typically, such thoughts remain at the level of fantasy or take shape as mutual role-playing.

If it stopped here, the pairing of sex and aggression would be relatively harmless. However, sometimes sexual excitement becomes associated with destructive aggression against others or even against *oneself.* A sadistic eroticism that thrives on inflicting pain as an end in itself is widely viewed in our culture as erotic rather than malevolent.

Most men are not really dangerous bullies. They fulfill the male role in other, less disturbing ways and know better than to get into physical fights. However, many in our culture associate masculine sex appeal with being rough, tough, and slightly uncivilized. The hint of danger from brute force is exciting.

An aura of violence is somewhat less basic to the male role in the present-day United States. Few people would consider someone a "real man" solely on the basis of aggressiveness and violence. These qualities are very useful, however, in bolstering a male image that doesn't quite make the grade on other dimensions.

One of the significant facts about gender roles is that real people cannot fulfill the idealized cultural prescriptions in every respect and are not expected to. Although there are a few men who are not at all affected by the male gender role at all, most men try to conform to some aspects of these expectations, even if they don't have much to work with. For adult males, financial success is the "royal road" to being a real man. Since adolescent males have little access to income as a means of achieving status, they may resort to athletic prowess, daring, or violence, as might adult members of ethnic groups that are shut out of high-income jobs through discrimination.

Machismo

In Hispanic families, men tend to play a dominant role, having power and authority over the wife and children. "Qualities that are collectively known as *machismo* include physical strength, sexual attractiveness, masculinity, aggressiveness, and the ability to consume an excessive amount of alcohol without getting drunk" (Comas-Diaz, 1988; Comas-Diaz & Duncan, 1985). To have machismo is to be able to command respect from others in one's culture. Men who are macho display strength, virility, and dominance. Such men are careful to restrain their feelings and to maintain emotional distance.

➤ THE TRADITIONAL AMERICAN FEMALE

To some extent, women have more latitude than do men in their self-expression. Generally speaking, it has been more acceptable for a woman to imitate a man than vice versa. This has not always been the case. At one time, the scope of activities considered appropriate for a woman was clearly spelled out and rather narrow. Traditionally, women were expected to be emotional, lacking in ambition, concerned with relationships, and dependent. Even today there are expectations as to what qualities one is likely to find in a woman.

Emotionality

Traditional women are permitted to show their feelings, but they pay the price of being considered weak for so doing. Women have a tendency to be emotional; excitable in a crisis, and are prone to having fears as well as feeling easily hurt. They are also supposed to be irrational, intuitive, sensitive, and sentimental. Sandra Bem referred to these qualities in women as "expressiveness."

However, women are not expected to express anger; they are especially supposed to avoid expressing anger to men (Lerner, 1985). Consequently, there are some feelings that a woman must hold in. Open displays of anger, contempt, impatience, hostility, or cynicism are distinctly unfeminine. The traditional woman was likely to be prone to idealism rather than to being cynical. She may channel angry feelings into depression.

Lack of Ambition

Women's socialization has traditionally downplayed the desirability of having aspirations in terms of achievement in the competitive world. A woman was expected to be uninterested in power. In the past, many women were concerned that they would be perceived as unfeminine if they were to strive for success with too much zeal. Culturally prescribed roles discouraged women from competing with men. Women who did compete and excel were in danger of "showing up" their perspective dates. The norm was for women to seek men as mates who were superior to them in intelligence, accomplishment, and income. An ambitious woman might inadvertently make herself undesirable as a marriage partner!

Bubbles and the Prince of Darkness.
By permission of Jerry Van Amerongen and Creatives Syndicate.

An Interest in Relationships

Women are interpersonally oriented. They tend to define themselves and to develop an identity on the basis of interpersonal relationships, and they are thus concerned with finding and keeping a secure relationship, usually with a male partner. "To have and to hold" is a part of the marriage vow. A traditional woman is supposed to *hold on* to her man. Some theorists maintain that this view motivates women consciously or unconsciously to regard sex as a bargaining chip. Sex is an asset to be rationed rather than merely an activity to be enjoyed for its own sake. This attitude is reflected in language, when people talk of a woman "giving herself" to, or "saving herself" for, a man (Wade & Tavris, 1990).

Traditional women were expected to care for their children and husbands. Women also tend to be the "kin keepers," in that they are the ones in the family who keep up ties with the extended family. They arrange for the celebrations and commemorations of special events. To nurture relationships, women are encouraged to cultivate the gentle, tender aspects of their personalities. Women are seen as exhibiting qualities of warmth and empathy. They are tactful. They are supportive and compassionate.

There is a difference between the two genders in what is communicated. Females are more willing than males to reveal their feelings and personal experiences (Dindia & Allen, 1992), because they value the discussion of emotions (Shields, 1994; 1995). Conversations with this type of content tend to maintain and deepen relationship ties. The discrepancy starts to appear early in life, as parents emphasize the discussion of emotions more with their daughters than with their sons (Kuebli & Fivush, 1992). Another gender difference is that women talk about men almost four times as much as men talk about women (Aries & Johnson, 1983; Bischoping, 1993; Levin & Arluke, 1985). Men are more likely than women to talk about leisure activities, such as sports and entertainment events.

Nonverbal cues have been found to be extremely important in transmitting social messages (Burgoon, 1991; Frances, 1979). There is often a substantial gender difference in ability to decode nonverbal behavior such as smiling, body position, and personal space (Brody & Hall, 1993; Hall, 1984). Women are particularly skilled at reading facial expression and body posture. The only facial expression for which females are less accurate than males is anger (Rotter & Rotter, 1988; Shields, 1995). As children, males are taught by their parents to attend to and understand anger (Fivush, 1989).

Passivity/Dependency

PASSIVITY   The traditional woman gives no evidence of an aggressive and independent spirit. She tends to be *submissive, passive, dependent;* she is *indecisive.* Women are supposed to harbor this sentiment: "I want a real man, someone I can lean on, depend on." Traditional wives are psychologically as well as economically dependent on their husbands. They want and expect to be cared for. In exchange, they accept their husband as the head of the household and agree in the traditional marriage vows to be obedient to him. Women are typically more religious than are men, a characteristic that could be considered a form of reliance on another outside oneself.

Erik Erikson described women as *enclosing, accessible, "expectant"* (Monte, 1991). Women are to be accepting and inclusive. In the area of psychoanalytic theory, women are sometimes referred to as *containers*. They hold troubling aspects of their loved ones, in order to enable those loved ones to be more secure and strong. This behavior suggests a receptive attitude. Women are yielding rather than courageous. Also, they are to be protecting, as are men, but a woman protects passively, by "holding" or "containing." Feminist artists have highlighted the things that women wait for, such as "wearing a bra, being asked to dance, the perfect man, an orgasm, and so forth" (Lifton, 1993, p. 71).

Other characteristics often associated with the traditional woman are a proneness toward a home orientation and a frustration associated with the housewife role. Erikson regarded the home as a container for the family, which the woman is instinctively inclined to set up and maintain as her nest. The frustration experienced by many housewives, however, suggests that in this more passive, dependent role, many women may have experienced facets within their personalities that were left untapped.

CODEPENDENCY   In 1987, Melody Beattie published *Codependent No More,* which identified a set of characteristics that have come to be known as "codependency." Beattie suggested that people can be addicted to love, sex, work, food, gambling, anger, and shopping, as well as to drugs and alcohol. She described the codependent person as anyone who has let another person's addictive behavior affect him or her and is caught up in an attempt to control that behavior. By equating any kind of self-control problem with addiction, Beattie made the notion of codependency applicable to a wide range of people, although perhaps at the price of trivializing the notion of addiction. Other theorists have offered some variations to Beattie's definition of codependency (Whitfield, 1991). Most of the definitions contain the idea that codependency involves becoming enmeshed in a dysfunctional relationship, marked by excessive preoccupation with another person's needs and problems, to the virtual exclusion of one's own.

Theorists suggest that many people unknowingly seek out relationships with troubled persons to satisfy an excessive desire to be needed (O'Brien & Gaborit, 1992; Wright & Wright, 1991). Women are assumed to be more vulnerable to codependency than men because the socialization process of women tends to place importance on selflessness, being emotionally supportive, and taking care of others (Haaken, 1990). In these relationships, codependents become caught up in trying to protect, control, and change their partners, and consistently subordinate their own needs to those of their mates. Hence they end up leading unfulfilling lives. The payoff for this self-sacrifice is avoidance of facing the decision-making involved in coming to terms with what to do with one's own life. The codependent person can also blame her (or his) partner for the disappointments in her or his own life.

Recovery groups, such as Codependents Anonymous, seek to provide participants with social support, which has well-documented value in helping people cope with stress (Leavy, 1983). Recovery groups also encourage participants to talk about their problems and vent their emotions. Research suggests that these are healthy coping strategies (Pennebaker, Colder, & Sharp, 1990; Spielberger et al., 1985). The personal stories shared in recovery groups obviously show participants that they are not alone in their misery. Research on group therapy suggests that this is a valuable insight (Yalom, 1985). Thus it is plausible that many people benefit from their participation in the recovery programs promoted by the codependency movement.

There are some limitations in the concept of codependency. One is that definitions of codependency are ambiguous. Researchers have only recently begun to develop reliable methods for determining who is codependent and who is not (Fischer, Spann, & Crawford, 1991). People who label themselves as codependent are making highly subjective self-diagnoses of dubious validity. In addition, controlled, scientific studies of codependency are virtually nonexistent, and there is little or no evidence to support many of the basic tenets of codependency theory (Wright & Wright, 1991).

PASSIVE AGGRESSION   There is considerable evidence that in our culture, boys are more aggressive than girls and that girls are more empathic than boys (Block, 1979; Maccoby & Jacklin, 1974). Empathy is one of the characteristics that is known to counteract aggressive tendencies, and is discussed elsewhere (Chapters 5 & 13). However, *passive* aggressiveness is a feminine characteristic.

Passive aggression encompasses a category of behaviors in which hostility is expressed indirectly, usually because the actor has discovered that he or she is powerless to protest directly and would be endangered by being directly aggressive. This behavior appears among people with little power or influence who have no other way of retaliating against their oppressors. Traditional women are in this situation with regards to their husbands. Direct aggression is too dangerous, so that an indirect approach is seen as the only defense against active aggression directed at him or her.

A person who is overly friendly and compliant to the extreme might also be exhibiting passive aggressive behavior. When a person is always available to help out, others may find it easy to take advantage of him or her. The friendly person's compliant and self-sacrificing manner may exhibit a kind of passive aggression known as "killing with kindness." Other types of passive aggressive behavior include sulking, withholding, and provocative behaviors (Averill, 1983). Those who sulk may be showing aggression by intending to make others miserable. Individuals who withhold their affection are also demonstrating passive aggressive behavior. Yet another way to be indirectly aggressive is by passively provoking others into behaving aggressively toward oneself. In doing so, the passive aggressive person reveals the other person's lack of maturity and self-control.

Marianismo

In traditional Hispanic families, women are expected to have *marianismo*, which means that they are to be submissive, obedient, dependent, timid, docile, sentimental, and gentle, and are to remain a virgin until marriage (Comas-Diaz, 1988; Comas-Diaz & Duncan, 1988; Martinez, 1988; Ruiz, 1981). The women's role is also to be centered around taking care of their husbands, children, and household. Women's needs are expected to be subordinate to those of their husbands and children. Although these women are considered morally superior to their men, they are also expected to endure with forbearance the burden of mistreatment. Women who suffer in silence are idealized. They are also viewed as the providers of joy. This cultural ideal of the wife as martyr derives its name from the Virgin Mary.

➤ THE LOOSENING OF GENDER ROLE CONSTRAINTS

Gender stereotypes still exist in our culture, although they have become less pronounced in the past three decades. Brannon (1988) concluded that the qualities assigned to our gender are imposed on us even if we have little interest in or aptitude for them. "Traditionally sex roles come in just two large and unwieldy packages: masculine and feminine. (We don't even get to choose which one fits us best.) What this arbitrary assignment discourages most of all is the option of choosing what sort of characteristics we want to have" (p. 312). When our behavior varies from those qualities viewed as being appropriate for our gender, we may be punished with overt criticism or covert measures, such as rude comments to or avoidance of social contact with us. Whereas a male's assertive behavior is called "bold," in a female it may be considered "aggressive." Nurturing may be labeled "warmth" in a woman but "softness" in a male. Vulnerability may be alluring in a woman but repelling in a man.

Many psychologists have concluded that gender roles are neither necessary nor beneficial and that our society would be more diverse, more interesting, and happier without them (Brannon, 1985; Bem, 1975a; 1975b). We are a long way from being a society without gender roles, but there is some movement toward redefinition of them, which calls for a greater flexibility and sharing of roles to permit better use of our individual strengths. For women, this new definition invites the expansion of the current female role to include positions of power and prestige outside the family that have traditionally been occupied by men. For men, the redefinition encourages a development of nurturing, tenderness, and emotional expressiveness (Balswick, 1988).

Within the past several years, both men and women have increasingly experimented with nontraditional attitudes, behaviors, and adornment. Men have lengthened and dyed their hair and have donned nail polish, earrings, necklaces, and bracelets. Some, though not many, have put on makeup and stuck curlers in their hair. Women have exchanged their skirts for slacks and their high heels for flats, or even heavy work boots. Although many of these changes may have begun as adolescent rebellion, they nevertheless have found their way into the majority culture, perhaps because of the enhanced personal freedom that they offer. Even so, there are more "traditional" constraints on men than on women (Cohen, 1996). For instance, whereas a woman in a gray flannel suit, white shirt, and tie might raise an eyebrow, a man in a dress and heels would still elicit more of a reaction than that.

Many women seem so caught up in their revolt against traditional expectations that they have difficulty accepting any of the qualities usually attributed to them as women, even when these are positive qualities. The rejection of everything traditionally feminine does not liberate women; in fact, such rejection is precisely how men have defined their own role! It is important that women choose what they *want* for themselves as individuals; however, women won't be entirely free to do so until further changes occur in society as a whole.

Some men and women might prefer a division of labor along traditional gender lines. Roles are reciprocal, in that they must be played opposite another person who takes on a complementary role. A man who wishes to be the leader in his household will have to find a partner who wishes to be guided. Even when such traditional partners find one another, they may discover disapproval among their neighbors and coworkers. A woman who desires to be supported financially while she rears children is likely to suffer low status as an adult. In the new way of interpreting sex roles this choice might be denounced as limiting and constricting for the woman.

Psychoanalytic theorists have typically argued that women are biologically predisposed and/or socialized as children to develop nurturant and dependent personalities. However, as the "traditional family" has given way to a variety of household forms (Gerson, 1987), it has become difficult to argue that the traditional division of labor between the sexes is natural and

inevitable. Today there is no single standard for family life. Social changes are promising women new sources of power but also are bringing about new insecurities. Especially for women, it is not possible to use previous generations as a model. The guidelines for composing a life are no longer clear for either gender. There is now a state of normlessness, a condition discussed earlier in the chapter.

The freedom to be oneself is purchased at the price of having to carve out a unique identity. Men who feel less pressure to be the sole source of their female partner's happiness and the only provider for the family are experiencing liberation. Ironically, to the extent that men rely on the masculine role to gain a sense of identity, they may suffer a loss of their sense of self. This false front supplied by adopting masculine role expectations denies most of the inner self. A man can get caught up in being the way he thinks he should be as a male, rather than figuring out who he really is. Remember that self-actualization involves achieving one's true inborn potential, daring to express oneself in one's own *unique* way and living an inner-directed life (Chapter 2).

Certainly, men and women have come a long way. Can there be any doubt of this accomplishment with Madeline Albright as the U.S. Secretary of State, or with the growing number of single fathers taking custody of their children rather than turning them over to their mothers? These are undeniable examples of cultural *change*; however, do they represent *progress*? Restructuring of the household has, to some extent, left dependent children in the lurch. As a society we shall have to come to grips with the question, Who is to bring up the next generation if Mommy and Daddy are at work?

➤ PSYCHOLOGICAL ANDROGYNY: ACHIEVING A BALANCE

Gender-role differences are becoming less pronounced, and there is controversy as to whether this process is desirable. Some psychologists and others have called for changes in society to produce more **psychological androgyny** (a word of Greek origin from *andro*, meaning "male" and *gyn*, which means "female"). Androgyny actually means having male and female parts. Sandra Bem (1974) used the term to identify those people who indicate that a plentiful number of "masculine" and "feminine" adjectives describe them. Psychological androgyny involves attributing to oneself both traditionally masculine and traditionally feminine characteristics. The androgynous person integrates qualities of both sexes. This person would feel relatively free of gender constraints, and thus be more likely to express his or her own unique personality.

Bem was interested in what it means to be "masculine" or "feminine" when she developed the *Bem Sex Role Inventory*. The inventory classifies people as *masculine, feminine, androgynous,* or *undifferentiated,* on the basis of how they describe themselves. Having masculine traits means that a person is independent, assertive, and self-confident. Having feminine traits indicates that a person is nurturant, sensitive, relationship-oriented, and is likely to enjoy marital satisfaction as well as greater social closeness with others. Masculine traits are sometimes summed up by the term "instrumental," whereas feminine traits are often characterized as being "expressive." Bem and others feel that being androgynous is valuable, because this type of person tends to be more flexible, letting his or her behaviors be appropriate to the occasion rather than being confined by gender-role stereotypes. The inventory's "undifferentiated" category is something of a leftover, in which young people do not register on the scale as one of the other types, generally because of failure to characterize themselves as clearly exhibiting many of the adjectives from which they must select. Sample items from the Bem Sex-Role Inventory are provided in the following box.

SAMPLE ITEMS FROM THE BEM SEX-ROLE INVENTORY

Directions: Below are a number of personality characteristics. Please use these characteristics to describe yourself. Indicate, on a scale from 1 to 7, how true of you each trait is. Please do not leave any unmarked.

1	2	3	4	5	6	7
never or almost never true	usually not true	sometimes but infrequently true	occasionally true	often true	usually true	always or almost always true

    1. Self-reliant   ____
    2. Yielding   ____
    3. Helpful   ____
    4. Defends own beliefs   ____
    5. Cheerful   ____

Scoring: Starting with item 1, every third item denotes a masculine quality; beginning with the second item, every third item is considered a feminine quality. Starting with the third item, every third item is a neutral quality.

Bem's conclusion, which is based on a number of studies, is that rigid gender roles can seriously restrict behavior, especially for men (Bem, 1974; 1975a; 1975b; 1981). She believes that masculine males have great difficulty expressing warmth, playfulness, and concern, even when these qualities are appropriate, because they view such traits as feminine. In the same way, feminine women have trouble being independent and assertive, even when these qualities are called for.

Some initial research suggested that androgynous people feel better about themselves than do gender-typed masculine men and feminine women. However, dozens of studies, from North America to India, revealed that for both men and women, masculine qualities were associated with high self-regard (e.g. Orlofsky & O'Heron, 1987; Whitley, 1988).

Strong masculine qualities seem to interfere with intimacy. In a study of 108 couples in Sydney, Australia, Antill (1983) found that when either the wife or the husband had traditionally feminine qualities such as gentleness, sensitivity, and affectionateness, marital satisfaction was higher. The highest satisfaction was found when *both* partners in the couple had feminine qualities. Masculine qualities may be good for self-esteem, but both husbands and wives report that it is much more satisfying to be married to someone who is nurturant, sensitive, and emotionally supportive. This finding suggests that when spouses adhere to traditional gender-role ideology, wives in such marriages will report less marital satisfaction than will husbands, as the husbands will lack nurturing skills.

Psychological characteristics account for the ability to establish intimacy rather than whether one is a man or a woman. Jones and Gembo (1989) tested the relative importance of *gender* as compared with *gender-role* differences in level of intimacy. It was predicted the traditional males would score lower on intimacy than females, but androgynous males would show no such difference. A sample of 217 children from ages 8 to 14 was given a version of the Bem Sex-Role Inventory modified for children and adolescents. Intimacy was assessed with a self-report measure of closeness to a best friend. The results were that females and androgynous males form a homogeneous high-intimacy group, whereas sex-typed males score significantly lower.

According to Carl Jung, we use the facets of our personality that are like those of the other gender to help us relate to people of the other gender. In accordance with Carl Jung's theory of what constitutes a healthy personality, the loosening of strict gender role constraints allows individuals more easily to achieve balanced personalities.

Other observers of gender-role blurring find androgynous notions incompatible with their idea of people's true nature. Some, like Ebeling (1993), call upon women to stop competing with men and to fulfill their own "child-bearing biology." Others, such as Bly, call upon men to stop being "soft males" and to assert their "primitive masculinity," which includes decisiveness, fierceness, and—somehow—sensitivity. Some observers make the case that our gender role is a part of our core identity and that we must learn this role before we can know who we are. In this view, boys and girls get support and assistance in self-definition by interacting with members of their own sex and by taking stances in relation to the other gender (Arkoff, 1993).

Whereas psychological androgyny advocates the combining of gender roles, Matlin (1996) suggests that the entire concept of gender roles may eventually be rendered obsolete. People will be free to express their talents and abilities without having to worry about being appropriate. In any case, the behaviors of men and women already overlap substantially, and many people do not display the behaviors that are characteristic of their gender.

Gender Roles over the Life Span

In early adulthood, American men are generally high in achievement motivation or mastery and are highly committed to their careers. Young women, though not without vocational ambition, tend to be high in affiliative needs and show a considerable interpersonal commitment. Yet, as men move beyond their middle years, they often become less aggressive and ambitious and more affiliative and nurturant. Women somewhat reverse this patterning, becoming more aggressive, assertive, or managerial (Fiske, 1980). Carl Jung was perhaps the first psychological theorist to point out this tendency (in Campbell, 1971).

➤ CARL JUNG'S THEORY OF A BALANCED PERSONALITY

Carl Jung (1875–1961) was among many psychological theorists who were influenced by Freud. Once revered by Freud as his most promising disciple, Jung bitterly disappointed his mentor by developing some ideas about human nature and personality development that substantially departed from Freud's model. Eventually, the two men parted company over these intellectual differences and became decided enemies. After the break with Freud, Jung founded a discipline called "analytic psychology."

Jung had a more positive view of human nature than did Freud. He believed that besides having instinctual urges, people develop potential. Our present personality is determined both by who and what we have been and by the person we hope to become. Part of human nature is to be constantly emerging, growing, and moving toward a balanced development. Jung conceptualized the human psyche as continuing to evolve throughout the life span.

The higher forces in humans were thought by Jung to be in conflict with our animal nature. Jung believed that the spiritual needs of humans are at least equally, if not more, potent than the basic biological needs and that these yearnings could be expected to be expressed differently in introverted people from the way they would be in extroverted people. The inwardly oriented introvert finds purpose in life by integrating the inner conflicts into a whole self, whereas the action-oriented, outwardly directed extrovert finds purpose in life by harmonizing the self with social reality.

Jung objected to Freud's heavy emphasis on childhood sexuality. In addition, he argued that neurotic symptoms were not always the residue of an unhappy childhood, as Freud maintained, but were often attempts on the part of the mind to restore its equilibrium and thus could serve as pointers to a more satisfactory synthesis.

The Collective Unconscious

Jung agreed with Freud on the importance of the unconscious mind. However, Jung conceptualized the unconscious as having two aspects. Jung's *personal* unconscious is comparable to Freud's notion of the unconscious, where the mind stores memories from childhood that remain outside conscious awareness. Jung also proposed the concept of a **collective unconscious.** For Jung, all that human beings are comes from the entire sweep of prior human experience. This storehouse of memories is transmitted genetically, so that each person inherits all of previous human history. Jung used as evidence for the existence of the collective unconscious the finding that people from different parts of the world and/or different eras have chosen the same symbols to represent an object or a situation. The universal awe of nature and love of trees among humans may stem from an earlier close link with forest life. Likewise, the very common fear of the dark in humans may hearken back to a time when humans had no fire, so that nighttime was very dangerous indeed.

Archetypes

The collective unconscious contains **archetypes.** These are deeply rooted, inherited ideas or images that are present in everyone. They are universal representations of a kind of person, a type of object, or a particular experience, and they reflect the common experiences of humanity in coping with nature, war, parenthood, love, and evil. Archetypes function as prototypes, molds, or models that organize and shape the person's interactions with the external world. They are flexible templates for shaping experience in certain directions. For instance, there are archetypes for the Mother and the Hero, meaning that these concepts evoke images common to every human psyche. We have preconceived notions of what is good mothering behavior and of what we can expect from a hero.

Jung undertook to identify the archetypes by studying dreams, paintings, poetry, folk stories, myths, and religions. He found that the same themes appear again and again. For instance, the story of Jack and the beanstalk is essentially the same as the story of David and Goliath. Both tell how a small, weak, good person triumphs over a big, strong, bad person. Archetypal themes were considered by Jung to be reflected in every aspect of human society. They are the substance of our literature, art, architecture, and religions. Archetypes are reflected in our laws, customs, etiquette, mores, taboos, value systems, and ideologies. How we deal with these themes forms the basis of our culture and civilization.

Two important archetypes are the **anima** and the **animus.** Each person has both male and female aspects, according to Jung. The anima is the female aspect in men, and the animus is the male aspect in women. Jung considered the expression of both our male and female qualities as necessary for balanced personality development. Existence of the anima in males and the animus in females enables us to relate to members of the other sex. A man who hates women would be considered by Jung to be at war with his own anima. A woman may project her ideal image of manliness (her animus) onto a potential mate and would be disappointed if that man did not live up to the masculine standards she carries internally.

The **shadow** archetype represents the denied portions of ourselves; the undesirable aspects of our personality. For Jung, both constructive and destructive forces coexist in the human psyche. To become integrated, we must accept the dark side of our nature with our primitive impulses, such as selfishness and greed. Acceptance of our dark side (or shadow) does not imply being dominated by this dimension of our being but rather recognizing that this is part of our nature. The shadow is both a personal and a collective unconscious phenomenon. The levels of shadow are the conscious part of shadow, the unconscious part projected onto others, and the evil of the ages, or the collective part.

The **self-archetype** is the most important archetype and represents unity and balance between the conscious and the unconscious, anima and animus, thinking and feeling, sensing and intuiting, persona and ego, introversion and extroversion. Jung viewed human nature as consisting of polarities: We might be male, but we also have female aspects to our psyches. We may be extroverted, yet we have an introverted side (though it will be an inferior, weaker aspect of ourselves than is the dominant end of the continuum). We may be essentially a thinking person, but we have reservoirs of feeling. We are conscious beings, but we have within our unconscious mind, raw material seeking outward expression. We live on a physical/material plane, yet we also have a spiritual self. Jung felt that we become richer and more completely human when a balance is achieved between these polarities.

The self-archetype is generally experienced as an inner guiding factor. A person can encounter the expression of the self-archetype in meditative moments, often as an inner voice. Having undertaken the exploration of the dark side of our nature and come to terms with our shadow aspects, followed by making conscious the opposite sex function within us (the anima or the animus), we are then prepared to begin the task of reconciling and integrating the opposites within us. The archetypal image of this unification, the mid-point common to both consciousness and unconscious is the self. This is the path to self-realization, although few people actually achieve this state of psychological development. Even so, the process of striving for self-realization is intrinsic to human nature (O'Connor, 1985).

Jung represented the self-archetype with a **mandala,** which is a circular creation that was used by Jung to represent the wholeness of one's being.

With symmetrically placed figures and patterns within the mandala, Jung represented the balancing of opposite human inclinations, which he deemed necessary to a healthy personality.

Individuation

Achieving **individuation** is a primary goal of each person, according to Jung. The process of individuation involves the reconciliation of opposites and their integration. This task is achieved by bringing into consciousness the unconscious aspects of our being. Through the process of individuation, the self is formed. For Jung, the overriding goal was always the achieving of a harmony between the conscious and the unconscious forces in the personality. That alone could make a person whole. The process of individuation is the central concept of Jungian psychology (O'Connor, 1985).

A person is individuated to the extent that he or she has a fully harmonious and integrated personality. It is desirable for a personality to have balance, meaning that all aspects of the self are developed, so that the person is not a fanatic about anything, and that the person does not have "inferior" (or undeveloped) aspects, which would be the opposite of the fanatic quality. For example, a person would not want to be either miserly or excessively generous. A balance between the two is desirable.

QUESTIONS: *How do you handle aspects of yourself that you do not find admirable? Are you able to acknowledge and accept some of them?*

A balance between thought and feeling is also desirable. When thought enhances feeling, and feeling enhances thought, we have a well integrated personality. When we are overdeveloped in our ability to think and are cut off from our feelings, we are more limited in our ability to experience the many facets of life. We tend to see and trust only facts. We undervalue relationships. Our spiritual needs may be neglected. Conversely, when we are overdeveloped in our ability to feel and are cut off from our ability to think, we often act impulsively. We can become overwhelmed and immobilized by our feelings. We may tend to see ourselves as helpless and needy. When we are more in balance, our feelings give us energy, and our minds give us the ability to channel that energy into productive ways of being.

Jung felt that this rational age of contemporary Western culture has gotten out of balance, in that the imaginative interest in mythology and poetry, which draws from the unconscious, has all but vanished. Modern life demands concentrated, directed conscious functioning, and this involves the risk of dissociation from the unconscious. Jung believed that only under ideal conditions, where one's life activities are simple and unconscious enough to follow the circuitous path of instinct without hesitation or misgiving, can the compensatory forces within the psyche work with complete success. Success would be defined as the conscious and unconscious aspects of the psyche operating in an integrated manner. The more civilized, the more conscious and complicated a person is, the less he or she is able to follow his or her instincts. The complexities of modern living conditions create environmental conditions so strong that they drown the quiet voice of nature (Campbell, 1971).

Personality Dimensions

INTROVERTED VERSUS EXTROVERTED   Jung's most widely accepted ideas have to do with the concepts of **introversion** and **extroversion.** He was convinced that personality types were inborn and that the most important innate tendency was that toward introversion or extroversion. Jung characterized the introvert as reserved or inscrutable. "The introvert's attitude is an abstracting one; at bottom, he is always intent on withdrawing libido from the object, as though he had to prevent the object from gaining power over him" (Jung, in Campbell, 1971, p. 179). The tendency of the introvert is to defend himself or herself against all demands from outside, to conserve his or her energy by withdrawing it from objects, thereby consolidating his or her own position. Introverts might rehearse things before saying them and prefer that others would do the same. They often respond with "I'll have to think about that" or "Let me tell you later." Introverts enjoy the peace and quiet of having time to themselves and find their private time too easily invaded. Shy people are thought to be introverted. They need to "recharge" alone after they've spent time socializing with a group. The more intense the encounter, the greater is the likelihood that they will feel drained afterward.

The extrovert is open and sociable. The extrovert has a positive relation to the outside world "to such an extent that his subjective attitude is constantly related to and oriented by [others]" (Jung, in Campbell, 1971, p. 179). Extroverts are "jovial people, or at least friendly and approachable characters who are on good terms with everybody, or quarrel with everybody, but always relate to them in some way and in turn are affected by them. The nature of the extrovert constantly urges him to expend and propagate himself in every way" (Jung, in Campbell, 1971, p. 180). Extroverts tend to know a lot of people, count many of them among their "close friends," and like to include as many people as possible in their activities. They are approachable and easily engaged by friends and strangers alike, though perhaps somewhat dominating in a conversation. Also, they find telephone calls to be welcome interruptions and don't hesitate to pick up the phone whenever they have something to tell someone. Extroverts like going to parties and prefer talking with many people instead of with just a few. They need affirmation from friends and associates about who they are, what to do, how they look, and just about everything else; they may think that they're doing a good job, but until they hear someone tell them that it is so, they don't truly believe it.

There are two other personality dimensions (of lesser importance) in Jung's theoretical model:

INTUITIVE VERSUS SENSING   Intuitive people tend to think in the abstract. They generally think about several things at once and are often accused by friends and colleagues of being absentminded. They consider the future and its possibilities more intriguing than frightening; they are usually more excited about where they are going than where they are. Intuitive people think that "boring details" are a redundancy. They believe that time is relative; so that no matter what the hour, they aren't late unless the meeting/meal/party has started without them. Also, they like figuring out how things work just for the sheer pleasure of doing so. They find themselves seeking the connections and interrelationships among most things rather than accepting them at face value and are always asking "What does that mean?"

Sensing types of people lean toward the concrete. They prefer specific answers to questions; when they ask someone the time, they prefer answers such as "three fifty-two" to "a little before four." They like to concentrate on what they're doing at the moment and generally don't wonder about what's next. Moreover, they would rather *do* something than think about it. They find most satisfying those jobs that yield some tangible result, so that as much as they may hate doing housekeeping, they would rather clean their office than think about where their career is headed.

THINKING VERSUS FEELING   Thinking types of people are objective and impersonal. They are able to stay cool and calm in situations in which everyone else is upset. Thinkers would rather settle a dispute on the basis of what is fair and truthful than what will make people happy. They enjoy proving a point for the sake of clarity and might argue both sides in a discussion simply to expand their intellectual horizons.

Feeling types of people are subjective and personal. They consider a "good decision" one that takes others' feelings into account. They feel that love cannot be defined, and are offended by those who try to do so. Feeling types put themselves in other people's moccasins; and they are likely to be the ones who in a meeting will ask, "How will this affect the people involved?" In fact, they may overextend themselves in meeting other people's needs, because they will do almost anything to accommodate others, even at the expense of their own comfort. They may find themselves wondering, "Doesn't anyone care about what I want?" although they may have difficulty actually saying this to anyone. They are often accused of taking things too personally.

The last dimension is the only one with gender-related preferences. About two-thirds of all males are thinking types, and about the same proportion of females are feeling types. Many people do not fit neatly into either extreme of these dichotomies. They may have definite tendencies toward one end of the continuum on some dimensions, yet be fairly well balanced on others. As with all other personality typologies, Jung's four personality dimensions inadequately take into account individual uniqueness.

Jungian Analysis

Jung promoted a more active interchange between the analyst and the patient than did Freud. Jung believed that when the analysis is going well, both analyst and patient experience the therapy as a growth process. In contrast to Freud, Jung erected a theoretical model in which the patient's past sexual and family histories played only a minor role.

A large part of analysis was devoted to the interpretation of the patients' dreams. Jung had an inclination to interpret patients' dreams as archaic residues from long-lost religious symbols or things they knew nothing about in their ordinary, everyday lives. Richard Noll (1997), author of a biography about Jung, commented that "this wild ride into mythological symbolism was indeed therapeutic. It helped make their individual, mundane lives seem much more interesting and even important on a cosmic level." Patients didn't seem to mind being told that they were a member of a holy order, a secret one that was doing important work that would ultimately redeem the entire world.

Jung's Approach to Dreams

Like Freud, Jung used dreams as vehicles for getting at unconscious material. Also in accord with Freud's views, Jung believed that the unconscious is the most powerful and determinative force in our lives. According to Jung, the unconscious is the source of both madness and creative inspiration. To be healthy, people must come to terms with their unconscious. The key to the unconscious, for neurotics and normal people alike, is dream analysis. Jung believed that dreams reflect not only an individual's personal unconscious but also the collective unconscious. In other words, some dreams deal with an individual's relationship to a larger whole such as the family, universal humanity, and generations over time (Hall, 1984).

Although Jung agreed with Freud that dreams provide a pathway into the unconscious, he differed with Freud on the causes of dreams. Jung wrote that dreams have two purposes: Dreams help people prepare themselves for the experiences and events that they anticipate in the near future, and they also serve a compensatory function, in that they work to bring about a balance between opposites within a person. Dreams compensate for the predominance of one facet of the individual's personality (Schultz, 1990).

How should dream images be interpreted? First, most dreams are compensatory and indicate that some portion of the psyche is being ignored. Jung believed that one of the most important tasks of psychic hygiene was to pay continual attention to the symptoms and symbols of unconscious content, because the conscious mind is always in danger of becoming one-sided or of keeping to well-worn paths and getting stuck in blind alleys (Campbell, 1971). The complementary and compensating function of the unconscious ensures that these dangers can in some measure be avoided. Second, a dream's meaning is usually not hidden. Third, if the dreamer finds an interpretation unacceptable, then it is probably wrong. Fourth, free association is a useful technique for discovering obscure meanings of dreams. Finally, dreams often contain hints concerning the advisability of intended actions.

Since dreams are often fragments of old (but universal) myths and legends, one must have considerable knowledge of anthropology, art history, linguistics, literature, and religion before one can understand these images. Jung believed in everything supernatural, from reincarnation and ghosts to telepathy and UFOs, from alchemy and astrology to parapsychology and the occult (McLynn, 1997). How do we know when we have correctly interpreted a symbol? The next dream may give the answer, or perhaps the interpretation will be followed by an upsurge of repressed emotion and energy. An incorrect interpretation causes doubt, resistance, deadlock, and a natural drying up of associations.

➤ MASLOW'S RESOLUTION OF DICHOTOMIES

In his study of self-actualized people, Maslow concluded that polarities or opposites that existed in ordinary people were somehow resolved by the healthier, self-actualized individuals. Many opposing forces—such as that between heart and head, reason and instinct, or thoughts and feelings—find synthesis and unity in self-actualizers. Maslow (1987) wrote that "St. Augustine's 'Love God and do as you will' can easily be translated 'Be healthy and then you may trust your impulses.'" (p. 149).

Maslow suggested that the polarity between selfishness and unselfishness disappears for healthy individuals, as every act is inherently both. Self-actualizers are both lusty, animal creatures and moral ones, and thus the sensual and sexual aspects of life can be a path to spirituality. Work and play may blend together, when a person takes pleasure in his or her work. Maslow addressed further false dichotomies:

> Similar findings have been reached for kindness-ruthlessness, concreteness-abstractness, acceptance-rebellion, self-society, adjustment-maladjustment, detachment from others-identification with others, serious-humorous, Dionysian-Apollonian, introverted-extroverted, intense-casual, serious-frivolous, conventional-unconventional, mystic-realistic, active-passive, masculine-feminine ... the war between the sexes turns out to be no war at all in matured people. (p. 149)

➤ SOCIAL LEARNING THEORY PERSPECTIVE

Social learning theorists believe that children acquire gender-typed behavior patterns according to the same principles that explain all learned behavior (Mischel, 1966; 1970). Thus, gender differences are at least in part brought about by differential socialization. Children are rewarded for "gender-appropriate" behavior and punished for "gender-inappropriate" behavior (Matlin, 1996). Children observe their parents and then use them, particularly the same-sexed parent, as models (Bussey & Bandura, 1984). In addition to immitating their parents, children use teachers, siblings, and even television and movie characters as role models. Thus, observational learning should result in having girls play with dolls and dishes, whereas boys would play with erector sets and cars, as long as the models whom children watch engage in a division of labor along traditional lines.

> ## ➤ SUMMARY

The terms *norm* and *role* refer to social rules that govern behavior. These rules are developed through consensus and serve the purpose of reducing anxiety over not knowing what to expect from others. Norms are rules concerning what is appropriate behavior in a given situation. A role can be defined as a set of norms that describe how people in a given social position ought to behave. Roles exert a powerful influence on behavior and may overpower individual differences in personality.

Over the centuries of human existence, social roles based on gender have developed, such that certain tasks and attributes have typically been assigned to men or to women. Gender roles still exist, although they have become less pronounced in many cultures during the past few decades.

There are a number of themes that define the male gender role in U.S. culture. Traditional men are careful to avoid appearing feminine in any way. Such men may find it difficult to express warmth, tenderness, and compassion, because they identify these characteristics as feminine. They strive to be successful and self-reliant, and tend to be competitive and aggressive compared with women. Men are socialized to believe that success at work is the measure of their value as men. Traditional men also value being self-reliant in all things. Masculinity may be seen as synonymous with aggressive striving; that is, the need to conquer, to outwit, or to defeat.

Women have more latitude in self-expression than do men. Traditionally, women were expected to be emotional, lacking in ambition, concerned with relationships, and dependent on men. Traditional women have a tendency to be emotional, are easily hurt, and are thought to be excitable in a crisis. Women are traditionally thought to be uninterested in achievement, competition, or power. They tend to develop an identity based on interpersonal relationships. The traditional woman tends to be submissive, passive, dependent, and indecisive.

There has been an interest in a cluster of characteristics which have come to be known as "codependency." The concept has been expanded to include becoming enmeshed in a dysfunctional relationship, marked by excessive preoccupation with another person's needs and problems, to the virtual exclusion of one's own. Women are assumed to be more vulnerable to codependency than men because the socialization of females typically places more emphasis on the importance of selflessness, being emotionally supportive, and taking care of others.

Psychoanalytic theorists have typically argued that women are biologically predisposed and/or socialized as children to develop nurturant and dependent personalities. The discovery that there are exceptions to traditional gender roles suggests that gender roles are not biologically predetermined, but can vary considerably depending on one's culture. As the "traditional family" has given way to a variety of household forms, it has become difficult to argue that the traditional division of labor between the sexes is natural or inevitable. Restructuring of the household has to some extent left society to come to grips with the question as to who will bring up the next generation if Mommy and Daddy are at work.

Gender-role differences are becoming less pronounced, and many psychologists have contended that gender roles are neither necessary nor beneficial. According to psychologist Sandra Bem, men and women who have developed a wide array of personal qualities within themselves are the most adaptable to new situations. Bem developed the *Bem Sex Role Inventory*, which classifies persons as *masculine, feminine,* or *androgynous.* Having "masculine" traits means a person is independent, assertive, and self-confident. Having "feminine" traits means a person is nurturant and relationship-oriented, and is related to marital satisfaction as well as greater social closeness with others. Research has suggested that androgynous people feel better about themselves than do gender-typed masculine men and feminine women. In general, masculine qualities are associated with high self-regard but reduced intimacy. When spouses adhere to traditional gender-role ideology, wives in such marriages report less marital satisfaction than do husbands. Bem and other psychologists have called for changes in society to produce more *psychological androgyny,* a term used to identify those people who attribute to themselves both masculine and feminine characteristics.

According to Carl Jung, we use the facets of our personality that are like those of the other gender to help us relate to the other gender. Jung believed that in early adulthood, men are generally high in achievement motivation and highly committed to their careers. Young women, though not without career ambition, tend to be high in affiliative needs and to show a considerable interpersonal commitment. Yet, as men move toward their middle years, they often become less aggressive and ambitious and more affiliative and nurturant. Women reverse this pattern, becoming more aggressive, assertive, and managerial.

Jung was among many theorists who were influenced by Freud, but he held a more positive view of human nature than did Freud, contending that part of human nature is to be constantly developing, growing, and moving toward a balanced development throughout the life span. Jung likewise objected to Freud's heavy emphasis on childhood sexuality.

Jung agreed with Freud on the importance of the unconscious mind. However, Jung conceptualized the unconscious as having two aspects: Jung's *personal* unconscious is comparable to Freud's view of the unconscious, in which the mind stores memories from childhood that remain outside conscious awareness. In addition, Jung proposed that all human beings share a *collective unconscious*, which is transmitted genetically and contains elements of all past human experiences.

The collective unconscious contains *archetypes*. These are deeply rooted ideas that are present in everyone and that reflect the common experiences of humanity. Two important archetypes are the *anima* and the *animus*. The anima is the female aspect in men, and the animus is the male aspect in women. Jung considered the expression of both male and female qualities as necessary for balanced personality development. He might be said to have anticipated Bem's concept of psychological androgyny.

The *self* archetype is the most important archetype, and represents unity and balance between the polarities of the self. Jung represented the self archetype with *mandalas*, which are circular creations used by Jung to represent the wholeness of a person's being. Another archetype, the *shadow*, represents the negative, denied portions of ourselves. To become integrated, we must accept this shadow side as part of our nature.

Achieving *individuation* is a primary goal of each person, according to Jung. A person is individuated to the extent that he or she has a fully harmonious, balanced, and integrated personality. For Jung, the overriding goal was always the achieving of a harmony between the conscious and the unconscious. That alone could make a person whole. Jung felt that contemporary Western culture has gotten out of balance, in that the imaginative interest in mythology and poetry, which draws from the unconscious, has all but vanished. The complexities of modern living in the rational age create environmental conditions so strong that they drown the quiet voice of nature.

INTROVERSION VERSUS EXTROVERSON   Jung's most famous idea is that the personality of human beings can be assessed along a dimension of introversion versus extroversion. He was accurate in his characterization of this dimension as being at least partly inherited.

Jung's personality type system included two lesser dimensions: (1) *Intuitive versus sensing:* Intuitive persons are abstract and are often absent-minded. They view the future and its possibilities as more intriguing than frightening; also, they are usually more excited about where they are going than where they are. Sensing types are concrete. They like to concentrate on what they're doing at the moment and generally don't wonder about what's next. Moreover, they would rather *do* something than think about it. (2) *Thinking versus feeling:* Thinking types are objective and impersonal. Feeling types are subjective and personal. This last dimension is the only one with gender-related preferences. About two-thirds of all males are thinking types and about the same proportion of females are feeling types.

JUNGIAN ANALYSIS   Jung promoted a more active interchange between the analyst and the patient than did Freud. He believed that when the analysis is going well, both analyst and patient experience the analysis as a growth process. A large part of analysis was devoted to the interpretation of patient dreams.

JUNG'S APPROACH TO DREAMS   Like Freud, Jung used dreams as vehicles for getting at unconscious material. He believed that the unconscious is the determinative force in people's lives. Jung thought that dreams help people prepare themselves for experiences that they anticipate in the near future and that dreams also compensate for the predominance of one facet of the individual's personality.

LEARNING THE LANGUAGE OF PSYCHOLOGISTS

norms	**shadow**
role	**self-archetype**
psychological androgyny	**mandala**
collective unconscious	**individuation**
archetypes	**introversion**
anima	**extroversion**
animus	

CHAPTER REVIEW QUESTIONS

1. What are social norms and roles, and what are their functions?
2. What did Professor Phil Zimbardo's Stanford Prison Experiment demonstrate about roles?
3. How might the discovery that assuming a role can dramatically influence subsequent behavior be used beneficially to help people get along?
4. What characteristics are traditionally associated with masculinity and with femininity?
5. How does Sandra Bem's concept of psychological androgyny relate to Jung's anima and animus archetypes?
6. What are the advantages of maintaining gender roles, and what is gained by loosening them or giving them up altogether?
7. What is Jung's concept of the collective unconscious, and how does it relate to his idea of archetypes?
8. According to Jung, what is the primary goal of each person?

ACTIVITIES

1. *LARGE GROUP EXERCISE:* ***Role-Reversal.*** Have the women in the class sit in an inner circle and the men sit in an outer circle. The men should observe silently while the women "become men" and talk among themselves as they imagine that men talk when they're together. Then the men move to the inner circle and "become women," expressing themselves as they imagine a group of women would do so. After both groups have had a

chance to become the other gender, an exchange can occur. This exercise can be a catalyst for an examination of the myths, stereotypes, and opinions that each gender holds concerning the other.

2. *SMALL GROUP EXERCISE: **Actual Role.*** In small groups, discuss the role you deem most important and the one least important in your life. Be aware of how much time you devote to each role. Share with others the degree of satisfaction or dissatisfaction that you derive from each role. Also, spend time in your group discussing possible competing roles. For example, you may be a mother of young children and a college student. Do you experience any conflict in these dual roles? Are both roles fulfilling for you?

3. *DYADS EXERCISE: **Ideal Role.*** Imagine yourself in an ideal role that would lead to good feelings about yourself. Now form dyads, and share with your partner what this role is and how it would be for you actually to be in this ideal role. For instance, you may want to see yourself as an accomplished athlete, one who is recognized by others. Share how you think your life would be different if this role were a reality. Do you have any ideas of how you can go about bringing your actual roles in line with your ideal roles?

4. *SMALL GROUP EXERCISE: **Personal Reflections on Gender Roles in My Life.***

5. *COMPLETE INDIVIDUALLY: **Introversion-Extroversion Scale.***

6. *COMPLETE INDIVIDUALLY: **A Jungian Strategy for Self-Understanding.***

Personal Reflections on Gender Roles in My Life

Directions: Read each of the following questions, and then write your answers in the blanks.

1. Traditional women were thought to be more open and vulnerable than traditional men. Describe your own experiences and observations in this regard. Are these qualities still more likely to be found in women than in men?

_____

_____

_____

_____

2. If you are a female, would you want a partner you could lean on and depend on? If you are a male, would you want a mate who leans on and depends on you? Why, or why not?

_____

_____

_____

_____

3. Do you think it is appealing for an American man today to have a hint of untamed aggressiveness about him? If you are a female, would you value this quality in a partner? If you are a male, would you cultivate this quality in yourself?

_____

_____

_____

_____

4. As a part of the male gender role, men are supposed to be knowledgeable, on top of things, and generally able to handle any situation that may arise. Describe your own experience and observations in this regard.

_____

_____

_____

_____

5. Since men are admonished not to be feminine in any way, how can you account for the trends in the past twenty years toward men's adopting feminine self-adornment strategies?

_____

_____

_____

_____

6. Do you feel that the roles of wife and mother, as they are traditionally defined, would be demeaning for you or for your spouse? Why, or why not?

_____

_____

_____

_____

7. Would you expect to have more rights, privileges, and prestige as a breadwinner than as a homemaker? Why, or why not?

_____

_____

8. What are five characteristics that, when encountered in another person, would cause you to take an immediate dislike to that person? After making your list, consider whether these qualities might be a part of your own "shadow." To what extent do you deny having any of these qualities yourself?

9. Which of the following emotions would you be willing to show openly in front of friends and acquaintances? If feasible, compare your answers with those of your classmates and look for gender differences.

a. _____ anxiety		k. _____ trust
b. _____ depression		l. _____ cynicism
c. _____ fear		m. _____ tenderness
d. _____ happiness		n. _____ hostility
e. _____ disgust		o. _____ envy
f. _____ love		p. _____ upset
g. _____ anger		q. _____ hurt
h. _____ contempt		r. _____ worry
i. ._____ impatience		s. _____ sadness
j. _____ surprise		t. _____ jealousy

10. State whether you agree or disagree with this statement, and why: "Since money is the most common source of power in this society and frequently symbolizes social power, it is not surprising that the person who brings economic resources into a family or a relationship has increased power. The partner who earns the greater amount of money holds the power in a relationship."

11. Complete one of the following sentences: "If I didn't have to worry about being feminine . . ." or "If I didn't have to worry about being masculine . . ."

_____

_____

_____

_____

12. What is your opinion about the likely outcome of efforts to reduce or eliminate gender-stereotypical attitudes and behavior? Are you optimistic or are you pessimistic, or do you stand somewhere in the middle? Why?

_____

_____

_____

_____

13. How do you think that marital partners should divide up family responsibilities?

_____

_____

_____

_____

14. Describe either one of your recent dream figures of the opposite sex or a memorable dream figure from the past. Was this figure friendly? Antagonistic? Dangerous? Helpful? Seductive? Does the demeanor of your dream figure suggest anything to you about your current ways of relating to the other gender?

_____

_____

_____

_____

15. Working as a group, use a separate piece of paper to list all of the adjectives you can think of to describe what it means to be "feminine" and "masculine." When the list has been completed, discuss whether there are aspects of each gender role that should be avoided by all healthy adults.

Introversion-Extroversion Scale

Directions: Circle "T" for true or "F" for false for each of the following statements.

1. T F I tend to keep in the background at social events.
2. T F I prefer to work with others rather than alone.
3. T F I get embarrassed easily.
4. T F I generally tell others how I feel regardless of how they may take it.
5. T F I really try to avoid situations in which I must speak to a group.
6. T F I am strongly motivated by the approval or interest of others.
7. T F I often daydream.
8. T F I find it easy to start a conversation with strangers.
9. T F I find it difficult to make friends of the opposite sex.
10. T F I particularly enjoy meeting people who know their way around the social scene.
11. T F I would rather read a good book or watch television than go out to a movie.
12. T F I would rather work as a salesperson than as a librarian.
13. T F I spend a lot of time philosophizing and thinking about my ideas.
14. T F I prefer action to thought and reflection.
15. T F I am often uncomfortable in conversations with strangers.
16. T F I am mainly interested in activities and ideas that are practical.
17. T F I would prefer visiting an art gallery over attending a sporting event.
18. T F I enjoy open competition in sports, games, and school.
19. T F I make my decisions by reason more than by impulse or emotion.
20. T F I have to admit that I enjoy talking about myself to others.
21. T F I like to lose myself in my work.
22. T F I sometimes get into arguments with people whom I do not know well.
23. T F I am very selective about who my friends are.
24. T F I make decisions quickly and stick to them.

Scoring:
1. Go through the odd-numbered items and add the number of true responses, and then add the number of false responses. Enter the two numbers on the appropriate lines below.
2. Go through the even-numbered items, adding the number of true as well as the number of false responses. Enter the numbers on the proper lines.
3. Add only the *ODD*-false items to the *EVEN*-true items.
4. The total thus obtained should be marked on the introversion-extroversion scale.

True: False:

ODD ITEMS _____ _____

True: False:

_____ _____EVEN ITEMS

Total: _____ (Total the numbers on the lines that are directly above this one.)

```
0———————6———————12———————18———————24
INTROVERT                              EXTROVERT
```

A Jungian Strategy for Self-Understanding

Background: Carl Jung found in his explorations of mythology that the self was often archetypically symbolized by a mandala. *Mandala* is a Sanskrit word meaning "circle." In various mythologies, in religious rituals, and in the dreams and fantasies of his patients, Jung observed a variety of mandala-like figures. Sometimes the mandala is divided into four segments around which is drawn the characteristic circular enclosure. Jung was occasionally seized with the compulsion to create mandala figures in paint:

> My mandalas were cryptograms concerning the state of the self which were pre-sented to me anew each day. In them I saw the self—that is, my whole being—actively at work . . . I had the distinct feeling that they were something central, and in time I acquired through them a living conception of the self. The self, I thought, was like the monad which I am, and which is my world. The mandala represents this monad [i.e., unity], and corresponds to the microcosmic nature of the psyche. (Jung, 1961, p. 196)

Accompanying is a reproduction of one of Jung's own mandala paintings. It shows a group of interlocking circles, with human figures in the four most peripheral circles. This mandala was intended by Jung to illustrate four complementary aspects of the self. To the right and the left of center are two female figures, with the left woman representing the "dark" side of the anima and the right one symbolizing the nurturing aspect. The top and bottom peripheral circles contain the "wise old man" archetype and the "trickster" archetype, respectively. The sixteen "globes" surrounding the center star are symbolic "eyes," which stand for "observing and discriminating consciousness" (Jung, 1950, p. 374).

Jung insisted that how we live our lives is how we confront the great archetypal themes of human existence. Archetypal themes deal with conception and birth, existence and nonexistence, joy and suffering, love and hate, crisis and resolution, dying and sorrow, and transcendence and rebirth. Some of the archetypes identified by Jung are listed here. These may be useful to

One of Carl Jung's mandala paintings.

you in creating your own mandala.

Trickster or Magician Archetype. Characteristics of the trickster or magician figure are his fondness for sly jokes, malicious pranks, and his dual nature: half animal, half human. (Jung, 1954, p. 256)

Wise Old Man Archetype. The personification of wisdom and maturity in life, the symbol of whom is the prophet.

Anima Archetype. The feminine qualities present in all men; symbols of anima are the woman, the Virgin Mary, and Mona Lisa.

Animus Archetype. The masculine qualities present in all women; symbols of animus are the man, Christ, Don Juan.

Persona Archetype. The artificial social roles that we enact in public the symbol of which is the Mask.

Shadow Archetype. The repressed animalistic urges that we would prefer not to recognize in ourselves and the disowned aspects of self, the symbols of which are Satan, Hussein, Hitler.

Self Archetype. The embodiment of unity, harmony, and wholeness within the personality, the symbol of which is the Mandala, or "magic circle."

God Archetype. The final realization of psychic reality projected onto the external world; the symbol of which is the Eye of the sun.

Hero Archetype. The Hero, and its opposite, the demon (e.g., Anti-Christ, Satan), are common symbols and myths in many cultures. The Hero defeats evil, slays the dragon or monster, usually near water, suffers punishment for another, or rescues the vanquished and downtrodden (Jung, 1917, p. 99).

Mother Archetype. The mother archetype may be symbolized by a wife, Divine Mother (Virgin Mary), and institutions such as one's Alma Mater or the Church; or any event, place, or person associated with fertility and fruitfulness. The Mother archetype includes both the loving and the terrible mother. For example, the goddess of fate (Moira) can be kind and generous, or remorseless and heartless. Evil-Mother archetype symbols abound: the witch, the dragon (or any devouring and entwining animal), and the wicked stepmother (Jung, 1938, p. 82).

Directions: Paint or draw your own mandala. Accompany your painting or drawing with a brief interpretation.

7

Work

A goal is a dream with a deadline.
—Joyce Brothers

> ➤ *PREVIEW QUESTIONS:* What sorts of psychological factors get in the way of people's accomplishing their career goals? What does Zen Buddhism have in common with high achievement motivation? Does your personality dictate what your career should be? A lack of what kinds of skills generally gets people into trouble at work?

➤ INTRODUCTION: WORK AS A DEFINITION OF SELF

To derive satisfaction in our work life and our interpersonal relationships is of utmost importance. Sigmund Freud once said that the goals in life for a person were to "lieben und arbeiten" (love and work). Later, his daughter Anna Freud (1945) said, "Healthy adults have the capacity to live a conflict-free love life and to work productively with satisfaction" (p. 15).

Work is more likely to be gratifying if it meshes well with who we are. The very question asked of children in our culture, What are you going to be when you grow up? seems to confirm how much our choice of occupation becomes a part of our self-concept and personal identity. Thus, career decisions play a significant role in settling the question, Who am I? The relationship between identity and career choice is reciprocal: The career selected will influence our subsequent personal development. Likewise, we would be wise to consider our existing personality and abilities when we consider career options.

Leisure time activities can also be sources of personal fulfillment. Finding a good balance between work and leisure can contribute to our personal vitality, and failing to do so may lead to burnout. If we are dissatisfied with our daily life activities, either at work or at play, we are unlikely to experience much in the way of personal happiness.

QUESTION: *What are some things to look for in a career?*

➤ CAREER PLANNING

Planning your career to fit your personality and lifestyle is extremely important. It is desirable to actively choose a career, rather than to fall into the first job slot that becomes available. If you merely drop into a job opening, you will probably be disappointed with the outcome. Just as you would want to spend time getting to know a prospective marriage partner before settling into a long-term relationship, you will also want to investigate alternative career possibilities to make sure you find one that is suitable. With your selection goes the responsibility of living with the consequences of your decision.

Although you can always change your mind, you will save time, expense, and some frustration by thinking ahead about how you want to make a living.

QUESTIONS: *How many careers would you be able to list if asked to? One hundred? Two hundred?*

One way to assume an active role in deciding on a career is to talk to other people about their job satisfaction. Another strategy involves using professional career search materials to look into available occupations in your areas of interest. There are approximately 40,000 career options listed in the *Dictionary of Occupational Titles*, a book used by career counselors to familiarize applicants with the array of available opportunities. Generally, career selection is needlessly limited by our lack of awareness as to what is available.

It may be a mistake to think in terms of selecting *one* occupation that will last a lifetime, because our society experiences a fast pace of technological and social change, which produces continual changes in the demand for workers. We might find it fruitful to consider a broad field of endeavor rather than a specific job within that field. It can be liberating to think of our current career choice as part of a developmental process rather than a monumental decision that must last a lifetime. More will be said on the subject of career changes later in this chapter.

► CAREER ASSESSMENT

Self-assessment is the key to the career planning process. Any assessment that you make of which careers might be satisfying for you should take into consideration your expectations and needs. What do you hope to get out of being a working person, other than enough money to live on? What do you need from your job in order to be happy? Perhaps you would be unbearably lonely if you had to work by yourself or horribly rattled if you were expected to work in an environment with loud music or machinery noise. Your motivation, abilities, interests, and values must be assessed to enable you to find a good fit with a work environment.

Motivation

Setting goals is central to the process of deciding on a career. If you have goals but do not have the energy and persistence to pursue them, then your goals will not materialize. Psychologist Robert Sternberg (1986) suggested that people tend to differ more in level of motivation than in intelligence level or any other type of ability. This finding implies that if you can motivate yourself to set and move towards a career goal, you have a distinct advantage in the job market.

As a way of recognizing what kind of activities you are motivated to pursue, reflect on any past achievements of which you are particularly proud. Identify those areas where your drive is the greatest. When you undertake an activity

I'm doing this because I like it.

for pure enjoyment, for demonstrating competence, or for gaining a skill, your motivation is usually intrinsic. **Intrinsic motivation** occurs when there is no obvious external reward or ulterior purpose behind your actions. The activity is an end in itself. Also, intrinsic motivation is closely related to the higher levels of Maslow's hierarchy. Maslow's self-actualizers sought to admire beauty for the sheer joy of the experience. Their "peak experiences" produced emotional and intellectual highs without any external reward being a factor.

Jacqueline Kennedy Onassis, widow of President John F. Kennedy and of the Greek multimillionaire Aristotle Onassis, did not need to work in order to make a living. Yet Mrs. Onassis worked for many years as a book editor at Doubleday Publishing Company. Clearly, people in Mrs. Onassis's situation work because of an internal motivation, such as a sense of accomplishment gained by a job well done, a creative outlet, or a way to feel useful. Participation in the workforce and the greater society is another possible motivation for those who do not need to work for economic reasons. Within the past generation, a great many women entered the job market as a means of gaining personal fulfillment.

In contrast to intrinsic motivation, **extrinsic motivation** stems from obvious external factors, such as financial incentives, grades, rewards, approval, obligations, and threats. Most of the activities we think of as "work" are extrinsically rewarded. However, since we tend to adapt to whatever level of compensation we are given for the work we do, the external rewards tend to lose their reinforcing effect after awhile. Consider, for instance, how happy we feel when first given a pay raise, yet how quickly we grow accustomed to it. Thus, in the long run, we are much better off looking for work that is also intrinsically rewarding.

Maslow (1987) viewed motivation as the result of five basic instinctual needs: physiological, safety, belongingness, esteem, and self-actualization (Chapter 2). According to Maslow, these needs are arranged in a hierarchy so that each need acts as a motivator only when the previous ones have been gratified. Moreover, with the exception of self-actualization (which is never completely satiated), once a need has been satisfied, it does not act as a motivator.

An implication of Maslow's need-hierarchy theory for organizations is that in order to maximize employee motivation and performance, employers should provide employees with opportunities to satisfy their unfulfilled needs. Within an organization, physiological and safety needs are satisfied by job security, pay, benefits, and certain characteristics of the work environment. Belongingness needs and esteem needs are fulfilled, respectively, by satisfactory relationships with supervisors and coworkers and by recognition and opportunities for self-control. Finally, the need for self-actualization is satisfied when a job is perceived to be interesting and challenging.

Maslow's theory is not clear about the impact of pay on motivation. Lower-level needs are more directly fulfilled by money than are higher-level needs, but many workers are most concerned about higher-level needs. Consequently, Maslow's theory seems to suggest that money is not a particularly potent source of motivation for many employees unless it can be used to satisfy higher-level needs.

Research on Maslow's theory has yielded mixed results. There is but little evidence that there are five distinct needs, that needs are always activated in the order described by Maslow, that only one need can be activated at a time, or that a need becomes less important once it is satisfied (e.g., Wahba & Bridwell, 1976). There is some evidence, however, that unfulfilled needs (especially physiological needs) do take precedence over other needs. Also, as implied by the theory, the importance of needs seems to be related to job level. Managers, for instance, rate esteem and self-actualization needs as most important, whereas nonmanagers rate lower-level needs as more important.

Abilities

Ability refers to your competence in an activity. Abilities may be inborn or acquired through experience. Aptitude is your ability to learn. Scholastic aptitude, or general intelligence (as measured by IQ tests), is an academic ability that helps determine who will be able to obtain the levels of education required for entrance into the higher-status occupations. Abilities imply performance, or what you do with your aptitudes. Your abilities can be measured and compared with the skills required of various professions and academic areas that are of interest to you.

A skill is something you can do. Skills can be expressed as verbs, like cook, skate, type, run. Skills show action and doing. There are three categories of skills: work content, adaptive, and transferable skills. Work content skills are learned and apply to a specific job. For example, knowing which wrench to use on an automobile, being able to type, and making floral displays are work content skills. Adaptive skills relate to self-management and temperament. Examples are punctuality, reliability, relating well to coworkers, or willingness to take direction and criticism. These skills, which are learned from family and society, often cause the worker more problems in performance reviews than doing the actual job itself. Transferable skills are related to our aptitudes and can be transferred to and used in many different occupations. Examples would be analyzing, organizing, public speaking, persuading, writing, explaining, or leading.

QUESTIONS: Can you take orders? Do you get to work regularly? Do you finish projects on time?

During your college years, you will be building several types of skills. There is a relationship between how you approach your college experience and how you will someday approach your career. If you are conscientious in getting your schoolwork done completely and on time, you are a good invest-

ment for prospective employers. If you find meaning in your college experience, then you are likely to assume responsibility for making your job satisfying. Thus, your educational training signals to prospective employers that you have probably acquired work content, adaptive, *and* transferable skills. Murnane and Levy (1996) expressed the value of education this way: ". . . people must see themselves as economic free agents, prepared to prove their market worth at any time. It is a world where you go to war everyday, and short of being a millionaire, a very good education is your best armor" (p. 229).

Interests

Surprisingly, there is only a slight relationship between a person's interests and his or her abilities. Your interests are things you like to spend time doing. Your "career interests" are the work-related activities that you like. Since you spend 65 percent of your adult life working, you might as well try to find a job that interests you!

Career interest inventories can be used to compare your interests with those of others who have found job satisfaction in a given area. These comparisons can help you identify general occupational areas where your interests overlap with those of people who have found success in a particular career. The most widely used interest inventories are the Strong-Campbell Interest Inventory and the Kuder Occupation Interest Survey. Also used are SIGI, a computerized interest test, and the Myers-Briggs Type Indicator. This latter tool assesses personality types, which have been related to career interests. The Myers-Briggs was based on Carl Jung's personality typology (Chapter 6). Some sources claim that interests are the best single predictor of career success, satisfaction, and persistence (a better predictor than abilities). Other sources indicate that interest tests are more valid for predicting job choice, satisfaction, and persistence than job success (Edwards, 1996; Layton, 1955; Levine & Wallen, 1954).

Research investigating the relationship between interest test scores and future occupational choice suggests that these tests have the highest predictive validity for middle-class people. Members of the middle class usually have the greatest latitude when it comes to choosing an occupation and, therefore, are most likely to choose jobs that coincide with their interests. Lower-class people do not always have the opportunity to pursue occupations that coincide with their interests and thus frequently choose those jobs that provide the greatest pay and security. Upper-class individuals often choose occupations on the basis of family tradition or societal expectations rather than on their interests.

Though interests are important, they must be considered along with ability in order to do a realistic assessment of appropriate career goals for a given individual. Young students may find that their interest patterns are not yet stable enough to predict job success and satisfaction.

Values

Your values refer to what is important to you, and thus influence what you want from life. You may even seek to answer the question, What value does my life have? It is worthwhile to clarify your values so that you may integrate them into your choice of career.

QUESTIONS: *Do you want to work with people or with products? Imagine that you have just received a compliment. What is it? These kinds of questions can help you sort out your values.*

Your "work values" refer to what you hope to accomplish through your career. Things you might hope to gain from your work are an adequate income, prestige, independence, an opportunity to help others, security, variety or stimulation, leadership opportunities, ample time off, working in your field of interest, and early entry into the position. Your pattern of work values can be a basis for matching you with career positions that are likely to be satisfying.

To the extent that you have trouble articulating what you hold sacred, you are lacking conscious awareness of your value system. The values clarification exercises that are in this chapter and throughout this text, can help you become aware of the beliefs that you prize and would be willing to stand up for. You might then consider whether your actions match your stated beliefs, and if not, how to bring the two into closer harmony. Research evidence suggests that after clarifying values, people feel more energetic and more critical in their thinking, and are more likely to follow through on decisions (Simon, Howe, & Kirchenbaum, 1972).

➤ DISPOSITIONAL APPROACH TO UNDERSTANDING PERSONALITY

What is personality? It is a hypothetical construct, which means it is something that cannot be directly observed. Personality refers to the unique combination of talents, attitudes, values, hopes, loves, hates, and habits characteristic of a person. It alludes to the consistency in what a person is, has been, and will become. Everyone has these unique and enduring behavior patterns.

There have been many psychologists who have believed that personality is best understood as an organization of "traits" within an individual. A trait is the unit of analysis and the basic focus of examination by personality psychologists; traits are somewhat analogous to the basic elements that make up the periodic table in chemistry. Trait psychologists believe that there are characteristics of individuals that remain consistent over time and across situations. For example, if you are an aggressive person, you will be aggressive in many different settings and will tend to be more aggressive than your peers over your life span (Harrington, Block, & Block, 1987).

Gordon Allport (1937) was the founder of the modern dispositional strategy. He believed that traits are the basic units of personality and that they can explain behavior. His theory is eclectic, borrowing concepts from learning theory, psychoanalysis, and existentialism. Allport saw personality as unified, constantly evolving and changing, and as caused by forces within the person. Although situational influences have an effect, it is the individual's own perception of these forces that determines his or her behavior.

Allport made a number of distinctions among various kinds of traits. The most interesting of these are the **cardinal traits,** which are characteristics that are pervasive and dominant in a person's life. Cardinal traits are ruling passions; for example, a person may have an overwhelming need to be powerful, and this need could be inferred from virtually all of his or her behavior. Such a person not only would strive to attain a position of power within society but would also interact with his or her golf partner, mail carrier, children, and marriage partner in a similar fashion.

Individuals with ruling passions would seem to have a straightforward answer to the question, Who am I? Life themes for such people might be summarized in a single phrase, such as "Christ-like," "Narcissistic," "Napoleonic," or "Machiavellian." The term Machiavellian is used to describe a person who espouses the philosophy that any means necessary is justifiably used to gain a noble objective. Niccolo Machivevelli, a 16th century Italian political philosopher advocated use of deception and cunning to gain advantage over others, and endorsed the idea that the end always justifies the means. This cardinal disposition was expressed in Machiavelli's personal as well as his political life. Very few people actually have single driving themes in their lives. Most people would be described in Allport's system as having **central traits** and **secondary traits.** Central traits control less of a person's behavior but do influence the person's actions in a variety of situations. Such traits are the ones that people mention when asked to write a letter of recommendation for someone or to describe that person in a different context. We might say that someone is intelligent, competitive, sincere, honest, or funny. Secondary traits are characteristics that are peripheral to the person, in that they are less important, less conspicuous, and less often called into play than are central traits. An affinity for certain colors, a liking for vigorous physical activity, or a preference for rich foods would be examples of secondary traits.

Dispositional theorists view traits as at least partially inherited, so that they are somewhat fixed within the individual. Thus, rather than emphasizing personality change, this approach looks at the stability of traits over time, implying that personal adjustment might better be achieved by helping people seek out situations to which they are temperamentally suited rather than to try to change to fit their environments.

Research on job satisfaction suggests that it is a relatively stable trait and is minimally affected by job changes. It appears that job satisfaction is directly related to the tendency toward positive or negative **affect** (emotion), which is a stable characteristic. People with negative affect tend to be dissatisfied with work; people with positive affect tend to be satisfied.

Personality psychologists emphasize the stability of personality. It follows that personality change would be difficult. Thus, it may be wise to keep the individual who is disposed to be very aggressive away from aggression-provoking situations rather than to try to change him or her into an nonaggressive person. By the same token, finding a career to fit your personality is easier than trying to make yourself fit a career that you have gotten into in a haphazard manner.

QUESTION: *If you could create a job tailored to you, what would that job be like?*

➤ CAREER ASSESSMENT USING PERSONALITY TRAITS

Psychologists have developed methods for using personality dimensions as career guidance tools (Tett, Jackson, & Rothstein, 1991). There is widespread agreement that personality factors are heavily implicated in many aspects of job-related performance. Intellectually capable individuals falter on the job when their personality traits do not fit with task requirements. Therefore, psychologists have been studying the relationship between personality dimensions and success in various career areas.

There has emerged some agreement among the many theorists that there are from five to eight basic elements of personality. Here is the most commonly used set, a list of five traits, that are known as the "Big Five" (McCrae & Costa, 1987):

1. FACTOR I: *Extroversion* versus *Introversion*. The core of this factor seems to be sociability, or the enjoyment of the company of others. The extremes of the continuum can be described as sociable versus retiring; fun-loving versus sober; affectionate versus reserved; talkative versus quiet; and assertive versus passive.

2. FACTOR II: *Agreeableness* versus *Antagonism*. The two ends of this spectrum can be described as soft-hearted versus ruthless and unsympathetic; trusting versus suspicious; mistrustful and skeptical; helpful and pleasant versus uncooperative; kind and warm versus hostile and selfish; and as showing friendly compliance versus hostile noncompliance.

3. FACTOR III: *Conscientiousness (having a will to achieve)*. This factor includes morality, hard work, and striving for excellence. Descriptions of the

WORKAHOLICS

THAT'S IT, PAL. NO MORE WORK FOR YOU.

two poles of this dimension are organized versus disorganized; careful and thorough versus careless; disciplined versus impulsive; dependable or reliable versus negligent and unreliable.

4. FACTOR IV: *Emotional Stability* versus *Neuroticism.* This factor captures the negative affect as well as the disturbed thoughts and behaviors that accompany emotional distress. Descriptions of the extremes of this continuum would be calm versus anxious or nervous; secure versus insecure; self-satisfied versus self-pitying; even-tempered versus moody and temperamental.

5. FACTOR V: *Openness (to Experience).* This dimension is associated with having broad interests and being daring. The opposites expressed along this dimension are imaginative versus practical; preference for variety versus preference for routine; independent versus conforming; curious and creative versus shallow and imperceptive.

There is disagreement about the specific nature of Factor V, which was initially called "Culture." It has also been interpreted as "Intellect" (e.g., Digman & Takemoto-Chock, 1981; Peabody & Goldberg, 1989).

Research has shown that some of the Big Five personality measures are systematically related to a variety of criteria of job performance (Goldberg, L. R., 1993). Measures associated with conscientiousness are most likely to be valid predictors of success for a variety of jobs from professional to semiskilled (Barrick & Mount, 1991). It is difficult to imagine a job in which the traits associated with the conscientiousness dimension would not contribute to job success. Likewise, personality measures related to agreeableness in the Big-Five model were most highly related to criteria of job performance (Tett et al., 1991).

Although the dimensions of the Big Five are to a certain extent inborn, we can still modify our behavior. To move in the direction of being more conscientious, we might keep in mind college president Dr. Jan Kehoe's (1998) advice: "Give what you do all that you've got; and the corollary to that is, don't take on too much."

Traits may be said to cluster together naturally to form personality types, which designate people who share similar patterns of personality traits. For instance, there are types of **personality disorder,** such as antisocial or narcissistic, in which a pattern of personality characteristics cause people to have troubled interpersonal relationships. Psychologists have been able to determine which traits tend to occur together and how patterns of traits are organized within an individual.

One drawback to personality type systems is that they oversimplify personality. Nevertheless, personality typologies do have value. For one thing, they can help us to explain to couples why they have difficulty appreciating or understanding each other. Consider this: A thrifty wife may have difficulty appreciating a husband who is a generous tipper at restaurants, and so forth. Both generosity and thriftiness can be considered virtues; however, having one partner lean toward thriftiness while the other emphasizes generosity will probably result in some initial conflict until a compromise is reached.

Job satisfaction can be predicted by matching personality types with career requirements. A consistent finding of the research is that we tend to affiliate with those who are similar in terms of attitudes, abilities, and personality characteristics (e.g., Antill, 1983; Barry, 1970; Boyden et al., 1984). John Holland's (1997) theory of career decision making is based on the assumption that career choices are an expression of personality, as well as of the person's motivation, knowledge, and ability. Holland believes that it is important for the work environment to match one's personality type. To facilitate this process, Holland developed six occupational themes that can aid individuals in the career planning process. Here is a summary of Holland's six themes:

Realistic Personality Types

These people are attracted to outdoor, mechanical, and physical activities, hobbies, and occupations. They like to work with objects and animals rather than with ideas, data, or people. They enjoy creating things with their hands. They tend to have mechanical abilities and like to work with tools, especially large, powerful machines. They are likely to be athletic and are usually physically strong and well-coordinated. They like to construct, shape, and restructure things around them, as well as to repair and mend things. Although they usually have good physical skills, they sometimes have trouble expressing themselves or in communicating their feelings to others. They generally have conventional political and economic opinions, and are usually cool to radical new ideas.

Examples of realistic career positions would be geologist, farmer, construction worker, forest ranger, industrial arts teacher, civil engineer, electrician, machinist, carpenter, tailor, motion picture projectionist, surveyor, dental technician, truck driver, draftsperson, barber, and aircraft mechanic.

Investigative Personality Types

Investigative persons are naturally curious and inquisitive. They are theoretical and analytic in outlook, with a need to understand, explain, and predict the things that go on around them. They are scholarly and scientific in their attempts to understand things and tend to be skeptical and critical when nonscientific, simplistic, or supernatural explanations are suggested by others.

Extremes of this type are task-oriented and not particularly interested in working around other people. Investigative types enjoy solving abstract problems and have a great need to understand the physical world. They prefer to think through problems rather than act them out. Such people find abstract and ambiguous problems and situations challenging and do not like highly structured situations with many rules. They frequently have unconventional values and attitudes and tend to be original and creative, especially in scientific areas.

Examples of career positions suitable to this type are scientist, engineer, architect, mathematician, experimental psychologist, computer operator, computer programmer, economist, actuary, physician, clinical psychologist, dentist, anthropologist, astronomer, marine biologist, optometrist, and quality control technician.

Artistic Personality Types

Artistic people are creative, intuitive, sensitive, emotional, and complicated. They like to be different and strive to stand out from the crowd. They prefer to work without supervision. Artistic types describe themselves as independent, original, unconventional, expressive, and tense. They place great value on beauty and aesthetic qualities.

This type of person likes to work in artistic settings that offer many opportunities for self-expression. Such people have little interest in problems that are highly structured or require gross physical strength, preferring those that can be solved through making a statement via artistic media. They resemble investigative types in preferring to work alone, but they have a greater need for individualistic expression and are usually less assertive about their own opinions and capabilities. They score higher on measures of originality than do any of the other types.

Examples of career positions in this area are painter, actor/actress, drama coach, critic, designer, decorator, composer, musician, music arranger, architect (listed here as well as under investigative careers), journalist, writer, editor, advertisement executive, art teacher, sculptor, literature teacher, and dancing teacher.

Social Personality Types

Social people are friendly, enthusiastic, and outgoing. They are cooperative and enjoy working with and being around other people. They like to be helpful to others by serving in facilitative roles. They like to deal with philosophical issues such as the nature and purpose of life, religion, and morality. They are sociable, responsible, humanistic, and concerned with the welfare of others.

These people usually express themselves well and get along well with others. They like attention and seek situations that allow them to be near the center of the group. They prefer to solve problems by discussion with

"Workaholic? Brokers and salesmen are workaholics. Artists are obsessed. There's a difference."

others and by arranging or rearranging relationships between others. They typically have little interest in situations requiring physical exertion or working with machinery. Such people describe themselves as cheerful, popular, and achieving, and as good leaders.

Examples of career positions in this area are teacher, mediator, adviser, counselor, career counselor, social worker, interviewer, job analyst, claims adjuster, educational administrator, training director, historian, college professor, political scientist, sociologist, nurse, minister, judge, and librarian.

Enterprising Personality Types

Enterprising people are outgoing, persuasive, and optimistic. They like to organize, direct, manage, and control the activities of groups to attain personal or organizational goals. These people are ambitious and like to be in positions of authority, power, and status. They are adventurous and impulsive. They are assertive and verbally persuasive in bringing others around to their point of view.

The extreme of this type has a great facility with words, especially in selling, dominating, and leading, a quality that makes these people qualify as charismatic. They see themselves as energetic, enthusiastic, adventurous, self-confident, and dominant, and they prefer social tasks in which they can assume leadership. They are impatient with precise work or work involving long periods of intellectual effort. Such people like material wealth and enjoy working in expensive settings.

Examples of career positions appropriate to this personality type are salesperson, entrepreneur, politician, broker, manager, market analyst, banker, insurance underwriter, realtor, real estate appraiser, florist, contractor, government official, systems analyst, attorney, or labor arbitrator.

LEADERSHIP STYLES   In the enterprising category, here are several types of leaders. *Transformational leaders* alter values, beliefs, and attitudes for their followers. They identify and articulate a vision, provide an appropriate model, foster acceptance of group goals, have high performance expectations, provide individualized support, and promote intellectual stimulation. They rely more on referent and expert power than informational power. *Transactional leaders* manipulate rewards and punishments to gain compliance. *Charismatic leaders* are viewed by their followers as having "exceptional powers."

Conventional Personality Types

Conventional people are well organized, persistent, and practical in their approach to life. They enjoy clerical and computational activities performed according to set procedures. Conventional types are dependable, efficient, and conscientious in accomplishing their tasks. They enjoy the security of belonging to groups and organizations and make good team members, but they do not seek leadership.

Extremes of this type prefer highly ordered activities, both verbal and numerical. These people fit well into large organizations. They respond to powerful others and are comfortable working in a well-established chain of command. Such people describe themselves as conventional, stable, well-controlled, and dependable. They have little interest in problems requiring physical skills or intense relationships with others, and are most effective at well-defined tasks. They dislike ambiguous situations, preferring to know precisely what is expected of them.

Examples of career positions in this area are accountant, theater stage manager, banker, bank teller, credit manager, secretary, business teacher, reservations agent, data processing worker, mail clerk, typist, receptionist, proofreader, finance expert, credit manager, time keeper, or time study analyst.

Essentially, we are treating careers as though they have personalities, just as people do. In the same way that couples with similar personalities and interests tend to have more satisfying relationships, so too will coworkers find it easier to get along and understand each other's priorities when they have common values and personality dimensions.

At the end of this chapter are several exercises calculated to help you identify the Holland codes that fit your values, interests and skills profile. Once you complete the summary sheet that follows the exercises by entering the results from each exercise, you can refer back to the chapter to find careers that match your Holland personality type. Finally, you may put these prospective careers as "alternatives" on the decision making worksheet that follows the summary sheet, and use the worksheet to decide how well each of the careers you are considering fulfills your idea of what a job should be.

➤ GOAL SETTING

You may not yet have had the inclination to stop and think about what you really want out of life or where you are going. You might consider making a list of your lifetime goals. Doing so should help you discover what you really want to do, help motivate you to do it, and give meaning to the way you spend your time. Having lifetime goals will provide a direction and a purpose to your life. You should feel more focused and in control of your destiny. You will also know what are your priorities, so that you will find it easier to balance the many aspects of your life.

Resistance to writing out lifetime goals can come in various forms. The task may feel overwhelming or confining, in that you'll be prematurely committed to a plan. You may worry that establishing a direction will spoil your fun in life by limiting your spontaneity and creativity.

Most people who try it find that the benefits of goal setting far outweigh any initially perceived drawbacks. Long-term goals help individuals feel clear about their purpose and thus counteract the sensory overload they often experience due to continual stimulation from the environment, which threatens to disorient them. People sometimes don't know which opportunities to pursue and which to let pass them by.

You have probably had lots of thoughts about what you would like to accomplish and experience in your lifetime. However, when you don't formally commit to goals by writing them down, you are likely to be aware of your dreams and wishes only as vague notions. Therefore, you will never consider whether these dreams would make realistic goals for you. Furthermore, writing down your goals prompts you to be specific and thus allows you to scrutinize them. Once you give them serious consideration, you may decide to refine or change your goals.

If you have never tried writing down your lifetime goals, you might do so by putting at the top of a sheet of paper, "What are my lifetime goals?" (Lakein, 1973). Spend five minutes trying to answer the question. Write down whatever comes to your mind, taking care to consider personal and family goals, as well as those in the realm of your social life, career, finances, community involvement, and the spiritual domain. Don't worry at this point about whether you truly want to commit to the goals that you are writing down. At this point, you are only generating ideas. Put down whatever occurs to you as a desirable goal. Do not be afraid to include some wild fantasies, such as singing the "Star-Spangled Banner" to open a Dodgers baseball game.

As you think about your current activities, you may become aware of additional goals. If you watch every cooking program on television and try out several new recipes each week, you might form a plan to become a chef, or at least to taste one dish from every country in the world.

A second phase of goal-setting involves spending another five minutes answering a second question, "How would I like to spend the next three years?" If you are over age 30, you may want to change the three-year time span to five years (Lakein, 1973).

Finally, devote another five minutes to answering the question, "If I knew my life would come to a sudden end in six months, how would I live until then?" As you think about squeezing everything important that you would want to do in your life into this time frame, imagine that your will and funeral arrangements have been taken care of, so that you need not attend to these details.

This last question gets you to think about whether there are some vitally important experiences that you are planning for yourself but have been putting off until later. Although you may still put them off after this exercise, you will have a greater awareness of their importance to you.

If you find that you would not change much of what you are doing, you should see this outcome as an affirmation that your current lifestyle is right for you. Naturally, you will discover some activities that are a means to an end that you hope to enjoy in the future. These activities, which involve a delay of gratification, might be discontinued if there were to be no "later." Did attending your college classes fall into the category of activities you would discontinue? If so, you now know that for the time being, your learning experience seems to you like a means to an end; the process itself is not rewarding to you. Do not be afraid to look at this reality. Your goal at this time is to find out who you are and what you want out of life.

If you have more goals than time to work on them, you will have to set priorities. You might select the top three goals from each list, rank them, and decide to work on them for now, recognizing that you can turn your attention to your other goals in due time. You might refine your top three goals from your lifetime goals list over the next several days or weeks. After that, you might want to revisit your lifetime goals on your birthday each year, since your perspective on your life is likely to change as you mature. By focusing on your goals, you begin to clear a path toward them. Keeping the end in mind provides you with a sense of purpose and enables you to pass by less important but perhaps momentarily enticing activities.

Zen and the Protestant Work Ethic

The United States has a tradition of embracing what has come to be known as the "Protestant work ethic." This ethic extols the virtues of striving towards goals in an all-out, full-steam-ahead fashion. A life of vigorous effort is advocated. Somehow, a diligently busy person is viewed as more virtuous than one who is idle. No doubt some people may view this approach as a bit one-sided.

Throughout the nations that make up "the East," several forms of Buddhism are practiced, one of which is Zen Buddhism. On the face of it, Zen promotes the spiritual practice of purposelessness and would thus seem to be in opposition to the theme of this book, which is that focusing on your purpose in life is desirable. Yet, Zen could be considered the other side of the same coin from intense focus on a goal. Both the practice of Zen and conscious goal-setting involve the ability to control attention. Zen seems to involve putting the engine of the mind in neutral, so that it isn't engaged in moving forward toward a specific destination, and then humming along with the engine on—to allow emotion, spirit, and ideas to emerge. One goes with the flow.

Zen and Western-style goal-setting have in common that both require patience and persistence. The "aimless" state which the student of Zen seeks is far from easy to attain. Eugene Herrigel (1989), author of *Zen in the Art of Archery*, reported spending three to four years in training before understanding how to lose the desire to make the shot and simply loose the arrow, allowing the shot to go off "effortlessly" at the right moment. To endure such training, the student must have a clear intention to persist until the desired state of mind is attained. Maslow's peak experiences (Chapter 2) and Csikszentmihalyi's sensation of flow (Chapter 14) also represent descriptions of the integration of zealous effort and spiritual abandonment.

There is a bit of Zen in the common childhood experience of learning to ride a bicycle. In the beginning, a child receives verbal instructions, such as "keep pedaling, even when it seems that you need to stop and catch your fall" and "turn the handlebars this way to keep from falling to the right and the other way to keep from falling to the left." In addition, the child needs to get "the feel" of correct riding. At first, the appropriate balance is achieved for only a few seconds. The child isn't sure how she or he managed it. Gradually, the balance can be achieved for as long as the cyclist wishes to ride. This achievement seems effortless, because it has been learned to the point of being automatic. The learning requires effort, whereas the accomplished practice of the skill does not.

What Zen and ordinary goal-setting would seem to have in common is self-discipline and a guidance of one's attention. Skill-building apparently requires a period of struggle wherein the trainee hasn't yet gotten the hang of it, an exciting phase during which the skill can be displayed sporadically, and a final phase in which the skill can be reliably brought into play, so that further practice will serve simply to polish and enjoy the art.

Likewise, creative endeavor requires a period of sitting in the midst of a problem, with no solution in sight. Active searching for the solution may or may not yield a favorable result. However, immersion in the parameters of the problem enables our minds to work on it even without conscious volition. We don't always succeed by pressing towards the goal, but might instead arrive at our desired end by waiting with expectation and openness. Both approaches—Zen and goal-setting—have their merits. Understanding these merits will help us know which mode to engage in any given situation.

> ## GETTING THROUGH ROADBLOCKS

Reality Factors

Reality factors refer to constraints on accomplishing our goals in life. All of us have some kinds of constraints with which we must contend in pursuing our dreams. Here are some obstacles that might keep us from attaining our career goals:

*

age
health
spouse
parents
children
intelligence
peer pressure
discrimination
negative attitude
lack of direction
physical handicap
grade point average
physical appearance
personal obligations
lack of assertiveness
family responsibilities
patchwork career history
lack of communication skills
lack of decision making skills
religious/cultural background
transportation or distance to job
lack of motivation (energy level)
inadequate pay in this career field
inability to project a corporate image
fierce competition in the desired field
physical limitations (size, weight, etc.)
lack of information about career fields
lack of self-confidence, poor self-image
lack of education, degrees, or certificates
no jobs in this area; layoffs, hiring freezes
lack of support (financial, emotional, mentor)

Some of the listed impediments are personal shortcomings. An effective strategy for dealing with disability is to think of some way that this apparent weakness might be an asset to your prospective employer. For instance, having a physical limitation may have made you more persistent (Sleek, 1997).

Notice that many of these obstacles are psychological in nature; that is, they can be overcome by changing how you think about your situation. There are many strategies available for overcoming psychological obstacles: (1) Turn negatives into positives. For example, although time pressure seems like a negative, it can get you motivated to start a task. Therefore, you can focus on how well you work under pressure, if this is the case, rather than how tense you feel in the process. (2) Restructure your belief system. (3) List things you want to accomplish. (You may want to consider this list a contract that you have made with yourself.) (4) Create and recite affirmations, which are assertions that something exists or is true.

Affirmations

Once you decide to make any kind of change in your life, the next step is to put the new decision into practice. If you don't, you haven't really made a decision—you have only expressed a wish. You must change your self-talk to change your self-image and thus bring about the reality.

Deciding to alter a habit, attitude, or personal situation will not bring about that change. That decision is only the first step. Further action is required to modify, first your self-image and then reality. Creating affirmations is one way to do this. Suppose your goal is to have more self-respect. You can encourage this transformation within yourself by creating and rehearsing a statement such as, "I like and respect myself, and I am worthy of the respect of others."

Affirmations are most effective when written out. By writing them out, you make them more concrete, public, and real. You can also help your goals come to pass by creating a visual picture of the end result you want. Doing so builds momentum by getting you to conceive of the outcome you want. The process goes like this: *Read* your affirmation. *Picture* vividly the end result. *Feel* the emotion that goes along with the accomplishment of the goal. *Repeat* this process several times each day. Following are a few simple guidelines for translating your mental desires or goals into a statement of affirmation.

Guidelines for Making Affirmations

1. *Be personal:* You can only affirm for yourself. You are changing your self-image. In most cases, your affirmation will be an "I" statement. (It might be "we" if you are working with a family member or as a team.)

   e.g., "I treat everyone with consideration and respect," rather than "You have to follow the Golden Rule and do unto others as you would have them do unto you."

2. *Avoid comparisons:* This is a personal process. Do not use statements indicating you are "as good as" or "better than" someone else.

   e.g., "I am keeping up with my homework," rather than "I've gotten more done than Jessie."

3. *Be positive:* Use positive sentence structure. Do not describe what you are trying to move away from or eliminate.

   e.g., "I am energetic," rather than "I am no longer lazy."

e.g., "I am fully occupied with a caseload of clients," rather than "I won't be able to get enough clients."

4. *Use present tense:* Always use the present tense—not "someday" or "to-morrow I will" or "maybe I will. Such statements tend to detach you from change.

    e.g., "I am a considerate person."

5. *Indicate achievement:* Do not indicate ability by using "I can" in your affirmations. You already have the ability. What you must indicate concretely is actual achievement with statements such as "I am" or "I have."

    e.g., "I am warm and friendly toward all" rather than "I can be friendly toward others."

6. *Use action words:* Describe the activity you are affirming in terms that create pictures of you performing in an easy and anxiety-free manner.

    e.g., "I *easily* keep my filing up-to-date so that information can be quickly found" or

    e.g., "I *enjoy* my life, my profession, and my relationships with other people."

7. *Use excitement words:* Put as much excitement into your wording as possible. Write in a manner that creates fun, pride, happiness, accomplishment, and joy.

    e.g., "Pressure is exciting and stimulating to me. I do an even better job when I am under pressure."

8. *Be realistic:* Affirm only whatever you can honestly imagine yourself becoming or performing. Don't overshoot; don't undershoot. Don't try to affirm perfection or place unrealistic demands on your performance. Don't say "I always" or "every time I" or "I never."

    e.g. "I am fair and just in dealing with people" as opposed to "I am always fair."

9. *Stay in balance:* Have affirmation statements that are keyed to growth in all areas, such as family, work, or leisure time.

    e.g., "I am a true professional in my approach to all my job activities."

10. *Keep them to yourself:* Your affirmations are for you only, because others may try to remind you of your "old" self. Change is sometimes upsetting to others.

QUESTION: *What "reality factor" most fits your situation? Write an affirmation that would help you rethink that obstacle. Check back through the ten requirements for an affirmation. Does your affirmation meet these criteria?*

Teaching Resilience in the Job Search Phase

Part of finding a suitable career is engaging in a job search. Since it's unlikely that we'll get the job we want on the first interview, we shall probably have to handle rejection from prospective employers. Many applicants give up too easily when their job search yields no immediate results. This reaction is understandable, because no one likes to feel unwanted.

You can help yourself from the outset by not having unrealistic expectations about getting work. One of the guru's of job search strategies, Richard Bolles (1999), estimated that a serious job search for a career type of position could take eight months. Another rule of thumb in industry is that you should allow one month for every $10,000 in annual salary you wish to earn. Therefore, you may have to settle in for the long haul. You can see why a classic piece of advice is not to quit the job you have before you have secured a new one! There is another reason for this advice, which is that you are demonstrating your employability by working while searching.

Since rejection is hard to take, part of your job search planning should involve ways to reward yourself for engaging in the activity of looking, whether or not it is fruitful at the moment. A good strategy is to consider the process a numbers game. As a good salesperson knows, the more contacts you make, the more sales you get. You can measure your accomplishment by meeting your goals in mailing out a designated number of résumés or by locating a small number of ads for job openings each day or week.

You can rehearse scenarios involving the setbacks you fear, so that you feel prepared for anything when you approach an employer. Don't overlook the usefulness of affirmations to keep yourself in a positive frame of mind.

➤ THE CHANGING FACE OF THE WORK LANDSCAPE

New Jobs and Obsolete Jobs

Your needs and wishes must be considered in light of the opportunities and constraints of the real world. Naisbitt and Aburdene (1990) indicate that the fast pace of social and technological change will continue to force people to adapt to a changing job market.

It is estimated that the average American who enters the workforce today will change careers, not just jobs, five to seven times. This means that training for work should emphasize transferable skills, not simply specific knowledge and particular job skills. Examples of nonspecific, and thus transferable, skills include time management, personnel management, and self-management skills. A specific skill, such as the ability to take dictation, can become outdated.

There is a shift from a manufacturing emphasis in the majority of jobs in this country to a growth in the service industry. Jobs in the future will increasingly be to provide service, from professionals such as attorneys and psychotherapists to housekeepers and gardeners. Some of these service jobs are being done from home through the Internet. Examples of such jobs are personnel recruitment, travel agent, newspaper salesperson, news publisher, secretarial service provider, researcher, and psychotherapist. Not only might an employee or consultant stay home and work, but also she or he might travel while working. For a growing number of people, working in transit is accomplished with the help of a cellular phone and a laptop computer.

Research on job satisfaction in the past two decades has generally found a trend toward increasing dissatisfaction at all job levels. The reasons for dissatisfaction, however, vary somewhat for different job levels and different types of workers. Studies have found that lack of opportunities for promotion to more prestigious jobs is a primary factor in the dissatisfaction of blue collar-workers (Sheppard & Herrick, 1972).

Maternal Employment and the Child-Care Debate

One recent trend in contemporary society is that for the past generation, large numbers of mothers with young children have been choosing to enter the workforce. In many situations, these women need to work, but also many like to work. No matter how much a person likes children, full-time child care is drudgery (Maccoby, 1998).

The question arises, Who should be responsible for the rearing of children, parents or society? Traditionally, parents were considered responsible for rearing and training, whereas society was responsible for the education of children. In a traditional family, the parental tasks were also divided, in that mothers did actual day-to-day rearing while father provided food and shelter, as well as other financial needs.

Yet, by the age of four months, three-fourths of all infants in the U.S. have some kind of child care that is nonmaternal for at least thirty hours per week. Incidentally, this nonmaternal care includes father care. Many of the parents who are caring for their children are likely to be very sleepy, because the parents often work different shifts to enable one parent to be at home with the children. Many of those who have watched this change in society have raised concerns about its effect on the development of children. There is a widespread feeling that parental care is the best care.

Psychologist Jerome Kagan and his colleagues (1978) set up a day-care center for very young children (four months to twenty-six months) in Boston, Massachusetts, to look at the effects of nonparental care on children. Later, children at this center were compared with home-reared children of the same age, social class, and ethnic background. The day-care children were no different intellectually, emotionally, or socially from their home-raised counterparts, nor did the children differ in the attachments they had formed with their mothers.

Maternal employment appears even to have some beneficial consequences for the family. Studies investigating the effects of maternal employment on the family have most consistently found that children of working mothers have more egalitarian concepts about sex roles and less traditional stereotypes of male and female activities than children whose mothers are full-time homemakers (see, e.g., Hoffman, 1989; Huston, 1983).

Overall, the research has been positive with regard to the effects of maternal employment on the development of children. Still, studies are not entirely consistent in their findings. For instance, in some situations, it does appear that middle-class boys do more poorly in school and obtain lower IQ scores when both parents work.

Kathleen Parker (1997), writing for *USA Today*, stated that

Very young children in day care do just about as well as those who stay at home with their mother. Provided, that is, the day care is good. This is an important qualifier, given the current bad news on the quality of day care in America. The Family and Work Institute found that more than three-quarters of children who spend their days in child care are receiving care that doesn't meet the needs for "health, safety, warm relationships and learning (p. 16A).

However, psychologist and researcher Sandra Scarr (1990), concluded that variations in the quality of care proves to have only small and short-term effects on children, except for "at risk" children. Self-selection seems to account for why children who are in better child care do better. More successful parents place their kids in better child-care facilities. What is needed is expanded quantity rather than expanded quality of care. In addition, child care is more expensive than many dual care families can afford, suggesting that it may become society's responsibility to ease the burden with policies such as parental leave and tax deductions for child-care expense.

Research indicates that fathers spend more time with their children when the mother is employed outside the home (Deutsch et al., 1993; Gottfried, et al. (1994); Gottfried & Gottfried, 1988). Interestingly, there do appear to be some gender differences with both mothers and fathers sharing more activities with boys than with girls in families in which the mother is employed outside the home.

> ## LEISURE

Historically, most people have not had an opportunity for much leisure time. A hundred years ago, twelve- to fourteen-hour workdays were the norm (Doyle, 1989). In the past several decades, however, shortened workdays have made leisure time activities possible. According to Yankelovich (1978), a majority of men reported that they derived more satisfaction from their leisure activities than from their work.

Leisure is an important component of life-career planning. People spend more time "at leisure" for a greater portion of the life span than at any other major life role (Super, 1980; 1990). Despite this fact, little is known about the psychological impact of leisure experiences on the individual (Tinsley & Eldredge, 1995). This is in part because very few psychologists have devoted time to studying leisure pursuits. The lack of attention to leisure should give way to intense interest in it, as increasing longevity of life carries with it the prospect that people may be spending more years in retirement than they did in the workforce.

Leisure activities differ in the needs that they satisfy (Tinsely, Barrett, & Kass, 1977; Tinsley & Johnson, 1984; Tinsley & Kass, 1978, 1979). It is believed that gratification of individuals' psychological needs through leisure experiences has a beneficial effect on their physical and mental health, life satisfaction, and psychological development (Tinsley & Tinsely, 1986). There is ample evidence supporting the need-satisfying properties of leisure activities (Driver, Brown, & Peterson, 1991; Schreyer, 1984; Tinsley, 1984; Tinsely, Hinson, Tinsley, & Holt, 1993).

Research has shown that among the psychological needs that are met by leisure activities are *agency* (this encompasses vigorous physical striving to achieve a difficult goal and reduced attention to intellectual and aesthetic stimulation); *novelty* (these activities satisfy the participants' needs for physical activity and their needs to experience enjoyment that is missing from everyday life); *belongingness* (this satisfies participants' needs to receive attention and feel important while coordinating their actions with others in a vigorous activity; often embodies teamwork); *service* (these activities gratify participants' sense of personal responsibility to assist and influence others in an accepted manner; there is an emphasis on helping and directing others and on conscientious behavior); *sensual enjoyment* (these activities satisfy participants' needs to be with people in ways that are intellectually or aesthetically stimulating and somewhat prestigious; they are enjoyed for the temporary pleasure they bring; they are immediately pleasurable and lacking in difficulty); *cognitive stimulation* (these activities require little physical exertion and emphasize intellectual and sensual stimulation; they tend to be solitary activities that afford little opportunity for affiliation or status); *self-expression* (these activities provide self-improvement benefits and opportunities for experiences missing from participants' everyday life; they tend to be restful, relaxing, and typically done alone); creativity, competition, vicarious competition, and relaxation.

6.22.95 THE PHILADELPHIA INQUIRER. UNIVERSAL PRESS SYNDICATE.

QUESTION: Which of the psychological needs discussed do you most consistently satisfy with your preferred leisure activities?

As with work environments, leisure activities can also be classified according to John Holland's six themes:

Leisure Activities for the Realistic Types

Realistic types tend to enjoy parachute jumping, mountain climbing, horse-back riding, backpacking, river rafting, swimming, jogging, walking, snowmobiling, scuba diving, skateboarding, dancing for exercise, skydiving, hang gliding, rollerblading, ice skating, cross-country snow skiing, downhill snow skiing, snow boarding, bicycling, car repairing, working out in a gym, remodeling a house, or training animals.

Leisure Activities for the Investigative Types

These types tend to seek activities such as studying Zen, meditation, astrology, prayer, reading tarot cards, genealogy tracing, fishing, bird-watching, kite flying, listening to music, flying by oneself, taking movies or photographs of nature, sailing alone, hunting alone, canoeing alone, sledding, taking nature walks, attending lectures and concerts, watching educational TV, attending theater or ballet, attending craft shows, and attending spectator sports such as football, baseball, boxing, or basketball, and reading.

Leisure Activities for the Artistic Types

Much of what artistic types regard as leisure is similar to activities they might select as paid employment. They tend to opt for candle-making, refinishing antiques, writing, playing a musical instrument, participating in choral singing, attending plays, reading popular fiction, sculpting, making pottery, photography, painting, drawing, calligraphy, interior decorating, or wine making.

Leisure Activities for the Social Types

Social types are drawn to community activities, engaging in volunteer work, cooking for others, entertaining at home, palm reading, working in political campaigns, activities with the family, giving a massage, performing magic acts, developing intimacy (flirtation, dating, courtship, making love), glee-club singing, letter writing, people watching, and traveling with others.

Leisure Activities for the Enterprising Types

Competitions of all types attract enterprising types. They like involvement in bowling, soccer, tennis, golf, skiing in competition, bicycle racing, racquetball, volleyball, handball, squash, baseball, football, basketball, badminton, Ping-Pong, billiards, pool, or shuffleboard. They enjoy gambling on a spectator sport, entering their work in competitions (craft shows, etc.), discussing politics, leading organizations, playing cards (especially bridge or poker), and playing chess.

Leisure Activities for Conventional Types

This type prefers flying model airplanes, organizing, arranging, collecting (stamps, etc.), reading, sewing, quilting, going to the movies, jigsaw puzzles, window-shopping, watching television, visiting family, flower arranging, gardening, amusement parks, and joining community service organizations.

➤ SUMMARY

CAREER PLANNING AND ASSESSMENT   Career planning is crucially important. It involves matching an individual's personality, values, interests and skills to prospective career areas. Generally, college students' career options are needlessly limited by their lack of awareness as to the availability of career options.

Self-assessment is the key to the career planning process. Taking into account the person's motivations, abilities, interests, and values helps with appropriate career selection. Setting goals is at the core of the process of deciding on a career. It can be liberating to think of a future career as part of an unfolding process rather than a monumental decision that must last a lifetime. This is a realistic approach since most people have several careers during the period of their lives when they are employed.

Motivation means having the energy or drive to engage in an activity. Those who are motivated to set and move towards a career goal, have a distinct advantage in the job market.

Ability refers to competence in an activity and can be measured and compared with the skills required of various professions and academic areas that are of interest to the person entering the job market. Skills can be divided into three categories: (1) work content skills that are specific to the job; (2) adaptive skills that relate to self-management and temperament; and (3) transferable skills that can be used in many different occupations.

Interests are those things an individual likes to spend time doing. Occupational interest surveys can be used to compare a student's interests with those of others who have found job satisfaction in a given area. These comparisons can help identify general occupational areas in which the applicant's interests overlap with those of people who have found success in a particular career.

Values refer to what is important to a person, and "work values" have to do with what that person hopes to accomplish through a career. Work values can be a basis for matching individuals with career positions that are likely to be satisfying.

DISPOSITIONAL APPROACH TO UNDERSTANDING PERSONALITY   Gordon Allport was the founder of the dispositional approach to the study of personality. The dispositional theorists believe that personality is at least partially inherited, so that it would be easier to find an environment to fit the existing personality than to change one's personality to fit the existing situation. Rather than emphasizing personality change, this approach looks at the stability of traits over time. This implies that personal adjustment might better be achieved by helping people seek out situations to which they are temperamentally suited rather than to try to change to fit their environments.

Intellectually capable individuals run into problems on the job when their personality traits are not suited to task requirements. Therefore, psychologists have been studying the relationship between personality dimensions and success in various career areas. Personality refers to the unique combination of talents, attitudes, values, hopes, loves, hates, and habits characteristic of a person, and implies a consistency in what a person is, has been, and will become. Everyone has unique and enduring behavior patterns, which are known as personality *traits*.

CAREER ASSESSMENT USING PERSONALITY TRAITS   Personality traits can be organized into five key dimensions, which are known as the "Big Five": Extroversion, agreeableness, conscientiousness, emotional stability, and openness to experience. An individual's personality profile can be assessed in terms of these dimensions, which can, in turn, predict career success. Of particular importance in predicting such success are conscientiousness and agreeableness.

1. *Extroversion* versus *Introversion:* Extroverts tend to be sociable, talkative, and assertive, while introverts are retiring, reserved, and passive.

2. *Agreeableness* versus *Antagonism:* Agreeable persons are helpful, trusting, pleasant, and kind while antagonistic individuals are ruthless, unsympathetic, suspicious, skeptical, and uncooperative.

3. *Conscientiousness:* Conscientious persons are hard working, organized, careful, disciplined, and dependable while unconscientious types are disorganized, careless, impulsive, negligent, and unreliable.

4. *Emotional Stability* versus *Neuroticism:* Those who are emotionally stable are calm, secure, and even-tempered as opposed to anxious, nervous, insecure, and moody (qualities which characterize neurotics).

5. *Openness:* Those who are open have broad interests, are daring imaginative, preferring variety; independent, curious, and creative versus practical, preferring routine, conforming, shallow and imperceptive.

John Holland has also devised a system to relate personality types with appropriate career choices, based on the assumption that career choices are an expression of personality, as well as the person's motivation, knowledge, and ability. Holland's Six Themes are: (1) Realistic: enjoys outdoors and physical activity, (2) Investigative: is curious, analytic, scholarly, skeptical, inquisitive, (3) Artistic: is creative, sensitive, unconventional, independent, expressive, (4) Social: is cooperative, helpful, sociable, humanistic, facilitative, (5) Enterprising: is outgoing, persuasive, ambitious, status-conscious, assertive, and (6) Conventional: is organized, persistent, practical, efficient, and conscientious. Holland believes that it is important for the work environment to match one's personality type.

Goal Setting   Defining lifetime goals provides direction and purpose to one's life, and provides a context for career plans.

Getting through Roadblocks   Sometimes emotional or practical obstacles get in the way of career goals. It is a good idea to be flexible and optimistic when thinking about career possibilities. There are many strategies available for overcoming psychological obstacles: (1) Turn negatives into positives; (2) restructure your belief system; (3) list things you want to accomplish; and (4) create and recite affirmations.

Affirmations are one strategy used to overcome these hurdles. They are positive statements about one's abilities that can be thought to oneself repeatedly to build confidence and motivation to move towards one's goals. Guidelines for making affirmations are as follows: Keep affirmations personal, avoid comparisons with others; keep them positive and in the present tense; indicate achievement; use action and excitement words, be realistic; stay in balance with goals in all areas of life; and keep the affirmations private.

CHANGING FACE OF THE WORK LANDSCAPE   The fast pace of social and technological change will continue to force people to adapt to a changing workforce. It is estimated that the average American who enters the workforce today will change careers, not just jobs, three to five times. This forecast means that training for work should emphasize *transferable skills*, not particular job skills, which become outdated.

Research on job satisfaction suggests that it is a relatively stable trait and is minimally affected by job changes. It appears that job satisfaction is directly related to the person's ongoing, stable sense of life satisfaction. Research on job satisfaction in the past two decades has generally found a trend toward increasing dissatisfaction at all job levels. The reasons for dissatisfaction, however, vary somewhat for different job levels and different types of workers.

One recent trend in contemporary society is that for the past generation, large numbers of mothers with young children have been choosing to enter the work force. Overall, the research has been positive with regard to the effects of maternal employment on the development of children. Studies on the effects of nonparental care on children have found that such children were no different intellectually, emotionally, or socially from their home-raised counterparts, nor did the children differ in the attachments they had formed with their mothers. Studies investigating the effects of maternal employment on the family have most consistently found that children of working mothers have more egalitarian concepts about sex roles and less traditional stereotypes of male and female activities than children whose mothers are full-time homemakers.

LEISURE   Leisure activities can also be organized in terms of Holland's six themes. Gratification of an individual's psychological needs through leisure activities apparently has a beneficial effect on physical and mental health, and overall life satisfaction. Finding a good balance between work and leisure can contribute to personal vitality, and failing to do so is likely to lead to burnout.

LEARNING THE LANGUAGE OF PSYCHOLOGISTS

intrinsic motivation   **secondary traits**
extrinsic motivation   **affect**
cardinal traits   **personality disorder**
central traits   **affirmations**

CHAPTER REVIEW QUESTIONS

1. Why might it be desirable to consider a broad field of interest rather than a specific job within that field?
2. How can you use knowledge of your skills, interests, and values to help you select a career?
3. What part does motivation play in having a successful career?
4. What is the relationship between enjoyment of your college experience and enjoyment of a career?
5. What suggestion was given for management of psychological barriers to achieving your desired job goal?
6. What are Holland's six occupational themes, and what are their characteristics?
7. How do the "Big Five" personality characteristics relate to Holland's six occupational themes?
8. How is Zen philosophy similar to and different from the Protestant work ethic?
9. How does maternal employment affect children?
10. To what extent do a career and one's leisure pursuits provide the same satisfactions?

ACTIVITIES

1. *SMALL GROUP EXERCISE*: **Personal Reflections on Work in My Life.**
2. *LARGE GROUP EXERCISE*: **What Do You Hold Sacred?** Go around the classroom, and ask class members to answer the following questions: "Is there anything you value so strongly that you would leave this city or country if it were taken away?" "If you had to leave and could take only one suitcase full of belongings, what do you prize so much that you would put into that suitcase?"
3. *SMALL GROUP EXERCISE*: **Work Values Auction.** (a value's clarification exercise)
4. *COMPLETE INDIVIDUALLY*: **What Are Important Job Satisfactions for You?** (a values clarification exercise)
5. *COMPLETE INDIVIDUALLY*: **What Is Important to You?** (a values clarification exercise)
6. *COMPLETE INDIVIDUALLY*: **Occupational Map.** (an interest inventory)
7. *COMPLETE INDIVIDUALLY*: **The Party** (an interest inventory)
8. *COMPLETE INDIVIDUALLY*: **Personality and Interest Mosaic** (an interest inventory)
9. *COMPLETE INDIVIDUALLY*: **Skills Checklist** (a skills inventory)

10. *COMPLETE INDIVIDUALLY:* **Most Satisfying Accomplishments** (a skills inventory)
11. *COMPLETE INDIVIDUALLY:* **Career Planning Summary Sheet**
12. *COMPLETE INDIVIDUALLY:* **Decision-Making Worksheet**
13. *COMPLETE INDIVIDUALLY:* Students may wish to complete the NEO Personality Inventory (NEO-PI-R), which was developed by Paul Costa and Robert McCrae (1992) to assess the Big Five Personality Dimensions.
14. *COMPLETE IN DYADS OR SMALL GROUPS:* **Mock Job Interviews:** From the class, recruit a volunteer interviewee and either a panel of interviewers or a single interviewer. Decide on a position that the interviewee might apply for. Conduct a practice interview.

Personal Reflections on Work in My Life

Directions: Read each of the following questions, and then write your answers in the blanks.

1. What meaning have you found in the work you've done so far? Has your work been a means of self-expression for you?

   _____

   _____

   _____

   _____

2. Some people feel that they have to play a role in order to keep their jobs, and that this role may necessitate being untrue to themselves. Do you feel this way? Is it possible to be honest, be yourself, and at the same time, to keep your job?

   _____

   _____

   _____

   _____

3. Discuss what you get or expect to get from work.

   _____

   _____

   _____

   _____

4. Do you see any way to incorporate your interests and hobbies into your career? Do some people make a career out of what are your leisure-time activities?

_____

_____

_____

_____

5. Do you think that you have been pressured to choose a career too soon? If so, where have these pressures come from?

_____

_____

_____

_____

6. It has been predicted that most people will change their jobs between five and seven times during their lives. What implication does this trend have for you personally?

_____

_____

_____

_____

7. Do you believe that you can choose your attitude toward work and thus change the meaning it has for you? Why, or why not?

_____

_____

_____

_____

8. Do you see most people as victims of meaningless work, or do you think that they have a choice and can change their work situations? Explain.

_____

_____

_____

_____

9. How are your relationships with others at work and/or school?

_____

_____

_____

_____

10. How satisfied are you with your work and/or academic situation?

_____

_____

_____

_____

11. Do you have time for recreational activities? Do you have leisure activities that are vastly different from what you do at school and/or work, or is there some overlap? What is you favorite leisure-time activity?

_____

_____

_____

_____

12. Do you anticipate there being adequate employment opportunities in your anticipated career area? How important is this consideration in your selection of a career goal?

_____

_____

_____

_____

13. Complete this sentence: "To me, work is . . ."

_____

_____

_____

_____

14. Complete this sentence: "My idea of a dream career is . . ."

_____

_____

_____

_____

15. Complete this sentence: "My dream vacation is . . ."

_____

_____

_____

_____

16. Did your parents or teachers make suggestions to you about jobs you should consider? If so, what were those suggestions?

_____

_____

_____

_____

17. When you were a child and adults asked you what you wanted to be when you grew up, what were some of your responses? Were the values and interests expressed by your childhood career ambitions similar to those you hold today? Write down some of your childhood interests, as well as your current interests, if different.

_____

_____

_____

_____

Work Values Auction

Directions: Divide into groups of four to five people. Select one group member to be the auctioneer. The rules for this exercise are that each participant has $5,000 to spend, and no more than $3,000 may be spent on any one item. Before beginning the auction, each person should privately create a spending budget, so that the allotted $5,000 is distributed across those items in the list that follows that he or she would like to procure from his or her work experience. Once each group member has had an opportunity to complete this process, begin the auction. Each person can use the second column to keep track of how much of his or her $5,000 has been spent so far in successfully bidding for items. After the auction, record the top five things *budgeted* for along with their codes shown at the right of the bid column to the *Career Planning Summary Sheet* on page 274.

Budget Bids

1. A job working with animals. _____ _____ R
2. Predicting the value, size, or cost of something. _____ _____ C
3. Having well-defined work responsibilities. _____ _____ C
4. Freedom to set your own work schedule. _____ _____ A, I
5. A month's vacation each year. _____ _____ R
6. Working outdoors. _____ _____ R
7. Being acknowledged as an expert in a given field. _____ _____ I
8. Complete job security. _____ _____ C
9. Good friendships or relations with coworkers. _____ _____ S
10. International fame and popularity. _____ _____ E
11. Work that seeks to understand the meaning of life. _____ _____ I, S
12. A job managing others. _____ _____ E
13. Traveling on the job and meeting new people. _____ _____ S
14. Work that involves perceiving intuitively. _____ _____ A
15. Work duties that involve risk and/or excitement. _____ _____ R, E
16. Feeling that my work adds meaning to the lives of others. _____ _____ S
17. Work near where you want to live. _____ _____ R
18. A career that involves observing, analyzing, and evaluating. _____ _____ I
19. Creating new programs, ideas, products, or artwork. _____ _____ A
20. A chance to influence other people. _____ _____ E
21. A job as a resource expert, an organizer of information. _____ _____ C
22. Being able to see some progress on what you're doing. _____ _____ C
23. A position that involves physical exercise. _____ _____ R
24. Having the power to decide courses of action and policies. _____ _____ E
25. Testing your abilities against others in a competitive situation. _____ _____ E

	Budget	**Bids**	
26. A career that calls for adapting, improvising.	_____	_____	A
27. Being able to apply your major interests to your job.	_____	_____	–
28. Having a large income, expense account, and company car.	_____	_____	E
29. Work that presents an intellectual challenge.	_____	_____	I
30. Having a variety of work responsibilities that often change in their content and setting.	_____	_____	I, A
31. Being able to determine the nature of your work without much direction from others.	_____	_____	I, A
32. Having a close working relationship with a group, working as a team toward common goals.	_____	_____	S
33. Using statistical procedures to analyze data or solve problems.	_____	_____	C

What Are Important Job Satisfactions for You?

Directions: Your task is to rank the 26 job factors listed here, in order of importance to you. In other words, your ranking should be a prediction of how motivated you are to acquire each of the following values from your job. Place a *1* by the factor you select as most important, a *2* by the next most important factor, and so on, up to *26*, which will be the least important item. Next, transfer the top five ranked items, along with the code letters (e.g., A, S, E) found next to your ranking, to the summary sheet on page 274.

1. Having the admiration of others.	_____	A, S
2. Recognition for doing a good job.	_____	S, E
3. Opportunity for promotion.	_____	E
4. A feeling of personal accomplishment.	_____	A, I
5. Freedom in doing your job, independence.	_____	A, I
6. Adequate compensation, financial reward.	_____	E
7. Company benefits.	_____	C, E
8. Leading others.	_____	E
9. Helping or training others.	_____	S
10. Learning new tasks	_____	I
11. Getting the opportunity to try new tasks.	_____	I, R

12. Job security.	_____ I
13. Having clear responsibilities.	_____ C
14. Pride in doing a good job.	_____ A, I
15. The kind of work you do (the work itself).	_____ A
16. Doing what is right.	_____ S, C
17. Striving for your own rights and the rights of others.	_____ S
18. Putting your own ideas into operation.	_____ A, I, E
19. Working conditions.	_____ C
20. People you work with.	_____ S
21. Having a good supervisor.	_____ C
22. A job involving physical activity.	_____ R
23. Creating things with your hands.	_____ A, R
24. Handling large, powerful machines.	_____ R
25. Job requiring physical skills, using tools.	_____ R
26. Working outdoors.	_____ R

What Is Important to You?

Directions: In the space to the right of the items listed here, indicate how important each item is to you by rank ordering the items from 1 to 22. Transfer the top five ranked items, along with the code letters found next to your ranking, to the summary sheet on page 274.

1. Status (high position, admiration from others)	_____ E
2. Recognition (praise, acknowledgment, respect)	_____ E & S
3. Accomplishment (achieving something meaningful)	_____ A, E, & I
4. Freedom (little or no control by others)	_____ A
5. Financial reward (money, possessing wealth)	_____ E
6. Power (leading, controlling the action)	_____ E
7. Serving others (helping, curing, training others)	_____ S
8. Knowledge (knowing, understanding)	_____ I
9. Adventure (change, risk)	_____ R
10. Security (little or no change, risk)	_____ C
11. Talents, skills utilization (doing something well)	_____ A
12. Responsibility (accountability for actions)	_____ C & E

13. Moral conviction (doing what is right)   _____ S

14. Justice (equality for all)   _____ S

15. Creativity (conceiving and using your own ideas)   _____ A

16. Wisdom (mature understanding of life)   _____ I

17. Daring (having courage)   _____ R

18. Self-control (restraint, self-discipline)   _____ C

19. Obedience (a sense of duty, respectfulness)   _____ C

20. Intellectualism (intelligence, reflection)   _____ I

21. Courage (self-reliance in times of peril)   _____ R

22. Leisure (having work that must not interfere with
    the most important satisfactions in life)   _____ R

Occupational Map Worksheet

Directions: Circle eight of the following activities that you think you would most enjoy. When you have done that, locate the same activities on page 264 and circle them again. Note the Holland codes related to the circled items. Transfer the three codes that have the most activities listed under them to the summary sheet on page 274.

design furniture	run a committee meeting
be a school counselor	work in a telephone office
work with salespeople	build cabinets
organize files and cabinets	work with scientists
work outside	be a musician
design electronic equipment	work in a day-care center
work in a photo studio	be a U.S. senator
study social problems	run office machines
work in a real estate firm	be a police officer
be an accountant	work with artists
run a bulldozer	study chemistry
work in a scientific laboratory	be a biologist
study drama	work with teenagers
teach children to read	study public speaking
work with office managers	work with farmers

Now, transfer your answers to the Occupational Map below.

Occupational Map

Realistic

work outside

build cabinets

run a bulldozer

work with farmers

be a police officer

Investigative

be a biologist

study chemistry

work with scientists

design electronic equipment

work in a scientific laboratory

Conventional

be an accountant

run office machines

organize files and cabinets

work in a telephone office

work with office managers

Artistic

be a musician

design furniture

work in a photo studio

work with artists

study drama

Enterprising

work in a real estate firm

run a committee meeting

work with salespeople

study public speaking

be a U.S. senator

Social

work in a day-care center

teach children to read

be a school counselor

study social problems

work with teenagers

Source: Campbell (1974).

Join a Club Day

Directions: Imagine that you are a student who wants to join a club on campus. You will have to decide from among several clubs, as you don't have time to join more than one. With this purpose in mind, you attend a "join a club day" event, at which the various clubs have put out tables with handouts to explain the nature of the club and photo albums to show off past club events. Also displayed on the table are club awards, mascots, T shirts, and other interesting paraphernalia. Several representatives from the club are sitting at the tables or standing around, ready to talk with perspective members.

You stand in the midst of the tables, trying to decide which one to approach first. Here are your choices:

SIERRA CLUB   This club goes on hikes, camping trips, snow and water skiing trips, picnics, horseback riding excursions, and bicycle trips. The club members are athletic. They like the outdoors, and tend to be animal lovers. They like to build all kinds of things, from birdfeeders to hiking trails.

DABBLER'S CLUB   This group likes to visit art galleries and museums, as well as attend plays and concerts. Once each semester, the club has permission to use the on-campus art gallery to put on an art show displaying club members' artwork. Some of the club members are amateur painters, sculptors, candle makers, or creators of folk art. Other club members simply appreciate the aesthetic side of life. Some of the members have formed a book club, in which each month they read the same book and then get together to discuss it. Quite a few theater majors have joined this club.

SCIENCE CLUB   This club sponsors evenings of star gazing, nature walks (they sometimes do this with the Sierra Club), visits to the museum of science and industry, the aquarium, and the local observatory. At times they invite scientists and even criminologists to speak on campus, and on occasion, the members carpool to an off-campus presentation that is of scientific interest. These club members like to investigate and analyze how things work in the physical world. They enjoy having formal debates among the club members on theoretical issues.

FUTURE ACCOUNTANTS AND BUSINESS MANAGERS CLUB   This club invites guest speakers from the business world and government organizations to talk about the kinds of work they do, in order to expose the club members to potential career areas that might interest them. The club members also arrange tours of various corporations, businesses, and government facilities to gather further information about career possibilities. These club members appear to be well organized, persistent and practical in their approach to life. They are detail-oriented, dependable, and conscientious.

POLITICAL SCIENCE CLUB   This club invites political candidates to the campus to speak, and hosts debates on hot political topics, either among the club members or among invited guests. The club members tend to be outgoing, energetic, self-confident and optimistic. They like leadership roles, and don't mind being put in charge of club events.

SOCIAL SERVICE CLUB   This club finds service projects to do such as feeding the homeless, campus clean-up, on-campus tutoring, visiting ill people in hospitals and hospices, and arranging outings for underprivileged children. In addition to their weekly meetings, the club has monthly potluck dinners at the club sponsor's home, simply to unwind and socialize.

Select the club that would be most likely to attract you. Indicate your choice in the following blank. _____

After you approach and talk to your first choice group, you learn that this club is very full, and isn't accepting any new members, as a school rule prohibits any club from having more than thirty members.

You decide to try another club. Which club table would you be likely to approach as your second choice? Put your selection in the following blank._____

You enjoy your chat with the second club, but are still in the mood to try another table before making up your mind. Indicate your third choice in the following blank: _____

Next, translate your choices into Holland codes, and put the codes on your "Career Summary Sheet."

Sierra Club = Realistic
Political Science Club = Enterprising
Social Service Club = Social
Dabbler's Club = Artistic
Future Accountants and Business Management Club = Conventional
Science Club = Investigative

Personality and Interest Mosaic

Directions: Circle the number of any of the following statements that clearly seems like something you might say or do or think, or that expresses how you feel. Circle as many as apply.

1. It's important for me to have a strong, agile body.

2. I need to understand things thoroughly.

3. Music, color, or beauty of any kind can really affect my moods.

4. People enrich my life and give it meaning.

5. I have confidence in myself that I can make things happen.

6. I appreciate clear directions so that I know exactly what to do.

7. I can usually carry/build/fix things myself.

8. I can get absorbed for hours in thinking something through.

9. I appreciate beautiful surroundings; color and design mean a lot to me.

10. I love company.

11. I enjoy competing.

12. I need to get my surroundings in order before I start a project.

13. I enjoy making things with my hands.

14. I find it satisfying to explore new ideas.

15. I always seem to be looking for new ways to express my creativity.

16. I value being able to share personal concerns with people.

17. Being a key person in a group is very satisfying to me.

18. I take pride in being very careful about all the details of my work.

19. I don't mind getting my hands dirty.

20. I see education as a lifelong process of developing and sharpening my mind.

21. I love to dress in unusual ways, to try new colors and styles.

22. I can often sense when a person needs to talk to someone.

23. I enjoy getting people organized and on the move.

24. A good routine helps me get the job done.

25. I like to buy sensible things I can make or work on myself.

26. Sometimes I can sit for long periods of time and work on puzzles, read, or just think about life.

27. I have a great imagination.

28. It makes me feel good to take care of people.

29. I like to have people rely on me to get the job done.

30. I'm satisfied knowing that I've done an assignment carefully and completely.

31. I like being on my own, doing practical, hands-on activities.

32. I'm eager to read about any subject that arouses my curiosity.

33. I love to try creative, new ideas.

34. If I have a problem with someone, I prefer to talk it out and resolve it.

35. To be successful, it's important to aim high.

36. I prefer being in a position where I don't have to take responsibility for decisions.

37. I don't enjoy spending a lot of time discussing things. What's right is right.

38. I need to analyze a problem pretty thoroughly before I act on it.

39. I like to rearrange my surroundings to make them unique and different.

40. When I feel down, I find a friend to talk to.

41. After I suggest a plan, I prefer to let others take care of the details.

42. I'm usually content where I am.

43. It's invigorating to do things outdoors.

44. I keep asking "why."

45. I like my work to be an expression of my moods and feelings.

46. I like to find ways to help people care more for each other.

47. It's exciting to take part in important decisions.

48. I'm always glad to have someone else take charge.

49. I like my surroundings to be plain and practical.

50. I need to stay with a problem until I figure out an answer.

51. The beauty of nature touches something deep inside me.

52. Close relationships are important to me.

53. Promotion and advancement are important to me.

54. Efficiency, for me, means doing a set amount carefully each day.

55. A strong system of law and order is important to prevent chaos.

56. Thought-provoking books always broaden my perspective.

57. I look forward to seeing art shows, plays, and good films.

58. I haven't seen you for so long; I'd love to know how you're doing.

59. It's exciting to influence people.

60. When I say I'll do it, I follow through on every detail.

61. Good, hard physical work never hurt anyone.

62. I'd like to learn all there is to know about subjects that interest me.

63. I don't want to be like everyone else; I like to do things differently.

64. Tell me how I can help you.

65. I'm willing to take some risks to get ahead.

66. I like exact directions and clear rules when I start something new.

67. The first thing I look for in a car is a well-built engine.

68. Those people are intellectually stimulating.

69. When I'm creating, I tend to let everything else go.

70. I feel concerned that so many people in our society need help.

71. It's fun to get ideas across to people.

72. I hate it when they keep changing the system just when I get it down.

73. I usually know how to take care of things in an emergency.

74. Just reading about those new discoveries is exciting.

75. I like to create happenings.

76. I often go out of my way to pay attention to people who seem lonely and friendless.

77. I love to bargain.

78. I don't like to do things unless I'm sure they're approved.

79. Sports are important in building strong bodies.

80. I've always been curious about the way nature works.

81. It's fun to be in a mood to try or do something unusual.

82. I believe that people are basically good.

83. If I don't make it the first time, I usually bounce back with energy and enthusiasm.

84. I appreciate knowing exactly what people expect of me.

85. I like to take things apart to see if I can fix them.

86. Don't get excited. We can think it out and plan the right move logically.

87. It would be hard to imagine my life without beauty around me.

88. People often seem to tell me their problems.

89. I can usually connect with people who get me in touch with a network of resources.

90. I don't need much to be happy.

Scoring: To score your answers, circle the same numbers in the following list that you circled on the Personality and Interest Mosaic.

Realistic	Investigative	Artistic	Social	Enterprising	Conventional
1	2	3	4	5	6
7	8	9	10	11	12
13	14	15	16	17	18
19	20	21	22	23	24
25	26	27	28	29	30
31	32	33	34	35	36
37	38	39	40	41	42
43	44	45	46	47	48
49	50	51	52	53	54
55	56	57	58	59	60
61	62	63	64	65	66
67	68	69	70	71	72
73	74	75	76	77	78
79	80	81	82	83	84
85	86	87	88	89	90

Now add up the number of circles in each column:

R_____   I_____   A_____   S_____   E_____   C_____

Which are your three highest scores?

1st_____ 2nd_____ 3rd_____

When finished, transfer your codes to the summary sheet on page 274.

Source: Michelozzi, 1998.

Skills Checklist

Directions: From the lists in this exercise, select your 15 strongest skills by placing a check mark in the blank. Ignore the category designations while doing so. When you have finished, find the three Holland codes under which you have put the most check marks. Transfer these codes to the summary sheet on page 274.

Realistic	Investigative	Artistic
__Ability	__Analyzing	__Adapting
__Adjusting things	__Appraising/Assessing	__Improvising
__Assembling/Producing	__Classifying	__Choreographing
__Building/Constructing	__Comparing	__Color discrimination
__Collecting things	__Determining/Diagnosing	__Composing
__Crafting objects	__Developing hypotheses	__Conceptualizing
__Cultivating/Growing	__Discovering/Detecting	__Creating art
__Distributing/Delivering	__Dissecting	__Creating products

Realistic

__Installing
__Lifting/Pushing/Balancing
__Maintaining
__Manual dexterity
__Making mechanical
drawings
__Mechanical reasoning
__Molding/Shaping
__Navigating
__Operating tools/Machinery
__Organizing outdoor
activities
__Physical coordination
__Precision working
__Repairing/Fixing
__Setting up equipment
__Skill at a sport
__Tending animals
__Touch sensitivity

Investigative

__Estimating
__Evaluating/Critiquing
__Experimenting/Testing
__Finding patterns
__Identifying/Defining
__Isolating
__Measuring
__Observing/Examining
__Monitoring
__Predicting
__Questioning
__Researching/Investigating
__Reviewing/Screening
__Seeing relationships
__Surveying
__Synthesizing
__Systematizing
__Troubleshooting

Artistic

__Creating techniques
__Decorating/Staging
__Demonstrating originality
__Designing/Styling
__Drafting/Making layouts
__Dramatizing/Acting
__Drawing/Illustrating
__Expressing emotion
__Form perception
__Generating ideas
__Imagining/Fantasizing
__Innovating/Inventing
__Mapping
__Model development
__Musical ability/Musical taste
__Perceiving intuitively
__Photographing
__Sculpting
__Visualizing

Enterprising

__Allocating resources
__Arranging/Scheduling
__Assigning tasks
__Conducting
__Confronting
__Conversing easily with
strangers
__Coordination/Organizing
__Decision making
__Delegating responsibility
__Demonstrating/Modeling
__Developing programs
__Enlisting/Recruiting
__Finding shortcuts
__Formulating ideas
__Influencing/Persuading
__Leading/Directing
__Managing
__Manipulating
__Mediating/Negotiating
__Motivating/Stimulating
__Planning
__Prioritizing
__Promoting
__Public Speaking
__Recommending
__Risk-taking
__Selecting courses of action
__Selling
__Setting/Meeting deadlines
__Supervising

Social

__Accepting others
__Advising/Coaching
__Assisting others
__Clarifying/Summarizing
__Conveying warmth
__Counseling
__Curing/Nursing
__Developing rapport
__Ear for languages
__Empathizing
__Encouraging
__Explaining
__Facilitating/Aiding
__Informing/Teaching
__Listening
__Offering support
__Protecting
—Raising others' self-esteem
__Rehabilitating
__Relationship building
__Responding to feelings
__Sensitivity to others' needs
__Serving others
__Sizing up people
__Teamwork
__Training
__Verbal ability
__Writing ability

Conventional

__Attention to detail
__Budget preparation
__Calculating
__Cataloging
__Checking
__Clerical ability
__Collecting information
__Compiling
__Computing
__Financial planning
__Following directions
__Implementing
__Memory for detail
__Money management
__Numerical ability
__Ordering/Purchasing
__Organizing/Simplifying
__Putting in order
__Preparing reports
__Processing
__Programming
__Record keeping
__Resource expert
__Retrieving
__Tabulating
__Taking inventory
__Transcribing

Most Satisfying Accomplishments

Directions: Think of the things you have done in your life that you thought were important and that represented a sense of accomplishment to YOU (not necessarily to anyone else). Now, on page 273, list ten of your achievements. No particular order is necessary for listing your accomplishments.

If you have difficulty thinking of ten achievements, then think of satisfying roles that you have been in, such as spouse, parent, grandchild, cook, housekeeper, athlete, student, friend, cheerleader, camp leader. In addition, think of jobs that you have held *if* these were jobs you enjoyed doing. The jobs can be paid or unpaid, full-time or part-time. For example, you may have been a baby-sitter, fast-food worker, newspaper carrier, volunteer worker, or salesperson.

Still stuck? Think of hobbies that you have enjoyed, a special school project that you have completed, activities that you enjoyed in the summertime or on weekends, or things that you have done frequently in your "alone" times.

You may find it difficult to remember your most satisfying experiences. However, in doing so, you will see that you have used a variety of skills in the activities on your list.

Turn to page 273 and complete the achievement/skills chart.

When you have finished that chart, add up the number of checks for each of the six career areas by referring to the letter next to the skill name.

Summary from the *Most Satisfying Accomplishments Chart:*

Total Rs: _____
Total As: _____
Total Ss: _____
Total Es: _____
Total Is: _____
Total Cs _____

Enter the top three career codes, in order, on your *Career Planning Summary Sheet* (page 274).

Source: Adapted from *PATH: A Career Workbook for Liberal Arts Students* by H. E. Figler. © 1979 by the Carroll Press. Reprinted by permission.

Most Satisfying Accomplishments Chart

I	Evaluating, Critiquing										
A	Drawing, Designing										
A	Appreciating Beauty/Music/Drama										
C	Organizing, Putting in order										
R	Repairing, Fixing things										
R	Physical coordination, Athletic ability										
C	Careful attention to detail										
C	Numerical ability, Money Management										
S	Facilitating, Aiding										
E	Ability to perform publicly										
E	Persuading, Motivating others										
S	Communication skills										
R	Operating tools or machinery										
S	Instructing, Guidance skills										
S	Human relations skills, Service										
A	Inventive, creative, artistic abilities										
I	Observational skills										
I	Investigation, Analyzing skills										
E	Ability to make hard decisions										
I	Problem-solving skills										
R	Farming, working with animals										
C	Persistence, Finishing what you start										
E	Leadership skills										
A	Perceiving intuitively										

1. 2. 3. 4. 5. 6. 7. 8. 9. 10.

Career Planning Summary Sheet

Values	*Interests*	*Skills*
What Are Important Job Satisfactions? (top five items)	**Occupational Map** (top three codes)	**Skills Checklist** (top three codes)
1.	1.	1.
2.		
3.	2.	2.
4.		
5.	3.	3.
What's Important to You? (top five items)	**Join a Club Day** (top three codes)	**Accomplishments** (top three skills)
1.	1.	1.
2.		
3.	2.	2.
4.		
5.	3.	3.
Values Auction Results (top five items budgeted for)	**Personality and Interest Mosaic** (top three codes)	**SUMMARY:** What are your three strongest Holland codes? List them here:
1.	1.	
2.		
3.	2.	1.
4.		2.
5.	3.	3.

Directions: Use the careers identified in the chapter that are associated with each Holland theme to locate promising career areas. If available in your college career center, you may also use Holland's *Occupations Finder* booklet from his self-directed search materials to find careers that fit your profile. List six of them on the Decision Making Worksheet (page 276) as alternatives.

Preparing a Decision Making Worksheet

Defining the Problem: The first step is the realization that a decision needs to be made. A decision making worksheet begins with a succinct statement of the problem, which will also help to focus on the precise issue at hand.

Generating the Alternatives: The next step is to write out in separate columns across the top of the worksheet all possible alternatives that could solve the problem. It is important to refrain from evaluating the alternatives at this stage of the process.

Listing the Considerations: Under this section, put the variables that will be affected by your decision. What is important to you? Is it to make a personal contribution to society? Having a large income? Having a leisurely lifestyle? You'll want to consider the impact of your decision on family and friends. Consult the values listed on your summary sheet to get an idea of your considerations.

Weighting the Considerations: It is almost always true that the considerations are not equally important to the decision maker and therefore need to be weighted accordingly. A 5-point scale, in which 1 = of slight importance, 5 = of great importance, and the numbers 2, 3, and 4 reflect gradations of importance between these end points, can be used to quantify the relative importance of each consideration. Weighting considerations is a personal matter. Only you can assign the weights for your decision making worksheet. Place your weightings in the box alongside each consideration.

Weighting the Alternatives: Assign each alternative a value from –2, –1, 0, +1, or +2, according to how well it satisfies each consideration. Put this value in the left-hand box in the same row as the consideration and the same column as the alternative.

Calculating a Decision: Now you need to determine how well each alternative satisfies your considerations. To calculate this guideline, multiply the weight previously assigned for each consideration by the value assigned to how well an alternative satisfies that consideration. Put the product in the right-hand box in the same row as the consideration and the same column as the alternative. This procedure is repeated for each alternative. The right-hand column for each alternative is then added, yielding a total score for each alternative.

2/3 Ideal Rule: Calculate the overall assessment total for an ideal alternative. To do this calculation, multiply each consideration weight by +2. Then sum the result, and divide by 3 and multiply by 2. If your best "realistic" alternative fails to measure up to 2/3 of an ideal solution, it may not be good enough to satisfy you. This outcome means that you need to generate further alternatives and to review your considerations.

Note: Students should use Holland's *Self-Directed Search Occupations Finder* to find alternative occupations to consider on the decision making worksheet. The *Self-Directed Search Occupations Finder* is a booklet that matches Holland's themes to a variety of career options. To get career ideas, students can take their top three Holland themes and look them up in this booklet. If this booklet is not available, use the information in your chapter identifying careers that belong to each of Holland's six themes.

Source: Adapted from "Preparing a Decision Making Worksheet" from *Thought and Knowledge* by Diane Halpern. Copyright © 1984 by Lawrence Erlbaum Asociates, Inc. Reprinted by permission.

Decision Making Worksheet

Problem Statement: _____

Alternatives →

↓ Considerations:

							ideal career alternative
☐							+2
☐							+2
☐							+2
☐							+2
☐							+2
☐							+2
☐							+2

Total score
for each alternative: __ __ __ __ __ __ __

8

Stress and Coping

A joyful heart is good medicine.
—Proverbs 17

Character is the result of two things, mental attitude
and the way we spend our time.
—Elbert Hubbard

> ➤ PREVIEW QUESTIONS: What effect does psychological distress have on the body? To what extent do we control the level of stress in our lives? Is having a sense of humor good for you? Does being married have health benefits?

➤ INTRODUCTION: WEAR AND TEAR FROM DODGING ROAD HAZARDS

Life can be wonderful, but often it isn't easy. Living in today's world requires that we manage a great many activities and concerns. We worry about everything from personal anxieties, such as the pressure to be successful, to global issues, which include worldwide pollution and the depletion of the ozone layer. Our emotional responses to these internal and external experiences play a role in the maintenance of our physical health. Health psychologists have found that stress and other psychological factors influence the immune system's ability to do its job of keeping the body well. We need to understand just how this process works, since safeguarding our immune system can be a matter of life and death!

In addressing the question, What is my goal in life? we generally would respond that we want to be healthy and happy. As long as we are healthy, our thoughts about how to attain happiness may include the desire for a college education, a good job, and a loving family. We might also wish to help others. These things are desired by us, because we expect them to make us happy and fulfilled. Relief from stress and ill health also enhance our opportunity for happiness. Freedom from troublesome anxiety should allow us to feel more at home in our world than is the case when we are overwhelmed. Thus, effective coping strategies benefit us by addressing our ultimate concerns.

➤ STRESS AND THE MIND-BODY CONNECTION

Stress can be defined as mental and physical strain resulting from demands or challenges to adjust to external reality. It has been characterized in two ways: (1) as exposure to life events that require adaptation, generally measured by a checklist of major events (e.g., divorce, death of a relative, job loss) and (2) as a state that occurs when people perceive that demands on them exceed their abilities to cope, usually measured by self-reports of subjective experience (Adler & Matthews, 1994). Attempts have been made to link systematically both types of stress with health. Life events presumably trigger perceptions of being overwhelmed, thus causing anxiety. These perceptions are known to alter neuroendocrine responses and immune responses that may put people at greater risk for a range of illnesses. The term **psychosomatic illness** means that the mind and body are interacting to cause illness. People experiencing recent stressful life events have been found to be at greater risk for gastrointestinal disorders (Harris, 1991), menorrhagia (excessive bleeding at the time of a menstrual period), secondary amenorrhea (absence or suppression of menstruation) (Harris, 1989), heart attacks (Theorell, 1974), heart disease (Byrne & Whyte, 1980; Tofler et al., 1990), stroke (Harmsen, Rosengreen, Tsipogianni, & Wilhelmsen, 1990), and susceptibility to infectious agents (Cohen, Tyrell, & Smith, 1991, 1993; Stone et al., 1992). There is evidence that severe life stresses frequently precede the appearance of some forms of cancer (Eysenck, 1991). A person's intrapsychic environment has also been linked to physical illness. A twenty-year longitudinal study of over 2,000 men revealed that depression scores on the Minnesota Multiphasic Personality Inventory (MMPI) predict the long-term likelihood of developing cancer.

➤ EARLY ATTEMPTS TO RELATE MENTAL STATES TO BODILY STATES

Freud's Accident-Prone Person

Sigmund Freud (1901) gave his views on the relationship between mental and physical health in his book *The Psychopathology of Everyday Life.* He characterized the accident-prone individual as one who is expressing unconscious conflict. When a person has repressed awareness of some sort of inner turmoil, he or she may inadvertently express that unconscious material by "accidentally" tripping a coworker or mistakenly slapping a loved one. The accident can be interpreted, along with other clues, to discover the unconscious conflict.

General Adaptation Syndrome

Hans Selye, a physiologist at the University of Montreal, was a pioneering stress researcher in the mid-1930s. His book *The Stress of Life* (1956) first introduced many people to the physiological and psychological complexities of stress. Selye noticed that the first symptoms of almost any disease or trauma (e.g., poisoning, infection, injury, or psychological distress) are almost identical. He concluded that the body responds in the same way to a variety of occurrences (e.g., infection, failure, embarrassment, adjustment to a new job, trouble at school, or a stormy romance). Selye referred to this nonspecific bodily reaction to any stimulus as **stress**. He also noted that part of the body's physiological response to a stimulus is specific to that stimulus. For example, if we are exposed to extreme heat, we perspire; if we are exposed to extreme cold, we shiver. If we are embarrassed, we blush.

Selye's original research was concerned primarily with the effects of physical **stressors** such as heat, cold, hemorrhage, X-rays, germs, and forced exercise on laboratory rats. Later, he came to realize that the stress response is often elicited by psychological stressors and that our stress response has both psychological and physical components, which may interact with and reinforce each other.

According to Selye, the body's response to stress occurs in three stages, which together are called the general adaptation syndrome. The three stages are as follows:

THE ALARM REACTION   During the alarm stage, the body mobilizes its resources to cope with stressors. When the brain perceives a stressor, it activates two interrelated physiological systems: the autonomic nervous system and the endocrine system. The activation of the autonomic nervous and endocrine systems increase the heart rate, blood pressure, and the amount of oxygen, glucose, cholesterol, and certain free fatty acids in the blood. It also raises the basal metabolic rate and alters the brain's electrical activity.

The hypothalamus, a key control center in the brain, activates the nerve fibers of the sympathetic division of the autonomic nervous system. The sympathetic system helps to control the involuntary muscles of the blood vessels and internal organs and also activates the glands of the endocrine system, particularly the adrenal glands, just above the kidneys. In response to the hypothalamic stress signal, the adrenal glands pour out the hormones epinephrine and norepinephrine into the bloodstream. As these hormones are added to the bloodstream, the blood supply to the digestive tract is reduced, and becomes concentrated in the skeletal muscles. At the same time, the hypothalamus activates the endocrine system directly by signaling the pituitary, the tiny master gland at the base of the brain, to secrete hormones that travel via the bloodstream to the adrenal, thyroid, and other glands.

All of these changes prepare the body for "fight or flight," which are the two most common behavioral responses to being frightened. During the alarm stage, people have symptoms such as headache, fever, fatigue, sore muscles, shortness of breath, diarrhea, upset stomach, loss of appetite, and lack of energy. They become alert and tense.

THE STAGE OF RESISTANCE   The symptoms of the alarm stage reaction disappear as the body's defenses are stabilized. The body increases its defense against the original stressor but becomes less resistant to other sources of stress. For example, animals placed in an extremely cold environment become more resistant to the cold but more susceptible to infection.

THE STAGE OF EXHAUSTION   At this stage, the body's resources are exhausted because the stress hormones are depleted. Continued exposure to the stressor can lead to psychosomatic illness, organ collapse, or death. Selye found enlargement and discoloration of the adrenal glands; intense shrinkage of the thymus, spleen, and lymph nodes; and deep bleeding stomach ulcers. Each overexposure to stressors causes permanent damage to the body, which cannot be repaired entirely by later rest. For instance, headaches become migraines, overreactivity may turn into chronic hypertension, and heart palpitations may become heart attacks.

Why is the experience of stress over a long period more damaging than over a short period? Our bodies are well equipped for emergency responses, which begin abruptly and are over quickly. Extended exposure to stressful life experiences, however, depletes the body's resources and may cause permanent tissue damage. Stress stimulates the production of steroids that suppress the functioning of the immune system. A weakened immune system increases susceptibility to disease (Adler & Cohen, 1993).

Social Readjustment Rating Scale

Holmes and Rahe's (1967) attempt to link stress and health produced the Social Readjustment Rating Scale. (See the end of the chapter for a reproduction of this scale.) This rating scale was developed in an attempt to quantify the relationship between stress and illness. Stress in a person's life can lead to psychological problems, illness, and accidents. The rating scale represented an effort to assess the way in which stressors reduce the body's natural defenses against disease and thus increase the likelihood of illness.

Holmes and Rahe assumed that any type of change could be stressful. The Social Readjustment Rating Scale contains "life change units," which are positive and negative events believed to place demands on people to adjust. It was a somewhat novel idea to consider stressful both positive and negative changes. After all, positive events such as Christmas are supposed to be fun, not harmful! Major life changes were expected to predict the person's state of health a year or two after the events took place.

As it turned out, there were limitations in this thinking. First, some of the items on the scale are the *result* of psychological problems or illness, not their *cause* (Hudgens, 1974). For example, problems at work or major changes in sleeping habits, while *causes* of further difficulties, are likely to be *effects* of other problems. Second, some events become more stressful once a person is already depressed or ill (Dohrenwend, 1979). Third, many expected changes, such as retirement or having the children leave home, are not especially stressful for most people. Fourth, later researchers have not found positive events to be related to illness or poor health (Taylor, 1986).

Perhaps the most important limitation in the approach taken by Holmes and Rahe is that people vary in their subjective reactions to stressors as well as in their coping behaviors. The damaging effects of stress are determined as much by how the individual decides to view it, as by what the objective life situation happens to be. An individual with effective coping strategies and a reliable social support system can be expected to fare better than a person without them, when both are exposed to the same external stressors.

A final limitation in the early attempts of Holmes and Rahe to quantify stressors and use them to predict illness is that the physiological predispositions of the people involved play a role in both the experience of stress and the onset of illness.

Type A Behavior Pattern

On the basis of a long-term study of heart problems, Friedman and Rosenman (1974) classified people into one of two categories: Those with a **Type A behavior pattern** and those with a Type B pattern. This study represented another early attempt to specify a correspondence between a psychological state and a physical ailment.

Type A personalities are those who are hard-driving, ambitious, highly competitive, achievement-oriented, hostile when encountering obstacles, and prone to strong reactions to stressors. They push themselves (and others) and tend to have an underlying animosity, probably from driving themselves to their limits of endurance. People with the Type A pattern of behavior were thought to run a high risk of heart attack. Some Type A indicators are yes answers to these questions: (1) Do you feel irritated when others are late? (2) Do you interrupt others often? (3) Do you feel rushed? (4) Do you eat, talk, and walk quickly? (5) Do you try to eat and shave, or drive and jot down notes, or talk on the phone while fixing dinner? (6) Do you feel guilty when you take time relaxing? (See the end of this chapter for a more complete list of Type A indicator questions.)

Type A people were advised to decrease their risk of having a heart attack by changing their behaviors and attitudes to fit the Type B pattern. Type B people, who are unlikely to have a heart attack, lead a more relaxed lifestyle but are not necessarily unproductive. They find meaning in both their work and leisure. They are able to have fun without feeling guilty, are calmer and less intense, and are able to relax.

Today, the enthusiasm over the discovery of the Type A behavior pattern as a causal element in heart disease has waned. It turns out that different tasks and situations produce different physiological responses in the same people and that being highly reactive to stress and challenge is not in itself a risk factor in heart disease (Krantz & Manuck, 1984). Type A people *do* set themselves a fast work pace and a heavy workload, but many cope better than Type B people who have a lighter workload, and without a high physiological price (Frankenhaeuser, 1980). People who are highly involved in their jobs, even if they work hard, have a low incidence of heart disease (Kobasa, Maddi, & Kahn, 1982).

One research team distinguished between two groups of ambitious, fast-moving people: (1) the "healthy charismatics," who are expressive, active, friendly, and relaxed, and (2) the "hostile competitives," who are angry, tense, and defensive (Friedman, Hall, & Harris, 1985). Other psychologists have proposed a concept called "flow," which relates to the healthy aspects of the Type A pattern. Flow refers to the capacity to be completely engrossed in one's work and is a reliable predictor of happiness with one's life in general (Csikszentmihalyi, 1990). Those with the Type A pattern, who also have qualities of *hardiness* (the hardy person will be discussed later in the chapter) are more resistant to heart disease and other illnesses (Kobasa & Puccetti, 1983).

Apparently the hazardous ingredients in the Type A personality are anger, anxiety, depression, and cynicism (Friedman & Booth-Kewley, 1987a;

1987b). For instance, men who are chronically angry and resentful and who have a hostile attitude toward others are *five times* as likely as nonhostile men to get coronary heart disease and other ailments, even when controlling for other risk factors such as smoking (Williams, 1989; Williams, Barefoot, & Shekelle, 1985).

In general, researchers have focused on whether individuals exhibit Type A or Type B personality. Robert Levine (1990) wondered whether it was also possible that these behavior patterns are triggered by environmental factors. He developed a method for measuring the pace of life in thirty-six American cities of various sizes, nine cities from each of four regions (Northeast, Midwest, South, and West). In each city, Levine determined the "pace of life" by combining four measures: (1) the walking speed of downtown pedestrians on a clear summer weekday, (2) the amount of time it took bank tellers to comply with a request for change, (3) the talking speed of postal clerks in response to a standardized question, and (4) the percentage of adults wearing wristwatches on the street. Levine also looked at health statistics on the local death rates from heart disease (adjusted in each city for the average age of the population) in order to determine whether the pace of life relates to the incidence of heart disease among the inhabitants of the cities under study.

The Northeastern cities that were sampled had the fastest pace of life, and the Western cities had the slowest (the fastest city was Boston, and the slowest was Los Angeles). It seems that there is some truth to the popular idea that New Yorkers and other Northeasterners live life in the fast lane and that Californians are laid back.

Levine found that those cities with a faster the pace had a higher incidence of death from heart disease. Levine's correlational data cannot explain why residents of fast-paced environments are more prone to heart disease; however, one possibility is that a city's pace causes its inhabitants to develop the kinds of personality traits that are necessary for survival. Perhaps one has to acquire a Type A behavior pattern in order to cope with life in the Northeast. Another way to explain the findings is to consider that people who are Type A by nature seek out fast cities, whereas those who are Type B tend to migrate to slower-paced lifestyles. Still other interpretations are that fast-paced cities are found in colder climates or that they may lead people to smoke cigarettes and engage in other stress-reducing but harmful habits. Whatever the explanation, the link between the pace of city life and heart disease prompted Levine to suggest that the environment in which we live can be combined with other factors to predict our health.

➤ BEHAVIORISM

Recall from Chapter 1 that behaviorism is a major school of thought in clinical psychology and is based on the idea that people are products of their past conditioning. The behavioral approach consists of three major strategies to understanding human personality: radical-behaviorism, social learning theory, and cognitive-behaviorism. Radical behaviorists John B. Watson and B. F.

Skinner began the school of behaviorism. Prominent social learning theorists include Julian Rotter and Albert Bandura. Two eminent figures in the area of cognitive theory are Albert Ellis and Aaron Beck.

Radical Behaviorism

In 1913, John B. Watson (1878–1958) began the behaviorist revolution by proposing that the concept of the "mind" be thrown out entirely. Watson wished to make psychology an objective science like biology and physics. To accomplish this, he thought that psychology should limit itself to the study of behavior. He considered introspection unscientific and had little use for terms such as "consciousness." Watson has been designated as the Father of Behaviorism.

Behaviorists view people as being controlled by their environments. The term environment refers to the sum of all external conditions influencing development. The behaviorists contend that the rewards and punishments that are the consequence of a person's past behavior, shape that person's future behavior. At one time, John B. Watson proclaimed the importance of environmental factors in shaping personality, saying,

> Give me a dozen healthy infants, well-formed, and my own special world to bring them up in and I'll guarantee to take any one at random and train him to become any type of specialist I might select—doctor, lawyer, artist, merchant-chief, and yes, beggarman and thief. (Watson, 1913)

People, he said, have no more voluntary control over their actions than does an adding machine. Just as you would not bother asking an adding machine to explain its actions, you should not bother asking people to tell you why they do what they do. According to Watson, your thoughts, feelings, and behaviors are completely determined by forces beyond your conscious control.

The second major founder of behaviorism, B. F. Skinner (1904–1990), took Watson's ideas on behaviorism and made them work in real-world situations. Skinner's contribution to behaviorism was his insistence that behavior is shaped and maintained by its consequences. Actions that have rewarding consequences will be repeated in the future, whereas conduct that does not yield desirable consequences will be discontinued. Behavior change in people and animals can be brought about by controlling the **reinforcement** that is sustaining their behavior. Those actions that are ignored do not pay off, and thus undergo **extinction.** Skinner's concern with overt behavior, and his tendency to ignore the subjective experience of people have led some to say that Skinnerian psychology has "lost consciousness." In spite of this apt criticism, the field of psychology recognizes that Skinner developed one of the most impressive technologies of behavioral change that the world has ever known.

Behavior therapy, which was derived from the principles of behaviorism, is based on the assumption that people have learned to be the way they are. Behaviorists define behavior as either adaptive or maladaptive. Some of the actions we have learned in the past may no longer be productive in our current life circumstances. Therefore, we may need to unlearn current behavior and relearn more adaptive conduct. Behavioral strategies differ from insight therapy (which is based on psychoanalysis or humanism) in that they focus on behavioral symptoms rather than on presumed underlying psychological sources of the problem.

Social Learning Theory

Most behaviorists today consider themselves to be social learning theorists. Albert Bandura's research is particularly central to this viewpoint. Social learning theory emphasizes the role of learning, social factors, and cognitive processes on how we interpret, process, and apply information to ourselves and others. As with behavior theory, social learning theory concludes that the ways we think, act, and feel are the result of our learning history. Therefore, reinforcement and punishment are important as determinants of our behavior. However, in contrast to radical behaviorism, social learning theory emphasizes that our behavior is influenced not only by consequences of our actions but also by our expectations of success and failure. Knowledge of our thought processes is useful in predicting what we are likely to do in the future.

Three types of beliefs are central to learning theory: locus of control, self-efficacy, and delay of gratification.

LOCUS OF CONTROL Rotter (1966) indicated that **locus of control** refers to our beliefs regarding how much control we have over given situations and reinforcement. "Internals" tend to see themselves as at the helm of their ship, free to direct their lives. Our beliefs that we have some control over given situations and rewards represents an internal locus of control. A job applicant who believes he or she can improve the chances of being hired by answering practice interview questions is demonstrating an internal locus of control. External locus of control occurs when a person believes that he or she does not have any control over given situations and rewards, but views what will happen as a matter of fate, or as in the hands of powerful others (e.g., Rosolack & Hampson, 1991). "Externals" view themselves as something like a cork floating in the ocean, being tossed wherever the waves send them. A locus of control scale is included in the back of this chapter.

SELF-EFFICACY **Self-efficacy** refers to our beliefs that we can perform adequately in a given situation (Bandura, 1977). We must have skills to successfully perform tasks with competence, but we also need to have the conviction that we know how to implement these skills in an effective manner. The strength of our convictions regarding our effectiveness determines whether we even try to cope with difficult situations. We tend to fear and avoid threatening situations when we believe ourselves unable to handle them, but we forge ahead when we judge ourselves capable of successfully managing the situation. The degree of self-efficacy that one has regarding one's performance also influences one's feelings of locus of control.

Delay of Gratification **Delay of gratification** involves the postponement of an immediate reward in order to gain a future reward or benefit that is greater than the one available in the immediate present. The ability to delay gratification in the present in order to obtain a greater reward later is a sign of maturity. Any college student represents a person who is delaying gratification by deferring whatever income could be earned now without a college degree, as well as leisure time that could be enjoyed now, in order to strive toward a degree. Of course, the degree should eventually bring a higher salary and a more enjoyable work experience.

Empirical evidence for the importance of delay of gratification was provided by Mischel, Shoda, and Peake (1988), who found that children who showed a high ability to choose delayed gratification at ages four and five years old were more successful and better adjusted adolescents ten years later. A later investigation found the children who were best able to delay gratification at four years had higher Scholastic Aptitude Test (SAT) scores when they applied to college (Shoda, Mischel, & Peake, 1990).

Many responsible adult behaviors entail delay of gratification. Saving money for a house, college tuition, or retirement requires us to forego the pleasure of spending the money now. The ability to overcome bad habits requires control of impulses, in order to gain a longe-range aim while tolerating short-range discomfort or sacrifice.

Cognitive Behavior Therapy

One of the earliest cognitive therapies was the rational-emotive therapy (RET) developed by Albert Ellis (1973). Ellis believes that people become unhappy and develop self-defeating habits because of faulty beliefs they embrace. The task of RET is to restructure the individual's belief system and self-evaluation, especially with respect to the irrational "shoulds," "oughts," and "musts" that are preventing a more positive sense of self-esteem and a creative, emotionally satisfying life. These admonishments might be directed at oneself, as in "I should be more sociable" or toward others, as in thinking "My friends ought to call me more often."

Ellis speaks of the ABC's of emotional responses, as a way of explaining the relationship between outside "stressors," our thoughts or reactions to those stressors, and our subsequent feelings:

> A = *activating* event
> B = unrealistic *beliefs* (about the activating event)
> C = emotional *consequence* (of our beliefs)

Activating events are considered relatively "neutral" by Ellis, in that we have a variety of ways we could think about them. If our beliefs tend to be of a negative or **catastrophizing** nature, we can make ourselves miserable in response to activating events that others may experience as benign or even positive. Our emotions, then, are a result of or consequence of our unrealistic beliefs about the activating event and are not actually "caused" by the event itself. What is irrational is to attribute our emotions to the activating event, over which we have no control.

For example, consider this situation: You are away at college, living in the dorms. Your mother, who lives alone, has an arrangement with you whereby she calls you each Sunday night, so that you both can stay in touch. Things proceed smoothly for the first couple of months of the semester, and then one Sunday evening your mother doesn't call. It is now Monday morning. What do you think about this "activating event"?

Activating Event: "Mother didn't call as expected."

Possible Beliefs	Emotional Consequences
"She's sick."	worry; dread
"She's in danger."	fear; anguish
"She's angry with me."	guilt; annoyance
"She forgot about me."	sadness; forlorness
("She doesn't love me.")	
"She found something so entertaining to do that she forgot to call."	happiness; relief

Depending on which belief you construct about the activating event, you could feel happy or forlorn, annoyed or worried. Some people habitually form negative thoughts and essentially make themselves miserable much of the time. RET trains people to alter this bad habit so that they can be happier. As John Milton put it, "The mind is its own place, and in itself / Can make a heav'n of hell, a hell of heav'n." In general, it is not the events of our lives that upset us, but rather the meanings and interpretations that we give to these events (Ellis, 1992).

There are some beliefs that are so irrational that they naturally have the consequence of producing negative feelings. Some of these unrealistic beliefs are common enough that Ellis included them in a list of basic irrational beliefs:

1. One should be loved by everyone for everything one does.
2. Certain acts are awful or wicked, and people who perform them should be severely punished.
3. It is horrible when things are not the way we would like them to be.
4. Human misery is produced by external causes, or outside persons, or events rather than by the view that one takes of these conditions.
5. If something may be dangerous or fearsome, one should be terribly upset about it.
6. It is better to avoid life problems, if possible, than to face them.

7. One needs something stronger or more powerful than oneself to rely on.
8. One should be thoroughly competent, intelligent, and achieving in all respects.
9. Because something once affected one's life, it will indefinitely affect it.
10. One must have certain and perfect self-control.
11. Happiness can be achieved by inertia and inaction.
12. We have virtually no control over our emotions and cannot help having certain feelings.

Ellis recommends a variety of therapeutic techniques to help individuals overcome irrational beliefs. A person's false beliefs can be disputed through rational confrontation. An example of this would be to ask questions, such as Why should your fiancée's changing her mind about marrying you mean that you are worthless? Sometimes homework assignments are given in order to encourage clients to have new experiences and to break negative chains of behavior. Clients might be instructed to reward themselves by an external reinforcement such as a food treat after working fifteen minutes at disputing their beliefs. Clients might also be taught self-reinforcement through covert statements, such as "You are doing a really good job."

Although Albert Ellis clearly marked the route between thinking and emotion, he did not delineate the particular kinds of appraisal that lead to specific emotions. Aaron Beck set out to determine which types of thoughts lead to what emotional consequences. He was able to determine that sadness is an emotional response to the belief that one has sustained a loss of something valuable. This could be the loss of self-respect, friendship, a tangible object such as one's automobile, or disappointment over some anticipated good thing that is not fully meeting one's expectations. On the other hand, happiness or excitement result from the perception of gain or the anticipation of it. The expectation of gain might be in the form of a new friendship, new clothes or other things, or accomplishing a goal. Anxiety is produced by perceived threat to one's safety or psychological well-being. Perceived danger to some valued institution or principle will also produce anxiety. Examples of this might be threat of physical harm, serious illness, social rejection, or a serious economic setback.

Beck (1976) first became well known for his use of cognitive therapy with depressed clients. According to Beck, depressed people engage in distorted thinking that maintains their depression. These illogical ideas are maintained even in the face of contradictory evidence, because these individuals typically engage in self-defeating and self-fulfilling behaviors. Beck's cognitive model of depression emphasizes that depressed people systematically and mistakenly evaluate ongoing and past experiences, leading to a view of themselves as losers, the world as frustrating, and the future as bleak.

Since their thought processes are distorted, depressed clients are encouraged to test out their beliefs by gathering evidence for and against their convictions, to enable them to challenge the validity of their negative ideas. They are also encouraged to keep a thought diary, in which they write down their negative thoughts, to enable them to become aware of how prevalent negativity is in their thinking. With the aid of the thought diary, the therapist helps his or her depressed client to identify and challenge **all-or-nothing thinking**, **overgeneralizations** and **selective perception**, which are unproductive thought patterns that Beck has identified as characteristic of depressed persons. When an individual engages in all-or-nothing thinking, he or she is categorizing events as good or bad, right or wrong, black or white. This is similar to the dualistic thinking discussed by Perry (Chapter 5). In personalizing this type of thinking, the person might think "I am either a success or a failure." Overgeneralization occurs when the person takes a single instance of a setback and makes a hasty generalization, such as "Since I failed this one text, I am all washed up as a college student" or "I must be totally worthless, because I was laid off from my job." Selective perception is illustrated by a person who attends only to negative events, ignoring the positive ones that he or she has also experienced. In Chapter 12, more will be said about the thought processes of depressed people.

Not only have cognitive interventions been successful with those who are depressed, but also with a broad spectrum of mental disorders as well as with ordinary problems in living. Cognitive therapy provides a trunk full of strategies for handling the upsetting thoughts that are a central component of the experience of stress.

➤ COPING STRATEGIES: MELTING ICY PATCHES ON THE ROAD

Reactions to Stress

Stress triggers three harmful responses, which are *physiological effects, upsetting thoughts,* and *ineffective behavior.* A person's cognitive evaluation of a stressor affects his or her bodily response to it. Much of the immediate discomfort of stress is caused by the body's "fight or flight" emotional response. The body is ready to act, with tight muscles and a pounding heart. In addition, stress is greatly affected by the view that we take of events in our lives. If we have "catastrophizing" thoughts, in which we build a mountain out of a molehill, we increase our distress. We can likewise decrease our anxiety with positive coping statements, such as, "I'll take just one step at a time," "Tomorrow I'll be through it," or "Nobody's perfect—I'll just do my best." Finally, stress can be made worse by our behavioral response to it. Unfortunately, many people cope with stress through ineffective and even self-destructive behaviors.

QUESTION: *What are one effective and one ineffective behavior that you tend to employ when stressed?*

Coping can be defined as the ability to manage the demands of the situation or to change our appraisal of the situation. In dealing with a high level of stress, we can safeguard our health either by changing our lifestyle or by adjusting some of our mental attitudes. Often, the most effective intervention entails changing upsetting thoughts, since these generally are responsible for our ineffective behavior, as well as our interpretation of our physiological state. Our conclusions about a given situation have the potential to escalate physiological arousal even to the point of panic. The interpretation we make of our physiological state results in the experience of an emotion. Ultimately, all harmful side effects such as negative feelings and destructive behaviors are brought about by anxious thoughts and can therefore be alleviated with calming thoughts.

In general, we have three behavioral choices in coping with dissatisfying life situations (Levine, 1988). First, we may either change ourselves or *adapt*. For instance, we may change our attitudes about what we are doing. If we are having trouble turning in schoolwork because we want to turn in nothing less than a perfect assignment, we may have to modify our thinking so that we find it acceptable to turn in a "good enough" assignment. Second, we may change our environment, or *shape* it. An example of this would be a harried mother, who may convince her family members to each wash their own clothes. Our third choice is to escape the current situation by finding a new environment. Levine called this third choice *selection*. Changing jobs when dissatisfied would be an example of selection. See the exercise at the end of the chapter for practice in identifying these three coping alternatives.

These three coping strategies involve changes in thinking or behavior. An adaptation may take place at the level of our thoughts, which, in turn, affect our feelings. Cognitive psychologists often treat thoughts as covert behaviors. On the other hand, we may adapt by altering our outward behavior. The remaining two alternatives, shaping or escaping our environment, are, of course, overt behaviors.

Adaptation: Coping with the Physiological Effects of Stress

If we cannot escape the stressors in our lives, we can at least reduce the physical effects that they cause. Three good ways to reduce the physical effects of stress are *relaxation, meditation,* and *exercise.*

RELAXATION: A PAUSE IN THE JOURNEY   Although in this text we use the metaphor of a journey, we do not mean to imply that one must be perpetually on the move. To be still is a sweet sensation in the midst of a busy life. Learning to take time for naps, to practice yoga, to do relaxation exercises, to meditate, to lie or sit quietly, or in some other way to banish worries of the day has a beneficial effect on the immune system. The relaxation response can be induced by a variety of techniques, including concentrating on one's breathing, repeating over and over a word or phrase, or making a sound, such as humming

(Benson & Stuart, 1991). Some people benefit from cognitive therapy or self-hypnosis, to learn to calm tense thoughts as well as relax tense muscles.

Napping is a productive form of relaxation for people leading a high-stress life. Rewards reaped from napping include improvements in stamina and judgment. Naps should be scheduled before extreme fatigue sets in, as a means to gain refreshment. They should last no less than twenty minutes, or the sleeper may awaken more tired than before, and no longer than sixty minutes, to avoid the stupor of "sleep inertia" (Sobel, 1993).

It is not necessary to lose consciousness in order to rest. Many people enjoy taking breaks from work or study, and find that they can be more productive when they return refreshed. Benson and Stuart (1991) explained that relaxation is the opposite of the inherent "fight or flight" response to stress that keeps chronically pressured people on edge. Their studies showed that relaxing for a mere ten to twenty minutes once or twice a day could counter the ill effects of a hectic life. Subjects in their studies experienced drops in blood pressure, decreased anxiety, better sleep patterns, and heightened immunity to disease.

Relaxation training may be necessary for people who have trouble getting rid of tension. A "deep relaxation" approach was developed in 1938 by the physician Edmund Jacobson, who taught this approach to his patients. He was convinced that a variety of diseases that he was treating were produced by the state of chronic tension his patients were enduring in their lives. By instructing his patients alternately to tense and then to relax the major muscles in the body, beginning with their toes, then moving to their feet, calves, thighs, buttocks, back, and so on throughout the muscle groups of the body, Jacobson enabled them to experience the difference between relaxed and tense muscles. He reported that his patients displayed a reduction in both psychological and physical symptoms as a result of using his relaxation method. Jacobson's deep relaxation technique is used today in the treatment of migraine headaches, phobias, insomnia, hypertension, test anxiety, and Raynaud's disease. In a sample of forty-five elderly people living in retirement homes, those who learned to reduce stress with relaxation techniques showed significant increases in natural killer (NK) cell activity and decreases in antibodies to herpes simplex virus, both signs of improved immune activity (Kiecolt-Glaser et al., 1985).

TOUCHING   Another way to achieve muscle relaxation and the psychological tension relief that can accompany it is through massage. Massage is a technique for relaxing both body and mind (e.g., Field, 1998). Studies have demonstrated that physical contact is essential for healthy development of body and mind. Therapeutic touch is recognized as a valuable tool in healing and is often a part of training for nurses and other medical personnel. Massage techniques have been developed for boxers, wrestlers, and other athletes. Healthy changes take place in both the one doing the touching and the one being touched. Hugging is a special type of touch that can contribute to healing and health at all ages (Hanna, 1995).

Touching is important for developing in healthy ways physically, psychologically, socially, and intellectually. Harlow and Harlow (1966) found

that infant monkeys reared in isolation during the first six months after birth showed serious inadequacies in their social and sexual behavior later in life. Similarly, Jane Goodall (1990) reported that young chimpanzees very often pine away and perish after losing their mothers. These youngsters seem to need close contact with their mothers even when well past the age when they could fend for themselves. Human babies also experience touch communication very early in life. Starting at birth, we are held and caressed by our parents and other caretakers. Cuddling and rocking a baby is the traditional human technique to soothe the child to sleep. Touch is among our first pleasant experiences, as well as our first means of receiving affection. Not only is it an important aspect of nonverbal communication in infancy, but also it plays a powerful role in the remainder of our lives.

Touching can express a variety of meanings, including support, consolation, and sexual intimacy (DeVito, 1992). Women are more apt than men to touch the people with whom they interact (Stier & Hall, 1984), and women generally respond more favorably to touching than do men (Henley & Freeman, 1981). This gender difference may depend on the status of the touch initiator. Support for this interpretation comes from the finding that both women and men react favorably to touching when the person initiating the touch is higher in status than the recipient (Major, 1981). In one experiment, women who were about to have surgical operations reported less anxiety and displayed lower blood pressure when nurses touched them on the arm as they explained the procedures (Whitcher & Fisher, 1979). However, men treated in this manner were more anxious and displayed elevated blood pressure. This gender difference may have been due to the men's interpreting the touching as a threatening sign of the nurse's assuming control over them or as an unwanted sexual advance. Since higher-status people are more likely to touch subordinates than the other way around, the touching may have served as a status cue for the men in this study.

MEDITATION   Some people learn to relax through meditation, a practice aimed at focusing one's attention and eliminating all distracting thoughts. An altered state of consciousness is brought about through a narrowing of attention and restricting incoming stimuli. The meditator may intend either to achieve a state of deep relaxation or to be able to look differently at himself or herself and the world.

A meditative state is attained by sitting in a comfortable position in a quiet setting. The person adopts one of two strategies, concentration or mindfulness. When practicing concentrative meditation, the person focuses on an object (such as a flower or stone), a sound, or an event. In mindful meditation, thoughts and sensations (e.g., colors, odors, tactile experiences) are allowed to arise spontaneously into awareness. Regardless of the type of meditation practice, the purpose is to achieve relaxation and expanded awareness of the contents of consciousness (Delmonte, 1990; 1995).

Research studies have found no differences between meditation and simple resting in terms of physiological or emotional states (D. Holmes, 1984; Holmes et al., 1983). Those who meditate do seem to report psychological benefits. Refer to the accompanying box for a personal account of a meditation experience.

A MEDITATION EXPERIENCE

At the age of 20, I was introduced to the techniques of meditation. Until that time, I had thought that meditation was primarily a method of relaxation. But there is so much more behind it than simple relaxation, and so much more you can learn about yourself. Being alone with yourself and just feeling so complete and in balance with nature and life was and is one of the greatest feelings a person can have.

At the age of 21, I meditated at the beach in Spain. I remember feeling confused at the time; it took me two hours just to stop my mind from talking to myself. What happened next was the greatest and most influential feeling in my life, but it's not easy to explain with words and it may be not easy to understand.

It was a passive state of seeing and feeling, and I could see into my heart. I saw my soul, and in it, the magic of life and absolute love, and I have found it in myself. I've felt stronger than I've ever been in my life and for a few moments, I understood the world. I wish everyone could have such an experience, because it can make life worth living.

I am no longer afraid of dying, because what I have seen in myself can't ever die. I am a strong believer, not in a particular religion, but in what religion attempts to do for mankind. What I have in myself is surely in every person, but I guess most of them just don't know that it's there, that they're a part of everything and that God is within us.

Likewise, I believe that when you help a person in need, you are not only helping him or her but you are also helping yourself because this person is a part of you, as you are a part of him. So, believing in meditation and the power in oneself, doesn't focus my life only on me. I love people and I want to know everything about them; what they believe, what they have to say to the world about life and the magic it contains. Having close relationships with people makes me happy and gives me a feeling of security. So I try to talk to people and build up relationships as much as I can.

Reported by Richard Wormstall, Long Beach City College Student, May 11, 1998

EXERCISE: OPEN THROTTLE   Many people prefer an exercise break to a nap or meditation session as a form of relaxation. Physical exercise, such as jogging, dancing, biking, and swimming, is very important in maintaining health and reducing stress (Hayden, 1984; Taylor, 1986). Research has suggested that maintaining an active life is one of the most important factors in longevity (Terman & Oden, 1959). An invigorating workout can leave a person feeling refreshed, energetic, and relaxed.

Besides reducing emotional tension, exercise combats anxiety and depression. Ornstein and Sobel (1989) cited a study in which a group of patients with mild to moderate depression, who were randomly assigned either to jog or to receive psychotherapy. Within a few weeks, the depressed runners felt significantly better, and the benefits lasted at least a year. In addition, the joggers fared as well as the short-term psychotherapy patients. Medical researchers attribute these effects to the brain's exercise-induced release of substances called **endorphins,** which are the body's natural opiates, or painkillers. Endorphins also apparently induce the experiences of elation. This euphoria, known as the runner's high, stems from this internal cascade of chemicals brought on by the vigorous activity of jogging. In addition, norepinephrine levels, which are low in some depressed people, may increase with exercise and thus help improve mood (Ornstein & Sobel, 1989). However, those who think angry, competitive thoughts while they are exercising are, in effect, adding fuel to the fire (France, 1984).

Ornstein and Sobel (1989) reported that in a long-term study of approximately 1,700 Harvard University alumni, health benefits were found for those who burned up as few as 500 calories a week. Another study, of 1,200 middle-aged men, revealed that those who used of 1,600 calories a week in leisure activities had nearly 40 percent fewer fatal heart attacks than did those who used less than 500 calories a week. In this same study, those who were physically active for more than two hours per day did not realize any further health benefits in terms of decreased deaths from heart disease.

Adaptation: Coping with Upsetting Thoughts

One way of coping with problems is to think about them in new ways. "The art of soothing ourselves is a fundamental life skill; some psychoanalysts such as John Bowlby and D. W. Winnicott see this as one of the most essential of all psychic tools" (Goleman, 1995 p. 57). One method of soothing ourselves is by **reframing** the problem situation. Reframing, which involves intentionally finding a new way to look at the problematic situation, has three goals: First, the person needs to find meaning in the experience. Essentially, you are asking, Why did this happen to me? or What does it mean for my life now? For instance, many people like to think of setbacks as "lessons" or "learning experiences." Second, a person facing a life crisis will need to regain mastery over both the event itself and his or her life. A person asks himself or herself questions, such as, How can I keep

Exercise Boosts Your Stress Resistance

this from happening again? or What can I do about it now? Finally, the individual needs to restore self-esteem, to feel good about himself or herself again in spite of the setback.

When people cannot eliminate a stressor, they can choose to rethink its implications and consequences. An example might be that losing a job gives one the motivation to find another, possibly more suitable one. Another instance of this is that reframing the motive behind the negative behavior of another person can change anger into acceptance. The aloof, standoffish behavior of a classmate might be seen as timidity, for instance. In the accompanying box you will find a story entitled, Good or Bad, Which Is It? which epitomizes the reframing coping strategy.

GOOD OR BAD, WHICH IS IT?

Once upon a time, there was a Chinese farmer who had just one horse, and one day the horse got out of the corral and ran away. The people in the village gathered around the farmer and sympathized with his loss. They said, "What bad luck!" But the farmer, who was older and wiser than many of the village people, answered, "Who knows? Maybe it is bad luck and maybe it isn't." The very next day the horse returned, followed by twelve wild horses. When all the horses were safely in the corral, the villagers came again and said, "What good luck you have had, old man!" But the farmer replied, "Maybe it is and maybe it isn't."

A few days later the farmer's only son was riding one of the wild horses and was thrown off. In the fall he broke his leg. The ever-present villagers wailed, "Oh, what bad luck you are having!" The old man just smiled and said, "Maybe and maybe not. How do you know it is bad luck?"

A few weeks passed and one day a Chinese war lord came riding through the village and drafted all the able-bodied young men, taking them off to fight in his little war. The farmer's son could not be taken because of his broken leg, and he lived a long, happy life on his father's farm.

That Chinese farmer was a very wise man, indeed! He truly believed that all things work out for good in the end, so he could face his good days and his bad days with calmness and faith.

Next time you are about to say or think, "That is good luck," or "Why did this happen to me?" just remember that everybody has some dark days, as well as lots of bright, happy days.

Source: Adapted from *Unconditional Life* by Deepak Chopra, pp. 49–50. Copyright © 1991 by Bantam Books.

THE FAR SIDE   By GARY LARSON

"You know, we're just not reaching that guy."

Social Comparisons We define ourselves and our situation in part by making comparisons with others. A reliable way to feel better fast is to compare ourselves with someone who is worse off than we are (Dermer, et al., 1979). People tend to cope with personal inadequacies by making comparisons with others who are less happy, less able, less successful, or less fortunate than themselves (Hakmiller, 1966; Pyszczynski et al., 1985; Wills, 1981). Such a reaction is referred to by psychologists as a downward comparison. Research by Gibbons (1986) found that the moods of mildly depressed subjects improved after they had read about the misfortunes of an accident victim. In the same way, when people in a depressed mood read about someone who is even more depressed, they feel somewhat better (Gibbons, 1986).

Those who are experiencing stressful life events, such as a crime, an accident, a disease, or the death of a loved one, often cope by making downward comparisons. Under these circumstances, people can benefit from keeping in mind that things could be worse. Among women who have had breast cancer, those who had lumpectomies (removal of the lump) compared themselves with women who had the whole breast removed and then felt better about their situation. Breast cancer patients may actively seek to compare themselves with others who are not adjusting well to the same illness (Taylor et al., 1983; J. V. Wood et al., 1985). Most of us have woes that fall far short of the threat of terminal illness, in which case, there are a wide range of comparisons to select from that will enable us to feel better about practically any situation.

Humor Martin & Lefcourt (1983) found that humor makes an excellent buffer between stress and negative moods. They demonstrated that although an abundance of negative life events predicted high levels of stress in college students, those students who mustered up humor in difficult situations were less affected by negative life events than were other students. People who can laugh at terrible news by transforming it into a sense of the absurd or the funny are less prone to depression, anger, tension, and fatigue than are people who give in to gloom.

Some theories of laughter emphasize its ability to reduce tension. Laughter can also help a person let go of negative emotions such as anxiety, fear, hostility, anger, and embarrassment (Long, 1987). Other theories emphasize the cognitive components of humor. The benefits of humor might be explained by its resulting in an abrupt cognitive shift, with an accompanying emotional change. When you laugh at a problem, you are putting it in a new perspective—seeing its silly aspects—and gaining control over it (Dixon, 1980).

There is evidence that laughter produces some beneficial biological responses, possibly stimulating the immune system or starting the flow of endorphins, the painkilling chemicals in the brain that were mentioned earlier (Cousins, 1991; Fry, 1986; Goldstein, 1987). A study in Canada found links between laughter and improved immune function, cardiovascular tone, and pain endurance (Pennebaker, 1991). As with physical exercise, laughter activates various internal organs through its vibrations and other movements. Fry (1986) estimated that thirty seconds of hearty laughter may even be equivalent breathing exercise to three minutes of rowing.

TRANSCENDING ONE'S OWN SITUATION   A person can be encouraged to turn the focus away from himself or herself. A psychologist who has worked with Holocaust survivors, prisoners of war, hostages, refugees, and other survivors of catastrophe believes that a key element in their recovering is compassion, "healing through helping" (Segal, 1986). Perhaps people gain strength by giving it to others.

Shaping

Whether or not you feel overwhelmed by the stress in your life will be influenced by your sense of being able to control it. People who feel that they are in charge of their lives often deal more effectively with problems and decisions than people who lack this sense of mastery. Extensive research has shown that having a feeling of personal control predicts happiness with one's life in general (Chapter 14).

Those who believe that they control their own destiny are considered to have an internal locus of control, whereas those who feel that chance or outside forces determine their fate are thought to have an external locus of control. "Internals" adjust their coping efforts to suit the problem, selecting the appropriate tactic from a range of possibilities (Parkes, 1984). Those who see themselves as internally controlled are more likely to do well in school, successfully stop smoking, wear seat belts, practice birth control, deal with marital problems directly, make lots of money, and delay gratification in order to achieve long-term goals (e.g., Findly & Cooper, 1983; Lefcourt, 1982; Miller et al., 1986). People who have an external locus of control feel powerless and tend to respond to stress with anger, depression, drug use, or physical symptoms (Langer, 1983). Negative emotions, pessimism, poor health habits, and an inability to cope may be related to not feeling in control of one's life.

Shaping: Attacking the Problem

In handling any stressful situation, both the emotions arising from the situation and the situation itself must be dealt with. Managing the emotions that a problem has caused is sometimes referred to as "emotion-focused coping." "Problem-focused coping," on the other hand, attacks the problem itself. We have discussed how emotional responses to stressful situations can be handled. For attacking the problem itself, having a general problem-solving model should be helpful. Following is a model that would be a useful tool to learn (Halpern, 1989).

A GENERAL PROBLEM-SOLVING MODEL   Of course, problem recognition is the first step in the problem-solving process. A problem cannot be solved if we deny that one exists. Sometimes the problem is clear, and sometimes it is uncertain. For example, problems that exist in relationships are generally not well-structured problems. They can be messy, persistent, and hard to identify. When people perpetually fight over the same issue, it is often because the problem is being defined by each participant in a different way (Sternberg, 1991). Each person is stuck in his or her own perception of what the problem is. Unless the participants can reach a point of agreement in their perceptions, it will not be possible for them to articulate a common problem and thus act to find a solution. The first step in problem solving when another person is involved is to examine it from each participant's points of view.

If the problem is ill-defined, try to restate it. In making a statement about the problem, we should do well to take a positive approach by viewing it as a challenge that must be addressed or a goal that must be achieved. The way the problem is expressed is an important step in the problem-solving process, since the way a issue is articulated determines the manner in which it will be addressed.

All problems can be viewed as having the same general structure. The general model starts with the *present state* or "what is" (Newell & Simon, 1972). Determination of the present state includes listing the "givens," that is, the information and rules that place constraints on the problem. This is not necessarily the best place to start solving a problem; sometimes working backward is more helpful.

The *goal state* must also be determined. This is "where we want to end up." Make sure the goal is clear. It is sometimes a good idea to broaden our goal as much as possible. For example, the goal "to lose weight" is broader than "to go on a diet," since a person can lose weight either by eating less or by exercising more. Also, How can I save money? can be changed to How can I have more money?

The *problem space* is the gap between the present state and the goal state. What is put into the problem space are the *solution paths*, which are the alternative solutions to the problem. In solving a problem (getting to the goal state from the initial state), people search through the problem space to find the best path. Sometimes the problem is the apparent absence of paths to the goal. When this absence occurs, a "brainstorming" procedure is used. Brainstorming, which can be done individually or in a group, consists of generating as many ideas as possible, without initially evaluating them as to their viability. It is important to put off the critiquing process, so that the idea generation will be as uninhibited as possible. In fact, wild and crazy ideas are entirely welcome, because they are likely to be creative and may contain useful ideas. After the flow of ideas has ceased, then an evaluation of the solution paths can begin. Sometimes the problem is deciding which of several paths is the best one to take. When solving a problem, we transform the given information into solution paths.

In problem solving, there are stages. *Familiarization* involves spending time understanding the nature of the problem, the goal, and the givens. During the *production stage*, solution paths are produced. The solution paths are judged during the *evaluation stage.* If we can't find a solution, the next step may be *incubation.* Incubation is a poorly understood but widely employed strategy that involves reviewing all the parameters of a problem and then putting the problem "on the back burner" so that we aren't focusing on it any longer. In this way, our mind is free to ponder the matter during moments of leisure and to notice possible solutions pertaining to the problem being incubated when we happen across them in our unrelated activities of the day. For practice in working with this model, turn to the exercise, A General Model for Problem Solving, at the end of this chapter.

Shaping: Getting Organized

Sometimes we are so busy that we feel we don't have time to plan, but in fact, no matter how busy we are, we should find it worthwhile to take time to plan our activities. Perhaps we don't have time to plan *and* do absolutely everything else we would like to get done. Yet, by neglecting to plan, we will free very little time; and by failing to plan, we shall probably not discriminate among the essential and nonessential activities. If we spend only ten minutes at the beginning or end of the day planning, our efforts will be repaid many times over. The less time we feel we have to spare, the more important it is to plan our time carefully.

Planning and making choices involve careful thinking and decision making. In the process, we learn to recognize what criteria we use in setting priorities. In all types of planning, we make lists and set priorities. A most useful planning strategy is to make a daily "To Do" list. Not all of the items on the list are of equal value. Once we have made a list, we need to set priorities on the basis of what is important to us on this particular day.

To make this task easier, we can use an ABC Priority System. Write a capital letter *A* next to those items on the list that have a high value, a *B* for those with medium value, and a *C* for those with a low value. As we do this, we'll be using our subjective opinion as to the relative value of each item. By comparing the items with one another, we'll help ourselves come up with the ABC priority choices for each entry on the list. If it seems necessary, the activities can be broken down further so that A-items become A-1, A-2, and A-3.

Our ABC priorities may change over time. Today's C may become tomorrow's A. For instance, grocery shopping may be a C activity for awhile, but eventually the cupboards become bare. Our priorities can be adjusted continually, according to the best use of our time right now. If we start with our A activities and always do them first, we can rest assured that we'll always be making the best use of our time. Our C activities may *never* get done, if they do not become more urgent with the passage of time. That's okay! If we chronically have more activities on our list than we can manage to get done, we may eventually discard some C items, realizing that we are simply too busy to get to them.

"To Do" lists are most effective when made each day, when the items are prioritized in an ABC fashion and when items are crossed off as each task is completed. The list should be kept in sight, so that we can look at it several times a day. We can make a game out of trying to plan just the right amount of activities for each day so that we can score a "bingo" at the end of each day. The bingo means that all of the items for the day get crossed off. It's a good idea to get started on top priority items right away before any unexpected events of the day crop up and interfere with our plan. Toward the end of the day, we can initiate whatever actions are necessary to finish up our "bingo card" for a perfect score (Lakein, 1973).

One of the important strategies to keep in mind is that getting panicky is never productive. It's amazing how much can be accomplished when one keeps plugging away, making little bits of progress toward the finish line. Be calm, and be relentless in your efforts.

Shaping: Seeking Social Support

There is a close relationship between close relationships and health, both mental and physical. The "individualism" of Western culture is implicated in the high incidence of depression in our society (Seligman, 1988). Personal identity is the focus today. We admonish people not to compromise themselves by getting too close to other people. However, excessive individualism makes for a life vulnerable to loneliness and depression. The more individual our pursuits, the more we are separated from social support, and social support has been shown to be a prime factor in the maintenance of psychological and physical health. Today, people are lonelier, more homicidal, more likely to divorce, and more likely to live alone than were their grandparents. In 1940, eight percent of adult Americans lived alone, whereas, in 1988, 24 percent of adult Americans lived alone (Myers, 1991). Close relationships, in which there is self-disclosure, predict happiness. Love and marriage are predictors of mental and physical health.

WHAT SOCIAL SUPPORT PROVIDES   Individuals may seek social support for emotional and instrumental reasons. Most of us find that it helps to talk to someone about how we feel. We receive sympathy and understanding, and might ourselves come to better understand our situation. We may also seek pragmatic advice about what to do. For this purpose, we ask people who have had similar experiences what they did. In turning to others, we may also find someone who can do something concrete about the problem we face.

MARITAL STATUS AND LONGEVITY   There is substantial evidence that marriage is correlated with longer life (e.g., House, Robbins, & Metzner, 1982; Hu & Goldman, 1990; Kotler & Wingard, 1989). This finding is often viewed as a protective effect of the social support of marriage. "Get married" appears on many lists of health recommendations. However, marriage brings the risk of divorce. Death of spouse, divorce, and marital separation are the top three most stressful events on the Social Readjustment Rating Scale, and there seems little doubt that marital dissolution is the most significant common social stressor in American society (with the possible exception of abject poverty). In addition, it is possible that an unstable marital history is the result of other psychological and behavioral problems rather than itself being a primary cause of premature mortality.

Researchers Friedman et al. (1995) followed up on Stanford Professor Louis Terman's (Terman & Oden, 1947) sample of gifted children who were subjects in one of the most famous longitudinal studies ever conducted by psychologists. A longitudinal study follows a group of people through time to note what changes take place as they age. In 1922, Terman embarked on a study of 1,528 California schoolchildren, whose average IQ score was 150. Terman's subjects have been kept track of since they were around age ten, and they will be studied until the last one dies. Friedman and his colleagues collected death certificates for the half of the sample that is now dead, and analyzed longevity and cause of death as a function of parental divorce during childhood, unstable marriage patterns in adulthood, childhood personality, adult adjustment, and possible mediating health behaviors. Psychosocial factors emerged as important risks for premature mortality.

Friedman found that the inconsistently married people were at higher risk for early death than the steadily married people and that the currently separated, widowed, or divorced people were at an even higher risk. Not only did those who were divorced tend to have shorter life spans, but so did those whose parents had divorced when the Terman subjects were children. In addition, the two life events had a cumulative effect, so that the Terman subjects who had experienced both a parental divorce and their own divorce had shorter life spans than either of the groups of subjects who experienced only parental divorce or their own. In addition, the negative health consequences of divorce are not erased by remarriage.

The consistently married Terman subjects had the fewest adjustment problems, a finding that could also mean that those with the fewest mental difficulties were most likely to remain married. Still, when level of adjustment was factored out of the analysis, it did not eliminate the relation between marital history and longevity. In other words, although mental adjustment seemed to play a role in poor health, a significant detrimental effect of divorce remained, even after taking psychological health in 1950 into account.

Whereas a stable marriage history is associated with increased longevity, getting married to promote health is not only impractical but also unjustified (Friedman et al., 1995). However, learning the social skills that foster close personal relationships should promote health and happiness.

LATINO LONGEVITY   The Latino culture stresses the importance of family, the maintenance of a work ethic, the role of religion, and the formation of community. These lifestyle factors may be play a role in the remarkable longevity enjoyed by the average Latino. Whereas an Anglo baby born in Los Angeles County has a life expectancy of 73.9 years (both sexes combined), a Latino baby has a life expectancy of 78.0 years, nearly four years longer (Hayes-Bautista, 1997). Elderly Latinos in this country have lower death rates than Anglos for heart disease, cancer, stroke, pneumonia, homicide, suicide, and cirrhosis. Latinos die of such causes at a rate nearly 40 percent lower than that of Anglos, except for diabetes. In Latinos, Type II diabetes (which does not require insulin injections) is apparently genetically based.

This health advantage of Latinos is not due to the result of greater use of hospitals and doctors. In 1990, the average Anglo senior generated $13,800 in hospital charges, whereas a comparable Latino generated $3,600. Even though Latino senior citizens use hospitals less, they live longer and fewer die of heart disease, cancer, or strokes.

For elderly Latinos, working longer, and thus retiring at an older age, is a way of life. The percentage of Latinos working past the standard retirement age of 65 far exceeds that of Anglos. Although they work more, they are more likely than Anglos to live in poverty and thus are more likely to lean on other family members. In Los Angeles County, 21 percent of the Latino seniors receive cash income from their adult children, whereas only 2 percent of elderly Anglos receive financial assistance from their adult children. The fact that Latinos in Los Angeles are more than twice as likely as Anglos to marry and have children may have some impact. Latino parents make personal sacrifices for their children, which seem to pay off in the form of productive and appreciative children. Today's working-age U.S.-born Latinos are 80 percent less likely to live in poverty than their parents.

Berkeley epidemiologist Len Syme has concluded that one's family and social networks are the best predictors of health status. Nearly a century ago, Emil Durkeim found that people with active family relationships were less likely to commit suicide. Stanford researcher Marilyn Winkleby has found that though Anglo adults demonstrate better knowledge of diet and nutrition than Latino adults, the latter tend to have healthier eating habits. Latino meals are richer in vegetables and legumes, as well as leaner in meats.

A religious life is another promoter of longer life. Compared with Anglo seniors, Latinos are twice as likely to be a member of an organized church. They are also twice as likely to attend weekly church services, and their church of choice tends to be Roman Catholic. Religious observance can reduce stress by, among other things, promoting a sense of belonging.

Selection (Escape)

Sometimes stress can be dealt with by modifying or removing its source. We can do this either by shaping our current environment or by moving to a new one. Sometimes the most reasonable way to cope with stressful situations in life is to leave them. We may simply decide to find a new job, a new neighborhood in which to live, even a new set of friends to enjoy. Many times, this is the most drastic of the three coping strategies, so we reserve it as a last resort. Certainly, if we were to find ourselves consistently selecting a new environment whenever problems arise, we might want to expand our assortment of coping strategies to include the other two.

DENIAL OR AVOIDANCE   Once we have all the necessary information to make a decision and that decision is out of our hands, letting go of worry is an excellent coping device. However, vigilance is called for when action is possible and necessary.

Use of denial as a defense against the pain of some life event can be either beneficial or destructive to the individual, depending on the situation. When direct coping behaviors are necessary to minimize harm, denial tends to make the situation worse (Lazarus, 1985). For instance, ignoring signs that one might need medical attention could prove fatal, and tragically so, if the problem is treatable. Likewise, if the stressful event is likely to be recurring, the person's denial will prevent the development of coping behaviors that would come in handy when the experience is repeated.

As mentioned earlier (Chapter 4), denial is sometimes employed when individuals receive news of terminal illness. In cases such as this, when the person's coping resources are likely to be inadequate for handling the full enormity of the crisis, denial can be helpful in "breaking the fall." On occasion, there are other times in life when nothing can been done about a problem situation. The skill to be developed here is in learning to recognize whether active coping efforts are appropriate in the situation, and if not, how to "let go," so that you don't endlessly ruminate about the problem. If, for instance, your kid brother is going to marry an absolute witch, but is of legal age to do so, and has turned a deaf ear to your warnings, you are in one of those situations where a passive stance is warranted.

Cultural Influences on Coping Strategies

In a research study comparing the coping styles of Caucasian American and Asian American college students, Chang (1996) discovered that Asians used problem avoidance and social withdrawal strategies more than do Caucasians. There were, however no significant differences between the two groups in the use of problem solving, cognitive restructuring, expressing emotions, seeking social support, self-criticizing, or wishful thinking.

➤ PERSONALITY FACTORS RELATED TO COPING

The Case for Selecting a New Environment

Psychologists who endorse the dispositional approach to studying personality development emphasize the stability of personality over time and across situations. Some of the rudiments of personality are thought to be biologically based. Thus, personality change is difficult, if not impossible. To help a person adjust, the dispositional psychologist looks for a life situation for which the person is already suited by virtue of his or her enduring characteristics. This viewpoint contrasts with that of clinicians, who often try to change the person to fit the situation that he or she is in.

Personality and Longevity

The Big Five personality dimensions were discussed in the last chapter (Chapter 7). The first dimension, extroversion, was generally thought by theorists and researchers to correlate with health. Resilient personalities were also considered to be emotionally stable and optimistic, whereas aggressive, excitable, impulsive, and neurotic people were thought to be prone to disease and mortality.

  The Terman study was used to shed some light on this matter (Terman & Oden, 1947; 1959). Terman and Oden collected ratings of personality traits of their 10-year-old subjects from the parents and teachers. Friedman and his colleagues (1995) constructed six personality dimensions from these ratings and used them to predict longevity and cause of death through 1986. The results were that childhood social dependability or conscientiousness predicted longevity. "Children, especially boys, who were rated as prudent, conscientious, truthful, and free from vanity . . . lived significantly longer. They were about 30% less likely to die in any given year" (p. 72). Furthermore, this increased longevity was not primarily due to a reduction in the risk of injury, as might be expected. Although there was some tendency for the unconscientious to be more likely to die a violent death, conscientiousness also lessened the likelihood of an early death from cardiovascular disease or cancer. Even though unhealthy behaviors explained some of the effect, the significant effect of conscientiousness remained after controlling for drinking and for smoking and other aspects of personality.

In the same study, no evidence was found that sociability or other aspects of extroversion were strongly related to health and longevity. Although the traits of neurotics, such as emotional instability, depression, and hostility, are thought to be correlated with poor health, in the Terman sample, the findings were mixed. For men, there was some tendency for emotional stability (as rated in childhood) to be related to increased longevity. In 1950, the Terman subjects were asked about tendencies toward nervousness, anxiety, or nervous breakdown. On the basis of this and previously related information dating back a decade, Terman categorized each on a 3-point scale from "satisfactory adjustment," to "some maladjustment," or "serious maladjustment." Almost one-third of this group of gifted adults experienced at least some mental difficulty at this point in their lives. For men, level of adjustment in 1950 predicted mortality risk through 1991, but this finding was not true for women. Poorly adjusted men were more likely to die from all causes investigated (cardiovascular disease, cancer, injury, or other diseases). There was a slight tendency for poorly adjusted men to die more from injury (including suicide), as well as from cardiovascular disease.

The Hardy Person

Suzanne Kobasa (1979) studied business executives who resisted illness while handling heavy workloads that would be expected to produce considerable stress. The researchers looked for differences among those executives who succumbed to illness and those who did not. They found that the hardy individuals differed in three ways: (1) They had a great deal of *commitment* to what they were doing; (2) they expected the *challenge* that they found in their work and found it stimulating; and (3) they had an internal *locus of control* (Kobasa, Maddi, & Kahn, 1982). They did not feel alienated, powerless, or threatened by their problems.

It seems that hardy people are less stressed by what is going on around them, because they believe that they have chosen to be in the situation and therefore feel in control of what is happening to them. They welcome the situation as a manifestation of what makes life interesting. If things were to get overwhelming, they perceive that they could exert some control over the situation or could successfully employ coping mechanisms, and thus they would be okay (Maddi & Kobasa, 1984).

A subsequent study looked at whether or not two other known buffers against the harmful effects of stress, exercise and social support, could be combined with hardiness to produce an especially potent effect in illness reduction among executives (Kobasa et al., (1985). When all three factors were present, the level of illness dropped dramatically.

More recently, psychologist Martin Seligman (1998) added to the qualities found in hardy persons. He included the following factors as human strengths that function as great preventatives, or protectors against mental disorders such as depression and excessive anxiety: courage, optimism, self-understanding, flow, a work ethic, hope, and rationality. We shall see that these are some of the same personal attributes that predict happiness in life (Chapter 14).

➤ INEFFECTIVE BEHAVIOR: SPEEDING UP ON THE ROAD'S ICY PATCHES

You probably already know the basic rules for protecting your health before reading any further. They are as follows:

1. Get enough sleep. (Most people require about eight hours of sleep per night.)
2. Get regular exercise.
3. Eat a nutritious diet.
4. Drink alcohol only in moderation.
5. Do not overeat.
6. Do not go on starvation diets.
7. Do not smoke cigarettes (or anything else).

Large numbers of Americans already know a great deal about how to stay healthy. A ten-year longitudinal study of nearly 7,000 people in Alameda County, California, found that each of the listed practices was independently related to good health and lack of stress symptoms (Matarazzo, 1984; Wiley & Camacho, 1980). The more of these practices that people followed, the better was their mental and physical health. It's perplexing to realize that although people know what is good for them, they often don't practice it. There are probably many reasons for this neglect. For one thing, many health habits are entrenched in childhood. It will be hard for someone to give up a high-cholesterol diet if the person associates it with home-cooked meals. People often have little incentive to change unhealthy habits. Smoking, drinking, eating junk food, and not exercising have no immediate negative consequences, and their effects might not become apparent for years.

Unfortunately, many people cope with stress through ineffective and even self-destructive behaviors. They may resort to the overuse of alcohol, cigarettes, or drugs. They may fall into other addictions, such as work, shopping, food, sex, sleep, exercise, and dependency on the company of other people. Notice that sleep and exercise are mentioned as both positive and negative coping strategies. Even healthy behaviors, such as engaging in a sexual relationship, can be transformed from a positive to a negative coping mechanism when practiced in excess and in a compulsive fashion. To assess your positive and negative coping mechanisms, turn to the back of this chapter, and complete the How Healthy Is My Lifestyle exercise.

Alcohol has been around since 2700 B.C. It was used to reward the pyramid builders in ancient Egypt, and has been an occupational hazard on construction sites ever since that time (Livingston, 1998). Alcohol consumption, which was seven gallons per capita per year in 1830, had decreased fourfold by 1990. Drinking is involved in 90 percent of deaths from cirrhosis, 50 percent of fatal car crashes, 50 percent of all murders, 40 percent of violent crimes (murders, rapes, sexual assaults, robberies and assaults), 20 to 30 percent of all suicides, and 40 percent of all admissions to mental institutions (Livingston, 1998; Reuters, 1997). According to essayist Ann Taylor Flemming (1997), college students spend more money on alcohol than on soft drinks and textbooks combined.

Cannabis, the active ingredient in marijuana, has been used for 10,000 years. The ancient Chinese used it for medicinal purposes, and George Washington grew cannabis on his plantation. It was declared illegal in 1937. There have been no reported deaths from marijuana.

Although the chemical alteration of one's brain chemistry is undeniably pleasant in the short run, regular use leads to chemical dependency. This is a highly undesirable state of affairs, because the need for the substance begins to interfere with normal functioning, and an increasingly greater proportion of one's waking life begins to revolve around procurement of the drug of choice. Substance dependence is considered by psychologists to exist if three or more of these criteria are met in the same 12-month period: (1) tolerance occurs (more and more of the substance is needed to produce the original effect); (2) withdrawal occurs (physiological repercussions when the drug is discontinued); (3) use is more or longer than intended; (4) the person desires or has made an effort to cut down; (5) the individual spends time getting, using and/or recovering from the substance; (6) the person gives up activities in order to continue using; and (7) the individual continues to use the drug regardless of the negative consequences.

➤ WELLNESS: A STURDY VEHICLE ON A SMOOTH, DRY STRIP OF ROAD

Travis and Ryan (1988), in their *Wellness Workbook*, include in their concept of wellness a decision to move toward optimal health by adopting a way of life designed to achieve one's highest potential for well-being. The individual has developed an awareness that health and happiness are possible in each moment, though the person doesn't arrive at an endpoint where these desirable ends are achieved once and for all. An integration of body, mind, and spirit—the appreciation that everything we do, think, feel, and believe—has an impact on our state of health. Finally, wellness comes from a loving acceptance of ourselves.

The Menninger Clinic (1996) proposes that optimal well-being is achieved through "emotional maturity," which consists of (1) the ability to deal constructively with reality, (2) the capacity to adapt to change, (3) the relative freedom from symptoms that are produced by tensions and anxieties, (4) the capacity to find more satisfaction in giving than receiving, (5) the capacity to relate to other people in a consistent manner with mutual satisfaction and helpfulness, (6) the capacity to sublimate, to direct one's instinctive hostile energy into creative and constructive outlets, and (7) the capacity to love. It seems that the "royal road" to physical well-being is through the psyche.

Schafer (1992), who wrote *Stress Management for Wellness*, believes that wellness is acquired and maintained by healthful daily habits, some of which are sleep, diet, exercise, ways of dealing with anger and tension, work satisfaction, and the presence of energizing visions for oneself and the world. Schafer suggested that we allow ourselves to have visions and dreams, some of which have social significance or will benefit others in significant ways. We reap health benefits when we work individually, as well as with others, to make these dreams a reality.

➤ SUMMARY

Stress has been characterized in two ways: (1) as exposure to life events that require adaptation and (2) as a state that occurs when persons perceive that demands on them exceed their abilities to cope. Health psychologists have found that stress and other psychological factors influence the immune system's ability to do its job of keeping the body healthy.

GENERAL ADAPTATION SYNDROME   Hans Selye noticed that the first symptoms of almost any disease or trauma are almost identical. He called this nonspecific, physiological response to any stimulus "stress." According to Selye, the body's response to stress occurs in three stages, which together make up the general adaptation syndrome: In the *Alarm Stage*, the body mobilizes its resources to cope with stressors. During the *Stage of Resistance*, the symptoms of the alarm stage reaction disappear as the body's defenses are stabilized. Finally, in the *Stage of Exhaustion*, the body's resources are exhausted. Continued exposure to the stressor will lead to psychosomatic illness, organ collapse, or even death.

SOCIAL READJUSTMENT RATING SCALE   Holmes and Rahe's attempt to link stress and health produced the Social Readjustment Rating Scale. It contained "life change units," which were positive and negative events believed to place demands on people to adjust. This rating scale was developed in an effort to quantify the relationship between stress and illness or accidents. Perhaps the most important limitation in the approach taken by Holmes and Rahe was that people vary in their subjective reactions to stressors as well as in their coping ability. It is not only important what happens to people but also how they view the event that determines how stressful they experience their lives to be. An individual with effective coping strategies and a reliable social support system can be expected to fare better than a person without them, when both are exposed to the same external stressors.

TYPE A BEHAVIOR PATTERN   Another early attempt to identify the relationship between a psychological state and a physical ailment was provided by Friedman and Rosenman who classified people as having either Type A or Type B behavior patterns. Type A people are those who are hard-driving, ambitious, highly competitive, achievement-oriented, and hostile when encountering obstacles. People with this pattern of behavior were thought to run a high risk of heart attack. Type B people (who are unlikely to have a heart attack) lead a more relaxed lifestyle but aren't necessarily unproductive. They are calmer and able to have fun without feeling guilty.

Subsequent research distinguished between two subtypes of Type A individuals, the "healthy charismatics," who are expressive, active, friendly, and relaxed, and the "hostile competitives," who are angry, tense, and defensive. Research also indicates that faster-paced environments may predispose individuals to exhibit Type A behavior.

BEHAVIORISM   In 1913, John B. Watson began the behaviorist revolution by proposing that psychology should limit itself to the study of behavior. Behaviorists view people as being shaped by the rewards and punishments received from their environments. The second major figure in the development of behaviorism is B. F. Skinner, who applied Watson's ideas and developed one of the most impressive technologies of behavioral change the world has ever known.

SOCIAL LEARNING THEORY   As with behaviorism, social learning theory concludes that the ways people think, act, and feel are the result of past learning. However, not only is a person's behavior influenced by its past consequences but also by that person's future expectations of success or failure. Three types of beliefs that are central to learning theory are *locus of control, self-efficacy,* and *delay of gratification*. Locus of control refers to the person's beliefs regarding how much control he or she has over given situations and reinforcement. Those with an internal locus of control believe that they have some control over their lives, whereas those with an external locus of control believe what will happen in life is a matter of fate or is in the hands of powerful others. Self-efficacy refers to a person's belief that he or she can perform adequately in a given situation. Delay of gratification refers to the ability to postpone an immediate reward in order to obtain a future reward that is greater than the one available in the immediate present.

COGNITIVE BEHAVIOR THERAPY   Albert Ellis, who developed rational-emotive therapy, believed that people become unhappy and develop self-defeating habits because of faulty beliefs. Ellis' ABC model of emotional responses explains the relationship between outside "stressors," the thoughts or reactions to those stressors, and the subsequent feelings: A stands for an *activating* event, B refers to the unrealistic *belief* that is sometimes formed about the activating event, and C stands for the emotional *consequence* of the belief. Cognitive therapists helps people restructure their belief system (the B level in the ABC system) in order to promote a more emotionally satisfying life. Aaron Beck identified specific beliefs that produce particular emotional consequences.

REACTIONS TO STRESS   Stress produces *physiological effects, upsetting thoughts,* and *ineffective behaviors.* All three responses can be handled through healthy coping mechanisms. In general, people have three choices in coping with dissatisfying situations in life. First, they may change themselves or *adapt.* Second, they may change their environment, or *shape* it. Their third choice is to *escape* the current situation by selecting a new environment.

ADAPTATION: COPING WITH THE PHYSIOLOGICAL EFFECTS   If individuals cannot escape the stressors in their lives, they can at least reduce the effects produced by their physical response to those stressors. Three good ways to reduce the physical effects of stress are *relaxation, meditation,* and *exercise.*

ADAPTATION: COPING WITH UPSETTING THOUGHTS   People can adapt to stressful events by rethinking the problem situation. Some of the more effective cognitive strategies that people use to reinterpret events are: reframing, making social comparisons, having a sense of humor, and transcending one's own situation.

SHAPING   Effective coping may involve seeking actively to change the properties of the situation itself. For attacking the problem directly, having a general problem-solving model is helpful. One such model starts with the *present state* or "what is," and the *goal state,* which is "where you want to end up." The *problem space* is the gap between the present state and the goal state. Into the problem space are put the *solution paths,* which are the alternative solutions to the problem.

There are stages in problem solving using the general model: *Familiarization* involves spending time understanding the nature of the problem. During the *production stage,* solution paths are produced. The solution paths are judged during the *evaluation stage.* If a solution can't be found, the next step may be *incubation.*

SHAPING: GETTING ORGANIZED   Getting organized only takes ten minutes at the beginning or the end of each day for planning. A most useful planning strategy is to make a daily "To Do" List, with an ABC priority system. In this system, activities are ranked in order of urgency and importance, with capital letters A, B, and C. The A activities are tackled first; then the B; and finally, if time permits, the C.

SHAPING: SEEKING SOCIAL SUPPORT   Close personal relationships, especially marriage, predict mental and physical health as well as satisfaction with life.

There is also evidence that marriage is correlated with longer life. Divorce and family conflicts have negative long-term health effects.

Latinos in this country enjoy a health advantage over Caucasians, which seems to be a result of lifestyle factors. The Latino culture stresses the importance of family, the maintenance of a work ethic, the role of religion, and the formation of community.

ESCAPE (SELECTION) The simplest way of coping with stress is to modify or remove its source either by shaping the current environment or moving to a new one. Since personality change is difficult, to help a person adjust, the dispositional psychologist looks for a life situation for which the person is already suited by virtue of his or her enduring characteristics.

PERSONALITY AND LONGEVITY Both personality and social stress factors are predictors of longevity. The Big Five personality dimensions have been linked to health. Extroversion, was generally thought by theorists and researchers to correlate with health. Childhood conscientiousness and emotional stability seem to predict longevity for men but not for women.

WELLNESS A combination of lifestyle factors contribute to our sense of well-being. These factors include (1) how we work and play, (2) how we relax, (3) how and what we eat, (4) how we keep physically fit, (5) how we think and feel, (6) whether we have good relationships with others, and (7) how we fulfill our spiritual needs. Although people know what is good for them, they often do not use their knowledge to guide their behavior. Instead, they often engage in unhealthy behaviors when experiencing stress.

The concept of *wellness* includes a decision to move towards an integration of body, mind, and spirit, out of an appreciation that everything a person does, thinks, and feels has an impact on his or her state of health. The Menninger Clinic proposed that optimal well-being is achieved through "emotional maturity." Schafer believed that wellness is acquired and maintained by healthful daily habits, some of which are enough sleep, a healthy diet, adequate exercise, ways of dealing with anger and tension, work satisfaction, and the presence of energizing visions for oneself and the world.

LEARNING THE LANGUAGE OF PSYCHOLOGISTS

psychosomatic illness
stress
stressors
Type A behavior pattern
reinforcement
extinction
locus of control
self-efficacy

delay of gratification
catastrophizing
all-or-nothing thinking
overgeneralization
selective perception
endorphins
reframing

CHAPTER REVIEW QUESTIONS

1. What are the two levels of stress mentioned in the chapter?
2. What did Holmes and Rahe consider the relationship to be between stressful life events and physical illness?
3. What characteristics differentiate the Type A and Type B behavior patterns?
4. How does the sense of having control over one's life affect one's health?
5. What is self-efficacy?
6. What are Albert Ellis's ABC's of rational emotive therapy?
7. Why does Ellis label bad things that happen to people as "neutral" events?
8. According to Aaron Beck, what are the characteristic thinking patterns of depressed people?
9. Relaxation and exercise are both aimed at reducing which aspect of stress?
10. What are some benefits of keeping a sense of humor during tough times?

ACTIVITIES

1. *COMPLETE INDIVIDUALLY:* **Social Readjustment Rating Scale.**
2. *COMPLETE INDIVIDUALLY:* **Type A Behavior Pattern Indicators.**
3. *SMALL GROUP EXERCISE:* **Practice Identifying the Three Coping Strategies.**
4. *SMALL GROUP EXERCISE:* **Practice Identifying Beliefs and Their Emotional Consequences.**
5. *COMPLETE INDIVIDUALLY:* **Locus of Control Scale.**
6. *INDIVIDUAL EXERCISE:* **The Worst Part of It.** Students fold a piece of paper in half. On the top, they write "the worst thing that has ever happened to me." (Students must respect their neighbor's privacy; responses can even be written in code.) On the bottom, they write "what I learned from it (the worst thing)." Students tear up the top half and keep the bottom half.
7. *COMPLETE INDIVIDUALLY:* **Premack's Principle.**
8. *SMALL GROUP EXERCISE:* **A General Model for Problem Solving.**
9. *COMPLETE INDIVIDUALLY:* **How Healthy is My Lifestyle?**
10. *SMALL GROUP EXERCISE:* **Personal Reflections on My Coping Ability.**

Social Readjustment Rating Scale

People's lives are continually changing. Changes require new coping strategies that create stress. According to T. H. Holmes and R. H. Rahe (1967), those who obtain a high score on the "Social Readjustment Rating Scale" have many changes in their lives, and thus have a greater chance of getting sick.

Directions: Write the life crisis units for those events that have happened to you in the last two years in the column at the right.

1. Death of spouse	100	___
2. Divorce	73	___
3. Marital separation	65	___
4. Jail term	63	___
5. Death of close family member	63	___
6. Personal injury or illness	53	___
7. Marriage	50	___
8. Being fired from job	47	___
9. Marital reconciliation	45	___
10. Retirement	45	___
11. Change in health of family member	44	___
12. Pregnancy	40	___
13. Sex difficulties	39	___
14. Gaining a new family member	39	___
15. Business readjustment	39	___
16. Change in financial state	38	___
17. Death of a close friend	37	___
18. Change to a different line of work	36	___
19. Change in number of arguments with spouse	35	___
20. Mortgage over $10,000	31	___
21. Foreclosure of mortgage or loan	30	___
22. Change in responsibilities at work	29	___
23. Son/daughter leaving home	29	___
24. Trouble with in-laws	29	___
25. Outstanding personal achievement	28	___
26. Spouse's beginning or stopping work	26	___
27. Beginning or ending school	26	___
28. Change in living conditions	25	___
29. Revision of personal habits	24	___
30. Trouble with boss	23	___
31. Change in work hours or conditions	20	___
32. Change in residence	20	___
33. Change in schools	20	___
34. Change in recreation	19	___
35. Change in church activities	19	___
36. Change in social activities	18	___
37. Mortgage or loan less than $10,000	17	___
38. Change in sleeping habits	16	___
39. Change in number of family get-togethers	15	___
40. Change in eating habits	15	___
41. Vacation	13	___
42. Christmas	12	___
43. Minor violation of the law	11	___

Total Score: ___

Compare your total life crisis units to the Holmes and Rahe findings:
   0–149   No significant problems
150–199   Mild life crisis (33 percent chance of illness)
200–299   Moderate life crisis (50 percent chance of illness)
300 or over Major life crisis (80 percent chance of illness)

Source: Holmes & Rahe (1967). Reprinted from *Journal of Psychosomatic Research,* vol. 11, "Social Readjustment Rating Scale," with permission from Elsevier Science.

Type A Behavior Pattern Indicators

Directions: Circle *Y* for yes and *N* for no for each of the following questions.

Y   N   1. Do you combine tasks, e.g., TV watching and eating, talking on the telephone and preparing dinner?

Y   N   2. Do you have nervous gestures or habits?

Y   N   3. Do you finish other people's sentences?

Y   N   4. Do you schedule yourself tightly, with little time allotted for unexpected delays?

Y   N   5. Do you feel guilty when you take off time, so that you feel compelled to be productive?

Y   N   6. Are you generally too rushed to enjoy beauty, to "smell the roses"?

Y   N   7. Do you think about something else when listening to others?

Y   N   8. Is it difficult for you to wait in line or in traffic?

Y   N   9. Do you think success is related to your ability to do things faster than everyone else?

Y   N 10. Do you believe that you're a type A person?

Y   N 11. Do you have a sense of time urgency about most things?

Y   N 12. Are you preoccupied with productivity and achievement?

Y   N 13. Are you competitive?

Y   N 14. Do you create deadlines for yourself and then try to beat them?

Y   N 15. Do you tend to get yourself trapped in several stressful situations at once?

Y   N 16. Do you find it hard to relax and have fun?

Y   N 17. Do you perceive life as being serious business?

Y N 18. Are you preoccupied with your work?

Y N 19. Do you find that you have little time for solitude or meaningful social relationships?

Y N 20. Are you "driven"?

Y N 21. Do you tend to speak rapidly?

Y N 22. Does your voice often sound irritated?

Y N 23. Does your speech have an explosive quality to it; do you
accentuate many of your words?

Y N 24. Do you walk and move fast most of the time?

Y N 25. Are you a fast eater?

Y N 26. Do you often feel that you have unfinished projects, even
though you work long and hard hours?

Y N 27. When others are speaking, do you often get impatient in
wanting them to make their point?

Y N 28. Are you at times afraid to stop, for fear that you won't get
enough done?

Y N 29. Do you measure your worth as a person by the number of
your accomplishments?

Y N 30. Do you have the urge continually to get ahead, so that
you're never satisfied with where you are?

Scoring: The more items you marked Y, the more you fit the Type A behavior
pattern.

Source: From *Type A Behavior and Your Heart* by Meyer Friedman and Ray N. Rosenman. Copyright © 1974 by Meyer Friedman. Reprinted by permission of Alfred A.
Knopf, Inc.

Practice Identifying the Three Coping Strategies

Directions: For items 1 to 3, select the coping strategy you would use by circling the appropriate letter. Then discuss your choice with your group members. For items 2 and 3, identify each coping strategy in the blank provided.
For items 4 to 6, provide strategies that would be examples of adaptation,
shaping, or escaping in each situation, and write the strategies in the blanks.

1. The nation of Dragonia is characterized by its authoritarian structure,
elitist culture, brutal repression of dissent, and general intolerance. Life
in this undeveloped, third-world nation is predictable, monotonous, and
gray. The small class of elites holds the bureaucratic and military power,

while an army of second-class citizens wrest a living working in urban factories and on collectivized farms. You are a young person of high birth who has just completed your education at a prestigious institution of higher learning in Europe. Upon returning to Dragonia, do you

a. accept the calling of your birth, resolving to perform your duties to the best of your ability?
(adaptation)

b. renounce the culture of elitism and seek to build a more just order? *(shaping)*

c. decide you cannot live amid such hypocrisy and moral depravity, and therefore move to a large cultural metropolis elsewhere, where you can live in relative freedom and obscurity? *(selection/escape)*

2. You are taken to a seat in a bar or restaurant that is not far from a very addicted smoker. The area around your seat is shrouded in a cloud of blue smoke, and your allergies are stifling you. To remedy the situation, do you

a. go to the bathroom every time the smoker lights up? (Identify coping strategy:_____)

b. ask the person not to smoke? (Identify coping strategy:_____ _____)

c. call for the waitress and ask for a new seat? (Identify coping strategy: _____)

3. You are currently in the midst of a midlife crisis. Your children disappoint you, your spouse is a bore, and your job is depressing. In order to improve the quality of your life, do you

a. leave home for a younger woman or man? (Identify coping strategy:_____)

b. seek psychiatric counseling? (Identify coping strategy:_____ _____)

c. explain to your family what you are going through and tell them that they must do their share to remedy the situation? (Identify coping strategy:_____)

4. Juan, a student living in an apartment, has for a neighbor, a fellow who parties and plays his stereo set at full volume almost every night into the wee hours of the morning. Juan, who is a serious student, is unable to sleep because of the noise. He clearly has a problem, one caused by another person.
Provide three choices for Juan:

a. *adaptation:*_____

b. *shaping:* _____

c. *selection/escape:* _____

5. Lin is miserable because her husband, whom she otherwise loves and who is a wonderful father, flirts openly with other women at parties. Provide three choices for Lin:

a. *adaptation:* _____

b. *shaping:* _____

c. *selection/escape:* _____

6. Fran's boss criticizes Fran's job performance in front of both Fran and board members of the organization where Fran works. Fran feels embarrassed, as well as angry, because she believes that the criticisms are unwarranted. Her boss seems to be deciding, after the fact, that there is more to Fran's job description whenever a board member asks why certain tasks have not been performed on behalf of the organization. The lapse in performance of these duties then falls on Fran's shoulders. Provide three choice for Fran:

a. *adaptation:* _____

b. *shaping:* _____

c. *selection/escape:* _____

Source: Examples 1, 3, and 4 are from Levine (1988).

Practice Identifying Beliefs and Their Emotional Consequences

Directions: After reading the following activating events, supply the missing belief or emotional consequence in the blank provided.

1. a. Someone pulls into the parking space you were waiting for.

   b. You think _____

   c. You get angry, roll down your window, and shout at the other driver.

2. a. Your parent yells at you for not doing your homework.

   b. You think, "I'm a lousy son/daughter."

   c. You feel (or do) _____

3. a. Your friend hasn't returned your phone calls.

   b. You think _____

   c. You're depressed all day.

4. a. Your friend hasn't returned your phone calls.

   b. You think _____

   c. You don't feel bad about the neglect, and go about your day.

5. a. You and your romantic partner have a fight.

   b. You think, "I never do anything right."

   c. You feel (or do) _____

6. a. You and your romantic partner have a fight.

   b. You think, "He/she was in an bad mood."

   c. You feel (or do) _____

7. a. You and your romantic partner have a fight.

   b. You think, "I can always clear up misunderstandings with my partner."

   c. You feel (or do) _____

8. a. Your boss called and left a message for you to call back as soon as possible.

   b. You think, "I'm getting fired."

   c. You feel _____

   b. You think, "I'm going to have to work on my day off."

   c. You feel _____

   b. You think, "I'm getting that raise I asked for."

   c. You feel _____

   b. You think, "Someone needs me; because he or she can't find or do something at work."

   c. You feel _____

Source: Adapted from Seligman, (1990), pp. 260–261.

Locus of Control Scale

Directions: Answer the following questions according to the way you feel. There are no right or wrong answers. Don't take too much time answering any one question. It's not unusual to feel that you could answer both yes or no to a question. If this happens, think about whether your answer is just a little more one way than the other. For example, if you'd assign a weighting of 51 percent to yes and assign 49 percent to no, circle *Y* for yes.

Y N   **1.** Do you believe that most problems will solve themselves if you just don't fool with them?

Y N   **2.** Do you believe that you can stop yourself from catching a cold?

Y N   **3.** Are some people just born lucky?

Y N   **4.** Most of the time, do you feel that getting good grades means a great deal to you?

Y N   **5.** Are you often blamed for things that just aren't your fault?

Y N   **6.** Do you believe that if somebody studies hard enough, he or she can pass any subject?

Y N   **7.** Do you feel that most of the time, it doesn't pay to try hard because things never turn out right anyway?

Y N   **8.** Do you feel that if things start out well in the morning, it's going to be a good day no matter what you do?

Y N   **9.** Do you feel that most of the time parents listen to what their children have to say?

Y N **10.** Do you believe that wishing can make good things happen?

Y N **11.** When you get punished, does it usually seem that the punishment is for no good reason at all?

Y N **12.** Most of the time, do you find it hard to change a friend's opinion?

Y N **13.** Do you think that cheering rather than luck helps a team to win?

Y N **14.** Do you feel that it's nearly impossible to change your parents' minds about anything?

Y N **15.** Do you believe that parents should allow their children to make most of their own decisions?

Y N **16.** Do you feel that when you do something wrong, there's very little you can do to make it right?

Y N **17.** Do you believe that most athletes are just born good at sports?

Y N **18.** Are most other people of your age stronger than you are?

Y N **19.** Do you feel that one of the best ways to handle most problems is just not to think about them?

Y N **20.** Do you feel that you have a lot of choice in deciding who your friends are?

Y N **21.** If you find a four-leaf clover, do you believe that it might bring you good luck?

Y   N   **22.** Do you often feel that whether or not you do your home-work has much to do with what kind of grades you get?

Y   N   **23.** Do you feel that when a person your age is angry at you, there's little you can do to stop him or her?

Y   N   **24.** Have you ever had a good-luck charm?

Y   N   **25.** Do you believe that whether or not people like you de-pends on how you act?

Y   N   **26.** Did your parents usually help you if you asked them to?

Y   N   **27.** Have you felt that when people were angry with you, it was usually for no reason at all?

Y   N   **28.** Most of the time, do you feel that you can change what might happen tomorrow by what you do today?

Y   N   **29.** Do you believe that when bad things are going to happen, they just are going to happen no matter what you try to do to stop them?

Y   N   **30.** Do you think that people can get their own way if they just keep trying?

Y   N   **31.** Most of the time, do you find it useless to try to get your own way at home?

Y   N   **32.** Do you feel that when good things happen, they happen be-cause of hard work?

Y   N   **33.** Do you feel that when somebody your age wants to be your enemy there's little you can do to change matters?

Y   N   **34.** Do you feel that it's easy to get friends to do what you want them to do?

Y   N   **35.** Do you usually feel that you have little to say about what you get to eat at home?

Y   N   **36.** Do you feel that when someone doesn't like you, there's little you can do about it?

Y   N   **37.** Did you usually feel that it was almost useless to try in school because most other students were just plain smarter than you were?

Y   N   **38.** Are you the kind of person who believes that planning ahead makes things turn out better?

Y   N   **39.** Most of the time, do you feel that you have little to say about what your family decides to do?

Y   N   **40.** Do you think it's better to be smart than to be lucky?

Scoring: Give yourself one point for each time that your answer agrees with the answers that follow. The higher the score, the more external the orientation.

1. Y	11. Y	21. Y	31. Y
2. N	12. Y	22. N	32. N
3. Y	13. N	23. Y	33. Y
4. N	14. Y	24. Y	34. N
5. Y	15. N	25. N	35. Y
6. N	16. Y	26. N	36. Y
7. Y	17. Y	27. Y	37. Y
8. Y	18. Y	28. N	38. N
9. N	19. Y	29. Y	39. Y
10. Y	20. N	30. N	40. N

Source: From "A Locus of Control Scale for Children" by S. Norwicki and B.R. Strickland. Copyright © 1973 by the American Psychological Association. Reprinted with permission.

Premack's Principle

Directions: Premack's Principle is based on the idea from behaviorism that those actions that are reinforced are more likely to recur again in the future. Premack's Principle states that any high frequency behavior can be used to reinforce a low frequency behavior. You can use this principle to modify your own behavior. Here's how: Simply identify an activity that you think you need to do more of but haven't been able to get yourself to do. Perhaps studying would fit the bill.

1. Write your low frequency behavior here (e.g., studying):

   _____

2. Next, identify a behavior that you like to do and thus do quite frequently. This could be something you think you should do less of, but it doesn't have to be. Write your high frequency behavior here:

   _____

3. Now, make an agreement with yourself that you will do a specified quantity of your low frequency behavior before engaging in a specified amount of your high frequency behavior. For instance, you agree to do a half an hour of homework for every half an hour of TV that you plan to watch. Write your agreement here:

   _____

A General Model for Problem Solving

Rationale: Newell and Simon (1972) have conceptualized all problems as being composed of the same basic parts. Their idea is that problems, like people, can be understood by reducing them to their anatomical parts. According to this view, the anatomy of a problem can be thought of as having a starting or *present state* and a final or *goal state*. The problem is the gap that separates where you are from where you want to be. All of the possible *solution paths* from the present state to the goal state comprise the *problem space*. In addition to the present and goal states, and the paths connecting them, there are givens or information and rules that place constraints upon the problem. The givens are the knowledge needed to reach the goal. When solving a problem, the given information is transformed into a solution. The givens can be things like age, height, time limitations, the number of people a car will hold, or emotional constraints, such as unwillingness to sneak into a concert (a possible solution path to the following problem).

Directions, part 1: Suppose that you finally work up the nerve to ask that special person out on a date. To entice him or her to agree to the date, you mention that you have tickets for a concert featuring a currently popular music group. Things go well, and you're on your date. The drive out to the concert is forty-five minutes long. It's ten minutes before the concert is due to begin and you realize that you have forgotten the tickets. Determine the goal state in this case, and then generate some solution paths.

PRESENT STATE (Where you are right now:)	PROBLEM SPACE (Put solution paths here:) e.g., sneak into the concert	GOAL STATE (Where do you want to end up?)

Directions, part 2: Pick a personal problem that you have and cast it into the model of a problem in general, i.e., present state, goal state, and solution paths.

a. Describe the present state, "what is." Include a list of the *givens*.

b. Describe the goal state, "what is desired."

c. Give some tentative solution paths that you might try (a minimum of five).

d. What might the future state be if no action is taken (i.e., if no solution path is taken)?

PRESENT STATE   PROBLEM SPACE   GOAL STATE

Directions, part 3: Repeat part 1, but with a social problem instead of a personal problem. Pick a problem of broad-reaching social consequence. Some examples might be population control, pollution, treatment of criminals, or distribution of wealth. Cast the problem into our model, with a present state, a goal state, and solution paths. Try to withhold judgment when generating solution paths, and make an extensive, even if not entirely practical, list. Then, narrow down your list to the most practical alternatives. Discuss the values of society that could affect your approach to a solution.

PRESENT STATE   PROBLEM SPACE   GOAL STATE

Source: "A General Model for Problem Solving" by A. Newell and H.A. Simon. From *Thought and Knowledge,* Second Edition, by Diane Halpern. Copyright © 1989 by Lawrence Erlbaum Associates, Inc. Reprinted by permission.

How Healthy Is My Lifestyle?

Directions: To estimate how healthy a lifestyle you have, fill in the appropriate numerical values in the blanks.

1. How did you feel yesterday? If you felt well, give yourself 2. If only so-so you score a 1. If terrible, write a 0. _____

2. If you did not take any medicine yesterday, not even an aspirin for a headache, give yourself 1 point. _____

3. If you have not had any illnesses during the past month, not even a cold or flu, give yourself 1 point. _____

4. If you have not had any accidents during the past month, not even minor mishaps, such as a cut finger or a scald, score 1. _____

5. How tired were you last night? If pleasantly tired, score 2. If a bit overtired, score 1. If exhausted, score 0. _____

6. If you slept well last night, score 1. _____

7. If you did not spend more than an hour last night watching television but were staring idly into space or dozing over a book, score 1. _____

8. If you practice yoga or set some time aside each evening for a hobby or some other form of relaxation, score 1. _____

9. Are you eating too much? If you are less than 13 pounds overweight, score 2. If less than 26 pounds overweight, score 1. If 26 pounds overweight or more, score 0. _____

10. If you take one spoonful of sugar or less in tea or coffee, score 1. _____

11. If you eat less than 8 ounces of butter a week, score 1. _____

12. If you do not average more than two large glasses of beer or a shot of liquor a day, score 1. _____

13. Do you make time for vigorous exercise in an average week? If your get an hour or more, score 2. If you get a half an hour, score 1. If none, score 0. _____

14. If you play any sports, score 1. _____

15. If you are not mainly deskbound at your job, score 1. _____

16. If you made love last week, score 1. _____

17. How many cigarettes a day do you usually smoke? If you smoked none, score 2. If less than ten, score 1. If more than ten, score 0. _____

18. If you have not smoked cigarettes for five years or more, score 1. _____

19. If you do not smoke a pipe, score 1. _____

20. If you do not smoke cigars, score 1. _____

TOTAL SCORE: ____

Scoring: The higher you score on this assessment, the more likely you are to be healthy enough to cope with stress. To assess how healthy your lifestyle is, add up your score and multiply it by four, which will give you a percentage. If you scored 0 to 25 percent, your lifestyle is in need of urgent improvement. If you scored 25 to 50 percent, you could do better. With 50 to 75 percent, you can feel reasonably satisfied. With 75 to 100 percent, you are doing well. It may not be possible to avoid stressful situations, but it would help to take a vacation, get more fit by exercising, cut down on your particular "vice," and learn to relax.

Source: Adapted from *Concern*, Vol. 2, No. 2.

Personal Reflections on My Coping Ability

Directions: Read each of the following questions, and write your answers in the blanks.

1. What psychosocial stressors are currently affecting your and/or your family?

_____

_____

_____

_____

2. What are the likely duration and severity of the stressors listed in item 1?

_____

_____

_____

_____

3. What resources (including coping resources) do you believe that you have and believe that you need in order to cope with the stressors listed in item 1?

_____

_____

_____

_____

4. What thought(s) do you have about the situation given in item 1?

_____

_____

_____

_____

5. What feelings might you experience as a consequence of the thought(s) mentioned in item 4?

_____

_____

_____

_____

6. Complete this sentence: "I worry most about . . ."

_____

_____

7. Complete this sentence: "The worst thing in life is . . ."

_____

_____

8. Finish this sentence: "My most frequent pleasure is . . ."

_____

_____

9. Finish this sentence: "I think touching . . ."

_____

_____

10. Finish this sentence: "What I want when I get sick is . . ."

_____

_____

11. Finish this sentence: "The way I help myself feel better when stressed is . . ."

_____

Love

*The measure of mental health is the disposition
to find good everywhere.*
—Ralph Waldo Emerson

> ➤ *PREVIEW QUESTIONS:* Can love be analyzed, and can its components be discovered? What is the typical process of falling in love and forming a relationship? Should one worry more about being loved or being capable of loving others? What is the role of commitment in loving relationships?

➤ *Introduction: The Importance of Love in Human Experience*

Sigmund Freud once said that "love and work" are the two activities that occupy the well-adjusted adult's life. The importance of one's work life has previously been discussed (Chapter 7). Freud's focus on love as a driving force behind adult activities is equally valid. Today, when asked, most people throughout the world say that they want to find a romantic partner and to form a committed, secure relationship. The accomplishment of this task is one of the greatest challenges in life, requiring both skill and effort. Although the topic of love has always been an integral part of human culture, it has perhaps never before in history held center stage to the extent that it does today (Hatfield & Rapson, 1996).

Psychologists and philosophers alike proclaim that loving relationships make life meaningful and thus worthwhile. In a sense, our relationships help us address the existential question, What is the purpose of my life? Maier (1991) believed that love comes into an imperfect world to make it livable. He wrote that love is a spirit that changes life. It is a way of life that is expansive and transforming. "Love is meant to bring meaning into life where nonsense appears to reign" (p. 47). Frankl (1963) said that love is one of a handful of ways to create meaning in one's life.

Robert Sternberg's (1988) model of love provides a useful way to look at this intangible experience, by distinguishing among three components of love: intimacy, passion, and commitment. Although Sternberg states that all three components must be present for the complete experience of love, most sociologists and psychologists note that in long-term love relationships, passion tamps down, while intimacy and commitment tend to grow. Thus, newly formed love relationships tend to emphasize **passionate love,** whereas enduring relationships are said to be characterized by **companionate love.** Because of the accent on romantic love in our culture, we tend to form relationships in a predictable series of stages, first romanticizing the relationship, then suffering the inevitable disillusionment that follows from our initial construction of the relationship, and finally, forming a mutual respect and affection based on a realistic appraisal and acceptance of the partner (Goldstine et al., 1988).

Love is one of the most inexplicable of all human experiences. It cannot be bought or sold, weighed or measured, captured or held. Love can only be given. As children grow up, the world that surrounds them and the people who interact with them, teach them what love means. We cannot give what we have not learned and experienced. Since love is not a thing, it is not lost when given. However, we show love by giving our attention to others, by looking at them and listening to them. Attention is a limited commodity. A loving person recognizes the need of others to be seen and to be heard. In order to have love in our lives, Eric Fromm recommends that we concentrate on learning to love others well.

QUESTION: *How would you define love?*

➤ STERNBERG'S TRIANGULAR THEORY OF LOVE

At one time or another, most people ask themselves, "Is this love or lust?" "Is it real love or infatuation?" This common type of confusion raises the question, What is love? Although many people feel that a quality of experience such as love cannot be defined, psychological researchers have made an effort to do so. One perspective has been offered by psychologist Robert Sternberg (1986; 1988), who has explored the nature of love and loving relationships. Sternberg has proposed that love is made up of *intimacy, passion,* and *commitment.*

Intimacy

Intimacy refers to the closeness in a relationship in which affection, sharing, communication, and support are present. Self-disclosure from one person begets return disclosure from another, in what is known as the "reciprocity effect" (Cozby, 1973). This mutual sharing of one's inner thoughts and feelings fosters understanding and friendship. The nature of intimacy will be discussed in greater detail elsewhere (Chapter 10).

Passion

Passionate love is a "hot," intense emotion that is typically described as a state of profound longing for union with another (Hatfield & Rapson, 1996). Passion applies mainly to physiological arousal, what is often called lust. The arousal may be sexual, but it doesn't have to be. No matter what its cause, arousal may be interpreted as passion in a romantic relationship (Bersheid & Walster, 1974). This property of physiological arousal, that it is relatively un-differentiated and thus can be interpreted in more than one way, is probably why passionate love often occurs against a backdrop of danger, adversity, or frustration. For instance, in a scene from the movie *Gone with the Wind*, heroine Scarlett O'Hara agreed to marry her first husband in a moment of high excitement over the declaration of war between the Southern and Northern States. Miss Scarlett was offered the proposal because of her beau's excitement over the war, and she accepted in a fit of jealousy in an attempt to make the man whom she *really* loved jealous over her.

Kahlil Gibran's (1976) poem "Love and Marriage" expresses the passionate aspect of love:

> Love have no other desire but to fulfill itself.
> But if you love and must needs have desires,
> let these be your desires:
> To melt and be like a running brook
> that sings its melody to the night.
> To be wounded by your own understanding of love;
> And to bleed willingly and joyfully.
> To wake at dawn with a winged heart
> And give thanks for another day of loving . . .

Source: From *The Prophet* by Kahlil Gibran. Copyright 1923 by Kahlil Gibran and renewed 1951 by Administrators C T A of Kahlil Gibran Estate and May G. Gibran. Reprinted by permission of Alfred A. Knopf, Inc.

Clearly, Gibran considers passion to be a significant aspect of love, perhaps the *defining* quality. Passion is the primary source of love's intensity. As the popular country and western song title suggests, passionate love is "No Thinkin' Thing."

Social psychologists and anthropologists, who have studied people throughout the world, have found evidence that passionate love and sexual desire seem to be universally felt and to have existed at all times and in all places (Brown, 1991; Buss, 1988a,b; Hatfield & Rapson, 1993). How we learn to express love will be somewhat determined by the society in which we grow up. Culture can have a powerful impact on how easily and how deeply people fall in love and how they try to deal with these feelings. For example, cultures vary in their attitudes about emotional demonstrativeness. In the United States, most children are taught to control their emotions and to internalize their feelings, because being demonstrative, laughing uproariously, or weeping bitterly are considered signs of immaturity.

Are there universal qualities that elicit passionate desires in people? David Buss (1989) traveled to thirty-seven countries and asked over 10,000 people what characteristics they would like to have in a potential mate. The respondents were given eighteen traits to rank order in terms of importance in choosing a partner. It seems that men and women throughout the world want much the same things. At the top of the list for both men and women was mutual attraction! Throughout the world, passionate love has become the number one prerequisite for mate selection. The next three most-sought-after qualities for men and women were also identical: dependable character, emotional stability and maturity, and a pleasing disposition.

Buss's Cross-Cultural Findings of Preference in Mate Selection

Men's Ranking of Various Traits[1]	Women's Ranking of Various Traits[1]
1. Mutual attraction—Love	1. Mutual attraction—Love
2. Dependable character	2. Dependable character
3. Emotional stability and maturity	3. Emotional stability and maturity
4. Pleasing disposition	4. Pleasing disposition
5. Good health	5. Education and intelligence
6. Education and intelligence	6. Sociability
7. Sociability	7. Good health
8. Desire for home and children	8. Desire for home and children
9. Refinement, neatness	9. Ambition and industriousness
10. Good looks	10. Refinement, neatness
11. Ambition and industriousness	11. Similar education
12. Good cook and housekeeper	12. Good financial prospect
13. Good financial prospect	13. Good looks
14. Similar education	14. Favorable social status or rating
15. Favorable social status or rating	15. Good cook and housekeeper
16. Chastity (no previous experience in sexual intercourse)	16. Similar religious background
17. Similar religous background	17. Similar political background
18. Similar political background	18. Chastity (no previous experience in sexual intercourse)

Source: Buss et al. (1990).

Hatfield and Rapson (1996) cited a study of three industrialized nations—the United States, Russia, and Japan—each of which varies in the extent to which it endorses a Western individualistic culture. The United States is the most individualistic society in the world, whereas Japan is very much an Eastern collectivist society. Russia would be somewhere in the middle of this continuum. Individualistic cultures tend to encourage pursuit of individual goals and personal fulfillment, whereas collectivist societies are likely to expect their members to put aside personal needs when necessary to further the interests of the larger group.

Nevertheless, the college students interviewed in these three countries were remarkably similar in what they sought in a prospective mate. They looked first for kindness and understanding, a sense of humor, expressiveness and openness, intelligence, and being a good conversationalist. Less critical but still desired traits were sociability, ambition, and physical attractiveness.

Surprisingly, perhaps, these qualities were considered less important: skillfulness as a lover; potential for success; money, status, and position; and athletic ability. The U.S. students, more so than the Japanese or the Russians, seemed to embrace the notion of an ideal mate and to think that they should be able to "have it all." The Japanese students were the least demanding of the three groups in their expectations of finding all the qualities that one might wish for in a partner.

Good looks are universally sought after in a prospective mate. Those who have researched what make human beings attractive to one another have discovered that people who are considered attractive in their own cultures are likely to be thought attractive in other cultures as well (Cunningham, Barbee, & Pike, 1990; Jones & Hill, 1993). The ancient Greek philosopher Aristotle proposed that "the Golden Mean" was the standard for beauty; that is, people with average features would be considered attractive. Contemporary research has borne out this ancient wisdom (Langlois & Roggman, 1990). Both in the United States and throughout the world, people show a preference for the appealingly average face (Gangestad, Thornhill, & Yeo, 1994).

Commitment

Commitment refers to our decision to love another person and to plan a long-term involvement with that person. Love often prompts commitment, and once made, commitment provides a safe harbor in which love can prosper and grow (Barbeau, 1988). Commitment also implies accepting responsibility for another. Should this person become disabled or terminally ill, we promise to stand by him or her. We agree to face the hardships of life together, rather than to abandon a mate who has become a burden. The popular radio talk show host and former psychotherapist Dr. Laura Schlessinger (1995) said that commitment is what holds partners together during times of strife, because, according to Schlessinger, we *don't love* our partner at these moments, at least in the sense of feeling positively towards him or her. Love is what we feel when things are going well.

An enduring love relationship, and perhaps *any* lasting relationship, requires caring enough about the other person to stay and work on breaking through any impasse. Each person has an obligation to the other. They both have an investment in their future together and thus are willing to stay with each other in times of crisis and conflict. We require commitment in our relationships and the assurance that we can disagree and struggle over issues without destroying the attachment (Peck, 1978). Couples who have this understanding are willing to struggle to develop a meaningful relationship. They share some common purposes and values and therefore have enough sense of security to be willing to look at what is lacking in their relationship and to work on changing undesirable situations.

Eric Fromm (1963), who wrote *The Art of Loving*, one of the classic books on the subject, expressed the commitment aspect of love in this way:

Erotic love, if it is love, has one premise. That I love from the essence of my being—and experience the other person in the essence of his or her being. In essence, all human beings are identical. We are all part of One; we are One. This being so, it should not make any difference whom we love. Love should be essentially an act of will, of decision to commit my life completely to that of one other person. This is, indeed, the rationale behind the idea of the insolubility of marriage, as it is behind the many forms of traditional marriage in which the two partners never choose each other, but are chosen for each other—and yet are expected to love each other. In contemporary Western culture this idea appears altogether false. Love is supposed to be the outcome of a spontaneous, emotional reaction, of suddenly being gripped by an irresistible feeling.

In this view, one sees only the peculiarities of the two individuals involved—and not the fact that all men are part of Adam, and all women part of Eve. One neglects to see an important factor in erotic love, that of *will*. To love somebody is not just a strong feeling—it is a decision, it is a judgment, it is a promise. If love were only a feeling, there would be no basis for the promise to love each other forever. A feeling comes and it may go. How can I judge that it will stay forever, when my act does not involve judgment and decision? (p. 47)

Some people believe that love is only temporary, probably because sooner or later, long-term relationships generally involve conflict. Conflict is a natural facet of intimacy. If our attitude is "I'll stay for the good times, but as soon as things get stormy or dull, I'll split and look elsewhere for something more fun," then we are probably not going to be willing to go through the effort that is involved in the maintenance of a long-term relationship.

For some of us, commitment has many negative connotations. It is associated with boredom, as well as the fear of being taken advantage of or being taken for granted. We may worry about getting derailed from our goals or may avoid the initial promise for fear of divorce later down the road. We may feel burdened by the responsibility of a relationship. Other people might want more from us than we are willing to give, so that we fear feeling suffocated. Some of us never seem to want to go beyond just meeting other people, for fear of becoming obligated to another person. As a result, we go through life in a series of superficial relationships, unable to initiate anything more substantial that runs the risk of leading to a commitment. We might also fear letting others down. We worry about not being able to live up to the expectations of others and to keep the needs of a partner in mind, or we might be reluctant to let go of other possibilities we are relinquishing by settling down into a serious relationship.

Sternberg (1991) suggests that commitment requires action, a form of investment; we must put something into the relationship in order to get something out of it. All investments entail risk, including the one that we make to achieve a successful relationship. If we decide to make the ultimate commitment and marry the person we are dating, we take on financial, emotional, and social obligations that involve risk. If we decide to stop dating this person and hope to find a more suitable partner, we hazard not finding such a one and experiencing the regret of losing this one. We must ask ourselves what we are willing to put on the line for the relationship. Commitments are risky, and they thus require an act of will.

Some people check their financial investments on a daily basis but fail to give the same attention to their most precious investment, which is in their romantic relationship. There is potential for both growth and loss in any relationship, and unless we monitor the direction in which things are going and intervene if difficulties arise, we may be unexpectedly caught losing out, because we were not paying attention. Sometimes small, initial changes in behavior by one or both partners beget larger changes over the long term. Every investment provides possibilities for growth and change. Not to be paying attention is to risk regret over missed opportunities.

The scary aspect of commitment is that, like any other decision, we make it knowing that things between us and the other person are bound to change. We have incomplete information about the other person and his or her potential. We are a surprise package both to ourselves and to our partner, and this characteristic is especially true for younger people. We both must have faith that things will work out and trust ourselves to be flexible enough to handle the twists and turns that the relationship takes. Attitudes change, feelings change, desires change. A great deterrent to commitment is the fear of change. Love dares us to commit ourselves to someone, to reach out into a future we cannot control with a person we must trust.

Because responsibility of any kind can seem intimidating, we may often be afraid of truly deep relationship with other human beings. The responsibility of a relationship implies a burden, a restriction of freedom. Although we may fear the demands that a relationship would make, we might be surprised to find that when we do get the courage to form a relationship, we actually become stronger. In joining forces with another person, we get twice the strength to grow, with twice as many alternatives.

QUESTION: *Do you have any concerns about making a commitment in a romantic relationship?*

Lasting love is sustained by continuing to pay attention to a person who has become familiar, rather than taking that person for granted, which is a major cause of deterioration of long-term relationships. The decision to pay attention to someone is a gift we give in the name of love. Making a study of the loved one enables us to know this person thoroughly, to become attached through understanding the life story and future dreams of the beloved one.

QUESTION: *To what extent do you think love is a pleasant sensation that we experience as a matter of chance, as opposed to something that we decide to do for another person? On a scale from one to ten (with one designating that love is a matter of chance and ten indicating that love is a decision requiring effort and commitment), indicate what your position is on this issue.*

Forms of Love

Sternberg (1988) describes several types of love, which consist of varying combinations of the three elements intimacy, passion and commitment: He stated that consummate (or complete) love contains all three elements, whereas romantic love consists of intimacy and passion but not commitment. Fatuous love is a combination of commitment and passion. It is possible to be "in love" without sharing intimacy, that is, without being friends. Friendship and love do not always coexist, though lasting love relationships tend to combine the two. Companionate love, commonly found in long-term marriages, is based on commitment and intimacy. Infatuation is founded on passion only; intimacy without either passion or commitment constitutes liking. Commitment alone would be considered an empty love.

Each of the preceding aspects of love, with the exception of consummate love, is incomplete, in that an element is missing. Clark and Reis (1988) have concluded that in most relationships, intimacy and commitment are a bigger part of love than is passion. Our culture tends to place a great deal of emphasis on passion as the main basis for "falling" in love, and the rest of the world seems inclined to follow suit (Hatfield & Rapson, 1996). However, the passionate, breathless stage of love typically lasts only about six to thirty months (Walster & Walster, 1978). The heat of passion inevitably calms down to a steady, warm afterglow often referred to as companionate love (Hatfield, 1988). Those who are caught up in expecting to maintain the passion at the original level of physiological arousal may neglect to build a more lasting relationship.

Some people assume that the fading of romance in the relationship is a sure sign that love never really existed. Unfortunately, American movies and folklore lead us to expect passion to last forever and to think that something is wrong when it subsides. Simpson, Campbell, and Berscheid (1986) suspect that "the sharp rise in the divorce rate in the past two decades is linked, at least in part, to the growing importance of intense positive emotional experience (e.g., romantic love) in people's lives, experiences that may be particularly difficult to sustain over time." The inclination to marry for love and then to divorce if love appears to have been lost is on the increase. Simpson and his colleagues found that 57 percent of men and 62 percent of women would find the disappearance of love a sufficient reason for ending a marriage. Researchers have suggested that liking for our marriage partner tends to lessen, because this person is no longer *exclusively* associated with

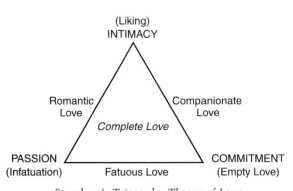

Sternberg's Triangular Theory of Love

From *Love the Way You Want It* by Dr. Robert J. Sternberg. Copyright © 1991 by Robert J. Sternberg. Used by permission of Bantam Books, a divison of Random House, Inc.

positive experiences as was the case during the courtship period (Aronson & Mettee, 1974).

If companionate love blooms, a relationship can survive the fading of intense passion. Continued high levels of passion may not even be desirable, since lovers exclude other social contacts, may be less productive in their work, and have less energy for other activities of life. Perhaps the most valuable human bond in society is friendship. The "common core" of a loving relationship has a high level of interpersonal communication, sharing, and support. People in companionate love tend to have deep friendships as well as a loving relationship, mutual respect, and commitment. Companionate relationships are intimate and tend to be characterized by self-disclosure. Berscheid and Walster (1978) suggest that people are more likely to maintain their relationship once the romance begins to fade if they have developed trust, loyalty, sharing of feelings, mutual respect and appreciation, lack of hypercriticality, and willingness to sacrifice. Companionate love is based on genuine knowledge of the other person, not on idealization. At this point, a couple can work together to meet each other's sexual as well as companionship needs. Security, understanding, acceptance, and faithfulness can substitute for the excitement of novelty.

Not all psychologists endorse the conclusion that the high flame of passion inevitably burns down to embers. Robert Sternberg (1991) disagrees with the notion that passion and sex are most important at the beginning of a relationship. He has collected data that indicate that the role of passion and sex increases in importance, so that two to five years into the relationship, passion and sex are even more important than they were at the beginning.

QUESTION: What qualities have psychologists found to be linked to lasting love relationships?

➤ THE THREE STAGES OF LOVE

Goldstine, Larner, Zuckerman, and Goldstine (1988) have developed a model to show how a typical romantic relationship unfolds. They have outlined three stages, *the sparkle, disillusionment,* and *mutual acceptance.*

Stage 1: The Sparkle

Falling in love produces intense feelings of passion, longing, affection, uncertainty, and fascination. Along with the initial blush of love goes a disturbing amount of unpredictability and vulnerability. The couple must shelve many of the defenses they rely on to protect themselves from hurt. In such a vulnerable state, a person may naturally fear rejection: "What if he/she doesn't love me back?"

"Let me take you away from all this and bring you over to all that."

Not everyone enters into a love relationship by falling in love. Some folks avoid the agony and the ecstasy of this process. Instead, they prefer to let love grow gradually. Yet these sensible types are going against the cultural norm that says that one falls in love as a result of chemistry, so that for most Americans, passionate stirrings are the awaited and hoped for cue that one is "in love."

Going along with the romantic ideal and falling in love necessitate self-disclosure, to achieve the closeness that is so desirable, yet often dreaded. Potential partners may feel some alarm over the prospect of the close-up scrutiny that intimacy entails. To be open is to risk rejection as one's physical, sexual, and psychological flaws are revealed. Withdrawal from the relationship by the very person whose opinion matters most would be painful indeed. The rejection by those who like us until they get to know us, bears the greatest sting. Rejection upon first sight, without our being known, hurts less.

Love makes a person feel cherished. Being in love tends to raise self-esteem. We feel lovable when we see the look of adoration in our partner's eyes, and we seem to have the power to make our partner feel just as wonderful. Initially, the couple forms a mutual admiration society. Each partner focuses on the desirable qualities of the other and shrugs off any shortcomings he or she finds. Each believes that over time, the rough edges of the other will be smoothed out. The couple becomes a cooperative unit and revels in a sense of being "us" rather than two separate persons. The intense desire for closeness temporarily subdues the fears that intimacy might typically awaken in them. Ambivalence about intimacy yields temporarily to the simple, childlike wish to be enfolded.

Being in love inclines people to treat each other with tender forbearance, which lessens the effect of whatever differences crop up between them. When falling in love, couples disregard each other's faults and failures. They wish to maintain their conception of each other and to protect their dreams for the relationship. If problems do surface that might endanger the relationship if discussed, they are likely to be painstakingly shied away from.

The romantic notion of falling in love so idealizes and enhances each partner's view of himself or herself and the other that each may succumb to the fantasy that this relationship will make all things possible. The relationship is thus burdened with the expectations of one partner or both partners that it will transform his or her life. This illusion may be encouraged by the fact that typically each person is on his or her best behavior. The partners groom themselves, use their best manners, tell their funniest jokes, and employ whatever other tools they may possess to be charming and stimulating. When they are falling in love, people are often deeply responsive to each other's needs. Both partners attempt to present their most appealing facets, and they are likely to succeed in being their most desirable selves at this time.

The initial experience of newness and discovery will, by definition, diminish as the relationship becomes more familiar. Although the partners may very well continue to take pleasure in each other's company, the intensity and longing for the other's continual presence lessens with time. It may well be that satiation, as well as confidence in the staying power of the relationship, allows the partners to be content with lapses in their togetherness. Other activities, such as work, school, and social ties, need to be attended to. With greater knowledge of each other, idealization gives way to aspects of the relationship that are not quite comfortable or perhaps even unpalatable. The sparkle begins to tarnish as dissatisfactions crop up.

Stage 2: Disillusionment

This stage entails disenchantment with one's partner. A couple must eventually face their inevitable differences. Each partner will notice aspects of the other that are undesirable. Since each person comes from a unique background, he or she will have different ways of doing things, some of which will clash with those of the partner. It is not easy to request behavior changes from a loved one, nor is it always a simple matter to accommodate change requests from another. There are some things about one's partner that cannot be changed and thus will have to be accepted or rejected as they are. When faced with the flaws and limitations of one's partner, one will possibly reconsider the wisdom of committing to that person.

When dissatisfaction is high, a partner may be tempted to use information that was shared by his or her partner, as a weapon to hurt the other. This behavior damages the relationship, because it inhibits future intimacy. On the other hand, a loved one who refrains from such unfair attacks is building trust in the midst of battle, an admirable course of action.

The mutual disapproval at this stage is particularly painful because it stands in contrast to the reciprocal admiration of the sparkle stage. The relationship was initially formed on a tacit agreement to help each other to feel better, be more appealing, and be more lovable than before the relationship's inception. Much of the feeling of rightness gained in a new relationship comes from the ability of each partner to provide an opportunity for the other to feel especially valued. Yet at this stage, the esteem turns to criticism. In the face of the disapproval of one's partner, one's self-esteem suffers. Now, rather than providing reciprocating compliments and other exchanges of rewards, the partners become locked into bouts of mutually punishing feedback.

THE FAR SIDE   By GARY LARSON

Same planet, different worlds

Part of the disenchantment comes from the realization that both partners have that the relationship is never going to give them all of the things they want. Those fantasies with which the relationship was burdened in the sparkle stage begin to evaporate, leaving a residue of disappointment and resentment. A couple's relationship cannot by itself ensure a lifetime of happiness. Nor can a relationship be expected to bring meaning to an unsatisfactory life. Problems between partners may be a symptom of problems in other areas of the partners' lives.

It is probably inevitable that two people experience friction in some points of contact. How does one know whether the criticisms received from one's partner are unjustly wounding or whether they are valuable, if painful, opportunities for growth? This dilemma seems to be a judgment call. Our perception that the other is intentionally inflicting harm will and should elicit a fierce defensiveness in us. We must guard our sense of ourselves as valuable, likable people. On the other hand, to the extent that we can feel basically worthwhile in the face of criticism, we'll be able to take in and make use of such feedback. It may help if our partner reminds us of those lovable qualities that he or she cherishes, at the same time that the corrective feedback is delivered. We are not likely to be able to see our own rough edges as clearly as does our partner. That being the case, criticisms, though aversive, can have value. If we can look at our partner as a person struggling to be close to us, even though he or she is complaining about a particular behavior, we might be able to view our mate as simply unhappy because this behavior gets in the way of closeness.

When dissatisfied, we tend to blame others. As relationship problems crop up, each partner is likely to focus on the behavior of his or her mate as the cause of the problems and to offer disapproval to the other. When this reciprocally punishing situation goes on too long without progress or resolution, one partner or both partners may withdraw. Neither experiences the relationship as a source of pleasure. The impasse feels hopeless. Although each harbors resentment that the other is so unwilling to change, the difficulty is more likely to lie in each person's reluctance to examine and alter his or her own behavior. Unless these entrenched positions are relinquished, the impasse remains. The partners may begin to entertain the idea that they might be in an unworkable relationship.

Goldstine and colleagues contend that the disillusionment stage is inevitable in *any* long-term relationship. One way out of the mire is for each partner to remind himself or herself of the lovable aspects of the other and of the pleasurable experiences that the relationship provides. When either person puts the difficulty in perspective by saying, essentially, "There is so much about this relationship that I value, and this is just one small part of it that I think we need to work on," this attitude instills hope again.

Stage 3: Mutual Acceptance

By an effort of will, the couple can convert disillusionment into a love that is durable. The partners have to strive to overcome the dissatisfaction and the mistrust that sometimes crop up in their relationship. Moving towards mutual acceptance requires not only effort but also optimism and skill. By comparison, the prior two stages seem "just to happen." If the partners persist in their efforts despite discouragement, they can gradually build a trusting and solid bond. This achievement entails patience with the slow pace of change in the relationship.

The couple will be content in a long-term relationship only if their expectations for it are realistic. The relationship will continue to be more comfortable in some ways than in others. There will be progress in some areas and backsliding in others. Frustrations and worries do not end, but as each partner experiences the commitment of the other, these difficulties cease to trigger doubts about their future as a couple. Each knows that they are both committed to working things out.

Mutual acceptance is the essence of Stage 3. Both partners feel at home with each other. The relationship allows each person to be himself or herself. The mates are sensitive to each other and accommodate each other. A gradually building reserve of trust over the years spent together prepares the couple to achieve mutual understanding, which is ultimately more satisfying than the shared illusion of the sparkle stage.

In a long-term relationship, the couple must find a way to balance individual and couple endeavors. There needs to be room for autonomy as well as acknowledgment of interdependence. Periods of closeness will arise as well as times when the partners are involved with their separate activities.

For their relationship to survive over the long term, not only must a couple retain a keen interest in each other, but they must also share the desire to seek each other out for enjoyment. They look forward to opportunities to spend time alone together. This sentiment stems from ongoing involvement in the life of the partner, which fosters a sense of shared history and extensive mutual knowledge.

The security provided by a long-term relationship accomplishes an essential function for the partners. Nothing allows a person to feel lovable so much as being embraced, warts and all, in an enduring relationship. The partners accept each other as fallible but essentially beautiful. By feeling known and appreciated, each partner feels strengthened by the secure nature of the love relationship. He or she can more freely and spontaneously explore who he or she is and what he or she might become.

A Stage 3 relationship can relapse into a Stage 2 under the strain of external stressors, such as illness, professional setbacks, or financial misfortune. However, the same combination of realistic expectations of the relationship and desire for its success that permitted the couple to achieve an equilibrium in the first place can empower them to restore the balance to their relationship. Stage 3 is more likely to be an achievement than a lucky accident.

➤ ## FEAR OF FORMING LOVING RELATIONSHIPS

On a daily basis, men and women buy self-help books and tune into radio and television talk shows looking for insight as to how to make their relationships work. Today, we no longer have to rely exclusively on other people's advice as to how to conduct our relationships, because we can turn to psychological research for answers and evidence.

Three common fears that people have concerning loving and being loved are discussed in the following sections:

Being Vulnerable to Getting Hurt Again

We fear being rejected or humiliated. We may fear losing the loved one through death.

Some of us give ourselves over completely to our first love. If that relationship isn't lasting, we may experience a sense of having lost ourselves when the partner leaves. Loss of a significant relationship can be so painful that we are reluctant to risk becoming vulnerable to further hurt. This devastation may leave us determined not ever to get so "carried away" again. This stance is not without merit. On the one hand, we do want to be willing to trust another again and to risk getting close. On the other hand, we want to keep enough of our self-possession so that we can sustain ourselves should disaster strike and our partner is lost through death or desertion.

This self-possession comes in part from realizing that we are half of the treasured relationship. If we were to lose the partner, yes, we would feel a significant loss, and yet, we would still have "half of the relationship" right here in our own person.

Even when a relationship ends, we can take heart in the knowledge that there is something to be gained from every relationship, whether or not it is permanent. We may become better at relating, listening, and articulating our own needs. We may learn a new sport that our partner was passionate about, may become interested in keeping up with the news, or may become a good cook, a theater critic, and so on. Finally, we have learned more about ourselves through the feedback from someone who got to know us.

Emotional closeness is scary, because it involves revealing our inner selves and thus being vulnerable. Deep-seated fear (Erikson's *mistrust* from infancy stage) may prevent self-disclosure. To the extent that our self-esteem is fragile, we would be unwilling to risk the vulnerability of emotional closeness. We might think to ourselves something like, "I couldn't take it if . . ." In order to be genuinely loved by another, we must make ourselves known and transparent to that person. Yes, that does mean risking either rejection or the tragic loss of someone to whom we have grown close. It takes courage to be a loving person.

Being Loved for the Wrong Reasons

Sometimes people discount the love that others give them as being contingent on a single characteristic of theirs, such as their easy-going personality, attractive looks or body, or their function as a good provider.

This attitude is likely to be a projection of our own feelings about ourselves onto others. We might try to realize that our body or our personality is *one* of our assets. We can learn to appreciate this asset without assuming that it is all there is to who we are. If we have trouble seeing any desirable characteristics besides our physical attractiveness, we are likely to be sending messages to other people that our primary value is bound up in appearances.

Ideally, we would come to accept that being a physically attractive person makes it easier for others to notice us and to want to initiate contact. However, we do not need to limit ourselves by depending exclusively on how we look because we can work at developing other traits. The danger consists of relying on physical attractiveness as a basis for building and maintaining a relationship. If we rely exclusively on physical attractiveness as a source of gaining love from others (or from ourselves), our ability to be loved is in a tenuous state. We cannot help but sense this situation.

Those of you who try to consciously portray an image or a persona will be bound to feel that you are effecting a snow job, thus leading to feelings of insecurity, because you may think that if you were truly known, you would be rejected. These kinds of worries are indicative of a poor relationship with yourself. It's time for some soul-searching to discover what is so unacceptable about you, in your own opinion. Once you get to the bottom of these feelings, you will realize either that those qualities aren't so bad (you're only human) or that you have the option of doing something about them.

Fear of Being Unlovable

We may have concerns that when other people get to know us, they won't want to have anything to do with us. We may feel unlovable. We may feel anxious about trying to look at ourselves as others do, because we might discover that we are shallow or empty. In fact, we may fear self-disgust.

This anxiety is caused by our own unwillingness to accept what we actually are, as opposed to what we think we should be. Our own inability to love and appreciate ourselves in spite of our limitations may block others from loving us. If we believe that nobody could possibly love us, we may subtly communicate this idea to others. We thus create a self-fulfilling prophecy (Chapter 2), which means that we make the very things we fear come true by telling ourselves and others that this is the way we are. Recall that a self-fulfilling prophecy is a prediction that, when made, influences the course of events toward fulfilling the prediction. Self-doubt—being convinced that no one could love us—leads to self-fulfilling prophecy as we project this out into our environment.

Having love for ourselves does not imply having an exaggerated picture of our own importance nor placing ourselves above others, or at the center of the universe. It does indicate that we respect ourselves, even though we are imperfect. It means caring about our lives and striving to become the persons we are capable of becoming. Once we can respect, appreciate, and care for ourselves, we open up the possibility of respecting, appreciating, and caring for others. Sometimes people cannot believe that they are lovable for who they are.

➤ MISTAKEN IDEAS ABOUT LOVE

Our culture, especially the media, influences the way that we conceive of love. If we hope to challenge myths, we will have to take a critical look at the messages that we have received from society about the essence of love. In the following sections are some common ideas about love, which research on relationships has shown to be flawed.

Those Truly in Love Desire Constant Togetherness

Some folks believe that if they love each other, then they should desire only the company of their partner. Love relationships are famous for their ability to elicit jealousy in the partners. Most of those who study love relationships insist that it is vital to express one's individuality and personal freedom within the relationship, so that the sharing and togetherness do not swallow up the parties involved, making them lose sight of their own uniqueness as persons. One partner or both partners might feel suffocated by constant to-getherness. The need for togetherness may stem not so much from love as from fear. Examples of these fears might be fear of abandonment, fear of having the other partner discover that he or she can get along without you, and fear of having the other partner meet someone more desirable than you. Erich Fromm (1963) wrote, "If I am attached to another person because I cannot stand on my own feet, he or she may be a lifesaver, but the relationship is not one of love" (p. 94).

People Fall in and out of Love, and It Just Happens

Although the notion of falling in love is popular, most serious writers on the subject deny that it can be the basis for a lasting and meaningful relationship. Although people say, "I love you," they may not be able to describe the active way in which they show this love.

Sometimes this unpredictable aspect of relationships is referred to as "chemistry." When we talk about chemistry in a relationship, we are often unaware of our predictable tendency to feel attraction for people who reinforce the patterns of relating that we learned early in life. However, psychological research has demonstrated that we tend to repeat the **attachment styles** that we developed in childhood in our relationships (Sternberg, 1991). If we mistakenly believe that our attraction to certain persons is entirely accidental, we may fail to recognize destructive patterns in our relationships and thus will not realize we can make changes in ourselves that will enable us to enjoy more fulfilling relationships. These patterns of relating are often unconscious and are very much a part of our identity. Even when we are aware of them, we may be reluctant to give them up.

As was discussed previously (Chapter 3), Mary Ainsworth (1989) studied infant-attachment patterns and found that an infant who is separated from his or her mother for a relatively brief period of time tends to react in one of three ways when the mother reenters the room. One type, the secure infant, seeks out the mother gladly, showing only minor distress at having been separated. Mothers of these children were consistently responsive to their infants' needs but also left them the freedom to play quietly alone when this seemed to be what the children desired. The secure infant contrasts to the avoidant infant, who, on the mother's return, actively avoids her. Mothers of avoidant infants typically rebuffed their infants' bids for comfort, especially for close bodily contact (Hatfield & Rapson, 1996). Both the secure and avoidant infants are in contrast to the anxious/ambivalent infant, who desperately seeks out the mother on her return, and has tremendous difficulty in dealing with the separation. The mothers of these infants were inconsistent in their reactions to their infants' signals. Sometimes they ignored their infants' cues but at other times were bossy and smothering.

There is growing evidence that we tend to repeat in adult romantic relationships the attachment style we developed in infancy (Hartup, 1989; Mikulincer & Nachshon, 1991; Shaver & Hazan, 1993; Shaver, Hazan, &

Bradshaw, 1988). The chemistry of a relationship, therefore, is at least some-what predictable. The adult who was secure as an infant will tend to be se-cure as an adult and thus will be able to form a stable and positive emotional bond with his or her partner. The secure adult is capable of being understand-ing, caring, intimate, and supportive with his or her partner. A person with a secure attachment regards himself or herself as friendly and likable, while viewing others as reliable and trustworthy.

The person who had an avoidant attachment style in childhood will, as an adult, demonstrate a fear of intimacy and a tendency to resist commitment to others. The avoidant adult is aloof and suspicious, thus regarding others as either unreliable or too eager to commit to the relationship. Both concerns re-sult in a reluctance of the avoidant person to get too close emotionally. In-stead, these skittish lovers tend to focus their attention on their work or to invest their energies in other nonsocial activities (e.g., Daniels & Shaver, 1991; Hazan & Shaver, 1987).

People who were anxious/ambivalent in infancy will also tend to reca-pitulate this pattern in adulthood, displaying mixed conflicting feelings of af-fection, anger, emotional turmoil, physical attraction, and doubt. They tend to regard themselves as misunderstood and unappreciated and to view others as undependable or unwilling to commit to a relationship. These adults are dependent, even clingy, and have low self-esteem, yet they idealize their ro-mantic partners. They have trouble finding a stable, committed relationship, because their insatiable demands seem to drive others away (e.g., Barthol-omew & Horowitz, 1991; Collins & Read, 1990).

Apparently, the first relationships of our lives become our mental mod-els for how to form affectionate adult relationships. Freud described the mother-child unit as the most critical for adult development, that it is "unique, without parallel, established unalterably for a whole lifetime as the first and strongest love-object and as the prototype of all later love relations—for both sexes" (1949, p. 45). When we reach adulthood, we use this model as a prototype for how to form, maintain, and break attachments to others.

People in Love Can Be Expected to Be Possessive

Some individuals may believe that they are capable of loving only one other person or that people *should* love only one person. This is particularly likely to be the sentiment about sexual expression within a love relationship. Two people may agree not to have sexual relationships with others, because they realize that doing so might interfere with their capacity to open up freely and trust each other. Even when this agreement has been made, couples can gen-uinely love others outside the couple, without including sexual expression as a manifestation of these other relationships.

The wish for exclusivity is sometimes caused by jealousy. One partner may fear being compared with others of his or her gender by the partner. The insecure partner may mistakenly conclude that something must be wrong with him or her in the partner's eyes or there would be no desire for these other relationships. The jealous guarding of the affection of one's partner can be disastrous. A person unable to deal in triads doesn't want to grow—he (she) wants only to be mirrored, like Narcissus. The couple who are able to have no friends besides each other may reflect this narcissistic disturbance.

Philosopher and author Sam Keen (1997) echoes this sentiment:

> First, our obsessive focus on intimacy heightens individualism and creates a form of egotism-à-deux, a style of alienated coupling in which we increasingly neglect the wider sphere within which we need to practice love—the family, the neighborhood, the polis, the land, the wilderness, the community of nonhuman sentient beings. *The terrible mistake of modern theories of love is to focus on two solitary individuals who join together to form an island in an alien sea of anonymous others and unknown neighbors.* The romantic myth is an integral component of the pathological individualism that has become a major threat to Western culture. (p. 15)

Genuine Love Is Demonstrated by Selfless Acts

When asked to define love, many college students say something to the effect that it means putting the other person ahead of our own needs. "Thinking of the other first" is a common response. Actually, this definition seems to describe altruism (Chapter 5) more so than the reciprocal give and take of a loving relationship. There are people who get their sense of being worthwhile primarily from giving to others. When others want to give to them, they tend to refuse these efforts to give back. These "selfish givers" create lopsided relationships, all in the name of trying to appear "selfless." They tend to become drained and resentful as a result of the types of relationships they set up with others. Those others also tend to feel uncomfortable in the relationship, because they feel inadequate or guilty about not being able to reciprocate the generosity to which they have been treated.

The discomfort with being a recipient of kindness may be an indication of having a fundamental sense of unworthiness on the part of the compulsive giver. The predicament of this person can shed light on the trite but true saying that love for others must be preceded by love and respect for oneself.

True Love Implies Not Getting Angry with One's Partner

People do not get married to fight; they marry to find a lifelong companion. When expectations for support are not met, conflict occurs. Learning to deal directly and honestly with anger is one of the most essential tasks in intimate relationships. Yet, many people believe that if they love someone, they must not get angry at the person. Belief that love and anger are incompatible is likely to make the one who accepts this idea uncomfortable in relationships. It may not be possible to negotiate an intimate, loving relationship and to feel happy with one's partner at all times. A person who feels guilty over getting angry is likely to deny the existence of anger. Denied anger results in the death of a relationship, because the blocking of anger actually destroys love rather than protecting it. Love requires an authentic self and an honest exchange with another self. Other people at times will fail to meet one's expectations, and this failure is undeniably frustrating. Frustration often results in anger, which is best dealt with when felt. Stuffing anger may also lead to the repression of positive emotions, such as joy and love. Angry feelings that are left festering breed resentment, which tends to poison the relationship. More will be said about the expression of anger in Chapter 13.

The Best Predictor of Happiness in a Relationship Is How Deeply You Feel about Each Other

A common myth about love is that the more deeply it is felt, the more "right" is the relationship, and therefore the longer it can be expected to last. Sternberg (1991) found that the best predictor of happiness in relationships is not how much you care for one another. Instead, it has to do with the difference between the way you would ideally like your partner to feel about you and the way you actually perceive your partner to feel. That is, it is the difference between what you think you want and what you think you are getting from the relationship.

Religion Is No Longer as Important to Marital Harmony as It Once Was

Sternberg (1991) discovered that the importance of a shared religion increases over the length of a marriage, more so than any other factor that was studied. When couples first marry, each partner may downplay religion as an issue, in order to please the other. However, when children are born, if this issue hasn't been settled, there is likely to be a tug-of-war to decide which religion will be primary. Dr. Laura Schlessinger cautions against parents' trying to teach *both* religions on an equal basis, because the traditions of the religions may come into conflict and unnecessarily confuse the child.

➤ LOVE AND MEANING IN ONE'S LIFE

We have thus far been discussing romantic love. Now we consider love in a broader context, as an orientation toward others and toward the possibilities available to a person for doing something with his or her life.

In part, love supplies meaning to one's life through the act of commitment to another person or to several others. In deciding to stand by another person (or persons), we give our lives a transcendent purpose; we have a goal, a dedication beyond ourselves. Philosopher Sam Keen (1997) makes a comparison between the word "encourage," which means to hearten and give courage to another, and the word "enjoy," which could be taken as the reciprocal infusing of sympathetic happiness that occurs when two or more people engage in a pleasurable activity together. When we love others, we both encourage and enjoy them. According to Keen, "Ultimately, the greatest gift we can give our children, our friends, or our lovers is to support and celebrate their own unfolding sense of purpose, vocation, and joy in living" (p. 110).

Even if we were not prepared to love *someone*, we can enjoy a sense of purpose through dedicating ourselves to *something* and thus can create a purposeful, if lonely, life. The famous philosopher Spinoza made such a choice. He was excommunicated because of questioning his religion, Judaism, and thus fled to the Netherlands, where he lived with a couple, rarely going out, and where he wrote his philosophical treatises. Erik Erikson considered the dedicating of oneself in middle age to something that furthers human endeavor to be an option for achieving generativity. Normally, generativity is achieved through direct nurturing of one's own children, mentoring a protégé at work, or in some other way taking an interest in helping others. An alternative would be to build buildings in which others will work and study, to write books for them to read and songs for them to sing, and so on.

Viktor Frankl believed that love is one of only three sources of meaning in life, the other two being creation and suffering. Arnold Toynbee, a history professor who devoted himself in the latter part of his life to the study of religion, believed that love, creation, and understanding give life meaning. His view coincides considerably with that of Frankl, especially since Toynbee suggested that we should be ready to sacrifice ourselves in the pursuit of these three endeavors, if sacrifice turns out to be demanded of us. Since these are the purposes to live for, we should be willing to devote our lives to them.

Toynbee considered love to be the highest purpose in life. For him, love involves expending oneself on people and on missions beyond that self. In loving, we overcome self-centeredness. Loving has a spiritual aspect, because the outpouring of love from the self forms a union with other people, and an end to separateness, which is what an individual is truly seeking as the ultimate fulfillment. It is up to us to select a loving way of relating to ourselves and others.

Although Toynbee believed that love is the highest calling for each of us, he acknowledged that we are also conscious and reasoning beings, and therefore we have the ability to make deliberate choices. Our capacity for reasoning is especially important, because humans are emotional creatures, not completely rational ones. In addition to being ruled by our passions, Toynbee concluded that we are also motivated by unconscious forces, which may be good or evil. We can use reason to bring unconscious motives into conscious awareness, so that we may choose to follow the good motivations and reject the bad. One core aspect of human nature is the struggle between the rational and the irrational forces within us.

As with Alfred Adler, who claimed that psychological health is dependent on having a social interest, Toynbee advises us to find meaning in life by being creative, that is, we should try to change our world for the better by adding good things to it, if possible. Alfred Adler believed that having the purpose of advancing one's society is what separates the healthy person from the neurotic. The world is imperfect and in many ways is unsatisfactory. We prey on one another, and upon the earth itself. Others prey on us, and natural disasters wreak destruction on humans, animals, and human creations. We should strive to supplement the natural environment with human innovations, in hopes of curtailing some of this destruction. The domestication of plants and animals enabled human beings to be more prosperous than they could ever hope to be as hunters and gatherers. Yet, such changes may have unintended consequences, sometimes in the form of unexpected benefits but at other times as occasions for regret. The human capacities to love and to create have allowed the human race to progress to a point where previously unimaginable blessings such as world peace and the end of world hunger are possibilities. We are all at the mercy of human potential and must endeavor to have human goodness to emerge the victor.

➤ ## PRACTICING THE ART OF LOVE: NOT YOUR BASIC THRILL RIDE

Erich Fromm (1963) contended that love is not something that you *have* so much as something that you *do.* Love is an art, which requires effort and practice, as well as the development of one's total personality. Love is not something you fall into. Most people see the problem of love as how to be loved and how to be lovable. Instead, we need to concentrate on how to love others well.

The loving of others is an art. The learning of an art which involves acquiring a set of skills. Fromm explained it thus:

> One does not begin to learn the art directly, but indirectly, as it were . . . an apprentice in the Zen art of archery begins by doing breathing exercises. One's own person becomes an instrument in the practice of the art, and must be kept fit, according to the specific functions it has to fulfill. With regard to the art of loving, this means that anyone who aspires to become a master in this art must begin by practicing discipline, concentration and patience through every phase of his life. (pp. 92–93)

We would not want to form a partnership with an architect who has only a little knowledge of building or with a broker who is new at gauging the stock market. Still, we form what we hope to be permanent relationships in love with people who have hardly any knowledge of what love is. Others may equate love with sex, attraction, need, security, romance, or attention. Love is all of these and yet not any one of them. Many people would reject the idea of studying the art of love, saying that love should not be pondered but that it must simply be experienced. The result is that people practice love in only a limited fashion and do not seem to relate the resultant confusion and loneliness to their lack of knowledge about love.

QUESTION: *On which of Sternberg's three components of love does Fromm appear to place most importance?*

Discipline

The practice of an art requires discipline. This might involve disciplining oneself to practice whatever one is attempting to learn for a certain amount of time each day, rather than waiting to be in the mood for it. In a larger sense, a person must have a well-disciplined life in order to be able to practice any art. According to Fromm (1956), people in contemporary society do not discipline themselves outside of work, and in fact, they are rather self-indulgent in the use of their leisure time. This tendency is partly a rebellion against the routine of regular work hours and partly a reaction against the need to submit to authority while on the job.

Self-discipline can be practiced in a variety of ways. One form is simply to arise early in the morning and go to bed at approximately the same time each night, in order to insure that we are well rested. We might take care not to overeat or drink alcohol to excess. Saving a certain portion of the money we earn each month is another form of self-discipline. We might decide to devote a certain amount of time each day to intellectual development through reading and/or physical development through an exercise program. We might consciously limit the amount of time allowed for escapist activities such as television.

Whatever form of self-discipline we choose, we want to experience it as an expression of our will, or inner drive, rather than something we are forced to do from without. Once attained, self-discipline is rewarding, and we would miss it if we stopped practicing it.

Concentration

Concentration is also necessary for the practice of love. The ability to concentrate is interfered with in modern life, because there are so many things for us to do and there is so much happening all around us. We so rarely sit alone with ourselves, that we can no longer do so comfortably. It is important to be able to be alone and to sit still, without doing any activity. We must stop being busy. We might close our eyes, focus on our breathing, and concentrate on experiencing ourselves as "I," as the center of our being. Imagine the source of creative power emanating from that center. To gain this self-awareness, Fromm recommended sitting alone for twenty minutes in the morning and again in the evening.

Concentration also involves giving ourselves over to whatever we are doing at the moment. We might practice focusing attention on the activity in which we are engaged as though nothing else in the world mattered. We should not think about yesterday or tomorrow when practicing being present. Those of us who habitually think about the next thing to be done may despair over ever simply being mindful of the present activity. Patience is needed in learning any new skill. New skills require practice, and so we cannot hurry ourselves into mastery of them.

Serious listening (Chapter 10) to another is one aspect of concentration. There are times when others attempt to talk something over with us in a genuine attempt to gain further understanding about a matter. Many of us find ourselves too impatient or distracted to concentrate for long periods of time on what another person is saying. Yet, attention is one of the most loving gifts we can give to another.

Part of learning to concentrate is becoming sensitive to ourselves. An automobile driver is sensitive to all relevant changes in the sound or feel of the automobile, as well to road conditions. When attending to our loved ones, we are sensitive to them in the same way. We can also be sensitive to ourselves, noting when we are irritated or tired, for instance. It is desirable to be open to our own inner voice.

Bodily sensitivity is relatively easy to experience, because most of us have a sense of what it means to feel well. However, many of us have never seen a genuinely loving person or have never felt what it is like to be loving or to receive from a loving person. So, we have a more difficult time measuring our feeling sensations against some optimal state. We can form a sense of optimal human functioning by learning about human beings who exemplify it. Through familiarity with the world's great literature and art, we can come to understand that there is consensus about the finest human functioning and thus to understand what represents a departure from it.

Narcissism is the greatest enemy to becoming a loving person, according to Fromm. For the narcissist, the only reality is his or her inner reality. As children, we are unable to see the world from the viewpoint of others, a condition Piaget referred to as **egocentrism.** It is healthy to begin to give this up around the age of 10. There is a certain humility involved in maturing out of narcissism, as we become aware that we are not the center of things, except for our own concerns. To be interested in what others feel, rather than how they affect us, is to overcome narcissism. The development of empathy is a good antidote to narcissism.

Faith

To practice the art of loving requires faith. This faith is rooted in the confidence in one's thoughts and judgment. Faith is indispensable in friendships and loving relationships. It involves faith in oneself, in our conviction that we know who we are. Only the person who has faith in himself or herself is able to be faithful to others. Our ability to promise is dependent on having faith in our own ability to love and in our ability to produce love in others. Without belief in our own ability to be faithful, we cannot commit to love another. To love means to commit oneself without guarantee; it is an act of faith.

The significant person in a child's life must have faith in that child's potentialities. Faith in others has its culmination in faith in humanity. It is based on the idea that given the proper conditions, human culture will be based on love, justice, truth, and equality. We have faith in the potentialities of ourselves and others to the extent that we have experienced our own growth and productivity. It takes faith to bring up a child, go to sleep, or begin any kind of productive work.

To have faith requires courage, the ability to take risks. To be loved and to love require courage. In deciding to love another, one commits oneself without guarantee, giving oneself completely in the hope that one's own love will produce love in the beloved person. Faith can be practiced at every moment, for example, in sticking to one's judgment about a person, even when public opinion has turned against that person. To practice faith, we can notice where and when we lose faith and act in a cowardly way, as well as how we rationalize the loss of faith.

An Orientation toward Productivity

The practice of love involves a constant state of active concern for the other. The capacity to love demands a state of vitality that can be accomplished only by productivity in other spheres. For Fromm, the good life entails productive activity. Whether we are envisioning something we want to accomplish at work or the kind of loving relationship we wish to create and maintain, we must have faith in our own ability in order to have the heart to move forward towards the goal. We need the faith to wish for something, the courage to embark on the journey towards the goal, and the discipline to persevere.

➤ SUMMARY

TRIANGULAR THEORY OF LOVE   Robert Sternberg's model of love provides a useful way to look at love by discussing three facets of this intangible experience: *intimacy, passion,* and *commitment*. Intimacy refers to the closeness in a relationship in which affection, sharing, communication, and support are present. Passion applies mainly to physiological arousal and is the primary source of love's *intensity*. Commitment refers to the decision to love and to plan a long-term involvement with another person.

Sternberg described several types of love, which consist of varying combinations of intimacy, passion, and commitment. He stated that consummate love contains all three elements, whereas romantic love consists of intimacy and passion, but no commitment. Fatuous love is a combination of commitment and passion. Companionate love, commonly found in long-term marriages, is based on commitment and intimacy. Infatuation is founded on passion only; intimacy without either passion or commitment constitutes liking. Commitment without passion or intimacy is empty love.

In long-term relationships, intimacy and commitment are thought to be a bigger part of love than is passion. Although U.S. culture tends to emphasize passion as the main basis for "falling" in love, the passion aspect of love does not seem to form the core of a lasting relationship. Long-term relationships tend to be companionate, and are characterized by communication, sharing, acceptance, trust, respect, and loyalty.

Some people interpret the fading of romance in the relationship as a sign that love between the partners never really existed. Simpson, Campbell, and Bersheid speculated that the increase in the divorce rate in the past couple of decades is linked, at least in part, to the growing importance of intense positive emotional experiences in people's lives, experiences that may be difficult to sustain over time.

A lasting love relationship requires commitment, or caring enough about the other person to stay and work on breaking through inevitable impasses. Those who fear commitment may go through life in a series of superficial relationships. Some of the fears associated with commitment are boredom, being taken advantage of or being taken for granted, getting derailed from pursuing other goals, having the responsibility for the welfare of another person, and divorce later down the road.

THREE STAGES OF LOVE   Goldstine, Larner, Zuckerman, and Goldstine have outlined three stages to explain how romantic relationships unfold in U.S. culture: *the sparkle, disillusionment,* and *mutual acceptance.*

STAGE 1: THE SPARKLE   Falling in love creates an emotional high, which includes elements of passion, longing, fondness, and uncertainty. People newly in love feel uncertain of the relationship and thus vulnerable. Love also makes a person feel cherished. Partners may believe that the relationship will realize their fantasies and transform their lives. Both partners strive to be their finest selves. When they are falling in love, couples disregard each other's faults in order to preserve their images of each other and to safeguard their hopes for the relationship.

STAGE 2: DISILLUSIONMENT   This stage entails disenchantment with one's partner. A couple must come to grips with their differences, thereby making inevitable the experience of some conflict in the relationship. As the flaws and limitations of one's partner surface, one may question the wisdom of making a commitment to that person.

STAGE 3: MUTUAL ACCEPTANCE   People can find satisfaction in a long-term relationship only if their expectations for it are realistic. Frustrations and anxieties do not stop, but they no longer trigger doubts about the couple's future together. The partners trust each other and feel at home with each other. Known and appreciated, each person is free to become most fully himself or herself.

FEAR OF FORMING LOVING RELATIONSHIPS   Three common fears that people have concerning loving and being loved are as follows:

GETTING HURT AGAIN   To have loving relationships, people must be willing to trust others again, even after being previously hurt. On the other hand, they need to keep enough self-possession to sustain themselves should disaster strike and they lose a partner through death or desertion.

FEAR OF BEING LOVED FOR THE WRONG REASONS   Sometimes people discount the love that others give them as being contingent on a single characteristic of theirs, such as their easygoing personality, their attractive looks or body, or their function as a good provider.

BEING UNLOVABLE   Individuals who are convinced that no one could love them, may set up a self-fulfilling prophecy as they project this fear out into the environment. Those who respect, appreciate, and care for themselves open up the possibility of respecting, appreciating, and caring for others.

MISTAKEN IDEAS ABOUT LOVE   Some common misconceptions about love that were discussed are as follows:

1. *Love implies constant closeness.* Most of those who study love relationships insist that it is vital to express one's individuality and personal freedom within the relationship, so that the sharing and togetherness do not cause the parties involved to lose sight of their own uniqueness as persons.

2. *People fall in love by chance.* When people talk about the accidental nature of falling in love, they are often unaware of the tendency to feel attraction for people who reinforce the patterns of relating that were learned early in life. Mary Ainsworth's study of infant-attachment patterns showed that infants who are separated from their mothers for relatively brief periods of time tend to react in one of three ways when the mother reenters the room. One type, the secure infant, seeks out the mother gladly, showing only minor distress at having been separated. The secure infant contrasts to the avoidant infant, who, on the mother's return, actively avoids her. Both of these infants are in contrast to the anxious/ambivalent infant, who desperately seeks out the mother on her return and has tremendous difficulty in dealing with the separation.

People tend to repeat in their adult romantic relationships the attachment style developed in infancy. The adult who was secure as an infant will tend to be secure as an adult. A person who was either avoidant or anxious/ambivalent in infancy will tend to recapitulate these patterns in adulthood.

3. *People in love can be expected to be possessive.* Even though two people may agree not to have sexual relationships with others, both partners may care deeply about others outside the couple. The jealous guarding of the affection of one's partner can harm the relationship. The partners who have no friends besides each other may suffer from a narcissistic disturbance—a wish to be mirrored, like that of Narcissus.

4. *Genuine love is demonstrated by selfless acts.* There are people who get their sense of being worthwhile primarily from giving to others and who tend to refuse efforts on the part of others to give back. They are likely to become drained and resentful as a result of the types of relationships they set up with others.

5. *Love and anger are incompatible.* Learning to deal directly and honestly with anger is one of the most essential tasks in intimate relationships. Yet, many people believe that if they love someone, they cannot get angry at them. Angry feelings that are left festering breed resentment, which tends to poison the relationship.

6. *The best predictor of happiness in a relationship is how deeply you feel about each other.* A common myth about love is that the more deeply it is felt, the more "right" is the relationship and the longer it can be expected to last. Instead, the best predictor of happiness in a relationship has to do with the difference between the way each partner would ideally like the other to feel about him or her and the way that other is actually thought to perceive him or her.

7. *Religion is no longer as important to marital harmony as it once was.* The importance of a shared religion tends to increase over the length of a marriage. When couples first marry, each partner may downplay religion as an issue, in order to please the other. However, when children are born, if this issue has not been settled, there is likely to be a tug-of-war to decide which religion will be primary.

Love and Meaning in One's Life   In part, love supplies meaning to one's life through the act of commitment to another or several others. In deciding to stand by another, we give our lives a transcendent purpose; we have a goal, a dedication beyond ourselves. Even if we were not prepared to love someone, we can enjoy a sense of purpose through dedicating ourselves to something to better the human condition, and thus we can create a purposeful life.

The Art of Loving   Erich Fromm wrote that love is not something we have, it is something we do. He suggested that the practice of love involves discipline, concentration, patience, faith, courage, and a productive orientation to life. In this sense, loving is an activity that we engage in, not a passive, expectant stance that we assume in relation to others.

Learning the Language of Psychologists

passionate love	**narcissism**
companionate love	**egocentrism**
attachment styles	

Chapter Review Questions

1. According to Sternberg, what are the elements that make up complete love?
2. In what way is love an act of will or a decision?
3. What is companionate love?
4. What are the three stages of love, as discussed by Goldstine et al., and what are the essential qualities of each stage?
5. What are common fears about forming loving relationships?

6. What makes emotional closeness scary?
7. According to the text, what are common but mistaken ideas about love?
8. What is the relationship, if any, between loving and possessing another person? Does a couple's profession of mutual love give them a claim on each other?
9. According to the text, is loving another a selfless act?
10. How are attachment styles in infancy related to adult relationships?

ACTIVITIES

1. *SMALL GROUP EXERCISE:* **Personal Reflections on the Love in My Life.**
2. *COMPLETE INDIVIDUALLY:* **The Sternberg Triangular Love Scale.**
3. *COMPLETE INDIVIDUALLY:* **Love Letters Straight from Your Heart.** One of the ways to demonstrate love is to be open to others. Otherwise, all of this talk about love is just poetry. This exercise provides an opportunity for you to communicate with each other. You are to write to five people in the group towards whom you have an unexpressed positive feeling. These notes may be anonymous. Please don't write to someone you knew before entering the group, unless you want to add to your list a sixth love letter for that person. If you have a message that might help that person get more out of the group, put it in the note also. You may write love letters to more people than the original five, if you wish. Here are some possible sentence beginnings for the love letters:

    I experience you as . . .

    One thing about you that I respect is . . .

    I think that one of your strengths is . . . A way that I see you are blocking your strength is . . .

    One more thing that I want to tell you is . . .

    The most meaningful interaction I've had with you is . . .

    My hope for you is . . .

    My greatest fear for you is . . .

    One thing that I hope you'll consider is . . .
4. *CLASS GO AROUND:* **"People love me only because I am . . ."**
5. *WRITE:* What's a Date? Write a one- to three-page essay on this topic: "What's a date?" Imagine that you are explaining your culture's dating practices to someone from a culture that doesn't have this practice.
6. *LARGE GROUP EXERCISE:* **What's in a Phrase; Would Any Other Sound as Sweet?** Go around the classroom, and ask class members to give examples of what is meant when a person says, "I love you." Ask about any difference in meaning for the statement, "I am in love with you."
7. *LARGE GROUP EXERCISE:* **The Three Choices.**

FIRST STEP: Make two lines or circles, with people facing those in the other line.

SECOND STEP: Face the next person, and make a decision about how you want to express yourself to this person.

a. A wish to nod to acknowledge the other is signaled by holding up one finger.

b. A wish to smile and wave to the other is signaled by holding up two fingers.

c. A wish to shake hands with the other is signaled by holding up three fingers.

d. A wish to hug the other is signaled by holding up four fingers.

THIRD STEP: Hold up the number of fingers appropriate to your decision in the second step, while the person facing you does the same.

FOURTH STEP: Do the activity with the lowest number of fingers shown by either of the two people.

FIFTH STEP: Move on to the next person in line, and start over. Go through until you've seen each person at least twice.

8. *SUGGESTED READING:* **"Love and Marriage"** in *The Prophet,* by Kahlil Gibran.

Personal Reflections on the Love in My Life

Directions: Read and then answer each of the following questions.

1. What have been the significant relationships in your life so far, and how have they made a difference?

   _____

   _____

   _____

   _____

2. How do you express your love to others? Check the following responses below that indicate ways that you express your love and affection.

   a. _____ by telling the one I love how I feel about him or her and by saying "I love you"

   b. _____ by listening to the person

   c. _____ by doing things for the person as special treats

   d. _____ by sharing my inner thoughts and feelings with the person

   e. _____ by trusting the person

   f. _____ by buying the person flowers, gifts, and/or cards

   g. _____ by touching and other body language

   h. _____ by accommodating the person's wishes

  i. _____ by making things for the person

  j. _____ by telling others how important this person is in my life

  k. _____ by taking care of errands or doing projects for the person

  l. _____ by telling the person how important he or she is in my life

  m. _____ by teasing and "bothering" the special person

  n. _____ by encouraging the person in his or her pursuits

  o. _____ by being faithful to my partner

  p. _____ _____

  _____

3. How do you express to another person your own need to receive love and affection? Check the appropriate responses.

  a. _____ by saying that I need to be loved

  b. _____ by seeking physical affection

  c. _____ by hinting, teasing, or questioning

  d. _____ by being emotional, moody, or pouting

  e. _____ _____

  _____

4. What are some specific fears or concerns that you have about loving others?

  _____

  _____

  _____

  _____

5. How can you become a more loving human being?

  _____

  _____

  _____

  _____

6. Are there any qualities within yourself that interfere with others' loving you or that prevent you from fully receiving their love? (Examples: Being moody, being overly suspicious, refusing to accept the love of others, feeling a lack of self-worth, needing to return the love of others.)

  _____

_____

_____

_____

7. List some of your lovable aspects. (Examples: Caring for others, having a sense of humor, being playful, being helpful in times of need.)

_____

_____

_____

_____

8. How might you become a more lovable person? (Examples: Paying more attention to others, trusting others more, taking better care of my physical appearance.)

_____

_____

_____

_____

9. Whom do you love?

_____

_____

_____

_____

10. By whom are you loved?

_____

_____

_____

_____

11. How satisfied or unsatisfied are you with your love life, considering all loving relationships, not just the one with your romantic partner?

_____

_____

_____

_____

12. What style of loving was practiced in your family? What was the vocabulary of love—touch, discipline, food, gifts, nurturing your talents?

_____

_____

_____

_____

13. Complete this sentence: "To me, dating . . ."

_____

_____

14. Complete this sentence: "Falling is love is . . ."

_____

_____

15. Complete this sentence: "When I fall in love, I . . ."

_____

_____

16. Complete this sentence: "Married life is . . ."

_____

_____

The Sternberg Triangular Love Scale

Directions: Consider the person with whom you are in a relationship. If you are not currently in a relationship, think of your last significant relationship. Rate each statement on a 1 to 9 scale, where 1 = not at all true, 5 = moderately true, and 9 = extremely true." Use intermediate points on the scale to indicate intermediate levels of feelings.

1	5	9
not at all true	moderately true	extremely true

1. I am actively supportive of my partner's well-being. _____

2. I have a warm relationship with my partner. _____

3. Just seeing my partner excites me. _____

4. I know that I care about my partner. _____

5. I find myself thinking about my partner frequently throughout the day. _____

6. I am able to count on my partner in times of need. _____

7. I am committed to maintaining my relationship with my partner. _____

8. I have confidence in the stability of my relationship with my partner. _____

9. My relationship with my partner is very romantic. _____

10. My partner is able to count on me in times of need. _____

11. I find my partner to be very personally attractive. _____

12. Because of my commitment to my partner, I would not let other people come between us. _____

13. I expect my love for my partner to last the rest of my life. _____

14. I idealize my partner. _____

15. I am willing to share myself and my possessions with my partner. _____

16. I cannot imagine another person making me as happy as my partner does. _____

17. I would rather be with my partner than with anyone else. _____

18. I could not let anything get in the way of my commitment to my partner. _____

19. I receive considerable emotional support from my partner. _____

20. I will always feel a strong responsibility for my partner. _____

21. I give considerable emotional support to my partner. _____

22. There is nothing more important to me than my relationship with my partner. _____

23. I especially like physical contact with my partner. _____

24. I communicate well with my partner. _____

25. I value my partner greatly in my life. _____

26. I feel close to my partner. _____

27. I view my commitment to my partner as a solid one. _____

28. I cannot imagine ending my relationship with my partner. _____

29. There is something almost "magical" about my relationship with my partner. _____

30. I have a comfortable relationship with my partner. _____

31. I adore my partner. _____

32. I am certain of my love for my partner. _____

33. I view my relationship with my partner as permanent. _____

34. I cannot imagine life without my partner. _____

35. I view my relationship with my partner as a good decision. _____

36. I feel that I really understand my partner. _____

37. My relationship with my partner is passionate. _____

38. I feel that my partner really understands me. _____

39. I feel a sense of responsibility toward my partner. _____

40. I feel that I can really trust my partner. _____

41. When I see romantic movies or read romantic books, I think about my partner. _____

42. I share deep personal information about myself with my partner. _____

43. I plan to continue in my relationship with my partner. _____

44. Even when my partner is hard to deal with, I remain committed to our relationship. _____

45. I fantasize about my partner. _____

Scoring:
(1) Write down the number you assigned to each statement.

1. __ intimacy	16. __ passion	31. __ passion
2. __ intimacy	17. __ passion	32. __ commitment
3. __ passion	18. __ commitment	33. __ commitment
4. __ commitment	19. __ intimacy	34. __ passion
5. __ passion	20. __ commitment	35. __ commitment
6. __ intimacy	21. __ intimacy	36. __ intimacy
7. __ commitment	22. __ passion	37. __ passion
8. __ commitment	23. __ passion	38. __ intimacy
9. __ passion	24. __ intimacy	39. __ commitment
10. __ intimacy	25. __ intimacy	40. __ intimacy
11. __ passion	26. __ intimacy	41. __ passion
12. __ commitment	27. __ commitment	42. __ intimacy
13. __ commitment	28. __ commitment	43. __ commitment
14. __ passion	29. __ passion	44. __ commitment
15. __ intimacy	30. __ intimacy	45. __ passion

(2) Add up the numbers in the intimacy category:_____
(3) Add up the numbers in the passion category:_____
(4) Add up the numbers in the commitment category:_____
(5) Divide each of the three numbers by 15. This will give you an average rating for each of the three components.

Source: Sternberg, R. J., 1991.

10

Intimate Relationships

*You can't control all aspects of the season, but you can control
the breadth and depth of your days, the contour of your face,
and the atmosphere of your mind.*
—Anonymous

➤ *PREVIEW QUESTIONS:* How might an "inferiority complex" interfere with the establishment of fulfilling relationships? What communication skills are necessary for maintaining satisfying relationships? In what ways do couples need to be similar, in order for their relationship to be compatible? Is it important for intimate relationships to be free of conflict?

➤ Introduction: The Sharing of Oneself with Another

According to Robert Sternberg's model of love (Chapter 9), intimacy is one of three components that make up complete love. Sternberg defines intimacy as "the feelings of closeness, connectedness, and being bonded" (1991, p. 66). Intimacy is brought about and maintained through self-disclosure (Chapter 1). When we achieve intimacy with another person, we feel known and understood. Indicators of intimacy are giving and receiving emotional support, a desire to further the welfare of the loved one, and a sharing of oneself and one's possessions with the significant other.

Any discussion of relationships addresses the question, Where do I fit in? Maslow's hierarchy of needs incorporated "love and belongingness" as a fundamental human requirement. The love needs involve giving and receiving affection. When belongingness needs are unsatisfied, a person will hunger for relations with people in general and for family and group affiliation, and will attempt to establish contact and closeness with others. Once an individual feels accepted and loved, she or he is encouraged to fulfill her or his human potential.

Closeness does not come about automatically. We earn it by letting others know us, instead of keeping our thoughts, feelings, and reactions to ourselves. Erik Erikson believed that the challenge of forming intimate relationships is the major task of young adulthood (Chapter 3). Intimacy implies that we are able to share significant aspects of ourselves with others. The closeness we enjoy with another person can be emotional, intellectual, physical, spiritual, or any combination of these. Erikson noted that in order to risk intimacy, one must be able to trust others and to have a strong enough sense of one's own identity to feel secure when being influenced by another person without fear of losing oneself. When we avoid intimacy, we cheat ourselves out of one of the very finest experiences in life: the feeling of being cared about by others and the feeling of being invested in others. We miss out on one of the most important factors in producing personal happiness as well as in preventing physical and mental illness. Unsatisfied hunger for contact leads to feelings of alienation and loneliness.

The Buss (1989) study of men and women from thirty-seven countries (mentioned in Chapter 9) indicated that potential mates were valued when they elicited mutual attraction and love. Both men and women wanted a partner with dependable character, emotional stability, and maturity, as well as a pleasing disposition. These are qualities that allow self-disclosure to be safe and thus make intimacy possible. Notice also that there are similarities between these wished-for qualities in a mate and the positive poles of the big five personality dimensions that were discussed in Chapter 7 as being relevant to predicting success on the job. Apparently these personality dimensions may also predict success in love and work relationships.

➤ Alfred Adler (1870–1937) and the Importance of Having a Social Interest

As with Jung, Alfred Adler began as an adherent of Freud's psychoanalytic theory, but Adler soon developed ideas that departed from Freud's, with the result that the two men parted company in considerable bitterness. Adler believed that Freud's emphasis on internal dynamics was too limited and, in particular, challenged Freud over the relative importance of the sexual drives. In general, Adler focused on conscious drives over unconscious forces. His theory emphasized self-determination: We are not the victims of fate but instead are creative, active, choice-making beings whose every action has purpose and meaning. In Addler's view, intelligence and personality were not inherited but were developed as the child matured. Viewing social interaction as a critical factor in human development, Adler looked at the role of social forces in shaping behavior. He accepted Freud's concept of an inborn aggressive drive, which tends toward cruelty, but proposed that the drive becomes converted through the demands of cultural and parental censure into altruism, charity, and sympathy. Adler considered this transformation to be the hallmark of healthy development. He believed that friendship, love, and work are the central concerns of adult life.

Inferiority Complex

Adler viewed each human being's struggle to overcome feelings of inferiority as a core problem in life. He theorized that every person experiences feelings of inferiority mainly because he or she begins life as a small, weak, and relatively powerless child surrounded by larger and more competent adults. Children feel inferior because they are little and are dependent on adults. Youngsters react to this inferior position of childhood by striving for superiority and power. Gradually, they learn to do the things that older people can do. Adler believed that throughout life the desire to overcome inferiority was the prime determining force in behavior. By gaining mastery in various areas, we achieve a primary goal in life of self-acceptance.

Adler coined the term **inferiority complex.** If one's childhood feelings of inferiority continue into adulthood, the person will develop an inferiority complex and would be motivated to prove himself or herself to family and peers. The adult experiencing an inferiority complex would have trouble with establishing mature relationships because of a constant struggle to show his or her worth to others. The specific ways an individual chooses to compensate for inferiority and to achieve superiority determines his or her **style of life.**

Style of Life

The term "style of life" was originated by Adler. It refers to the uniqueness of each individual's goal in life and to the meaning that a person gives to his or her existence. To the degree that people have developed healthy social interests, their striving for superiority will be shaped into a style of life that is warmly receptive of others and focused on friendship. Such individuals will assume that other people are likewise warmly receptive of them and are therefore sources of satisfaction and pleasure.

Adler described his meaning of "style of life" with the following analogy:

> Perhaps I can illustrate this by an anecdote of three children who were taken to the zoo for the first time. As they stood before the lion's cage, one of them shrank behind his mother's skirts and said, "I want to go home." The second child stood where he was, very pale and trembling, and said, "I'm not a bit frightened." The third glared at the lion fiercely and asked his mother, "Shall I spit at it?" The three children really felt inferior, but each expressed his feelings in his own way, consonant with his style of life. (1931, p. 50)

The development of a style of life represents an individual's creative endeavor to overcome feelings of inferiority. The person decides to shape his or her life in the direction of that goal because that person's feelings of inferiority form a unique constellation with his or her own striving for superiority.

According to Adler, a person's earliest childhood recollection should be able to provide some clues as to the style of life that individual has adopted. Here is an illustration of the impact of an early childhood memory on English biologist Rupert Sheldrake, who took part in the documentary, *A Glorious Accident:*

> I was staying at the family farm house and I was outside with an uncle. And I saw a row of willow trees with rusty wire hanging between them. So I said to my uncle, why is that row of rusty wires hanging between those trees? And he said, well, we made a fence out of willow stakes and the fence came to life. And I looked and, of course, could see that each . . . had been a fence post and these wooden posts had formed shoots and roots and it wasn't a fence anymore. It was a fence of living trees . . . And this made a really tremendous impression on me, this sense of dead things coming to life in such a vivid way that you could directly see . . . this particularly vivid incident . . . in this childhood memory was summarized [in] much of my subsequent scientific career. I spent years working

on plant development on the behavior of isolated stem cuttings. And a lot of what I did subsequently was foreshadowed in this particular memory.

Source: A Glorious Accident, KCET.

Social Interest

Adler believed that people are motivated primarily by an innate **social interest** and that the goal in life is to act in ways that fulfill social responsibilities. He distinguished between a healthy and an unhealthy (mistaken) style of life, proposing that social interest is the primary characteristic that differentiates the two. Whereas a healthy style of life is marked by goals that reflect optimism and confidence and that entail contributing to the welfare of others, a mistaken style of life is characterized by goals reflecting self-centeredness, competitiveness, and striving for personal power.

Unlike Freud, who regarded society as a limitation on the individual, Adler came to see social interaction as essential to mental health. Social interest can be described as a striving for a form of community, as it could be envisioned if humanity had reached the goal of perfection. This striving implies respect and consideration for all human beings. We remain open to the other person, welcoming that individual as a host would welcome a guest. The life of this individual is respected as equally valid as our own.

Social interest can be equated with identification and empathy with others. For Adler, our happiness and successes are largely related to a sense of belonging and an interconnectedness. As social beings, we need to be of use to others and to establish meaningful relationships in our community. Adler asserted that only when we feel united with others can we act with courage in facing and dealing with life's problems.

Adler's social interest bears some resemblance to the Hispanic notion of *individualismo* (individualism), which emphasizes what is unique about each member of the community and how this uniqueness leads to cooperation rather than to competition (Canino & Canino, 1993). *Individualismo* means that everyone has something to offer to the Hispanic community. Each person is expected to share his or her unique offerings with the rest of the community. In contrast, American individualism emphasizes competition among people, leading to an individual's ability to obtain economic and professional success without the assistance of other members of the community (Sandoval & De La Roza, 1986).

Like Hispanics, Native Americans reject the traditional sense of individualism that leads to competition among family members and between American Indians and other people (Richardson, 1981). Among Native Americans, the emphasis is on working together to achieve common goals among all members of the tribe. A recognition of the qualities of the individual and his or her independence is also apparent, though there must be harmony between the desire of a person for self-actualization and the welfare of the tribe (O'Brien, 1989; Paniagua, 1994).

Since we are embedded in a society, we cannot be understood in isolation from our social context. Self-actualization is thus not an individual matter; it is only within the group that we can actualize our potentialities. Social interest is the key difference between the neurotic's and the normal person's striving for superiority.

QUESTION: *What are some ways in which having a social interest would be reflected in someone's style of life?*

Adler's Approach to Dreams

As with Jung, Adler did not agree with Freud's perspective that dreams fulfilled wishes or revealed deeply hidden conflicts. Instead, he thought that dreams involve the meaning surrounding current life problems. Adler's theory focuses on what people's intentions are and what they are striving to accomplish. Adler viewed dreams as an expression of an individual's unique strivings toward goals.

For Adler, dreams were not to be interpreted as the fulfillment of unacceptable wishes; rather, they represent dreamers' attempts to resolve problems that they are unwilling or unable to master with their conscious power of reason (Adler, 1973, p. 214). In this sense, Adlerians view dreams as rehearsals for possible future courses of action.

Dreams clarify our views of ourselves and the world. They remind us of our life goals and guide us toward accomplishing these goals. Like Freud, Adler believed that the dream was disguised, but in contrast to Freud, Adler was convinced that the purpose of the dream was to be incomprehensible. The intention of the dream is to deceive the dreamer. It is the purpose of a dream to create a mood. No attempt should be made to clarify the mood, because the dream represents an effort to bypass rational problem solving, which is not expected to be effective. The dreamer's unconscious strives to create a mood or an emotional state upon waking that will force the person to take action that he or she is reluctant to attempt. The dream provides the person with an excuse and the momentum to actualize true feelings.

View of Psychopathology and Therapy

Adler rejected the idea that troubled individuals are psychologically sick. For him, mental disorders represent a mistaken style of life, which is characterized by maladaptive attempts to compensate for feelings of inferiority, a preoccupation with achieving personal power, and a lack of social interest. According to Adler, psychotics, criminals, and addicts all share a lack of social interest. He viewed clients as "discouraged" rather than sick and felt that a therapist's primary task was to provide their clients with encouragement so that these people can grow to become what they were meant to be. Adler also believed that therapists should offer advice by suggesting alternative courses of action from which the client can then choose. Therapists teach people better ways to meet the challenges of life tasks, provide direction, help people change unrealistic assumptions and beliefs, and offer encouragement to those who are discouraged.

➤ CHARACTERISTICS OF HEALTHY RELATIONSHIPS

There are perhaps dozens of concepts that could be discussed as guidelines for maintaining healthy relationships. Following are six ideas for your consideration:

Establishing a Separate Identity

It is important for each person in a close relationship to have a separate identity. Making relationships work involves creating and maintaining a balance between separateness and togetherness. It's common to fear both abandonment and loss of identity when growing close to another person. If there is not enough togetherness in a relationship, people in it typically feel isolated and do not share feelings or experiences. They tend to grow apart and feel alienated from one another. People outside the relationship who do share common interests with one or both of the partners tend to be drawn in to alleviate the loneliness that results from the estrangement between the partners.

On the other hand, if there is not enough separateness, the partners give up a sense of their own identity and control. They may devote their efforts toward becoming what the other person expects, rather than to revealing themselves to their partner. Lerner (1985) wrote that women often define their own wishes and preferences as being the same as those of their partners. This is particularly likely to be the case in a relationship in which partners adhere to traditional gender roles, with the result that there is no equality in the relationship. It is also not unheard of for men to take on the role of molding themselves to their partner's wishes. To establish a more balanced relationship, both parties will need to look at aspects of inequality and to demonstrate a willingness to negotiate changes. The stronger partner can promote this balance by drawing out the attitudes and preferences of the more reticent partner.

The quality of interactions with one's partner is enhanced when each person finds meaning and sources of nourishment outside the relationship. Sometimes people become very possessive in their friendships and love relationships. Although we may experience jealousy at times, we should not demand that our partner numb his or her feelings for others. To do so saps vitality from the bond between the two intimates.

A healthy couple cultivates a group of friends and family, acknowledging that no one person is capable of filling all of their needs. Sometimes the presence of a close friend can serve as an important balancing force that functions to strengthen the primary relationship. We may well consider our romantic partner to be the one we like and love most, and trust that he or she feels the same way about us. We do not, however, want to introduce a flavor of "ownership" into the relationship, since doing so can breed jealousy and fear.

An important aspect of having a separate identity is that each person allows the other a sense of privacy and freedom. Both partners recognize the need for solitude and are willing to create time in which each person can be alone. Also, each avoids prying into every thought of the partner or manipulating the other to disclose what he or she wants to keep private.

Hopefully, we can experience ourselves as wanting rather than as needing our partner. Our lives did not begin when we met our partner, nor will our lives end if the relationship fails to continue. Although loss of intimacy with our partner would be regrettable, each of us can survive without the other. Should anything happen to our significant other, those of us who have close friendships are likely to recover more easily from the loss and to feel less anxious while in the intimate relationship. When we depend on our partner to fill all our needs, we necessarily feel excruciatingly vulnerable to the ever present possibility of loss of this person, and we exclude other people who can be important in our lives.

Kahlil Gibran's (1976) poem "Love and Marriage" advises us to "let there be spaces in your togetherness." Partners should not be so tightly bound together that if they are separated, one or the other becomes lost and empty. Dependency should not be interpreted as love but as the seeking of an object to make one feel complete. Neither person should depend on the other for confirmation of his or her personal worth, nor should one walk in the shadow of the other.

When an adult has an excessive need to be taken care of by another, he or she may be considered to have a **dependent personality disorder.** This condition leads to submissive and clinging behavior and fear of separation. The dependent behaviors are designed to elicit caregiving and arise from the self-perception of being unable to function adequately without the help of others. Individuals with this disorder tend to be unrealistically preoccupied with fears of being left to take care of themselves. They are likely immediately to seek another relationship as a source of care and support when a close relationship ends.

Coping with Conflict and Anger

Couples need to be able to handle anger in their relationship. It is unrealistic to expect that an intimate relationship will be without conflict. Rather than having as a goal the absence of fighting, the couple might be better served to learn how to fight cleanly and constructively. Doing so entails an ongoing process of expressing annoyance and frustration while the events that stimulated these negative feelings are still fresh and while the level of feeling remains mild. It is the buildup in intensity of these potentially destructive emotions that creates trouble. If anger is not expressed and dealt with appropriately, it will sour the relationship. Bottled-up irritation may be let out indirectly through sarcasm and hostility; it may be displaced onto an inappropriate target; or it can turn to resentment and thus destroy love. There seems to be no "statute of limitations" on such resentment. Anger is best expressed in a direct manner, yet there is an art to doing so appropriately. For instance, a couple might agree to abide by rules such as allowing each partner "time out" to cool off before discussing the problem. A good predictor of long-term relationship satisfaction is having a mutually agreeable strategy worked out for handling disagreements and other sources of hard feelings.

Many people do not know when they are feeling upset or angry. If they were to perceive their anger, these people would find the upset feeling unacceptable and so repress knowledge of it. Even if consciously aware of our anger, most of us aren't willing to bring it out into the open for fear of not being agreeable to others. We may also conclude that since we don't know how to resolve conflicts, there is no point in bringing them up. Therefore, we hold in our anger and rely on our training in how to be polite to maintain us in interpersonal relations.

Often a partner will strive at any cost to avoid a conflict, saying "I don't see a problem." The fear behind this defensive strategy is that if the more confrontive person starts talking about a problem, the avoidant partner may end up having to make embarrassing admissions, which will evoke feelings of shame and unworthiness. However understandable the desire to avoid such feelings might be, pretending that a conflict does not exist won't make it go away. Typically, during relationship struggles, partners fail to acknowledge the validity of one another's concerns. Yet, if one person is distressed about a particular situation, then that situation automatically becomes an issue for the relationship. The nature of an intimate relationship is that it involves reciprocal concern for the well-being of the other. When viewed in this light, the concerns of one partner are likewise a problem for the other partner as well.

Some people who customarily avoid conflict are convinced that if they give in one more time, their mate will come around. This belief is sometimes known as the Chamberlain fallacy. Neville Chamberlain was the British Prime Minister who again and again pacified Hitler prior to the outbreak of World War II. Chamberlain mistakenly concluded that if he made just one more gesture of appeasement, then the dictator would be satisfied. Instead, Chamberlain empowered Hitler to continue and expand on his early aggressive strategy. Essentially, Hitler found that his predatory conduct was positively reinforced; therefore, he had no reason to stop, because he was getting what he wanted.

Compliance with the status quo is generally a strategy aimed at keeping the peace. Often the compliant partner feels somewhat dependent on the relationship and thus is reluctant to challenge his or her partner. The compliant partner may kid himself or herself into believing that he or she is simply an "agreeable" person. If that person were to examine his or her feelings, the individual would probably find that he or she is harboring resentment. Sooner or later, this resentment will diminish the positive feelings in the relationship.

People who are submissive are sometimes matched with partners who are aggressive and persistent. There is give-and-take in every relationship, but when one person does all of the giving in, it is an unhealthy sign for continued intimacy. Without meaningful dialogue, the intimacy that is the foundation of a good relationship is eventually destroyed. The avoidant partner can make a change for the better in the relationship by learning to negotiate his or her rights. Sometimes doing so means saying no to one's partner and not giving in to pressure, so that one's partner learns to take one seriously. In Chapter 13, more will be said about healthy strategies for getting through disagreement.

NOTE: *See the Practice Identifying Response Styles at the end of this chapter.*

Assuming Responsibility for One's Own Happiness

In a good relationship, neither partner blames the other when experiencing unhappiness. We cannot expect other people to make us feel alive, take away our boredom, assume our risks, or make us feel valued and important. Ideally, each of us is working on our own personal growth and thus changing and opening up to new experiences. Our relationship should benefit from the vitality we bring to it as a by-product of such growth experiences. A good way to build solid relationships with others is to work on developing ourselves.

Since personal growth always holds within its potentialities the possibility of growing in a different direction from our loved ones, we may feel frightened as we notice ourselves changing. Unless our loved ones are also enthusiastic about their own plans, they may not look favorably on our joy over our own goals and adventures. Thus, we should not be surprised if we encounter resistance to our growth and change on the part of our significant others. Also, the achievement and joy of others will make uncomfortable any of us who aren't also moving in the direction of personal development. Unfortunately, we may be tempted to block our partner's progress out of fear that the change will upset the delicate balance of the relationship. This is not a viable strategy; we cannot hold onto others by restricting their freedom.

Ultimately, we are responsible for defining our goals and can take action to change what we are doing if we are unhappy with our situation. A person who relies on others for personal fulfillment and confirmation is in trouble. Even the most loving and devoted partner is incapable making his or her loved one happy. Anyone who passively waits for another to provide her or him with a sense of fulfillment in life will eventually recognize the futility of such an expectation.

Each person must be free to move in a direction in life that is personally meaningful. When this is the case, both partners will be excited about the quality of their lives and their projects. Both can feel that their needs are being met within the relationship, but they also feel a sense of engagement in their work, play, and relationships with other friends and family members.

Demonstrating Active Concern for the Other

A sense of being emotionally supported by one's partner is a principal contributor to marital satisfaction, relationship stability, personal growth, and sexual enjoyment. Matthews and Clark (1982) describe this kind of support as having two dimensions: Our partner understands our true identity, and our partner accepts and appreciates who we really are. Such validation fills a deep void in one's life.

Partners encourage each other to become all that they are capable of becoming. They have an interest in each other's welfare and a desire to see that the other person is fulfilled. In a close relationship, the unhappiness of the other person is bound to affect us. Although the way others feel will influence our lives, they do not cause our feelings. We allow our happiness to be dampened by concern for those we care about.

In *The Art of Loving*, Erich Fromm wrote, "The most fundamental kind of love, which underlies all types of love is . . . the sense of responsibility, care, respect, knowledge of another human being, the wish to further his life" (1963, p. 47). The two intimates avoid manipulating, exploiting, or using one another. Also, each respects and cares for the other and is willing to see the world through the other's eyes. Each person has a desire to give to the other.

Sometimes partners believe that by being in a committed relationship, they have adequately demonstrated their love for one another. They do not understand the need to protect and nurture a relationship over time. If we give our relationship less than the care it needs, its value in our lives is likely to decrease. Without being nurtured, it may well go into decline.

Our partners feel validated when they receive supportive comments from us. Such compliments contribute to our partners' sense of personal worth. Our loved ones may also learn how to be caring by observing our supportive behavior and recognizing how good it feels. Initiating positive input can be one way to break the negative exchanges that tend to characterize unhappy couples (Schaap & Jansen-Nawas, 1987).

Self-Disclosing

As was discussed elsewhere (Chapter 1), self-disclosure involves telling others what is going on inside our heads. A willingness to divulge our thoughts and feelings is needed to achieve and sustain emotional intimacy with others.

Each person reveals himself or herself to the other, particularly with regard to thoughts and feelings about the quality of the relationship and other matters pertaining to the relationship. The two intimates can openly express grievances and let each other know the changes they desire. They can ask for what they want, rather than expecting the other intuitively to know and provide for their needs.

When we disclose ourselves to one another, we become vulnerable. Just because we have the advantage of having hurtful information about the other person doesn't mean that we ought to use it to clobber him or her. The most commonly mentioned principle for guiding interpersonal relationships is the Golden Rule, which admonishes us to do unto others as we would have them do unto us.

Sometimes couples expect that their ability to communicate will improve as they get to know one another better. This is not necessarily the case, according to Robert Sternberg (1991). In relationships, the closer we become, the more that we may feel we have to lose by communicating openly with one another. At the beginning of a relationship, we typically self-disclose slowly and carefully. As we feel more comfortable, we may share ever more deeply, perhaps telling our partners about matters that we have until now kept private. As the relationship becomes more serious, however, there is a tendency to close up again because we feel vulnerable to our partner's opinion of us. Sternberg states that if communication and trust are not established early in the relationship, we cannot hope that they will develop later when the stakes are much higher.

Withholding pertinent information about ourselves in an effort to be self-protective in a relationship is potentially damaging. Sometimes we lie about or cover up feelings. At other times, we may force significant others into mind reading in order to please us. We may keep silent when angry, hurt, or afraid, so that loved ones have no idea that there is something endangering the relationship. The good feelings among intimates are both precious and fragile, and they must be cared for. Usually those who withhold information are reluctant to feel vulnerable by putting themselves on the line. What if those things that were disclosed were later used against them? What if, when we make ourselves known, we are rejected as unacceptable? The possibility seems devastating.

Even while trying to be so careful to make a good impression, those who withhold self-disclosure are generally regarded by others as cold and unfeeling. Others may attempt to provoke them, simply to gain some kind of emotional response. It seems that the most painful reaction we can possibly receive from another person is no reaction, that is, indifference.

A new twist on self-disclosure has been interaction with strangers on the Internet. A significant number of people have been forming human connections over this anonymous electronic medium. The anonymity of the Internet chat rooms allows people to give free reign to fantasy and to speak their minds with impunity. Those seeking more personal relationships eventually arrange to meet their cyber-partners in person. Although for some people, the romance fades on meeting face-to-face, many others apparently decide to accept the appearance of those they have grown close to through a mental connection. If Internet "dating" were to become the norm, the stage theory of love relationships discussed in Chapter 9 would have to be revised, because Internet relationships begin with intimacy instead of passion.

Having Shared Activities, Interests, and Values

Just as one's values, interests, and skills are important career considerations, so, too, are the couple's compatibility in terms of these qualities. For a relationship to work, shared activities are important, as well as agreement about what is important in life, so that the couple may work as a team in deciding how to invest their time, money, and talents.

We tend to be attracted to those who share our beliefs and interests. Similarity forms a basis for sharing activities and makes communication with our partner easier. Those whose attitudes differ from ours challenge our views and can produce in us uneasiness, hostility, and even avoidance. Although we may have heard that "opposites attract," in fact, we are generally attracted to people of similar backgrounds, interests, attitudes, and beliefs. This tendency may occur partly because it is reinforcing to see our views confirmed by others, thus showing how "right" we are to embrace our beliefs and implying that our significant others are sensible people as well.

Similarity in other areas makes for compatible relationships, too. One of the most consistent findings in the research on interpersonal attraction is that similar people are attracted to each other (Carli, Ganley, & Pierce-Otay, 1991). We tend to marry a person like us in almost every way (Caspi & Herbener, 1990). Most married couples are similar in age, education, race, religion, and ethnic background. In addition, they share common attitudes and opinions, mental abilities, and, to a lesser extent, socioeconomic status, height, weight, and eye color.

A couple's ability to play together can be enhanced if the pair enjoy a similar energy level. Two energetic partners are more likely to feel compatible than are a couple with one partner who is energetic and one who is laid-back. Although to some extent, energy level can be influenced by factors such as a healthy diet, plenty of rest, and an optimistic life philosophy, it is probably also controlled in part by heredity.

Research indicates that couples who have a great deal in common, from similar leisure time activities to shared core values, tend to have greater marital satisfaction (Antill, 1983; Byrne, 1971). Even in a society such as ours, which reveres romantic love, a systematic look at what values and interests partners share or do not share can be helpful. Marriage contracts (these are not "prenuptial agreements," which are legally binding contracts, but rather are informal agreements) can help couples spell out their marital values and goals, so that they don't enter a legal marriage without a good understanding between them ahead of time. By discussing before they get married who will do what, couples gain insight into potential sources of conflict and have an opportunity to resolve them, or to reevaluate the wisdom of continuing with their marital plans. Refer to the end of this chapter for a sample marriage contract.

Mate selection on the basis of similarity is probably a good thing. It is easier to understand someone who is very much like us. We find it rewarding to talk with a partner who shares our views. We may learn more when we discuss matters with those who hold different opinions, but we are likely also to feel a bit defensive and uncomfortable. Personality traits tend to be similar in the most stable marriages (Kim, Martin, & Martin, 1989). Couples who have closely matched MMPI profiles (the Minnesota Multiphasic Personality Inventory is the most widely used personality test used by psychologists) are the most happily married (Richard, Wakefield, & Lewak, 1990). On the other hand, couples with large discrepancies in age or level of education run the greatest risk of divorce (Tzeng, 1992).

➤ IMPROVING RELATIONSHIPS THROUGH EFFECTIVE COMMUNICATION

The word "dialogue" comes from the Greek *dia logos*, which means "flow of meaning" (Senge, 1990). In order to be heard by others, we must develop a speaking style that is comfortable for others, rather than making them defensive and guarded. In the following sections are suggestions for how we might express ourselves in a manner that is likely to create a positive interpersonal climate, conducive to mutual self-disclosure.

Strive for Honesty

Others can sense whether we are being genuine or disingenuous. Without being needlessly hurtful, in order to be effective communicators, we must disclose our true thoughts and feelings to those with whom we care to have an authentic relationship. Naturally, there are times when to speak our mind would be unproductive and unnecessarily rude. Good communicators learn to discriminate between the times when openness is desirable and occasions when the tactful strategy would be to hold one's tongue.

One aspect of being honest with others involves conveying our sense of ourselves as fallible human beings. Consider a classic study conducted by Aronson (1969) in which college students listened to one of four tapes of supposed candidates for a "College Quiz Bowl." On two of the tapes, the person was represented as highly intelligent; on the other two, he was depicted as average in ability. One of the "intelligent" and one of the "average" tapes included an incident in which the candidate clumsily spilled coffee on himself. Those listening to the tapes rated as most attractive the superior candidate who spilled, and as least attractive the average student who was clumsy. It seems that when our positive qualities speak for themselves, we can make ourselves more appealing to others by acknowledging and otherwise displaying our imperfections.

Approach Others as Equals

As much as our culture embraces the concept of equality, people do not have the same status or ability in all areas. Those who have the advantage of higher status or greater ability would do well to disregard their advantage in conversation. People don't like being reminded of the greater accomplishments of someone else. Accomplished people who refrain from mentioning their attainments exhibit graciousness.

If one person in a conversation is more articulate or more informed than the other, that person is more likely to win his or her point. However, a good communicator who is interested in furthering mutual understanding between the involved parties rather than in winning his or her point will draw out the other person and thus encourage that person's self-expression.

Express Your Opinions Tentatively

Rather than giving the impression that we know all the answers, we want to convey to others that our beliefs and attitudes are flexible and subject to revision. We can do this by using qualifying words or phrases. Perhaps Benjamin Franklin said this best in his *Autobiography*:

> My list of virtues contain'd at first but twelve; but a Quaker friend having kindly informed me that I was generally thought proud; that my pride show'd itself frequently in conversation; that I was not content with being in the right when discussing any point, but was overbearing, and rather insolent, of which he convinc'd me by mentioning several instances; I determined endeavouring to cure myself, if I could, of this vice or folly among the rest, and I added *Humility* to my list, giving an extensive meaning to the word.

> I cannot boast of much success in acquiring the *reality* of this virtue, but I had a good deal with regard to the *appearance* of it. I made it a rule to forbear all direct contradiction to the sentiments of others and all positive assertion of my own. I even forbid myself, agreeably to the old laws of our Junto, the use of every word or expression in the language that imported a fix'd opinion, such as *certainly, undoubtedly,* etc., and I adopted, instead of them, *I conceive, I apprehend,* or *I imagine* a thing to be so or so; or it *so appears to me at present.* When another asserted something that I thought an error, I deny'd myself the pleasure of

contradicting him abruptly, and of showing immediately some absurdity in his proposition; and in answering I began by observing that in certain cases or circumstances his opinion would be right, but in the present case there *appear'd* or *seem'd* to me some difference, etc. I soon found the advantage of this change in my manner; the conversations I engag'd in went on more pleasantly. The modest way in which I propos'd my opinions procu'd them a readier reception and less contradiction; I had less mortification when I was found to be in the wrong, and I more easily prevail'd with others to give up their mistakes and join with me when I happened to be in the right.

And this mode, which I at first put on with some violence to natural inclination, became at length so easy, and so habitual to me, that perhaps for these fifty years past no one has ever heard a dogmatical expression escape me. And to this habit (after my character of integrity) I think it principally owing that I had early so much weight with my fellow-citizens when I proposed new institutions, or alterations in the old, and so much influence in public councils when I became a member; for I was but a bad speaker, never eloquent, subject to much hesitation in my choice of words, hardly correct in language, and yet I generally carried my points.

In reality, there is, perhaps, no one of our natural passions so hard to subdue as *pride.* Disguise it, struggle with it, beat it down, stifle it, mortify it as much as one pleases, it is still alive, and will every now and then peep out and show itself; you will see it, perhaps, often in this history; for, even if I could conceive that I had completely overcome it, I should probably be proud of my humility.

Source: The Autobiogaphy of Benjamin Franklin, edited by Charles W. Eliot, pp. 87–88. Copyright © 1937 by P.F. Collier & Son, Corp.

Do Not Try to Change the Other

We may sometimes entertain these thoughts: "*I* am not really in need of any improvement. It's the other person in my life who is causing me grief. What I need is for him/her to change. If only this would happen, things could be so great." It's easy to get hung up on how we wish others would change, rather than working on changing ourselves. Our lives seem as though they would be so much more comfortable, if only our parents, siblings, children, friends, employers, lovers, and so on would change in a particular way.

If we blame others for the fact that we are not as happy or as comfortable as we'd like to be, we diminish our power fully to control our own lives. The good news is that by changing ourselves, we can prevent others from continuing with negative behavior towards us. In that regard, we can have an indirect, though effective impact on the behavior of others. Essentially, we have the power that we need in order to change our relationships, by altering our own thoughts, feelings, and behavior.

In any intimate relationship, we can expect at times to experience feelings of awkwardness, unexpressed desires, and fears of rejection. We don't need to feel helpless in the midst of these feelings. We can make decisions about how we can assume increased control of our relationships. We have the power to bring about change if we alter our own thoughts or behavior and if we do not need to insist that the other person make changes to accommodate us. It is appropriate to focus on our own wants and to look at what we are doing that makes us a participant in the undesirable situation. In doing so, we can have a positive influence on our relationships. For example, "I messages" allow us to assert our wants and needs in the relationship without directly attempting to change the other person.

This realization should bring some measure of relief, in that we generally have more ability to control ourselves than we do to influence other people. When we begin to feel upset over the "outrageous" behavior of others, we can remind ourselves to refocus on our own conduct and on the way that we might be participating in the situation. Turning our attention to our own actions can allow us to discover what we can do to improve the outcome. As difficult as changing our own habits might be, attempting to alter the conduct of others is even more problematic. Sternberg (1991) advises, "When you are considering a commitment, your best course is to ask yourself whether you love and accept your partner as he or she is at that moment—not as you hope the person will be at a distant point in the future" (p. 92). Often in relationships, we hope that the other person will learn to behave differently, and we may even develop the intention to help the other person change. We may believe that if we love the other enough, he or she will "blossom." However, it is a mistake to overestimate our ability to bring about change in others.

In relationships, a review of past behavior is a reasonable way to make predictions about what future behavior is likely to be. Such predictions are possible, because long-term behavior patterns are difficult to alter, so that even if the person wants to change, doing so cannot generally be accomplished overnight. For the most part, people are not all that interested in becoming substantially different from who they are. For all of these reasons, past behavior is a fairly reliable indicator of future behavior.

Listen

Our self-exploration will be facilitated by sharing our thoughts with others and by having others share their thoughts and feelings with us. The quality of this exchange will depend on our skill in both listening and self-disclosure. Listening is a crucial aspect of interpersonal communication. Despite the importance of listening, most of us have had little training in this skill, and many of us attend poorly to what others have to say. Either failure to listen or selective listening is a significant block to communication.

In order to be a good listener, we must give the other person our undivided attention. We must move into a position of acceptance, so that we refrain from prejudging the person and from making assumptions as the individual speaks that will keep us from hearing everything that person has to say.

Humanistic psychologist Carl Rogers (1961) found that in his work as a therapist, very attentively listening to his clients was an important way of being helpful. He developed that strategy of simply listening whenever he was in doubt as to what he should do. It seemed surprising to Rogers that this ordinary kind of interaction could be so useful in bringing about understanding among people.

From Rogers's discovery, a therapeutic strategy has been developed known as **active listening.** Active listening is considered to be far more effective than the more typical passive type, because it involves the listener in a manner that improves the chances that the sender's message will be understood. To understand why active listening is more effective than is passive listening, we must delve into the communication process itself. In order to communicate something to another person, we need to translate an internal state, a thought or feeling we have, into language, a tone of voice, and body language. Our listener must accurately interpret the signals that we send. If the receiver decodes the message accurately, he or she will understand the speaker. If, however, the listener decodes the message inaccurately, he or she will misunderstand the speaker. The communication process will have broken down. What is unfortunate is that neither party will realize that there has been a miscommunication. The speaker cannot observe how the message was decoded inside the listener's head! This is quite a common communication difficulty among people: The speaker's message is misunderstood by the listener, and neither party is aware of the problem.

If the listener, however, informs the speaker of how the message has been decoded, by repeating back the essence of what the listener has understood the speaker to be saying, the speaker can either confirm that the intended meaning has been received or can correct the misunderstanding. This feedback by the listener to the speaker is active listening. The active listening process allows any misunderstanding to be noticed and cleared up before the conversation resumes. In addition, the speaker is reassured on an ongoing basis of having been listened to and understood.

Withhold Judgment

There is some confusion about what it means to be judgmental of others. We do have a right, and perhaps a need, to be discerning—to have opinions and make judgments. Yet, to the extent that we manage to interact with people in ways that do not put them down or make them feel inadequate, we create a climate conducive to effective communication.

Carl Rogers (1961) proposed that the main block to effective communication is our tendency to evaluate and judge the statements of others. He believed that what gets in the way of understanding another person is our tendency to approve or disapprove of the other's position, and our unwillingness to put ourselves in the other person's frame of reference. Rogers noted that the stronger are the feelings of those who are trying to relate, the more likely

By permission of Johnny Hart and Creators Syndicate, Inc.

it is that there will be no mutual element in the communication. There will be just two ideas, two feelings, and two judgments, missing each other in psychological space. This tendency to react to someone else's emotionally meaningful statement by forming an evaluation of it from our own point of view is a major barrier to interpersonal communication.

Telling others how they are rather than telling them how they affect us is likely to create resistance and defensiveness in the other person, and for good reason. It is seldom advisable to try to characterize someone else in order to get him or her to change. Instead, we must state what our needs are, rather than expecting others to know those needs intuitively or to make changes after we have criticized them.

Learn to Feel and Communicate Empathy

Empathy means adopting another person's frame of reference in order to comprehend his or her viewpoint. Empathy includes being sensitive to the needs of others and accepting of their feelings. Being tolerant of another person does not necessarily extend to approving of that person's behavior. One can be supportive of a friend's struggle to be faithful to his or her partner, while regretting the times when the friend is unfaithful.

A good listener also uses empathy to understand how the other person experiences his or her life. There is an old saying, "Never judge someone until you have walked a mile in his moccasins." Development of an empathic understanding means that we try to put ourselves in that person's place and to see the world as she or he does. Empathy is a skill that takes a great deal of practice. We don't set ourselves apart from others, and then sympathize with or pity them. Neither should we overidentify with others. When we walk a mile in the other person's moccasins, we must keep one foot in our own world.

Part of the difficulty in responding with empathy comes from our natural and habitual tendency to view the world from our own frame of reference. Each of us has a belief structure that functions as a template superimposed on the events that occur around us. This template was constructed from past experiences as well as from assumptions we have formed about why things are the way they are. An empathic stance requires us to lift our own template and attempt to adopt that of the person whose viewpoint we wish to understand. Essentially, we ask ourselves, How would I view this situation if I were this other person instead of me?

NOTE: To try this listening strategy, refer to the exercise at the end of this chapter, entitled Active Listening Practice.

Sometimes we may fear being changed ourselves if we really listen to and understand a person with a viewpoint different from our own. This situation is particularly likely if we sense that the other is good at arguing and is better at articulating his or her thoughts and feelings than we are.

As was mentioned previously, when two people are in an argument, a good rule to put in place is that each person must restate the ideas and feelings of the other speaker before making his or her next point. This active listening procedure elicits empathy, which is the necessary foundation for all intimate relationships. This strategy also requires each person to listen with enough care to enable him or her to represent the position of the other person. Both qualities—empathy and attentiveness—are guaranteed to soften any argument.

Apologize When Appropriate

Failure to offer an apology when an apology is appropriate represents another roadblock to effective communication (Lazare, 1995). An authentic apology offered and accepted can repair injured relationships. If done correctly, an apology can heal humiliation and generate forgiveness. For want of a heartfelt apology, relationships become strained. Such relationships may deteriorate to a place beyond repair or may create lasting ill will and resentment. To be effective, an apology must be offered with genuine understanding of the harm done to the victim of the affront. To be capable of offering an apology, a person has to have the security and strength to admit fault.

The basis of any personal insult is that we've bruised another person's self-esteem. Self-esteem is our evaluation about who we are and about how close we come to being the way that we would like to be and the way that we want to be viewed by others.

There are four basic motives for apologizing: The first motive is to save or reestablish the relationship. The second arises from feelings of empathy; we are sorry to be the reason for someone else's pain and consequently apologize to lessen the person's suffering. The third motive is to avoid retribution. The last motive is to alleviate a guilty conscience.

By apologizing, we take the shame of our offense and redirect it to ourselves. We admit to hurting or diminishing someone and, in effect, say that we are really the one who is degraded. In admitting our guilt, we give the wounded one the prerogative to forgive. This interchange is fundamental to the healing process.

There are several elements of an apology: First, we have to concede that a social norm or an ethical principle was violated or that we ignored some private understanding agreed to in the context of the relationship. We also must acknowledge responsibility for the violation. We need to be specific about the wrongdoing we committed; otherwise, the apology will not be effective. We must show not only that we understand the nature of the offense but also that we recognize the impact it had on the person. Additional components to an acceptable apology are an explanation of why we engaged in the misconduct in the first place and a reassurance that it will not happen again. This treatment lets the offended person know that he or she can feel safe with us now and in the future. Finally, we want to communicate our embarrassment and disappointment with ourselves over the situation.

The biggest obstacle to apologizing is our conviction that apologizing is a sign of weakness and an acknowledgment of guilt. To the extent that we prefer winning to maintaining relationships, we are likely to be unwilling to admit our own blunders. We have the mistaken idea that we are better off by overlooking or denying our offenses and hoping that no one notices. In fact, an apology is a show of strength. It is an act of sincerity because we admit that we misbehaved; and it is an act of generosity because it restores the self-concept of those we offended. An apology offers hope for a more authentic and sturdy relationship. By offering an apology, we commit ourselves to cultivating the relationship and to working on our own development. Since all of us make frequent mistakes when relating to others, we will inevitably have a great deal of apologizing to do along the way in life.

QUESTION: *How often do you find it necessary to offer an apology?*

► *MARRIAGE*

In spite of contemporary threats to the institution of marriage, it is still the dominant relationship in our society. Bellah and his colleagues (1985) found that in today's society, most people still want to marry, even though many of them no longer see it as a life requirement. Most of those interviewed believe in love as a basis for an enduring relationship. Social psychologist Ellen Bersheid (1998) said, "There is nothing people consider more meaningful and essential than close interpersonal relationships."

Yet, the news about the durability of marriage is bleak. Approximately 54 percent of newlywed couples fail (Bradbury, 1998). Today, the average marriage lasts seven years (Harvey, 1998).

A survey of 300 couples who had been happily married for fifteen years or more provides some clues to a successful marriage. The most frequently named reason for an enduring and a happy marriage was having a generally positive attitude toward one's spouse, that is, viewing one's partner as one's best friend and liking him or her as a person. Among the characteristics that the partners liked in each other were qualities of caring, giving, integrity, and a sense of humor. In essence, they said, "I am married to someone who cares about me, who is concerned for my well-being, who gives as much or more than he or she gets, who is open and trustworthy and not mired down in a somber, bleak outlook on life" (Lauer & Lauer, 1985, p. 24). They also liked the fact that their spouses had changed and grown more interesting over the years.

Other elements important to a lasting marriage were a belief in marriage as a long-term commitment, agreement on common goals, and the ability to communicate with each other and to resolve problems calmly without venting anger. As is usually the case with surveys of marital satisfaction, sexual fulfillment was far down the list of reasons for a lastingly happy marriage. Although most people were generally satisfied with their sex lives, few listed it as a major reason for their happiness. Those who were dissatisfied felt that sex was less important than understanding, friendship, and respect (Lauer & Lauer, 1985).

➤ DIVORCE AND SEPARATION

The divorce rate has tripled since 1960. The number of single-parent families in the United States has quadrupled since 1960, so that in 1998, there are over 20 million such families. The estimated number was 1 million in the United States in 1998. Of the 1 million divorces predicted for 1998, at least 150,000 were expected to involve custody battles. Out of the approximately 260 million people who currently live in the United States, over 70 million have been divorced at least once (Harvey, 1998).

People feel more free than they did in the past to leave a marriage that is not working. Many couples may not be committed enough to each other to stay together in times of crisis and struggle. Economic prosperity has enabled dissatisfied couples to split up, more so than in times past when making ends meet was a more crucial issue. Marital counseling and individual therapy are both valuable for those who are considering divorce or separation. Each person might explore what he or she expects from the divorce. It's helpful for us

"I don't believe it. That's my ex-wife."

to know as clearly as possible why we are divorcing and to look at the changes we need to make in ourselves as well as in our circumstances.

Unless there are some alterations within the individuals, the problems that they experienced may not end with the divorce. Without an insight into ourselves, we tend to find new partners who are very similar to the ones we divorced and to repeat the same dynamics. We need to understand why we "choose" to align ourselves with this sort of person.

➤ ## CHOOSING THE SINGLE LIFE

Although they may enjoy their single lifestyle, many people eventually marry because they begin to wonder what is wrong with them. This phenomenon occurs because even today, society is more accepting of marriage as a lifestyle than of a single life.

Even so, many adults today are electing to remain single, more so than in the past. In 1940, 8 percent of adults lived alone. In 1988, 24 percent lived alone. In 1990, 28 percent were single-parent families. Marriage rates have declined, and the happiness level of married partners has declined as well. There has been a quadrupling of the rate of unwed motherhood. Today, people are lonelier, more homicidal, and more likely to divorce. Marriage rates are decreasing even though marriage is a predictor of life satisfaction. This trend seems unfortunate in light of research findings that close relationships (where there is self-disclosure) predict happiness. Love and marriage are also predictors of mental and physical health. Twenty-five percent of those who are unmarried describe themselves as very happy, whereas 40 percent of those who are married say they are very happy (Myers, 1991).

Why are so many adults choosing to remain single? This phenomenon has multiple determinants. First, women are finding that they have more educational and career opportunities than was the case in the past, meaning that women have more economic independence and thus don't need to marry in order to make a living. A career also provides an alternative source of satisfaction to the enjoyment of investing in children, though most adults who are invested in their work still wish to have children. An additional source of economic independence for women who are mothers is the advent of government-sponsored welfare. Many critics of current welfare programs point out that the availability of Aid to Dependent Children benefits has enabled young women to consider husbands unnecessary as providers for their children.

An alternative explanation of the rise in the number of single adults might be that the social stigmas against premarital sexuality, cohabitation, and unwed motherhood have been relaxed, so that the motivations of securing a sexual partner and being able to have a family have lessened as reasons to marry. Finally, adults choosing a homosexual lifestyle would be an another reason for remaining single, since most in our society are not in favor of permitting same-sex marriages.

➤ FRIENDSHIP

According to Robert Sternberg's model of love that was discussed in the previous chapter, intimacy alone produces liking. This is the stuff of friendship. Friendships supply intimacy in addition to or in lieu of romantic partnerships. An example of how intimacy enriched the lives of two teen-age friends was provided by White (1972):

> Ben, whose school experience had been so unstimulating that he never read a book beyond those assigned, discovered in Jamie a lively spirit of intellectual inquiry and an exciting knowledge of politics and history. Here was a whole world to which his friend opened the door and provided guidance. Jamie discovered in Ben a world previously closed to him, that of confident interaction with other people. Each admired the other, each copied the other, each used the other for practice. In Ben's words: "You see how I was almost consciously expanding my image of myself to include attributes which he already had, so that I felt extended, both of us felt extended by the intimacy. (pp. 303–304)

Particularly in an age when more and more people are deciding to remain single, friendships play an important role in buffering them against distress in the face of adversity. Likewise, a loosening of family ties contributes to the significance of friendships. As with marriage partners and family members, we share a sense of history with longtime friends. We share our triumphs with those who know us and thus can appreciate what our accomplishments mean in the context of our lives.

There are some differences among men and women as to how they carry on friendships. Men tend to form friendships with other men that are based around activities they do together (Hays, 1985; Sherrod, 1989). Shared activities provide men with companionship without the vulnerability that comes from self-disclosure. Women tend to rely on women friends for emotional support and thus spend much of their shared time talking. The topic of conversation is likely to be personal problems, feelings, and people (Caldwell & Paplau, 1982; Davidson & Duberman, 1982). Women are more likely to bring up and resolve tension that arises in their friendships, whereas men are more inclined to avoid addressing relationship problems and simply tolerate the inevitable tension that crops up in friendships. Men tend to report less intimacy in their same-gender friendships than do women, and to perceive their friends as less available for emotional support than is the case for women in their same-gender friendships (Sherrod, 1989). However, for men who don't adhere to traditional male personality and behavior patterns, these trends do not hold up. Nontraditional men report friendship patterns more similar to those of women (Lavine & Lombardo, 1984).

QUESTIONS: *Do you have both male and female friends? If so, how do they differ, and in what ways are they similar?*

➤ SUMMARY

ALFRED ADLER   An early theorist who appreciated the role of social relationships in human development was Alfred Adler. He viewed human beings as creative, active, choice-making beings whose every action has purpose and meaning, and he believed that friendship, love, and one's occupation are the central concerns of adult life.

The term *inferiority complex* was coined by Adler. He asserted that each human being's struggle to overcome feelings of inferiority is a core problem in life. People react to the experience of being incompetent as children by striving for superiority and power throughout their lives. Through gaining mastery in various areas, individuals achieve self-acceptance. If the childhood feelings of inferiority continue into adulthood, the person will develop an inferiority complex and will have trouble with establishing mature relationships because of a constant struggle to show her or his worth to others.

The specific ways that individuals choose to compensate for inferiority and to achieve superiority determine their *style of life*. To the degree that people have developed healthy social interests, their striving for superiority will be shaped into a style of life that is focused on interpersonal ties.

Adler believed that people are motivated primarily by an innate *social interest* and that the goal in life is to act in ways that fulfill social responsibilities. He distinguished between a healthy and a mistaken style of life, and he proposed that social interest is the primary characteristic that differentiates the two.

ADLER'S APPROACH TO DREAMS   Adler viewed dreams as an expression of an individual's unique strivings toward goals. Dreams represent a dreamer's attempt to resolve current life problems that the person is unwilling or unable to master with her or his conscious power of reason. Adlerians view dreams as rehearsals for and guides to possible future courses of action.

VIEW OF PSYCHOPATHOLOGY AND THERAPY   Adler looked upon clients as "discouraged" rather than sick and felt that a therapist's primary task is to provide a client with encouragement so that the client can grow to become what she or he was meant to be.

CHARACTERISTICS OF MEANINGFUL RELATIONSHIPS

1. *Establishing a separate identity.* In order to feel safe in an intimate relationship, each partner has to have established a separate identity. Making relationships work involves creating and maintaining a balance between separateness and togetherness. If there is not enough togetherness in a relationship, those in it typically feel isolated and do not share feelings and experiences. If there is not enough separateness, the intimates give up a sense of their own identity and control. Each partner allows the other a sense of privacy and freedom. Partners should not be so tightly bound together that if they are separated, one or the other feels lost and empty. Dependency should not be interpreted as love but as the seeking of an object to make oneself feel complete.

2. *Coping with conflict and anger.* It is unrealistic to expect conflict to be absent from intimate relationships. If anger is not expressed and dealt with constructively, it will damage the relationship. Without meaningful dialogue, the intimacy that is the foundation of a good relationship is eventually destroyed. Instead, rules for appropriately presenting grievances should be agreed to.

3. *Assuming responsibility for one's own happiness.* Each person refrains from blaming the other person if he or she is unhappy. Neither expects the other person to make him or her feel alive, take away boredom, assume the other's risks, or make the other person feel valued and important.

4. *Demonstrating active concern for the other.* Feeling supported by one's partner is a principal contributor to marital satisfaction, relationship stability, personal growth, and sexual enjoyment. Partners have an interest in each other's welfare and a desire to see that the other person is fulfilled.

5. *Self-disclosing.* Each person discloses himself or herself to the other, particularly about the quality of the relationship and other matters of significance to the relationship. The two persons can openly express grievances and let each other know the changes they desire.

6. *Having shared activities, interests, and values.* For a relationship to work, shared activities are important, as well as agreement as to what is important in life, so that the couple may work as a team in deciding how to invest their time, money and talents. Similarity in every way contributes to marital happiness.

EFFECTIVE COMMUNICATION   Strategies for expressing oneself in a manner that is likely to create a positive interpersonal climate, conducive to mutual self-disclosure, include the following:

1. *Strive for honesty.* Without being needlessly hurtful, effective communicators disclose their true thoughts and feelings to those with whom they care to have an authentic relationship.

2. *Approach others as equals.* It is wise for anyone enjoying greater status or power in a relationship to disregard the status difference when trying to communicate with others.

3. *Express your opinions tentatively.* Rather than giving the impression that we know all the answers, seek to get across that our beliefs and attitudes are flexible and subject to revision.

4. *Do not try to change the other.* We do not need to insist that the other person make changes. In focusing on our own desires and actions, we can have a positive influence on our relationships. By changing ourselves, we can prevent others from continuing with negative behavior towards us. In that regard, we can have an indirect, though effective, impact on the behavior of others.

5. *Listen.* Failure to listen or selective listening are common blocks to communication. In order to be a good listener, we must give the other person our undivided attention. We must move into a position of acceptance, so that we refrain from prejudging the person and from making assumptions as the person speaks that will keep us from hearing everything he or she has to say.

6. *Practice withholding judgment.* Our tendency to evaluate and judge the statements of others hinders communication. To the extent that we manage to interact with people in ways that do not put them down or make them feel inadequate, we create a climate conducive to effective communication.

7. *Learn to feel and communicate empathy.* A good listener uses empathy to understand how the other person experiences his or her life. Empathy means adopting another person's frame of reference in order to comprehend his or her viewpoint.

8. *Apologize when appropriate.* Another block to communication is failure to offer an apology when appropriate to do so. A sincere apology has the power to restore damaged relationships. A successful apology requires empathy as well as the security and strength to admit fault.

MARRIAGE In spite of contemporary threats to the institution, marriage is still the dominant relationship in our society. The most frequently named reason for an enduring and happy marriage is having a generally positive attitude toward one's spouse. Other qualities found in long-term successful marriages are viewing one's partner as one's best friend and liking him or her as a person, and viewing the partner as caring and giving, as well as having integrity and a sense of humor. Other elements important to a lasting marriage are a belief in marriage as a long-term commitment, agreement on common goals, and the ability to communicate with each other and to resolve problems calmly without venting anger.

DIVORCE AND SEPARATION People feel more free than they did in the past to leave a marriage that is not working. Women are more financially independent than in the past, making it easier for them to leave an unsatisfactory marriage. Unless there are some changes within the individuals, the problems they experienced may not end with the divorce.

REMAINING SINGLE   Many adults today are electing to remain single, more so than in the past. Adults are choosing to remain single for a variety of reasons, including economic independence, lower birth rates, and lessened social stigmas against both unwed motherhood and a homosexual lifestyle.

FRIENDSHIP   In an age when more and more people are deciding to remain single, friendships play an increasingly important role in buffering people against painful isolation. As with marriage partners and families, friendships enable people to have a sense of shared history with friends. Friends are reliable sources of material and emotional support.

Men and women differ in how they carry on friendships. Men tend to form friendships with other men that are based around activities they do together, whereas women tend to rely on friends for emotional support.

LEARNING THE LANGUAGE OF PSYCHOLOGISTS

inferiority complex
style of life
social interest

dependent personality disorder
active listening

CHAPTER REVIEW QUESTIONS

1. What is the relationship between self-disclosure and intimacy?
2. What did Adler mean by an "inferiority complex"?
3. How does one develop a style of life, according to Adler?
4. According to Adler, why must a healthy person have "social interest"?
5. How do Freud, Jung, and Adler differ in their approaches to the interpretation of dreams?
6. What are the characteristics of healthy relationships, according to the text?
7. Which characteristic of a healthy relationship is most addressed in Kahlil Gibran's recommendation to "let there be spaces in your togetherness," in his poem "Love and Marriage"?
8. What is the relationship between conflict and intimacy?
9. Why do friends and loved ones sometimes interfere with each other's pursuit of happiness?
10. How can you best change an unsatisfactory relationship?
11. According to Carl Rogers, how does our tendency to judge and critique others affect our personal relationships?

ACTIVITIES

1. *DYADS EXERCISE: **Role-Play***. This role-play exercise is designed to help you understand your partner more fully. Here's how it works: Joan wishes to increase her ability to understand how her husband, Fred, feels in their marital life. She begins by "becoming" Fred and talking for Fred. She may say anything that comes to mind. She may tell the class about Joan through Fred's eyes. Students can try this by forming into pairs and "becoming" their romantic partner or a family member.
2. *COMPLETE INDIVIDUALLY: **A Strategy for Conflict***.
3. *COMPLETE IN PAIRS: **Active Listening Practice***.
4. *SMALL GROUP EXERCISE: **Personal Reflections on Intimacy in My Life***.
5. *COMPLETE INDIVIDUALLY: **Marriage Contract***.
6. *COMPLETE INDIVIDUALLY: **Apology letter***. Write an apology letter to someone you have hurt. You do not have to send it, but you may do so if you like.

A Strategy for Conflict

Problem: Most psychological difficulties involve problems between people. Marriage counselors, for example, often help people resolve conflicts by helping them realize that the things they fight about are not usually the "real" problem. The real problem is often a continuing power struggle in which each party tries to win at the other's expense. Couples must develop strategies for handling conflict in order to get through problem situations without damaging the relationship.

Even when the difficulty is unmasked, getting out of a power conflict is not easy. Have you ever noticed that in most arguments, no one really listens to the other person's point of view? That is, while one person talks, the other uses that time to rehearse his or her own side of the argument. This project suggests one effective technique for short-circuiting this power game.

Directions: Form a small group with three or four of your classmates, and proceed as follows:

1. Find two people in your group who strongly disagree on some issue. It doesn't make any difference who the people are or what the disputed issue is. If you have any trouble finding something on which to disagree, try one of the following topics. Write the topic you choose in the blank provided.

   banning abortion
   allowing children with AIDS in public school
   promoting gun control
   discontinuing affirmative action
   legalizing euthanasia
   dismantling welfare
   allowing gay marriages
   abolishing capital punishment
   spanking children as a reasonable means of discipline

   Your Subject of Disagreement:_____

2. Select one of the two disputants to present her or his side of the question first. Give this person about two minutes, during which time *no one else may say anything* and *everyone else writes down the main points that this person makes.*

Name of First Speaker: _____

Main Points: _____

_____

_____

_____

The person representing the other side of the issue must repeat back to the group what the first person said. (Doing this forces the second person to listen to what the first person is saying.) The crucial part is that *this paraphrase must be said in such a way that the first person can accept it as a fair representation of what she or he said.*

3. As soon as the paraphrased statement has been "accepted," reverse the process: The other person states her or his side, and the first person must paraphrase correctly.

Name of Second Speaker:_____

Main Points: _____

_____

_____

_____

4. Everyone summarizes this exchange. What is your opinion of this approach to discussing controversial issues? Are there advantages? Disadvantages?

_____

_____

_____

Active Listening Practice

Directions: Arrange yourselves into dyads, and choose the person who will begin the exercise by talking about some experience that he or she has been having in the past week. The second person will give the first person his or her undivided attention. In order to show that he or she is listening and to make sure that the listener understands what is being said, the second person will rephrase what is being said and will say it back to the speaker. The listener is to use tentative phrases such as, "You seem to be saying . . . is that it?" or "If I understood you, what you mean is . . . did I get that right?" or "There's a lot on your plate this week, and maybe you're not sure if you can manage it all."

The listener should not ask questions, because to do so would be to direct the conversation. A question requires the speaker to stop pursuing his or her own train of thought in order to answer the question. The exception to this instruction is that the listener may ask whether he or she has understood the speaker correctly. "You seem excited about going off to college, yet sad to leave your family and friends. Is that what you are telling me?"

In addition, to indicate that he or she got the gist of what was being said, the listener should try to convey back to the speaker the feelings that the speaker is receiving with the rest of the message. This impression might be communicated with comments such as, "You seem very hurt about that" or "You are excited about it, aren't you?" or "You sound sad when you say that" or "Your boss really got you upset by doing that!"

In essence, the listener mirrors back to the speaker both the thoughts and the feelings that are being expressed.

After ten minutes or so, change places so that the listener has a turn to speak and be heard.

Personal Reflections on Intimacy in My Life

Directions: Read each of the following questions, and then write your answers in the blanks.

1. Would you like to have the same kind of relationship as your parents? What are some of the things you like best about that relationship? What are some features of their relationship that you would not want to have in your own marriage?

   _____

   _____

   _____

   _____

2. Other than your parents, name a couple whose relationship you most admire. What are some of the things you like best about their relationship? What are some features of their relationship that you would not want to have in your own intimate relationship?

   _____

   _____

   _____

   _____

3. Why do you think a person might want an intimate relationship with you?

_____

_____

_____

_____

4. How would you hope to benefit from being involved in a significant relationship?

_____

_____

_____

_____

5. How do you feel about spending time apart from your significant others?

_____

_____

_____

_____

6. How do you handle the situation when you are angry with those with whom you have an intimate relationship?

_____

_____

_____

_____

7. What are some of the things you do to let others close to you know that they are important to you, that you value the relationship, and that you are a loyal partner or friend?

_____

_____

_____

_____

8. Discuss how much this statement describes you: "I always have time for my partner/close friend."

_____

_____

_____

_____

9. Discuss how much this statement describes you: "I am eager to hear about my partner's successes."

_____

_____

_____

_____

10. For each person in the group who is involved in an intimate relationship, try this as a go-round: "If only my partner were not _____, then I _____." Another version of this you can try comes from Eric Berne: "If it weren't for you . . ."

_____

_____

_____

_____

11. Imagine that you are the person with whom you are most intimately related. As you sit in silence for a time, "become" your own partner. Would you get along well with yourself? Would there be anything missing in the relationship? In what ways would the relationship be satisfying?

_____

_____

_____

12. On the basis of what you have read in this chapter, how would you advise a friend to change an unsatisfactory relationship, in which your friend feels mistreated by the other person?

_____

_____

_____

_____

13. Often we engage in unacknowledged conspiracies with another person in order to keep a relationship secure. Assume, for the sake of this exercise, that there are some conspiracies occurring in your relationships, and see whether you can detect them. Some examples are winner/loser or nurse/patient; helpless/powerful (or strong one/weak one); parent/child; and social activities coordinator/willing participant. Are you the other person's security blanket? Are you the other person's police officer? Write your observations in the blanks.

_____

_____

_____

_____

14. What are your current interpersonal relationships like? For instance, do you find them nurturing, draining, abusive, etc.? How do you view yourself in these relationships? Do you feel taken advantage of, or conversely, do you take advantage of your friendships?

_____

_____

_____

_____

15. What roles do friends play in your life? What qualities do you look for in friends?

_____

_____

_____

16. Do you believe that you have close and reliable friendships? In general, do you trust others?

_____

_____

_____

_____

17. How would you describe your relationship history?

_____

_____

_____

_____

_____

18. Alfred Adler believed that an important goal in life is overcoming perceived inferiority. Can you recall any early feelings of helplessness, weakness, or inferiority? Do you feel that the attempt to overcome these feelings has played a significant role in your personality development? Explain.

_____

_____

_____

_____

19. Close your eyes, and attempt to identify your earliest concrete single memory. It should be something that you actually remember, not something that you were told about. Spend a few minutes recalling the details and reexperiencing the feelings associated with this early event. Write down your earliest recollection:

_____

_____

_____

_____

20. Do you have any hunches about how this early memory may still be having an impact on the way you think, feel, and behave today?

_____

_____

_____

_____

21. Does your life reflect your having a social interest?

_____

_____

_____

_____

Marriage Contract

Directions: What should a couple discuss and agree on before marriage or living together? Considering this question could save considerable unhappiness. Think about the issues that follow.

1. Will the name of either partner be changed?
2. How will finances be handled?
   a. Who will earn income for the family?
   b. Who will pay the bills?
   c. How will economic decisions be made?
3. Will the couple rent or buy a place to live; will residential decisions accommodate the husband's or the wife's career plans? (Will either the husband or the wife be willing to move to another city so that one spouse may take advantage of a better job offer?)
4. What type(s) of contraception will be used, and who will take the responsibility for birth control measures?
5. How many children does the couple plan on having, if any?
   a. At what time in the marital life cycle will the couple plan to have children?
   b. How will the care of the children be handled?
   c. Will one parent be more active if the child happens to have special needs?
   d. What techniques will the partners employ in rearing their children?
   e. What would be appropriate custody arrangements, should the couple separate?
   f. Who will be asked to care for the children, should something happen to both parents?
6. How will the housework be divided? Who will be responsible for which everyday activities, such as cleaning, washing, cooking, and minor home repairs? Will a paid housekeeper be employed?
7. What part will religion play in the relationship?
8. How will decisions be made when the partners disagree?
9. What will be the limitations on relationships with others, notably,
   a. with friends of the same gender?
   b. with friends of the other gender?
   c. with in-laws? For example, will vacations be spent visiting relatives?
   d. with former spouses or lovers (if any)?
10. What proportion of leisure activities will be spent together? Will a portion be spent apart from the spouse?
11. How will the couple's sexual relations be negotiated? Will fidelity be preserved?

12. What procedure will be used if one partner wants to renegotiate part of the contract?

It may be interesting to view the preceding project in light of how we get into relationships in the first place. On a separate sheet of paper, write down ten qualities that you find attractive in another person whom you might consider dating.

11

Sexuality

Freud is the father of psychoanalysis. It has no mother.
—Germain Greer

➤ *PREVIEW QUESTIONS:* Is it important to master techniques of love-making in order to be a good lover? What are the most common worries that people have about sexual expression? How does one develop sexual values? What are the psychological effects of sexual abuse?

➤ INTRODUCTION: THE TOLL GATE

For most people, sexual expression is a valued aspect of life, providing a source of pleasure and joy through human connection. As discussed earlier (Chapter 9), the typical desire expressed by young adults is to find a romantic partner to form a committed relationship. A committed relationship generally implies one that is sexually exclusive. For those cultures that embrace the romantic ideal, sexual attraction provides the basis for forming an intimate relationship.

Although sexual attraction is an important part of life for most of us and provides the impetus for initiating pair-bonding, we do not find it socially acceptable to talk about sex. Unfortunately, sex education, which could promote optimal sexual functioning, is not widespread. Many of us have difficulty in talking openly about our sexual concerns and are thus hindered from becoming knowledgeable about sex through informal channels. This communication difficulty often extends to talking with our lovers in order to convey our sexual desires. The result is that in spite of the fact that we live in an age of greater sexual liberation than in the past, many people do not experience genuine satisfaction in their sexual relationships. There are a substantial number of myths and misconceptions about sexual functioning, which remain unaired. Inhibitions surrounding sex hamper our ability to establish a sexual identity, which forms a significant portion of our answer to the question, Who am I?

Sexual relations can be a vehicle through which others are mistreated. Among men and women, sexual relations sometimes become intermingled with the assertion of power and dominance. When this event happens, sexual abuse is often the result. Unfortunately, children are not universally protected from such sexual "power plays."

➤ FORMING A SEXUAL IDENTITY

There is a great deal of variety in the ways people choose to express their sexuality. Some individuals expend considerable energy suppressing sexual thoughts, feelings, and behaviors. Others indulge in frequent sexual fantasies

and are preoccupied with gaining sexual stimulation. Some people confine their sexual expression to long-term monogamous relationships, whereas others prefer casual encounters with numerous partners. Some are content with the missionary position in their own bed with their one-and-only partner in complete darkness, whereas others like a variety of settings with special attention being given to lighting and with the liberal use of sexual props or equipment as foreplay.

In general, one's identity refers to having a stable sense of oneself. Sexual identity, then, specifies a person's characteristic way of perceiving himself or herself as a sexual being and the person's habitual forms of sexual expression, as well as the person's attitudes about his or her own sexuality and that of others. Our sexual identity encompasses our **sexual orientation,** our body image, our sexual values, and our preferred ways of achieving sexual arousal.

Sexual orientation has to do with an individual's preference for a sexual partner of either one gender or the other. For any given individual, sexual preference seems to fall somewhere on a continuum from the person's being exclusively heterosexual to being exclusively homosexual. Male homosexuals are often referred to as being "gay," whereas female homosexuals are known as "lesbians" (although the term "gay" is sometimes used inclusively to refer to homosexuals of both genders).

Our body image has to do with how we view ourselves as physical beings, and it includes not only what we think we look like but also our evaluation of how attractive we are. Individuals who feel attractive are more likely to be sexually active, and they report greater sexual satisfaction than do those people who see themselves as less attractive (Hatfield & Rapson, 1996).

We tend to adopt the basic sexual values of our culture. All cultures teach their members that certain sexual practices are acceptable, whereas others are wrong (Rubin, 1984). What constitutes acceptable sexual practices is conveyed by the media, schools, family, friends, and one's religion.

Whereas all those existing within one culture share some common sexual values, individuals within a particular culture have different sexual likes and dislikes. Our erotic preferences consist of our attitudes about masturbation, dating, oral sex, intercourse, birth control methods, safe sex practices, sources of sexual stimulation, and the like.

The preceding aspects of sexual identity are apparently influenced by a host of factors, including our genetic endowment, our gender-role socialization, our sexual attitudes acquired from the media, our families, and our peers.

➤ GUILT OVER SEXUAL THOUGHTS AND FEELINGS

Many of us have learned that certain sexual thoughts and feelings are bad. We then feel guilty when we have these thoughts and feelings, even when we don't act on them. Guilt is commonly experienced in connection with homosexual fantasies and impulses, with feelings of sexual attraction toward members of one's family, with sexual feelings toward people other than one's spouse, with enjoyment of sexuality, and with too much (or too little) desire for sex.

Whereas not all guilt is unhealthy and irrational, there is value in challenging guilt feelings and getting rid of ideas that are unrealistic. A common concern is that if we recognize or accept our sexual thoughts and feelings, our impulses will sweep us away, leaving us out of control. Sometimes we fear that we'll be more likely to act on our feelings if we fully acknowledge them. This is not likely to be the case. Instead, becoming fully aware of thoughts and feelings should allow us a greater opportunity to exercise conscious control over them. If there is a problem with **rumination,** which refers to obsessive pondering of the same thoughts, a thought-stopping technique (described in Chapter 8) might usefully be implemented.

It is important to realize that we can accept all of our sexual thoughts and feelings as helpful messages to ourselves about our sexual self-definition. We are responsible for appropriate behavior, but we do not have to worry about having "appropriate" thoughts and feelings. It is unrealistic to expect that we can or should suppress our thinking to the same extent that we can control our actions. After we accept our sexual thoughts and feelings, we can decide what to do about them. By being master of our own behavior, we define what kind of person we are, whereas by trying to deny or banish our inner life, we risk becoming alienated from ourselves. Corey (1993) has suggested the following questions to use as guidelines for acting on sexual feelings:

1. Will my actions hurt another person or myself?
2. Will my actions limit another person's freedom?
3. Will my actions exploit another person's rights?
4. Are my actions consistent with my commitments?

If our behavior passes inspection when we use the preceding criteria, we can probably proceed with a clear conscience.

➤ DEVELOPING SEXUAL VALUES

Most of us form our initial values by automatically accepting the standards of significant others, such as those of our church leaders or our parents. This process, which is called **introjection** by many psychologists, means swallowing whole, without question, what is taught us through the socialization process.

Typically, during adolescence we reexamine these values and internalize a subset of them that we decide we can live with. This is part of the individuation process that was discussed earlier in the text (in Chapters 3 and 6). We are unlikely to shed all our past beliefs or values, but after this process of reexamination, we have made those that we do keep more fully our own.

It is relevant to add the caution that many introjected attitudes go unexamined, because they remain outside the individual's awareness. It can be tempting to sidestep the reflective process that is entailed in reexamining what we have been taught at an earlier time and to allow someone besides ourselves to make our decisions for us; then we don't have to wrestle with sorting out our own values for ourselves. However, the price we pay is that of surrendering our autonomy. We run the risk of being estranged from ourselves. We fail to mature and individuate, and instead, we experience a personality foreclosure rather than personal growth.

In a rapidly changing society such as ours, values and behaviors may shift dramatically from one generation to the next. The famous "generation gap" of the 1960s represented an acknowledgment of this phenomenon. Nowhere has the transformation in values and behaviors been more pronounced than in the way to view one's sexuality. The baby boomers, who may be said to have had parents who viewed sexuality as the prerogative only of married couples, espoused a view that free love, without commitment, was a legitimate way to go about conducting sexual relationships. "If it feels good, do it," a slogan in the early 1970s, suggests that we can trust our emotions to give us good direction in life.

Ideally, our sexual values should fit in with our view of ourselves in other areas of life. Otherwise, we are likely to feel realistic and appropriate guilt when we engage in sexual practices that are not in accordance with our value system. An example of a typical guilt-inducing situation would be having an affair when one is married and has promised to be faithful to one's spouse.

Some college students may not as yet be sexually active. Others may have elected to be abstinent until marriage. A few individuals even prefer to go without sex throughout their lives. Today, in what is sometimes referred to as the "postmodern era," some young adults are returning to celibacy, while others have progressed further along the continuum of "dispassionate sex." By this apparent oxymoron is meant sex without a caring relationship.

If we pay attention to how we feel about ourselves in regard to our past and present sexual experiences, we can use our level of self-respect as one important guide to our future behavior. McCarthy and McCarthy (1984) offer these values for your consideration as guidelines for a healthy sex life:

1. Sexuality is a basic part of life and is not to be considered inherently evil.

2. Our sexuality is a positive and integral part of our personality.

3. It is our responsibility to choose how we will express our sexuality. Since sexuality can enhance our life, it should not contribute to anxiety and guilt.

4. At its best, a sexual relationship involves trust, respect, and concern for our partner.

5. An intimate relationship is the most satisfying way to express our sexuality.

➤ SEX AND INTIMACY: PARKING ON LOVERS' LANE

In current dating practice, couples are likely to become physically intimate prior to becoming emotionally intimate. Through the classical conditioning process, we would thus tend to grow attached to those with whom we have sexual relations. This is so because our many pleasurable experiences become associated with our partners, and we consequently form a positive emotional attachment to them. Partners may feel pressured by their sexual familiarity to declare love for one another and to move toward a commitment. As was discussed in Chapter 9, this action might better be interpreted as a declaration of passion. At any rate, early sexual intimacy puts partners in the position of hoping to get along with the person with whom they are sleeping.

A mutually pleasurable sexual relationship can supply the "cement" to keep a couple bonded enough to get through crises. As we have discussed, partners do not like each other much while in the midst of an argument. When mutual sexual gratification is an ongoing aspect of the relationship, the intimates are likely to be kindly disposed toward one another, thereby making conflict resolution easier. Any fight that crops up can be about the issue at hand, rather than a way to displace sexual frustration.

Rollo May (1981) has observed that people who engage in sex without intimacy have little capacity for feelings and become detached, robotlike sex machines that function mechanically instead of lovingly. The danger is that these persons, who are afraid of intimacy, will experience the drying up of their emotions not only on sexual levels but also on all levels. Dr. May contends that the trend toward sex without intimacy in our culture is closely associated with the loss of the capacity to feel any emotions. His perspective is that love is a state of physical and emotional sharing: "Intimacy is a sharing between two people not only of their bodies, but also of their hopes, fears, anxieties and aspirations" (p. 149).

➤ THE ROLE OF TECHNIQUE IN SEXUAL ENJOYMENT

Technique Can Get in the Way

There is a common belief that the more people know about the mechanics of sex, the more they will be satisfied with their sexual relationship. Today, numerous books devoted to enhancing one's sexuality are available in bookstores. However, people's increased awareness of what is normal for women and men may not have the intended effect of helping to improve their sex life. A possible side effect of concentration on learning and implementing techniques is that attention will be focused on the mechanics of sex rather than on establishing a sense of emotional closeness with one's partner. The intimates may develop expectations of what their sex life *should* be like rather than relaxing and enjoying the experience of exploring physical intimacy with another human being. Performance standards and expectations often get in the way of people's sensual and sexual pleasure, and this is particularly the case with men. For some men, the fact that their partner experiences an orgasm signifies that they have performed adequately. They may expect her always to have an orgasm during intercourse, partly out of their need to prove their sexual prowess, but also from consideration for their partner's gratification.

Although there is something to be said about decreasing one's ignorance about the mechanics of sex, there is more to it than this. Technique and knowledge are important but not sufficient for an emotionally intimate sexual relationship. Each person has slightly different sexual preferences, and the techniques explained in self-help books and the like are, to some extent, suggestions that may or may not be compatible with the wishes of one's partner. What technique seems to supply is some degree of self-confidence, so that a person can relax. Whereas increased self-confidence is a desirable outcome, heightened *self-consciousness* is not. A tense person will have difficulty experiencing sensual or sexual pleasure. Anxiety over performance and technique can only impede sexual enjoyment and can rob an individual of the experience of genuine intimacy and caring. Psychological relaxation in the midst of sexual tension can make for optimal sexual enjoyment. A person who is much too serious in approaching sexuality may come across to his or her partner as unnatural or mechanical; in other words, overemphasizing technique can cause us to become oblivious to our sexual partner. Sex is adult play. To the extent that we become preoccupied with technique, we may find it difficult to be spontaneous.

Some Techniques to Consider

Even though a preoccupation with technique can get in the way of sexual enjoyment, some knowledge of sexual functioning is beneficial. Sexual difficulties fall into two categories: arousal dysfunction and orgasmic dysfunction. Following are some techniques that can be helpful in enhancing sexual pleasure and in overcoming both types of sexual problems.

KEGEL EXERCISES   Kegel exercises are intended to help women achieve orgasm during intercourse. Women with weak pubococcygeus muscles generally have little or no vaginal sensation during intercourse, whereas women with strong pubococcygeus muscles typically report pleasurable vaginal sensation (Kegel, 1952). This is the case because the vagina is surrounded by the pubococcygeus muscle. Strengthening this muscle can help women experience greater pleasure during intercourse (Barbach, 1976).

Kegel exercises are used by women to increase muscle tone and thus also to help increase sensitivity during intercourse as well as to enhance orgasmic responsiveness (Graber, 1982; Perry & Whipple, 1981). Arnold Kegel actually developed this exercise for another purpose: that of helping women to regain control over urination after childbirth. The pubococcygeus muscle becomes stretched and weak during pregnancy, causing many women to suffer from urinary incontinence. Kegel exercises reduce incontinence as well as increase vaginal sensitivity.

The first step to doing a Kegel is to learn what it feels like to contract the pubococcygeus muscle. A woman can accomplish this by stopping herself in the middle of urinating with her legs apart. After she recognizes what it feels like to contract the pubococcygeus muscle, she should insert a finger into her vagina and bear down until she can feel the muscle squeeze her finger. Once she can do this, she is ready to start doing daily Kegels without the inserted finger. A recommended frequency for Kegel exercises is ten contractions of three seconds each three times a day (King, 1996).

THE FEMALE-SUPERIOR POSITION   In the standard missionary position for intercourse, where the man is on top (also known as the male-superior position), the woman has relatively little clitoral stimulation and thus not much opportunity to achieve orgasm, since many women are unable to achieve orgasm through penile thrusts alone. In addition, since the man typically supports himself with his hands to take some of his weight off his partner, he will probably find it difficult to caress his partner or offer her manual clitoral stimulation during intercourse. Between 50 percent and 75 percent of women who have orgasms by other means of stimulation such as masturbation do not have orgasms when the only form of stimulation is penile thrusting during intercourse (Reinisch, 1990).

Since men tend to find the male-superior position highly stimulating, they may have difficulty delaying orgasm long enough to provide satisfying stimulation for their mates. Consequently, habitual use of the missionary position has obvious disadvantages for the woman. Even so, at the time that Alfred Kinsey and his colleagues (1948) published their classic study on male sexuality, as many as 70 percent of the male respondents reported using the male-superior position exclusively. Today couples use a greater variety of positions for intercourse.

With the woman-above position (or female-superior position), the woman sits or lies on top of her partner, with the two facing each other. By straddling the man from above, the woman is able to control the angle of penile entry as well as the depth of thrusting. This freedom of movement allows her to find a position that allows her maximum stimulation and a minimum of discomfort. With little effort, she can move as rapidly or as slowly as she wishes. Each partner can stroke and kiss the other since they are facing one another. This position thus facilitates orgasm in the woman. Since it tends to be less stimulating for the man, he is more able to delay ejaculation until his partner has received adequate stimulation.

QUESTION: *Why is the female-superior position recommended for treatment of both female orgasmic dysfunction and premature ejaculation in the male?*

The Lateral Position   This is a variation of the woman-above position, and it is recommended by Masters and Johnson (1966; 1970) as the most effective position for mutual satisfaction. The woman lies at roughly a 30-degree angle across the man, with her head beside his on a pillow and with her right leg extending between his legs on the bed. This position offers the greatest control of male ejaculation. The man can stop pelvic thrusting at any time, and the woman has total freedom of pelvic movement against the erect penis. In fact, each partner has freedom of movement and easy access to the other. This position allows for prolonged **coitus,** as both partners rest easily on the bed. Masters and Johnson report that the position can be learned fairly easily, and couples who become comfortable with it use this position at least 75 percent of the time. It is also an excellent position when couples are fatigued.

Sensate Focus   When men and women have difficulties with sexual arousal, they may desperately attempt to will themselves to be aroused. However, sexual arousal is an involuntary reflex and thus must be coaxed with an inviting atmosphere rather than willed into existence.

Sensate focus exercises are intended to give a couple an opportunity to enjoy each other without fear of failing to perform properly. It is a procedure developed by Masters and Johnson (1970) for use when partners are having sexual difficulties, particularly male arousal dysfunction (failure to get an erection) due to performance anxiety. One partner gives the other a massage or engages in other types of stroking while both partners are nude. In order to create an undemanding atmosphere, an agreement is made that the fondling will not include stroking of the genitals or the woman's breasts. The person receiving the touching is allowed to give feedback to the active partner regarding what feels good, and so on. The purpose of this exercise is to arrange for each partner in turn to enjoy physical stimulation without feeling obligated to reciprocate immediately or to become sexually aroused. The partner being fondled is simply to relax and enjoy it. This undemanding situation allows the partners to get back to an experience of mutual enjoyment, without performance anxiety and without having either partner feeling rushed into intercourse.

During the first sessions, touching genitals and intercourse are prohibited. With the pressure off, many men spontaneously have erections in response to the pleasant stimulation. With repeated erections, the man's confidence in his sexual response returns. In subsequent sensate focus sessions, genital stimulation and intercourse can gradually be reintroduced.

Sensate focus exercise are also effective for arousal dysfunction in women. Whereas a man's arousal is evidenced by an erection, arousal in a woman is demonstrated by lubrication of the vagina. Both parties must be aroused for effective penetration. The creation of an undemanding atmosphere, in which the point is merely to provide one another with pleasurable sensations, enables the woman to relax and attend to both her partner's external stimulation, as well as her own sexual thoughts and feelings.

QUESTION: *What makes the sensate focus exercise effective in treatment of arousal dysfunction?*

SQUEEZE TECHNIQUE   The squeeze technique is a method commonly employed to prevent premature ejaculation in the male. While the couple lies in bed, the woman stimulates her partner's penis until he is about to ejaculate. Just before ejaculation, she squeezes the tip of the penis to temporarily prevent ejaculation. This process is repeated a couple of times before the man intentionally ejaculates. The technique must be done with care and only after the couple has received instruction from a sex therapist. The woman holds the penis with one hand between her thumb and first two fingers. Her thumb presses against the frenulum (the sensitive strip of tissue that connects the underside of the penile glans or head to the shaft), while her fingers are spread apart to hold the penis by the coronal ridge. Ejaculation is prevented by squeezing the thumb and forefingers together with fairly strong pressure for about twenty seconds or until the man's urge to ejaculate passes. Although some of the erection may be lost in the process, this technique is not painful. The erect penis can withstand fairly strong pressure without discomfort.

After several sessions of practice with the squeeze technique, the couple can try coitus using the female-superior position because it creates less pressure to ejaculate. The woman can insert the penis and then remain motionless. If the man feels that he is about to ejaculate, the woman can ease the penis out and apply the squeeze technique. The couple can try again in a few minutes. When the man can withstand the stimulation of having his penis inside his partner's vagina, the woman can begin gently thrusting. The man will gradually learn to control his urge to ejaculate for a time while experiencing the stimulation of normal intercourse.

BRIDGE TECHNIQUE   When the female partner has problems getting to an orgasm during intercourse, the couple can be taught the "bridge" technique. This involves intercourse and simultaneous manual stimulation of the clitoris. It is more easily accomplished when the couple is in the female-superior coital position (with the woman on top of the man, while each is facing the other) and the rear-entry coital position (where the man faces the woman's rear), than in the more common male-superior position (with the couple facing and the man on top).

The bridge technique provides a good transition from a combination of manual and coital stimulation to coital stimulation alone as a means for reaching orgasm. Manual stimulation during intercourse is used until the woman senses that she is about to achieve orgasm. Manual stimulation is then discontinued and the woman thrusts with her pelvis to provide the stimulation needed to reach orgasm. Gradually, the manual clitoral stimulation can be discontinued earlier and earlier in the process. Whereas some couples prefer getting to the place where the woman can reach orgasm through vaginal stimulation alone, there is no need to discontinue manual stimulation. The Freudian distinction between clitoral orgasms as "immature" in comparison with "mature" vaginal orgasms has been discredited by research evidence (Masters & Johnson, 1966).

➤ COMMON MISUNDERSTANDINGS ABOUT SEXUAL RELATIONSHIPS

My Partner Should Know How to Please Me

We may believe that if our partner really cares for us, we shouldn't have to tell him or her what we like. The partner should intuitively know what is needed without our request or explanation. This notion is impractical. No matter how much our partner takes the trouble to read up on how to please a mate, he or she will still have to contend with the reality that not all men and women like the same thing.

Both men and women tend to keep their sexual preferences and dislikes to themselves instead of sharing them with their partner. To ask for what one wants sexually is often seen as diminishing the value of what is received. The intimates fear that their lovemaking will become mechanical or that their partner will only be trying to please them and not enjoying the experience. Nevertheless, it is unrealistic to think our partner should know intuitively what we like and don't like. We need to let them know.

I'll Hurt My Partner's Feelings If I Give Instructions

Couples are often uncomfortable communicating their sexual likes and dislikes, their fears, and the shame, guilt, and embarrassment that they sometimes have about sex. We worry that out partner would be offended and hurt if we gave her or him instructions on how to please us. Many people are reluctant to send a message to their partners that they are not adequate in providing pleasure. We sense that our partner is fragile in this area.

Some people might be concerned with spoiling the moment, the romantic atmosphere, or the sense of innocence or wonderment between the partners by discussing sexual preferences. When this is the case, waiting until a conversation can take place outside the bedroom may be preferable.

Even though we may at first feel embarrassed in doing so, we can learn how to express to our partners specifically what our sexual likes and dislikes are. An example of an especially articulate lover was provided by Shere Hite (1976) in her book *The Hite Report*:

> I like: a romantic mood, being undressed, stroking my entire body, putting pressure to my pelvic area with hands and fingers, his nude body held tightly to mine, talking to me about our bodies and feelings while I watch in the mirror, then oral stimulation, soft, wet kisses, rectal stimulation while having my vagina stimulated with fingers, biting all over, blowing in my ear, then finally penis penetration and intercourse with close contact of our pelvic areas. (p. 290)

Although some of us would probably not care to go into quite so much detail, we might want to consider providing our partner with hints as to our preferences.

Most couples with sexual problems do not communicate well, either inside or outside the bedroom (Moore, 1989). Communication skills that are focused on nonblaming and on nonaccusatory expression of feelings, desires, needs, and dislikes, are often useful.

The Source of My Gratification Is Outside Myself

We may believe that we are not responsible for the level of our sexual satisfaction. "Am I responsible if my partner is dissatisfied?" "Is my partner responsible if I am not satisfied?" There seem to be two extremes in this regard: We can be overly concerned with pleasing our partners and therefore take too much responsibility for their sexual gratification, or we can become so involved with our own pleasure that we don't concern ourselves with our partner's feelings or needs. How can we discover a balance between being self-focused enough to get our own needs met and being sensitive enough to meet our partner's needs? Having genuine concern for both ourselves and our partners will help. It is possible to shift one's focus back and forth between self and partner until mutual concern becomes second nature.

► COMMON FEARS THAT PEOPLE HAVE CONCERNING SEXUALITY

Unintended and Unwanted Consequences of Sexual Behavior

Fear of getting AIDS may keep some people from being involved in sexual relationships. Even if our partner has been tested for the AIDS virus, we may still feel uneasy because of the possibility that he or she will have sex with others. We might also be concerned about nonfatal sexually transmitted diseases, as well as with pregnancy.

These are certainly legitimate concerns. In an age when a casual sexual relationship can have lifelong consequences and can shorten or redirect the course of one's life, sex is a serious matter. The practices and guidelines provided by the generation of "free love" do not make much sense today when the stakes are so high. A good rule of thumb to consider is that one might not want to become physically involved with someone with whom a trusting relationship has not been established.

Concern over Being an Inadequate Lover

There may be times when we feel that our partner is bored with sex, and that makes us wonder whether we are sexually attractive to her or him. We wonder whether our partner has had more enjoyable mates than we are. If we are concerned about this, we should ask ourselves whether we have any behavioral evidence of boredom that we might be able to ask our partner about. In addition, such concerns are a good place to begin a conversation with our partner about the sexual relationship. If, in fact, our partner has had a more enjoyable mate, he or she can teach the pleasurable behaviors to us.

Couples need to be able to have fun together. To the extent that they enjoy doing things with each other, they are likely to feel satisfied with the relationship. Each partner will want to remain sensitive to the quality of their sexual contact and to monitor whether both partners continue to experience this aspect of the relationship as fulfilling. Couples in long-term relationships may go places that they haven't been to before or otherwise vary their routine in some way in order to keep the interaction lively. Both partners need to be alert to recognize when their life is getting dull so that they can look for ways to eliminate its boring aspects. In their lovemaking, caring partners are sensitive to each other's needs and desires; and at the same time, they are able to ask each other for what they want and need.

Concern over Being Physically Attractive

Physical attractiveness is a major determinant of interpersonal and sexual attraction (Hatfield & Sprecher, 1986; Hensely, 1992). Indeed, attractive people are better off than their less attractive counterparts in many areas of life (Allen, 1990; Hatfield & Sprecher, 1986). With so much emphasis on physical appearance, it is understandable that many of us wonder whether our physical appearance is acceptable or pleasing to others. We may wonder whether we are normal; that, is whether our body parts have standard dimensions. How do we compare with others? Are we too big? Too small? Are we proportioned properly? Do others find us attractive? Do we find ourselves attractive? What can we do to increase our own appeal to ourselves and to others?

As very small children, we are oblivious to nudity and our bodies. However, we are soon made self-conscious about our bodies on the basis of other's comments. Naturally, any shame related to our bodies is likely to interfere with our ability to be physically intimate with another person.

Given the importance placed on physical beauty, we might be surprised to learn that what people look like is actually unrelated to their level of self-esteem (Hatfield & Sprecher, 1986). Instead, self-esteem is related to what we *think* we look like. People who are content with their looks also tend to be satisfied with themselves generally, and those who are unhappy with their bodies tend to have low self-esteem in other areas as well. In addition, beautiful people tend to pay more attention to physical appearance and to rely on their attractiveness as a source of self-esteem, whereas less attractive people are likely to focus on their other attributes and to develop other competencies as sources of self-esteem.

Fear about Initiating Sex

Sometimes when we desire sex and initiate it, our partner lets us know that he (she) isn't interested. At those times we are vulnerable to feeling almost like a beggar or to feeling completely rejected. This kind of experience would make anyone not want to initiate anymore. However, let us consider this occurrence in light of Albert Ellis's ABCs of rational emotive therapy (Chapter 8). What was the activating event? Our partner was not responsive to our sexual overtures. Was *that* what actually made us feel bad? Not really. We formed a belief about that activating event, namely that we were being rejected. Perhaps we carried this further and told ourselves that we are *entirely resistible*, and perhaps even repulsive to our partner. Those beliefs are what precipitated our unhappy emotional state. What other, more positive beliefs about the situation are possible? Try this one: "How nice that my partner feels comfortable enough with me to let me know she (he) is too tired tonight to accept my offer. My partner must trust that I am secure enough to handle rejection once in a while, without taking it personally." If this viewpoint seems unrealistic, try coming up with one that fits your situation.

In spite of television shows, films, and radio talk shows that today depict women as sexual initiators, in the trenches of day-to-day living, women are still generally expected to be passive and receptive in dating and sexual relations. There is a discrepancy between theory and practice in terms of who can initiate sexual relations and related sexual behaviors. For instance, even though today most college students say that it would be acceptable for a woman to ask a man out on a date, when the same group is asked about their actual behavior, relatively few women report that they do request dates from men.

Women may worry about being seen as sexually undesirable when they initiate intercourse. They may harbor concerns that if they initiate sexual contact, they will appear demanding and put their partner in an embarrassing predicament if the man can't get an erection. Even when the sexual approach is not for intercourse but for a date or a kiss, a man who refuses may experience his masculinity as being on the line, rather than merely his preference for a particular partner. His thought process might run something like this: "This is an offer that no healthy man would refuse."

Concern about Being Impotent, Frigid, or Not Having an Orgasm

Both men and women are subject to performance anxiety when it comes to sex. As mentioned earlier in this chapter, the two types of sexual problems are inability to become aroused and inability to reach orgasm. A man's inability to maintain an erection, often referred to as impotence, may have a variety of causes. It could be merely a symptom of a strained relationship. In addition to the lack of desire to have sex with a certain person at a certain time, impotence may result from feelings of guilt, prolonged depression, hostility or resentment, anxiety about personal adequacy, or a generally low level of self-esteem. Fatigue may be the cause of impotence. There are also physiological reasons for impotence that may need to be looked into if the problem seems to be ongoing. For many men, lack of erection can be conquered by use of the sensate focus exercise described earlier.

Many of the same factors that produce impotence in men can cause a woman to have difficulty becoming lubricated, a condition commonly referred to as frigidity. In addition, when women reach menopause, they tend to have decreased vaginal lubrication during sexual arousal, and vaginal dryness is sometimes a side effect of certain types of oral contraceptives (Reinisch, 1990). Masters and Johnson (1980) found that teaching women and their partners to pay greater attention to the physical indicators of sexual arousal helps women to overcome arousal problems.

Yet another point to make is that there may be no deep significance in a man's not having an erection or a woman's inability to become lubricated. Sometimes our bodies don't respond. An analogous situation might be the surprise felt at not being able to wake up easily after what seemed to be an adequate night's rest or amazement over being hungry an hour or two after we have eaten a meal. Cultivating a cooperative attitude with our body rather than fighting against it can lead to a sense of mental and physical harmony.

Homophobia

Males in our society are under pressure to avoid any behavior that might be considered feminine, and they can become concerned that they possess or are seen as possessing feminine qualities that may reflect negatively on them (O'Neil et al., 1986). For some males, this fear of femininity may create a feared homosexual self along with an abhorrence of and intolerance for any behavior that might be considered homosexual. At least one study has provided evidence that homophobia in heterosexual men is positively related to their tendency to be aroused by homosexual stimuli (Adams et al., 1996). Although it is less common among women, they also have homophobic tendencies, especially when it comes to lesbians (Libbee, 1996). It seems that with both men and women, the probability of homophobia is greater with exposure to a homosexual of the same gender.

Occasionally, young men or boys who wish very much to lead a heterosexual lifestyle find that they are not attracted to women, but rather to men. Sometimes men marry first and later decide that they are better suited to a gay lifestyle, or they may marry to test their sexual orientation. An even higher proportion of women who later turn to a lesbian lifestyle first marry than is the case for gay men (Chapman & Brannock, 1987; Garnets & Kimmel, 1991).

HOW CAN I BE GAY?

Matthew (not his actual name) came into my office one day. I had had him in my Introductory Psychology class a couple of years before, and we now greeted each other in the halls. Occasionally, he would pop his head into my office, and we would speak briefly, until he had to go.

This time, Matthew said he wanted to ask me something and had been wanting to do so since I brought something up in class two years earlier. I had referred to an old disorder, which appeared in prior versions of the DSM, the diagnostic manual used by psychologists and psychiatrists to identify disorders. There used to be a disorder known as Ego-Dystonic Homosexuality, which referred to men who were gay and didn't want to be. Matthew asked me to tell him more about it, because he thought it applied to him.

At the time, Matthew was engaged to be married to a woman with whom he had lived for the past three years. The relationship had grown, in spite of disastrous sexual relations. Matthew confided that the young couple had sexual relations about once a month, often less. Although Matthew found his girlfriend to be beautiful, loved her dearly, and wanted her to have his children, he did not feel aroused in her presence. Nor did other women arouse him. Men did.

Matthew let me know that he had been aware of something to this effect since the age of *three!* Apparently, his mother and grandmother noticed also. His mother announced once at a family gathering for Easter dinner that she was happy Matthew wasn't gay, as she had always thought he was. At the occasion of this announcement, Matthew was seated at the table with his girlfriend! Matthew mentioned that his grandmother had expressed a similar sentiment on a separate occasion.

The question Matthew put to me was, what should he do? It didn't seem ethical to marry his girlfriend without telling her. She had asked him more than once whether he was gay, and he had always denied it. She was worried that he didn't find her attractive. He desperately wanted not to lose her.

What would you say to him? What would you do if you were Matthew?

➤ SEXUAL ABUSE

At its best, sex can be a source of pleasure, can enhance one's overall well-being, and can express love, caring, and affection. At its worst, sex can be used to hurt others. Sex is abusive when it is used to manipulate, to be a punishing force, to get favors, to be a tool of aggression and control, to dominate or humiliate another, or to evoke guilt. Inappropriate sexual behavior takes several forms, four of which are discussed in the following sections.

Incest

Incest refers to having sexual relations with a blood relative. At least one out of ten children is molested by a trusted family member (Forward & Buck, 1988). Incest is sexual behavior that is usually perpetrated by an adult family member with a minor child and that involves inappropriate touching, fondling, oral sex, and/or intercourse. The most common type of adult-child incest is that between father and daughter.

When daughters relate to their fathers, the daughters need caring, affectionate responsiveness. Daddy serves as the prototype for future interactions with men in dating situations. When the father is unable to maintain appropriate boundaries and expresses his affection towards his daughter in a sexualized form, he is likely to cause her substantial psychological injury. This harm might take several forms, including anxiety, anger, depression, guilt, eating disorders, inappropriate sexual behavior, aggressive behavior, self-destructive behavior, substance abuse, suicide attempts, post-traumatic stress disorder, low self-esteem, and sexual dysfunction (Finkelhor, 1990; Goodwin et al., 1990; Kendall-Tacket et al., 1993; Trickett & Putnam, 1993).

Children who have been sexually abused by someone in their family feel betrayed and typically develop a mistrust of others who are in a position to take advantage of them. The woman's ability to form sexually satisfying relationships may be impaired, because she may come to resent all men, associating them with the father or other man who initially took advantage of her. If she couldn't trust her own father, then what man can she trust? She may have a hard time trusting men who express affection for her, thinking that they, too, will take advantage of her.

She may keep control of relationships by not letting herself be open with men, or she may be sexually playful and free with them. Since many incest victims detach from their feelings as a survival tactic, part of the recovery process involves regaining the ability to feel, as well as getting in touch with buried memories. Sharing the experience with others generally has a therapeutic effect for a variety of reasons, including the discovery that she is not alone in having had this happen.

The issue of child abuse has created a major controversy among psychotherapists. When children experience mistreatment early in life, they sometimes repress any memory of it. They may, however, recall the experience later, even after reaching adulthood, if something elicits the recollection. A typical trigger for such recollections is the reexperiencing of emotions similar to those felt at the time of the incident. The difficulty comes from attempting to determine whether the recollections during adulthood are likely to be false memories or genuine ones. Some researchers assert that such memories are likely to be genuine (e.g., Bass & Davis, 1988; Briere, 1993), whereas others argue that people can be encouraged to create false memories (e.g., Loftus, 1993; Loftus et al., 1994). Probably each of these explanations would fit some of the people who have had such memories. After many years have elapsed, there is no reliable way to determine the veracity of a particular person's recollection. Therapists are frequently stuck with attempting to help clients deal with past traumatic events that may or may not have actually happened.

Rape

Rape is generally defined as vaginal, anal, or oral penetration accomplished by force or threat of harm, either when the victim does not consent or when the victim is incapable of giving consent (Koss, 1993). Many who have studied rape view it as an expression of power over another person or of anger, not an act prompted by sexual passion (Ellis, 1991; Malamuth et al., 1991; Matlin, 1996). The distinction must be understood in order to get a complete understanding of this violent crime. In general, women are aware of being less physically strong than are men; however, after being raped, women are left feeling even less powerful.

Women are reluctant to report rapes for fear of being further violated by the court proceeding, where every detail will be revisited and her possible culpability will be examined. The perpetrator's defense typically involves accusations that the rape victim was seductive and willing. Often, with only two people present, the court is left to decide whether her word is good against his. Under these circumstances, the rape victim's character is almost inevitably on trial, along with that of the perpetrator.

In one study, a majority of Americans over the age of 50 believed that when a woman dresses provocatively, is under the influence of alcohol, or agrees to go to the man's home, she is partially responsible for the occurrence of rape (Yankelovich et al., 1991). Among those under age 50, approximately one-third of respondents thought that any of these behaviors made the woman a contributor to her own victimization.

Because of the reluctance of the victim to report rape, estimating the prevalence of this crime is difficult. It appears that between 14 percent and 25 percent of U.S. women will be victims of rape at some point during their lives (Calhoun & Atkeson, 1991; Michael et al., 1994; Muehlenhard & Linton, 1987). This is only an estimate, since it is expected that only about 10 percent to 50 percent of rapes are reported (Gostin et al., 1994; Koss, 1985).

Acquaintance and Date Rape

Acquaintance rape takes place when a woman is forced to have unwanted sex with someone she knows. **Date rape** occurs in situations in which a woman is forced to have unwanted intercourse with a person in the context of dating. The vast majority of rapes are perpetrated by acquaintances or dates rather than by strangers (Gibbs, 1991). Estimates are that only one rape in five is committed by a complete stranger.

Our society links sex with domination and submission. In U.S. culture, masculinity is equated with power, dominance, and sexual aggressiveness, whereas femininity is associated with pleasing men, sexual passivity, and lack of assertiveness (Basow, 1992). Rape can be viewed as an outgrowth of a culture that glorifies sex and violence and that often links them. Some researchers have asserted that U.S. culture socializes men into becoming sexual aggressors to the point of ignoring partner resistance (Malamuth et al, 1991; Prentky & Knight, 1991). Dominance over women by men in the sexual arena is not merely culturally accepted and but even expected. Men often interpret their date's oppositional behavior as a part of the adversarial sex play (Celis, 1991). Women are *expected* to protest, so that their dates will respect them. The majority of American men and women think that some women like to be talked into having sex.

Getting men and women to agree to one rule between potential sexual partners would clear up a great deal of confusion: If at any time, including being on the brink of **intromission** or even in the midst of intercourse, one of the partners no longer wants to continue, the sexual behavior should be discontinued. There is no point at which consent has been tacitly given and thus cannot be revoked. Ongoing mutual consent is the only basis on which sexual contact should move forward toward greater intimacy.

Sexual Harassment

Sexual harassment is considered to be repeated and unwanted sexually oriented behavior in the form of comments, gestures, or physical contacts. Sexual harassment includes unwelcome sexual jokes; suggestive comments; subtle pressure for sexual activity; remarks about a person's clothing, body, or sexual activities; leering at a person's body; unwelcome touching, patting, or pinching; brushing up against a person; and the like. Both men and women can be the perpetrators of or the objects of sexual harassment. However, women experience sexual harassment more frequently than do men, as a function of the power differential that tends to exist between men and women. The person doing the harassment is typically someone with power in a work or an academic setting. Sexist remarks, sexual bribery, seductive behaviors, and sexual coercion serve as reminders to women that they are not viewed as equals by male coworkers who engage in these behaviors. In fact,

© 1991 by S. Kelly. Reprinted by permission from Copley News Service.

some researchers contend that sexual harassment may have more to do with the abuse of power than with sexual desire (Goleman, 1991).

Men sometimes make the assumption that women like sexual attention, when in fact many women resent being related to in strictly sexual terms. Harassment reduces people to objects to be demeaned. Even when the intention of the initiator is to admire rather than to demean, the victim is conscious of being related to on only one channel, as it were.

When men make observations about women's bodies, they are often seen as behaving "like a normal male" (Riger, 1991). Men are expected to be dominant, controlling, and aggressive. Women are expected to be passive and compliant. The woman who asserts her right to not be the focus of unwanted sexual attention may be viewed as being inappropriate and as taking normal behavior the wrong way.

QUESTION: *How do social norms perpetuate sexual abuse of women?*

➤ *AIDS Prevention*

AIDS (Acquired Immuno-Deficiency Syndrome) is one of many sexually transmitted diseases. To date there is no cure for AIDS, so that people who develop it eventually die as a result. In the past few years, an expensive drug treatment has been developed that dramatically retards the progress of AIDS in many patients. Even so, the only available remedy for the AIDS problem at this time is prevention.

People infected with HIV (Human Immuno-Deficiency Virus) may spread the virus through sexual contact or by contact with an open wound of another person, so that the body fluids of the infected person have an opportunity to reach the bloodstream of the contacted person. The virus has also been spread through direct infusion of contaminated blood or blood products. Other sources of the viral spread are organ transplants or shared needles (Stine, 1995). A woman infected with HIV who becomes pregnant or breast-feeds can pass the virus to the baby.

To stay safe from this dangerous virus, you merely need to control your own behavior. Talk to your partner(s) about past and present sexual practices and drug use. Whereas it is a good practice to ask potential partners about past sexual behavior, research suggests that you should not necessarily trust your potential mate's response, since 34 percent of the men and 10 percent of the women in their samples said that they had lied about their behavior in order to have sex (Cochran & Mays, 1990). Avoid sex with someone whom you don't know well or with someone whom you know has had several sexual partners. Avoid having sex with multiple partners. The more partners you have, the more you increase your risk. Avoid sex with persons with AIDS, with those at risk for AIDS, or with those who have had a positive result on the HIV antibody test. Avoid anal sex, with or without a condom. Use condoms and spermicidal barriers to reduce the possibility of transmitting the virus, but realize that they are not 100 percent effective. The only "safe" behavior consists of choosing not to be sexually active or of restricting sex to one mutually faithful, uninfected partner, and not injecting drugs. If you use intravenous drugs, don't share needles.

➤ *Same-Sex Intimacy: What's the Difference?*

Homosexuals in our society endeavor to come to terms with their sexual identity against a background of social condemnation and hostility. For years, a societal attitude against homosexuality was reflected in and fostered by the psychological and psychiatric communities. The official mental health position used to be that homosexuality amounted to a sexual perversion. This stance began to change when, in the mid-1950s, Evelyn Hooker, Ph.D., undertook a controlled study of the psychological characteristics of heterosexual men. She found that the psychological view of homosexuality as a mental disorder was unfounded. In 1973, as a result of this study and subsequent ones, the American Psychiatric Association removed homosexuality from its diagnostic manual as a mental disorder. The association reported its findings as follows:

> Whereas homosexuality per se implies no impairment in judgment, stability, reliability, or general social or vocational capabilities, therefore . . . the (APA) deplores all public and private discrimination against homosexuals . . . (National Gay Task Force, 1977, p. 4).

Although the personalities of homosexual individuals have been shown not to differ from those of their heterosexual counterparts, same-sex relationships differ from opposite-sex relationships in significant ways. Homosexuals face external and internal homophobia, discrimination, and AIDS (Tessina, 1989). Establishing a gay or lesbian identity involves two levels, that of acknowledging one's orientation to oneself and that of going public with one's sexual orientation, a process often referred to as coming out of the closet. Homosexuals may have problems in both recognizing and accepting their sexual orientation as a part of their self-definition. They also face stigmatization from the rest of society.

Homosexuals and bisexuals do not have many role models and thus lack some of the social norms that allow heterosexuals to understand what is expected of them in a given social setting (Wohlfarth, 1995). Role models are available to heterosexuals through family, community, educational institutions, or mass culture. This is not the case for the homosexual person. If gays search out role models, they are likely to be barraged with sexually explicit ads and articles, and/or media caricatures of homosexuals as woman-haters, child-molesters, drag queens, and the like.

Fortunately, a few gays have stepped forward as highly publicized role models, such as Martina Navratilova, the tennis star; k.d. lang and Melissa Etheridge, both musicians and vocalists; and Greg Louganis, a U.S. Olympic gold medalist in the diving competition. Somewhat less visible, but still influential, are authors such as Deb Price and Joyce Murdoch, who wrote a chronicle of the day-to-day realities of a monogamous gay relationship. Thus, while there is a lack of representation of the gay lifestyle in the media, there are some positive role models emerging in our culture.

Another difficulty for a gay person is in dating. Beginning a same-sex relationship is problematic because of the lack of social models or the presence of inappropriate ones (e.g., bars, sex clubs, and cruising areas). Gays face an arduous process involved in searching out a mate. Heterosexuals can meet at church, work, or community gatherings. Although these options are now becoming available to gays, lesbians, and bisexual people, these options are still not the norm. When homosexuals do find partners, they find that public displays of affection are uncomfortable and may even be dangerous.

It may be a myth that most gay relationships are not lasting (Wohlfarth, 1995). Relationships are typically fleeting when one is young, whether heterosexual or homosexual. There is a distinct emphasis on youthfulness and an attractive physical appearance in the gay community, which may outstrip that of the heterosexual community. There is also a great deal of changing of partners among gays. However, many homosexual relationships last just as long as "straight" relationships. Whereas Wohlfarth views this longevity as a result of the arduous nature of the mate selection process, others attribute it to the same commitment, respect, nurturing, and understanding that characterize satisfying, long-term heterosexual couples (Libbee, 1996). Gay male couples who live together in stable relationships have been found to have similar adjustment levels to married heterosexuals (Bell & Weinberg, 1978). In general, the psychological adjustment of homosexuals tends to mirror that of heterosexuals, with adjustment reflecting lifestyle rather than sexual orientation (Bell & Weinberg, 1978).

As described earlier in this chapter, homophobia refers to the fear of being homosexual or of being around homosexuals. It is a condition that can be experienced by heterosexuals and gays alike, and it involves an irrational fear of contagion. The U.S. culture itself is sometimes characterized as homophobic. Society's prejudices against gays and others who don't fit in with the norm may well create a "self-fulfilling prophecy." The homosexual who even as a child must grapple with inadequate treatment often does not adjust well within the strict guidelines of our culture.

Violent attacks continue to be made against lesbian and gay people. In recent years, organized statewide political initiatives have tried to limit or deny civil rights protection to gay people by any local or state governmental entity. Lesbians and gay men feel constantly threatened because they rarely have any legal protection against discrimination in employment, child custody, or housing.

One stereotypical view is that homosexuals are child molesters. Some research estimates are that about 10 percent of the world population is gay, lesbian, or bisexual (Gonsiorek & Weinrich, 1991; Kinsey, 1953), although other surveys have reported lower estimates (Johnson et al., 1992; Laumann et al., 1994). About 10 percent of all reported molestation is perpetrated by homosexuals (Falk, 1989; Koss et al., 1994). Here, again, is evidence suggesting that gays are pretty much like heterosexuals in their likelihood to engage in this type of criminal activity.

Added to the strain of coming to terms with a homosexual identity in a largely hostile social context is the menace of AIDS, a disease that threatens young gay males more so than any other subgroup in our culture (Baker, 1990).

As yet, we don't know exactly how human sexual orientation is determined (Ellis & Ames, 1987; Money, 1988). There is evidence that the tendency runs in families (LeVay, 1992; Pillard, 1990). Gay or lesbian children may be aware at an early age of being different. They generally become aware of their sexual orientation during adolescence or early adulthood (Troiden,

1989), although many are slow to recognize their sexual orientation (Garnets & Kimmel, 1991; Hencken, 1984). About two-thirds of gay males report evidence of gender role nonconformity during childhood, such as preferring girls' toys, although the remaining one-third describe themselves as having had typical gender role behavior as children (Adams & Chiodo, 1983; Green, 1987).

Gay persons lead lives as varied as those of heterosexuals. They establish stable, long-lasting relationships, work for a living, watch TV, vote, and pay taxes. They are not predominantly hairdressers, a one-time stereotype about gay men. They are found distributed throughout the community of employed persons in the same manner as heterosexuals. Gays and lesbians come from all occupations and all levels of education. They are teachers, nurses, doctors, ministers, and members of congress. They are also clerks, artists, athletes, accountants, and city planners. They work in heavy industry. Some gay people fit stereotypes often attributed to homosexuals, but others look and act like individuals from the heterosexual community. Physical appearance and mannerisms are not reliable cues in determining a person's sexual orientation. There are masculine women and effeminate men who are heterosexual. Gay men and lesbian women share the same amount of interest in sexual activity as heterosexual persons, neither more nor less (Bell & Weinberg, 1978).

► *Summary*

In spite of the fact that we live in an age of sexual liberation, many people do not experience genuine satisfaction in their sexual relationships. This difficulty may in part be due to the reluctance that many people have to talk openly about sexual concerns.

Forming a Sexual Identity   A person's sexual identity, an aspect of his or her overall identity, consists of the individual's sexual orientation, body image, sexual values, and his or her preferred manner of reaching sexual arousal.

Guilt Over Sexual Thoughts and Feelings   Many people have learned that certain sexual thoughts and feelings are bad, even though they are not acted on. Guilt is commonly experienced in connection with homosexual fantasies and impulses, feelings of sexual attraction toward members of one's family, sexual feelings toward people other than one's spouse, enjoyment of sexuality, and too much (or too little) desire for sex. Although not all guilt is unhealthy and irrational, there is value in challenging guilt feelings and getting rid of ideas that are unrealistic.

Developing Sexual Values   Most people form values by accepting external standards, such as those of their church leaders or parents. Typically, during adolescence these values are reexamined. Some are discarded, and others are retained. After this process of reexamination, the retained values are more fully one's own. This is part of the process of *individuation.*

Sexual and dating practices have changed dramatically in the past fifty years. Ideally, sexual values should fit in with values held about other aspects of life. Otherwise, people are likely to feel realistic and appropriate guilt when engaging in sexual practices that are not in accordance with their value system.

SEX AND INTIMACY   In current dating practice, couples often become physically intimate prior to becoming emotionally intimate. Through the classical conditioning process, lovers are expected to grow attached to one another. The partners may consequently feel pressured by their sexual familiarity to declare love for one another. Early sexual intimacy puts partners into the position of hoping to get along with the person with whom they are sleeping.

Rollo May observed that people who engage in sex without intimacy have little capacity for feelings and that they function mechanically instead of lovingly. He contended that the trend toward sex without intimacy in western culture is closely associated with the loss of the capacity to feel any emotions.

THE ROLE OF TECHNIQUES IN SEXUAL ENJOYMENT   There is a common belief that the more people know about the mechanics of sex, the more they will be satisfied with their sexual relationships. An unintended consequence can be a focus on learning and implementing techniques rather than attention paid to relaxing and enjoying the sexual experience with one's partner. Technique and knowledge are helpful, but they are not sufficient to achieve an emotionally satisfying sexual relationship. What technique seems to supply is some degree of self-confidence.

There are some techniques that might improve one's sexual experience: (1) Kegel exercises (for women), (2) the woman superior position, (3) the lateral position, (4) sensate focus, (5) the squeeze technique, and (6) the bridge technique.

COMMON MISUNDERSTANDINGS ABOUT SEXUAL RELATIONSHIPS   Some common misunderstandings about sexual relationships are the following: (1) *My partner should know how to please me:* Many individuals have the unrealistic belief that their partner should intuitively know what is needed or desired without being told. (2) *I'll hurt my partner's feelings if I give instructions:* Some individuals fear sending a message to their partners that they are not adequate in providing pleasure. (3) *The source of my gratification is outside myself:* There is sometimes confusion between partners as to who is responsible for whose orgasm; a balance is needed so that each sexual partner takes some responsibility for his or her own sexual experience, while also being attentive to the other partner's needs.

COMMON FEARS THAT PEOPLE HAVE CONCERNING SEXUALITY   Typical concerns that people have about sexual relations are as follows:

Unintended and unwanted consequences of sexual behavior: Fear of getting AIDS may keep some people from being involved in sexual relationships. Even if their partners have been tested for the AIDS virus, they may still feel uneasy because of the chance that the partner will have sex with others. They may also be concerned about other sexually transmitted diseases, as well as with pregnancy.

Concern over being an inadequate lover: There are times when lovers feel that their partner is bored with sex and thus wonder whether they are sexually attractive to their partners. Such feelings can be overcome by communicating the concerns to one's partner and by taking care that the sexual relationship is nurtured and has variety.

Concern about being physically attractive: We may wonder whether we are normal, how we compare with others, and whether others find us attractive.

Fear about initiating sex: One partner may be reluctant to initiate sex for fear of being rejected or putting the partner on the spot.

Concern about being impotent, frigid, or not having an orgasm: Men's inability to maintain an erection or a woman's not becoming lubricated may have a variety of causes. Some causes are emotional, such as guilt, depression, hostility or resentment, and anxiety. There are also physical causes, such as fatigue and certain medications. Whereas men worry about becoming sexually aroused, women worry more about inability to achieve orgasm.

Homophobia: Men experience pressure to avoid any behavior that might be considered feminine, since possession of feminine qualities may suggest homosexual leanings. This fear may lead to homophobia. A similar, though less common, fear may be found in women.

SEXUAL ABUSE   Sexual behavior is abusive when it is used to manipulate, to be a punishing force, to get favors, to be a tool of aggression and control, to dominate or humiliate another, and to evoke guilt.

INCEST   Incest involves inappropriate touching, fondling, oral sex, and/or intercourse, usually perpetrated by an adult family member with a minor child. Children who have been sexually abused by someone in their family typically develop a mistrust of others who are in a position to take advantage of them.

RAPE   Rape is generally defined as vaginal, anal, or oral penetration accomplished by force or threat of harm, either when the victim does not consent or when the victim is incapable of giving consent. Rape is an expression of power over another person, not an act prompted by sexual passion. *Acquaintance rape* takes place when a woman is forced to have unwanted sex with someone she knows. *Date rape* occurs in situations in which a woman is forced to have unwanted intercourse with a person in the context of dating. Women are much more likely to be raped by someone they know than by a stranger.

Sexual Harassment Sexual harassment is considered to be repeated and unwanted sexually oriented behavior in the form of comments, gestures, or physical contacts. Sexual harassment is typically an issue of abuse of the power differential between men and women.

AIDS Prevention The AIDS virus can be transmitted by sexual intercourse with a person infected with the virus, as well as under other circumstances in which body fluids are exchanged. Risk of contracting AIDS is under the control of each individual. Safe behavior consists of choosing not to be sexually active, restricting sex to one mutually faithful, uninfected partner, and of not injecting illegal drugs.

Same-Sex Intimacy For years, a societal attitude against homosexuality was reflected in and fostered by the psychological/psychiatric community. The official mental health position was that homosexuality amounted to a sexual perversion. In 1973, as a result of several studies, the American Psychiatric Association removed homosexuality from its diagnostic manual as a mental disorder. As yet, we don't know exactly how human sexual orientation is determined.

Although the personalities of homosexual individuals have been shown not to differ from those of their heterosexual counterparts, same-sex relationships differ from opposite-sex relationships in significant ways. Homosexuals do not have many role models and thus lack social norms. They also face external and internal homophobia, the necessity of being secretive, AIDS, and denial of their civil rights. Public and private displays of affection are usually uncomfortable and may be dangerous. Gays face an arduous process involved in searching out a mate.

LEARNING THE LANGUAGE OF PSYCHOLOGISTS

sexual orientation	**acquaintance rape**
rumination	**date rape**
introjection	**intromission**
coitus	**sexual harassment**

CHAPTER REVIEW QUESTIONS

1. What is sexual identity?
2. What aspects of sexuality commonly cause people to experience guilt, and how might a person free himself or herself from such a feeling?
3. How might a person avoid feeling guilty about his or her sexual behaviors?

4. What are some guidelines suggested in the text for developing sexual values?
5. What is Rollo May's view on the relationship between physical and emotional intimacy?
6. In what ways might sexual techniques be helpful and in what ways might they be harmful in promoting satisfying sexual relations?
7. What are some of the misconceptions about sex that are mentioned in the text?
8. What are some of the common fears that people have about their bodies, when it comes to feeling adequate as sexual partners?
9. What are some likely causes of impotence in a man and of frigidity in a woman?
10. How is the AIDS virus spread?
11. What are some of the misconceptions about homosexual relationships that are described in this chapter?

ACTIVITIES

1. *WRITE INDIVIDUALLY:* **Everything You Ever Wanted to Know about Sex, but Were Afraid to Ask.** Each class member composes a questionnaire on gender-role identity, sexual feelings, and/or behavior. Write one or more questions that you would like your fellow students to answer or discuss. The questions will be answered in class. You may include questions on love and intimacy.
2. *SMALL GROUP EXERCISE:* **Personal Reflections on My Sexuality.**
3. *COMPLETE INDIVIDUALLY:* **Is It Sexual Harassment?**

Personal Reflections on My Sexuality

Directions: Read each of the following questions, and then write your answers in the blanks.

1. How did you first learn about sex?

   _____

   _____

   _____

   _____

2. What is your earliest memory about sex?

   _____

   _____

_____

_____

3. Try completing this sentence: "One verbal sexual message that I received from my parent(s) was . . ."

_____

_____

_____

_____

4. Now try completing this sentence: "One nonverbal sexual message I received from my parent(s) was . . ."

_____

_____

_____

_____

5. Check off those concepts in the following list that you associate with sex. Then add any other words that you may think of in association with sex.

___ fun	___ ecstasy	___ conquest	___ vulnerability
___ performance	___ duty	___ guilty	___ spiritual
___ anger	___ depression	___ regret	___ suspicion
___ bonding	___ release	___ sport	___ animalistic
___ dirty	___ trust	___ giving in	___ pressure
___ pregnancy	___ embarrassment	___ sharing	___ sinful
___ closeness	___ risk	___ enjoyment	___ routine

___ (other)_____

6. How have you developed your attitudes and values regarding sex? What factors have influenced your attitudes? Have you tried to form your own standards?

_____

_____

_____

_____

7. Is there a double standard of "acceptable" sexual behavior for women and men? If so, how do you feel about it? Is there any reason to have a double standard?

_____

_____

_____

_____

8. Compare the sexual attitudes and behavior of contemporary youth with those of their parents' generation. Do you see any real differences? If so, what are they? In the long run, are these changes constructive or destructive?

_____

_____

_____

_____

9. Differentiate between sensuality and sexuality. What do the two have in common? How are they different?

_____

_____

_____

_____

10. Discuss your thoughts about this statement: "Sexuality is a part of our identity as a person and should not be thought of as merely an activity divorced from our feelings, values, and relationships."

_____

_____

_____

_____

11. What kind of sexual ethics would you like your children to develop? Do you want them to have your sexual values? If not, why not? In what ways do you hope that their values might be different?

_____

_____

_____

_____

12. In going forward with a sexual relationship, what responsibility do you think you might have to the other person and what responsibility might you have to yourself?

_____

_____

_____

_____

13. Have you ever thought that you were the target of sexual harassment? If so, how did you cope with it? If not, have any of your friends or family members been victims of sexual harassment, and if so, how did they handle the situation?

_____

_____

_____

_____

14. In your own view, what is the difference between sexual harassment, flirting, and just being nice to someone while at work or at school?

_____

_____

_____

_____

15. Complete this sentence: "My nude body is . . ."

_____

_____

_____

_____

16. Complete this sentence: "Women's bodies are . . ."

_____

_____

17. Complete this sentence: "After making love, a man . . ."

_____

_____

18. Complete this sentence: "When I see a couple kissing in public, I . . ."

_____

_____

19. Complete this sentence: "Men's bodies are . . ."

_____

_____

20. Complete this sentence: "After making love, women . . ."

_____

_____

Is It Sexual Harassment?

Directions: Consider the following vignettes, and then rate them as to whether you agree or disagree that they constitute sexual harassment by writing in the blank the number that expresses your opinions. (There is no right or wrong answer.) Then compare your responses with those of your classmates, and use your differences of opinion as a basis for discussion.

    1 = Strongly Disagree
    2 = Disagree
    3 = Agree
    4 = Strongly agree

1. Todd and Katie had a preplanned lunch meeting in the staff lounge at Todd's request, and he expected Katie to pay for her own meal. _____

2. Dr. Smith walked up to nurse Johnson in the staff lounge and started rubbing her shoulders, saying, "You're so tense, let me help you relax." _____

3. Margaret, the college dean, shows obvious preference for the input of male faculty members, and she more frequently assigns them special projects that entitle the male faculty members to stipends and to release time from their classroom teaching assignments. _____

4. A district attorney said to his female paralegal, "Have you lost weight? Your pants look loose. You're looking great!" _____

5. Waitress Melissa bends down to pick up her pen. While she is doing so, her manager, Jeff, jokingly remarks, "While you're down there . . . !" _____

6. David walked up to his secretary, Dawn, and said, "You look beautiful in that dress! You should wear it more often." _____

7. Maria's boss complimented her on a job well done. He slapped her on the buttocks, telling her that she's a good team player. _____

8. Greg commented to his coworker Denise, "Wow! That dress really accentuates your figure." _____

9. While attending a business meeting, Mr. Summers placed his hand on Mrs. Perell's upper thigh, in order to get her attention. _____

10. Jessica wore a tight sweater to the office. When her colleague Jose walked into the room where she was sitting, he blatantly stared at her breasts. _____

11. Mr. Jones, an account manager, stares up and down at Ms. Adam's body when she walks by him. _____

12. Bill approaches Sara in her office and asks her for her phone number. _____

13. Mrs. Robinson, Benjamin's boss, showed an obvious preference for him over her other subordinates. One day as they were discussing a project, she reached over and brushed his hair off his forehead. _____

14. As Sashi is walking down the hall at work, her boss walks up behind her, and as the boss passes Sashi, the boss pats her on the fanny and smilingly says, "Hurry up or you'll never get everything done today." _____

12

Loneliness and Solitude

Whosoever is delighted in solitude is either a wild beast or a god.
—Francis Bacon

> PREVIEW QUESTIONS: What can be done to alleviate loneliness? Does U.S. culture foster loneliness? What are the benefits of seeking solitude? How is depression related to loneliness?

> ## INTRODUCTION: MISSING OUR CONNECTION

In a sense, all of us are alone in life, or so say the existentialists. Being alone, we may feel lonely, but this result is not a given, just as the presence of others will not necessarily alleviate our loneliness.

Although the company of others can surely enhance our life, no one else can completely share our unique world of feelings, thoughts, hopes, and memories. We come into the world alone, and we must face death on our own. Understanding this condition of separateness can actually enrich our experience of life. If we accept that no one can take away *all* our loneliness, we can deal more effectively with the times when we long for human companionship. This acceptance enables us to choose freely to give ourselves to our projects and relationships rather than to immerse ourselves in them out of the dread of sensing our isolation from others.

The inevitability of our having some sense of there being an unbridgeable gap between ourselves and others is what is referred to as existential isolation (Chapter 1). Occasional awareness of our aloneness can be expected, no matter how much we seem to have satisfactorily formed relationships and answered the fundamental question, Where do I fit in?

To be alone is neither bad nor good in itself. "Loneliness" and "solitude" are terms that are frequently used to denote negative and positive aloneness, respectively. **Loneliness** implies unhappiness over our separateness from others. **Solitude** denotes the positive experience of having time to oneself for recuperation or reflection.

PEANUTS reprinted by permission of United Features Syndicate, Inc.

➤ LONELINESS: WISHING FOR A TRAVELING COMPANION

Human beings are naturally social. We seek a sense of belongingness with others. Loneliness is a painful awareness that our social relationships are less numerous or meaningful than we desire. To be lonely is to feel excluded from a group, unloved by those around us, unable to share our private concerns with others, and/or alienated from those in our surroundings (Beck & Young, 1978). Some researchers have estimated that as many as one-quarter of the population at any given time feels intensely lonely (Russell, Peplau, & Cutrona, 1980). Dr. Albert Schweitzer (in Buscaglia, 1972) said, "We are all so much together, but we are all dying of loneliness." When we are lonely, we suffer because of our longing for human companionship.

The frustration, isolation, and anxiety brought about by unmet emotional needs can produce a degree of psychological starvation. Even so, people often neglect to meet their own emotional needs. Each of us has psychological requirements to be seen, recognized, appreciated, heard, embraced or touched, and sexually satisfied. Nevertheless, lonely people tend to spend time by themselves. They eat dinner alone, spend weekends alone, and participate in few social activities, such as dating (Russell, 1982).

QUESTION: *How would you describe the opposite of loneliness?*

Attempts to Avoid the Experience of Loneliness

Human beings are amazingly resourceful in developing strategies to escape the feelings of loneliness. Some people stay in unsatisfactory relationships to avoid being lonely. Control of our environment is an important strategy for coping with the possibility of unexpected bouts of loneliness. We busy ourselves in work and activities, so that we have little time to reflect on our emotional state. We schedule every moment, so that we have no opportunity to think about ourselves and what we are doing with our lives. We go to bars, trying to lose ourselves in a crowd or to escape our problems through alcohol. By keeping active, we endeavor to avoid coming to terms with deeper layers of our inner world. We immerse ourselves in helping others and in our "responsibilities." We eat compulsively, hoping that doing so will fill our inner emptiness and protect us from the pain of being lonely. We try to numb ourselves with television, loud music, or drugs, and distract ourselves with radio talk shows, compulsive shopping, Internet chat rooms, sex, or video games. We make ourselves slaves to routine, becoming stuck in a narrow and predictable rut, turning into machines that don't feel much of anything.

Thoughts and Behaviors That Foster Isolation

Chronically lonely people seem caught in a vicious cycle of self-defeating thinking and social behaviors. Some people who are afraid of being rejected make themselves unapproachable. They may be convinced that others won't like them, and thus they make the prophecy self-fulfilling by displaying avoidance behavior. The self-fulfilling prophecy is operating when belief in their social unworthiness and pessimism about others inhibits lonely people from behaving in ways that would reduce their sense of deprivation.

Lonely people blame themselves for their deficient social relationships, and they harbor expectations of failure in relating to others, particularly the fear of being rejected by others (Anderson, Horowitz, & French, 1983; Lear, 1987; Snodgrass, 1987). They also perceive others in negative ways. For example, Jones, Freeman, and Goswick (1981) paired lonely and nonlonely students with a stranger of the same sex. The lonely students were more likely to form a negative perception of the other person than were the nonlonely ones. Wittenberg and Reis (1986) found the same phenomenon when pairing either a lonely or a nonlonely student with a college roommate: The lonely students felt more negatively about their roommates. This unfavorable perception may stem in part from the lonely person's demand for too much too soon from others in the early stages of a relationship, resulting in a misperception of other people as cold and unfriendly (Lear, 1987).

The negative self-perceptions and negative views of others by lonely people may have a basis in reality, because they tend to lack social skills, in particular the interpersonal skills needed to make friends or to cope with disagreements (Rubin, 1982). They often find it hard to introduce themselves, make phone calls, and participate in groups (Rook, 1984; Spitzberg & Hurt, 1987). When talking with a stranger, they have been observed to spend more time talking about themselves and to take less interest in their conversational partners than do nonlonely people (Jones et al., 1982). Thus, it is not surprising that new acquaintances often come away with negative impressions of the lonely people (Jones et al., 1982).

QUESTIONS: *Do you decide in advance that the other students and professors want to keep to themselves? Do you assume that there already are well-established cliques at school or work to which you cannot belong?*

Personality Factors Implicated in the Experience of Loneliness

Lonely people are disposed to be self-conscious and low in self-esteem. They are unlikely to self-disclose to others. Consequently, their friendships are likely to be shallow. Lonely people tend to have an external locus of control (Jones, 1982), so that they do not see themselves as being capable of taking their lives into their own hands and achieving through their own efforts the goals that they set. They are inclined to be cynical and pessimistic about life in general (Nevid, Rathus, & Rathus, 1995).

It seems that the more devastated an individual becomes as a result of life experiences, the more he or she builds defenses and rationalizations, and creates walls behind which to grumble. The person feels misunderstood, unloved, abused, and exploited. The more she or he needs loving understanding, the more the person moves away from any possibility of receiving it. Pouting is a good example of this. If an individual needs something, he or she must let others know what the need is. Some people are so loving and empathic that they can spot a need in another person, but most people aren't quite so astute. Even so, the vast majority of people are well-meaning and will provide something when asked for it directly. Often, when lonely or shy people muster up the courage to express a need, they are surprised at the response they receive. Others may say, "I had no idea you were lonely" and "You always seem so self-sufficient, so composed. I'm really pleased to know you're human." Even lovers aren't reliable mind readers. We cannot assume that people, even those close to us, will know and understand our unexpressed needs and feelings. If we want people to know us, we are responsible for communicating about ourselves to them.

Mental Disorders Related to Loneliness

Mental disorders represent extreme deviations from normal or optimal functioning. Social anxiety and avoidance of social situations are associated features of many mental disorders, such as major depressive disorder, dysthymic disorder (an ongoing experience of depression for years), and schizophrenia. Three mental disorders particularly related to loneliness are schizoid personality disorder, avoidant personality disorder, and social phobia.

Those with schizoid personality disorder are "loners" who are detached from human relationships. Whereas most of us miss the company of others when we do not enjoy it on a regular basis, schizoid people don't particularly feel this way. If a person with this disorder were to receive either praise or criticism from others, he or she wouldn't have a strong reaction to it, as most of us would. Such persons lack warmth and have minimal emotional needs. Although they are usually content to do activities on their own, schizoid people are not immune from occasional pangs of loneliness.

A person suffering from avoidant personality disorder may act somewhat like a schizoid person, in that both tend to avoid the company of others; however, the avoidant person has a different motivation. This individual fears being embarrassed, humiliated, criticized, or rejected by others. With the anticipation of such punishing consequences from interacting with others, this person prefers to steer clear of the company of people. Thus, those who suffer from this disorder withdraw from situations where they would be required to interact with others.

Whereas the prior two mental disorders represent deeply ingrained, enduring aspects of the individual's core personality, a social phobia does not. Those suffering from social phobia have a marked and persistent fear of certain social situations, especially those that involve some sort of performance, such as public speaking. These people dread scrutiny by others, since they anticipate acting in a manner that will be humiliating or embarrassing. Their fear may be great enough to lead to a panic attack. The person recognizes that the fear is excessive, an awareness that can add to the distress. People suffering from social phobia are more likely than those with personality disorders to seek help for their timid condition. Those with a personality disorder of any kind are likely to experience their way of relating to others as being "just the way I am."

Cultural Factors That Promote Loneliness

Markus and Kitayama (1991) contended that culture has a significant impact on the way an individual relates to others. Some cultural changes in the United States within the past few decades have contributed to interpersonal isolation. Family relations have become less stable, partly because of the increased mobility of the society. Residential neighborhoods, churches, independently owned stores located in the neighborhood, and private physicians who make house calls have declined in number or have disappeared. In the early days of television, families all over the community would watch the same few programs and talk about them with friends the next day. Now, with hundreds of channels to choose from, we are challenged to find *anyone* who watched the same program as we did on the previous evening, thus leaving little opportunity to enjoy this particular type of shared activity.

Cultures vary in the amount of privacy and contact they provide and foster. The United States is a highly individualistic culture, in which there is a belief in the inherent separateness of people. Cultures such as ours value individuality, uniqueness, and independence. Citizens within such a culture focus on personal goals, and they are self-reliant. Individual behavior is shaped by one's personal preferences, by a private cost-benefit analysis of what will work for oneself and what won't (Hatfield & Rapson, 1996).

In competitive societies, privacy is valued. Both competition and personal achievement are stressed in the United States. Children are encouraged to be self-reliant. Thus, asking for help may provoke anxiety or feelings of inadequacy in U.S. children and adolescents. American culture is more competitive and individualistic than many other cultures, including that of Mexico. Conversely, in traditional Chinese culture, independence is not so highly prized, and asking for help is not so likely to produce feelings of inferiority.

Most cultures provide physical arrangements and mechanisms for ensuring privacy, such as locks on doors, curtains, and Do Not Disturb signs. Societies that require economic cooperation and shared decision making tend to have physical arrangements that reduce opportunities to spend time alone. In an Israeli kibbutz, privacy is hard to come by. A kibbutz is a community typically located in a rural part of Israel in which members live collectively. A Western visitor to an Indonesian household reported that except in the front doorway, there were to be found within the house no doors to shut; there were only curtains hanging in the archways between rooms (Feshbach & Weiner, 1991).

Individuals within a culture also vary in their contact needs. In the United States, there are both forces that encourage us to affiliate and pressures that encourage us to maintain our privacy. There has been considerable emphasis among young people in the American culture on "popularity," "fitting in," and "getting along". As children, we are taught the importance of being likable and sociable, of presenting a pleasant public face or persona. For punishment, we are sent alone to a corner or to our room, whereas by contrast, happy events are typically shared with family, friends, and classmates. We may come to consider aloneness an undesirable experience and thus go to great lengths to avoid it. Whereas members of individualistic societies are good at getting along with a wide range of people, including strangers, they are less adept at managing long-term relationships than are members of collectivist societies (Hatfield & Rapson, 1996).

Antidote for Loneliness

Psychologists encourage lonely people to develop more adaptive ways of thinking and behaving. Generally, the way to bring about improvement in our lives is to make changes in ourselves. Two ways to recover from the predicament of not having as many social relationships as we would like will be discussed: (1) giving something back—for example, being good company so that others will like being around us; and (2) learning better social skills so that we'll know what to do with people once we attract them.

GIVE SOMETHING BACK   We might ask ourselves whether we are good company, accepting of others, and possessing goals, projects, thoughts, and feelings that we are willing to share with others. If we do not like our own company, why should others want to be with us? Our experience of loneliness may stem from self-rejection.

Sociologist Peter Blau (1967) asserts that we end up with the friends and lovers that we deserve. If we want to enjoy the benefits of social relationships, we must offer other people enough value to make association with us worth their while. The more we have to offer, the greater demand there will be for our company. Other people are not our mother, so we can't expect them to be the gift that keeps on giving, without expectation of our reciprocating in some form.

Social-exchange theory asserts that human interactions are guided by a trading of material and social goods, and that people form and remain in relationships in which they feel that they get a good bargain. That is, the benefits of the relationship outweigh the costs. **Social exchange theory** uses an economic model to understand human relationships. The theory suggests that people are aware of the costs and benefits of a relationship and are motivated to "profit" from their associations by pursuing a **minimax strategy.** Minimax, a term that comes from game theory, means that we seek to minimize costs and maximize rewards (Blau, 1964; Homans, 1961; Thibaut & Kelly, 1959). Although we almost certainly do not consciously think about our relationships in this way, these factors do predict relationship satisfaction and longevity. Expressions such as "I'm not getting a lot out of this relationship" or "This friendship isn't worth the trouble anymore" reflect this cost/benefit analysis.

There are three categories of benefits that intimates provide for one another, which are stimulation value, utilitarian value, and emotional support. Interesting or imaginative people with new ideas provide stimulation value for their friends, coworkers, and family members. Being well-read, taking classes, or keeping up with current events furnishes some of the ammunition for supplying others with this kind of entertainment. Alternatively, companions may also have utility value, that is, they provide tangible services. A cooperative and helpful friend has such value. This person will show up to help us move, pick up our car at the shop, do baby-sitting for our kids, or tutor us in an academic subject with which we have trouble. Furthermore, this person is likely to accompany us to that movie we have been wanting to see, even though action thrillers are not his or her favorite genre, and might even loan us the money for our movie ticket. Even elevating the status of one's partner or friends by association with our own prestige is a utilitarian service (Foa & Foa, 1975). Financial security is another utilitarian benefit that relationships sometimes provide. Finally, friends and intimates who give us love, attention, affection, feedback, approval, recognition, consolation in times of distress, sexual gratification, advice, gratitude, and companionship are supplying us with emotional support. The exchange of value in a relationship does not have to be of the same type. For instance, a stimulating partner might receive recognition for being clever as well as gratitude from his or her mate for the satisfying entertainment. Both parties feel rewarded.

Through the framework of social exchange theory, we can examine our work, school, and personal associations to determine how we might benefit others and thus to make friends. As long as the participants in a relationship find profit in the social interaction, they are likely to continue it. When the expected benefits are no longer forthcoming, the relationship may end.

A healthy approach to relationships might be summed up this way: Don't try to *find* the right person, *be* the right person. Reach out by sending a note or card to someone you know. Do something nice for someone else, as a way to shift the focus from your feelings of longing. It is likely that if we sit back and wait for others to come to us, we shall have few friends. Only outgoing people who take the initiative to get to know us will become our friends.

QUESTION: *Would you be your own best friend?*

THIS IS YOUR CAPTAIN SPEAKING . . . DEVELOP SOME SOCIAL SKILLS . . . MAKE IT SO   We may sense that something is wrong with the way we are relating to others, but we cannot figure out what it is. If we are desperate for the company of others,

"My wife and I are deeply in love, my children are a delight, my career is exciting, I find solace and inspiration in my religion, I'm as healthy as anybody I know. But, still, something is missing."

others might experience us in that way, and so they may be put off. Creating this perception of ourselves is not conducive to beginning a new relationship, because we are likely to attract only an individual who teams up with needy people. A psychotherapist can help us gain understanding of how we relate to others and how we might decide to change our patterns of relating in order to have more satisfactory relationships. Later in this chapter, some specific strategies for developing social skills will be discussed as a way of overcoming shyness. Development of these skills should help alleviate loneliness.

QUESTION: *Might a period of loneliness provide an opportunity for personal growth or a greater sense of comfort with oneself?*

➤ SOLITUDE: ALONE ON THIS STRETCH OF ROAD

Being alone is a potentially valuable human experience. Viktor Frankl (1969) wrote, "We need new types of leisure, which allow for contemplation and meditation. To this end, man needs the courage to be lonely" (p. 98). In order to develop satisfying relationships with others, we might start with being good company for ourselves. We do not have to seek and find company in order to get over loneliness. Self-acceptance is a prerequisite for meaningful interpersonal relationships. Once we have mastered our reluctance to be alone, we can approach others without a feeling of being desperate for contact.

Time spent alone has a number of functions, including the opportunity for self-evaluation, reflection, and planning. We spend much of our time alone thinking about our relationships with others. We try to figure out why a particular person did something that bothers us. We examine our attitudes and compare them with the positions of other people we know. We wonder why we dislike those we do, and conversely, what make us so fascinated by those who charm us.

We might use time alone to reflect on whether there is at least one person whom we feel we can talk to, someone who really listens to us. If so, we might be able to cultivate this relationship by suggesting get-togethers. If not,

we'll have to settle for our own company for now. Later, we can develop acquaintances into friendships or get to know new people by attending social functions on or off campus.

We might think about how we have coped with lonely times in the past. We may be able to use positive coping methods from the past as reliable strategies for the future. We can also look at some of the decisions that we made during past times of extreme loneliness and ask whether these decisions are still appropriate. Sometimes strategies that we adopted as children remain with us into adulthood, when they are no longer workable. We might benefit from trying to discover some of the ways in which the person we are now is a result of our experiences of loneliness in the past.

We can use times of solitude to look within ourselves and renew our sense of direction in our life. We can better pay attention to our own intuitions, feelings, and thoughts when we are not attending to input from others. Solitude can thus provide us with the opportunity to sort out our lives and gain a sense of perspective. Dwelling within ourselves can be like being in an oasis, a refuge, or a retreat. We can let down our guard.

Abraham Maslow noted that self-actualized people prefer to spend some time alone. This kind of separation is self-chosen and comfortable, and it can be enriching. Self-actualizing people are also inclined to be uninterested in social "chatting" or party-going. They resist the distractions and petty influences imposed by other people, and they value being completely themselves over placating others. They invest their time and effort in maintaining a few close friendships, preferring a small number of intimate personal relations to a wider circle of friends.

Taking time to be alone gives us the opportunity to think, plan, imagine, and dream. It allows us to listen to ourselves and to become sensitive to what we are experiencing. We can learn to find direction from within ourselves. Solitude can bring a sense of serenity that Walt Whitman aptly described when he wrote,

> I exist as I am, that is enough
> If no other in the world be aware
> I sit content
> and if each and all be aware
> I sit content.

For these reasons, the absence of sufficient time alone can have serious psychological consequences. We may be distracted and overstimulated by a busy life. As Ralph Waldo Emerson put it,

I see not any road of perfect peace which a man can walk, but to take counsel of his own bosom. Let him quit too much association; let him go home much, and establish himself in those courses he approves. (1991, p. 133)

Some of us resist spending time alone. Silence may be experienced as threatening, because it forces us to reflect and to touch deep parts of ourselves. We may also fear that we will alienate others if we ask for private time. Instead, we alienate ourselves. Both privacy and contact can be enriching. We need to learn the value of each and to arrive at a balance that is right for us.

➤ USING COGNITIVE BEHAVIOR THERAPY TO ALLEVIATE LONELINESS

As was discussed in Chapter 8, cognitive behavior therapists apply learning principles to thoughts and feelings just as behavior therapists apply them to actions. Whereas the goal of behavior therapy is to change a person's maladaptive behaviors, the aim of cognitive therapy is to modify negative or unrealistic beliefs.

Albert Ellis, one of the pioneers of cognitive therapy, developed rational-emotive therapy (Chapter 8), which is based on the assumption that emotional problems arise when a person has unrealistic beliefs about life. Ellis noticed that people say things to themselves in an ongoing flow of internalized sentences. This internal dialogue contains both positive and negative messages. Suppose that a student is considering asking a question in class. She may have thoughts such as "I might make a mistake and look silly in front of my classmates. Wouldn't it be awful if I did say something dumb? How could I even face the class again if I were humiliated like that?" When we say these catastrophizing sentences to ourselves, we begin to feel anxious. If the student were instead to tell herself, "So what? If I make a mistake and look silly, it won't be great, but it still won't be awful. In fact, my classmates might be grateful that I asked a question they wanted to ask but were afraid to," she could avoid feeling excessively anxious at the prospect of speaking up in class. In other words, Ellis discovered a way that each of us can manage our emotional state by changing our internal dialogue. He encouraged his clients to challenge their irrational beliefs through **rational confrontation.** With this procedure, a person learns to dispute his or her illogical thoughts about a given situation.

Aaron Beck has been the other central figure in the development of cognitive therapy. According to Beck, the principles underlying cognitive therapy start with the premise that perception of reality is not the same as reality itself (Beck & Freeman, 1990). A person's sampling of reality is restricted by the inherent limitations of his or her sensory functions—seeing, hearing, and so on. Furthermore, the individual's interpretations of his or her sensory input are dependent on inherently fallible thought processes through which he or she filters incoming information. Thus, the appraisal of reality can be flawed by unrealistic patterns of thought. Finally, the cognitive therapist tries to help people to accept the distinction between external reality and their psychological perception of it (e.g., the appraisal of danger).

One of the best known techniques used in cognitive therapy is the **dysfunctional thought diary.** The client is encouraged to keep a journal in which he or she identifies and labels **automatic thoughts,** which are the beliefs we form in response to life events. We are often unaware of our automatic thoughts, because they are fleeting and thus we do not usually attend to them. Yet these thoughts, and not external events, are responsible for our mood.

Once the automatic thoughts are noticed and recorded in the thought diary, the client and therapist can challenge any faulty beliefs. **Cognitive restructuring** of maladaptive thoughts is the central goal of cognitive therapy. This procedure involves modifying illogical ideas that maintain a person's maladaptive behaviors. Through cognitive restructuring, people change what they say to themselves about what is going on in their lives. Specifically, they learn to change negative self-statements, which interpret the situation in such a way that nothing can be done to cope with it, into positive self-statements that are optimistic and that point to some constructive, realistic course of action (Spiegler, 1983).

QUESTION: *Do you expect others to reach out to you, even though you don't initiate contacts yourself?*

> ## THOUGHT PROCESSES IMPLICATED IN PROBLEMS RELATED TO LONELINESS: DEPRESSION AND SHYNESS

Depression

Depression is the most pervasive mental affliction (Blazer et al., 1994). Whereas periods of sadness are an inherent aspect of human experience, prolonged periods of gloom, during which all pleasure has gone out of life, may signal a depression (DSM-IV).

How do the attributions, expectations, and other thought patterns of troubled and untroubled people differ? Thought processes are implicated in depression. Like lonely people, depressed people are negative thinkers. Beck (1972) wrote that depressed people magnify bad experiences, minimize good ones, and become unrealistically pessimistic. They tend to engage in selective perception (Chapter 8). Depressed individuals tend to have three negative views, which have been referred to as "the cognitive triad." First, they feel negative about themselves; second, they are negative about the world; and third, they are pessimistic about the future.

Depressed people are negative, but they are not always unrealistic in their thinking. Alloy and Abramson (1979) studied college students who had scored as either mildly depressed or as nondepressed on a depression inventory. The students had to observe whether or not their pressing a button was linked with whether or not a light came on. Surprisingly, the depressed students were quite accurate in estimating their degree of control. It was those who were *not* depressed whose judgments were distorted, by exaggerating the extent of their control over the light. Subsequent experiments have consistently confirmed this phenomenon of **depressive realism.** Nondepressed people overestimate the degree to which they are responsible for positive events and underestimate their responsibility for negative events; depressed people do not have this characteristic (Alloy & Abramson, 1988).

Although these studies have refuted the common presumption that depressed people are unrealistic, they have revealed a specific way in which depressed people think differently from those who are nondepressed. Depressed people have a **negative attributional style.** Compared with people who are not depressed, those who are depressed engage in more self-blame, interpret and recall events in a more negative light, and are less hopeful about the future.

Sweeney, Anderson, and Bailey (1986) conducted over a hundred studies involving 15,000 subjects. The researchers found that depressed people were more likely than nondepressed people to attribute failures and setbacks to causes that are *stable* (It's going to last forever) and *global* (It's going to affect everything I do). Depressed people also make *internal* attributions (It's my fault). This pessimistic, overgeneralized, self-blaming type of thinking leads to a sense of hopelessness (Abramson et al., 1989), and hopelessness has consistently been linked to depression.

Consequences of Depression

Is the attributional style of depressed people the *cause* or the *consequence* of their depressed mood? Depressed thinking has consequences for the depressed person's behavior, and that behavior in turn helps maintain a self-defeating cycle. Sacks and Bugenthal (1987) created an awkward social situation by asking some young women to get acquainted with a stranger who sometimes acted in a cold and unfriendly manner. Unlike the optimistic women, those women with a more pessimistic explanatory style reacted to the social failure by becoming somewhat depressed. They then behaved more antagonistically toward the next person they met. Thus, their negative thinking predisposed a negative (depressed) mood response that resulted in negative behavior, thereby activating depression's vicious cycle.

Research on the social thinking of people who are vulnerable to depression indicates that they tend to see their future successes and failures as uncontrollable even when they are *not* in a depressed state. Another way of saying this is that these people tend to have an external locus of control, a concept discussed earlier (Chapter 8). The social learning theorists have found that many depressed people suffer from "learned helplessness," or lack of self-efficacy. That is, depressed people have had experiences in which their efforts to better the situation failed, causing them to conclude that they are helpless to do anything to improve their circumstances. For these reasons, depression is viewed as both a cause and a consequence of negative thoughts.

Depressed people withdraw from society. They may not have the energy to groom themselves, clean their homes, or prepare meals. Existing under such conditions is indeed depressing. Thus, another aspect of depression's vicious cycle emerges.

Overcoming Depression

Psychologist Martin Seligman (1991) contended that one consequence of having an extremely individualistic society such as ours is having to cope with an epidemic of depression. Seligman also pointed to meaninglessness in life as a common cause of depression in this type of culture. A necessary condition for meaning is the attachment to something larger than we are. Seligman argues that our society has moved toward making the self the repository of all our hopes. No longer do larger institutions such as family, workplace, nation, or religion provide a context of meaning for individuals. He asserts that the self is a very poor site for meaning and that depression stems from an overcommitment to self and an undercommitment to the common good. What is needed is a change in orientation from a self-focus to a greater attentiveness to others.

Cognitive therapy seeks to change the way depressed people consciously think about failure, defeat, loss, and helplessness. First, depressed people are taught to recognize the automatic thoughts that flit through their consciousness at the times when they feel the worst. Second, they learn to dispute the automatic thought by marshaling contrary evidence. Third, they learn to make different explanations, or reattributions, and use them to dispute the old automatic thoughts. Fourth, once they realize that thinking negative things is not inevitable, depressed people can learn how to distract themselves from depressing thoughts. Finally, depressed people learn to recognize and dispute the depression-causing assumptions that govern much of their behavior. Assumptions such as "Unless I do everything perfectly, I'm a failure" can be replaced with ideas like "Success is doing my best" (Seligman, 1991, p. 90).

Since the 1950s, a vast array of medications have been developed for alleviating psychological problems such as anxiety and depression. Currently, there are dozens of antidepressants available through prescription, the most well known of which goes by the brand name of Prozak. Antidepressants do not work for everyone, however. In addition, many people object to using such medications. The good news is that recent research has shown that cognitive therapy—essentially working on the negative thought patterns—is as effective as antidepressant medication in relieving depression (e.g., Beck et al., 1985; Blackburn, Eunson, & Bishop, 1986).

Even with both medication and therapy available for treatment of depression, there are many people who wage a lifelong battle with clinical depression.

Shyness

Shyness refers to the tendency to feel tension in social situations and thus to withdraw from them or to avoid them altogether. Shy people show restraint and signs of strain when socializing (Buss, 1980). They seem to be afraid of people. Approximately fifty percent of American college students consider themselves shy (Carducci & Stein, 1988). Seventy-five percent of people who say they are shy don't like being that way.

A genetic basis for shyness has been suggested by the differences found among infants on this personality dimension. Some children are consistently timid and emotionally restrained in the presence of a stranger or in an unfamiliar setting, whereas other children in the same situation are uninhibited and even display pleasure over the novelty of the situation (Kagan & Snidman, 1991). In addition, most children retain their characteristic style of relating at least through the eighth year of life. Relatives of the shy children also show a greater degree of social anxiety than do relatives of the more social children. These findings show the stability of a child's position on the shy versus sociable continuum and suggest a genetically mediated condition (Kagan et al., 1991). Although estimates vary, researchers generally ascribe no more than 40 percent to 50 percent of personality dimensions such as shyness to genetic factors (Plomin, Chipeur, & Loehlin, 1990; Plomin & Rende, 1991). The environment also plays a significant role in the development of personality dimensions such as shyness. Many children with a shy disposition can learn not to act shyly, although subtle signs of their inherent tendency to be inhibited in strange situations may still be observed (Feshbach, Weiner, & Bohart, 1996).

Shy people tend to lack social skills. They avoid eye contact and are inclined to withdrawal when spoken to. They show little interest or vitality, and they pause too long in conversations. Many have not learned how to meet others; for instance, they have not learned how to start a conversation and keep it going or how to end social encounters. Most shy people have social anxiety. They fear being evaluated, embarrassed, ridiculed, rejected, and found inadequate.

Thought patterns are also implicated in social anxiety (shyness). The fears of shy people tend to cause self-defeating thinking. Shy individuals are filled with self-blame when social encounters do not go smoothly. As with lonely and depressed people, those who are shy tend to be pessimistic when anticipating future outcomes, an attitude that can become a self-fulfilling prophecy. Shy people tend to see incidental events as somehow relevant to themselves (Fenigstein, 1984). They overpersonalize situations. This inclination breeds anxious concern and, in extreme cases, paranoia.

Shyness is generally triggered by unfamiliar social situations; for example, shy people dread meeting strangers, being in formal settings, meeting high-status people, being the focus of attention, or being different from others. Shy people are observers of themselves in public and thus feel acutely self-conscious. They see themselves as social objects. We are all eager to present ourselves to others in ways that make a good impression and that avoid making a bad impression. Those who are shy are motivated to impress others, but they feel anxious because they are doubtful of their ability to do so.

Consequences of Shyness

The natural tendency of shy individuals is to be guarded, to talk less than nonshy people, and to avoid topics that reveal their ignorance. Shy people misinterpret the actions of others as rejection. They have a lasting sense of their own shyness, even when their behaviors are modified.

Those who are shy have difficulty in making new friends or meeting people, and thus they experience feelings of isolation, loneliness, and depression (Schmidt & Fox, 1995). They are misperceived by others in that a shy person may strike others as vain, bored, aloof, unfriendly, or disinterested. A general lack of self-projection and confidence in social settings is typical of shy individuals. However, unless shyness is intense and quite painful, it is a mistake to think of it as a major problem. Shyness does have its costs, but it tends to lessen with age as we become more experienced with others.

Overcoming Shyness: Learning Social Skills

Probably the single greatest cause of both shyness and loneliness is the lack of social skills. Many children seem to "outgrow" shyness as they gain interpersonal skills and wider social experience. A more proactive way to tackle shyness than waiting to outgrow it is to work on changing one's thought processes. As with loneliness and depression, shyness is often sustained by a number of irrational or unproductive ideas. Here are some of these faulty beliefs along with positive self-statements that might replace them (adapted from Girodo, 1978):

1. *Faulty belief:* "Popular individuals get invited to do things with others because they are lucky enough to know a lot of people."

   Rational confrontation: "Those whose companionship is sought after by other people are popular because they make an effort to meet and spend time with others: They don't leave it to luck to meet people but instead join clubs, invite others to do things, and strike up conversations with them."

   Alternative positive self-statement: "Even individuals who are popular and socially skillful don't always win people over. I don't have to take it to heart if a particular interaction goes poorly."

2. *Faulty belief:* "You can be successful at a social gathering by passively waiting for something to happen or for someone to approach."

   Rational confrontation: "Although something could happen with this strategy, it might well be that nothing good will come of it. You may go the entire evening without talking to anyone. On the other hand, if you approach someone yourself, you are guaranteed to have at least this minimal amount of social interaction."

Alternative positive self-statement: "I need to do my part in initiating social interaction."

3. *Faulty belief:* "Since practically everywhere you go, there are human beings, the likelihood of meeting people who are looking for social interaction is the same everywhere."

Rational confrontation: "Although there are people practically everywhere, many of them are busy and thus uninterested in socializing. It pays to select settings and events that have a high probability of leading to association with people who are unhurried and intent on enjoying themselves through some kind of recreation. Drama clubs, hiking clubs, sports teams, school events, dance groups, and so forth often serve as a convenient way to bring together people who are interested in meeting and talking with others."

Alternative positive self-statement: "I can set attainable goals for enlarging my circle of friends and acquaintances by planning a few activities each week."

4. *Faulty belief:* "If people don't seem to like you immediately, they in fact don't like you and won't ever like you."

Rational confrontation: "This conviction results in unnecessary withdrawal and isolation. Someone's initial failure to pay attention to you doesn't mean that he or she holds you in disfavor. It takes time and opportunity to grow fond of someone. Perhaps the other person doesn't approach you because he or she is also shy."

Alternative positive self-statement: "It is unrealistic to expect *everyone* to like me, but there are bound to be people who will like me the way I am. When I think other people are judging me harshly, I am probably just being hard on myself."

Source: Adapted from *Shy! (You Don't Have to Be!)* by Michel Girodo. Copyright © 1978 by Pocket Books. Reprinted by permission from the author.

Learning such skills, first by rehearsing and then by employing them in actual encounters, should work just as it does for learning to play golf or to paint a portrait. We aren't born with a natural ability to effectively initiate and keep up a dialogue with another person.

There are many ways in which social skills can be practiced. You might tape-record and then listen to your conversations. As you listen to the recording, you may wonder at the way you pause, interrupt, fail to respond to others, or lack animation. If you watch yourself in a mirror while practicing exaggerated facial expressions of surprise, dislike, interest, and enjoyment, you can create a more lively way of presenting yourself. You might also practice looking attentive and noting how your face feels when you are doing this, so that you'll know by feel what your facial expression must look like to convey interest in others.

One way to become more comfortable in social situations is to learn to ask questions of others. Questions that shift attention to the other person show that you are interested in her or him. The best questions are often open-ended: (1) "Do you get a chance to travel much?" as opposed to "Have you ever been to Oregon?" (2) "What's it like living at the beach?" as opposed to "Do you like living at the beach?" (3) "What kinds of music do you like?" is preferable to "Do you like classical music?" Open-ended questions require several words for an answer rather than a "yes" or "no." It takes only a few questions to keep a conversation alive. Also, in replying to open-ended questions, people often give additional information about themselves. This knowledge can then be used to maintain the conversation by asking further questions that may to lead into other topics (adapted from Coon, 1998).

Conquering shyness calls for taking pains to learn new social skills and to challenge old convictions about ourselves and others. It also entails mustering the courage to hazard new social interactions. Although overcoming shyness is likely to include a few clumsy attempts at conversation along with uncomfortable moments of not knowing what to say, the benefits are human fellowship and a sense of self-efficacy.

Overcoming Shyness: Role-Playing

Psychologist Philip Zimbardo (1977) recommended getting the best of shy tendencies by role-playing. He contended that shy people worry too much about whether their behavior reflects their "real" selves. Zimbardo developed a shyness institute at Stanford University, where he encouraged shy people to initiate

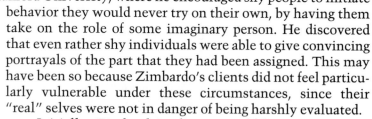

behavior they would never try on their own, by having them take on the role of some imaginary person. He discovered that even rather shy individuals were able to give convincing portrayals of the part that they had been assigned. This may have been so because Zimbardo's clients did not feel particularly vulnerable under these circumstances, since their "real" selves were not in danger of being harshly evaluated.

Initially, Zimbardo's clients would be given a script of what to say when acting out their part. Not only were the shy students capable of performing their roles, but also many of them found that they enjoyed themselves while doing so. Often as they carried out their assigned role, the students were able to extend their behaviors beyond the specifications of the assignment and to begin to merge their role-playing assignment with their other roles, or in other words, with their real selves.

It seems that being cast in a particular role allows the shy person to "forget" herself or himself. Without the burden of self-consciousness, the shy person can show what she or he would be like if the shy individual weren't herself or himself. Once having played the role, however, the role *is* a part of the shy person; the new role becomes part of the person's repertoire of behaviors. The shy individual cannot deny that she or he is capable of feeling and doing what she or he managed to do as "someone else." Research has confirmed that acting out a new role results in changes in privately held attitudes and values (Festinger, 1957; Festinger & Carlsmith, 1959).

➤ SUMMARY

The existentialists assert that each human being is ultimately alone in life. Appreciating this condition of aloneness can actually enrich one's experience of life. The words "loneliness" and "solitude" have, respectively, negative and positive connotations of aloneness.

LONELINESS   Loneliness stems from awareness that one's social relationships are less numerous or meaningful than desired. Human beings long for relationships with others.

ATTEMPTS TO AVOID LONELINESS   People develop strategies to avoid the awareness of loneliness, such as staying in unsatisfactory relationships or keeping busy with work and other activities. People also escape awareness through alcohol, drugs, overeating, loud music, television, sex, compulsive shopping, or surfing the Internet.

THOUGHTS AND BEHAVIORS THAT FOSTER ISOLATION   Lonely people blame themselves for their lack of social relationships and expect failure in relating to others. Chronically lonely people seem caught in a vicious cycle of self-defeating thinking and social behaviors. Their conviction that others won't like them may become a self-fulfilling prophecy, because they make themselves unapproachable through defensive behaviors. They also perceive others in negative ways.

People who are lonely tend to lack social skills. They often find it hard to introduce themselves, make phone calls, and participate in groups. Lonely people are unlikely to self-disclose to others, so that as a consequence, their "friendships" are likely to be shallow. Lonely people tend to spend a fair amount of time by themselves. They eat dinner alone, spend weekends alone, and participate in few social activities. They tend to be self-conscious and low in self-esteem, and they are likely to be cynical and pessimistic about life in general.

MENTAL DISORDERS RELATED TO LONELINESS   Social anxiety and avoidance of social situations are associated features of many mental disorders, such as major depressive disorder, dysthymic disorder, and schizophrenia. Three mental disorders related to loneliness are schizoid personality disorder, avoidant personality disorder, and social phobia.

Those with schizoid personality disorder are "loners" who are detached from human relationships. Although a person suffering from avoidant personality disorder may act somewhat like a schizoid person, in that both tend to avoid the company of others, the avoidant person does so only because he or she fears being embarrassed, humiliated, criticized, or rejected by others. Those suffering from social phobia have a marked and persistent fear of certain social situations, especially those that involve some sort of performance, such as public speaking.

Cultural Factors That Promote Loneliness   Cultures vary in the amount of privacy and contact they provide and encourage. Societies that require economic cooperation and shared decision making tend to have physical arrangements that reduce opportunities to spend time alone. On the other hand, in competitive and individualistic cultures such as the United States, privacy is valued and thus protected.

Antidote for Loneliness   Psychologists encourage lonely people to develop more adaptive ways of thinking and behaving. Social exchange theory suggests that individuals who are rewarding to be with will have companions. Learning to accept others and to find ways to take an interest in them should help. Doing something nice for someone else is a way to shift the focus from feelings of loneliness toward behavior aimed at making friends. Social functions are ideal settings for the cultivation of new acquaintances.

Self-acceptance is a prerequisite for meaningful interpersonal relationships. Once we have mastered our reluctance to be alone, we can approach others without a feeling of desperation. Finally, a psychotherapist can help a person who is isolated gain an understanding of how to change his or her patterns of relating in order to have more satisfactory relationships.

Solitude   Time spent alone has a number of positive functions, including the opportunity for self-evaluation, reflection, and planning. Without having an opportunity to be alone, individuals may be distracted and overstimulated by a busy life.

Using Cognitive Behavior Therapy to Alleviate Loneliness   The aim of cognitive therapy is to modify negative or illogical beliefs. Albert Ellis developed rational-emotive therapy, which is based on the assumption that emotional problems arise when a person has unrealistic beliefs about life. Ellis noticed that people say things to themselves in an ongoing flow of internalized sentences. He discovered a way that individuals can manage their emotional states by changing this internal dialogue. Aaron Beck investigated the typical thought patterns of depressed and anxious persons.

One of the best-known techniques used in cognitive therapy is the *dysfunctional thought diary*. The client is encouraged to keep a journal in which she or he identifies and labels automatic thoughts. Once the automatic thoughts are noticed and recorded, they can be challenged. *Cognitive restructuring* of maladaptive thoughts is the central goal of cognitive therapy.

DEPRESSION   There is a common denominator in the experience of loneliness, shyness, and depression. As is the case with lonely or shy people, depressed individuals are pessimistic thinkers. Those who are depressed are more likely to attend to negative experiences than to positive ones, to magnify bad experiences, to minimize good ones, and to become unrealistically pessimistic.

Depressed people are not always unrealistic in their thinking. Research has consistently confirmed the phenomenon of *depressive realism*. Nondepressed people overestimate the degree to which they are responsible for positive events and underestimate their responsibility for negative events, whereas depressed people do not have this characteristic.

Depressed individuals have a *negative attributional style.* Compared with nondepressed people, those who are depressed engage in more *self-blame.* They interpret and recall events in a more negative light, and they are less hopeful about the future. Depressed people are more likely than nondepressed people to attribute failures and setbacks to causes that are *stable* and *global.* They also make internal attributions. This pessimistic, overgeneralized, self-blaming thinking leads to a depressing sense of hopelessness.

Research on the social thinking of people vulnerable to depression indicates that even when they are not in a depressed state, they tend to see their future successes and failures as uncontrollable. Another way of saying this is that these people tend to have an external locus of control.

OVERCOMING DEPRESSION   There are dozens of antidepressant medications available to combat depression. In addition, cognitive therapy is as effective as antidepressant medication in relieving depression.

SHYNESS   Shyness refers to avoidance of others. Shy individuals show signs of strain when socializing. They fear being evaluated, embarrassed, ridiculed, rejected, or found inadequate.

Shy people tend to lack social skills. They fail to make eye contact and tend to withdrawal when spoken to. They show little animation and pause too long in conversations. Shyness is likely to be triggered by unfamiliar social situations.

Shy people engage in self-defeating thinking. They are filled with self-blame when social encounters do not go smoothly. As with lonely and depressed people, shy people tend to be pessimistic when anticipating outcomes, an attitude that can become a self-fulfilling prophecy.

CONSEQUENCES OF SHYNESS   Shy people have difficulty in making new friends or meeting people. They experience feelings of isolation, loneliness, and depression. They are misperceived by others; a shy person may strike others as vain, bored, unfriendly, or disinterested.

OVERCOMING SHYNESS   Overcoming shyness requires making an effort to learn new skills and to test unrealistic beliefs. It also requires a willingness to take social risks.

LEARNING THE LANGUAGE OF PSYCHOLOGISTS

loneliness	dysfunctional thought diary
solitude	automatic thoughts
social exchange theory	cognitive restructuring
minimax strategy	depressive realism
rational confrontation	negative attributional style

CHAPTER REVIEW QUESTIONS

1. What do humanistic existentialists mean when they remark that we are ultimately alone?
2. What are typical methods used by people to escape awareness of their loneliness?
3. What mental disorders are related to loneliness?
4. How do people's thoughts and perceptions create their sense of loneliness?
5. How might lonely people inadvertently create and perpetuate their lack of meaningful connection with others?
6. What are some advantages to spending time alone?
7. According to Albert Ellis, what causes us to feel emotionally upset or depressed?
8. What do loneliness, shyness, and depression have in common?
9. What is "depressive realism"?
10. What are common characteristics of shy people?
11. Is shyness caused merely by a lack of social skills? What about loneliness?

ACTIVITIES

1. *COMPLETE INDIVIDUALLY:* ***Personal Reflections on Loneliness and Aloneness in My Life.***
2. *COMPLETE INDIVIDUALLY:* ***Loneliness Scale.***
3. *COMPLETE INDIVIDUALLY:* ***Shyness Inventory: How Shy Are You?***

4. *LARGE GROUP EXERCISE:* **Go Around.** Start a group story about loneliness. Go around the classroom, and have each person project his or her own lonely time or experience onto the main character(s).

5. *LARGE GROUP EXERCISE:* **Internet Debate.** Have a discussion of Internet chat rooms; divide the class into two camps, and then debate whether the chat rooms decrease or increase loneliness.

Personal Reflections on Loneliness and Aloneness in My Life

Directions: Read each of the following questions, and then write your answers in the blanks.

1. Think of the time in your life when you were the most lonely. Relate when that was, how it felt to you, and what you did to cope.

   _____

   _____

   _____

   _____

2. First, close your eyes and imagine being rejected by the entire group. See each person in your fantasy rejecting you. What does this experience feel like? After a few minutes of silence, limit each person to three minutes of sharing what it felt like to be totally rejected by every group member. How did you imagine responding? Consider the things that we do (and don't do) because of our fear of group rejection. Use the following blanks to record any new awareness about yourself.

   _____

   _____

   _____

   _____

3. Now, imagine what it might be like to be condemned always to be with others. Have each person share what it would be like if he or she could never experience solitude. How much do you need private time? What happens to you when you don't recognize your need for distance from people?

   _____

   _____

   _____

   _____

4. Do you try to escape from your loneliness? In what ways? Check any of the following statements that you think apply to you.

a. _____ I bury myself in work.

b. _____ I constantly seek to be with others.

c. _____ I drink excessively or take drugs.

d. _____ I schedule every moment so that I'll have very little time to think about myself.

e. _____ I attempt to avoid my troubles by watching television or listening to music.

f. _____ I eat compulsively.

g. _____ I sleep excessively to avoid the stress in my life.

h. _____ I become overly concerned with helping others.

i. _____ I rarely think about anything if I can help it; I concentrate on playing and having fun.

5. List here some specific ways in which you sometimes try to avoid loneliness:

_____

_____

6. Would you like to change any of the patterns you've just identified? If so, what are those patterns? What might you do to change them?

_____

_____

_____

_____

7. List a few of the major decisions you've made in your life. Did you make these decisions when you were alone or when you were with others?

_____

_____

_____

_____

8. Complete the following sentence: "The time in my life when I most enjoyed being alone was when . . ."

_____

_____

9. Complete the following sentence: "I usually deal with my loneliness by . . ."

_____

_____

10. Complete the following sentence: "I escape from loneliness by . . ."

_____

_____

11. Complete the following sentence: "If I were to be left and abandoned by all those who love me . . ."

_____

_____

12. Complete the following sentence: "One value I see in experiencing loneliness is . . ."

_____

_____

13. Complete the following sentence: "My greatest fear of loneliness is . . ."

_____

_____

14. Complete the following sentence: "I have felt lonely in a crowd when . . ."

_____

_____

15. Complete the following sentence: "I feel loneliest when . . ."

_____

_____

16. Complete the following sentence: "For me, being with others . . ."

_____

_____

17. Complete the following sentence: "The thought of living alone the rest of my life . . ."

_____

_____

18. To what extent do you feel nervous when talking to strangers? Do you feel comfortable in approaching your professors? What about other authority figures or people of high status?

_____

_____

_____

_____

Loneliness Scale

Directions: Circle *T* for true or *F* for false for each of the following statements, depending on whether it accurately describes you or your situation. If an item is not applicable because you are not currently involved in the situation, score it *F*.

T   F   1. I do not feel that I can turn to my friends living around me for help when I need it.

T   F   2. I allow myself to become close to friends.

T   F   3. I do not have many friends in the city where I live.

T   F   4. I get plenty of help and support from my friends.

T   F   5. Few of my friends understand me the way I want to be understood.

T   F   6. I feel close to members of my family.

T   F   7. I have little contact with members of my family.

T   F   8. I do not get along very well with my family.

T   F   9. I have a good relationship with most members of my immediate family.

T   F   10. My family really seldom listens to what I say.

T   F   11. I have a lover, friends, or a spouse with whom I can discuss my important problems.

T   F   12. I am not involved in a romantic or marital relationship in which both of us are making a genuine effort at cooperation.

T   F   13. I seldom get the emotional security I need from a good romantic or sexual relationship.

T   F   14. My lover, friend, or spouse senses when I am troubled and encourages me to talk about it.

T   F   15. I feel valued and respected in my current romantic or marital relationship.

T   F   16. I feel I really do not have much in common with the larger community in which I live.

T   F   17. No one in the community where I live seems to care much about me.

T   F   18. I feel that I have "roots" (a sense of belonging) in the larger community or neighborhood I live in.

T   F   19. I do not have any neighbors who would help me in a time of need.

T   F   20. I know people in my community who understand and share my views and beliefs.

Scoring: Examine the subscale to determine which area needs the most work in your life. Each of your answers that match those that follow indicates loneliness. Give yourself one point for each answer that matches.

Friendship:	1 - T	2 - F	3 - T	4 - F	5 - T
Family relationships:	6 - F	7 - T	8 - T	9 - F	10 - T
Romantic/Sexual relationships:	11 - F	12 - F	13 - T	14 - F	15 - F
Larger group relationships:	16 - T	17 - T	18 - F	19 - T	20 - F

The mean score for college students is between 5 and 6. Higher scores indicate greater loneliness.

Source: "Loneliness Scale" by Schmidt and Sermatt. From *Journal of Personality and Social Psychology,* 44, pp. 1038–1047. Copyright © 1983 by the American Psychological Association. Reprinted with permission.

Shyness Inventory: How Shy Are You?

Directions: Read each item carefully, and decide to what extent it is characteristic of your feelings and behavior. Answer each question by choosing a number from the key that follows.

1 = very uncharacteristic or untrue, strongly disagree
2 = uncharacteristic
3 = neutral, neither characteristic nor uncharacteristic
4 = characteristic
5 = very characteristic or true, strongly agree

1. I feel tense when I'm with people I don't know well. _____

2. I am socially somewhat awkward. _____

3. I find it difficult to ask other people for information. _____

4. I am often uncomfortable at parties and other social functions. _____

5. When in a group of people, I have trouble thinking of the right thing to say. _____

6. It takes me a long time to overcome my shyness in new situations. _____

7. It is hard for me to act natural when I am meeting new people. _____

8. I feel nervous when speaking to someone in authority. _____

9. I have doubts about my social competence. _____

10. I have trouble looking someone right in the eye. _____

11. I feel inhibited in social situations. _____

12. I find it hard to talk to strangers. _____

13. I am more shy with members of the opposite sex. _____

Scoring: Add up your score. If it is over 50, you are very shy; if it is between 36 and 50, you are somewhat shy; if it is below 36, you are probably not shy.

Source: Cheek & Buss (1979).

13

Anger, Antipathy, and Aggression

The beginning of strife is like letting out water,
So abandon the quarrel before it breaks out.
—Proverbs 17

> ➤ PREVIEW QUESTIONS: What are the potential benefits and costs of letting others know that we are angry? How does one go about having a good, clean fight? Is anger expression involuntary? Is it healthy to "ventilate" anger?

➤ INTRODUCTION: THE NATURE OF ANGER

Those of us who have more than one pet of the same species have no doubt noticed that they get on each other's nerves periodically, so that a squabble ensues. So it is with human beings. The wonder of it is that with animals, the fight is over and the pair may be found fifteen minutes later nestled up together and fast asleep. Although this outcome likewise occasionally happens with human beings, we are as likely to hold a grudge over the incident, perhaps for years. The author is not imbuing animals with a special virtue over human beings. The difference in behavior probably stems from our larger human brains that can remember the offenses of others for a lifetime. Even though we *can* do this, we probably don't want to.

Wondering about the nature of anger takes us back to the question, Who am I, *really*? According to Charles Darwin (1872), anger is one of seven innate emotions in the human species. If so, it follows that human beings cannot avoid experiencing anger at times. Wilkinson (1995) believes that people who interact intensely and continuously, whether or not in a hostile or cooperative fashion, belong to the same civilization, since they are associating with one another rather than living in isolated groups. This antagonistic bonding can be observed on all levels of social life. A primary way that social beings relate is in opposition and competition. It behooves us to learn skills to negotiate through the inevitable tensions of such relationships.

According to the majority of psychologists, it is not appropriate to judge emotions as being good or bad. That is, we need not feel guilty for getting angry over something or with someone. Angry feelings are neither right nor wrong, neither legitimate nor illegitimate. Our upset feelings deserve attention and respect, from ourselves, if from no one else. What is appropriately judged, however, is the behavior motivated by any emotion. Aggressive actions resulting from inappropriate expression of anger fill our daily media. We read about, hear about, and see violent acts leading to the brutal slaughter of defenseless human beings. Thus, anger is considered one of the most negative forces on the planet, because its expression sometimes takes a destructive form. The issue of how to deal with anger cuts to the heart of what it means to be human, because it concerns a basic conflict between self-expression and being socially agreeable.

In contemporary Western society as well as in the East, the open display of anger is not typically encouraged. At an early age, children get the message that anger must be controlled. From childhood, most of us learn that when something happens to make us upset so that we act on our initial emotions (e.g., break the toy that frustrated us), the results are quite often damaging and a cause for remorse. We may hurt someone's feelings, destroy property, or physically hurt ourselves and others. Eventually most of us learn not only to control our aggressive behavior but also to contain, and even to deny, our angry feelings. However, learning too well to control anger may be as disadvantageous as the indiscriminate venting of anger (Sterns & Sterns, 1986). Lack of overt anger does not necessarily mean lack of conflict. Unresolved anger turns to resentment and destroys love, and there seems to be no "statute of limitations" on such resentment. Philosopher Sam Keen (1997) gave a definition of resentment as "a poison we take in the hope that it will kill the other guy" (p. 108). Close on the heels of resentment, a person experiences antipathy. Antipathy refers to a habitual dislike of or aversion to something or someone. Suppressed anger can turn warm feelings towards others into indifference.

Unexpressed anger may also be released as hostility or sarcasm. Furthermore, a person may be **passive aggressive** (Chapter 6), meaning that indirect, disguised ways are found to express displeasure. When this behavior occurs, getting to the bottom of interpersonal conflict is difficult and often requires the skill of a psychotherapist. A further possibility is that hostility may be displaced onto an inappropriate target. Some physical maladies may also be linked to chronic anger. Finally, psychoanalysts have theorized that repressed hostility is turned against oneself in the form of depression. It might be far better to teach socially acceptable expressions of anger, that is, anger communicated in a direct and controlled manner, so that the inevitable irritations we experience with one another might be dealt with as bumps in the road rather than impassable chasms.

QUESTION: *Do you think that anger needs to be expressed?*

➤ A CASE FOR GETTING HOT UNDER THE COLLAR

A case can be made for viewing anger as a constructive force in relationships. In order for anger to be seen as having a positive role in human interaction, we must begin to view anger as natural and acceptable. As was noted in Chapter 10, it may be unreasonable to suppose that human relationships will be free of conflict. Since anger is a part of the human condition and cannot be removed, we must learn the best way to handle it. More important than avoiding fights is developing skills that enable us to fight cleanly and constructively. Clean anger expression refers to sticking to the point of what has just now aroused one's ire. For instance, the statement that "I feel very annoyed when I get up in the morning and see dishes in the sink, when I was so careful to leave the kitchen clean after dinner last night" is a clear and direct message. It would not be helpful to throw in past grievances, unless they are explicitly relevant to the present complaint. For example, we wouldn't follow up on the last statement with "You have been messy as long as I have known you." This comment is a criticism of the person's character and also makes the problem seem hopeless. If anger is not expressed and dealt with constructively, it will sour the relationship. Therefore, after a complaint has been expressed, the person against whom it is lodged must be given some way of making things okay. The person who committed an offense might be asked to make an apology, to make a simple change in behavior, or merely to explain himself or herself. What might suffice is for the "offender" to acknowledge that offense might legitimately be taken to his or her remarks or behavior, even if no offense was intended. Practical benefits from anger expression also may entail relief of tension and frustration. It can be astonishing how much merely having one's say soothes upset feelings over being mistreated. It is the buildup of these emotions that creates trouble.

Anger as an Aspect of Self-Awareness

Socrates observed that true wisdom comes to each of us when we realize how little we understand about life, ourselves, and the world around us (Smith, 1975). Although we may never fully understand ourselves, we do well to work continually to increase our self-awareness. Since we are taught as children to control our feelings, we may be relatively unaware of them.

We need to monitor our emotional state, since it provides a valuable signal as to what is going on inside us. When we feel guilty for having negative emotions, we generally try to suppress them. This reaction leaves us out of touch with ourselves, a condition that is not only undesirable but also perhaps dangerous. The danger lies in the possibility of unexpected and uncontrolled explosions of rage that can end in physical violence. If emotions are ignored, we can't use them to guide us, to help us decide what we want and need. It is both possible and desirable to be in touch with angry feelings without letting them control us. There is a significant difference between accepting a feeling and letting it rule our behavior. When we are in touch with our feelings, we know where we stand. Our emotions won't boil over and surprise us, because we have monitored their increasing intensity as the negative situation developed. Finally, people who are open with their anger can ultimately be more comfortable to be around, since we know where they stand and we can trust them to let us know if we have offended them.

Carl Rogers (1951) wrote about a transition in a client's way of experiencing her anger:

> In the discussion of her feelings about anger there appears to be an astonishingly clear description of what it feels like, from an internal frame of reference, to let experience come freely into awareness. Where heretofore anger was denied until

it broke forth in an uncontrolled burst which was not a part of self, now anger rises at once into consciousness. But where experience is freely symbolized in awareness, it is also far more subject to control. Expression of anger becomes a choice, feelings of anger can be considered along with feelings of friendliness, and either may be consciously chosen for expression. This is not necessarily more pleasant; it is simply that there is less of experience which is denied or distorted, and hence a greatly reduced bill to pay in the form of defensive tension. (p. 126)

According to Rogers, a person has good personality integration when all sensory and visceral experiences, impulses, and perceptions are admitted to conscious awareness. The person has the possibility of exerting conscious control over such inner experiences to the extent that he or she is aware of them.

Viewing anger on a continuum with mild irritation at one end and rage at the other can assist us in determining the point at which this emotion moves from a constructive to a destructive force. Two people can debate, even heatedly, without getting to the point of extreme displeasure, hostility, indignation, or exasperation. Such rage is sometimes a manifestation or reenactment of earlier conflicts that have not been resolved. Psychotherapist Harville Hendrix (1992) uses the expression of anger by his patients to get to their unresolved issues and to promote personal and interpersonal growth between couples who are in his private practice. He contends that anger is a response to a threat to the self-concept and that it is thus essential that partners assist each other in identifying the source of the threat, as well as dealing with feelings of inadequacy and anxiety. According to Hendrix, irritation can reveal inner needs and issues that have to be resolved in order to continue growing and maturing in a healthy manner.

Anger is an effective form of communication. It is often triggered by two emotions: fear and frustration. We get frustrated when we do not get what we want or need. Lerner (1985) wrote, "In using our anger as a guide to determining our innermost needs, values, and priorities, we should not be distressed if we discover just how unclear we are. If we feel chronically angry or bitter in an important relationship, this is a signal that too much of the self has been compromised . . ." (p. 106). Chronic anger or resentment is an indication that we need to reevaluate our participation in a particular relationship. We may need only to change the way we are relating, rather than to leave a worthwhile relationship.

Although the situation of finding oneself angry when on the job or when among strangers is something of a different story, it generally calls for application of a similar set of behaviors. Again, self-awareness is the key to adopting an effective coping strategy. If we find ourselves frequently indignant and outraged by the petty infractions of others, we'll want to alter our own perspective on such things. However, if we encounter a quarrelsome, overbearing person who habitually intimidates smaller, weaker, or lower-status people, we may find that a confrontation is necessary. In general, it's probably best to avoid confrontation whenever possible, but this isn't always feasible. When such an encounter is in order, the "I" messages, which will be explained later in this chapter, are one form of assertive behavior that can be usefully employed.

Anger as a Motivator

Anger is an intense emotion that serves as a warning sign. It points to there being something wrong with what is going on in the environment. When a person expresses anger, everyone around her or him feels defensive, alarmed, or concerned. In this way, anger is powerful and may enable a person to get her or his way. Because anger is forceful, it can also protect us from being taken advantage of by others.

Anger provides a powerful motivation for cultural change. It was the anger over social, political, and religious issues that motivated the Pilgrims to board the *Mayflower* and set forth to a new land. Anger also motivated the American colonists to revolt against Great Britain and form a new sovereign nation. Thus, although anger has many negative aspects, it can be a powerful catalyst for change if it is appropriately channeled. In order for this process to happen, people have to view themselves as competent to bring about improvements in the current situation. Philip Zimbardo (1969), a noted social psychologist, wrote that "emotions serve a motivational function by arousing us to move and to take action with regard to some experienced or imagined event. Emotions then direct and sustain our actions toward specific goals that benefit us" (p. 237). When we ignore emotions such as anger, we are not allowing ourselves to be directed toward a more beneficial situation. For example, since anger is often the result of some outside stress factor, the anger therefore motivates us to get away from or to reduce the effect of the stressful situation. When we disregard our anger, the stimulus that caused the anger is not reduced and thus often increases. When stressors persist or increase, our behavior begins to be affected. We sometimes hear stories about disgruntled employees who enter their workplace or former workplace with a gun and indiscriminately kill people. It was reported in 1996 that in this country, homicide is now the second leading cause of death in the workplace, behind auto accidents. In these cases, the stress went unrelieved and continued to build until the anger became too much to control, and the individual "lost it."

QUESTION: *What are some potentially positive effects of anger expression?*

Control of Anger

How does one effectively use anger to motivate oneself to create a better situation without "losing it"? The constructive use of anger requires a certain degree of self-control. The positive and negative aspects of anger expression derive from its power. One way to maintain self-control is that each of us needs to become familiar with our own anger signals and those of our significant others. When anger is aroused, we can monitor it carefully. In some ways, anger is analogous to fire in that it is helpful for survival and comfort, yet it can ruin us if we are not careful with it. There is an art to appropriately expressing anger. Displeasure is best disclosed in a direct manner and before it intensifies. Rules or guidelines such as allowing each partner "time out" to cool off should be agreed to.

Self-control can be attained through cognitive and behavioral strategies by (1) refraining from taking immediate action to allow sufficient time to think through a proper course of action, (2) focusing on the positive elements of the situation, (3) trying to relax to avoid the buildup of too much physical tension, and (4) maintaining self-rewarding, positive thoughts such as "I am okay" and "I can successfully cope with this situation" (Allcorn, 1994). These coping strategies should seem familiar to those who have read the earlier chapter on stress and coping.

Some of us have a problem controlling our anger in response to the frustrations and irritations of daily life. A step toward reducing our own hostility is first to admit to ourselves and perhaps to a close friend or trusted family member that we want to learn to better regulate our feelings of irritation. Next, we can become aware of our angry thoughts by recording them in a notebook. When we have a cynical thought about someone, we might silently look for ways in which the thought is irrational and unreasonable. We can look for assertive alternatives to our habitual aggressive reaction.

QUESTION: *What are some strategies for constructively expressing anger?*

Rules for a Good Fight

Ground rules for a good fight start with a realization as to the purpose of the argument. The purpose is to gain better understanding, not to win the fight by defeating one's partner or coworker.

KEEP YOUR COMMENTS CLEAN   We can learn "clean" expression of dissatisfaction, such as the use of "I" messages, which is a behavioral technique that involves beginning a complaint by saying, "I feel . . ." rather than saying, "You lousy so-and-so . . ." Few people are able to listen well when they are being criticized or told what is wrong with them. An angry invective, such as "You're a no-good, mean-spirited, manipulative no-good loser!" could be transformed into "I am furious with you, because I don't feel heard when I complain to you about your not doing your share of the work around here!" It may be hard to imagine that these two sentences are referring to the same grievance, but they well could be. The first statement will probably elicit

CALM YET DEADLY

Those who practice martial arts embrace an intriguing combination of maintaining control of one's emotions while being capable of using deadly force. The various martial arts, such as judo and karate, are examples of well-controlled, defense aggression, which stands in contrast to offensive aggression.

Generally speaking, jujitsu (which later developed into the more familiar judo) may be defined as an art of attack and defense without weapons against an opponent, who may be with or without weapons. Special methods, such as hitting, poking, or chopping with the hand, fingers, elbow, and fist; kicking with the kneecap, heel, or ball of the foot; or bending and twisting the joints, were studied and developed so that an unarmed person could subdue an adversary.

The tenets of jujitsu stem from the idea in a famous old book on strategy selected by the Chinese strategist Hwang-Shihkon, which was the bible of his warriors in the feudal age, namely, "In yielding is strength" ("oaks may fall when reeds brave the storm"). The principles also carry echoes of the Chinese philosophy represented in the *Book of Lao-tsu*, who preached nonresistance and gentleness, or the *Yi-King* (or *I Ching*), *Book of Changes*.

Draeger and Smith (1981) add the following note:

"Ju" is a Chinese character meaning "pliable," "submissive," "harmonious," "adaptable," or "yielding." The common translation of "ju" as "gentle" is usually misinterpreted by the westerner as suggesting the complete lack of functionally applied strength. This was never the case with combat "jujutsu," where frequently great strength was needed to insure the defeat of an enemy. "Jujutsu" techniques are not all gentle, though sometimes they are made with such swiftness and efficiency that they appear to be so. They seek to blend with the enemy's direction of strength, which is then controlled. This "gentleness" is thus more correctly spoken

defensiveness in the other person, making it less likely that the person voicing a complaint will be heard. The second expression is superior to the first in that the speaker takes responsibility for bringing up an issue to be discussed because of his or her own discomfort. This strategy avoids blaming and shaming the other person for misbehavior or lack of consideration. In addition, we implicitly acknowledge that it is not up to the other person to fix our problem. The second approach is also preferred since the grievance is focused rather than being a blanket indictment of the other person's character. This treatment is what makes the expression "clean."

Another aspect of clean communication involves avoiding demagoguery. To demagogue is to use emotionally inflammatory language or stirring rhetoric to evoke an emotional response in others. This term is generally used in connection with politicians, who, for example, might fight against cutting government programs by talking about how those who wish to rein in federal spending are trying to "starve our children" and "throw our elderly out into of as "flexibility," meaning that mind and body adapt to a situation and bring it to advantage for the defender. Furthermore, the principle of "ju" is not as all-pervading as exponents of systems who have taken it at its face value would have us all believe. "The willow does not break under the load of snow," reads an old Oriental maxim. From this, some systems extend this limited philosophy to cover the absolute range of mechanical actions for their systems. While some snow may not "break the willow," a correctly applied force will. An enemy who attacks with such forces cannot be turned aside by "ju." (p. 137)

The process of the evolution of judo from jujitsu began about one hundred years ago. Professor Kano was one of the early advocates of the training. After realizing its effectiveness in developing both body and mind, Kano decided to try to disseminate it far and wide. He found that it was necessary to improve the old jujitsu to a certain degree in order to popularize it, because the old style was not developed for physical education or moral and intellectual training but was exclusively devised for winning. Combining all the good points he had learned from the various schools and adding his own devices and inventions, he founded a new system for physical culture and mental training as well as for winning contests. He called this "kodokan judo."

Everyone admired the tenets, slogans, and high idealism of the new judo. Draeger and Smith (1981) noted, "Classical judo represented a quasi-fighting art with consideration being given primarily to training of mind and body through prescribed exercises; included were aspects of physical education, self-defense, and competition. Kano substituted the word 'opponent' for the word 'enemy' of 'jujitsu' . . ." (p. 138).

Judo is an example of exquisitely controlled aggression, accompanied by a mental training in impulse control and the like. As such, martial arts training might provide a model for appropriate anger regulation.

the street." It's also very easy to wax poetic and hurtfully articulate when describing the offenses of our adversary in the midst of a heated argument. We might be tempted to describe the other as a Nazi who is bullying us into submission, a characterization that won't go over well.

Avoid Blaming and Shaming   Analyzing the other person is another poor strategy. Although such analysis can be motivated by a desire to provide helpful insight, more often it is a projection of blame, one-upmanship, or an attempt to manipulate. We are presumptuous when we suggest that we are an expert on someone else's experience and thus know what that person thinks, feels, or wants. It is difficult enough to be aware of our own thoughts, emotions, and desires.

There is one legitimate reason for not listening during an argument. To the extent that the other person is denigrating us through name-calling or is making a general assessment of our character, we do a disservice to ourselves by listening. Such personal attacks should not be permitted as a part of the agreed-upon ground rules for conducting an argument. Every person has weak spots or vulnerabilities, which eventually become known to her or his partner. A caring mate will not intentionally violate these vulnerable areas. A partner who takes advantage of such weaknesses shows himself or herself to be untrustworthy. If one partner treads on an area so sensitive that it feels "bellow the belt" to the other partner, that partner should stop the discussion, claim the comment to be "unfair," and explain why. Nothing allows one to feel quite so well taken care of as having one's partner treat vulnerabilities with consideration.

Handicap the Heavyweight   Bach and Wyden (1968) say that rarely are two people equal combatants in a fight, so that the "heavyweight" will need to abide by different rules than will the "lightweight." For example, the lightweight partner might be allowed to bring up an issue at any time, whereas the heavyweight would be more restricted and might need to agree to choose times when the lightweight is feeling confident. A heavyweight partner might be an especially articulate person, such as an attorney, who is in essence a professional arguer. If only one partner has attended college or has some other knowledge base or has a wider range of experience, these would be advantages and would qualify the person as a heavyweight. A partner who is physically much larger has a natural ability to intimidate. Lightweights would be shyer, smaller, younger, less self-confident, and less experienced people.

Think Before You Act   Healthy means of anger expression can be incorporated into our behavioral repertoire. Preferred ways of handling anger include such processes as the following: (1) evaluating the angry feelings: "What is making me angry?" "Am I jumping to conclusions?" "Is my anger legitimate?"; (2) making sure that you know what the other person means by what is being said and done; (3) recalling past situations and then reviewing them for indications of how best to handle the current situation; and (4) developing a list of alternatives to being angry (Allcorn, 1994).

Engage in Active Listening   One source of exasperation in arguments with intimates is a conviction that one is not being listened to. A good listener uses empathy to understand how the other person experiences his or her life. As mentioned in Chapter 10, there is an old saying, "Never judge someone until you have walked a mile in his moccasins." Development of an empathic understanding means that we try to put ourselves in that person's place and to see the world as he or she does. Sometimes a request for the opponent to take one's own side of the argument and to display a comprehension of the various points supporting it is a good way to defuse anger on both sides. This strategy has the benefit of helping each person feel listened to. Explaining the other person's side of an argument, or at least showing an awareness of what the other is feeling and thinking, builds empathy. By intentionally playing a new role, we can sometimes change our viewpoint through empathy with the other person. This role-reversal in the argument should be reciprocal, with both sides repeating the points made by his or her opponent, to that opponent's satisfaction (see also Chapters 6 and 10 for an explanation of role-reversal). A good rule of thumb for getting through any argument is to search for the kernel of truth in what the other side is saying.

QUESTION: Why is reminding ourselves of the purpose of a fight or argument beneficial?

Humanistic View on Anger Expression

Carl Rogers (1961), one of the early humanistic theorists (Chapter 2), contended that in therapy, clients learn that they can allow their anger to surface when it is the authentic reaction (and not a cover-up for another emotion) and that this transparent anger is not destructive. Just as clients find that their fear does not dissolve them, likewise, clients can see that their hostile feelings do not cause the roof to fall in. The reason seems to be that the more the person is able to permit these hostile feelings to flow and to be experienced, the more these emotions take their appropriate place in the total harmony of the individual's feelings. The person discovers other emotions with which the hostile ones mingle and find a balance, because she or he becomes aware of feeling loving, tender, considerate, and cooperative, as well as hostile, lustful, or angry. The individual's feelings, when she or he accepts the experience of them with all of their complexity, operate in a constructive harmony rather than sweeping their owner into some uncontrollably evil path.

Rogers asserted that when human beings are allowed to function freely, by nature they are constructive and trustworthy. We do not need to worry about healthy people controlling their aggressive impulses, because for those who have become more open to all of their impulses, their need to be liked by others and their tendency to give affection will be as strong as their impulses to strike out or to seize some advantage for themselves. Healthy people will be aggressive in situations in which **aggression** is realistically appropriate, but they will not experience a runaway need for aggression. For Rogers, those who are moving towards becoming fully functioning persons will find that they "live more intimately with their feelings of pain, but also more vividly with their feelings of ecstasy; that anger is more clearly felt, but so also is love; that fear is an experience they know more deeply, but so is courage" (p. 195). Rogers felt that this keen awareness of clients' feelings came about because of the development of an "underlying confidence in themselves as trustworthy instruments for encountering life" (p. 195).

Humanistic psychologist Leo Buscaglia (1972) echoed the Rogersian faith in people:

> We tend to suspect man of evil more readily than of good. The evil about him makes the news media, the good seldom does. Considering the word's population, there are relatively few murders, robberies, rapes or major crimes. But when

a crime does occur, we are certain to hear of it. Not simply because it's news, but rather because it sells newspapers. People seem to enjoy the sensational and find some pleasure in revulsion. But, in reality, the greater number of men are like ourselves. They do not voluntarily hurt another human being, steal from him or kill him. They can usually be trusted, are concerned and are friendly. Most live their lives without having to deal with polices, courts or law or lawyers. This fact is taken, rather, as what is to be expected of man. The evil he does, on the other hand, is magnified. It is of interest for it is the deviation. But we act, often, as if the deviation is the rule. (p. 124)

In contrast to the preceding views, humanistic existentialist Irving Yalom (1980) considered losing control in a fit of anger to be a form of denial of responsibility for one's own behavior. A person may excuse his or her own impulsive actions as not being deliberate, thus making a self-deceptive maneuver to avoid the necessity of checking one's aggressive behavior. In an ongoing, intimate relationship, the explosive person can tyrannize his or her partner with his or her propensity for furious, irrational behavior.

➤ EXISTENTIAL CONCERNS AND AGGRESSION

As explained in Chapter 1, human beings have a series of concerns that stem from their well-developed intellect. Two of these concerns are discussed in the following sections, because they relate to aggressive acts.

The Need for Excitation and Stimulation

Fromm (1973) considered excitation to be a basic need characteristic of healthy human functioning. Surveying neurological and behavioral evidence, he concluded that the human brain is constantly active, continually functioning even in the presence of reduced external stimulation. From this evidence, he inferred that human beings need a constantly stimulating, interest-provoking environment. Fromm did not mean that people require a chronic succession of novel stimuli. Rather, they need stimulation that induces them to *actively* construe their worlds, to *actively* participate in life.

Even if human beings have all the security they want, enough to eat, and access to sexual partners, they still seek more, namely drama and excitement. Fromm (1973) proposed that some types of stimulation are good for people but that others are not. A *simple stimulus* is junk food for the brain. It does not engage human reason but rather is a passive form of entertainment. For a person to avoid boredom, simple stimuli must constantly change or continually increase in intensity. An *activating stimulus* provides good psychological nourishment for the brain and the soul, eliciting creative energies within the person. This kind of stimulation prompts the person to strive actively for a goal.

Contemporary technological society provides many simple stimuli that foster passivity and boredom. One consequence of continuous simple stimulation is that people living today are driven to seek methods of escaping boredom. Thus alcohol, drugs, television, Internet cruising, and sexual promiscuity can all be the means of avoiding an overwhelming sense of boredom in the face of the continual barrage of simple stimuli. The trouble with these escape mechanisms is that in themselves, they are further sources of simple, boredom-producing stimulation that supply only temporary and superficial relief.

In times past, boredom was a bane of human existence. The author recalls reading Richard Henry Dana's classic book *Two Years Before the Mast*, in which a Harvard graduate decides that he doesn't have anything better to do with himself than to hire on as an ordinary deckhand aboard a merchant ship. He survives a harrowing journey around the continent of South America and eventually arrives in California. There his job is to help load the ship with tanned hides. His life is excruciatingly dull, and he has to rely on humdrum activities for entertainment. Many classic novels and narratives relay a similar sense of the characters' fighting the crushing impact of having too little amusement.

Fast-forward to today. Life is so full of entertainment that we have to worry more about overstimulation than boredom. We have succeeded beyond our wildest dreams in banishing monotony from modern life—or have we? Fromm contends that over-indulgences in simple stimulation, such as action thriller movies and music videos, causes us to **habituate** to ever more tantalizing or shocking forms of entertainment. Habituation refers to a physiological mechanism in which the senses acclimate or get used to a stimulus that is repeatedly or continuously presented. For instance, when we first step into a bathtub full of hot water or a pool filled with cool water, we will have to get used to the temperature. After we habituate, we may find that we don't notice the water temperature any longer. Fromm worried about the type of chronic boredom and irritation that comes from habituating to higher and higher levels of stimulation.

Author Sven Birkets (1994) remarked on a similar modern phenomenon, that of being overloaded with information to the degree that we may not be able to make sense of it or to organize it in a way that is useful. According to Birkets, two factors—the explosion of data and the general collapse of society-wide philosophies, such as the Christian, Marxist, Freudian, or humanistic perspectives—have all but destroyed our ability to think about our lives as an organized whole. Inundated both by multiple perspectives and by huge, indigestible quantities of information, we are not able to assemble a complete picture of the world. Instead of trying to discover the truth of things—the ancient project of philosophy—we direct our energies to managing information.

Another, and more pathological, consequence of contemporary human boredom, according to Fromm, is "malignant" aggression. Fromm developed a theory of aggression that divides it into two types: "benign" aggression and "malignant" aggression. Benign aggression is biologically adaptive and life-serving, whereas malignant aggression is biologically maladaptive. Defensive (benign) aggressiveness, which is "built into" the animal and human brain, serves the function of defense against threat to vital interests. It aims at the removal of the threat, either by destroying it or by removing its source. The aim of defensive aggression is not lust for destruction but the preservation of life. Unlike animals that use aggression for defense, human beings are unique in their capacity to be violent, cruel, and destructive for no apparent defensive purpose.

Fromm described malignant aggression as a uniquely human quality, concluding that humans are the only animals who destroy members of their own species without any rational gain, either biological or economic. In humans, destructiveness and cruelty can produce intense satisfaction. Animals, on the other hand, do not appear to relish inflicting pain and suffering on other animals, nor do they kill "for nothing." In human beings, individuals and groups may have a character structure that makes them create situations that permit the expression of destructiveness. Human cruelty cannot be explained either in terms of animal heredity or in terms of a destructive instinct but must be understood on the basis of those factors by which human beings differ from their animal ancestors. The malignant part of human aggression is not inborn, according to Fromm, but it is more than a learned pattern of behavior.

Fromm (1973) examined how the conditions of human existence are responsible for human lust for killing and torturing. He concluded that although malignant aggression does not serve the physiological survival of humanity, it is an important part of our mental functioning. Destructiveness is one of the possible answers to psychological needs, such as that for excitement or stimulation, that are rooted in the human condition. Another apparent requirement of human beings is to have impact on other people—to be seen and to be noticed. Such existential needs are shared by all human beings, and their fulfillment is as necessary for our remaining sane as the satisfaction of organic drives is necessary for remaining alive. However, these needs can be satisfied in different ways, which vary according to the peculiarities of our social conditions. These different ways of satisfying the existential needs manifest themselves in passions, such as love, tenderness, striving for justice, independence, truth, hate, sadism, masochism, destructiveness, and narcissism. According to Fromm, such passions as the strivings to love and to be free, as well as the drives to destroy, to torture, to control, and to submit, form the basis of our interest in life, our enthusiasm, our excitement; they are the stuff from which are made not only our dreams but also art, religion, myth, drama—all that makes life worth living. When we cannot gratify our need for stimulation on a higher level, with rich food for thought, we create for ourselves the drama of destruction.

These existential needs do not become powerful only *after* the more elementary ones have been satisfied. People have committed suicide because of their failure to realize their passions for love, power, fame, or revenge.

To escape the tedium and irritation that result from chronically passive forms of entertainment offered by technological culture, such as hours of television viewing, people may resort to active aggression and violence. In a life without meaning, violence and destructiveness can provide individuals with some measure of distorted mastery. For example, in the classic movie *Taxi*, Robert DeNiro played a character who was aimlessly hanging around, until he hit upon the idea of assassinating a politician he happened to see on television. Suddenly his directionless life had meaning, purpose, and excitement. Such aggression is malignant because it subverts the very essence of human character; it solves the individual's sense of despair at the meaninglessness of his or her life by allowing malevolent control over the life of another person. In short, boredom (a life without meaning or value) provokes malignant aggression.

Conversely, having projects that capture our interest and imagination satisfies our need for meaning and removes the temptation to have impact through destructive routes. George Konrad, author of *Antipolitics*, proclaimed that "creative intellectuals don't want to be bosses; they want to tinker, to invent, to create what they have imagined" (Lifton, 1993, pp. 242–243). That is, those who are thoroughly entertained are less interested in controlling others.

Fromm's (1973) view is that all human passions, both the "good" and the "evil," can be understood as a person's attempt to make sense of his or her life. Change is possible only if the person is able to "convert" himself or herself to a new way of finding meaning in life by mobilizing his or her life-furthering passions and thus experiencing a sense of vitality and integration that is superior to the one that the person had before. Fromm believed that help for individuals can come only through changes in our social and political structure. We need to create conditions that would make the personal growth of human beings the supreme goal of all social arrangements. Genuine freedom and independence, the end of all forms of exploitive control, are the conditions for mobilizing the love of life, which is the only force that can defeat the inclination towards destructive activities. Unless we understand these human passions, we have no way to recognize how they may be reduced and what factors tend to increase them.

The Denial of Death

Ernest Becker (1975) maintained that aggression is a form of death denial; one way that human beings attempt to come to terms with their mortality. Killing may give the killer a feeling of invulnerability and power over death. The widespread practice of human sacrifice in ancient times was an affirmation of godlike power over life and death. Ervin Staub (1989) contends that people seek strength and control through the exercise of power over others to compensate for the feelings of insecurity, incomprehension, and lack of control brought on by some combination of cultural background, personality, and life problems. The ultimate exercise of power over others is, of course, killing. People are less prone to murder when they feel valued and significant, when they find life comprehensible, and when they feel capable of influencing their circumstances in life.

➤ A Case for Keeping a Cool Head

Of course, there are dangers in encouraging anger. When anger intensifies to the point of rage, it can create cloudy and irrational thinking. University of Alabama psychologist Dolf Zillman (Goleman, 1995) refers to this state as "cognitive incapacitation." An angry individual is more inclined to take an extreme ground on an issue, is also more likely to become defensive about his or her opinion, and may be less willing to negotiate a compromise. In an angry state, an individual may even be unwilling to recognize the other's opinion. When this condition occurs, those who are involved must take time to calm down and develop a better frame of mind in which to think rationally about the situation. A time-honored way to do so is to take a long walk or otherwise to wait out the adrenal surge in a setting where there are not likely to be further triggers for rage.

Paying attention to our own warning signals entails taking the time to become familiar with our feelings so that we can tell when we are getting to an unproductive point. We might say something like "I am so angry with you that I realize I don't care what you have to say right now." A statement like this makes it obvious that a time-out is needed. There isn't much point in continuing an argument if we are aware of being too furious to hear the other person's side. For this reason, friends and family members might very well find it useful to develop a set of rules about time-outs and other necessary arrangements for careful expressions of anger.

The point has already been made that suppressed anger can be counter-productive if, in not revealing our feelings, we enable a stressful situation to continue. Expressed anger can likewise be unwise if in revealing our feelings, we make the situation worse. One example of harmful expression of hostility is through emotionally wounding remarks, a behavior that invites retaliation. Blunders such as this are likely if we are not skilled in clean, direct, and con-trolled anger expression.

An economical use of anger makes it more potent when we do express it. A frequently angry person is viewed as someone with poor impulse control (and rightly so). A chronic, habitual use of anger is undesirable in a compan-ion in any sphere of life. Anger is to be used sparingly; it is the nuclear bomb in one's arsenal.

Sometimes the best thing we can do about anger is nothing, according to Carol Tavris (1989). Tavris advised that if we want our anger to dissipate and the relationship in question to remain friendly, we should keep quiet. If we want to stay angry so that we can use the anger to motivate us, we should keep talking. As a rule, she suggests that we cool down—practice "keeping a cool head"—and let life's small indignities pass but that we stand and fight against the larger ones. Of course, the tricky part of this advice is learning to tell the difference! An alternative to this passive, grin-and-bear-it approach to handling irritation will be discussed later in this chapter in the section on **assertiveness.**

Behavioral Perspective on Anger Expression

Anger may be defined as a feeling or an emotion that is a learned means of neutralizing or avoiding the anxiety that arises in response to an interpersonal threat. The behaviorist perspective on the expression of anger is that this emotion will be converted into action when the person perceives that there is an advantage in doing so. Almost any behavioral expression of anger translates into aggression, which can be defined as the intention to harm another individual. As with any other type of behavior, aggressive acts will continue and grow more frequent if reinforced.

Hokanson (1970) believed that aggressive **catharsis** (a venting of anger) is a learned reaction to anger, not an instinctive one. The learned aspect of catharsis works like this: Someone irritates us and provokes us beyond the edge of self-control. Now we do something aggressive, and this reaction lessens both our physiological arousal and the psychological sensation that we are furious. In the future when we are angry, we'll tend to do whatever worked for us before, whether it was swearing, yelling, hitting the person who angered us, writing a letter, or having a drink.

Anger as a Strategy for Winning   When we are young, we learn a variety of means to get our way, some of which would be considered attempts to manipulate others. Most techniques aimed at getting one's way can be categorized as either helplessness, suffering, or anger (Narciso & Burkett, 1975). These are behaviors that we learned to use in past interpersonal situations that weren't going the way we wanted them to go. All get-our-way behaviors are used because they work in relation to some or all of our significant others.

Helplessness.   Although we may actually find ourselves in a truly helpless predicament from time to time, we often pretend to be helpless in interpersonal relationships in order to manipulate other people into doing what we want them to do or into not doing what we don't want them to do. Offering excuses to others for our misbehavior or our failure to perform an expected behavior is a form of acting helpless. Those who habitually feign helplessness have learned to explain their behavior rather than to change it.

Suffering.   By suffering, we can sometimes manipulate others. "You've hurt my feelings" is a statement motivated by a desire to make the other person responsible for our reactions to the person and to get the person to change a behavior that we find unacceptable. Once the other person changes her or

I think I'll just Stonewall rather than get into a fight.

his behavior to make it more to the speaker's liking, the speaker won't have to hurt any longer. It's also true that once the other party accepts responsibility for the speaker's feelings and thus complies, the speaker has used her or his "feelings" to gain control of the other person.

Anger. Anger is the last-resort technique in getting our way. We attempt to demand that others comply with our wishes when we are overtly angry. Alternatively, we may present an angry silence, in which we withdraw from the other person as a means of calling attention to our displeasure. Anger may take the form of silence or of overt behavior such as shouting, gesturing, swearing, slamming doors, driving erratically, throwing things, or physically attacking.

Behaviors aimed at getting our way will continue as long as they are rewarded, that is, as long as they allow us to get what we want. The problem is that these behaviors are inappropriate because they require submission by another person. One person loses and the other one wins. This result causes the loser to become frustrated, angry, depressed, or resentful—responses that may lead to a break in the relationship.

A more desirable alternative would be for the parties involved to enter a dialogue with the understanding that each person's needs and wants will be made clear before any decisions are made. Then, a solution will be sought to which all parties can agree. The negotiations will not be over until the solution is reached, even if a discussion must be postponed because the participants are fatigued. This type of negotiation is for a "win-win" solution, a term that suggests that an agreement can be reached in which the wishes of both (or all) parties are respected.

QUESTION: *Is the expression of aggression cathartic?*

Psychoanalytic View of Anger

Alfred Adler (1931/1992) agreed with the behaviorist position that anger is a device used to dominate a person or situation. He viewed an individual's level of anxiety, cheerfulness, sadness, or anger as relating to the person's lifestyle. For instance, a person who accomplishes his or her goal of superiority through sadness cannot be cheerful and satisfied with his or her accomplishments. The person can only be happy when miserable. Neurotic people avoid aspects of life in which they do not feel strong enough to achieve dominance. For Adler, an outburst of temper indicates that the person wishes to overcome his or her difficulties as quickly as possible and has decided that the best way to do so is to hit, accuse, or attack another person. Anger can be as much an expression of an inferiority complex as can tears or excuses. Perhaps the angry individual feels inferior in his or her ability to be patient and persuasive.

Freud (Jones, 1953) proposed that human aggression emanates from our redirecting toward others the energy from our inborn aggressive drive, which he sometimes referred to as the "death instinct." As the impulse builds up within a person over time, the individual must find ways to channel it into outside activities, or it may harm the person himself or herself in the form of depression.

CATHARSIS THEORY OF PSYCHOANALYSIS   Can pent-up aggression be drained off through aggressive activity, viewing of aggression, or aggressive fantasy? Many people believe that it is psychologically and physically healthy to ventilate their anger at the first person, pet, or piece of property that gets in the way or through competitive sports activity or some other means.

Catharsis is the theory that one can purge emotions by experiencing them. The concept of catharsis usually is credited to Aristotle. Although Aristotle actually said nothing about aggression, he did argue that one can purge emotions by experiencing them and that viewing the classic tragedies therefore enabled a catharsis ("purgation") of pity and fear. To have an emotion excited, he believed, is to have that emotion released (Butcher, 1951). Freud (Jones, 1953) believed that human beings need to find ways of draining off the aggressive drive through catharsis, lest this inner destructive urge become turned against oneself. Most Americans seem to endorse this notion of "blowing off a little steam."

The idea of catharsis implies a hydraulic model of emotions or drives. The hydraulic model claims that pressure to express certain urges builds up over time and must be drained off periodically. This view does not hold up in the face of research, because participating in aggressive activities has been shown either to increase aggressive behavior or to maintain it at the same level, rather than to reduce it (Nelson, 1969). Berkowitz (1962) found that ventilation-by-yelling does not reduce anger. He discov-

ered that frequently when we tell someone off, we stimulate ourselves to continued aggression; for example, swearing increases anger and hostility rather than relieving it. The reason for this phenomenon may be that hearing ourselves curse gives us feedback that we are indeed quite angry. Researchers also report that Canadian and American spectators of football, wrestling, and hockey exhibit more hostility after viewing the event than before (Arms et al., 1979; Goldstein & Arms, 1971; Russell, 1983). Not even war seems to purge aggressive feelings. After a war, a nation's murder rate tends to jump (Archer & Gartner, 1976). The near consensus among social psychologists is that catharsis does not occur as Aristotle, Freud, and others supposed (Geen & Quanty, 1977).

Aggression tends to breed more aggression rather than reducing subsequent aggression. One reason for this effect is that little aggressive acts can breed their own justification, thus facilitating further aggressive behavior. Social psychologists have found that cruel acts give rise to cruel attitudes. We are likely to justify our cruelty by denigrating our victim, which makes us feel more hostile and facilitates further aggression. Another reason is that retaliation reduces physical tension, and this result is experienced as reinforcing. Retaliation may thus increase the likelihood of future retaliation.

Actually, years of research in many different fields suggest that sometimes expressing anger is beneficial but that often it is not. Expressing anger frequently makes the angry person angrier, makes the target of the anger angry back, lowers everybody's self-esteem, and fosters hostility and aggression. Anger is sometimes said to be contagious. For this reason, it is somewhat dangerous, in that interactions among people who are in conflict can escalate out of control. Unfortunately, violence is often the result. Yet despite the lack of evidence to support it, the belief persists that expressing anger purges it out of one's system.

Should we therefore bottle up anger and aggressive urges? Silent sulking is hardly more effective, because it allows us to continue ruminating over our grievances as we conduct conversations in our head. Fortunately, there are other ways to express our feelings and to inform others about how their behavior affects us. Assertive statements communicate the nature of what is bothering us while our level of upset is still mild. Stating "I'm angry," "When you talk like that, I feel irritated," or "I have a bone to pick with you," communicates our feelings in a way that leads the other person to hear us out rather than defensively to fight back and in doing so, to escalate the aggression. It is possible to be assertive without being aggressive.

Cognitive Behavioral View of Anger

Recall (Chapter 8) that cognitive therapy takes the view that the meaning we attach to the events in our lives are what precipitate our emotional reactions. Aaron Beck (1976) asserted that people are unlikely to respond with anger to a frustrating situation if they judge the frustrating agent to be justified, nonarbitrary, or reasonable. We are not annoyed with a friend who has promised to do an errand for us but has failed to do so, after finding out that the friend has been sick.

DIRECT OFFENSES OF INTENTIONAL AND UNINTENTIONAL TYPES   Different kinds of anger-producing situations have a common denominator: The offended person perceives a threat to her or his safety, self-esteem, or desires, and judges the encroachment to be intentional. Suppose that an adult woman is intimidated by a gang of teenage boys; that one student is singled out by a teacher and criticized for talking, when several students were doing so; that a person dutifully waiting in line for theater tickets finds the tickets are sold out, after noticing that several people cut in front of him or her; or that a young executive's new idea is rejected by more established employees who have no ideas of their own to offer instead.

What these examples have in common is that the offended person is subjected to an unpleasant experience by one or more adversaries. The unpleasantness is deliberate on the part of the perpetrator, who is seen by the offended one as deliberately infringing on his or her domain. Even when the perpetrator's action is not motivated by the wish to injure, it may be perceived that way by the person who is the object of that behavior.

Another type of anger-producing situation occurs when we believe that someone else's demands or restrictions trespass on our rights. The attempts of another person to confine our activities will annoy us, even if we had previously had no desire to engage in the forbidden behavior. The "rights" that we are protecting may be our freedom of action; freedom of expression; or expectations of respect, consideration, or loyalty from other people.

INDIRECT OFFENSES   We may become upset because the behavior of others indirectly threatens to lower our self-esteem. Following are some examples of these kinds of scenarios: A hostess feels annoyed with a guest who insists on bragging about his accomplishments; a young man is jealous after hearing his girlfriend rave about the fine qualities of an actor in a film they just finished viewing; a student is very pleased at receiving a straight A grade until she learns that fully one-quarter of the class also earned As; a wife is enraged at her husband after receiving only a faint acknowledgment from him for what she considers to be an important career promotion. All of these situations expose the offended person with self-devaluation. To revisit the earlier examples: The hostess feels envy: "Why is this guest demanding so much attention?" The young man feels deflated on noticing that his girlfriend is so enamored of another man. The student's esteem over getting a good grade is diminished when the grade is cheapened by being given out so freely by the professor. The wife feels devalued and patronized when her husband fails adequately to acknowledge her achievement.

Those who experience a loss of self-esteem might be expected to become sad or depressed as a result, rather than to grow angry. However, anger can be used to ward off loss of self-esteem by redirecting the negative attention to the offender. The other person is viewed as a show-off, as superficial, or as envious. If the offended person accepts the indirect blow to her or his ego, then the person will indeed feel sad.

HYPOTHETICAL OFFENSES   Beck noted that people may have angry reactions to occurrences that seem to be neither direct nor indirect offenses. For example, a pedestrian may become irate over seeing a motorist fail to make a complete stop at a crosswalk; a mother might be quite critical when her child displays poor manners in public; a man who is dedicated to the law might become furious over an article in the paper reporting on a crime in another state. Although none of these situations represents a direct encroachment on the offended person's domain, the perpetrator has broken a rule or standard that the offended person holds as important. Thus, the violation causes the offended person to see himself or herself as vulnerable. The offended person may readily see that she or he is in no way *actually* personally damaged but that she or he could have been harmed. The pedestrian might entertain the thought "I could have been walking across the street in the crosswalk and been run into." The mother might wonder whether others will consider her to be an incompetent parent, since her child does not behave well in public. Beck contends that hypothetical infringements account for a large proportion of the strife in human relations.

The preceding examples show quite clearly that individuals may become angry as a result of their internal dialogue. Thus, it is not unusual for a person not to react to an external event until he or she has time to ponder it. Then, and only then, does the person become angry. What is a poor bystander to do? What helps in this situation is for the angry person to reveal his or her thought process, to explain the beliefs that he or she has developed about the past incident. Anger management, then, would involve forming the habit of thinking differently about the situations that arise, so that they are viewed in a more benevolent light.

➤ ASSERTIVENESS

Anger, which is a signal worth attending to, may indicate that we are being hurt, that our rights are being violated, or that our needs or wants are not being adequately met. Once mobilized by anger, we can use assertive strategies to correct what is amiss.

Assertion refers to the expression of one's rights without interfering with the rights of others. When we are assertive, we stand up for ourselves and express our thoughts and feelings directly, honestly, and appropriately. We show respect for ourselves, but at the same time we demonstrate consideration for those with whom we are involved. As it is written in the Talmud, "If I am not for myself, who will be for me? But if I am for myself only, who am I?" Assertiveness is typically prompted by some form of anger, from mild irritation to well-disciplined outrage.

The alternatives to assertiveness are submissiveness and aggression. We are submissive or nonassertive when we fail to express our rights or when we hold back and neglect to present our wishes out of fear of incurring disapproval. We may also put forth our position in such a self-effacing way that we may be disregarded.

Submissive people are sometimes matched with partners who are aggressive and persistent. There is give-and-take in every relationship, but when one person does all the giving in, it is an unhealthy sign for the couple. Without meaningful dialogue, the affectionate bond is eventually destroyed by resentment. The submissive partner can make a change for the better in the relationship by learning to negotiate to have his or her needs taken seriously.

Aggression is frequently confused with assertive behavior but differs in that the aggressive person's rights are enforced at the expense of another person. When we are aggressive, we lash out verbally or physically in an attempt to belittle or overpower others or to put them down. When we use aggression, we do not show respect for others, and we invite retaliation rather than cooperation. Use of intimidation to coerce compliance in others is aggression rather than assertion.

In order to be assertive, we must know what we want, thus perhaps necessitating clarifying our goals and beliefs. It takes a certain level of self-esteem to be willing to evaluate our lives and ourselves in preparation for becoming more assertive. We need to have the conviction that our value systems, beliefs, wants, and needs are valid and acceptable. When assertively stating our position, we must accept responsibility for the consequences of taking that position. For example, Martin Luther King, Jr., broke a segregation law in order to protest its unfairness, and he expected to be arrested and jailed as the consequence. King accepted this outcome as a means to his intended end.

Becoming assertive isn't always an easy undertaking. Asking for what we want involves taking a risk, because there is a possibility that the other person will not give it to us. The assertive person is willing to take the chance that his or her request will be rejected and is able to recognize that rejection of a request is not necessarily a personal rejection.

To be assertive means not to let others control us. Assertive people make decisions about their lives on the basis of their intentions for themselves, not on other people's expectations of them. Once we have determined that we deserve to have our needs met, then we can make decisions about our lives without feeling guilty because we are disappointing someone else.

Assertive Rights

In order to give people guidelines for developing assertive behavior, psychologist Manuel Smith (1975) proposed a list of assertive rights as a basic framework for healthy participation in any kind of human relationship:

1. You have the right to judge your own behaviors, thoughts, and emotions, and to take the responsibility for their initiation and consequences upon yourself.

Explanation: We are the ultimate judge of all we are and do. This is our primary right, from which all those that follow are derived. If we have the sole jurisdiction over our own behavior, we'll decide which of the rules and standards that other people try to impose on us are ones we agree to be guided by. Other people need to have our cooperation if they are to succeed in manipulating us. Otherwise, their attempts to control us will be unsuccessful.

2. You have the right to offer no reasons or excuses for justifying your behavior.

Explanation: We do not need to explain our behavior to someone else in order for the person to determine whether it is right or wrong. Other people have the assertive right to tell us what they think of our behavior, and we have the option either to listen to or to disregard their input. People may try to demand reasons from us for our behavior in order to show us that we are wrong. We don't have to cooperate. One advantage to being an adult rather than a child is that others are generally not entitled to make decisions about the appropriateness of our behavior.

3. You have the right to judge whether you are responsible for finding solutions to other people's problems.

Explanation: In spite of our compassion for the troubles of others, we must acknowledge the reality of the human condition, that each of us must come to terms with the problems of living by learning to cope on our own. The person with a problem has the responsibility to solve it himself or herself. In business settings, this attempt at manipulation can take the form of people's trying to get us to place the well-being of ineffective systems above our own well-being. A salesclerk may attempt to stop us from complaining about a defective item that we wish to return by pointing out that we are holding up the line. Other people want to be served, too, after all. In reality, we have no responsibility to see to it that the store runs smoothly. An assertive response might be to suggest that the clerk take care of our complaint promptly so that the other people in line behind us won't have to wait any longer than necessary.

4. You have the right to change your mind.

Explanation: If we change our mind, other people may resist our new choice and attempt to discourage us by trying to convince us that we are committed to the old course of action. They may pressure us to consider ourselves irresponsible. At any rate, they want us to satisfy them that we are sufficiently remorseful over our change of heart. Nevertheless, we are entitled to change our mind and still to be comfortable with ourselves. Naturally, since we accept responsibility for our own behavior, we'll expect to handle the consequences, which might be serious if we are breaking a contract or in some other way refusing to do what we promised.

5. You have the right to make mistakes—and to be responsible for them.

Explanation: None of us is perfect. As human beings, we are going to make mistakes, so that when someone else pretends that we are not entitled to err, we are the object of that person's attempt to manipulate. Naturally, we are responsible for the consequences of our errors, but this does not mean that we need to feel guilty or to atone for our mistakes in a manner that someone else specifies. It also doesn't imply that we have shown ourselves to be incompetent in general, so that someone else should supervise our actions from now on.

6. You have the right to say, "I don't know."

Explanation: We do not have to supply an immediate answer to whatever question someone might ask us. Many of us who are still stuck in the childish belief that unless we have an answer to any possible question that could be asked about the potential consequences of our behavior, we are irresponsible and need to be controlled. This belief allows other people to manipulate us. Questions that might be intended to manipulate generally start like this: "What would happen if . . ." or "What kind of person . . ."

7. You have the right to be independent of the goodwill of others before coping with them.

Explanation: We do not need the goodwill of others in order to deal with them effectively and assertively. Other people often threaten to withdraw their goodwill in order to manipulate us. As children, we needed the cooperation of other people in order to survive, but that isn't the case for adults. Adults are capable of functioning, being safe, and even being happy without the goodwill of any one person. If we live in terror of having other people take offense at our actions, we won't feel free to do what we want with our time and our lives.

8. You have the right to be illogical in making decisions.

Explanation: Logic isn't much help in dealing with our own and other people's wants, motivation, and feelings. Logical reasoning may not provide us with much understanding of why we want what we want or in solving problems created by conflicting motives. Others may sometimes use logic to manipulate us into doing what they want us to do. For example, our roommate may point out that if we stay up into the wee hours of the morning to watch the federal election returns, we'll be tired at school the next day. That prediction does logically follow. However, from our perspective, the delight in staying up to learn the election results may be worth the next day's tiredness. We take responsibility for making the choice to stay up.

9. You have the right to say, "I don't understand."

Explanation: We don't always understand what another person means or wants. Some individuals try to manipulate us into doing what they want us to do by hinting, implying, or suggesting; or they may subtly act as if they expect us to do something for them or to refrain from doing something. They may have the attitude that we should automatically understand what behavior pleases or displeases them, and in the latter case, that we should change that behavior so that they will no longer be hurt, angry, or disappointed.

10. You have the right to say, "I don't care."

Explanation: Since we are flawed human beings, we probably believe that we should strive to better ourselves. However, if someone else points out how we can improve ourselves, we are not obligated to follow that person's direction. We have the right to assert ourselves by saying that we don't care to live up to anyone's definition of how we should be. If we fall into the trap of agreeing with others that we should want to improve our behavior, we are then forced to explain our failings to others and thus to allow others to be the ultimate judge of our acceptability. One way to stop this manipulation is to ask ourselves whether we are satisfied with our own performance and then to make our own decision about whether or not we wish to change.

Source: From *When I Say No, I Feel Guilty* by Manuel J. Smith. Used by permission of Doubleday, a division of Random House, Inc.

Cultural Issues and Teaching Assertiveness

In Hispanic families, in which the traditional beliefs are in *machismo* and *marianismo*, assertive behaviors may seem out of place. They can sometimes be implemented in a softened version, by offering the *respeto* (respect) due to the head of the household. A wife might say to her husband, "With all of the respect you deserve, I believe . . ." rather than, "I disagree with the position you have taken" (Comas-Diaz & Duncan, 1985).

➤ AGGRESSION AS AN EXPRESSION OF CULTURE: IS AGGRESSION AS AMERICAN AS APPLE PIE?

How the United States Compares with Other Countries

The United States has a higher rate of violent crime than does any other industrialized nation. The risk of being murdered in the United States is now 7 to 10 times that in most European countries (Lore & Schultz, 1993). Comparable differences exist between the United States and Europe for rape and robbery. In Japan, individual acts of aggression are exceedingly rare, and the murder rate is about 1 per 100,000 people. The murder rate in the United States is nearly 6 times that of England (Washington Post, 1998). A similar comparison can be made with Canada, where the 1991 murder rate was 2.8 per 100,000 population. The 1997 murder rate in the United States was 6.8 per 100,000 (Los Angeles Times, 1999).

Murder Often Hits Close to Home

Both murder, which is the rarest of criminal offenses, and assault, which is the most common violent offense, are generally unplanned and unintended. Both crimes arise from similar circumstances: (1) They tend to evolve out of spontaneous quarrels between neighbors, drinking partners, and family members; and (2) roughly 60 to 80 percent of those who assault or murder are relatives or acquaintances of their victims. Forty percent of killings occur in homes or apartments, between family members or acquaintances. These parameters suggest that murder falls largely into the category of domestic violence. In 1991, one-third of all women treated in emergency rooms in the United States were injured by their husbands (KCBS, 1992). An analysis of the

PEANUTS reprinted by permission of United Features syndicate, Inc.

most prominent prevalence studies in the field suggests that between 21 percent and 34 percent of women in this country will be physically assaulted— slapped, kicked, beaten, choked, or threatened or attacked with a weapon—by an intimate adult partner (Browne, 1993). These estimates are bound to be conservative, because the national surveys of violence perpetrated by intimates typically do not include in their samples groups such as very poor, non-English speaking, hospitalized, homeless, institutionalized, or incarcerated women (Browne, 1993). When a woman is the murderer, she is likely to kill her husband or lover.

QUESTIONS: *Do the findings that murders tend to be unplanned and unintended and that they occur between people who know each other suggest any ways to curb this type of violent behavior? If so, what?*

➤ REDUCING AGGRESSION

There is considerable evidence that aggressive behavior can readily be eliminated by adjustments in environmental and social factors, and by helping individuals with anger management. Lore and Schultz (1993) claim that all animals have evolved strong inhibitory mechanisms that enable them to suppress aggression when it is in their interest to do so. As a result, aggression in even the so-called primitive or violence-prone species is always an optional strategy. Its expression is largely determined by an animal's previous social experiences and the current social context. The role of experience and learning becomes more powerful as one ascends the evolutionary ladder (Feshbach & Weiner, 1991).

Reducing Factors That Evoke Aggression

The social learning approach suggests controlling aggression by counteracting the factors that provoke it. First, we could teach people how to minimize aversive stimulation. Instead of probing the inner lives or motives of violent people, behaviorally oriented psychologists research the sorts of situations that promote violence and the kinds of payoffs that violence earns for its perpetrators. For example, studies find that aggressiveness in children increases when a teacher unwittingly rewards the child with attention (Serbin & O'Leary, 1975). Violent behavior can be reduced or eliminated by withdrawing rewards for it and by rewarding cooperative, friendly behavior instead (Fixsen et al., 1978).

Modeling Nonaggression and Prosocial Attitudes

Reduction in aggression can be accomplished by rewarding and modeling nonaggressive behavior. People are more likely to help when they have observed someone else helping a person in distress. Bryan and Test (1967) found that Los Angeles drivers were more likely to offer help to a female driver with a flat tire if a quarter mile earlier they had seen someone helping another woman change a tire. In another study, Bryan and Test observed that New Jersey Christmas shoppers were more likely to drop money in a Salvation Army kettle if they had just seen someone else do the same. Rushton and Campbell (1977) also found that British adults were usually unwilling to donate blood unless they were approached after observing a role model, who had been set up by the researcher, consent to donating.

Lore and Schultz (1993) have proposed a variety of social changes that should reduce aggression in American culture, among which is a reduction in the almost continuous exposure to glorified, unrealistic violence in the entertainment media. Television teaches aggressive styles of conduct through observation of an aggressive model, and it reduces restraints on aggressive behavior. It desensitizes viewers to violence and shapes their assumptions about social reality. Moreover, television increases arousal and also distorts views about conflict resolution. On television or movie screens, interpersonal conflicts are resolved by physical aggression much more often than by any other means (Gerber & Gross, 1976).

QUESTION: How would you explain the greater popularity of movies and television programs depicting people's inhumanity to each other than that of people engaging in altruistic acts?

However, as producer Sean Daniel (McLaughlin Group, 1995) pointed out, Canada has essentially the same media, television, and radio as does the United States; in fact, most of Canada's programs are generated from the United States. Yet, Canada has one-third the murder rate and one-half the crime rate of the United States. The picture is mixed. When Williams (1986) observed children in a rural Canadian town, he found that playground aggression doubled after the introduction of television. After Schutte et al. (1988) had five- to seven-year-old children play a violent (karate) video game, they found that the physical aggression doubled during a subsequent free-play period.

Beyond media violence, we need research on more subtle effects of entertainment. For example, television typically displays utterly fanciful and grandiose lifestyles that may raise the expectations of the entire population to unrealistic levels. The inevitable contrast with reality might prompt violence in susceptible persons, under the principle of "relative deprivation," which is the principle explaining that whether we feel well off or deprived has everything to do with whom we are making the comparison.

QUESTION: One possible source of frustration caused by the sense that we are less well off than those with whom we are comparing ourselves is the affluence depicted on television. If comparing ourselves with the wealthy characters who are portrayed causes us to feel relatively deprived, what is the appeal of these programs?

Eliciting Reactions Incompatible with Aggression

EMPATHY   The human capacity to experience empathy, to perceive the perspective and feelings of another, may be one mechanism that helps restrain an aggressor from continuing an attack, though empathy is not automatic and requires experience and training (Feshbach, 1979). It was Batson (1991) who suggested that our capacity for empathy may well be what prompts our altruistic acts. His theory of altruism suggests that the sight of someone in distress may produce "empathic sympathy" in the observer. That is, the observer suffers along with the victim. For this reason, coming to the aid of another person alleviates not just the victim's distress but also the observer's empathic suffering. Seeing things from another person's perspective may lead us to feel genuinely sympathetic and compassionate, and therefore to want to help the person for his or her own sake.

Batson tested the notion that helping another who is suffering is motivated by our wish to relieve our own distress. He set up an experiment in which it was easy for subjects to escape the situation and thus to relieve their own discomfort without helping. He found that once the subjects' feelings of empathy were aroused, they usually would help rather than escape the scene. This finding lends support to the theory of empathic sympathy. Through empathy, we enter into another person's self-understanding and to some extent, appreciate the other in the same way and for the same qualities that this person views and enjoys his or her own existence.

QUESTION: How can the evidence that empathy seems to be at the core of altruism and that low empathy is linked with aggression be a part of individual and collective responses to violence in our culture?

RELAXATION   Relaxation is another state of being that is incompatible with aggression. As was discussed in Chapter 8, relaxation is effective in counteracting stress. On the other hand, busy, hurried people are undesirable companions who are sometimes abrupt and surly in their social interactions.

In addition to feeling hostile, people in a hurry are unlikely to engage in altruistic behaviors. This phenomenon has been well researched by social psychologists. For instance, Darley and Batson (1973) conducted an experiment with Princeton Theological Seminary students who were expecting to be recorded giving a brief extemporaneous talk on the Good Samaritan parable. The researchers directed the students to a recording studio in a nearby building. On their way to the studio, they passed a man sitting slumped in a doorway, head down, coughing and groaning. Some of the students had been sent off nonchalantly: "It will be a few minutes before they're ready for you, but you might as well head on over." Of these, almost two-thirds stopped to offer help to the slumped-over man. Other students were told, "Oh, you're late. They were expecting you a few minutes ago . . . so you'd better hurry." Of these, only 10 percent offered help.

Reflecting on these findings, Darley and Batson remarked,

> A person not in a hurry may stop and offer help to a person in distress. A person in a hurry is likely to keep going. Ironically, he is likely to keep going even if he is hurrying to speak on the parable of the Good Samaritan, thus inadvertently confirming the point of the parable. (Indeed, on several occasions, a seminary student going to give his talk on the parable of the Good Samaritan literally stepped over the victim as he hurried on his way!)

A person in a hurry is less likely to take the time fully to grasp that the situation is an emergency. In addition, the person is liable to perceive that the costs of helping are high in terms of missed appointments and neglected commitments to others. For Type A people (Chapter 8), a "chronic sense of time urgency" may produce an underlying hostility that causes them to view other people as impediments. To the extent that our entire society steps up the pace of life, we can anticipate a decline in empathy for our fellow citizens.

QUESTION: Given that the pace of life will probably increase steadily during the next several decades, how might individuals be influenced to remain mindful of the need to be courteous and helpful toward others?

➤ SUMMARY

Anger is considered one of the most negative of human emotions, because its behavioral expression sometimes takes a destructive form. The question of how to deal with anger cuts to the heart of what it means to be human, since it concerns a basic conflict between self-expression and being socially agreeable.

In contemporary Western society, most people are taught to control, and even to deny, their anger. However, learning to stifle anger may be as disadvantageous as the indiscriminate venting of anger. Suppressed anger is likely to be expressed eventually in a deleterious form. It may turn to resentment and destroy love or may be released as sarcasm. It may be expressed in a *passive aggressive* form, meaning that indirect, disguised ways are found to express hostility. A further possibility is that hostility may be *displaced* onto an inappropriate target. Psychoanalysts have theorized that repressed hostility is turned against oneself in the form of depression. Some physical maladies may also be linked to chronic anger.

A Case for Getting Hot Under the Collar   Anger is a natural emotion, which can be effective when communicated and acted upon in a controlled manner. The predominant danger inherent in anger lies in the possibility of unexpected and thus uncontrolled explosions of rage that can lead to physical violence.

Anger provides a powerful motivation for social, political, and cultural change. Anger can also protect people from being taken advantage of by others. When anger is a result of some outside stress factor, the negative emotion motivates people to get away from or to reduce the effect of the stressful factor. If human beings ignore their anger, the stress that caused it is not reduced and thus often increases. When stress factors persist or increase, the result may be a continued buildup of anger until the individual loses control of his or her behavior.

Rules for a Clean Fight   A caring mate will not intentionally take advantage of his or her partner's vulnerable areas. Personal attacks should be prohibited as part of the agreed-on ground rules for conducting an argument.

One source of exasperation in arguments with intimates is a conviction that one is not being listened to. A good listener uses empathy to understand how the other person experiences his or her life.

The constructive use of anger requires a certain degree of self-control. A way to maintain self-control is for each person to become familiar with his or her own anger signals and those of his or her significant others. Anger is best disclosed through the use of "I" messages, which are direct, focused on a particular topic, and effective in reducing the listener's defensiveness.

Humanistic View on Anger Expression   Carl Rogers contended that when anger is an authentic reaction (and not a cover-up for another emotion), it is not destructive. Rogers believed that human beings are basically constructive and trustworthy, and need to be liked by others. Anger is often denied until it breaks forth in uncontrolled bursts; however, in the fully functioning person, anger rises at once into consciousness. It is also far more subject to control, so that its expression becomes a choice. When emotions, including anger, are ignored, they cannot be used as guides to help decide what is wanted and needed.

EXISTENTIAL CONCERNS AND AGGRESSION   People have an inborn need for a stimulating environment. Fromm proposed a distinction between a *simple stimulus*
and an *activating stimulus:* Simple stimulation that does not engage human
reason results in passive reactions. To avoid boredom, simple stimuli must
constantly change or continually increase in intensity. Activating stimuli
nourish the mind and soul, inducing people to actively participate in life.

Contemporary technological society provides many simple stimuli that
foster passivity and boredom. One consequence of continuous simple stimulation is that people living today are driven to seek methods of escaping boredom. Thus, alcohol, drugs, food, television, Internet cruising, and sexual
promiscuity can all be means of avoiding an overwhelming sense of boredom
in the face of the continual barrage of simple stimuli. People may resort to
gaining stimulation through violence. In a life without meaning, destructiveness provides such individuals with some measure of distorted mastery. Aggression of this sort solves the individual's sense of despair at the meaninglessness of his or her life by allowing malevolent control over the life of
another person.

A CASE FOR KEEPING A COOL HEAD   Anger that intensifies to the point of rage
can create cloudy and irrational thinking. Suppressing anger can be counter-
productive if a stressful situation continues; likewise, expressing anger can be
unwise if revealing one's feelings makes the stressful situation worse. Paying
attention to one's own warning signals entails taking the time to become familiar with one's feelings so that a person can tell when he or she is getting to
an unproductive point. Couples and family members might very well find it
useful to develop a set of rules about time-outs and other necessary arrangements for careful expressions of anger.

BEHAVIORAL PERSPECTIVE ON ANGER EXPRESSION   Behaviorists contend that aggressive behavior is a learned reaction to anger, not an instinctive one. People
learn to be aggressive, because that kind of behavior is rewarded.

Most techniques aimed at getting one's way can be categorized as helplessness, suffering, or anger. These actions are used because they worked in
the past for the person using them, but they are inappropriate because they require submission by another person. This behavior causes the loser of the
struggle to become frustrated and resentful, an outcome that may lead to a
break in the relationship. A more desirable alternative would be for the parties involved to enter a dialogue with the understanding that each person's
needs and desires will be made clear before any decisions are made. Then, a
solution will be sought to which all parties can agree.

PSYCHOANALYTIC VIEW OF ANGER   Catharsis is the theory that one can purge emotions by experiencing them. Freud believed that human beings need to find
ways of draining off the aggressive drives through catharsis, lest this inner destructive urge be turned against oneself.

The notion of catharsis implies the hydraulic model of emotions. This
view does not hold up in the face of research, because participating in aggres-

sive activities has been shown either to increase aggressive behavior or to maintain it at the same level, rather than to reduce it.

Aggression tends to breed more aggression rather than to reduce subsequent aggression. Years of research in many different fields suggests that sometimes expressing anger is beneficial but that more often it is not.

Cognitive Behavioral View of Anger Cognitive theorists contend that anger is a result of what a person thinks about the events of his or her life. Anger management entails rethinking the situation, so that it is viewed in a more benign light.

Assertiveness Assertion refers to the expression of one's rights without interfering with the rights of others, and it is the preferred alternative for communicating one's needs to significant others. The choices that are less desirable than assertiveness are submissiveness and aggression. Submission refers to failure to assert one's rights; aggression means that one's rights are expressed at the expense of another person. Ten assertive rights were listed and explained.

Aggression as an Expression of Culture The United States has a greater volume of violent acting out than does any other industrialized nation. Both murder and assault are generally unplanned and unintended, and both crimes tend to arise from spontaneous quarrels between neighbors, drinking partners, and family members. Roughly 60 to 80 percent of those who assault or murder are relatives or acquaintances of their victims.

Reducing Aggression There is considerable evidence that aggressive behavior is learned and can be eliminated by adjustments in environmental and social factors. Research suggests that all animals have evolved strong inhibitory mechanisms that enable them to suppress aggression when it is in their interest to do so.

One method of curbing violence is by reducing factors that evoke aggression. Aggressiveness increases when rewarded; it is reduced or eliminated when rewards for it are withdrawn and when cooperative, friendly behavior is rewarded instead. People might be taught how to minimize aversive stimulation. Violence on television teaches aggressive styles of conduct through observation of an aggressive model.

The human capacity to experience empathy—to perceive the perspective and feelings of another—may be one mechanism that helps restrain an aggressor from continuing an attack, though empathy is not automatic and requires experience and training.

People in a hurry are not likely to be helpful, whereas people who are relaxed and in a good mood are inclined to offer help.

Learning the Language of Psychologists

passive aggressive	**assertiveness**
aggression	**catharsis**
habituate	

Chapter Review Questions

1. How are the emotions of unresolved anger, resentment, and antipathy related?
2. How might "getting hot under the collar" be beneficial? Is the "hot" person benefited, or the recipient of the anger (the one who is the appropriate object), or are both people benefited?
3. How can anger be handled constructively, so that it functions as a positive force in a person's life?
4. When should an individual *not* be a good listener during an argument?
5. What did Erich Fromm have to say about the need for humans to have stimulation and excitation? What happens when people don't have enough excitement in their lives?
6. What did Fromm mean by "malignant aggression," and how does it differ from "defensive aggression"?
7. What is the humanistic view of anger? The behavioral? The psychoanalytic? The cognitive?
8. What were the main points presented in favor of keeping a "cool head"?
9. What are "get-my-way" behaviors?
10. What does it mean to be assertive? What makes assertiveness preferable to submissive or aggressive behaviors?
11. What are some of the recommendations that have been made by psychologists to reduce aggression?
12. What is the relationship between empathy and aggression?

Activities

1. *COMPLETE AS A GROUP:* **Personal Reflections on Anger and Aggression.**
2. *COMPLETE AS A GROUP:* **Practice Identifying Response Styles.**
3. *COMPLETE AS A GROUP:* **Assertiveness Training Practice.**
4. *COMPLETE AS A GROUP:* **Is It Aggression?**
5. COMPLETE AT HOME: **Anger Journal.**
6. *COMPLETE AT HOME:* **Role Reversal Exercise.** Consider a conflict that you are currently having with your romantic partner, your parents, or your child that never seems to be resolved. Instead of either defending

your own position or criticizing, attacking, or blaming your "loved" one, switch sides and become the advocate for your intimate adversary.

7. *COMPLETE AT HOME: **"Gifting" up a Grudge: Behaving Your Way into a New Attitude.*** Send an anonymous gift to someone whom you find difficult, and then imagine the pleasure that he or she will get on receiving it.

8. *COMPLETE AS A GROUP: **Debate.*** Divide the class into two groups and debate this issue: "Resolve: Anger is a useful tool in negotiating relationships."

9. *COMPLETE IN GROUPS OF TWO OR FOUR: **The Red/Black Game.***

Personal Reflections on Anger and Aggression

Directions: Read each of the following questions, and then write your answers in the blanks.

1. What gets you angry? How frequently do you become angry? How do you handle your anger?

   _____

   _____

   _____

   _____

2. Do you feel guilty when you have gotten angry? If so, what do you do about the feeling? If not, what do you tell yourself that makes you feel okay about your anger?

   _____

   _____

   _____

   _____

3. How was anger expressed by your immediate family members as you grew up?

   _____

   _____

   _____

   _____

4. Whom do you most admire in respect to the manner in which he or she manages his or her anger? Why?

   _____

   _____

_____

_____

5. Try to think of an occasion when you were influenced to engage in an altruistic act after observing another person's doing so. Explain.

_____

_____

_____

_____

6. Do you have friends from a different culture who handle anger differently from the way that your family handles it? If so, how?

_____

_____

_____

_____

7. Given the information in this text, what are some suggestions that you might make to an irritable peer as to how to handle his or her anger?

_____

_____

_____

_____

8. Social psychologists have said that Americans are particularly prone to feeling "relatively deprived" because the American Dream is to be upwardly mobile, so that we tend to use as our reference group those "one rung up from us on the ladder." With whom do you compare yourself to decide how competent or successful you are? Do we as a culture need to reorient our thinking as to what it means to be successful in life?

_____

_____

_____

_____

9. Identify an area in your life where you need to be assertive but where you have been either too submissive or too aggressive. Describe a good way to handle that situation.

_____

_____

_____

_____

10. What is your favorite "get-my-way" behavior? With whom does it work best?

_____

_____

_____

_____

11. Complete this sentence: "My most frequent feeling is . . ."

_____

_____

_____

_____

12. Complete this sentence: "The thing I hate most is . . ."

_____

_____

_____

_____

13. Complete this sentence: "When someone is angry, I . . ."

_____

_____

_____

_____

14. What is your most successful relationship at present? (It could be with a parent, a friend, an employer, a coach, or a romantic partner.) What strategy have you worked out between the two of you for handling disagreements?

_____

_____

_____

Practice Identifying Response Styles

Directions: In the blanks at the right, write the letter of the answer choice that most fits what you think would be the appropriate behavior in the given situation.

1. You're shortchanged at the supermarket. What do you do? _____
   a. Walk away quietly to avoid imposing on the clerk.
   b. Angrily point out the error to the clerk, accusing the clerk of trying to take advantage of you.
   c. Calmly point out the error, and ask for the correct change.

2. You've just finished three loads of laundry when your teenager asks you to wash his favorite shirt. You should _____
   a. Wash it, postponing the shopping excursion you had been looking forward to.
   b. Tell him you'd have been happy to do it if he had asked when you were starting the laundry, but now you're finished with the laundry and want to go shopping.
   c. Refuse, barking at him that you've tired, he's old enough to take care of his own damned shirt, and you're not a servant.

3. You're alone at a party and know very few people who are there. What do you do? _____
   a. Find someone who appears to be alone, introduce yourself, and comment on how good the refreshments are.
   b. Sit quietly, hoping someone will approach you.
   c. Interrupt the conversation of a small group to introduce yourself, and start a new topic of conversation.

4. Your spouse hasn't paid much attention to you lately, and you feel neglected. What do you do? _____
   a. Tell your spouse that if you're going to be ignored at home, you'll go somewhere else.
   b. State matter-of-factly that you feel ignored and that his or her attention makes you feel good.
   c. Think that your spouse is justifiably bored with you and that you have no right to feel bad.

5. Your college roommate leaves clothes and dishes all over the apartment in spite of an agreement that the two of you made to keep the place tidy. Should you _____
   a. Throw your roommate's clothes in the trash, and dump the dirty dishes on his or her bed?

    b. Make a statement about your disappointment over the agreement's not being kept?

    c. Clean some yourself, and ignore the rest of the clutter?

6. Your friend has twice stood you up for a lunch date, each time without calling afterwards to explain. When you called, your friend apologized for forgetting the date. Should you   _____

    a. Tell your friend that you value your time and that you feel reluctant to agree to any further get-togethers unless he or she can assure you that the appointment will be kept?

    b. Let your friend know how inconsiderate he or she has been and "cool" the friendship?

    c. Try again, and see whether your friend shows up this time?

Scoring: The *assertive* responses in each choice were 1c, 2b, 3a, 4b, 5b, and 6a. The *aggressive* responses were 1b, 2c, 3c, 4a, 5a, and 6b. The *submissive* responses were 1a, 2a, 3b, 4c, 5c, and 6c. Did you see a pattern in the style of choice you tend to select?

Assertiveness Training Practice

Problem: Much of the stress that we experience comes from problems we have with other people. The difficulty is that many people see only two alternatives: aggression or submission. (*Note:* These two alternatives are related to the fight or flight responses.)

    Assertiveness represents a third alternative, but one that is often confused with aggression. Assertive statements are not attacks (as aggressive statements often are); rather, they communicate one's own perceptions and emotions. Such responses often take the form of "I statements," which describe your view of the situation and your emotions:

    "I feel _____ when _____, because _____."

I FEEL (say whatever the feeling is, and try to avoid using "angry," which is usually a cover-up for another feeling) WHEN (give a nonjudgmental account of the situation, and avoid using the pronoun "you" when possible) BECAUSE (give a statement telling how it affects you, the message-sender).

    Being assertive tends to defuse conflict situations, and therefore helps lift stress.

Directions: Divide into groups of from four to six people. With the members of your group, construct assertive, aggressive, and submissive responses to each of the following situations.

    1. Someone is crowding in front of you in the supermarket line.

submissive_____

aggressive_____

assertive _____

2. A boyfriend or girlfriend wants to end your relationship.

submissive_____

aggressive_____

assertive _____

3. You have received a grade that is much lower than you feel you deserved on an essay examination.

submissive_____

aggressive_____

assertive _____

4. Your boss tells you that your work has been of poor quality and that you should shape up or you'll be fired.

submissive_____

aggressive_____

assertive _____

5. After a physical examination, your doctor gives you a prescription without telling you what the diagnosis is, what the prescription is for, or what the side effects might be. When you ask for this information, the doctor seems evasive.

submissive_____

aggressive_____

assertive _____

Is It Aggression?

Directions: Decide whether or not each of the following examples represents aggressive behavior. Place a check mark in either the Yes or the No column, depending on your answer.

	Yes	No
1. A murderer is executed under Utah's capital punishment law.	____	____
2. A father spanks his disobedient six-year-old.	____	____

3. A woman shoots mace at her would-be rapist. _____ _____

4. A batter's line drive hits the pitcher in the knee. _____ _____

5. A frustrated wife yells at her "messy slob of a husband." _____ _____

6. A smoldering destroyer at Pearl Harbor in 1941 manages to shoot down a Japanese plane. _____ _____

7. A professor lowers a student's grade on a late paper. _____ _____

8. A man passes along rumors about his rival's sexual transgressions. _____ _____

9. A teenager tells his proud little sister that her art project is "dumb and ugly." _____ _____

10. Two girls sneak out at night and toilet-paper their mutual friend's front yard. _____ _____

11. A person commits suicide. _____ _____

12. Out of frustration, a girl kicks a wastebasket. _____ _____

13. A soldier shoots an enemy at the front line. _____ _____

14. Iraqi soldiers set fire to the oil wells of Kuwait as they retreat from battle. _____ _____

15. A farmer beheads a chicken and prepares it for supper. _____ _____

16. A physician gives a flu shot to a screaming child. _____ _____

17. A boxer gives his opponent a bloody nose. _____ _____

18. A Girl Scout tries to assist an elderly woman but trips her by accident. _____ _____

19. A bank robber is shot in the back while trying to escape. _____ _____

20. A tennis player smashes his racket after missing a volley. _____ _____

21. An angry son purposely fails to write to his mother, who is expecting a letter and will be hurt if none arrives. _____ _____

22. A man daydreams of harming his antagonist but has no hope of doing so. _____ _____

23. An enraged boy tries with all his might to inflict injury on his antagonist, a bigger boy, but is not successful. His efforts simply amuse the bigger boy. _____ _____

24. A senator does not protest the escalation of bombing to which he is morally opposed. _____ _____

25. A hunter kills an animal and mounts it as a trophy. _____ _____

26. A spider eats a fly.　　　　　　　　　　　　　　　　　　____ ____

27. Two men fight for a piece of bread.　　　　　　　　　　____ ____

28. A dog snarls at a mail carrier but does not bite her.　____ ____

29. A cat kills a mouse, parades around with it, and then
    discards it.　　　　　　　　　　　　　　　　　　　　　____ ____

30. A politician intentionally misrepresents his opponent's
    position on an issue.　　　　　　　　　　　　　　　　____ ____

After completing the exercise, can you come up with a definition of aggression?

Source: From "Defining Aggression: An Exercise for Classroom Discussion" by L. T. Benjamin. From *Teaching of Psychology,* 12, p. 41. Copyright © 1985 by Lawrence Erlbaum Associates, Inc. Adapted with permission.

Anger Journal

Directions: For the next couple of days, carry around a little notebook, and record in it every time you have a painful feeling. Indicate the kind of feeling; are you uncomfortable, frightened, angry, or regretful? Note what the time of day is; what caused the feeling to happen; what you were doing; and what kind of loss it was. What did you do about it? Was this a new pain or an old pain? If you have experienced it before, what did you do about it before?

At the end, you'll have an array of feelings. Look at the record as though it were that of a person you didn't know. What do you think of this person? How important are the things that this person is pained about? Does the other person know about the pain? Is that person afraid of something? If so, what—telling the truth, being rejected?

Make a list of all of the people who hurt you during these few days, and add any others who have hurt you in the past. Make a list of all of the people who need to know that they have hurt you. The pain of these pages is what keeps you from giving your best to the world. These hurts are opportunities to get better. Each pain you suffered was an opportunity to be open. What excuse do you give for not sharing your pain? Did you deny the impact of the pain in yourself?

Write a letter to each person who hurt you; you don't have to mail it, though. "You hurt me when . . ." Some of the pain you are feeling with each person may be pain that's very old. You need to be clear about what the original injury was. What could have been done to make it better? What would you like the person to do to make amends? Give the other person the benefit of knowing what's going on inside you. Other people have to realize that their actions prompted you to feel that way; let the people in your life know how their actions affect you. The object of clarifying your feelings is to express them when your perceptions are clear. You will have completely dealt with the pain so that it doesn't intrude on the world as displaced anger.

Forgive as many people as possible after you have let the pain out. Ask forgiveness of those whom you have hurt.

Think of the people in your life who are no longer here, with whom you have unfinished business. You have to hear yourself expressing the hurt. You might take your letter to the graveside and read it there.

If concern that the other person will be crushed stops you from expressing yourself, make sure your message is assertive, not aggressive, but do not permit that person's weakness to control you. If you are lost and don't know what you should be doing with your life, then you have been hiding your feelings.

If passion is missing from your relationship, then hurt and anger may be blocking it. You don't have to hurt the other person to get your hurt out. Express the hurt, not the anger. Those feelings that you will not look at in the present will build up within you. What stands between you and loving yourself are the negative feelings you haven't expressed.

The Red/Black Game

Directions: Divide the class into either two or four groups. Each group plays opposite another group. The game has four rounds. On each round, your group must secretly decide whether it will cooperate with the other group, by voting green, or whether it will compete, by voting red. Use the following chart to calculate your payoff. Your payoff will depend on how you vote as well as on how the other group votes.

For example, if your group decides to vote green (a cooperative response) and the other group does the same, both groups win two points (as indicated in the upper-left-hand quadrant of the payoff table). If, however, your green vote is matched against a competitive red vote from the other group, you will

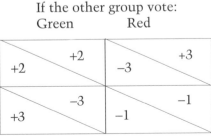

lose three points and they will win three points. If both groups give a competitive response in a given round, both lose one point.

To play each round, select someone to record your vote on a piece of paper. Then, at the instructor's signal, both groups will show each other their vote at the same time.

After each round, in the following chart (1) indicate how your group voted, (2) give the number of points won or lost, and (3) write one or two adjectives that come to mind to describe the members of the other group.

	How you Voted	Points Won/Lost	Description off Other Group
Round 1			
Round 2			
Round 3			
Round 4			

Total Points _____

14

Happiness

One is happy as a result of one's own efforts, once one knows the necessary ingredients of happiness—simple tastes, a certain degree of courage, self denial to a point, love of work, and above all, a clear conscience. Happiness is no vague dream, of that I now feel certain.
—George Sand

Happy is the man who has all that he desires, providing he desires nothing amiss.
—St. Thomas Aquinas

➤ *PREVIEW QUESTIONS:* Ultimately, is there anything people want from life other than happiness? Does happiness depend more on one's life circumstances or on one's personality? What makes people happy? How can one's habitual way of thinking promote or reduce a pleasant mood?

➤ INTRODUCTION: THE HUMAN SEARCH FOR JOY

The scientific study of emotional well-being is relatively new, but theories about the secrets of happiness have developed throughout human history. The ancient Greeks wrote about the roots of happiness. Philosophers from Aristotle in 400 B.C. to contemporary philosopher and writer Mortimer Adler (1988) have described happiness as "the ultimate good." That is, happiness is something desired for its own sake and not for the sake of anything else. According to both Aristotle and Adler, people do not say, "I want happiness because . . ." It is an end in itself.

Although happiness is the end that we strive for, it is not the end of our travels. We cannot attain happiness once and for all time, forever after. According to Aristotle, it comes from a life that is well lived. With an investigation into the nature and the causes of happiness, we may be approaching an answer to the questions, Where am I going? and Why am I here? Each of us is ultimately responsible for our own psychological well-being, happiness, and success in life.

The ancient philosophers believed that happiness arises from a life of leisurely and intelligent reflection. "There is no fool who is happy, and no wise man who is not," wrote the Roman statesman Cicero (106–43 B.C.). For the Greeks, as well as for the Roman Cicero, the pleasures of life have less to do with physical pleasures than mental stimulation. Other routes to happiness that have been proposed are (1) engaging in the pursuit of excellence, (2) leading a virtuous life, (3) knowing the truth, (4) practicing restraint, (5) purging pent-up rage, and (6) living in the present.

Psychologists have historically occupied themselves with the analysis of misery and the way to relieve it. During most of psychology's first century, studies of negative emotions—depression, anxiety, and stress—have overshadowed studies of positive emotions. In fact, the study of such emotions as love and joy strike some people as a trivial area of research. During the past several decades, however, psychologists have become increasingly interested in discovering what factors promote psychological health. In *Psychological Abstracts*, the number of articles pertaining to happiness, life satisfaction, or well-being mushroomed from 150 in 1979, to 780 in 1989 (Myers, 1991). Such studies have been helpful in illuminating the road to happiness.

QUESTION: *If the pursuit of excellence is one route to happiness, why do people try to avoid being perfectionists?*

➤ PHILOSOPHICAL PERSPECTIVES ON HAPPINESS

Aristotle (384–322 B.C.)

Aristotle was a philosopher in Athens, Greece, who was a student of Plato and a teacher of Alexander the Great. Aristotle set out to determine what is the ultimate goal of life.

According to Aristotle, most people would agree that happiness is the highest of all realizable goods (Jacobus, 1994). Ordinary people equate happiness with pleasure, wealth, or fame. They want merely a life of enjoyment. Besides this approach to happiness, Aristotle saw two other routes: the political and the contemplative life. Political people identify happiness with honor. However, Aristotle believed this view to be mistaken, because people generally pursue honor in order to assure themselves of their own merit, as well as to have others appreciate them and see them as virtuous. Since honor is sought in order to gain virtue, then honor cannot be the highest goal of life.

For Aristotle, wealth was clearly not the highest good. Indeed, he viewed the life of money-making as unnatural. Money should be considered only a means to an end.

Aristotle was interested in what good conduct did for the person who engaged in it, and he believed that being virtuous contributed to leading a good life. For a human being, happiness is the effect of good functioning, though not necessarily the test of good functioning. This is the case because a person who acts virtuously might well be happy as a result, but if misfortune plagues him or her and results in unhappiness, this circumstance does not mean that the person was not virtuous.

The highest occupation of human beings is an activity of the soul in accordance with virtue and reason. By activity, Aristotle meant not just the possession of reason but the exercise of reason. He did not think of the supreme good as the mere possession of virtue but instead as its employment. A person might be of good character but without producing any good result from it. In life, those who win the prizes are those who manifest their excellence in their deeds. Also, since animals and children are not able to conduct virtuous lives, they are not capable of happiness, as defined by Aristotle.

Aristotle called virtues praiseworthy dispositions. Virtues consist of intellectual attributes, such as wisdom, understanding, sagacity, and healthy pride; and of moral ones, such as generosity, courage, tolerance, temperance, and gentleness. Moral virtue, according to the ancients, consisted of right aim and right habit. We can pursue our own happiness in pursuing ideal ends such as knowledge and self-improvement. Even virtue will not guarantee happiness, though. A person might be virtuous and yet suffer great misfortune. A person in such a circumstance could not be expected to be happy.

An individual may be a good person in the sense of being virtuous, but a good person does not always succeed in the pursuit of happiness, in making a good life for himself or herself. Virtue by itself does not suffice for the attainment of the ultimate good. There is a bit of luck or good fortune involved, according to Aristotle.

Aristotle wrote that happiness is a complete life, lived in accordance with virtue and attended by whatever moderate supply of external goods are necessary for good fortune (Adler, 1988). The life of people who are actively expressing virtue, that is, who enjoy doing noble actions, is intrinsically pleasant. Therefore, the life of virtuous people requires no superfluous pleasure but finds its own pleasure within itself. Aristotle maintains that to live well and to do well are the same as being happy.

Happiness requires external goods as well, since we cannot act nobly without the proper equipment. There are activities that can be carried out only with the help of friends, wealth, or political influence. Being born into a prosperous or otherwise good family was thought by Aristotle to add to happiness, as well as having children one can be proud of. Personal beauty may also be a source of happiness. A person who is repulsively ugly or who has worthless children and friends could hardly be considered happy. In addition to having a degree of external prosperity, a person needs a measure of good fortune to be happy; for instance, having good friends but then losing them through premature death would detract from one's happiness.

A person's happiness must be assessed in the completeness of her or his life. Life brings many vicissitudes so that a person who is prosperous at one time may suffer great misfortunes at another. When a person is thus buffeted by misfortune, he or she is bound to be unhappy. Still, Aristotle did not consider it reasonable to regard a person's happiness as wholly dependent on the person's good fortune. Although good fortune is a necessary ingredient in a complete human life, it is virtuous activities that constitute happiness, because they are more abiding than anything else about life. When a person is engaged fully and continuously in virtuous acts and contemplation, these pursuits will produce stability and will enable the person to bear with nobility any changes of fortune. Small misfortunes will not mar an individual's happiness, but a multitude of great ones might still overwhelm even a virtuous person, diminishing happiness and hindering the individual's normal activities. A person with moral excellence will bear even this calamity with calmness, with noble suffering. A truly wise and good person will bear with dignity whatever fortune sends and will make the best of his or her circumstances.

According to Aristotle, except for those whose capacity for virtue has been stunted, everyone has the ability to acquire the virtues that ordinarily lead to happiness. Since is it our activities that give life its character, then no virtuous person will be miserable, since this individual will avoid doing unworthy and mean things. Though without good fortune, this person will not be completely happy, he or she will at least not be miserable.

QUESTIONS: *Does happiness stem from feeling lucky and gratified? Was Aristotle correct in saying that happiness comes from living a morally virtuous and intellectual life?*

John Stuart Mill (1806–1873)

John Stuart Mill was a nineteenth-century British moral philosopher of the utilitarian school. For Mill, the main constituents of a satisfied life are tranquillity and excitement. If a person enjoys a great deal of tranquillity, he or she may then be content with only a little pleasure. If, on the other hand, an individual lives a life of excitement, that individual may accept a considerable amount of pain. In fact, these two attributes of happiness are compatible, since whenever a person has had too much of one, he or she generally desires some of the other. Only those who are lazy do not want some excitement and activity after an interval of repose. Likewise, there is something amiss with those who find tranquillity after a period of excitement to be dull rather than restful.

When people who are tolerably well off, in terms of their lot in life, do not find enough enjoyment to make life seem worth living, the cause is generally that they care for nobody but themselves. For those who have only selfish interests, excitement and interest in life fades as the person approaches death. On the other hand, those who have cultivated a fellow feeling with the rest of of humanity retain a lively interest in life and even the vigor of youth right up to their death. Genuinely affectionate personal relationships and a sincere interest in the public good are possible for every rightly brought-up human being.

According to Mill, next to selfishness, the principle cause of unhappiness in life is the lack of mental cultivation. A mind that has been exposed to knowledge and that has been taught to think and reason finds inexhaustible sources of interest everywhere. There is much in nature, art, poetry, history, and humanity's prospects for the future in which to become engrossed. However, a person might become uninterested in such things if she or he sought in them only the gratification of curiosity, rather than embracing knowledge with moral or human concern.

In a world in which there is so much to interest a person, so much to enjoy, and so much to correct and improve, everyone who has a moderate amount of moral and intellectual sensibility is capable of an enviable existence. Mill acknowledged that there are exceptions to this enviable existence, such as when happiness is marred by physical and mental suffering, including poverty, disease, and either enduring the death of those with whom our happiness is involved or being treated unkindly at the hands of our loved ones. Finally, discovering that one's friends or loved ones are worthless would be expected to detract from one's happiness.

Nevertheless, Mill (1987) was quite optimistic about the ability of humanity to improve the level of happiness for all humanity:

> No one whose opinion deserves a moment's consideration can doubt that most of the great positive evils of the world are in themselves removable, and will, if human affairs continue to improve, be in the end reduced within narrow limits. Poverty, in any sense implying suffering, may be completely extinguished by the wisdom of society, combined with the good sense and providence of individuals. Even that most intractable of enemies, disease, may be indefinitely reduced in dimensions by good physical and moral education, and proper control of noxious influences, while the progress of science holds out a promise for the future of still more direct conquest over this testable foe...[and] every mind sufficiently intelligent and generous to bear a part, however small and inconspicuous, in the endeavour will draw a noble enjoyment from the contest itself, which he would not for any bribe in the form of selfish indulgence consent to be without. (pp. 286–287)

Without question, it is possible to do without happiness, wrote Mill. Those who sacrifice their personal enjoyment of life in order to secure happiness for others or to increase happiness in the world are engaging in the highest virtue to be found in human existence. Paradoxically, it is the conscious ability to do without happiness that provides the best prospect of attaining it. This is the case because once a person decides that no matter what fate brings, the person intends to pursue his or her chosen ends; this conscious decision allows the person to be free of fear resulting from inescapable uncertainty about the future. Under these conditions, an individual does not have to be preoccupied with the evils of life and the fickleness of fortune.

According to Mill, the ethical principle of the golden rule of Jesus of Nazareth—to do to others as you would have them do to you and to love one's neighbor as oneself—also paves the road to happiness. To realize that one's own happiness and self-interest are intertwined with the good of humanity is to have gained true wisdom. This realization should make unthinkable any conduct that works against the general good of one's community.

QUESTION: *Does happiness mean having lots of fun and pleasure?*

Bertrand Russell (1872–1970)

Bertrand Russell was a British philosopher who was profoundly affected by the atrocities of World War I. With death so present and familiar, he acquired a new love for what is living. He decided that most human beings were unhappy and that they displaced their misery in destructive rages against convenient targets. The only way to create a good world would be to suffuse it with instinctive joy. Russell became suspicious of those who administered stern discipline, having become convinced that puritanism did not promote human happiness. A puritan education teaches children to meditate on their sins and shortcomings. Such a preoccupation with oneself limits happiness and can produce self-disgust. Instead, one should focus on external affairs, such as the state of the world, gaining knowledge, and paying attention to loved ones.

Over the course of his life, Russell observed in himself changes in his attitude about what would make him happy. As a young man, he wanted to be unencumbered so that he could embark on personal adventure. He desired to think his own thoughts, select his own house, and choose his own friends without having to consider tradition, his elders, or anything else except his own tastes. Later, Russell concluded that such a stance in life requires boundless vitality. As a young man, he had felt strong enough to stand alone, without any kind of outside support.

As an older man, Russell no longer found enchantment in the notion of standing alone. Rather than adventure, he longed for the companionship of his children, his hearth and home, and the prosperity of his beloved country. The very ordinariness of these desires staved off loneliness and separateness, since he was embedded by his longings in the norms of his culture.

Russell (1951) decided that aging makes us feel vulnerable and afraid. Motivated by anxiety, we become conciliatory and endeavor to win the approval and affection of others. We seek "some human warmth to keep away the chill of the cold universe" (p. 220). Not only do we fear decrepitude and death, but also we feel fear on a metaphysical scale. With advancing age, we become more aware of the major evils that can befall a person. We dread such things as the cruelty of human nature, the betrayal of friends, and the loss of loved ones through death.

Russell warned that enjoyment of domestic bliss as well as of the other little joys of life could sap the will and destroy courage. An awareness of human folly and wickedness should be a sobering reminder not to let our idealism falter. It is sometimes necessary to sacrifice indulgence in the softer pleasures of life in order to protect and promote the advancement of civilization. Russell proclaimed that he did not live for human happiness but instead focused on the life of the mind and its value to civilization. He took an abiding interest in furthering the emergence of humanity away from a brutish existence and considered this purpose to be the ultimate pursuit that a person should have.

In 1930, Russell published *The Conquest of Happiness,* a book consisting of commonsense advice as to what an individual can do to overcome temperamental causes of unhappiness, as opposed to what can be done to further happiness by changes in social and economic systems. Russell believed that the cause of unhappiness was embedded partly in the social system and partly in the psychology of the individual. As to the latter, unhappiness is due largely to erroneous views of the world, misguided morals, and mistaken habits of life, all of which tend to eliminate a person's natural zest for living and the appetite for the things that naturally bring pleasure.

A life out of balance produces unhappiness. A person who wants power above all is unhappy and even disturbed, whereas keeping power within its proper bound may add greatly to happiness. Russell suspected that such one-sidedness comes from being deprived in childhood of some normal satisfaction, with the deprivation then becoming disproportionately important to the person.

Russell identified two kinds of happiness: one animal and the other spiritual. The former stems from the heart, and the latter from the head. The first kind of happiness is based on physical vigor. Anyone who does something that engages all his or her abilities and that is considered important by both the person and society is bound to be happy. "Pleasures of achievement demand difficulties such that beforehand success seems doubtful although in the end it is usually achieved" (pp. 114–115). The pleasure of work is available to anyone who can develop some specialized skill.

A sense of well-being can also have spiritual origins. Fundamental happiness depends more than anything else on a friendly concern for people and things. Such interest in others is affectionate yet neither possessive nor demanding. To like and enjoy people without effort is perhaps the greatest of all sources of well-being. An interest in things is important, though not as relevant to personal happiness as is an enjoyment of people. Belief in a cause is a reliable source of happiness for a great many people. An individual's interests should be as wide as possible and of a friendly, rather than a hostile, nature.

➤ PSYCHOANALYTIC PERSPECTIVE ON HAPPINESS

Since Freud's focus was on psychological problems rather than on healthy, contented living, it would be difficult to say what constituted happiness from the psychoanalytic viewpoint. Certainly, human beings were thought to be better off when they had achieved a balance between the pleasure principle and the reality principle. In other words, when the ego is able to achieve a reduction in tension produced by the unconscious drives of the id and when at the same time it is able to satisfy the superego demands, the person achieves a homeostasis that is experienced as satisfying.

Freud maintained that the healthy adult enjoys both love and work. Sexual release enhances happiness and mental health, whereas repression of the sexual drive is a source of psychopathology. Freud believed that we delude ourselves as to the nature of our unhappiness by repressing painful feelings (Myers, 1992). Repressed feelings sap energy needed for productive life pursuits and sometimes manifest themselves in symptoms of mental disorder.

Alfred Adler (1931/1992) believed that through cooperation with others, a person's work life, friendships, and love life can be successfully negotiated. People who lack fellow feelings or social interest have as their goal a fictitious personal superiority, so that their triumphs are meaningful only to themselves. Adler points out that even genius is defined as supreme *usefulness,* so that only when a person's life is recognized by others as having significance is he or she regarded as a genius. The true meaning of life is expressed by making a contribution to the whole. The person who meets the problems of human life successfully acts on her or his understanding that the fundamental meaning of life is interest in and cooperation with other people. Everything that the individual does is guided by the interests of fellow human beings; and where difficulties are encountered, they are overcome in ways that do not impinge on the welfare of others. Happiness resides not in asking, "What can I get out of life?" but rather in asking, "What can I contribute to further human well-being?"

This cooperation with others is not accomplished at the sacrifice of individual development. In selecting a contribution that the person would like to make to further the good of society, the individual is prompted to develop himself or herself. In equipping himself or herself to achieve the particular goal that has been set, this person will develop personal abilities and will learn to solve the problems of life.

➤ HUMANISTIC PERSPECTIVE ON HAPPINESS

The humanists ascribe more lofty motives to human beings than do the psychoanalysts. The key figures in humanistic psychology share a belief in the individual's inherent self-actualizing tendency. Maslow and Rogers thought that human beings have an inherent drive for a high level of personal and interpersonal functioning. Buscaglia (1972) also wrote that perhaps the only peace and joy in life lies in the pursuit and development of one's inborn potential.

Abraham Maslow's self-actualized person characteristically has "peak experiences." These experiences represent moments of bliss for which Maslow (1962) himself considered the word "happiness" too weak to be an adequate description. These were moments of great joy when all doubts, fears, and inhibitions were left behind. Although peak experiences are always transient, they may leave the person with gifts of seeing life in a new perspective and of knowing the degree of happiness of which human beings are capable.

Peak experiences cannot be brought about at will. Maslow thought that, as with happiness, peak experiences are brought about indirectly. Both are byproducts of doing a good job at a worthy task in which the individual is invested. Seeking out the highest values in the world helps to produce or strengthen them in us. Maslow speculated that almost any situation in which perfection may be attained, hope may be fulfilled, perfect gratification may be reached, or affairs may go smoothly, can produce a peak experience.

Whereas a healthy human being has a strong will, that is, the ability to develop a purpose and to focus energy on its accomplishment, in order to have peak experiences, a person also must be able to relax the will and to become receptive to new experiences. Those who do not like to encounter anything out of the ordinary may brush off peak experiences. These experiences are deeply moving, such as when people shed tears at the happy ending of a movie, have goose bumps during an exceptional musical performance, or feel ecstasy over some especially fine acting in a play. Some treasure such moments for their emotional and intellectual impact, whereas others might find the loss of composure suffered as peak experiences take hold of them embarrassing.

To some, the idea of "letting go" suggests that a person's egotism or pride must be broken, that the individual must surrender and be passive so that he or she will be open to a new experience, such as in some forms of religious conversion. For Maslow, it is only unhealthy pride or arrogance that must be gotten through, whereas healthy pride goes very well with healthy receptivity. Both a clear intention (an expression of the will) and a state of trusting expectation are necessary for creative endeavor, good thinking or theorizing, effective relating to others, enjoyable sexual relations, and peak experiences.

Maslow's subjects who reported on their peak experiences seemed to identify striving for excellence or perfection as an aspect of such experiences. Robert M. Pirsig (1974), in his inquiry into values when writing *Zen and the Art of Motorcycle Maintenance*, expressed a similar sentiment. He examined the concept of "quality," by which he meant "excellence," "worth," and "goodness" (p. 208). He further explained "that care and Quality are internal and external aspects of the same thing. A person who sees Quality and feels it as he works is a person who cares. A person who cares about what he sees and does is a person who's bound to have some characteristics of Quality" (p. 247). For Pirsig, care is the means through which quality is obtained.

Many psychologists work with people to get them to refocus on the joy of the moment. To ruminate excessively about past mistakes or to occupy oneself exclusively with anticipation of the future is to miss the opportunity to be present, to immerse oneself in the pleasures of the moment. Humanist Leo Buscaglia (1972) provides a perspective on enjoying life by living in the moment through relating a Buddhist *koan*, or paradox, that tells the story of a monk who is running from a hungry bear:

> He runs to a cliff and is required to jump or be eaten. As he falls, he grabs hold of a small clump of wood extending from the wall of the cliff. He looks down to find a starving tiger awaiting his fall. At that moment from the side of the cliff, come two hungry gophers who start at once to gnaw at the clump of wood from which he is suspended. There he is, hungry bear above, starving tigers below, and gophers to the side. Looking beyond the gophers, he sees a bush of wild strawberries and a giant, red, ripe, juicy one facing him, ready to be eaten. He plucks it and puts it in his mouth and eats it, exclaiming, "How delicious!" (p. 107)

Carl Rogers (1961) believed that when human beings are inwardly free to move in any direction they like, they tend to move in the direction of the good life. A characteristic of the good life involves an increasing tendency to live fully in each moment, meaning that there is an absence of rigidity or of the imposition of structure on one's experience. Instead, a person living the good life discovers the structure of what is going on at the moment in the process of living the experience. There is a flexibility about the person leading the good life, a mature life. With this sensitive openness to the world, the individual can develop his or her ability to form new relationships with the environment. This responsiveness to the environment is creative, spontaneous, and harmonious.

Another quality of the good life is an increasing openness to experience. This openness is the direct opposite of defensiveness, which is a natural response to threat. We defend ourselves by distorting and denying reality. A healthy person does not feel the need to do this and can thus take in the outside world without distorting it. Such openness also applies to an awareness of one's own thoughts and feelings.

A person moving toward the good life has an increasing trust in allowing what feels right to be a competent guide to behavior. Since this person is open to experience, all the information from her or his sense impressions, memory, previous learning, and internal states can be integrated and used to inform the person of an appropriate course of action. The individual is able to put more trust in her or his inner knowing, not because the inner knowing is infallible but because it is fully open to the consequences of her or his behavior, so that the behavior can be changed if the action proves to be less than satisfying.

Carl Rogers (1961) also discussed how the good life is related to happiness:

> I believe it will have become evident why, for me, adjectives such as happy, contented, blissful, enjoyable, do not seem quite appropriate to any general description of this process I have called the good life, even though the person in this process would experience each one of these feelings at appropriate times. But the adjectives which seem more generally fitting are adjectives such as enriching, exciting, rewarding, challenging, meaningful. This process of the good life is not, I am convinced, a life for the faint-hearted. It involves the stretching and growing of becoming more and more of one's potentialities. It involves the courage to be. It means launching oneself fully into the stream of life. Yet the deeply exciting thing about human beings is that when the individual is inwardly free, he chooses as the good life this process of becoming. (pp. 195–196)

➤ COGNITIVE BEHAVIORAL VIEW OF HAPPINESS

Aaron Beck (1976) attributes euphoria or excitation to the perception or expectation of gain. Forming new friendships, getting tangible objects such as new clothes, or attaining a goal—all improve our situation by adding something positive to it. Tangible objects are perceived as extensions of ourselves, so that we feel enhanced in much the same manner as we do when we receive a compliment. Expectation of future enrichments also leads to immediate pleasure. Such anticipatory thinking may explain how optimistic individuals maintain an ongoing state of happiness. A person may make the most of anticipating a future event and may even elaborate on the future prospects, so that an escalating level of pleasure results. For instance, suppose that a student gets her photograph in the school newspaper, along with a piece of artwork she created in class. Her initial enjoyment is magnified when she imagines other students' reading the paper and noticing her photograph. She might imagine that some of her professors will see the newspaper or will visit the local art gallery. She might even become known through this bit of publicity, so that somehow her career might be launched.

Whether or not the person experiences happiness depends on the meaning attached to a particular situation or object. Positive evaluations result in corresponding elevations in mood. Any event or idea that represents a meaningful addition to one's life is sufficient to produce happiness. Once an individual becomes aware of those things that bring about the experience of pleasure through enhancing his or her situation, the person develops an active desire to replicate the experience. This principle has been useful in helping depressed people overcome their inertia. Even modest efforts generally bring about an improvement in one's situation and thus an elevation in one's mood.

QUESTION: *Does happiness arise from being good-looking, popular, and intelligent?*

➤ Who Is Happy, and Why?

In the past couple of decades, psychologists have looked for research evidence to support or refute existing notions as to just what is the royal road to happiness. The remainder to this chapter reports on such findings. Whereas dozens of studies will be cited, much of the evidence comes from social psychologist David Myers (1991; 1992), who integrated and reported on a large number of studies conducted during the 1980s. The research reported on by Myers includes a sample of sixteen countries: the United States, Canada, Great Britain, Ireland, Spain, Portugal, France, Belgium, West Germany, Hungary, Italy, Greece, Japan, the Netherlands, Denmark, and Luxembourg. Hundreds of thousands of people were selected through careful sampling procedures. There were 169,776 interviews conducted.

For the purpose of research, happiness or well-being has generally been defined as a pervasive sense that life is good, meaningful, and satisfying. The researchers considered these two questions: (1) What are the experiences and circumstances that enable people to be happy? (This question refers to the situation in which people find themselves.) (2) What traits and attitudes enable some people to experience well-being but others not? (This question refers to the disposition of the person.) In general, people gave positive reports on their perceived level of well-being: 80 percent said that they are from "very" to at least "fairly" happy (Myers, 1991). About one-third of Americans reported that they were "very happy."

Do Life Circumstances Create Happy People?

AGE   Are the young, the middle-aged, or the old happier? There is remarkably little variation in the level of satisfaction with life as a function of age (Myers, 1992). Key factors influencing subjective well-being may shift somewhat as people grow older; for instance, work becomes less important, health more so, but people's average level of happiness tends to remain remarkably stable over the life span.

Cameron (1972) also found that young adults, the middle-aged, and the aged reported the same degree of life satisfaction. However, the middle-aged were considered by the other two groups to be the happiest. Nevertheless, adults over 30 in the United States generally would prefer to be somewhat younger (Kastenbaum et al., 1972).

Among the elderly, the degree of activity and social engagement is positively related to their reports of satisfaction with life (Havinghurst, Neugarten, & Tobin, 1968). There was no empirical support for the notion of a "midlife crisis" or the "empty-nest" syndrome. Most men in their midforties exhibit no decline in happiness, no increase in the incidence of suicide, no increase in career dissatisfaction, and no increase in divorce rate. Most divorces occur when the partners are in their twenties. Most mothers are glad to have their children grow up, leave home, marry, and begin careers (Neugarten et al., 1963).

GENDER   What makes for happiness in women and men? Since women are treated for depressive disorders, anxiety disorders, and phobic disorders about twice as often as men, we might expect that women are less happy on the average than are men. However, no difference has been found between men and women on their level of happiness and global well-being (Myers, 1992), despite very substantial objective differences in career opportunities, personal income, and opportunities for self-expression throughout the industrial societies included in the study. Furthermore, whereas women suffer more so than do men from the previously mentioned mental disorders, men have a fivefold greater risk of suffering alcoholism than do women.

Women have been steadily entering the workforce. Myers reported that in 1890, one in seven married women were in the workforce; in 1940, one in four were employed; and in 1990, that number rose to six in ten. Myers (1992) found that employed married women tended to be only slightly happier than wives who were not employed, apparently because both roles are similar in the level of satisfaction they provide. Even though housework is routine and potentially boring, so are many low-skilled and low-paying jobs.

The strain from the dual roles of wage earner and motherhood does hinder some women's sense of well-being, according to Myers. Even so, working wives report feeling neither more nor less understood by their husbands than do unemployed wives, and husbands of either employed or unemployed wives do not differ in their reported marital satisfaction.

Many women and men believe that women's moods fluctuate along with their menstrual cycles. During the days prior to, and in some cases a few days after onset of, menstruation, women are supposed to experience increased irritability, tension, tiredness, or depression. Researchers have looked for the alleged mood fluctuations in large groups of women and have been unable to find evidence that such changes exist (e.g., Alagna & Hamilton, 1986; Kato & Ruble, 1992). Women's irritability, loneliness, fatigue, and depression did not increase during their premenstrual and menstrual phases, although the women themselves were convinced that their moods did fluctuate according to the cycle. Apparently, the women's belief in the effect of menstruation on mood causes **confirmation bias.**

Confirmation bias occurs when we notice only those occurrences that provide evidence that our beliefs are correct and when we fail either to look for or to notice **disconfirming evidence.** Disconfirming evidence is any observation that could show our existing belief to be false. Suppose it is our job to hire employees for a large firm. We find that of the fifty employees we hired last year, forty have remained and are doing a good job. We may conclude that our hiring strategy is working out well. However, we have failed to discover how those prospective employees that we did *not* hire might have worked out. Perhaps we could contact them a year after rejecting them and investigate whether our competitors have hired them and whether those whom we did not hire have worked out well somewhere else! Similarly, if a woman notices that she is feeling hostile, she might ask herself whether she is anywhere near time for her menstrual period. If she is, she is likely to smile grimly and think, I *knew* it. If she is nowhere near the expected place in her cycle, she may offer an alternative explanation and not count this episode as disconfirming evidence for her first hypothesis. Thus, women's perceptions of their own emotional ups and downs are influenced by their expectations and menstrual myths (Parlee, 1973).

Ethnicity There were no differences in blacks or whites on level of happiness. African Americans do not exhibit lower self-esteem than do white Americans. Many studies conclude that African Americans have levels of self-esteem equal to or higher than that of Caucasians (Crocker & Major, 1989). People of color may suffer somewhat less depression than whites.

People from disadvantaged groups (whether because of gender, ethnicity, or disability) tend to maintain their self-esteem by valuing things at which they excel. They also are likely to attribute their problems to prejudice. The result of blaming external causes for one's lack of success is that one's self-esteem isn't damaged by the unsuccessful outcome. Finally, disadvantaged groups compare themselves with others who are like themselves.

A Sound Body Disabled individuals describe themselves as no less happy than do able-bodied people. Likewise, people describe their disabled friends as about as happy as their able-bodied friends. Argyle (1987) found that on a happiness scale from 1 to 9, where 1 is "not at all happy" and 9 is "very happy," the average rating of people in our society turns out to be approximately 6.5.

People who have been involved in accidents in which they become paraplegic are understandably distraught immediately after the event, but a year later they rank at 6.0 on the same happiness scale—nearly as high as the societal average. Their level of happiness dropped only about one-half point!

Conversely, those who won the lottery were quite elated immediately after winning, but a year later, their happiness level on the same scale was 6.8. Thus, happiness appears to change very little after people adjust to either devastating or delightful life events.

MONEY   Does money buy happiness? We all know that a person "who has everything" may feel sad and that another person "who has nothing" may be content and happy. According to research, Americans *believe* that if they had more money, they would be happier; that is, they believe that there is a relationship between well-being and being well-off (Myers, 1991). Americans at every income level, except at the very top, insist that just 10 to 20 percent more income would make them happier (Strumpel, 1976).

This tendency to believe that money is a major source of happiness is on the increase. In 1967, 83 percent of Americans agreed that a meaningful life philosophy would make them happy, whereas 41 percent felt that being very well-off would make them happy. In 1990, 40 percent felt that a meaningful life philosophy would make them happy, whereas 75 percent felt that being very well-off financially would make them happy (Myers, 1991). Over these decades, greater importance has been placed on achieving money, power, and status, while the emphasis on altruism and other social concerns has declined (Astin et al., 1992; Astin, Green, & Korn, 1987).

There is a positive correlation between wealth and happiness, up to a point. However, once the basic life needs are met, there are diminishing returns. The second $50,000 doesn't do much, compared with the first $50,000 in earnings (Myers, 1991). Beyond poverty, increased wealth doesn't increase happiness (Argyle, 1987). On average, wealthy people are only marginally happier than those in the middle class. The problem with money is that in this era of voracious consumption, most of us find a way to spend all of it and come out short, no matter what our income. Complaints about not having enough money are commonplace, even among affluent people earning six-figure incomes.

Even so, the less expensive (and generally more involving) a leisure activity is, the happier people are while doing it. Most people get a greater sense of well-being from gardening than from steering a power boat and are happier after talking to a friend than after watching television (Myers, 1992).

Does the happiness of people rise with their affluence? Galbraith (1958) wrote in *The Affluent Society* that in 1957, the per capita income was $7,000. In 1990, the per capita income was $14,000 (Myers, 1991). Yet the level of happiness has been constant since 1957. In that year, 35 percent reported themselves "very happy," whereas in 1987, 32 percent reported themselves "very happy." Moreover, the percentage of Americans who are happy with their financial situation has dropped since 1957, from 42 percent to 30 percent in 1990. Over the last thirty years, there has also been an increase in the proportion of delinquent and suicidal youth coming from more affluent families. Younger adults now more so than in the past report being disabled by depression.

Why hasn't increased wealth brought happiness? One explanation can be derived from the adaptation-level phenomenon, which refers to the tendency of people to adapt to a given level of stimulation and thus to notice and react only to changes from that level. Happiness is relative to our prior experience.

A second explanation comes from social comparison theory. Happiness is relative to others' attainments. We define ourselves in part by making comparisons with others, according to what Leon Festinger (1954) proposed in his social comparison theory. Festinger maintained that when people are uncertain about their abilities or opinions because objective information is not available, they evaluate themselves by drawing comparisons with others whom they see as similar to themselves. In our effort to evaluate ourselves with regard to our taste in music, or our value on the job market, or our athletic ability, most of us wouldn't compare ourselves with royalty, Olympic gold medalists, Donald Trump, or others with whom we have little in common. To make accurate self-appraisals, people look toward others who are similar in relevant ways (Goethals & Darley, 1977; Miller, 1984; Wheeler, Koestner, & Driver, 1982).

We may feel overshadowed by the success of others and so experience social comparison jealousy, a mixture of feelings that includes envy, resentment, and a loss of self-esteem (Salovey & Rodin, 1984). When those whom we know surpass us in ways that are important to our self-concept, we feel envious. When we are surpassed in ways that are not important to our self-concept, we can take pride in the achievements of those close to us (Tesser & Collin, 1988; Test et al., 1988).

Happiness can be viewed as related to both accomplishments and expectations. It can be represented as an equation, with "attainments" in the numerator and "expectations" in the denominator. We might enjoy several accomplishments, yet not realize an increase in happiness if our expectations as to how much we *should* accomplish keep pace with our actual attainments. In fact, we could be better off but *less* happy if our expectations rise faster than do our attainments. One way to enhance happiness would then be to lower our expectations. Another solution would be to accumulate accomplishments, without allowing expectations to outpace our attainments.

$$\text{Happiness} = \frac{\textbf{attainments}}{\textbf{expectations}}$$

INTELLIGENCE Intelligence has been shown to predict the ability of children from disadvantaged environments to select prosocial and work ethic values from the mainstream culture. Intelligence also correlates with outstanding achievement (Terman et al., 1925). However, researchers have not found an association between IQ scores and happiness. Educational attainment also appears to be unrelated to subjective well-being (Diener, 1984). Happiness is independent of academic intelligence. There is no relationship between grades or IQ and people's emotional well-being (Goleman, 1995).

COMMUNITY   According to Freedman (1978), when asked where they would most like to live, people show a clear preference for the stereotype of the tranquil, pastoral life believed to exist in rural areas. However, when actual reported happiness is related to community types, people living in urban, suburban, and rural areas are found to be equally happy.

PARENTHOOD   Children can be a tremendous source of joy and fulfillment, but they are also a major cause of worry, headaches, and hassles. Compared with childless couples, parents worry more and have more marital problems (Argyle, 1987). Even so, people who have children are neither more nor less happy than people without children. Several studies have actually shown a marked increase in marital happiness when the last child leaves home (e.g., Feldman, 1964; Gilford & Bengtson, 1979; Myers, 1992); however, other studies show a more mixed picture, with some marriages getting better after the child-rearing stage but others getting worse (e.g., Swenson, Eskew, & Kohlhepp, 1981).

Predictors of Well-Being: The Traits of Happy People

HEALTH   Good physical health is moderately correlated with subjective well-being (Diener, 1984). Physical health would seem to be a vital component of happiness, yet Myers (1992) discovered that people who have serious, disabling health conditions aren't as unhappy as might be thought. In addition, Freedman (1978) contends that good health alone doesn't account for personal happiness, because people tend to take good health for granted.

Moderate exercise can make people feel strong and healthy. Those who begin an exercise program find that their mood improves and that they feel more confident, have an improved body image, and have a sense of self-mastery (Ornstein & Sobel, 1989). People report more positive feelings

"Ah-ha! You are not happy."

when interrupted while doing something active (Myers, 1992). One study indicated that 3 percent of people who were asked to report their mood while watching television reported experiencing flow (a very positive emotional state), whereas 39 percent reported feeling apathetic. For those who were actively engaged in a hobby or an artistic pursuit, the pattern was just the opposite, with 47 percent reporting flow and only 4 percent indicating that they were experiencing apathy (Massimini & Massimo, 1988). In terms of play activities, it turns out that people who are engaged in the most costly leisure activities report the least happiness (Myers, 1991).

PERSONALITY   Personality refers to enduring patterns of behavior, over time and across situations (Chapter 7). A great deal of evidence suggests that happiness does not depend on external circumstances, such as having a nice house, good friends, and an enjoyable job, as much as it does on internal factors, such as one's outlook on life and personality dimensions. For this reason, the best predictor of a person's future happiness is his or her past happiness (Myers, 1992). Other sources have confirmed that there is a very high correlation between people's reports of *positive affect* in the moment and their general level of happiness as an ongoing trait (MAACL). The limited influence of life events was apparent in the study previously mentioned that found only marginal differences between lottery winners and quadriplegics in overall happiness (Argyle, 1987). Just as the best predictor of happiness is the person's level of happiness in the past, likewise, the best predictor of future grades is past grades, and the best predictor of violent tendencies is past violent behavior. Thus, with human beings, there seems to be a remarkable degree of stability in both internal states and external behaviors.

SELF-ESTEEM   Happy people like themselves. Self-esteem is one of the best predictors of happiness with life in general. According to Myers (1992), people with high self-esteem "are less vulnerable to ulcers and insomnia, less likely to abuse drugs, more independent of pressures to conform, and more persistent at difficult tasks" (p. 108).

Self-Esteem and Social Class. Among children there is virtually no relationship between social class and self-esteem. In general, people tend to gauge their self-worth by comparing themselves with others. Children are likely to believe that their external environment is homogeneous and that others are like themselves. However, among adults, those of the higher social classes at times score higher in sense of self-esteem than those of the lower classes (Rosenberg & Pearlin, 1978). Those of lower social class may maintain their self-esteem by ascribing their relative failure in life to barriers imposed by others. They may also devalue material gains and value other characteristics that they do possess, such as friends.

Self-Esteem and Educational Attainment.   It has been reported that the overall self-esteem of college graduates was no higher than that of high school graduates (Luck & Heiss, 1972), again suggesting that people compare themselves with others in the same category.

In Western societies, life satisfaction is evaluated in terms of the extent to which one achieves one's ideals. Traditionally, the similarity between a person's actual self-concept and ideal self-concept has been used as an index of life satisfaction. The more similar they are, the more satisfied people feel about themselves. Ogilvie (1987; 1988) proposed another measure of personal satisfaction, which looks at the discrepancy between one's actual self-concept (the way that one sees oneself) and one's undesirable self-concept (the personality characteristics and behaviors that one considers undesirable in oneself). The greater the difference between the actual and undesirable self-concepts, the more satisfied people would feel about themselves.

In a study with college students, Ogilvie (1987) found that life satisfaction can be predicted better by the discrepancy between actual and undesired self-concepts than by the similarity between actual and ideal self-concepts. Ogilvie suggested that this finding may indicate that "the implicit standard individuals use to assess their well-being is how close (or how distant) they are from subjectively being like their most negative images of themselves" (p. 383). The reason that life satisfaction may not be predicted as well from comparing actual and ideal self-concepts as has been thought may be explained by the discovery that the actual self may, in fact, be closer to the ideal self than has been previously assumed. People who are well adjusted tend to view themselves as more attractive, more intelligent, and the like than they really are, as assessed by objective measures and the opinions of others (Brown, 1991; Dunning, Meyerowitz, & Holzberg, 1989; Taylor & Brown, 1988). A better term for the actual self, then, would be the *perceived* self.

This favorably distorted view of ourselves has been referred to by social psychologists as the **self-serving bias,** which is present in nondepressed people and helps to keep them happy. Self-serving bias can be defined as the tendency to perceive oneself favorably. It involves taking credit for good things that happen and shirking responsibility for negative events. It seems that we function best when we have a slightly distorted view of reality.

PERSONAL CONTROL   Happy people believe that they choose their destinies. This finding relates directly to the locus of control discussion in Chapter 8. People with an internal locus of control generally achieve more in school and work, cope better with stress, and live more happily than people who believe that outside forces have relatively more control over the course of their lives. Research by Campbell (1981) found that of those studied, 15 percent felt in control of their lives *and* felt satisfied with themselves. This group had exceptionally positive feelings of happiness, being more than twice as likely as others to say that they were very happy and having three in five of them reporting this level of happiness.

Older people who are confined to nursing homes tend to do better when they have some control over what happens to them (Rodin, 1988). In an experiment in which one group of senior citizens was allowed to have an influence on their environment, that group became more alert, active, and happy than the more passive group. In addition, when old people feel that they have a purpose in life, their well-being flourishes (Baum & Boxley, 1983).

The benefits of being a hardy person (Chapter 8) are largely accounted for by an internal locus of control (Cohen & Edwards, 1989). Psychologically, there is a big difference between having a lot to handle but still feeling on top of things, and conversely, feeling overwhelmed and unable to cope with what we are expected to handle.

Even though we don't actually control everything that happens to us, it works well to operate as though we do. Then, whenever we run into a circumstance in which something "just happens," we can remind ourselves that occasionally we do not control the outcome of an event. Developing the ability to "let go" under these circumstances and then to turn right back to managing our other affairs as though they were practically under our complete control, works very well as a life strategy.

OPTIMISM   Happy people are hope-filled. A *Psychology Today* survey (Freedman, 1978) revealed that although people might have jobs that they don't like, may have less income than they would like, and may not be in the relationships they want, if they have *great expectations* of getting these things, they are likely to be happy. Conversely, a cardinal characteristic of the thinking of depressed people is the belief that their situation is hopeless and that the prospects for things improving in the future are dim.

Research by Weiner (1986) showed that well-adjusted people attribute success to *internal* causes, that is, to their ability and effort; and that they attribute failure to *external* and uncontrollable causes, such as task difficulty and luck. People who take responsibility for both successes and failures are likely to feel pride after success but to be vulnerable to feelings of shame after failure, when they attribute those outcomes to their own lack of ability or effort, rather than to external factors. These different kinds of attributions can have important motivational and emotional consequences when people explain their performance to themselves.

Weiner also noted that people can attribute outcomes to either *stable* or *unstable* factors, and to either *controllable* or *uncontrollable* factors. When individuals attribute an outcome to stable factors, that is, to factors that do not change from one moment to the next, they raise and lower their hopes according to the outcome. However, when they attribute the same outcome to unstable factors such as effort or luck, their hopes for the future are relatively unaffected by this particular outcome. For instance, if our study partner's poor performance on the first exam of the semester is attributed to his or her lack of ability, we may be alarmed and conclude that we aren't going to receive much benefit from further study with this person. If the same poor grade is attributed to our partner's severe cold during the week prior to the exam, we should have no such misgivings about the prospects for future study sessions. Finally, when people attribute negative outcomes to factors within another person's control such as a lack of effort, they become angry. When they attribute these same outcomes to uncontrollable factors such as a lack of ability, they tend to react with pity or sympathy (Weiner, Graham, & Chandler, 1982).

Psychologist Martin Seligman (1990) is well-known for his research on learned helplessness, depression, and optimism. As had Weiner, Seligman concluded that our **explanatory style** has a great deal to do with our characteristic level of optimism. Explanatory style refers to the way we habitually explain to ourselves why events happen. An optimistic explanatory style can protect us against depression, raise our level of achievement, and enhance our physical well-being. A person with an optimistic style explains negative life events as if the event happened for external reasons (it's not about me), is a temporary setback, and is limited in scope.

Pessimists explain unfortunate occurrences in a manner that is systematically more permanent, pervasive, and personal. Suppose a major client pulls his or her business out of the pessimist's firm. The pessimist would be less likely than the optimist to start thinking about how to woo the client back, since the pessimist views the situation as permanent. The unfortunate event is also seen by the pessimist as "signaling" the possible loss of other clients and perhaps is the result of some fatal flaw in the firm's operation, thus setting off a cascade of negative emotions within the pessimist. Finally, the pessimist will tend to blame himself or herself, rather than looking for a more benign rationale for the loss of the client.

For good events, the situation is reversed: The pessimist expects them to be temporary and unlikely to be repeated. For example, the gain of a prestigious new account is seen as a fluke: "These kinds of things don't usually happen to me." "Why would they want *me* to service their account?" "How long can I expect to hang onto such a great account?" Pessimists would also see the gaining of a new client as limited to this one positive event and as not particularly a result of their own doing.

Optimistic people tend to behave differently and fare better in stressful situations than do those who are more pessimistic (Scheier & Carver, 1985; Scheier, Weintraub, & Carver, 1986). Optimists are likely to focus more on the problem and to generate and then to try possible solutions. They are also more likely to seek help from others than are pessimists. Optimists have a higher expectation of being successful in resolving the problem, and they don't give up at the first sign of a setback (Carver & Scheier, 1987; Peterson & Barrett, 1987). In other words, optimists use a variety of methods to resist helplessness. Pessimists are more prone to getting caught up in the emotions aroused by the situation rather than concentrating on how to solve the problem. They disengage from the problem, thus reducing the likelihood that it will get resolved. In sum, optimists tend to be problem-focused rather than emotion-focused; the reverse is true for pessimists.

Whereas the past twenty years of research have shown that a pessimistic style of thinking in children and young adults makes them more vulnerable to depression, quite the reverse may be true of adults beyond age 65 (Isaacowitz & Seligman, 1998). It may be that realistic acceptance of end-of-life issues, such as the death of a friend or spouse, as permanent and something that one cannot control, is an adaptive strategy for seniors.

Seligman (1990) agreed that there are times when pessimism is a good strategy. When the cost of failure in the situation is high, such as failing to maintain the brakes or other important features of our car or thinking that we can drive after drinking alcohol, it's best to be a pessimist. Unrealistic optimists can fail to take precautions: Those who don't practice safe sex expose themselves to the risk of developing AIDS; those who don't wear seat belts are at greater risk of fatality in case of a car accident; and those who don't study risk failure in college. Pessimism is also the preferred strategy when we want to appear sympathetic over the misfortunes of others. At such times, we should not try to get those suffering a setback to look immediately at the optimistic possibilities in the situation.

In most situations, however, optimism is the preferred strategy. High degrees of pessimism are associated with impaired immune activity and increased illness (Rodin, 1988), even when the pessimists were no more depressed or sicker to begin with than were the optimists. A confident attitude, on the other hand, promotes health (Ornstein & Sobel, 1989). The optimistic beliefs we have about our own health can be more important than the reality of our situation.

Cognitive therapy has been quite successful in teaching depressed people new explanatory styles, although there is some controversy over the benefits of teaching people to look for external sources to blame for mishaps. Whereas Seligman has no problem encouraging people to view bad events as temporary and confined to a specific aspect of their lives, he as more trouble with teaching people to externalize the causes of these events. Psychologists generally try to help people to see how they participated in the outcomes of their lives in order to help them recognize that they might change things to bring about better results. In general, assuming personal responsibility for what happens in our lives is an effective strategy, as we look for ways to actively engage problems in order to remove them. Optimism can be associated with the projection of blame, a defense mechanism that tends to stunt personal growth and hamper one's ability to negotiate successful relationships with others. With these cautions in mind, Seligman proposed that perhaps only depressed people should be encouraged to externalize the causes of their misfortunes, because depressed people tend to assume too much responsibility for unfavorable occurrences.

EXTROVERSION Optimism tends to breed sociability, which in turn predicts happiness. Happy people are outgoing (Emmons & Deiner, 1985). Extroverts are sociable, active, outgoing, and optimistic; they enjoy the company of others. Introverts tend to be passive, quiet, careful, and unsociable. This personality dimension, one's tendency to be introverted or extroverted, seems to be largely inherited. Extroverts are simply temperamentally more cheerful and high-spirited (Costa & McCrae, 1988).

Extroverts are likely to have a larger circle of friends than introverts, which is in itself a predictor of happiness. Social support is less available to an introverted person, because he or she is not likely to have made the effort to cultivate and maintain friendships. Extroverts experience more affection (Myers, 1992); they report finding more meaning in life (Addad, 1987); they tend to interpret stressful events as challenges (Gallagher, 1990); they respond better to efforts to elevate their mood (Larsen & Ketelaar, 1989; 1991); and they are simply happier than are introverts (Argyle & Lu, 1990; Furnham & Brewin, 1990).

SOCIAL ACTIVITY AND SOCIAL SUPPORT People who are content with their friendship networks and those who are socially active report above-average levels of happiness (Cooper, Okamura, & Gurka, 1992; Diener, 1984). Apparently endorphins (Chapter 8) are released as a result of the pleasure of social contact.

In contrast, people troubled by loneliness tend to be very unhappy (Argyle, 1987). The individualism of Western culture is implicated in loneliness and depression (Seligman, 1990). Today, people are lonelier, more homicidal, and more likely to divorce. In 1940, 8 percent of adults lived alone, whereas in 1988, 24 percent lived alone. In 1990, 28 percent were single-parent families. This is an unfortunate situation, since close relationships (where there is self-disclosure) predict happiness (Myers, 1991).

LOVE AND MARRIAGE Marriage is a predictor of mental and physical health. Being in love is consistently rated by research participants as a critical ingredient of happiness (Diener, 1984). Four out of five adults of all ages rate love as an important ingredient in their personal happiness (Myers, 1992). An excellent predictor of happiness in the United States and Europe is a very happy, close marital relationship. Among both men and women, married people are happier than people who are single or divorced. Marriage is a predictor of mental and physical health. Only 25 percent of those who are unmarried describe themselves as *very happy*, whereas 40 percent of those who are married say that they are *very happy*. Married people also report a high degree of fidelity to their partners. A 1988 Gallup survey found that nine out of ten married Americans indicated that they had not had sexual relationship with anyone other than their partner during their present marriage (Myers, 1992). Other studies have reported similar findings.

People who say that they are still in love with their partner and that they find their marriage satisfying rarely report being depressed or discontented with life (Myers, 1992). Among those who are married in the United States, two-thirds indicate they are happily married; three out of four maintain that their spouse is their best friend; and four out of five report that would marry the same person again.

However, the causal relations underlying this correlation are unclear. It may be that people who are happy tend to have better intimate relationships and more stable marriages, whereas people who are unhappy may have more difficulty finding and keeping partners. Myers (1992) asserts that marriage does indeed enhance happiness. Married people reap the benefit of a stable, supportive relationship and are thus less subject to suffering loneliness. In addition, the role of spouse offers status and a source of self-esteem. When things don't go well in other aspects of our lives, we may be able to comfort ourselves with the assurance of our marital role.

Unfortunately, the happiness level of married partners has declined. Compared with the percentage of younger married people in the mid-1970s who reported that they were "very happy," those surveyed in the middle and the late 1980s were nearly ten points lower (Myers, 1992). Myers offered the following research-based predictors (but not necessarily causes) of marital success: marrying after age twenty, dating for a long while before marrying, getting an education, obtaining a well-paying job, living in a small town or on a farm, avoiding cohabitation or becoming pregnant before marriage, and both spouses being religiously committed.

WORK   Although work is less critical than love and marriage as a source of well-being, job satisfaction is strongly related to general happiness (Argyle, 1987). Studies also show that unemployment has devastating effects on subjective well-being (Diener, 1984). It is difficult to determine whether job satisfaction causes happiness or whether the causal relationship works in the other direction, but evidence suggests that causation flows both ways (Argyle, 1987).

In his book *Excellence,* John Gardner (1984) wrote, "The best kept secret in America today is that people would rather work hard for something they believe in than live a life of aimless diversion" (p. 155). Gardner holds that happiness stems from striving toward meaningful goals. Indeed, there is considerable research evidence to support Gardner's view (Myers, 1991). "Flow" in work and play predicts happiness. The term "flow" was coined by Mihaly Csikszentmihalyi (1990), who wrote *Flow: The Ultimate Human Experience.* When a person undertakes activities that are challenging but that are also attainable because that individual has good skills to apply to the task, the person is experiencing flow. Meaningful work is a predictor of well-being.

The accompanying diagram shows four quadrants, one of which indicates the combination of the two qualities that produce flow. When challenging work is undertaken by an individual with low skills, anxiety is the typical result. When a person has low skills and unchallenging work, he or she feels apathy. A highly skilled person will be bored with unchallenging work. Finally, the combination of highly challenging work and high skills produces flow.

```
                High challenge

        Anxiety              Flow

Low     ────────────┼────────────    High
skills                                skills

        Apathy              Boredom

                 Low challenge
```

It appears that job satisfaction is a relatively stable trait, even when the individual changes jobs. Apparently, job satisfaction is directly related to the tendency toward positive or negative emotions, which is a stable characteristic. People with negative emotions tend to be dissatisfied with work; people with positive emotions tend to be satisfied. Researcher Faye Crosby (1990) reported that satisfaction in one's love life and in one's work reinforce each other. Working outside the home enhances a sense of contentment with home life, and likewise, having important roles outside work enhances job satisfaction.

Faith, Hope, and Joy

Spiritual commitment (or a religious experience) is correlated with being very happy (Argyle, 1987; Myers, 1991). This finding is true for both Americans and Europeans. Weekly church attendance is positively correlated with well-being. Among the elderly, religious belief and health are the strongest predictors of happiness. Among atheists and nonreligious people, only about 15 to 30 percent say that they are "very happy." Among religious individuals, 25 to 40 percent say that they are "very happy" (Myers, 1992).

Religious people have more favorable mental health records, such as less delinquency, less alcoholism, lower divorce rates, and lower incidence of suicide. Faith seems to offer (1) social support, (2) meaning and purpose, (3) ultimate acceptance, (4) focus beyond the self, and (5) an eternal perspective. Myers (1992) suggested that religion can give people a sense of purpose and meaning in their lives, help them to accept their setbacks gracefully, connect them to a

"But, in the end, you will become bored with that, too."

caring, supportive community, and comfort them by putting their ultimate mortality in perspective. Hillary Clinton (1993) put it this way: "Faith is a wonderful gift of grace. It gives you a sense of being rooted in meaning and love that goes far beyond your own life. It gives you a base of assurance as to what is really important and stands the test of time day after day, minute after minute, so that many of the pressures that come to bear from the outside world are not seen as that significant."

Although religious faith helps people handle great losses (probably because of the belief in eternal life), religious individuals also feel less in control of what happens to them (Myers, 1992). For some, religion produces feelings of guilt and may produce feelings that any unhappiness experienced is deserved. For most people, though, a religious faith promotes a sense of well-being.

➤ CONCLUSION

There is remarkable agreement among philosophers as to what factors promote human happiness. Furthermore, the observations of philosophers throughout the ages are essentially validated by the research evidence of psychologists. These research findings suggest that happiness is related to self-esteem, loving relationships, extroversion, good health, satisfying and challenging work, a sense of control over our good fortune, an optimistic outlook, being helpful to others, and making an effort to do new and fun things (Diener, Sandvik, & Pavot, 1990). To a surprising extent, control over our state of happiness resides within us rather than in external events. No single factor discussed is either necessary or sufficient for happiness.

➤ SUMMARY

The scientific study of emotional well-being is relatively new, but many theories about the secrets of happiness are very old. Greek philosophers wrote about the roots of happiness, indicating that well-being arises from a life of leisurely and intelligent reflection. Other routes to happiness that have been proposed are the pursuit of excellence, leading the virtuous life, knowing the truth, practicing restraint, purging pent-up rage, and living for the present.

ARISTOTLE ON HAPPINESS Aristotle maintained that happiness is the ultimate goal of life. A person who practices intellectual and moral virtues is likely to have a good life but will need, in addition, good fortune and whatever amount of external assets are required to enable the individual actively to express these virtues.

JOHN STUART MILL ON HAPPINESS Excitement and peaceful contentment are the two sides of happiness, according to Mill. Two impediments to happiness are selfishness and lack of mental cultivation.

BERTRAND RUSSELL For Russell, unhappiness is fostered by envy, mistaken morals, and bad habits. Happiness can be gained by cultivating a friendly interest in people and things.

HUMANISTIC PERSPECTIVE ON HAPPINESS Carl Rogers believed that the good life is not for the fainthearted, because it involves the courage to continue to actualize one's potential. Launching oneself fully into the stream of life is enriching and meaningful. To lead the good life, one must be open to experience, be able to live in the moment, and be willing to trust oneself to be capable of determining an appropriate course of action.

In agreement with Rogers, Buscaglia proposed that happiness can be attained by personal development and living in the moment. Maslow equated happiness with openness to peak experiences.

COGNITIVE BEHAVIORAL VIEW OF HAPPINESS Aaron Beck attributed euphoria to the perception or expectation of gain. Such anticipatory thinking may explain how optimistic individuals maintain an ongoing state of happiness. Whether or not a person experiences happiness depends on the meaning attached to a particular situation or object. Positive evaluations result in corresponding elevations in mood. Any event or idea that represents a meaningful addition to one's life is sufficient to produce happiness.

WHO IS HAPPY, AND WHY? Psychologists throughout the world have carried out research in order to determine what causes people to be happy. Researchers define well-being as a pervasive sense that life is good, meaningful, and satisfying. According to several studies, 80 percent of people say they are at least "fairly" happy.

AGE There is little variation in the level of satisfaction with life as a function of age.

GENDER No difference has been found between men and women on their level of happiness and global well-being.

ETHNICITY There are no differences between blacks and whites on level of happiness.

A SOUND BODY Disabled people describe themselves as being as happy as able-bodied people do.

MONEY There is a positive correlation between wealth and happiness, up to a point. However, once the basic life needs are met, increased wealth doesn't increase happiness.

INTELLIGENCE   Researchers have not found an association between IQ scores and happiness. Educational attainment also appears to be unrelated to subjective well-being.

COMMUNITY   People living in urban, suburban, and rural areas are found to be equally happy.

PARENTHOOD   People who have children are neither more nor less happy than people without children.

Research has identified several factors that appear to have an impact on subjective well-being:

HEALTH   Good physical health is moderately correlated with subjective well-being. However, sound health alone doesn't account for personal happiness, because people tend to take good health for granted.

PERSONALITY   The best predictor of a person's future happiness is his or her past happiness. Much evidence suggests that happiness does not depend on external circumstances, such as having a nice house, good friends, and an enjoyable job, as much as it does on internal factors, such as one's outlook on life.

SELF-ESTEEM   Self-esteem predicts happiness. In Western societies, life satisfaction is evaluated in terms of the extent to which one achieves one's ideals. The similarity between a person's actual self-concept and ideal self-concept has also been used as an index of life satisfaction.

PERSONAL CONTROL   Happy people believe that they choose their destinies. Even though this isn't entirely true in reality, operating as though it is the case works well as an orientation in life.

OPTIMISM   Happy people are hope-filled. Conversely, a cardinal characteristic of the thinking of depressed people is their belief that the current situation is hopeless and that things will not be any better in the future.

EXTROVERSION   Happy people are outgoing. Extroverts are sociable, active, outgoing, and optimistic, whereas introverts tend to be passive, quiet, careful, and unsociable.

SOCIAL ACTIVITY AND SUPPORT   People who are content with their friendship networks and those who are socially active report above-average levels of happiness. In contrast, people troubled by loneliness tend to be very unhappy.

LOVE AND MARRIAGE Being in love is consistently rated by research participants as a critical ingredient of happiness. Among both men and women, married people are happier than people who are single or divorced.

WORK Job satisfaction is strongly related to general happiness. Happiness comes from striving toward meaningful goals and having meaningful work. Activities that are challenging yet attainable create happiness.

FAITH, HOPE, AND JOY Spiritual commitment (or a religious experience) is correlated with being very happy.

LEARNING THE LANGUAGE OF PSYCHOLOGISTS

confirmation bias
disconfirming evidence

self-serving bias
explanatory style

CHAPTER REVIEW QUESTIONS

1. Did the philosophers Aristotle, Mill, and Russell have any common observations on the sources of happiness and unhappiness for human beings?
2. Before psychologists started doing research on happiness, what did philosophers think comprised the routes to achieving a sense of well-being?
3. Why did Carl Rogers think that the "good life" was not for the faint-hearted?
4. What did Aaron Beck maintain is the source of happiness?
5. Which characteristics of a person predict his or her level of satisfaction with life, and which characteristics do not?
6. What is the relationship between being wealthy and being happy?
7. What is "flow"?
8. Why is it that people who are disabled and those who have been subjected to prejudice are about as happy as people who are able-bodied and those who have not suffered from prejudice?
9. What suggestions have been offered to explain why religious faith correlates positively with happiness?
10. How did the recent research evidence of psychologists confirm or disconfirm the ideas of Aristotle, Mill, and Russell as to the sources of human happiness?

ACTIVITIES

1. *COMPLETE INDIVIDUALLY:* **Joy Quiz.**
2. *COMPLETE AS A GROUP:* **Personal Reflections on My Own Happiness.**
3. *COMPLETE INDIVIDUALLY:* **Gratitude Journal.** For one week, at the end of each day, write down five things that you felt thankful for on that day.
4. *COMPLETE INDIVIDUALLY:* **Martin Seligman's Optimism Test from his book** Learned Optimism.

Joy Quiz

Directions: Indicate whether you agree or disagree with the following statements by circling *T* for true or *F* for false.

T   F   **1.** The ancient Greeks felt that happiness arose from a life of leisurely and intelligent reflection.

T   F   **2.** About half of the people in Western industrialized countries report that they are happy.

T   F   **3.** Middle-age adults are happier than both younger and older adults.

T   F   **4.** Adults over 30 in the United States generally would prefer to be younger.

T   F   **5.** Women have a higher incidence of alcoholism than do men.

T   F   **6.** There is no difference in level of happiness for blacks or whites.

T   F   **7.** There is a positive correlation between level of intelligence and life satisfaction.

T   F   **8.** The best predictor of a person's future happiness is the happiness of that person in the past.

T   F   **9.** Suburban dwellers are happier than are city dwellers.

T   F   **10.** Being a parent is a predictor of life satisfaction.

T   F   **11.** Self-esteem is a predictor of happiness with life in general.

T   F   **12.** More-educated people are happier than less-educated people.

T   F   **13.** There is a relationship between well-being and being well off.

T   F   **14.** People who are not depressed tend to view themselves and their future prospects in an unrealistically favorable light.

T   F   **15.** Happy people believe that they choose their own destinies.

T   F   **16.** Happy people are realistic rather than optimistic.

T   F   **17.** Happy people tend to be extroverted rather than introverted.

T   F   **18.** An excellent predictor of happiness is a close marital relationship.

T   F   **19.** Able-bodied people are more content than are disabled persons.

T   F   **20.** Challenging work that is taken on by a skillful person is a predictor of well-being.

T   F   **21.** In general, men report more life satisfaction than do women.

T   F   **22.** Weekly church attendance is unrelated to well-being.

T   F   **23.** Having a social support network is related to a sense of well-being.

T   F   **24.** People are happier doing less expensive leisure activities than more costly ones.

T   F   **25.** Exercise increases one's sense of well-being.

Personal Reflections on My Own Happiness

Directions: Read and answer each of the following questions.

1. In general, how happy have you been? (Consider your overall state of being, without worrying about specific parts of your life.)

    a. How happy have you been over the past few months? The point of this question is to consider how you are feeling now—not just this one day, but over the recent period in your life. Place a check mark beside your choice.

        _____ extremely unhappy
        _____ moderately unhappy
        _____ slightly unhappy
        _____ neutral
        _____ slightly happy
        _____ moderately happy
        _____ very happy
        _____ extremely happy

    b. How happy have you been over the past five years? Determining this may be difficult, but try to assess your average level of happiness over this period. Place a check mark beside your choice.

        _____ extremely unhappy
        _____ moderately unhappy
        _____ slightly unhappy
        _____ neutral
        _____ slightly happy
        _____ moderately happy
        _____ very happy
        _____ extremely happy

    c. How happy have you been during your life up to now? This question is the hardest of all to answer, because it is difficult to combine events and feelings from years ago with those of today, but try to assess your whole life. How happy would you say it has been? Place a check mark beside your choice.

        _____ extremely unhappy
        _____ moderately unhappy
        _____ slightly unhappy

_____ neutral
_____ slightly happy
_____ moderately happy
_____ very happy
_____ extremely happy

2. Some people seem to be "good" at being happy. They enjoy life regardless of what is going on and get the most out of everything. Others are the opposite—they are never as happy as they might be. Where do you fall on this continuum? Place a check mark beside your choice.

_____ very good at happiness
_____ pretty good at it
_____ fair at it
_____ poor at it
_____ very poor at it

3. Some people seem to have everything that *should* make them happy, but they are less happy than you might think they would be. Others are the opposite; although they don't have much, they are happier than you might expect. Where do you fall? Place a check mark beside your choice.

_____ much happier than might be expected
_____ somewhat happier than might be expected
_____ about as happy as might be expected
_____ somewhat less happy than might be expected
_____ much less happy than might be expected

4. What is happiness? You have already answered several questions about happiness, but now take a moment to think about what this question means: not what produces happiness, not what specific things bring it, but what it actually is. Write your answer in the blanks.

_____

_____

_____

5. What three elements of life are most important in producing happiness for you? What is most essential for happiness, what brings it, and what makes it impossible if absent? The items on your list can be parts of life that you have (and that bring happiness) or that you don't have and wish that you did. Write your answer in the blanks.

a._____

b._____

c._____

6. Here are parts of life that other people have considered important to their happiness. Consider each one, and decide how important it is to you. Rate each according to the five-point scale that follows, and write the number in the blank.

   1 = not important
   2 = slightly important
   3 = somewhat important
   4 = moderately important
   5 = very important

   a. _____ financial situation

   b. _____ job or occupation

   c. _____ the place where you live (your community)

   d. _____ the home where you live (your house or apartment)

   e. _____ friends, people you see socially and who are close to you

   f. _____ romantic relationship in general

   g. _____ being in love and being loved

   h. _____ sex life

   i. _____ marriage

   j. _____ children, being a parent

   k. _____ recognition as a person, achievement of any kind

   l. _____ success or feeling of accomplishment in career or other aspects of life

   m. _____ health

   n. _____ religious or other spiritual beliefs

7. How often do you think about happiness and about how happy you are? Place a check mark beside your choice.

   _____ every day
   _____ every few days
   _____ weekly
   _____ twice a month
   _____ once a month
   _____ rarely, if ever

8. How optimistic or pessimistic are you about your life? Place a check mark beside your choice.

   _____ very optimistic
   _____ moderately optimistic

_____ slightly optimistic
_____ neutral
_____ slightly pessimistic
_____ moderately pessimistic
_____ very pessimistic

9. How happy do you think most of your friends are, compared with you? Place a check mark beside your choice.

_____ much happier
_____ somewhat happier
_____ about the same
_____ somewhat less happy
_____ much less happy

10. What single thing do you think could increase your happiness most? Write your answer in the blanks.

_____

_____

_____

_____

Source: Excerpts from "Some Questions" in *Happy People: What Happiness Is, Who Has It, And Why,* copyright © 1978 by Jonathan Freedman, reprinted by permission of Harcourt Brace & Company.

15

Meaning and Values

He who has the why to live can bear with almost any how.
—Friedrich Nietzsche

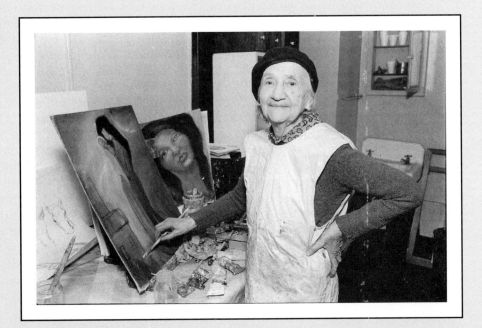

➤ INTRODUCTION: THE ILLUMINATED LIFE

By being aware of our values and living in concert with them, we can find meaning in our lives. Values can be defined as what is important to us, what the rules are that we live by, and what we cherish and respect. We may not have a clear idea as to what we hold most dear and as to what is guiding our behavior unless we spend time thinking about the matter. Since values can be embraced at an unconscious level, it is possible for people to deceive themselves about their real values or simply to be oblivious to them. Yet, if we look within ourselves and observe our own behavior, we can become aware of that which we deem to be truly worthwhile.

It is up to us to engage in a search for our values in order to construct a purpose in life. By now, you probably recognize this search as the questions, Why am I here? and Where am I going? Each of us also needs to answer the questions, What is the value of my life? and What is my contribution to the world?

Many who enjoy physical attractiveness, who achieve power, fame, success, and material comfort, nevertheless experience a sense of emptiness. Rollo May (1973) considered this inner emptiness to be the chief problem in contemporary society. Whether or not this view is accurate in general, a lack of meaning in our lives will be a problem for us, because we cannot be effective when we do not know what our purpose is. Examples of famous persons who struggled with a sense of meaninglessness are rock-and-roll star Elvis Presley, musician Kurt Cobain, and novelist Ernest Hemingway. Although Presley skyrocketed to fame as a rock-and-roll singer, he was haunted by something missing in his life. He turned to drugs and eventually died of an overdose. Cobain was a rising star as lead singer for the musical group, Nirvana. Although he had fame, fortune, and an apparently bright future, Cobain committed suicide and left a note indicating he saw no point in living. Hemingway, one of the great American authors of this century, committed suicide, seemingly to put an end to his inner conflict. Although people who are suffering in this manner may not be able to articulate what is lacking in their lives, they know that something is wrong. The widespread use of pills, drugs, alcohol, and cigarettes, as well as excessive use of video games, compulsive shopping, and continuous television viewing, provides evidence that many of us are unable to find pursuits that express our values and allow us to make sense of our place in the world. These are ways of escaping awareness of ourselves and our current situation. On the other hand, the contemporary musician Yanni seems to be filled with a sense of optimism and purpose that he expresses with obvious delight in his musical compositions and performances.

A need for meaning is one of the existential concerns discussed earlier in this text (Chapter 1). Recall that psychologists and philosophers have examined "human nature" in order to discover some general principles that guide people in their search for a fulfilling life. The existentialists have contended that because we human beings have highly developed brains, which enable us to have self-awareness, we must endeavor to cope with certain "concerns" we have about our very existence. The concerns that were selected for discussion in this text, in addition to the need to create meaning in one's life, were these: We must find our identity. At times we feel isolated from people and even from parts of ourselves. The awareness of our own inevitable death causes us to dread facing our mortality and to wonder what happens after death. We also feel anxious as we become aware of our responsibility for our actions.

➤ THE NEED FOR A SENSE OF IDENTITY

The discovery of our values is related to our achievement of identity as a person. Through his experience in a therapeutic situation with many clients, Carl Rogers (1961) concluded that each person faces one central problem in life, which is to address the questions: "Who am I, *really*? How can I get in touch with this real self, underlying all my surface behavior? How can I become myself?" (p. 108).

Likewise, Erich Fromm declared that among the existential needs of human beings is the requirement of a sense of identity: "Man may be defined as the animal that can say 'I,' that can be aware of himself as a separate entity" (Fromm, 1963, p. 62). People must feel in control of their fate. In short, each person must make decisions, reflect on them, and feel that his or her life is truly his or her own. Armed with self-awareness, we are able to feel in charge of our destiny. Psychologist Joe Livingston (1998) expressed the need for self-awareness this way: "All of us are looking for peace of mind, happiness, pleasure, a sense of well-being. To achieve this, we go within or we go without."

Pathways to Self-Understanding

Throughout this text, you have been trying various means of self-exploration for the purpose of better knowing yourself. Hopefully, you have found this process enjoyable and plan to continue moving in the direction of greater self-awareness. There are several ways of becoming aware of your values. Some of your options for pursuing this goal are described in the following sections.

SELF-MONITORING OF BEHAVIORS AND INTROSPECTION   Since our daily behaviors are expressions of our basic values, it's possible to gain insight into ourselves by examining *any* of our actions. For instance, we can probably tell something about a person's values by looking at his or her checkbook, to see where the money goes. From this behavior we can infer the importance that we attach to things.

In order to become self-aware, we must also be willing to look within ourselves to discover through introspection how to live (Chapter 1). We need to develop the ability to listen to our interior guidance system and to trust what we hear. Remember that Carl Rogers suggested that we can trust our inner knowing (Chapter 2). In fact, according to Rogers, we must rely on intuition to guide us toward self-fulfillment.

Self-help books, seminars, and courses can be helpful in assisting with introspection. They provide suggestions as to avenues of exploration. People often discover when they make self-observations that their actions and internal reactions do not follow their preconceived ideas of who they are (Ornstein, 1993).

PUBLIC EXPRESSION   We learn about ourselves by listening to what we tell others about our life circumstances. We can come to know our own minds by explaining ourselves to others (Lasch, 1995). Until we have to discuss and possibly defend our opinions in public, these opinions remain half-formed convictions based on random impressions of which we are only partially aware. Having a good friend who is realistic to bounce our thoughts off of is useful, because we sometimes get "crazy" ideas about ourselves and others. By asking us questions about our suppositions, friends help us spot faulty logic. This public airing of our ideas represents another strategy for enhancing self-awareness. Valuable extensions of this process could be relating to others in a self-help group setting and/or seeking out individual therapy.

DREAMS   From ancient times and from every civilization and culture, human beings have wondered about the meaning of dreams and the extent to which they can be useful. To the ancients, particularly the Greeks, dreams were a link between the present day and the future. Likewise, in biblical literature, dreams are considered predictions of the future. A famous dream book, which included interpretations, was produced by Artemidorus Daldianus, who lived in the second century A.D.

Dreams have been interpreted variously as divine messages, as the experiences of disembodied souls roaming heaven and earth during sleep, as visitations from the dead, as prophecies of the future, as the sleeping person's perceptions of external stimuli or bodily disturbances (what Thomas Hobbes called "the distemper of inward parts"), as fulfillment or attempted fulfillment of wishes (Freud), as attempts by the dreamer to discern his or her psychic development in order to plan for the future (Jung), as expressions of one's style of life (Adler), as attempted resolutions of conflicts (Stekel), and as existential messages about oneself and one's current struggles (Perls).

If we train ourselves to recall our dreams and learn to explore their meanings, we can get a sense of our struggles, wants, goals, purposes, conflicts, and interests. The value of dreams may be that they are expressions of what occupies our psyche when we are not consciously directing our thought process. We can consult our dreams for clues as to what is bothering us, and perhaps as to things that we wish for but are not attending to.

JOURNALS Keeping a journal is another good avenue for seeking insights. We may write personal observations in a journal as a means of fostering introspection. During one period of his life, Sigmund Freud spent the last half hour of each working day analyzing himself. The American President, John Quincy Adams, also kept a daily journal. A colleague recently told the author about a friend the colleague very much admires, who for thirty years has gotten up at 4:30 A.M. almost every morning to spend from that time to 5:45 A.M. by herself, either taking a walk, writing in her journal, or meditating. This woman also takes about twenty minutes each evening for herself to watch the sun go down. These respites from the ordinary flow of daily activity apparently give her the serenity to navigate her life successfully.

You might try this technique of sitting down each day to reflect on your day by writing about it. Pay particular attention to anything in your own thoughts, feelings, or behaviors that surprised or mystified you. Keeping a journal will help you gain self-awareness as well as provide you with a forum for working on current issues in your life. People get perspective on their lives but then lose it again. Journal writing is a good way to regain perspective.

Let's not pretend that everyone must proceed to arise at the crack of dawn for daily self-exploration in order to be a fulfilled person. Norman Vincent Peale suggested that we take a minute here and there throughout the day

to pause and check within ourselves or our higher power, as a means of reflecting on our lives. What is desirable is introspection, or periodic self-monitoring, with the goal of heightened self-knowledge. There is no need to become discouraged if we are not leading the kind of orderly life that would allow for daily self-examination. We can take the essence of this idea and tailor it to our own situation.

As you review in your journal your feeling states during the day, you may want to look for thoughts that preceded them. By doing so, you may become more aware of the links between your thoughts and their feeling consequences. Try thinking about the events of the day as neutral, as capable of being construed in a variety of ways.

THERAPY   Although many people who seek out therapy are troubled by recognizable symptoms of mental disorders such as depression, anxiety, or obsessions, others may elect to try therapy as a route to enhanced self-awareness. What may underlie the obvious symptoms distressing the therapy client is an unfulfilled existential need. The client seeks a sense of coherence, a renewed belief that his or her life matters. Among other things, the therapist offers an explanation, a way for the person seeking help to meaningfully interpret adversity or suffering. With the client's assistance, the therapist constructs a narrative to explain the client to himself or herself.

Along with finding help with their troubles, people might discover in therapy a source of peak experiences (Maslow, 1967). As a result of therapy, individuals may develop goals, and gain the sense that they know what they are about, and become conscious of what they are going toward. The breaking up of symptoms such as anxieties and rigid defenses at the same time promotes spontaneity and courage, as well as sensory and body awareness. Those seeking therapy for relief from symptoms should also find themselves gradually experiencing these other benefits.

➤ EXISTENTIAL ISOLATION

Existential isolation is a human concern that addresses the question, Where do I fit in? It refers to the occasional experience of feeling cut off or alienated from the rest of the world. We may experience this detachment as unfathomable loneliness. We may feel sad; lost.

Social Interest

Discomfort that arises from awareness of existential isolation can be transcended in part through satisfying connections with others. Alfred Adler theorized that in order to have a healthy personality, an individual must have "social interest," by which he meant the desire to consider the needs of others along with one's own (Chapter 10). A person with social interest feels united with others, and desires to act with their interests in mind. Social interaction was viewed by Adler as essential to mental health.

The same idea about the need for ties with people has been echoed by other psychologists and philosophers. Erik Erikson (1963) contended that middle-aged people have a need for "generativity," or caretaking of others. Either by mentoring others, or by indirectly benefiting them through one's efforts, the adult in mid-life achieves generativity. Psychologist Gordon Allport (1937) included this notion in his concept of the mature person, that is, the mature individual is capable of relating warmly to others. Such a person also realizes that all of us are in the same human situation, trying to survive and be happy. This realization paves the way for a compassionate and respectful relating to others. Bellah, et al. (1985) suggested that intense relationships with others rather than pursuit of self-realization is what ultimately makes life meaningful. Milton Mayeroof (1990), author of *On Caring*, wrote that we are ultimately at home through caring and being cared for.

Philosopher Ernest Becker (1971) suggested that what constitutes our sole means of achieving meaning in life is through our interactions with others:

> The basic question the person wants to ask and answer is "who am I?" "What is the meaning of my life?" "What value does it have?" And we can only get answers to these questions by reviewing our relationships to others, what we do to others and for others, and what kind of response we get from them" (p. 70).

At our best, we experience humanity as a single community. According to Fromm (1955), our mental health depends upon developing ties with our fellow human beings, and thus achieving a union with somebody or something outside of ourselves. Without strong emotional links to the human community, we suffer from utter isolation, and a feeling of being lost in a vacuum. A primary means of overcoming the fear of separateness, according to Eric Fromm (1963), is through love, whether its form is brotherly, motherly, erotic, or for God.

We need to be able to relate to others as a part of a family or group. In the past, the extended family and nuclear family provided a sense of connectedness and permanency. Though instability in the contemporary nuclear family has been much discussed, family relations still afford a sense of belonging for most individuals. Family ties are consistently ranked as most important by national surveys of Americans over the age of 18 years (*1991 American Family Values Study*). College students living away from home for the first time, as well as persons who move their residences for other reasons, are vulnerable to suffering loneliness and depression as they adjust to the loss of familiar surroundings and relationships.

Many forces in contemporary society have disrupted family ties. For the past half century, ours has been a mobile society, so that many people do not put down roots for very long. With increased economic prosperity, family members have had less need to rely on one another. That same prosperity has afforded a greater number of entertainment activities than before, with the result that individuals spend less time at home with the rest of the family. Lessened sanctions against working mothers and divorce have enabled unhappy wives to leave their marriages. Government aid programs to help the indigent have also lessened reliance on family members. In the past, more so than today, need for one another motivated conflict resolution, or at least tolerance of difficult family members.

For some generations of Americans, the workplace also provided a familial-like stability. In past times, people's jobs supplied a major sense of identity and continuity. Corporate downsizing and the seasonal nature of some forms of employment are current limitations on an individual's ability to rely on work as a stabilizing influence. Even so, one's work life can be a source of anchoring. Many find that friendships with coworkers furnish a major source of intimacy. Enduring friendships may be compared with one's convoy through life. Each type of "ship" in the fleet has a different supportive function. Such friendships may be either in lieu of a marriage relationship or as a compliment to it.

Church affiliation and civic organizations also provide opportunities for association and attachment (Chapters 5 & 14). These groups tend to develop altruistic projects for their members to work on together. Such community ties are also interfered with as individuals and families become more mobile.

The Need for Rootedness

Not only do we want to fit in with others, but also we want to be in sync with the rhythm of daily life itself. Most of us seek some measure of stability and continuity in our lives. Without some kind of foundation, we feel lost, rootless, aimless.

The existentialists contend that throughout life, human beings are torn from their roots in one fashion or another. In the birth process, the infant relinquishes the security and passivity of the womb existence. In late childhood, the youngster must give up the safety of the mother's care. Throughout adulthood, each person faces the prospect of being torn from life itself as he or she faces the reality of death. To counter these sources of insecurity, human beings have a need for roots, for a sense of stability, permanency, and predictability similar to the security they experienced in the mother-child relationship (Fromm, 1963; 1973).

Fromm believed that one's original dependence on one's mother is transformed in later life to a symbolic substitute, such as "the earth," nature, god, one's country or government, or the organization for which one works. The individual becomes a subject of and a devotee to a larger cause. This devotion can become fanaticism, brought about as a defense against the anxiety rooted in existential isolation. A healthier alternative is to progress towards individuation and to find new roots in the world by our own efforts. We thus learn to think for ourselves, reflect on our purpose, and determine the path we wish to take. To help us feel anchored, we establish ties with other people.

Self-Development

By social interest, Adler (1964) did not exclusively mean warm relationships with others. Having social interest implies working towards the advancement of one's society. We can improve social conditions in our corner of the world simply by making ourselves the best we can be. By being responsible, kind, and by taking care of ourselves rather than being a burden on society, we make an invaluable contribution. We can help our community by being tolerant of the foibles of others, and by being accepting of those with whom we disagree or from whom we differ in some way. We can decide to be a cooperative and ethical member of society. Notice the sentiment about focusing on self-improvement while avoiding comparisons with others in the two philosophical statements that follow.

A national social service association, Optimist International, has developed the following creed:

The Optimist Creed

Promise yourself . . .
To be so strong that nothing can disturb your peace of mind.
To talk health, happiness, and prosperity to every person you meet.
To make all your friends feel that there is something in them.
To look at the sunny side of everything
and make your optimism come true.
To think only of the best, to work only for the best,
and expect only the best.
To be just as enthusiastic about the success of others
as you are about your own.
To forget the mistakes of the past
and press on to the greater achievements of the future.
To wear a cheerful countenance at all times
and give every living creature you meet a smile.
To give so much time to the improvement of yourself
that you have no time to criticize others.
To be too large for worry, too noble for anger, too strong for fear,
and too happy to permit the presence of trouble.

Reprinted by permission from Optimist International.

A second philosophy of life is embodied in a prose poem written by Max Ehrmann (1927), which became a beloved statement for the birth cohort known as the baby boomers when they were adolescents. This philosophy also addresses the importance attending to one's own development without becoming critical of others:

Disiderata

Go placidly amid the noise and haste, and remember what peace there may be in silence. As far as possible without surrender be on good terms with all persons. Speak your truth quietly and clearly; and listen to others, even the dull and ignorant; they too have their story. Avoid loud and aggressive persons, they are vexations to the spirit. *If you compare yourself with others, you may become vain and bitter; for always there will be greater and lesser persons than yourself.* Enjoy your achievements as well as your plans. Keep interested in your own career, however humble; it is a real possession in the changing fortunes of time. Exercise caution in your business affairs; for the world is full of trickery. But let this not blind you to what virtue there is; many persons strive for high ideals; and everywhere life is full of heroism. Be yourself. Especially, do not feign affection. Neither be cynical about love; for in the face of all aridity and disenchantment it is perennial as the grass. Take kindly the counsel of the years, gracefully surrendering the things of youth. Nurture strength of spirit to shield you in sudden misfortune. But do not distress yourself with imaginings. Many fears are born of fatigue and loneliness. Beyond a wholesome discipline, be gentle with yourself. You are a child of the universe, no less than the trees and the stars; you have a right to be here. And whether or not it is clear to you, no doubt the universe is unfolding as it should. Therefore be at peace with God, whatever you conceive Him to be, and whatever your labors and aspirations, in the noisy confusion of life keep peace with your soul. With all its sham, drudgery and broken dreams, it is still a beautiful world. Be careful. Strive to be happy.

Social Responsibility

Finding meaning, in part, involves transcending our personal interests, which are ultimately not separate from the interests of others. Other people help us with our projects, and we need in turn to be concerned with their projects.

According to Adler (1964), a healthy person has a sympathy of feeling for his or her fellow human beings as well as an interest in society at large. An extroverted individual might express social interest by offering assistance directly to others. An introverted person might produce a work of art or technological improvement to benefit others without interacting with them. Erik Erikson (1963) suggested that generativity could be achieved by either directly caring for or by indirectly advancing the interests of others (Chapter 3).

Helping the condition of others by finding a way to shape our culture for the better might seem like an overwhelming task. We may be tempted to turn away and save ourselves from empathic suffering. However, if we keep in mind as role models other people who have made simple yet profound contributions, we may be encouraged about our own ability to influence the shape of events in the world. Consider Robert Fulghum, who wrote "All I Ever Needed to Know I Learned in Kindergarten." Here is an example of a "humble masterpiece" that touches the heartstrings of grown-up children. Through simple rules of life that could be taught to a five-year-old, Fulghum makes observations about the meaning and wonder of life.

Mother Theresa also provided us with an example of a modest activity that brought to her unanticipated and unsought world renown and admiration. Her daily life simply consisted of caring for the poor and the sick. She represented a style of life guided by a single principle, to see Jesus in the face of each poverty-stricken, ailing person whom she helped.

When contemplating social change, many of us are overwhelmed by the scope of the task. The quantity of human need seems infinite, while our resources are limited in terms of time, energy and money. The result is that although we can care for some people, in doing so, we necessarily neglect others. Whatever contribution we make to alleviate the suffering of others will make only a small difference relative to the total magnitude of suffering in the human community. This would be the case even if we were to devote our entire lives to the task, as did Mother Teresa. So, we suffer from our own

ALL I EVER NEEDED TO KNOW I LEARNED IN KINDERGARTEN

Most of what I really need to know about how to live and what to do and how to be, I learned in Kindergarten. Wisdom was not on top of the graduate mountain but there in the sandbox at the nursery school.

These are the things I learned: Share everything. Play fair. Don't hit people. Put back things where you found them. Clean up your own mess. Don't take things that aren't yours. Say you're sorry when you hurt someone. Wash your hands before you eat . . . Flush. Warm cookies and cold milk are good for you. Live a balanced life. Learn some and think some and draw and paint and sing and dance and play and work everyday some.

Take a nap every afternoon. When you go out into the world, watch out for traffic, hold hands and stick together. Be aware of wonder. Remember the little seed in the plastic cup. The roots go down and the plant goes up and nobody really knows how or why but we are all like that.

Goldfish and hamsters and white mice and even the little seed in the plastic cup—they all die. So do we.

And then remember the book about Dick and Jane and the first word you learned—the biggest word of all: LOOK. Everything you need to know is there somewhere. The golden rule and love and basic sanitation, ecology and politics and sane living.

Think of what a better world it would be if we all—the whole world—had cookies and milk about three o'clock every afternoon and then lay down with our blankets for a nap; or if we had a basic policy in our nation and other nations to always put things back where we found them and clean up our own messes.

And it is still true, no matter how old you are: when you go out into the world, it's best to hold hands and stick together.

Source: From *All I Ever Needed To Know I Learned in Kindergarten* by Robert Fulghum. Copyright © 1986, 1988 by Robert Fulghum. Reprinted by permission of Villard Books, a division of Random House, Inc.

compassion, and our caring threatens to bring us despair. We are faced with the dilemma of caring about people whom we cannot take care of. Through the media, we become aware of vast oceans of suffering due to poverty and violence. How tempting it would be to look away and fend off painful compassion. As philosopher and author Sam Keen (1997) wrote,

> It is only when we begin to face the impossibility of eliminating suffering and tragedy from the human condition that we discover the link between faith, hope, and love. To be a lover means to refuse to despair and to decide to care even when it breaks the heart. In the final analysis caring is not so much a matter of doing good works as it is the gift of attention and concern to another, whether or not there is anything we can do. (p. 120)

Although a focus on becoming the best person you can be would indeed go a long way toward creating a better world, you may decide to make a more direct impact on others by becoming a social activist. You might even lead a movement aimed at social change. One example of an individual effort to change societal norms was the creation of M.A.D.D. (Mothers Against Drunk Driving) in 1980 by Candy Lightner, following the death of her 13-year-old daughter who was killed by a drunk driver.

In order to effect change as a social activist, you might need to develop leadership skills. Good leaders have been shown to have many of the characteristics of healthy people in general, such as a high energy level, stress tolerance, integrity, emotional maturity, and self-confidence (e.g., Bass, 1990; Kirkpatrick & Locke, 1991). Effective leaders are able to recognize the need for change, create a vision of that change, give meaning to the change, and outline actions that followers must take to achieve it.

A contemporary role model for social activism is General Colin Powell. He has become the spokesperson for "America's Promise," an organization dedicated to nurturing the nation's children, while instilling in them what has come to be called "family values." Powell (1998) has said that the nation's children need more "laptop" time, although he didn't mean it in reference to computers.

In *To Love and Be Loved,* Sam Keen observed that:

> Caring liberates us from the self-encapsulation of modern individualism, where "I do my thing, you do your thing," and it carries us beyond the sweet spontaneity and intoxication of the romantic adrenaline-endorphin cocktail into the realm of consideration and thoughtfulness (p. 114).

If the preceding examples are too awe-inspiring to take in, then think about this: The author has a friend who is a runner. As this fellow jogs along the beach, he occasionally stoops to pick up trash, and then pops it into the next trash can that he comes to. Most of us are careful not to litter, yet we don't think to pick up trash when we see it. You, too, can be a light in a dim corner of the world.

➤ COSMIC AND PERSONAL MEANING

Among the existential questions asked by humans beings, one is, Why am I here? In order to be content with our lives, we must experience them as meaningful and worthwhile. The quest for a purpose is a basic element of human self-consciousness; the discovery of such a mission is a fundamental source of happiness.

Achieving Transcendence through Spirituality or Creative Endeavor

Many people find a reason for existence in developing goals or projects. According to Fromm (1973), human beings need a sense of effectiveness.

"Because individuals are aware of themselves and their world, they sometimes recognize how overpowering and frightening the vastness of the universe is. They may thus easily be overcome with a sense of their own helplessness and impotence" (p. 235). Yalom (1980) indicated that "deep loneliness is inherent in the act of self-creation" (p. 357). When people become conscious of nature's cosmic indifference, they need to surpass their own fear and uncertainty in the face of this impersonal and intimidating universe. Human beings may accomplish this end by actively striving to master their world and themselves.

An individual needs to master his or her own potential passivity: "He is driven by the urge to transcend the role of the creature, the accidental aspect and passivity of his existence, by becoming a 'creator'" (Fromm, 1955, p. 41). In short, human beings psychologically overcome their insignificance by being *effective*, saying essentially, "I am because I effect."

People can also answer the question, Why am I Here? by creating projects that reach beyond their own personal interests. These are sometimes referred to as transcendent goals.

There are at least two routes to the satisfaction of the need for transcendence. This desire is typically satisfied by the development of a spiritual basis to one's life and through creative endeavor. Forming a religious affiliation, or developing a spiritual sense independent of an organized religion apparently helps people conquer their fear of uncertainty and their angst over the prospect of an indifferent universe (Chapter 6). Faith seems to offer cosmic meaning and purpose, as well as access to a power greater than oneself. These elements fulfill our need to defeat helplessness and powerlessness. A spiritual belief also allays anxiety over the realization of one's inevitable death, in that many spiritual belief systems assert that earthly existence is only one phase of spiritual life. A spiritual belief and/or philosophy of life provide an internal source of continuity.

We humans also combat a sense of powerlessness by being creative, effective, and proactive. We can compensate for being only a small part of the world by striving to be competent at something, to influence others, or to "make a dent" some way. It is fulfilling to feel effective at what we do. A capable person can set and accomplish goals, and through this process can overcome a sense of impotence instilled by his or her position as a tiny speck in the cosmos. Groos (1901), who studied children's play, wrote that the essential motive in the child's play was the "joy in being a cause." This was his explanation of the child's pleasure in making a clatter, moving things around, playing in puddles, and so on. Piaget (1952) also observed children's special interest in objects that they affect by their own movements. Alfred Adler (1973) used a similar concept in describing the basic motivation in human beings as a striving for competence or superiority. Adler said that when all goes well, one's style of life embraces a striving toward mastery or competence, and an interest in directing one's talents toward contributing to the betterment of society at large. At the core, such activity represents the proof that one *is*.

Meaning through Achievement, Experience, and Love

Viktor Frankl (1963) believed that we can discover meaning in life in three different ways: first, by doing a deed, that is, through achievement or accomplishment; second, by encountering a value, that is, something such as a work of nature or culture; and third, by experiencing someone through loving that person. He concluded that the only way we can comprehend the essence of another person is through love. The spiritual act of love allows us to sense the potential in the other and enable the beloved person to actualize that potential.

Meaning through Suffering

Meaning in life can also be found through suffering, according to Frankl. He became an authority on the subject by surviving a World War II concentration camp. Frankl believed that when a person is confronted with an inescapable situation and thus has to face a fate that cannot be changed, such as a terminal illness or unjust imprisonment, that individual has a chance to salvage some dignity in life by finding meaning in suffering. To Frankl, what matters is the attitude we take toward inescapable suffering, the manner in which we handle adversity. We can ennoble our lives by finding a purpose in our misfortune.

By way of example, Frankl relates a story of a physician who sought out Frankl for help with a depression caused by grief over the death of his wife of many years. The man had been unable to recover from his loss. Frankl asked the physician what would have happened if he had been the first to go and his wife had survived him. This husband was sure that her agony would have been even harder for her to bear. Frankl pointed out that the husband had been able to spare his wife this pain, but in so doing, he paid the price of suffering in her place. This comment enabled the widower to find meaning in his misery, the meaning of sacrifice. Though his fate was unchanged, his attitude toward his lot was very much changed. People may be quite willing to suffer, if they are sure that their misfortune has meaning.

One can learn from adversity. Suffering can teach us patience, endurance, and self-mastery (Lifton, 1993). It forces us to decide how we are going to react. Will Durant (1961), in *The Story of Philosophy*, wrote that suffering can make us either bitter or gentle. Those who maintain their humanity in the face of adversity may develop the ability to give meaning to the fundamental contradictions and schisms in the human condition. Mahatma Gandhi was prompted by suffering to create a movement promoting independence from British rule for India. His nonviolent approach to protesting social ills transformed voluntary suffering into a noble endeavor.

➤ The Need for a Frame of Orientation

Humans beings achieve meaning by answering the question Where am I going? According to Fromm (1973), "Man needs the map of his natural and social world, without which he would be confused and unable to act purposefully and consistently" (p. 230). Because a person is enveloped in a universe of puzzling phenomena and frightening realities, he or she has the drive to make sense of life. A person needs to be able to predict the complexities of existence. A frame of orientation is a set of beliefs about the ultimate course of one's destiny. Fromm believed that a frame of orientation is an absolute necessity for the maintenance of sanity (Fromm, 1955).

Life as a Coherent Story

One way to make sense of one's life is to translate it into a coherent story or narrative. Doing so wards off the feeling of being fragmented and promotes integration. Since a story has a plot and a resolution, we arrive at an answer to the question of where we are headed. Creation of a narrative enables us to "make our existence into a whole by understanding it as an expression of a single unfolding and developing story" (Polkinghorne, 1988, p. 150). This narrative integrates what we have been with our current unfolding and the anticipation of what we will become.

Ernst Becker (1971) has said that each person desires to be the hero of his or her life story and that "to become conscious of what one is doing to earn his feeling of heroism is the main self-analytic problem of life." (p. 4) Becker proposed that one of the key concepts for understanding the urge to heroism is the idea of "narcissism." In its more negative connotation, narcissism implies that practically everyone is expendable except ourselves. Its more positive side is that humans have an undeniable urge to have cosmic significance. This desire, if positively channeled, provides citizens within a culture who are willing to work hard for a goal, once convinced that the goal matters. The quest to be heroic satisfies our natural narcissism, our need for self-esteem as *the* condition for our lives.

All who live within a society embrace a shared belief system regarding the significance of human life and of the way that one attains heroism. Becker contends that the crisis of modern society is that young people no longer feel heroic in the plan of action set out for them by their culture. When effective, this mythical hero-system induces people to serve in order to feel they are:

> of primary value, of cosmic specialness, of ultimate usefulness to creation, of unshakable meaning. They earn this feeling by carving out a place in nature, by building an edifice that reflects human value: a temple, a cathedral, a totem pole, a sky-scraper, a family that spans three generations. The hope and belief is that the things that man creates in society are of lasting worth and meaning, that they outlive or outshine death and decay, that man and his products count. (p. 5)

It is not only younger people who are affected by the need to have the sum total of their lives add up to something. When older people conduct a life review, they tend to fit the events of their lives into the overall saga of the decades gone by. Past events are construed less randomly than they may actually have occurred. Seniors who engage in the life review process report enhanced satisfaction with their lives.

Members within a culture endorse a shared myth. In American Westerns, the lone hero rode out "toward the horizon in complete individual freedom, no longer constrained by any social rules or requirements" (Lifton, 1993, p. 223). According to Sam Keen (1994), we have come of age and have left myth behind, and now we enter the age of enlightenment. Scientific method and reason are relied on to answer our questions. Carl Jung (1965) warned humanity not to abandon myth and art in favor of science, but instead, to maintain a balance between them. He wrote that mythic statements are needed to "frame a view of the world which adequately explains the meaning of human existence in the cosmos" (p. 340). According to Jung, meaninglessness is equivalent to illness, whereas meaning makes many things, and perhaps everything endurable. Writer Sven Birkerts (1994) agrees with the perspective that the electronic age has given us greater access to information, while stripping the information of its context and thus depriving it of meaning. We expect the world of artificial intelligence and computerized data banks to tell us everything we need to know. What they provide is information, but we must create some kind of context for those data, and in doing so, explain to ourselves why we need the information and what is the meaning of our life.

Birkerts (1994) suggested that in the earlier days of human history, people lived out their lives pretty much in one place, being greatly limited by lack of mobility. This way of life allowed a person to get to know intimately a small corner of the world and a narrow slice of human activities, and to make sense of his or her world through familiarity with it. This in-depth knowledge of one's own world, combined with a spiritual faith, may have allowed this person a sense of meaning.

However, such a narrow scope of existence would also be limiting, in that this person would be unaware of other possibilities about how to live. Lack of this larger perspective creates provincialism, conservatism, and a suspiciousness of the unfamiliar, according to Birkerts:

> But by the same token, the constant availability of data and macroperspectives has its own diminishing returns. After a while the sense of scale is attenuated and a relativism resembling cognitive and moral paralysis may result. When everything is permitted, Nietzsche said, we have nihilism; likewise, when everything is happening everywhere, it gets harder to care about anything. How do we assign value? Where do we find the fixed context that allows us to create a narrative of sense about our lives? (p. 73)

Wisdom comes from the ability to grasp a sense of the natural connectedness of things. We must construct a life story for ourselves that will help us make sense out of our lives. Our narrative should help us see some purpose to our being here. Birkerts makes the case that reading continuously provides us with new perspectives and "truths about human nature and the processes of life" (p. 74). On the other hand, the media and high tech information swamp us with data, without providing a context from which to put them into perspective. For instance, if we learn of some gang killings in the inner city, those who read extensively know that this event does not mean that the 1990s in the United States are the bloodiest, most violent period of human history. Quite the contrary, these are the best of times in so many ways, and the most humane of times, in comparison to the entire sweep of human history.

Every occurrence in a book has significance; it is there for a reason. The meaning of all of the parts come together at the end, in a significant pattern. The reader gets a perspective on life that is imbued with meaning. A second benefit of reading that Birkerts sees is that while the physical self remains rooted in the world, the inner self moves away from its reliance on the immediate. One can exist in two realms simultaneously, with each enriching and informing the other. This inner life gives a tremendous feeling of freedom and control. The book is one's secret life, waiting to be reentered, a treasure of enjoyment.

Just as the reader of a novel lives in two worlds, that of the plot as well as that of everyday life, so also it is true that as the hero of our own life's purpose, we may partake in everyday life, with meaningful agenda as a backdrop.

An Outward Frame of Reference

Many of us do not have a solid sense of self, because we have directed our search for identity outside ourselves. Paying attention to what others expect from us can distract us from attending to our own inner desires and feelings. Indeed, the point of getting others to direct us or of allowing them to do so is to escape the risk, angst, and responsibility of growing ourselves into mature persons.

Horoscopes provide "meaning" and "purpose" from the outside. Their popularity is one expression of our desire for a frame of orientation, of guidance from an external source. This tendency amounts to being other-directed. Whereas we certainly want to be responsive to others, and external reality in general, we are capable of considering our options and making decisions informed by our philosophy of life.

The Value of a Personal Vision: Developing a Philosophy of Life

A philosophy of life is a system of motivating beliefs, that encourages us to live our lives in accordance with a set of rules of our own choosing. A goal of this text has been to promote consideration of what enduring guidelines might be incorporated into a personal vision. A meaningful philosophy can become a self-fulfilling prophecy. It serves as a compass on your journey. We can expect our philosophy of life to undergo gradual transformation as we continue to have new experiences. Even so, it performs a tremendous service in orienting our everyday behaviors toward an overall purpose.

➤ SUCCESS

According to psychologist Mike McCaffrey (1986), success is knowing your values and goals and conducting your life in accordance with them. Individuals develop values over the course of a lifetime. They are not born with them. Human beings are born with innate intelligence, and are thus motivated by a handful of needs stemming from their awareness of being mortal, of wanting to affiliate with and to have impact on others, of requiring alleviation of boredom, of knowing who they are, and of seeking answers to explain their very existence.

Sometimes people do not know what their values are. They are without purpose or direction. Many in our culture have embraced the idea that success in life is measured by achieving wealth, power, glamour, or fame. For Ernest Holmes (1988), success does not necessarily mean the acquisition of a million dollars. Subjectively, it means a state of well-being, a sense of happiness— objectively, an environment that reflects this inner state of consciousness. To complement such external achievements as financial success, people need inner development. You need to consider the things worth being as well as those worth having. You can delineate internal states which are important to you, such as an optimistic outlook or concern for others, as well as external goals, which are made up of things you would like to accomplish, such as a college degree and landing a job in a particular field. If you really know what is important in your life, you will be able to marshal your abilities toward accomplishing them. In order to be successful, you need knowledge, self-esteem, and commitment or resolve.

Here is one more philosophical outlook for your consideration, in which a poet expresses some of the existential needs and the sources of contentment discussed in this text:

Success

To laugh often and much;
To win the respect of intelligent people and the affection of children;
To earn the appreciation of honest critics and endure the betrayal of false friends;
To appreciate beauty;
To find the best in others;
To leave the world a bit better; whether by a healthy child, a garden patch or a redeemed social condition;
To know even one life has breathed easier because you lived.
This is to have succeeded.

➤ CONCLUSION: THIS JOURNEY'S END

Psychology has a great deal to offer in enabling us to understand and tackle both our personal and our interpersonal problems. In general, as we become more aware of who we are, what motivates us, how we have formed the attitudes and values that we hold, we become better able to chart our course through the rough terrain of life. Although we can get through life without becoming self-aware, this state is well-worth achieving.

During the past several decades, the rather disparate theories of personality development, psychopathology, and cure have been researched and, to some extent, integrated. Each orientation is as yet incomplete in its substantiation and provision of explanations for the array of human thoughts, feelings, and behaviors that must be explained. Portions of these theories have been referred to throughout this text, by way of explanation of everyday human experiences. For instance, we have been introduced to the defense mechanisms, which serve to ward off anxiety at the cost of distorting or denying reality. We have considered how unconscious motivations may inspire our behavior, and that environmental influences shape our actions as well. We have also learned that to a certain extent, we were born with the personality that we have. We have considered how these inborn qualities have combined with our childhood experiences to create our style of life. Although the most dramatic personality development occurs during childhood, most psychologists would agree that this development process continues throughout life.

As with personality, development of an ethical sense may result from a combination of inherited potential and socialization by parents and society. Genetic factors are evidenced by research such as family adoption studies that have shown the criminal behavior patterns of children adopted at birth to be more similar to those of their biological parents than to those of the adoptive parents who reared them. This finding argues for inherited qualities that indirectly affect later moral behavior. Even so, the bulk of the evidence seems to suggest that a moral sense is something that human beings need to be taught. There is research evidence that indicates adults who display exceptional altruism recalled special emphasis by their parents during childhood on the importance of such acts. We have seen that theorists explaining moral development tend to agree that making a commitment to a set of values, while acknowledging that alternative points of view exist, is the hallmark of a mature ethical sense. In addition, the characteristics of cooperation, generosity, caring, empathy, respect, and civility are generally regarded as highly desirable behaviors to cultivate in members of society.

Since our personality is partially inborn, and is substantially shaped throughout childhood, it makes sense to seek a career to fit who we are. Psychologists have linked personality types with job performance and job satisfaction. They have also used personality types to match student profiles with those of people in various career areas who are successfully functioning in their professions or occupations. When an individual is performing in a suitable career, his or her preferred leisure activities are likely to be in a similar domain. For many who have accomplished this synthesis, the line between leisure and work activities may become blurred. At its best, a person's career provides ongoing opportunities for creative expression. When this is so, one's work becomes a source of peak experiences and self-actualization.

We have seen that Western culture increasingly endorses gender equality. The economic attainments of women during the past few decades have had the effect of allowing women greater freedom in their selection of romantic partners. In former times, women were inclined, out of necessity to seek out a good provider, to focus more on income earning capacity of potential mates than on physical attractiveness, compatible interests, or pleasing personality traits. Today, men and women are moving towards psychological androgyny and away from traditional gender roles. This is considered a healthy trend by many psychologists, the foremost among them being Sandra Bem.

Psychologists and philosophers alike proclaim that loving others makes life meaningful and thus worthwhile. Robert Sternberg's model of love provides a useful way to look at this intangible experience by identifying three components of love: intimacy, passion, and commitment, all of which must be present for the complete experience of love. Intimacy grows through reciprocal self-disclosure. This process entails making oneself relatively "transparent" to at least one other person. In fact, this is an effective approach to interpersonal relating in a more general sense. Passion refers to the attraction towards a potential partner. Commitment involves a decision to build an ongoing relationship with another.

Success in our love life requires many of the same characteristics that we employ in other aspects of life: self-awareness, self-discipline, and motivation to make the relationship work. A good relationship provides a transcendent purpose for each participant, a goal that is larger than oneself.

Most people want to find a romantic partner and to form a committed, secure relationship. The accomplishment of this task is perhaps the greatest challenge in life, which takes both skill and effort. Because of the emphasis on romantic love in our culture, we tend to form relationships in a predictable series of stages, first romanticizing the relationship, next suffering the inevitable disillusionment that follows from our initial construction of the match, and finally, arriving at a mutual respect and affection based on a realistic appraisal and acceptance of the partner.

One consequence of romanticizing the formation of partnerships is that many of us "lead" into relationships with our sexual attraction. For most people, sexual expression is an important part of life, providing a source of pleasure and joy through human connection. Ironically, although sex is a vital part of life for most of us, and it is what we use to initiate pair-bonding, we don't find it socially acceptable to talk about sex. This situation is problematic, as many of us are left feeling fearful and inept with regard to sexual expression. As with success in other aspects of interpersonal relations, a good sex life requires self-knowledge and effective communication.

Adler's contention that an overriding goal for human beings is to gain self-acceptance is considered valid today. Self-esteem has been described as a sense of personal competence and worth, and enables one to feel competent to meet life's challenges. Having the experience of the setting of goals and accomplishing them builds self-confidence. Likewise, successfully tackling challenges builds self-esteem. To help us along, we have been given decision-making, problem-solving, time management, and goal-setting strategies.

One's degree of personal happiness seems to be a stable characteristic, a part of one's personality. Level of happiness correlates with several other personality characteristics, such as self-esteem, optimism, extroversion, and having an internal locus of control. In addition, having a spiritual faith, challenging work, along with the skills to meet the challenge, and a social support network predict one's level of happiness.

Although the presence of others can surely enhance our lives, a liking of our own company is the prerequisite for overcoming loneliness. The more introverted types among us require alone time to recharge after negotiating the intricacies of human relationships. All of us can benefit from time alone, to sort out our feelings, our desires, and otherwise get our bearings.

For more than half a century, psychologists and physicians have been investigating the link between physical and mental health. Our interactions with physical, social, and psychological environments can interact with our unique physiology to ensure health or to precipitate disease. One major breakthrough is our understanding of how our interpretation of external events can affect us. We are able to control our emotional lives by modifying our thoughts about external phenomena. In addition, our available coping mechanisms have a great deal to do with whether or not we interpret adverse external circumstances as catastrophic or relatively benign. Negative thinking has been linked with the experience of loneliness, depression, and ill health.

As with personality, predictors of physical health and longevity are partially inherited and partially predicted by lifestyle. The factors that contribute to a sense of well-being are widely known and include how we work and play, how we care for ourselves physically (diet, rest and exercise), how we think and feel, how we relate with others, and how we tend to our spiritual/existential needs.

Our uncomfortable relationship with our mortality seems to be a component of this latter need. Death anxiety is considered one of the fundamental human concerns, and it can be an ongoing stressor if not integrated into one's life. Encountering the time-limited nature of our existence can give us the motivation to make the most of the time we have. As with the confrontation of any fear, this encounter can also release energy previously used to ward off awareness and can allow us to engage life with a realistic appreciation of its parameters.

Freedom to express one's individualism is a highly prized ideal in the United States. Sometimes this value is purchased at the expense of a sense of

community. Along this road, we have been given the rationale and tools for getting along with our fellow human beings. One skill required for smooth human relationships is an ability to deal with the inevitable irritations that people experience with one another, so that behaviors that create minor annoyance in others don't get deferred until they explode as rage. Likewise, fear and depression make affiliation with others more difficult. A counter force, loneliness, prompts action toward the goal of being close to others.

If Adler and others are to be believed, one cannot experience fulfillment in life without negotiating relationships with others in a satisfying manner. People create meaningful lives for themselves by loving others, creative endeavor, embracing a spiritual belief, and even through suffering.

This tour is over. In the first chapter of this text, you were invited to get perspective on your life by looking back at your past, thinking about your current situation, and by projecting yourself into the future to envision where you might like to end up. A good understanding of yourself, as well as self-acceptance and a sound life philosophy, can be your guideposts to a happy life. Once you have a comfortable life philosophy, all actions and decisions can be made in light of your individual understanding of the purpose of your personal journey. This awareness should help you to understand better both your life and your mortality. May you have a long and successful journey, with many a lamp to guide you along your way!

So many truths about the human experience are inspiring when discussed, yet it is no easy matter deciding how to live according to the ideals one has embraced as worthwhile. Be patient, but steadfast in your attempts to get focused on what you want in your life. Be open to suggestions from a variety of sources, some of which may be unexpected. No one source is likely to have all that you could find useful. In Bertrand Russell's words,

> *I am sorry that I have had to leave so many problems unsolved. I always have to make this apology, but the world is rather puzzling and I cannot help it.*

➤ SUMMARY

One's values are what one considers important, the rules guiding one's life, and what makes life worth living. By being aware of one's values and living in accordance with them, we can find meaning in our lives. Due to their importance, time is well spent clarifying one's values.

Psychologists have examined "human nature" in order to learn what fundamental principles guide people in their quest for a fulfilling life. The existentialists have concluded that human beings struggle with certain "concerns" about their existence. Individuals must define who they are. People fear death and dread isolation from others. According to the existentialists, it is up to us to search for meaning in life. The relationship between freedom and responsibility must be understood.

THE NEED FOR A SENSE OF IDENTITY   Discovery of one's values is related to achievement of identity. One's search for identity involves asking several questions, the most important of which is: "Who am I?" Several practical steps can be taken to foster self-awareness.

1. *Self-monitoring of behaviors and introspection.* Since one's daily actions are expressions of one's basic values, it is possible to learn about oneself by examining one's behaviors. Introspection is another way to increase self-awareness.

2. *Public expression.* One can come to know one's own mind by explaining oneself to others. Until one's beliefs and attitudes are expressed in public, they remain half-formed convictions, of which one may be only partially aware.

3. *Dreams.* Dream content may be useful in heightening awareness as to one's own wants, goals, and conflicts.

4. *Journals.* Keeping a journal is an excellent way to gain self-awareness and to work through current issues in one's life.

5. *Therapy.* Although people who seek out therapy are often troubled by recognizable symptoms of mental distress, they may also try therapy as a route to enhanced self-awareness. What the therapist offers much of the time is a way to meaningfully interpret one's turmoil or suffering.

EXISTENTIAL ISOLATION   To overcome their feelings of isolation from nature and from themselves, people need to love, and care for others. Love is a union with somebody or something outside of self. Although self-awareness and self-acceptance are prerequisites for a meaningful existence, human beings also have a need to establish connections with others in society, and make a contribution to that society.

Improving the condition of others and finding a way to shape one's culture for the better may seem to be an overwhelming task. No one person will eliminate the suffering of all of humanity. The challenge is to refuse to despair, and find some way to express concern for others.

Becoming the best person one can be would itself help create a better world. One can help by looking to one's own self-development and being tolerant of the foibles of others.

THE NEED FOR ROOTEDNESS   Throughout life people have a need for roots, for a sense of security similar to what they experienced in the mother-child relationship. In the past and to some extent today, the extended family and the nuclear family provide a sense of continuity and connectedness. For some, the workplace has also provided a familial-like stability. Church affiliation and social organizations likewise provide an opportunity for affiliation and attachment.

Cosmic and Personal Meaning Individuals sometimes feel insignificant and fearful in the face of the vastness of the universe. They may overcome this feeling to some extent by actively striving to master their world and themselves. There are at least two routes to the satisfaction of this need for mastery: through the development of a spiritual basis to one's life or through creative endeavor. Forming a spiritual belief helps people overcome their fear of uncertainty and their dread over the prospect of an indifferent universe. Faith seems to offer meaning and purpose, as well as access to a power greater than oneself. People also combat a sense of powerlessness by being creative. Individuals can compensate for being only a small part of the world by striving to be competent at something, by influencing others, or by "making a dent" in some way.

Viktor Frankl believed that people can discover meaning in life in three different ways: first, through achievement; second, by experiencing a value, that is, something such as a work of nature or culture; and third, by experiencing someone through loving that person. Frankl also believed that meaning in life can be gained through suffering. Suffering can teach individuals patience, endurance, and self-mastery.

The Need for a Frame of Orientation: Developing a Style of Life A *frame of orientation* is a set of beliefs about the ultimate course of one's destiny. People can guide themselves toward a fulfilling style of life by first developing their philosophy of life.

Another way to make sense of one's life is to view it as a coherent story. Ernst Becker wrote that each person desires to be the hero of his or her life story and that to become conscious of what one is doing to earn one's feeling of heroism is the main problem of life. Becker contends that the crisis of modern society is that young people no longer feel heroic in the plan of action set out for them by their culture. Ordinarily, this mythical hero-system allows people to feel valuable and special.

Many of us do not have a solid sense of self, because we have directed our search for identify outside ourselves. Paying too much attention to what others expect from us can distract us from attending to our own inner desires and feelings. Indeed, the point of getting others to direct us or of allowing them to do so is to escape the risk, angst, and responsibility of developing into mature persons.

Success While many people measure success by external standards such as power and wealth, success can also be defined as using one's values and goals to guide everyday behavior.

Conclusion Knowledge of psychology enables us to understand and tackle our personal and interpersonal problems. As we become more aware of who we are, what motivates us, how we have formed the attitudes and values, we hold, we become better able to chart our course through life. Each theoretical orientation in psychology provides some explanation for the array of human thoughts, feelings, and behaviors that must be explained.

An overriding goal for human beings is to gain self-acceptance. However, most of us cannot experience fulfillment in life without negotiating relationships with others in a satisfying manner. Although good relationships with others can surely enhance our lives, a liking of one's own company is the prerequisite for overcoming loneliness. A person gains self-esteem by feeling competent to meet life's challenges. We demonstrate such competence to ourselves by setting goals and accomplishing them.

Inborn aspects of personality combine with life experiences to form one's personality and style of life. As with personality, development of an ethical sense may result from a combination of inherited potential and socialization by parents and society. Since personality is partially inborn and is gradually shaped through childhood, it makes sense to seek a career to fit who we are. Work is one avenue for fulfilling the fundamental need for a transcendent purpose.

Loving others is a basic route to experiencing life as worthwhile. Successful relationships require self-awareness on the part of the involved individuals, as well as a willingness to self-disclose to loved ones. For some time, relationships between men and women have been moving toward an egalitarian model.

Our interactions with physical, social, and psychological environments can combine with our unique physiology to ensure health or to precipitate disease. We are able to control our emotional lives by modifying our thoughts about external phenomena. Negative thinking has been linked with the experience of loneliness, depression, and poor health. As with personality, predictors of physical health and longevity are partially inherited and partially predicted by lifestyle. The factors that contribute to a sense of well-being are widely known and include how we work and play, how we care for ourselves physically (diet, rest, and exercise), how we think and feel, how we relate with others, and how we tend to our spiritual/existential needs. Our uncomfortable relationship with our mortality seems to be a component of this latter need. Facing one's mortality can prompt an interest in making the most of one's life.

Pursuit of excellence is a time-honored route to happiness. One's level of personal happiness seems to be a stable characteristic, a part of one's personality. Happiness with one's life correlates with several other personality characteristics and supports, such as self-esteem, optimism, extroversion, having an internal locus of control, a spiritual faith, successful mastery of challenging work, and a social support network.

While individual freedom is a strong value in the United States, it must be balanced with an appreciation of one's fundamental need for affiliation with others. Many negative emotions, such as anger, fear, and depression, interfere with the wish to be close to people. It is another unpleasant feeling, loneliness, which motivates us to form bonds with one another.

CHAPTER REVIEW QUESTIONS

1. What does Rollo May mean by his statement that a major problem that people face in today's society is inner emptiness?
2. What are some strategies that we might use to become aware of motivations we might have that currently lie outside conscious awareness?
3. How is having a sense of meaning in life related to Adler's concept of "social interest"?
4. How is it possible for us to improve the human condition simply by changing ourselves?
5. How does finding one's roots counteract existential isolation?
6. What concept does the Optimist Creed have in common with the prose poem, Disiderata?
7. According to Sam Keen, what makes caring for others difficult?
8. What suggestions does Viktor Frankl offer for finding meaning in life?
9. What is the value in viewing one's life as a heroic story?
10. What are some non-material standards of success delineated in the chapter?

ACTIVITIES

1. *SMALL GROUP EXERCISE:* **Personal Reflections on My Values.**
2. *INDIVIDUAL PROJECT:* **Ways to Live.** Read the choices, and select one of them to be the basis for your own written description of your "philosophy of life."
3. *INDIVIDUAL PROJECT:* **Goal-Setting.** Make a list of five things you plan to accomplish in the next year. You may include goals that will further you toward a career goal, or something that you would like to work on regarding your social life. Then prepare a self-addressed, stamped envelope, and place a copy of your list inside. This list will be mailed to you by your instructor one year from now.

Personal Reflections on My Values

Directions: Read each of the following questions, and then write your answers in the blanks.

1. What in your life gives you a sense of purpose? Name the five most important things in your life, the things that provide your sense of purpose.

_____

_____

_____

_____

_____

2. Are you an inner-directed person who acts out of values that you've examined and made your own? Do you find yourself simply reflecting what others expect of you? Are you living your life by becoming what others expect you to become? Are your values merely your reflections of others' values? Write your thoughts on these questions below.

_____

_____

_____

_____

3. How often do you tune into your private thoughts and feelings? Do you have any process to help you with this, such as journal writing, or talking to your best friends or a relative? Explain your process of self-reflection.

_____

_____

_____

_____

4. How is your philosophy of death related to your philosophy of life? Can you separate these two philosophies? Are you able to describe them?

_____

_____

_____

_____

5. Is there some cause that you would die for?

_____

_____

_____

_____

6. When you look at what you were like five years ago, how do you perceive that you have changed? Do you truly like the kind of person you are becoming?

_____

_____

_____

_____

7. What are some of the major struggles you are now experiencing in regard to making sense out of life?

_____

_____

_____

_____

8. What changes would you like to implement in your life by the time five more years have passed?

_____

_____

_____

_____

9. Do you set aside even a few minutes each day to reflect on the meaning and quality of your life, and to examine the direction you are taking? Do you seek solitude so that you are able to reexamine the values that give your life meaning, as well as what you most want from life? Do you ask yourself what you are doing, or not doing, to get what you want from life?

_____

_____

_____

_____

10. Think of one crucial turning point in your life. It might be a decision you made, a struggle you were involved in, or some other significant experience. Share with the group in what ways who you are now is a result of this critical turning point. What might be different in your life now if you hadn't had this experience or if you had made a different decision?

_____

_____

_____

_____

11. Spend some time exploring activities that you engage in that seem meaningless. Does everything you do have to be grounded in meaning?

Why do you engage in experiences that have little or no personal meaning or value to you?

_____

_____

_____

_____

12. Socrates asked, "How should one live?" What, if anything, has the study
of psychology taught you about this question?

_____

_____

_____

_____

13. Who are the five people you most admire, and what do you suppose each
would describe as his or her purpose in life?

_____

_____

_____

_____

_____

14. Complete this sentence: "I think spending money on _____
is foolish and wasteful."

15. What are your roots? In other words, what aspects of your life give you a
sense of groundedness?

_____

_____

_____

_____

16. Think of yourself *without* some of the people and projects that give your
life a sense of purpose and direction. What are you without these people
or projects? If you take away some of the sources of meaning in your life,
what is left to you? How much do you derive your identity from other
significant people?

_____

_____

_____

_____

Ways to Live

Directions: Formulate your own philosophy of life by responding to the following 13 scenarios that represent alternative life styles. Rank order all 13, from your first preference to your last. Write about this. Then, write out your own way of life, borrowing ideas from any of the 13 scenarios, or using your own ideas. Finally think of things you have done in the last year that are consistent with the life style you have described. Cite any instances where your behavior in the past has radically departed from your philosophy of life. (This bridges the gap between a general philosophical statement and the way you actually live.)

> *Way 1:* You actively participate in the social life of your community, not primarily to change it but to understand, appreciate, and preserve the best that human beings have attained. Social changes are to be made slowly and carefully, so that what has been achieved in human culture is not lost. In this lifestyle, excessive desires are avoided, and moderation is sought. Indulgence and even great enthusiasm are to be avoided. You want the good things in life, but not vulgarity, irrational behavior, or impatience. Life is to have clarity, balance, refinement, control, and order. Friendship is to be esteemed, but not easy intimacy with many people. Life is marked by discipline, good manners, and predictability. You are active physically and socially, but not in a hectic or radical way. Restraint and intelligence give order to your life.

> *Way 2:* For the most part, you go it alone, assuring yourself of privacy in living quarters, having plenty of time to yourself, attempting to control your own life. Your emphasis is on self-sufficiency, self-knowledge, reflection and meditation. You avoid intimate associations and relationships with social groups, as well as attempts to control the physical environment by the physical manipulation of objects. You believe that one should aim to simplify one's external life, to moderate desires that depend on physical and social forces outside oneself. You concentrate on refinement, clarification, and self-direction. Not much is to be gained by living outwardly. You must avoid dependence on other people or things; the center of life should be found within yourself.

> *Way 3:* This way of life centers on sympathetic concern for other people. Affection is the main thing in life, affection that is free from all traces of the imposition of yourself upon others or of using others for your own purpose. You avoid greed in possessions, emphasis on sexual passion, striving for power over people and things, excessive emphasis on intellect, and undue self-concern. These things hinder the sympathetic love among people that alone gives significance to life. Aggressiveness blocks receptivity to the forces that foster genuine personal growth. You believe that one should purify oneself, restrain one's self-assertiveness, and become receptive, appreciative, and helpful in relating to other people.

> *Way 4:* Life is something to be sensuously enjoyed, enjoyed with relish and abandonment. The aim in life should not be to control the course of the world or to change society or the lives of others, but to be open and receptive to things and persons, and to delight in them. Life is a festival, not a workshop or a school for moral discipline. To let yourself go, to let things and people affect you, is more important than to do good. Such enjoyment requires that you be

self-centered enough to be keenly aware of what is happening within yourself in order to be free for new happiness. You believe that you should avoid entanglements, should not be too dependent on particular people or things, and should not be self-sacrificing. You should spend ample time alone, should have time for meditation and self-awareness. Both solitude and sociability are necessary for the good life.

Way 5: This way of life stresses the social group rather than the individual. You think that a person should not focus on himself or herself, should not withdraw from people, should not be aloof and self-centered. Rather, you want to merge yourself with a social group, enjoy cooperation and companionship, and join with others in resolute activity for the realization of common goals. People are social, and people are active; life should merge energetic group activity and cooperative group enjoyment. Meditation, restraint, concern for your self-sufficiency, abstract intellectuality, solitude, and stress on your possessions—all cuts the roots that bind people together. You live outwardly with gusto, enjoying the good things of life, while working with others to secure the things that make possible a pleasant and energetic social life.

Way 6: You believe that unless a person strives to be dynamic, his or her life continuously tends to stagnate, to become comfortable, with too much time to ponder. Against these tendencies, you must stress the need for constant activity—physical action, adventure, the realistic solution for specific problems as they appear, the improvement of techniques for controlling the world and society. The future of human beings depends primarily on what you do, not on what you feel or on your speculations. New problems constantly arise and always will arise. Improvements must always be made if people are to progress. You can't just follow the past or dream of what the future might be. You should rely on technical advances made possible by scientific knowledge. You should find your goals in the solution of your problems.

Way 7: At various times and in various ways, you accept something from all other paths of life, but give no particular path your exclusive allegiance. At one moment, one way may be more appropriate; at another moment, another is the more appropriate. Life should contain enjoyment, action and contemplation in about equal amounts. When any one way is carried to extremes, you lose something important for your life. Therefore, you must cultivate flexibility; admit diversity in yourself; accept the tension that this diversity produces. You find a place for detachment in the midst of enjoyment and activity. The goal of life is found in the dynamic integration of enjoyment, action, and contemplation, and in the dynamic interaction of the various paths of life. You should use all of them in building a life, and not one alone.

Way 8: Enjoyment should be the keynote of life: not the hectic search for intense and exciting pleasures, but the enjoyment of the simple and easily obtainable pleasures; the pleasures of just existing, of savoring food, of comfortable surroundings, of talking with friends, of rest and relaxation. A home that is warm and well stocked with food, a door open to friends—this is the place for you to live. Your body at ease, relaxed, calm in its movements, not hurried, breathing slowly and easily; a willingness to nod and to rest, feeling gratitude to the world that feeds the body—so should it be. Driving ambition and the fanaticism of ascetic ideals are the signs of discontented people who have lost the capacity to float in the stream of simple, carefree, wholesome enjoyment.

Way 9: Receptivity should be the keynote of life. The good things of life come of their own accord, and they come unsought. They cannot be found by resolute action. They cannot be found in the indulgence of the sensuous desires of the body. They cannot be gathered by participation in the turmoil of social life. They cannot be given to others by attempts to be helpful. They cannot be garnered by hard thinking. Rather, they come unsought when the bars of the self are down. When your self has ceased to make demands and waits in quiet receptivity, you become open to the powers that nourish you and work through you; sustained by these powers, you will know joy and peace. When you are sitting alone under the trees and the sky, open to nature's voices, calm and receptive, then can the wisdom from without enter within you.

Way 10: Self-control should be the keynote of life: not the easy self-control that retreats from the world, but the vigilant, stern, vigorous control of a self that lives in the world and knows the strength of the world and the limits of human power. The good life is rationally directed and firmly pursues high ideals. It is not bent by the seductive voices of comfort and desire. It does not expect social utopias. It is distrustful of final victories. Too much should not be expected. Yet you can, with vigilance, hold firm the reins of yourself, can control unruly impulses, can understand your place in the world, can guide your actions by reason, and can maintain self-reliant independence. And in this way, though you finally perish, you can keep your human dignity and respect, and die with cosmic good manners.

Way 11: The contemplative life is the good life. The external world is no fit habitat for human beings. It is too big, too cold, too pressing. It is the life turned inward that is rewarding. The rich internal world of ideals, of sensitive feelings or reveries, of self-knowledge, is your true home. By the cultivation of the self within, you become human. Only then does there arise deep sympathy with all that lives, an understanding of the suffering inherent in life, a realization of the futility of aggressive action, the attainment of contemplative joy. Conceit then falls away, and austerity is dissolved. In giving up the world, you find the larger and finer sea of the inner self.

Way 12: The use of the body's energy is the secret of a rewarding life. Your hands need material to make into something: lumber and stone to build, food to harvest, clay to mold. Your muscles are alive to joy only when in action: in climbing, running, skiing, and the like. Your life finds its zest in overcoming, dominating, conquering some obstacle. It is the active deed that is satisfying, the deed that meets the challenge of the present, the daring and the adventuresome deed. Not in cautious foresight, not in relaxed ease does your life attain completion. Outward energetic action, the excitement of power in the tangible present—this is the way for you to live.

Way 13: A person should let himself or herself be used: used by other people in their growth, used by the great objective purposes in the universe, which silently and irresistibly achieve their goal, since the purpose of people and the world are basically dependable and can be trusted. You should be humble, constant, and faithful, and grateful for affection and protection; but you should also be undemanding. Close to people and to nature, you are willing to be second. You nourish the good by your devotion. You should be a serene, confident, quiet vessel and instrument of the great dependable powers that move to fulfill themselves.

Source: Adapted from Simon, Howe, & Kirchenbaum (1972).

GLOSSARY

Acquaintance rape: A woman being forced to have unwanted sex with someone she knows.

Active euthanasia: A practice involving the administration of a lethal injection by a physician, for the purpose of ending the suffering of a terminally ill or gravely injured patient, who is judged to have no hope of recovery nor remaining quality of life.

Active listening: A technique of listening that improves communication between two people over and above the usual level of understanding gained through passive listening. The listener repeats back to the speaker the essence of what the listener has understood the speaker to be saying. The speaker can either confirm that the intended meaning has been received or can correct the misunderstanding. This feedback by the listener to the speaker is active listening. The active listening process allows any misunderstanding to be noticed and cleared up before the conversation resumes. In addition, the speaker is reassured on an ongoing basis of having been listened to and understood.

Affect: Visible signs of emotion.

Affiliation: The desire to be with others of one's own kind; to belong to a group.

Affirmations: Assertions that something exists or is true that are put in writing and rehearsed to foster a change in thinking within the individual. Such an exercise builds momentum toward positive change by setting up a self-fulfilling prophecy in the direction of the desired outcome.

Aggression: Verbal or physical behavior intended to do harm to another person, an animal, or property.

All-or-nothing thinking: Dualistic thinking that categorizes events as good or bad, right or wrong, black or white.

Altruism: Behavior performed on behalf of another person, without benefiting the one performing the act in any obvious way.

Analysis of resistance: Unconscious behaviors on the part of patients undergoing psychoanalysis that serve to defend the patient against the discovery of painful unconscious material. The psychoanalyst notices and interprets the resistance displayed by patients in order to uncover unconscious material of which the patients are reluctant to become aware.

Analysis of transference: Transference occurs when the patient relates to the psychoanalyst as though he or she were a significant person from the patient's past, such as a rejecting father or an overprotective mother. The psychoanalyst notices such patterns of behavior and brings them to the attention of the patient. When made aware of the transference, the patient has an opportunity to discontinue this automatic, unconscious way of relating. Through this reexperiencing of old relationship patterns in a safe environment, the patient learns better ways to relate to others.

Anima: According to Jungian theory, each person's personality has both male and female aspects or archetypes. The anima is the female aspect in men. Existence of the anima in males enables men to relate to members of the other sex. A man who hates women would be considered by Jung to be at war with his own anima, and is projecting this internal conflict onto women. As they approach age 40, Jung believed that men become more comfortable with their anima qualities.

Animus: The animus is the male aspect in women, according to Jungian theory. A woman may project her ideal image of manliness (her animus) onto a potential mate and would be disappointed if that man did not live up to the masculine standards she carries internally. Toward middle age, women tend to show more of their animus side, and thus have more balanced personalities.

Antipathy: This refers to a habitual dislike or aversion to something or someone.

Antisocial behavior: Behavior that displays a disregard for the needs and rights of other people. It can be contrasted with prosocial behavior. Antisocial individuals seem to have inadequate conscience development, which allows them to harm others without remorse.

Archetypes: According to Jungian theory, archetypes are deeply rooted, inherited ideas that are present in everyone. They are universal representations of a kind of person, a type of object, or a particular experience, and they reflect the common experiences of humanity in coping with nature, war, parenthood, love, and evil. Archetypes are reflected in literature, art, architecture, religions, laws, customs, etiquette, mores, taboos, value systems, and ideologies.

Assertiveness: Assertiveness refers to the expression of one's rights without interfering with the rights of others. Assertive people stand up for themselves, expressing their thoughts and feelings directly, honestly, and appropriately. Assertiveness is typically prompted by some form of anger, from mild irritation to well-disciplined outrage.

Assisted suicide: Doctor-assisted suicide has been used in cases involving individuals who are suffering from terminal illness or whose quality of life has been irreparably damaged. When life has become unbearable and has no prospect of returning to a tolerable condition, people who may wish to end their own lives are often unable to do so. For this reason, Dr. Kavorkian, a physician, developed a procedure for assisting terminally ill patients to end their lives.

Attune: To bring into harmony or sympathetic relationship. Theorist and psychotherapist Heinz Kohut used the term "empathic attunement" to describe the natural and appropriate sympathetic relationship that develops in healthy mother-infant bonding, wherein each responds easily to the cues of the other.

Automatic thoughts: The beliefs people form in response to life events that are fleeting and thus not usually attended to. These thoughts, and not external events, are responsible for a person's mood.

Behaviorism: A form of psychotherapy that treats maladaptive behaviors without resorting to an investigation of internal mental processes.

Blame the victim: The inclination to justify the harm that befalls another person by rationalizing that the victim did something to cause or to deserve that harm. This thinking serves to enable people to continue a common but irrational belief known as the "just world hypothesis," which is the conviction that life is fair and that people get what they deserve. Such a belief allows people to feel safe, thus denying the legitimacy of everyday observations that bad things happen to good people.

Cardinal traits: Characteristics that are pervasive and dominant in a person's life. Cardinal traits are ruling passions that organize an individual's behaviors toward one purpose or theme. In Gordon Allport's theory, personality traits are categorized as cardinal, central, or secondary.

Catastrophizing: An irrational way of thinking identified by Albert Ellis that involves blowing things out of proportion so that they seem worse than they are.

Catharsis: An emotional release through overt expression of that emotion; a venting, cleansing or purifying. In psychoanalysis, the expression of strangulated feeling was linked to the alleviation of neurotic symptoms.

Central traits: Central traits control less of a person's behavior than do cardinal traits but do influence the person's actions in a variety of situations. Such traits are the ones that people mention when asked to write a letter of recommendation for someone, characterizing the person as intelligent, competitive, sincere, honest, or funny.

Client-centered therapy: A form of humanistic therapy developed by Carl Rogers. The goal of client-centered therapy is to release the inherent capacity in a potentially competent individual. This therapy emphasizes the client's current life circumstances rather than the person's childhood experiences. Client-centered therapy focuses on the client's conscious thoughts and feelings, as well as removing obstacles to full functioning. The therapist offers the client unconditional positive regard by accepting the client for his or her true self, without criticisms or demands for change. This acceptance leads to a dissolving of conditions of worth. Total acceptance by the therapist is the first step toward self-acceptance by the client.

Cognitive: Having to do with thinking; mentally processing information.

Cognitive restructuring: Changing maladaptive thoughts is the central goal of cognitive therapy. The cognitive restructuring procedure involves modifying illogical ideas that maintain a person's maladaptive behaviors. Through cognitive restructuring people change what they say to themselves about what is going on in their lives. They learn to change negative self-statements, which interpret the situation in such a way that nothing can be done to cope with it, into positive self-statements that are optimistic and that point to some constructive, realistic course of action.

Coitus: Sexual intercourse.

Collective unconscious: A storehouse of memories is transmitted genetically, so that each person inherits all of previous human history. For Carl Jung, all that human beings are comes from the entire sweep of prior human experience. Jung used as evidence for the existence of the collective unconscious the finding that people from different parts of the world and/or different eras have chosen the same symbols to represent an important object or a situation.

Compensation: A defense mechanism involving compensatory reactions against feelings of inferiority. A person who has a defect or weakness (real or imagined) may go to unusual lengths to overcome the weakness by excelling in other areas. The perceived weakness may be compensated for in a different area or in the same realm as gave rise to the initial feelings of inferiority.

Conditioning: Learning, the modification of behavior as the result of experience.

Conditions of worth: The conviction that one is worthy and acceptable only under conditions specified by one's parents and society. Conditional positive regard, the acceptance of a person that is dependent on the positive or negative evaluation of that person's actions, leads to the development of conditions of worth.

Confirmation bias: The tendency to notice only occurrences that provide evidence that one's beliefs are correct, and the failure to either look for or notice disconfirming evidence.

Congruence: Agreement among an individual's ideal self, which represents who the person want to be; the true self, which is who the person really is; and the self-image, which reflects the way the person sees himself or herself as being. If these three aspects do not correspond with one another, inner conflicts arise within a person.

Date rape: Forced sexual intercourse that occurs in the context of dating.

Defense mechanisms: A means of protecting the ego or self at the cost of distorting reality. If a person cannot deal with reality as it actually is, he or she can try to alter it and make it appear to be in agreement with his or her wishes. Although these unconscious strategies falsify reality, they are effective in affording protection from the disabling effects of anxiety and frustration. In psychoanalytic theory, anxiety is thought to arise when the ego tries to resolve the conflicting demands made by the id, the superego, and the reality of the external environment.

Deindividuation: The experience of anonymity that comes from being a part of a large group or crowd. A temporary experience of loss of self-consciousness, self-awareness, and personal responsibility that results from an individual's being immersed in a group the tends to occur when people are emotionally aroused and their sense of responsibility is diminished.

Delay of gratification: Involves the postponement of an immediate reward in order to gain a future reward or benefit that is greater than the one available in the immediate present.

Denial: A primitive, infantile defense mechanism that denies the existence of any external reality that is too unpleasant to face. Denial is typically elicited by the death of a loved one, terminal illness, and similar painful or threatening experiences.

Dependency: The seeking of an object to make one feel complete. Dependent behaviors are designed to elicit caregiving and arise from the self-perception of being unable to function adequately without the help of another person. Dependent individuals tend to be unrealistically preoccupied with fears of being left to take care of themselves.

Depressive realism: Depressed people are often more realistic in their thinking than are nondepressed individuals. Nondepressed people overestimate the degree to which they are responsible for positive events and underestimate their responsibility for negative events; depressed people do not have this characteristic.

Determinism: The assumption that all behavior is caused by factors in the individual's environment, within his or her unconscious mind, or some other source not under the person's conscious control.

Disconfirming evidence: Any observation that could show one's existing belief to be false.

Displacement: The transference of emotions produced in one situation to another. What takes place is a redirection of an emotional attachment away from its original object and toward another, less threatening object. It can involve the expression, in a new situation, of feelings that one is afraid to show in the original situation.

Disposition: Coming from the person; usually referring to the personality.

Dispositional: Emphasizing the role of inherited predispositions in shaping human behavior. This approach focuses on enduring characteristics of the person that can be seen in different situations and over time.

Dream analysis: A fundamental tool of psychoanalysis, the purpose of dream analysis is to uncover the unconscious conflicts, which are believed to cause mental illness. The objects and events that are conjured up in dreams represent attempts to fulfill some impulse of the id, usually in disguised ways. Freud contended that dreams represent, in hidden or symbolic form, repressed desires, fears, conflicts, and wishes, and were particularly likely to be expressions of repressed sexual impulses and fears, as well as aggressive wishes.

Dysfunctional thought diary: A journal that cognitive therapy clients are encouraged to keep in which automatic thoughts are recorded, as well as the life events that prompted them. Clients are often unaware of their automatic thoughts, because such thoughts are fleeting and are not usually attended to. Yet these thoughts, and not external events, are responsible for client's emotional responses to life experiences.

Ego: The rational, problem-solving part of personality. The ego is said to operate on the reality principle. Its role is to test mental images for their reality. Such images or wishes do not satisfy needs; reality must be considered. The ego, the "executive" of the personality, plans how to achieve satisfaction of id drives. It decides what actions are appropriate and thus determines which id instincts will be satisfied and in what manner. The ego must counteract the wishful thinking of the id as well as the moralistic thinking of the superego, in order to avoid a distortion of reality.

Ego ideal: In psychoanalytic theory, the portion of the superego that encompasses those actions for which the child is rewarded.

Emotion: A state characterized by physiological arousal and subjective thoughts about (interpretations of) that arousal.

Emotional insulation: The tendency to submerge feelings, a practice that enables a person to avoid experiencing psychological pain, although closing off negative feelings dampens positive feelings as well. Emotional insulation functions as a blanket over all feelings.

Empathy: The ability to see things from the perspective of another person.

Empirical: Based upon observable evidence; data derived from experience or verifiable by experiment.

Endorphins: A neurotransmitter found in the brain that acts as a natural pain killer, and plays a role in the pleasure of social contact.

Enmeshment: This term comes from family therapy, and refers to family members who have not achieved enough individuation to experience themselves as separate from other family members.

Environment: Anything external to oneself; one's surroundings.

Ethical nihilism: The denial of the existence of any possible bases for the establishment of an ethical or moral philosophy.

Ethical relativism: The view that moral standards and principles are relative to the nature of the particular society in which they exist and admit of no outside criticism or evaluation.

Existential isolation: The recognition that no matter how close an individual feels to others, he or she must face life alone and can never be completely understood by another person. It refers to the occasional experience of feeling cut off or alienated from the rest of the world.

Existentialism: A branch of humanistic psychology formed around the idea that human beings are set apart as a species by their awareness of certain predicaments brought about by simply being alive. There are some basic existential concerns that address each person's "situation" in the world and that cut beneath any individual's personal life history.

Explanatory style: The characteristic way people explain to themselves why events happen.

Extinction: In learning theory, operant extinction is the eventual discontinuance of a voluntary behavior that does not produce the desired outcome. Classical extinction is the eventual failure of the conditioned stimulus to produce the conditioned response.

Extrinsic motivation: A reward offered by the environment that motivates the individual to take some action.

Extroversion: Openness and sociability. The extroverted person is friendly, approachable, and eager to relate to others and be affected by them. Extroverts tend to know a lot of people, and like to include as many people as possible in their activities. They are easily engaged by friends and strangers alike.

Feedback: Information about what effect a response has had.

Fixation: In psychoanalytic theory, disturbances in development during childhood were believed to result in being stuck, or fixated. The person could not continue to grow until he or she returned to this childhood predicament and mastered it.

Flow: Involves having the competence successfully to handle challenging tasks. When a person undertakes activities that are challenging, but that are also attainable because that individual has good skills to apply to the task, the person experiences the happiness brought on by a sense of accomplishment.

Free association: A psychoanalytic therapy technique in which the patient verbalizes all thoughts and feelings that come to mind. The purpose of free association is to lower defenses so that unconscious material can emerge and be dealt with in therapy.

Free will: The philosophical and religious position that behavior is ultimately directed by volition regardless of external influences.

Fully functioning person: An individual who has achieved an openness to feelings and experiences and who has learned to trust inner sensations and intuitions, feelings, thoughts, as well as to the external environment. The fully functioning person experiences congruence between the true self, the ideal self, and the self-image.

Generativity: Erik Erikson used this term in referring to the task during middle-age of finding a way to give to others, particularly younger people, who can benefit from the nurturing of mature adults. Generativity can also be attained by helping others indirectly through creative works, such as constructing buildings or authoring a book.

Gerontologist: A person who studies the aging process.

Habituate: A physiological mechanism in which the senses acclimate to a stimulus that is repeatedly or continuously presented.

Halo effect: A phenomenon in which physically attractive people are viewed more positively than are less attractive people on a variety of dimensions that are unrelated to physical attractiveness.

Homeostasis: A steady state of bodily equilibrium normally maintained automatically by various physiological mechanisms.

Humanism: An approach to psychology that focuses on subjective human experience, free will, and human potential.

Id: One of three structures in Freud's model of the mind. The id is the original source of personality, present at birth. It consists of a collection of basic biological drives that provides the energy for the operation of the entire personality, for the id itself, and for both the ego and the superego. The id and its motivations are unknown to the conscious self.

Ideal self: In Rogersian therapy, an aspect of the self representing whom the person wants to be.

Identification: The earliest expression of an emotional tie with another person. The process of incorporating the goals and values of another person into one's own behavior prompted by the wish to be like the other person.

Identity: The condition of being oneself and not another. The establishing of a separate self from one's family and society, a process that is referred to by psychologists as "individuation."

Identity crisis: According to Erik Erikson, adolescents worry about who they are. This self-confrontation involves physical elements such as the awakening of sexual drives; cognitive developments associated with the attainment of logical thought; and social elements. The identity crisis is often successfully resolved with the adoption of an ideology that restores personal and social meaning.

Individuation: The formation of a distinct identity, separate from one's family of origin. Through the process of individuation, the self is formed. A person is individuated to the extent that he or she has a fully harmonious and integrated personality. Carl Jung contended that it is desirable for a personality to have balance, meaning that all aspects of the self are developed, so that the person is not a fanatic about anything, and that the person does not have "inferior" (or undeveloped) aspects, which would be the opposite of the fanatic quality.

Inferiority complex: Alfred Adler viewed each human being's struggle to overcome feelings of inferiority as a core problem in life. People experience feelings of inferiority mainly because they begin life as small and relatively powerless children surrounded by larger and more competent adults. People react to this inferior position of childhood by striving for superiority and power. Adler believed that throughout life the desire to overcome inferiority was the prime determining force in behavior. By gaining mastery in various areas, individuals achieve self-acceptance, their primary goal in life. If childhood feelings of inferiority continue into adulthood, the person will develop an inferiority complex and will be motivated to prove himself or herself to family and peers. The adult experiencing an inferiority complex would have trouble with establishing mature relationships because of a constant struggle to show his or her worth to others.

Intrapsychic: Occurring within the mind, as in an internal conflict.

Intrinsic motivation: A source of motivation that comes from within the individual.

Introjection: A swallowing whole, without thoughtful reflection, some principle modeled or taught.

Intromission: The admission or the letting in of; usually referring to the insertion of the penis into the vagina.

Introspection: Introspection involves observation or examination of one's own mental and emotional state. It is the act of looking within oneself.

Introversion: A personality dimension involving an inclination to be reserved and reticent to interact with others.

Latent content: The hidden aspect of a dream. The latent content of a dream can be arrived at only by careful interpretation of the manifest content. The latent content is deciphered through dream analysis, which involves making associations to the content of the remembered dream.

Libido: The psychic energy hypothesized by Freud. In psychoanalytic theory, one of two major instincts are thought to operate in all people at an unconscious level. These instincts are the libido, the life (or sexual) instinct and its opposite, the death (or aggressive) instinct.

Life review: The tendency, when looking back over the events of one's life to fit events into an overall pattern. Past events are construed less randomly than they may actually have occurred.

Locus of control: Refers to a person's belief regarding how much control he or she has over given situations in life. The belief that an individual has substantial control over given situations and rewards represents an internal locus of control. External locus of control occurs when a person believes that he or she does not have much control over given situations and rewards, but views what will happen as a matter of fate, or as in the hands of powerful others.

Loneliness: A painful awareness that one's social relationships are less numerous or meaningful than one desires. To be lonely is to feel excluded from a group, unable to share one's private concerns with others, and/or alienated from those in one's surroundings.

Maladaptive: A term from the school of behaviorism, referring to any behavior that works against the person's survival interests.

Mandala: A circular creation that was used by Carl Jung to represent the self-archetype, the wholeness of a person's being. With symmetrically placed figures and patterns within the mandala, Jung represented the balancing of opposite human inclinations, which he deemed necessary to a healthy personality.

Manifest content: The remembered version of the dream. It consists of all those recalled sights, images, ideas, sounds, and smells that compose the story of the dream.

Mental disorder: A significant impairment in psychological functioning that has occurred commonly enough to have been labeled and the symptoms identified.

Minimax strategy: A term that comes from game theory, and means that people seek to minimize costs and maximize rewards in their relationships and other experiences.

Negative attributional style: Compared with people who are not depressed, those who are depressed engage in more self-blame, interpret and recall events in a more negative light, and are less hopeful about the future.

Neuroendocrine response: The brain has two ways of sending messages to the rest of the body: the nervous system and the endocrine system. A neuroendocrine response involves a combination of these communication systems.

Nihilism: Refers to the philosophical doctrine that all values and beliefs are unknowable and worthless, and that therefore existence is meaningless.

Norms: Rules for accepted and expected behavior. They are culturally based rules concerning what is appropriate or inappropriate action. Norms are developed through consensus, meaning that people living within a culture typically set and enforce the norms because they agree with them.

Normlessness: Pertaining to a new situation without existing behavior standards.

Overgeneralization: A phenomenon that occurs when an individual takes a single instance of a setback and applies it inappropriately to predict similar setbacks.

Peak experience: Mystic states characterized by Abraham

Maslow as a feeling of limitless horizons opening up for the person. One who has undergone such moments comes away from them feeling that the world "looks different." Peak experiences change one's frame of reference. The person feels more integrated, whole, and unified—more at one with the world, as if the person were at the peak of his or her power, more fully himself or herself. Such an individual may feel free of inhibitions, blocks, doubts, and self-criticisms.

Persona: From Jungian theory, it refers to the aspects of oneself that one shows to the world.

Personality: A hypothetical construct that refers to the unique combination of talents, attitudes, values, hopes, loves, hates, and habits that are consistent in an individual through time and across different situations.

Personality disorder: A pattern of personality characteristics that cause people to have troubled interpersonal relationships.

Pleasure principle: A principle on which the id is said to operate, in which the id seeks to avoid pain and obtain pleasure, regardless of any external considerations.

Proactive: Taking the initiative in some activity rather than passively waiting to see what transpires and then reacting to it.

Projection: This defense mechanism involves the transfer of blame from oneself to others, who are seen as responsible for one's own mistakes or misdeeds. Others may also be perceived as harboring one's own unacceptable impulses, thoughts, and desires. Projection works very well to reduce anxiety, but it does so at the risk of completely distorting the truth about oneself and others.

Prosocial: Positive behaviors and attitudes toward others that can be contrasted with antisocial behavior.

Psychoanalysis: A form of psychotherapy originated by Sigmund Freud, in which mental disorders were viewed as stemming from childhood trauma, especially relating to the repression of sexual impulses.

Psychological androgyny: Androgyny derives from a word of Greek origin, *andro*, meaning "male" and *gyn*, which means "female." Androgyny actually means having male and female parts. The term psychological androgyny is used to describe individuals who attribute to themselves both traditionally masculine and traditionally feminine characteristics. The androgynous person integrates qualities of both sexes, and is thus relatively free of gender constraints.

Psychosis: A condition of mental disorder in which the person has lost contact with reality.

Psychosomatic illness: Disorders in which psychological factors contribute to bodily damage or to harmful changes in physiological functioning.

Rational confrontation: Albert Ellis discovered a way to teach patients to manage their emotional state by changing their internal dialogue. He encouraged his clients to challenge their irrational beliefs through rational confrontation, a procedure that involves learning to dispute illogical thoughts about a given situation. According to Ellis, the criteria for rational thinking are that it is based on objective reality, preserves one's life, furthers one's goals, eliminates significant emotional conflicts, and keeps the person out of trouble with other people.

Rationalization: This defense mechanism involves thinking up logical, socially approved reasons for past, present, or future behaviors. It helps justify specific behaviors, and it softens the disappointment connected with unattainable goals. Rationalization is also used in an attempt to cover up one's failures or mistakes.

Reaction formation: This defense mechanism involves the development of a personality trait that is the opposite of the original, unconscious trait. The more socially unacceptable a motive, the more likely it is to be expressed indirectly, and the most indirect way to express a motive is as its opposite.

Reality principle: In Freudian theory, the ego aspect of personality decides how id instincts will be satisfied, as well as how superego demands will be met. The ego takes reality into account when planning a course of action.

Reframing: Making reattributions, or different explanations, usually more positive ones, about an event.

Regression: This defense mechanism refers to a reoccurrence of behavior or other response patterns long since outgrown. It involves a return to an earlier level of development, with less mature responses and typically a lower level of aspiration.

Reinforcement: Any event that brings about learning or increases the probability that a particular response will occur.

Repetition compulsion: In Freudian theory, repetition compulsion is the wish to enact again and again, to go through the process over and over in an attempt to master it.

Repression: This defense mechanism involves selective remembering. It is unconscious forgetting and should not be confused with suppression, which is intentional, conscious forgetting. Impulses, thoughts, or memories that are threatening are actively excluded from conscious awareness. The personality is thus protected from being overwhelmed by anxiety.

Role: A set of norms that describe how people in a given social position ought to behave. Roles are expected behavior patterns connected with various social positions and are analogous to a script in a play.

Rumination: Obsessive pondering of the same thoughts over and over again.

Secondary traits: Characteristics that are peripheral to the person, in that they are less important, less conspicuous, and less often called into play than are central traits.

Selective perception: Attending only to negative events and experiences while ignoring the positive ones that are also experienced, or doing the reverse.

Self-actualization: The fulfillment of one's human potential. In Abraham Maslow's hierarchy of needs theory, self-actualization encompasses the pinnacle of human experience.

Self-archetype: This is the most important archetype in Jungian theory and represents unity and balance between the conscious and the unconscious, anima and animus, thinking and feeling, sensing and intuiting, persona and ego, introversion and extroversion. The self archetype is generally experienced as an inner guiding factor. Through this archetype, a person reconciles and integrates the opposite sides of personality within the self. This is the path to self-realization, although few people actually achieve this state of psychological development.

Self-boundary: A person's sense of an invisible self-boundary separating himself or herself from other people and the rest of the environment. The idea of boundaries is based on a definition of what is "self" and what is "not self." It is the region separating these two psychological constructs.

Self-concept: Who and what people think they are.

Self-disclosure: Refers to the sharing of private thoughts and feelings with another person.

Self-efficacy: A person's view as to whether he or she can perform adequately in a given situation. Individuals may have skills to successfully perform tasks with competence, but must also have the conviction that they know how to implement these skills in an effective manner. The strength of one's convictions regarding one's effectiveness determines whether one will even try to cope with difficult situations.

Self-esteem: A sense of personal competence and worth.

Self-fulfilling prophecy: A prediction that prompts people to act in ways that tend to make the prediction come true.

Self-image: The way one perceives oneself. It reflects who one sees oneself as being.

Self-serving bias: The tendency to perceive oneself favorably. It involves taking credit for good things that happen and shirking responsibility for negative events, and is a tendency characteristic of normal people, as well as being noticeably absent in depressed people.

Self-transcendence: The need to rise above narrow absorption with the self. One achieves self-transcendence by overlooking oneself and by giving of oneself to other people and good causes.

Sexual harassment: Repeated and unwanted sexually oriented behavior in the form of comments, gestures, or physical contacts, usually occurring in a work setting. Sexual harassment includes unwelcome sexual jokes; suggestive comments; subtle pressure for sexual activity; remarks about a person's clothing, body, or sexual activities; leering at a person's body, unwelcome touching, patting, or pinching; brushing up against a person, and the like.

Sexual orientation: An aspect of one's sexual identity that has to do with an individual's preference for a sexual partner of one gender or the other.

Shadow: This archetype represents the denied portions of oneself; the aspects of one's personality shunned as undesirable. It represents the dark side of human nature, the realm of primitive impulses, such as selfishness and greed. Acceptance of one's dark side (or shadow) does not imply being dominated by this dimension, but rather recognizing that this is part of human nature.

Social exchange theory: A theory that uses an economic model to understand human relationships. The theory suggests that people are aware of the costs and benefits of a relationship, and are motivated to "profit" from their associations by pursuing a minimax strategy, minimizing costs and maximizing rewards.

Social interest: Alfred Adler theorized that in order to have a healthy personality, an individual must have social interest, the desire to consider the needs of others along with one's own. Adler believed that through cooperation with others, one's work life, friendships and love life can be successfully negotiated. The person who meets the problems of human life successfully acts on his or her understanding that the fundamental meaning of life derives from an interest in and cooperation with other people. Everything the individual does is guided by the interests of his or her fellow human beings, and where difficulties are encountered, they are overcome in ways that do not impinge on the welfare of others. A person with social interest feels united with others, and desires to act with their interests in mind.

Solitude: The positive experience of having time to oneself for recuperation or reflection.

Stress: Mental and physical strain resulting from demands or challenges to adjust to external reality. Stress has been characterized as exposure to life events that require adaptation, generally measured by a checklist of major events and as the state that occurs when people perceive that demands on them exceed their abilities to cope, usually measured by self-reports of subjective experience.

Stressors: Environmental stimuli to which a person reacts with increased alertness or worry, as though in danger.

Style of life: Refers to the uniqueness of each individual's goal in life, and the meaning that a person gives to his or her existence. To the degree that people have developed a healthy social interest, their striving for superiority will be shaped into a style of life that is warmly receptive of others and focused on friendship. Such individuals will be characteristically expectant that other people are likewise warmly receptive of them and are therefore sources of satisfaction and pleasure.

Subjective discomfort: A person's sense that he or she should be happier, less depressed, less anxious, or less lonely.

Sublimation: Considered to be one of the most mature of the defense mechanisms, sublimation involves channeling energy away from a motive that causes anxiety and into a more noble action in terms of its value to society. The primitive (id) impulses of love and hate are converted into activities that are socially acceptable, and thus bring credit to the person.

Superego: In psychoanalytic theory, the seat of a person's moral self. The superego is the internalized representation of societal values, as taught to the child by parents and others. The superego judges whether an action is right or wrong. It sits in judgment of the ego. The superego is composed of the "conscience," which incorporates all the things the child is punished or reprimanded for doing, and the "ego ideal," which encompasses those actions for which the child is rewarded. The conscience punishes by making the person feel guilty, and the ego-ideal rewards by making the individual feel proud.

True self: In Rogersian theory, the true self is who the person really is.

Type A behavior pattern: A hard-driving, ambitious, highly competitive, achievement-oriented, hostile behavior pattern. Those affected push themselves (and others) and tend to have an underlying animosity, probably from driving themselves to their limits of endurance. People with the Type A pattern of behavior were thought to run a high risk of heart attack.

Unconditional positive regard: A sense of being valued for oneself regardless of the degree to which specific behaviors are approved or disapproved by parents or significant others. Positive regard means that the person receives acceptance, respect, sympathy, warmth, and love from significant others.

Universality: A term used by Irwin Yalom to describe a benefit specific to group psychotherapy, in which group members experience their concerns, anxieties and wishes as held in common with most other human beings.

Weltanschauung: The German concept used to describe a world view that solves all the problems of human existence on the basis of one overriding hypothesis, which leaves no question unanswered and in which everything that interests human beings finds its fixed place. By embracing the world view, one can feel secure in life, can know what to strive for, and how one can deal most expediently with one's emotions and interests. A world view is one's basic outlook on the meaning and possibilities of one's life.

Wish fulfillment: In Freudian theory, the id engages in wish fulfillment, where the id attempts to reduce tension by forming a mental image of its desires. According to Freud, the objects and events conjured up in dreams represent attempts to fulfill some impulse of the id, usually in disguised ways. However, the id cannot fulfill its wishes and dreams and therefore needs the ego structure of the personality to negotiate with the real world in order to satisfy the id impulses.

REFERENCES

Abramson, L. Y., Metalsky, G. I., & Alloy, L. B. (1989). Hopelessness depression: A theory-based subtype. *Psychological Review, 96*, 358–372.

Adams, H. E., & Chiodo, J. (1983). Sexual deviations. In H. E. Adams & P. B. Sutker (Eds.), *Comprehensive handbook of psychopathology*. New York: Plenum Publishing.

Adams, H. E., Wright, L. W., Jr., & Bethany, A. L. (1996). Is homophobia associated with homosexual arousal? *Journal of Abnormal Psychology, 105*, 440–445.

Addad, M. (1987). Neuroticism, extraversion and meaning of life: A comparative study of criminals and noncriminals. *Personality and Individual Differences, 8*, 879–883.

Adelson, J. (1979). Adolescence and the generation gap. *Psychology Today, 12*, (February), 33–37.

Aderman, D. (1972). Elation, depression, and helping behavior. *Journal of Personality and Social Psychology, 24*, 91–101.

Adler, A. (1973). *Superiority and social interest: A collection of later writing.* H. L. Ansbacher and R. R. Ansbacher (Eds.). New York: Viking Compass.

———. (1931/1992). *What life could mean to you.* Oxford: Oneworld.

Adler, M. (1988). *Six great ideas.* [sound recording of a 1981 seminar]. Ashland, OR: Classics on Tape.

Adler, N. E., Boyce, T., Chesney, M. A., Cohen, S., Folkman, S., Kahn, R. L., & Syme, S. L. (January 1994). Socioeconomic status and health. *American Psychologist,* Vol. 49, No. 1, 15–24.

Adler, N., Matthews, K. (1994). Health psychology. *Annual Reviews of Psychology, 45*, 229–259.

Adler, R., & Cohen, N. (1993). Psychoneuroimmunology: Conditioning and stress. In L. W. Porter and M. R. Rosenzweig (Eds.), *Annual Review of Psychology, 44*, 53–85.

Ahrons, C. (Summer 1989). Personal communication.

Ainsworth, M. D. (1989). Attachment beyond infancy. *American Psychologist, 44*(4), 709–716.

Ainsworth, M. D. S. (1973). The development of infant-mother attachment. In B. M. Caldwell & H. N. Ricciuti (Eds.), *Review of child development research* (Vol. 3). Chicago: University of Chicago Press.

———. (1989). Attachments beyond infancy. *American Psychologist, 44*(4), 709–716.

Ainsworth, M. D. S., Blehar, M., Waters, E., & Wall, S. (1978). *Patterns of attachment.* Hillsdale, NJ: Erlbaum.

Alagna, S. W., & Hamilton, J. A. (1986). Science in the service of mythology: The psychopathologizing of menstruation. Paper presented at the annual meeting of the American Psychological Association, Washington, DC.

Albert, E. M. (1963). The roles of women: Question of values. In B. Farber & E. Wilson (Eds.), *The potential of women.* New York: McGraw-Hill.

Allcorn, S. (1994). *Anger in the workplace: Understanding the causes of aggression and violence.* Westport, CT: Quorum Books.

Allen, B. P. (1990). *Personality, social and biological perspectives on personal adjustment.* Pacific Grove, CA: Brooks/Cole.

Alloy, L. B., & Abramson, L. Y. (1979). Judgment of contingency in depressed and nondepressed students: Sadder but wise? *Jour-*

nal of Experimental Psychology: General, 108, 441–485.

———. (1988). Depressive realism: Three theoretical perspectives. In L. B. Alloy (Ed.), *Cognitive processes in depression.* New York: Guilford Press.

Allport, G. (1937). *Personality: A Psychological Interpretation.* New York: Henry Holt.

American Heritage Dictionary. (1978). Boston: Houghton Mifflin.

Anderson, C. A., Horowitz, L. M., & French, R. D. (1983). Attributional style of lonely and depressed people. *Journal of Personality and Social Psychology,* 45, 127–136.

Andrews, D. A., & Bonita, J. (1994). *The psychology of criminal conduct.* Cincinnati: Anderson Publishing.

Annual Review of Psychology, 39, 609–672.

Antill, J. K. (1983). Sex role complementarity versus similarity in married couples. *Journal of Personality and Social Psychology,* 45, 145–155.

Archer, D., & Gartner, R. (1976). Violent acts and violent times: A comparative approach to postwar homicide rates. *American Sociological Review,* 41, 937–963.

Argyle, M. (1987). *The psychology of happiness.* London: Metheun.

Argyle, M., & Lu, L. (1990). The happiness of extraverts. *Personality and Individual Differences,* 11, 1011–1017.

Aries, E. J., & Johnson, F. L. (1983). Close friendship in adulthood: Conversational content between same-sex friends. *Sex Roles,* 9, 1183–1196.

Arkoff, A. (1993). *Psychology and personal growth.* Needham Heights, MA: Simon & Schuster.

———. (1995). *The Illuminated Life.* Needham Heights, MA: Allyn and Bacon.

Arms, R. L., Russell, G. W., & Sandilands, M. L. (1979). Effects on the hostility of spectators of viewing aggressive sports. *Social Psychology Quarterly,* 42, 275–279.

Aronfreed, J. (1964). The origins of self-criticism. *Psychological Review,* 71, 193–218.

———. (1970). The socialization of altruistic and sympathetic behavior: Some theoretical and experimental analyses. In J. R. Macaulay

& L. Berkowitz (Eds.), *Altruism and helping behavior.* New York: Academic Press.

Aronson, E. (1969). Some antecedents of interpersonal attraction. In W. J. Arnold & D. Levine (Eds.), *Nebraska Symposium on Motivation.* Lincoln: University of Nebraska Press.

Aronson, E., & Mettee, D. R. (1974). Affective reactions to appraisal from others. *Foundations of interpersonal attraction.* New York: Academic Press.

Astin, A. W., Dey, E. L., Korn, W. S., & Riggs, E. R. (1992). *The American freshman: National norms for fall, 1991.* Los Angeles: Higher Education Research Institute, Graduate School of Education, University of California, Los Angeles.

Astin, A. W., Green, K. C., & Korn, W. S. (1987). *The American freshman: Twenty year trends, 1966–1985.* Los Angeles: Higher Education Research Institute, Graduate School of Education, University of California, Los Angeles.

Averill, J. R. (1983). Studies on anger and aggression: Implications for theories of emotion. *American Psychologist,* 38, 1145–1160.

Azar, B. (April, 1997). Environment is key to serotonin levels. *APA Monitor.* Washington, DC: American Psychological Association.

Babad, E., Bernieri, F., & Rosenthal, R. (1991). Students as judges of teachers' verbal and nonverbal behavior. *American Educational Research Journal,* 28, 211–234.

Bach, G. R., & Wyden, P. (1968). *The intimate enemy.* New York: Avon Books.

Bachman, J. G., O'Malley, P., & Johnston, J. (1978). *Youth in transition* (Vol. 6: *Adolescence to adulthood—Change and stability in the lives of young men*). Ann Arbor: Institute for Social Research, University of Michigan.

Baker, J. N. (Summer/Fall 1990). Coming out (Special Issue). *Newsweek,* pp. 60–61.

Baldrige, L. (1978). *The Amy Vanderbilt complete book of etiquette.* New York: Doubleday.

Balswick, J. (1988). *The inexpressive male.* Lexington, MA: Lexington Books/Heath.

Bandura, A. (1977). Self-efficacy: Toward a unifying theory of behavioral change. *Psychological Review, 84,* 191–215.

——. (1986). *Social foundations of thought and action: A social cognitive theory.* Englewood Cliffs, NJ: Prentice-Hall.

Bandura, A., & McDonald, F. J. (1963). Role of symbolic coding and rehearsal processes in observational learning. *Journal of Personality and Social Psychology, 26,* 122–130.

Barbach, L. G. (1976). *For yourself: The fulfillment of female sexuality.* New York: Anchor/Doubleday.

Barbeau, C. (1988). Fidelity: The creative vow. In A. Arkoff (Ed.), *Psychology and personal growth* (3rd ed.). Boston: Allyn & Bacon.

Barnett, M. A., Matthews, K. A., & Howard, J. A. (1979). Relationships between competitiveness and empathy in 6- and 7-year-olds. *Developmental Psychology, 15,* 221–222.

Barrett, W. (1958). *Irrational man.* Garden City, New York: Doubleday Anchor Books.

Barrick, M. R., & Mount, M. K. (1991). The big five personality dimensions and job performance: A meta-analysis. *Personnel Psychology, 44,* 1–26.

Barry, W. A. (1970). Marriage research and conflict: An integrative review. *Psychological Bulletin, 73,* 41–54.

Bartholomew, K., & Horowitz, L. M. (1991). Attachment styles among young adults: A test of a four-category model. *Journal of Personality and Social Psychology, 61,* 226–244.

Basow, S. A. (1992). *Gender: Stereotypes and roles* (3rd ed.). Pacific Grove, CA: Brooks/Cole.

Bass, B. M. (1990). Bass and Stogdill's handbook of leadership: Theory, research, and managerial applications. New York: Free Press.

Bass, E., & Davis, L. (1988). *The courage to heal.* New York: Harper & Row.

Batson, C. D. (1987). Prosocial motivation: Is it ever truly altruistic? *Advances in Experimental Social Psychology, 20,* 65–122.

——. (1990). How social an animal? The human capacity for caring. *American Psychologist, 45,* 336–346.

——. (1991). *The altruism question: Toward a social-psychological answer.* Hillsdale, NJ: Lawrence Erlbaum.

Baudry, F. (1988). Character, character type, and character organization. *Journal of the American Psychoanalytic Association, 37,* 655–686.

Baum, A. (1988). Disasters, natural and otherwise. *Psychology Today, 22*(4), 57–60.

Baum, S., & Boxley, R. (1983). Age identification in the elderly. *The Gerontologist, 23,* 532–537.

Baumeister, R. F. (1989). *Masochism and the self.* Hillsdale, NJ: Erlbaum.

Beattie, M. (1987). *Co-dependent no more.* New York: HarperCollins.

Beck, A. T. (1972). *Depression: Causes and treatment.* Philadelphia: University of Pennsylvania Press.

——. (1976). *Cognitive therapy and the emotional disorders.* New York: Meridian.

Beck, A. T., & Freeman, A. (1990). *Cognitive therapy of personality disorders.* New York: Guilford Press.

Beck, A. T., & Young, J. E. (September 1978). College blues. *Psychology Today,* pp. 80–92.

Beck, A. T., et al. (1985). Treatment of depression with cognitive therapy and amitriptyline. *Archives of General Psychiatry, 42,* 142–148.

Becker, E. (1971). *The birth and death of meaning* (2nd ed.). New York: Free Press.

——. (1973). *The Denial of Death.* New York: Free Press.

Bell, A. P., & Weinberg, M. S. (1978). *"Kinsey," homosexualities: A study of human diversity.* New York: Simon and Schuster.

Bellah, R. N., Madsen, R., Sullivan, W. M., Swidler, A., & Tipton, S. M. (1985). *Habits of the heart: Individualism and commitment in American life.* New York: Harper & Row.

Bem, S. L. (1974). The measurement of psychological androgyny. *Journal of Consulting and Clinical Psychology, 42,* 155–162.

———. (1975a). Sex-role adaptability: One consequence of psychological androgyny. *Journal of Personality & Social Psychology, 31,* 634–643.

———. (1975b, September). Androgyny vs. the tight little lives of fluffy women and chesty men. *Psychology Today,* 58–62.

———. (1981). Gender schema theory. A cognitive account of sex typing. *Psychological Review, 88,* 354–364.

Benjamin, L. T., Jr. (1985). *Teaching of psychology.* Hillsdale, NJ: Lawrence Erlbaum.

Benson, H., & Stuart, E. (1991). The wellness book. Carol Publishing Group.

Berkowitz, L. (1962). *Aggression: A social psychological analysis.* New York: McGraw-Hill.

Bernard, J. (1981). The good-provider role: Its rise and fall. *American Psychologist, 36,* 1–12.

Berscheid, E., & Walster, E. (1974). A little bit about love. In T. L. Huston (Ed.), *Foundations of interpersonal attraction.* New York: Academic Press.

———. (1978). *Interpersonal attraction.* Reading, MA: Addison-Wesley.

Bersheid, E., & Walster, E. (1972). A little bit about love. In T. L. Huston (Ed.), *Foundation of interpersonal attraction.* New York: Academic.

Berzonsky, M. D. (1989). Self-construction over the life span: A process perspective on identity formation. In G J. Neimeyer & R. A., Neimeyer (Eds.), *Advances in personal construct psychology* (Vol. 1, pp. 155–186). Greenwich, CT: JAI Press.

Birkerts, S. (1994). *The Gutenberg elegies: The fate of reading in an electronic age.* New York: Fawcett Columbine.

Bischoping, K. (1993). Gender differences in conversation topics, 1922–1990. *Sex Roles, 28,* 1–18.

Black, T. E., & Higbee, K. L. (1973). Effects of power, threat, and sex on exploitation. *Journal of Personality and Social Psychology, 27,* 382–388.

Blackburn, I. M., Eunson, K. M., & Bishop, S. (1986). A two-year naturalistic follow-up of depressed patients treated with cognitive therapy, pharmacotherapy, and a combination of both. *Journal of Affective Disorder, 10,* 67–75.

Blasi, A. (1980). Bridging moral cognition and moral action: A critical review of the literature. *Psychology Bulletin, 88,* 1–45.

Blau, P. M. (1964). *Exchange and power in social life.* New York: Wiley.

Blazer, D. G., Kessler, R. C., McGonagle, K. A., & Swartz, M. S. (1994). The prevalence and distribution of major depression in a national community sample: The national comorbidity survey. *American Journal of Psychiatry, 151,* 979–986.

Block, J. H. (1979). Another look at sex differentiation in the socialization behaviors of mothers and fathers. In J. H. Block (Ed.), *Psychology of women: Future directions of research.* New York: Psychological Dimensions.

Block, J. H., & Block, J. (1980). The role of ego-control and ego-resiliency in the organization of behavior. In W. A. Collins (Ed.), *Minnesota Symposium on Child Development* (Vol. 13). Hillsdale, NJ: Lawrence Erlbaum.

Bly, R. (1990). *Iron John: A book about men.* Reading, MA: Addison-Wesley.

Blyth, D. A., & Traeger, C. M. (1983). The self-concept and self-esteem of early adolescents. *Theory and Practice, 22,* 91–97.

Bolles, R. N. (1999). *What color is my parachute?* Berkeley, CA: Ten Speed Press.

Borkenau, F. (1965). The concept of death. In R. Fulton, (Ed.), *Death and identity.* New York: John Wiley & Sons.

Boyden, T., Carroll, J. S., & Maier, R. A. (1984). Similarity and attraction in homosexual males: The effects of age and masculinity-femininity. *Sex Roles, 10,* 939–948.

Bradbury, T. N. (1998). Essential strategies for building stronger marriages. Paper presented at the American Psychological Association Convention, San Francisco.

Bradshaw, J. (1988). *Healing the shame that binds you.* Pompano Beach, FL: Health Communications.

Branden, N. (1984). New York: Bantam Books.

———. (1986). *The psychology of high self-esteem: A life-changing program for personal growth.* [sound recording].

———. (1994). *Six pillars of self-esteem.* New York: Bantam Books.

Brannon, R. (1976). The male sex role: Our culture's blueprint of manhood, and what it's done for us lately. In D. S. David & R. Brannon (Eds.), *The forty-nine percent majority: The male sex role.* Reading, MA: Addison-Wesley.

———. (1985). Dimension of the male sex role in America. In A. G. Sargent (Ed.), *Beyond sex roles.* St. Paul, MN: West.

———. (1988). The male sex role. In A. Arkoff. *Psychology and personal growth* (3rd ed.), Boston, MA: Allyn and Bacon.

Breuer, J., & Freud, S. (1893–1895). *Studies on hysteria.* In James Strachey (Ed. and Trans.), *The standard edition of the complete psychological works of Sigmund Freud (Vol. 2).* London: Hogarth, 1955.

Briere, J. (1993). *Invited debate: Repressed memory controversy and sex abuse cases.* Paper presented at the annual convention of the American Psychological Association, Toronto, Canada.

Brock, J. W. (1996). Personal communication.

———. (1998). Personal communication.

Brody, L. R., Hall, J. A. (1993). Gender and emotion, In. M. Lewis & J. M. Haviland (Eds.), *Handbook of emotions* (pp. 447–460). New York: Guilford Press.

Brothers, J. (September 17, 1992). KCBS radio program.

Brown, D. E. (1991). *Human universals.* Philadelphia: Temple University Press.

Brown, H. (1973). *How I found freedom in an unfree world.* New York: Avon Books.

Brown, J. D. (1991). Accuracy and bias in self-knowledge. In C. R. Snyder & D. F. Forsyth (Eds.), *Handbook of social and clinical psychology: The health perspective.* New York: Pergamon Press.

Browne, A. (1993). Violence against women by male partners: Prevalence, outcomes, and policy implications. *American Psychologist, 48,* 1077–1087.

Bryan, J. S., & Test, M. A. (1967). Models and helping: Naturalistic studies in aiding behavior. *Journal of Personality and Social Psychology, 6,* 400–407.

Burgoon, J. K. (1991). Relationship message interpretations of touch, conversational distance, and posture. *Journal of Nonverbal Behavior, 15,* 233–259.

Buscaglia, F. L. (1972). *Love.* New York: Fawcett Crest.

Buss, A. H. (1980). *Self-consciousness and social anxiety.* San Francisco: Freeman.

Buss, A. H., & Plomin, R. (1984). *Temperament: Early developing personality traits.* Hillsdale, NJ: Erlbaum.

Buss, D. M. (1988a). Love acts: The evolutionary biology of love. In R. J. Sternberg & M. L. Barnes (Eds.), *The psychology of love.* New Haven: Yale University Press.

———. (1988b). The evolution of human intrasexual competition: Tactics of mate attraction. *Journal of Personality and Social Psychology, 54,* 616–628.

———. (1989). Sex differences in human mate preferences: Evolutionary hypotheses tested in 37 cultures. *Behavioral and Brain Sciences, 12,* 1–49.

Buss, D. M., & 49 colleagues. (1990). International preferences in selecting mates: A study of 37 cultures. *Journal of Cross-Cultural Psychology, 21,* 5–47.

Bussey, K., & Bandura, A. (1984). Influence of gender constancy and social power on sex-linked modeling. *Journal of Personality and Social Psychology, 47,* 1292–1302.

Bussey, K., & Bandura, A. (1992). Self-regulatory mechanisms governing gender development. *Child Development, 63,* 1236–1250.

Butcher, S. H. (1951). *Aristotle's theory of poetry and fine art.* New York: Dover Publications.

Butler, R. N. (1963). The life review: An interpretation of reminiscence in the aged. *Psychiatry, 26:* 65–76.

Butler, R. N. (1971). The life review. *Psychology Today, 5* (December): 49–51.

Byrne, D. (1971). *The attraction paradigm.* New York: Academic Press.

Byrne, D. G., & Whyte, H. M. (1980). Life events and myocardial infarction revisited: The role of measure of individual impact. *Psychosomatic Medicine, 42,* 1–10.

Caldwell, M. A., & Peplau, L. A. (1982). Sex differences in same-sex friendship. *Sex Roles, 8,* 721–732.

Calhoun, K. S., & Atkeson, B. M. (1991). *Treatment of rape victims: Facilitating psychosocial adjustment.* Elmsford, NY: Pergamon Press.

Cameron, P. (1972). Stereotypes about generational fun and happiness vs. Self-appraised fun and happiness. *Gerontologist, 12,* 120–123.

Campbell, A. (1981). *The sense of well-being in America.* New York: McGraw-Hill.

Campbell, D. P. (1974). *If you don't know where you're going, you'll probably end up somewhere else.* Niles, IL: Argus Communication.

Campbell, J. (Ed.) (1971). *The portable Jung.* New York: The Viking Press.

———. (Ed.) (1987). *The portable Jung.* New York: Viking Penguin, Inc.

Canino I. A., & Canino, G. I. (1993). Psychiatric care of Puerto Ricans. In A. C. Gaw (Ed.), *Culture, ethnicity, and mental illness* (pp. 467–499). Washington, DC: American Psychiatric Press.

Carducci, B. J., & Stein, N. D. (April 1988). *The personal and situational pervasiveness of shyness in college students: A nine-year comparison.* Paper presented at the meeting of the Southeastern Psychological Association, New Orleans.

Carli, L. L., Ganley, R., & Pierce-Otay, A. (1991). Similarity and satisfaction in roommate relationships. *Personality and Social Psychology Bulletin, 17*(4), 104–113.

Carter, S. L. (August 5, 1998). *The news hour.* On public television, KCET interview about his book, *Civility: Manners, moral and the Etiquette of Democracy.* New York: Basic Books.

Carver, C. S., & Scheier, M. F. (1987). Dispositional optimism, coping, and stress. Paper presented at the annual meeting of the American Psychology Association, New York.

Caspi, A., & Herbener, E. S. (1990). Continuity and change: Associative marriage and the consistency of personality in adulthood. *Journal of Personality & Social Psychology, 58*(2), 250–258.

Castenada, C. (1972). *Journey to Istlan.* New York: Simon & Schuster.

Celis, W. (January 2, 1991). Students trying to draw line between sex and an assault. *The New York Times,* pp. 1, B8.

Chang, E. C. (1996). Cultural differences in optimism, pessimism, and coping: Predictors of subsequent adjustment in Asian American and Caucasian American college students. *Counseling Psychology, Vol. 41, No. 1,* 113–123.

Chapman, B. E., & Brannock, J. C. (1987). A proposed model of lesbian identity development: An empirical investigation. *Journal of Homosexuality, 14,* 69–80.

Cheek, J. M., & Buss, A. H. (1979). Scales of shyness, sociability and self-esteem and correlations among them. Unpublished research, University of Texas. (Cited by Buss, 1980).

Chodorow, N. (1978). *The reproduction of mothering: Psychoanalysis and the sociology of gender.* Berkeley, CA: University of California Press.

Chopra, D. (1991). *Unconditional life.* New York: Bantam Books.

Clark, M. S., & Reis, H. T. (1988). Interpersonal processes in close relationships. *Annual Review of Psychology, 39,* 609–672.

Clinton, H. R. (May 23, 1993). *Los Angeles Times Magazine.*

Cochran, S. D., & Mays, V. M. (1990). Sex, lies, and HIV. *New England Journal of Medicine, 322,* 774–775.

Cocores, J. (1987). Co-addiction: A silent epidemic. *Psychiatry Letter, 5,* 5–8.

Cohen, A. (July 1996). Personal communication.

Cohen, R. J. (1979). *Binge! It's not a state of hunger . . . It's a state of mind.* New York: MacMillan.

Cohen, S., & Edwards, J. R. (1989). Personality characteristics as moderators of the relationship between stress and disorder. In R. W. J. Neufeld (Ed.), *Advances in the investigation of psychological stress.* New York: Wiley.

Cohen, S., Tyrrell, D. A. J., & Smith, A. P. (1991). Psychological stress in humans and susceptibility to the common cold. *New England Journal of Medicine, 325,* 606–612.

———. (1993). Negative life events, perceived stress, negative affect, and susceptibility to the common cold. *Journal of Personality and Social Psychology, 64,* 131–140.

Collins, N. L., & Read, S. J. (1990). Adult attachment, working models, and relationship quality in dating couples. *Journal of Personality and Social Psychology, 58,* 644–663.

Collins, W. A., & Gunnar, M. R. (1990). Social and personality development. *Annual Review of Psychology, 41,* 387–416.

Comas-Diaz, L. (1988). Cross-cultural mental health treatment. In L. Comas-Diaz & E. E. H. Griffith (Eds.), *Clinical guidelines in cross-cultural mental health.* New York: John Wiley.

Comas-Diaz, L., & Duncan, J. W. (1985). The cultural context: A factor in assertiveness training with mainland Puerto Rican women. *Psychology of Women Quarterly, 9,* 463–476.

Coon, D. (1998). *Introduction to psychology.* Pacific Grove, CA: Brooks/Cole.

Cooper, H. (1983). Teacher expectation effects. In L. Bickman (Ed.), *Applied social psychology annual,* Vol. 4. Beverly Hills, CA: Sage.

Cooper, H., Okamura, L., & Gurka, V. (1992). Social activity and subjective well-being. Personality and Individual Differences, 13, 573–583.

Corey, G., & Corey, M. S. (1993). *I never knew I had a choice.* Belmont, CA: Brooks/Cole.

Costa, P. T., & McCrae, R. R. (1988). Personality in adulthood: A six-year longitudinal study of self-report and spouse ratings on the NEO Personality Inventory. *Journal of Personality and Social Psychology, 54,* 853–863.

———. (1992). *NEO-PI-R professional manual.* Odessa, FL: Psychological Assessment Resources.

Costrich, N. (1975 Nov.). When stereotypes hurt: Three studies of penalties for sex-role reversals. *Journal of Experimental Social Psychology. 11*(6), 520–530.

Cote, J. E., & Levine, C. G. (1989). An empirical test of Erikson's theory of ego identity formation. *Youth & Society, 20,* 388–415.

Cousins, N. (1991). *The celebration of life.* New York: Bantam Books.

Cozby, P. C. (1973). Self-disclosure: A literature review. *Psychological Bulletin, 79,* 73–91.

Crawford, H. J. & Christensen, L. B. (1985) *Developing Research Skills.* Newton, Massachusetts: Allyn & Bacon, Inc.

Crocker, J., & Major, B. (1989). Social stigma and self-esteem: The self-protective properties of stigma. *Psychological Review, 96,* 608–630.

Crosby, F. J. (1990). Divorce and work life among women managers. In H. Y. Grossman & N. L. Chester (Eds.), *The Experience and Meaning of Work in Women's Lives.* Hillsdale, NJ: Erlbaum.

Csikszentmihalyi, M. (1990). *Flow: The ultimate human experience.* Chicago: Harper Perennial.

Cunningham, M. R., Barbee, A. P., & Pike, C. L. (1990). What do women want? Facial-metric assessment of multiple motives in the perception of male facial physical attractiveness. *Journal of Personality and Social Psychology, 59,* 61–72.

Daniel, S. (August 19, 1995). The McLaughlin Group, a KNBC television program.

Daniels, T., & Shaver, P. R. (1991). *Unpublished manuscript, Department of Psychology, State University of New York at Buffalo.*

Darley, J., & Batson, C. (1973). "From Jerusalem to Jericho": A study of situational and dispositional variables in helping behavior. *Journal of Personality and Social Psychology, 27,* 100–108.

Darwin, C. (1872). *The expression of emotion in man and animals.* Chicago: University of Chicago Press.

Davidson, L. R., & Duberman, L. (1982). Friendship: Communication and interactional patterns in same-sex dyads. *Sex Roles, 8,* 809–822. New York: P. F. Collier & Son.

Davis, F. B. (1968). Sex differences in suicide and attempted suicide. *Diseases of the Nervous System, 29,* 193–194.

Delmonte, M. M. (1990). Meditation and change: Mindfulness versus repression.

Australian Journal of Clinical Hypnotherapy and Hypnosis, 11, 57–63.

———. (1995). Silence and emptiness in the service of healing. *British Journal of Psychotherapy, 11,* 368–378.

Dermer, M., Cohen, S. J., Jacobsen, E., & Anderson, E. A. (1979). Evaluative judgments of aspects of life as a function of vicarious exposure to hedonic extremes. *Journal of Personality and Social Psychology, 37,* 247–260.

Deutsch, M. (1949). An experimental study of the effect of cooperation and competition among group processes. *Human Relations, 2,* 199–231.

———. (1980). Fifty years of conflict. In L. Festinger (Ed.), *Retrospections on social psychology.* New York: Oxford University Press.

DeVito, J. A. (1992). The interpersonal communication book. New York: Harper-Collins.

Diagnostic & Statistical Manual of Mental Disorders, 4th Edition (DSM-IV), (1994). American Psychiatric Association.

Diener, E. (1984). Subjective well-being. *Psychological Bulletin, 93,* 542–575.

Diener, E., Sandvik, E., & Pavot, W. (1990). Happiness is the frequency, not the intensity, of positive versus negative affect. In F. Strack, M. Argyle, and N. Schwarz (Eds.), *The social psychology of subjective well-being.* Oxford: Pergamon Press.

Digman, J. M., & Takemoto-Chock, N. K. (1981). Factors in the natural language of personality: Re-analysis, comparison, and interpretation of six major studies. *Multivariate Behavioral Research, 16,* 149–170.

Dindia, K., & Allen, M. (1992). "Sex differences in self-disclosure" A meta-analysis. *Psychological Bulletin, 112,* 106–124.

Dixon, N. F. (1980). Humor: A cognitive alternative to stress? In I. G. Sarason & C. D. Spielberger (Eds.), *Stress and anxiety* (Volume 7). Washington, DC: Hemisphere.

Dodd, D. (1985). Robbers in the classroom: A deindividuation exercise. *Teaching of psychology, 12,* 89–91.

Dohrenwend, B. P. (1979). Stressful life events and psychopathology: Some issues of theory and method. In J. E. Barrett et al. (Eds.), *Stress and mental disorder.* New York: Raven Press.

Douglass, F. (1994). *Narrative of the life of Frederick Douglass, an American slave.* In L. A. Jacobus (Ed.). *A world of ideas.* Boston, MA: Bedford Books of St. Martin's Press.

Dowling, C. (1981). *The Cinderella complex: Women's hidden fear of independence.* New York: Summit Books.

Doyle, J. A. (1989). The male experience. (2nd ed.) Dubuque, Iowa: Wm. C. Brown.

Draeger, D. F., & Smith, R. W. (1981). *Comprehensive Asian Fighting Arts.* Publisher is Tokyo, Palo Alto, CA: Kodansha International.

Driver, B. L., Brown, P. J., & Peterson, G. L. (Eds.) (1991). *Benefits of leisure.* State College, PA: Venture Publishing.

Dunning, D., Meyerowitz, J. A., & Holzberg, A. (1989). Ambiguity and self-evaluation: The role of idiosyncratic definitions in self-serving assessment of ability. *Journal of Personality and Social Psychology, 57,* 1082–1090.

Durant, W. S. (1961). *The Story of Philosophy. The lives and opinions of the great philosophers of the western world* (2nd ed.) New York: Simon & Schuster.

Dusek, J. B. & Flaherty, J. F. (1981). The development of the self-concept during the adolescent years. *Monographs of the Society for Research in Child Development 46,* (No. 191).

Eagly, A. H. (1987). *Sex differences in social behavior: A social role interpretation.* Hillsdale, NJ: Erlbaum.

Ebeling, K. (1993). Casualties on the road to equality. In A. Arkoff (Ed.), *Psychology and personal growth* (4th ed.), Boston, MA: Allyn and Bacon.

Edwards, J. R. (April, 1996). An examination of competing versions of the person-environment fit approach to stress. *Academic Management Journal, 39(z),* 292–339.

Ehrmann, M. (1927). *Disiderata.*

Eisenberg, N., Shell, R., Pasternak, J., Lennon, R., Beller, R., & Mathy, R. M. (1987). Prosocial development in middle childhood: A longitudinal study. *Developmental Psychology, 23,* 712–718.

Eisenberg, W., & Miller, P. A. (1987). The relation of empathy to prosocial and related behaviors. *Psychological Bulletin, 101,* 91–119.

Ellis, A. H. (1973). Rational-emotive therapy. In R. J. Corsini (Ed.), *Current psychotherapies.* Itasca, IL.: Peacock.

———. (1992). Secular humanism and rational-emotive therapy. *The Humanistic Psychologist,* 20(2–3), 349–358.

Ellis, L. (1991). A synthesized (bisocial) theory of rape. *Journal of Consulting and Clinical Psychology, 59,* 631–642.

Ellis, L., & Ames, M. A. (1987). Neurohormonal functioning & sexual orientation. *Psychological Bulletin, 101,* 233–258.

Emerson, R. W. (1991). In R. Whelan (Ed.), *Self-Reliance.* New York: Bell Tower.

Emmerich, W., Cocking, R. R., & Sigel, I. E. (1979). Relationships between cognitive and social functioning in preschool children. *Developmental Psychology, 15,* 495–504.

Emmons, R. A., & Diener, E. (1985). Personality correlates of subjective well-being. *Personality and Social Psychology Bulletin, 11,* 89–97.

Enzle, M. E., Hansen, R. D., & Lowe, C. A. (1975). Causal attribution in the mixed-motive game. Effects of facilitory and inhibitory environmental forces. *Journal of Personality and Social Psychology, 31,* 50–54.

Erikson, E. H. (1950). *Childhood and society.* New York: Norton.

———. (1963). *Childhood and society.* (Rev. ed.) New York: Norton.

———. (1968). *Identity: Youth and Crisis.* New York: Norton.

———. (Ed.) (1980). *Themes of work and love in adulthood.* Cambridge, MA: Harvard University Press.

Evans-Wentz, W. Y. (1960). *The Tibetan book of the dead.* London: Oxford University Press.

Eysenck, H. J. (1991). Personality, stress, and disease: An interactionist perspective. *Psychological Inquiry, 2,* 221–232.

Falk, P. J. (1989). Lesbian mothers: Psychological assumptions in family law. *American Psychologist, 44,* 941–949.

Feldman, H. (1964). *Development of the husband-wife relationship.* Ithaca, NY: Cornell University.

Fenigstein, A. (1984). Self-consciousness and the overperception of self as a target. *Journal of Personality and Social Psychology, 47,* 860–870.

Fermaglich, M. (May, 1986). *Mollie's Rules for the Socially Inept.* (Quill). Working Women.

Feshbach, N. D. (1975). The relationship of child rearing factors to children's aggression, empathy, and related positive and negative social behavior. In J. de Wit and W. W. Hartup (Eds.), *Determinants and origins of aggressive behavior.* The Hague: Mouton.

———. (1978). Studies on empathic behavior in children. In B. A. Maher (Ed.), *Progress in experimental personality research.* New York: Academic Press.

———. (1979). Empathy training: A field study in affective education. In S. Feshbach and A. Fraczek (Eds.), *Aggression and behavior change: Biological and social processes.* New York: Praeger.

Feshbach, N. D., & Feshbach, S. (1969). The relationship between empathy and aggression in two age groups. *Developmental Psychology,* 1(2), 102–107.

Feshbach, N. D., & Roe, L. (1968). Empathy in six- and seven-year-olds. *Child Development, 39,* 133–145.

Feshbach, S., & Weiner, B. (1991). *Personality.* Lexington, MA: D. C. Heath and Company.

Feshbach, S., Weiner, B., & Bohart, A. (1996). *Personality.* Lexington, MA: D. C. Heath.

Festinger, L. (1954). A theory of social comparison processes. *Human Relations, 7,* 152–163.

———. (1957). *A theory of cognific dissonance.* Stanford, CA: Stanford University Press.

Festinger, L., & Carlsmith, J. M. (1959). Cognitive consequence of forced compliance. *Journal of Abnormal and Social Psychology, 58,* 203–210.

Field, T. M. (1998). Massage therapy affects. *American Psychologist, 53* (12), 1270–1281.

Figler, H. E. (1979). PATH: *Career workbook for liberal arts students.* Cranston, RI: The Carroll Press.

Findley, M. J., & Cooper, H. M. (1983). Locus of control and academic achievement: A literature review. *Journal of Personality and Social Psychology, 44,* 419–427.

Finkelhor, D. (1990). Early and long-term effects of child sexual abuse: An update. *Professional Psychology: Research and Practice, 21,* 325–330.

Fischer, J. L., Spann, L., & Crawford, D. W. (1991) Measuring codependency. *Alcoholism Treatment Quarterly, 8(1),* 87–100.

Fiske, M. (1980). Changing hierarchies of commitment in adulthood. In N. J. Smelser & E. H. Erikson (Eds.), *Themes of work and love in adulthood.* Cambridge, Ma: Harvard University Press.

Fivush, R. (1989). Exploring sex differences in the emotional content of mother-child conversations about the past. *Sex Roles, 20,* 675–691.

Fixsen, D. L., Phillips, E. L., et al. (1978, November). The Boys Town revolution. *Human Nature. 1,* 54–61.

Flemming, A. T. (December 11, 1997). *The News Hour.* KCET Public Television.

Foa, U. G., & Foa, E. B. (1975). *Resource theory of social exchange.* Morristown, NJ: General Learning Press.

Forward, S., & Buck, C. S. (1988). *Betrayal of innocence: Incest and its devastation.* New York: Penguin.

France, K. (1984). Competitive versus noncompetitive thinking during exercise: Effects on norepinephrine levels. Paper presented at the annual meeting of the American Psychological Association, Toronto.

Frances, S. J. (1979). Sex differences in nonverbal behavior. *Sex Roles, 5,* 519–535.

Frankenhaeuser, M. (1980). Psychological aspects of life stress. In S. Levine & H. Ursin (Eds.), *Coping and health.* New York: Plenum.

Frankl, V. E. (1955). *The doctor and the soul.* New York: Alfred A. Knopf.

———. (1963). *Man's search for meaning.* New York: Simon & Schuster.

———. (1969). *The will to meaning.* New York: Meridian, division of Penguin Books.

Franklin, B. (1868/1937). The autobiography of Benjamin Franklin. In C. W. Eliot (Ed.), *The Harvard classics.* New York: P. F. Collier.

Freedman, J. L. (1978). *Happy people.* New York: Harcourt Brace Jovanovich.

Freud, S. (1900). *The interpretation of dreams.* In J. Strachey (Ed. and Trans.), *The standard edition of the complete psychological works of Sigmund Freud (Vols 4 and 5).* London: Hogarth, 1953.

———. (1901). *The psychopathology of everyday life.* Bergenfield, NJ: The New American Library.

———. (1908). Character and anal eroticism. In J. Strachey (Ed. and Trans.), *The standard edition of the complete psychological works of Sigmund Freud* (Vol. 9). London: Hogarth, 1959.

———. (1925). "Some Additional Notes on Dream-Interpretation as a Whole." In James Strachey (Ed. and Trans.), Vol. 19 of *The Standard Edition of the Complete Psychological Works of Sigmund Freud.* London: Hogarth, 1961.

———. (1927). Some psychological consequences of the anatomical distinction between the sexes. *International Journal of Psycho-Analysis, 8,* 133–142.

———. (1930). *Civilization and its discontents.* In J. Strachey (Ed. and Trans.), Vol. 21 of The standard edition of the complete psychological works of Sigmund Freud. London: Hogarth, 1961.

———. (1933). *New introductory lectures on psychoanalysis.* New York: W. W. Norton.

———. (1949). *An outline of psycho-analysis.* New York: Norton.

———. (1965). *Group psychology and the analysis of the ego.* Translated and edited by J. Strachey. New York: W. W. Norton.

Friedman, H. S., & Booth-Kewley, S. (1987a). The disease-prone personality: A meta-analytic view of the construct. *American Psychologist, 42,* 539–555.

———. (1987b). Personality, Type A behavior, and coronary heart disease: The role of emotional expression. *Journal of Personality and Social Psychology, 53,* 783–792.

Friedman, H. S., Hall, J. A., & Harris, M. J. (1985). Type A behavior, nonverbal expressive style, and health. *Journal of Personality and Social Psychology, 48,* 1299–1315.

Friedman, H. S., Tucker, J. S. Schwartz, J. E., Tomlinson-Keasey, C., Martin, L. R., Wingard, D. L., & Criqui, M. H. (1995). Psychosocial and behavioral predictors of longevity. *American Psychologist, 50* (2), 69–78.

Friedman, M., & Rosenman, R. H. (1974). *Type A behavior and your heart.* New York: Knopf.

Frodi, A. M., Macauley, J., & Thome, P. R. (1977). Are women always less aggressive than men? A review of the experimental literature. *Psychological Bulletin, 84,* 634–660.

Fromm, E. (1955). *The sane society.* Greenwich, CT: Fawcett Books (also published by Holt).

———. (1963). *The art of loving.* New York: Bantam Books/Harper & Row.

———. (1973). *The anatomy of human destructiveness.* New York: Holt.

Fry, W., Jr. (1986). Humor, physiology, and the aging process. In L. Nahemov, K. A. McCluskey-Fawcett, & P E. McGhee (Eds.), *Humor and aging.* Orlando, FL: Academic Press.

Fulghum, R. (1993). All I really need to know I learned in kindergarten: Uncommon thoughts on common things. New York: Ivy Books.

Furnham, A., & Brewin, C. R. (1990). Personality and happiness. *Personality and Individual Differences, 11,* 1093–1096.

Galbraith, J. K. (1958). *The affluent society.* Boston: Houghton Mifflin.

Gallagher, D. J. (1990). Extraversion, neuroticism and appraisal of stressful academic events. *Personality and Individual Differences, 11,* 1053–1057.

Gangestad, S. W., Thornhill, R., & Yeo, R. A. (1994). Facial attractiveness, developmental stability, and fluctuating asymmetry. *Ethnology and Sociability, 15,* 73–85.

Gardner, J. W. (1984). *Excellence: Can we be equal and excellent too?* New York: Norton.

Garfield, C. A., & Bennett, H. Z. (1989). *Peak performance: Mental training techniques of the worlds greatest athletes.* New York: Warner Books.

Garnets, L. D., & Kimmel, D. C. (1991). Lesbian and gay male dimensions in the psychological study of human diversity. In J. D. Goodchilds (Ed.), *Psychological perspectives on human diversity in America.* Washington, DC: American Psychological Association.

———. (1993). *Psychological perspectives on lesbian & gay male experiences.* New York: Columbia University Press.

Geen, R. G., & Quanty, M. B. (1977). The catharsis of aggression: An evaluation of a hypothesis. In L. Berkowitz (Ed.), *Advances in experimental social psychology* (Vol. 10). New York: Academic Press.

Gerber, G. L. & Gross, E. (1976). Conflicts in values and attitudes between parents of symptomatic and normal children. *Psychological Reports, 38*(1), 91–98.

Gerson, K. (1987). What do women want from men? Men's influence on women's work and family choices. In M. S. Kimmel (Ed.), *Changing men: New directions in research on men and masculinity.* Newbury Park, CA: Sage Publications.

Gibbons, F. X. (1986). Social comparison and depression: Company's effects on misery. *Journal of Personality and Social Psychology, 51,* 140–148.

Gibbs, N. (June 3, 1991). When is it rape? *Time,* pp. 48–54.

Gibran, K. (1976) *The prophet.* New York: Alfred A. Knopf.

Gilford, R., & Bengtson, V. (1979). Measuring marital satisfaction in three generations: Positive and negative dimensions. *Journal of Marriage and the Family, 44*(2), 15–50.

Gilligan, C. (1982). *In a different voice.* Cambridge, MA: Harvard University Press.

Gilligan, C., & Attanucci, J. (1988). Two moral orientations: Gender differences and similarities. *Merrill-Palmer Quarterly, 34*(3), 223–237.

Girodo, M. (1978). *Shy? (You don't have to be!).* New York: Pocket Books.

Godden, R. (1986). *The peacock spring.* New York, NY: Viking Press.

Goethals, G. R., & Darley, J. (1977). Social comparison theory: An attributional approach. In J. M. Suls & R. L. Miller (Eds.), *Social comparison processes: Theoretical and empirical perspectives.* Washington, DC: Hemisphere.

Goldberg, H. (1987). *The inner male: Overcoming roadblocks to intimacy.* New York: New American Library.

Goldfarb, L. A., Dyken, E. M. & Gerrard, M. (1985). *Journal of Personality Assessment, Vol. 49*(3).

Goldstein, J. H., & Arms, R. L. (1971). Effects of observing athletic contests on hostility. *Sociometry, 34,* 83–90.

Goldstein, M. J. (1987). The UCLA high risk project. *Schizophrenia Bulletin, 13,* 505–514.

Goldstine, D., Larner, K., Zuckerman, S., & Goldstine, H. (1988). In A. Arkoff (Ed.), *The psychology of personal growth.* Boston: Allyn & Bacon.

Goleman, D. (1995). *Emotional intelligence.* New York: Bantam Books.

———. (October 22, 1991). Sexual harassment: It's about power, not lust. *The New York Times,* pp. C1, C12.

Gonsiorek, J. C., & Weinrich, J. D. (1991). The definition and scope of sexual orientation. *Homosexuality: Research Implications for Public Policy.* Thousand Oaks, CA: Sage.

Goodall, J. (1991). *Through a window.* Boston, MA: Houghton Mifflin.

Goodwin, J. M., Cheeves, K., & Connell, V. (1990). Borderline and other severe symptoms in adult survivors of incestuous abuse. *Psychiatric Annals, 20,* 22–32.

Gorer, G. (1967). *Death, grief and mourning.* New York: Doubleday.

Gostin, L. O., Lazzarini, A., Alexander, D., Brandt, A. M., Mayer, K. H., & Silverman, D. C. (1994). HIV testing, counseling, and prophylaxis after sexual assault. *JAMA, 271,*1436–1444.

Gottfried, A. E., & Gottfried, A. W. (1988). Maternal employment and children's development. In A. E. Gottfired & A. W. Gottfried (Eds.) *Redefining Families: Implications for Children's Development.* New York: Plenum Press.

Gottfried, A. E., Bathurst, K., Gottfried, A. W. (1994). Role of maternal and dual-earner employment status in children's development: A longitudinal study from infancy through early adolescence. In A. E. Gottfried & A. W. Gottfried (Eds.) *Redefining families: Implications for children's development.* New York: Plenum Press.

Gould, S. J. (1987). Justice Scalia's misunderstanding. *Natural History, 96,* 14–21.

Graber, B. (1982). *Circumvaginal musculature and sexual function.* New York: Krager.

Green, R. (1987). *The "sissy boy syndrome" and the development of homosexuality.* New Haven: Yale University Press.

Greer, G. (1989). *The female eunuch,* in *The Macmillian dictionary of quotations.* New York: Bloomsbury Publishing.

Groos, K. (1901). *The Play of Man.* New York: D. L. Appleton.

Haaken, J. (1990). A critical analysis of the co-dependence construct. *Psychiatry, 53,* 396–406.

Hakmiller, K. L. (1966). Threat as a determinant of downward comparison. *Journal of Experimental Social Psychology* (Suppl. 1), 32–39.

Hall, C. S. (1954). *Primer of Freudian Psychology.* New York: Mentor.

Hall, C. S. (1984). *Dreams.* In R. J. Corsini (Eds.), *Encyclopedia of Psychology: Vol. 1* (pp. 388–390). New York: Wiley.

Hall, C. S., & Lindzey, G. (1970). *Theories of Personality* (2nd ed.). New York: John Wiley & Sons, Inc.

Hall, J. A. (1984). *Nonverbal sex differences: Communication accuracy and expressive style.* Baltimore: Johns Hopkins University Press.

Halpern, D. F. (1984). *Thought and knowledge.* Hillsdale, New Jersey: Erlbaum.

———. (1989). *Thought and knowledge.* (2nd ed.) Hillsdale, NJ: Lawrence Erlbaum Associates, Inc.

Hamacheck, D. E. (1990). Evaluating self-concept and ego status in Erikson's last three psychosocial stages. *Journal of Counseling and Development, 68,* 677–683.

Hanna, S. L. (1995). *Person to person.* Englewood Cliffs, NJ: Prentice Hall.

Harlow, H. F., & Harlow, M. K. (1966). Learning to love. *American Scientists, 54,* 244–272.

Harmsen, P., Rosengreen, A., Tsipogianni, A., & Wilhelmsen, L. (1990). Risk factors for stroke in middle-aged men in Göteborg, Sweden. *Stroke, 21,* 23–29.

Harrington, D. M., Block, J., & Block, J. H. (1987). Testing aspects of Carl Rogers's theory of creative environments: Child-rearing antecedents of creative potential in young adolescents. *Journal of Personality and Social Psychology, 52,* 851–856.

Harris, M. J., & Rosenthal, R. (1985). Medication of interpersonal expectancy effects: 31 meta-analyses. *Psychological Bulletin, 97,* 363–386.

———. (1986). Four factors in the mediation of teacher expectancy effects. In R. S. Feldman (Ed.), *The social psychology of education.* New York: Cambridge University Press.

Harris, T. O. (1989). Physical illness: An introduction. In G. W. Brown & T. O. Harris (Eds.), *Life events and illness.* New York: Guilford Press.

———. (1991). Life stress and illness: The question of specificity. *Annals of Behavioral Medicine, 13,* 211–219.

Harshoren, H., & May, M. A. (1928). *Studies in the nature of character* (Vol. 1. Studies in deceit.) New York: Macmillan.

Hart, K., & Ollendick, T. H. (1985). Prevalence of bulimia in working and university women. *American Journal of Psychiatry, 142*(7), 851–854.

Hartup, W. W. (1989). Social relationships and their developmental significance. *American Psychologist, 44,* 120–126.

Harvey, J. H. (August 15, 1998). Personal communication. American Psychological Association Annual Convention.

Harvey, J. H. (1998). Recent developments in close relationships theory and research. Paper presented at the American Psychological Association Convention, San Francisco.

Hatfield, E. (1988). Passionate and companionate love. In R. J. Sternberg & M. L. Barnes (Eds.), *The psychology of love.* New Haven: Yale University Press.

Hatfield, E., & Rapson, R. L. (1993). *Love, sex, and intimacy: Their psychology, biology, and history.* New York: HarperCollins.

———. (1996). *Love and sex: Cross-cultural perspectives.* Boston: Allyn & Bacon.

Hatfield, E., & Sprecher, S. (1986). Measuring passionate love in intimate relationships. *Journal of Adolescence, 9,* 383–410.

Havinghusrt, Neugarten, & Tobin, (1968).

Hawkins, S. A., & Hastie, R. (1990). Hindsight: Biased judgments of past events after the outcomes are known. *Psychological Bulletin, 107,* 311–327.

Hay, D. F. (1979). Cooperative interactions and sharing between very young children and their parents. *Developmental Psychology, 15,* 647–653.

Hayden, R. M. (1984). Physical fitness and mental health: Causal connection or simply correlation? Paper presented at the annual meeting of the American Psychological Association, Toronto.

Hayes-Bautista, D. E. (May 18, 1997). Los Angeles Times, Section M. *Want to Live Longer? Look to the Latino Lifestyle.*

Hays, R. B. (1985). A longitudinal study of friendship development. *Journal of Personality and Social Psychology, 48,* 909–924.

Hazan, C., & Shaver, P. R. (1987). Romantic love conceptualized as an attachment process. *Journal of Personality and Social Psychology, 52,* 511–524.

Heatherton, T. F., Herman, C. P. , & Polivy, J. (1992). Effects of distress on eating: the importance of ego involvement. *Journal of Personality and Social Psychology, 62,* 801–803.

Helmering, D. W. (1995). Scripps Howard News Service.

Helson, R., Mitchell V., & Moane, G. (1984). Personality and patterns of adherence and nonadherence to the social clock. *Journal of Personality and Social Psychology, 46,* 1079–1096.

Hencken, J. (1984). Conceptualizations of homosexual behavior which preclude homosexual self-labeling. *Journal of Homosexuality, 9,* 53–63.

Hendrix, H. (1992). *Getting the love you want: A guide for couples.* Chicago: Harper Perennial.

Henley, N. M., & Freeman, J. (1981). The sexual politics of interpersonal behavior. In S. Cox (Ed.), *Female psychology: The emerging self.* New York: St. Martin's Press.

Hensely, W. E. (1992). Why does the best-looking person in the room always seem to be surrounded by admirers? *Psychological Reports, 70,* 457–458.

Herrigel, E. (1989). *Zen in the art of archery.* New York: Random House.

Hesse, H. (1905). *On little joys.*

Hindelang, M. J. (1981). Variations in sex-race-age-specific incidence rates of offending. *American Sociological Review, 46,* 461–474.

Hite, S. (1976). *The Hite report.* New York: Dell Publishing.

Hoffman, L. W. (1989). Effects of maternal employment in the two-parent family. *American Psychologist, 44,* 283–292.

Hoffman, M. L. (1970). Conscience, personality, and socialization techniques. *Human Development, 13,* 90–126.

———. (1975). Altruistic behavior and the parent-child relationship. *Journal of Personality and Social Psychology, 31,* 937–943.

Hokanson, J. E. (1970). Psychophysiological evaluation of the catharsis hypothesis. In E. I. Megargee & J. E. Hokanson (Eds.), *The dynamics of aggression; individual, group, and international analyses.* New York: Harper & Row.

Hokanson, J. E., & Burgess, M. (1962). The effects of three types of aggression on vascular process. *Journal of Personality and Social Psychology, 51,* 389–395.

Holland, J. L. (1996). *Occupations Finder.* Palo Alto, CA: Consulting Psychologists Press.

———. (1997). Making vocational choices: A theory of vocational personalities and work environments. Psychological Assessment Resources.

Holmes, D. S. (1984). Meditation and somatic arousal reduction: A review of the evidence. *American Psychologist, 39,* 1–10.

Holmes, D., Solomon, S., Cappo, B., & Greenberg, J. (1983). Effects of transcendental meditation versus resting on physiological and subjective arousal. *Journal of Personality and Social Psychology, 44,* 1245–1252.

Holmes, E. (1988). *The Science of Mind.* New York: G. P. Putnam's Sons.

Holmes, T., & Rahe, R. (1967). The social readjustment rating scale. *Journal of Psychosomatic Research, 11,* 213–218. Pergamon Press.

Homans, G. C. (1961). *Social behavior.* New York: Harcourt Brace.

Horney, K. (1939). *New ways in psychoanalysis.* New York: Norton.

House, J. S., Robbins, C., & Metzner, H. L. (1982). The association of social relationships and activities with mortality: Prospective evidence from the Tecumseh community health study. *American Journal of Epidemiology, 116,* 123–140.

Hu, Y., & Goldman, N. (1990). Mortality differentials by marital status: An international comparison. *Demography, 27,* 233–250.

Hudgens, R. W. (1974). Personal catastrophe and depression. In B. S. Dohrenwend & B. P. Dohrenwend (Eds.), *Stressful life events: Their nature and effects.* New York: Wiley.

Huston, A. C. (1983). Sex-typing. In P. H. Mussen (Ed.), *Handbook of child psychology: Vol. IV* (4th ed.). New York: Wiley.

Isaacowitz, D.M., & Seligman, M. E. P. (September 1998). *APA Monitor.*

Isabella, R. A. (1993). Origins of attachment. *Child Development, 64(2),* 605–621.

Isabella, R. A., & Belsky, J. (1991). Interactional synchrony and the origins of infant-mother attachment. *Child Development, 62,* 373–384.

Isen, A. M., & Levin, P. A. (1972). Effect of feeling good on helping: Cookies and kindness. *Journal of Personality and Social Psychology, 21,* 384–388.

James, W. (1902). *The Varieties of Religious Experience.* New York: Harper & Row.

Johnson, A. M., Wadsworth, J., Wellings, K., Bradshaw, S., & Field, J. (1992). Sexual lifestyles and HIV risk. *Nature, 360,* 410–412.

Johnson, R. L. (1983) Instructor's manual with transparency masters to accompany *Understanding Human Behavior.* Holt, Rinehart & Winston: New York, NY.

Jones, A., & Crandall, R. (1986). Validation of a short index of self-actualization. *Personality and Social Psychology Bulletin, 12,* 63–73.

Jones, D. & Hill, K. (1993). Criteria of facial attractiveness in five populations. *Human Nature, 4,* 271–296.

Jones, E. (1953). *The life and work of Sigmund Freud: The formative years and the great discoveries* (Vol. 1). New York: Basic Books.

Jones, G. P., & Gembo, M. H. (1989). *Age and sex roles; Differences in intimate friendship during childhood and adolescence.* Merril Psalmer Quarterly. October, Vol. 35(4) pp. 445–462.

Jones, W. H. (1982). Loneliness and social behavior. In L. A. Paplua & D. Perlman (Eds.), *Loneliness: A sourcebook of current theory, research, and therapy.* New York: Wiley.

Jones, W. H., Freemon, J. E., & Goswick, R. A. (1981). The persistence of loneliness: Self and other determinants. *Journal of Personality, 49,* 27–48.

Jourard, S. M. (1971). *The transparent self.* (2nd ed.). New York: D. Van Nostrand Company.

Jung, C. G. (1950). On mandalas. In *The collected works of C. G. Jung Vol. 9.* Princeton, NJ: Princeton University Press, 1959 and 1969.

———. (1917). *Two essays on analytical psychology.* In *The collected works of C. G. Jung (Vol. 7).* Princeton, NJ: Princeton University Press, 1953 and 1966.

———. (1935). The relations between the ego and the unconscious. In *The Collected Works of C. G. Jung.* (Vol. 7) Princeton, NJ: Princeton University Press, 1953 and 1966.

———. (1938). *Psychological aspects of the mother archetype.* In Vol. 91 of *The collected works of C. G. Jung.* Princeton, NJ: Princeton University Press, 1959 and 1969.

———. (1954). *On the psychology of the trickster figure.* In *The collected works of C. G. Jung, (Vol. 9i).* Princeton, NJ: Princeton University Press, 1959 and 1969.

———. (1961). *Memories, Dream, Reflections.* Aniela Jaffe (Ed.). New York: Pantheon.

———. (1965). *Memories, Dreams, Reflections.* New York, NY: Vintage Books.

Jussim, L. (1986). Self-fulfilling prophecies: A theoretical and integrative review. *Psychological Review, 93,* 429–445.

Jussim, L., & Eccles, J. (1992). Teacher expectations. *Journal of Personality & Social Psychology, 63*(6), 947–961.

Kagan, J., Kearsley, R. B., and Zelazo, P. R. (1978). *Infancy: Its Place in Human Development.* New York: Wiley.

Kagan, J., & Snidman, N. (1991). Infant predictors of inhibited and uninhibited profiles. *Psychological Sciences, 2,* 40–44.

Kagan, J., Snidman, N., Julia-Sellers, M., & Johnson, M. O. (1991). Temperament and allergic symptoms. *Psychosomatic Medicine, 53,* 332–340.

Kastenbaum, Derbin, Babatini, & Artt, (1972).

Kato, P. S., & Ruble, D. N. (1992). Toward an understanding of women's experience of menstrual cycle symptoms. In V. Adesso, D. Reddy, & R. Flemming (Ed.), *Psychological Perspective on Women's Health.* Washington, DC: Hemisphere.

Keen, S. (1994). "Tell your stories, discover life's meaning." *Science of Mind.* Oct. Vol. 67, No. 10.

———. (1997). *To love and be loved.* New York: Bantam Books.

Kegel, A. (1952). Sexual functions of the pubococcygeus muscle. *Western Journal of Surgery, Obstetrics, and Gynecology, 60,* 521–524.

Kehoe, J. (March 18, 1998). *How to really be a leader: what the text books never told you.* Talk was a part of a series of leadership workshops at Long Beach City College, sponsored by the student senate.

Keith-Spiegel, P., & Spiegel, D. (1967). Affective states of patients immediately preceding suicide. *Journal of Psychiatric Research, 5,* 89–93.

Kelley, D. M. (1972). *Why conservative churches are growing.* New York, NY: Harper & Row.

Kendall-Tackett, K. A., & Williams, L. M., & Finkehor, D. (1993). Impact of sexual abuse on children: A review and synthesis of recent empirical studies. *Psychological Bulletin, 113,* 164–180.

Kenrick, D. T. (1987). Gender, genes, and social environment: A bisocial interactionist perspective. In P. Shaver & C. Hendrick (Eds.), *Sex and gender: Review of personality and social psychology* (Vol. 7). Beverly Hills: Sage.

Kiecolt-Glaser, J. K., Glaser, R., Williger, D., & Stout, J. C. (1985). Psychosocial enhancement of immunocompetence in a geriatric population. *Health Psychology, 4,* 25–41.

Kim, A., Martin, D., & Martin, M. (1989). Effects of personality on marital satisfaction. *Family Therapy, 16(3),* 243–248.

King, B. M. (1996). *Human sexuality today.* (2nd ed.). Upper Saddle River, NJ: Prentice Hall.

Kinsey, A. C., Pomeroy, W. B., Martin, C. E. (1948). *Sexual behavior in the human male.* Philadelphia: W. B. Saunders Co.

Kinsey, A. C., Pomeroy, W. B., Martin, C. E., & Gebard, P. H. (1953). *Sexual behavior in the human female.* Philapelphia: W. B. Saudners Co.

Kirkpatrick, S. A. & Locke, E. A. (1991). Leadership: Do traits matter? *The Academy of Management Executives, 5(2),* 48–60.

Klein, R. (1970). *Some factors influencing empathy in six and seven year old children varying in ethnic background.* Unpublished doctoral dissertation, University of California, Los Angeles.

Kobasa, S. C. (1979). Stressful life events, personality, and health: An inquiry into hardiness. *Journal of Personality and Social Psychology, 37,* 1–11.

Kobasa, S. C., & Puccetti, M. C. (1983). Personality and social resources in stress resistance. *Journal of Personality and Social Psychology, 45,* 839–850.

Kobasa, S. C., Maddi, S. R., & Kahn, S. (1982). Hardiness and health: A prospective study. *Journal of Personality and Social Psychology, 42,* 168–177.

Kobasa, S. C., Maddi, S. R., Puccetti, M. C., & Zola, M. (1985). Relative effectiveness of hardiness, exercise, and social support as resources against illness. *Journal of Psychosomatic Research, 29,* 525–533.

Kohlberg, L. (1968). "The Child as a Moral Philosopher." *Psychology Today, 1,* 25–30.

———. (1969a). Stage and sequence: The cognitive-developmental approach to socialization. In D. Goslin (Ed.), *Handbook of socialization theory and research.* Chicago: Rand McNally.

———. (1969b). *Stages in the development of moral thought and action.* New York: Holt.

———. (1976). Moral stages and moralization: The cognitive-developmental approach. In T. Lickona (Ed.), *Moral development and behaviors: Theory, research and social issues.* New York: Holt.

———. (1981). *Essays on moral development.* (Vol. I. The philosophy of moral development). San Francisco: Harper.

Kohlberg, L., Levine, C., & Hewer, A. (1983). *Moral stages: A current formulation and a response to critics.* New York: Karger.

Kohn, A. (1992). *No contest: The case against competition* (rev. ed.) Boston: Houghton Mifflin.

Kohn, M. L., & Schooler, C. (1983). *Work and personality: An inquiry into the impact of social stratification.* Norwood, NJ: Ablex.

Koss, M. P. (1985). The hidden rape victim: Personality, attitudinal, and situational characteristics. *Psychology of Women Quarterly, 9,* 193–212.

———. (1993). Rape: Scope, impact, interventions, and public policy responses. *American Psychologist, 48,* 1062–1069.

Koss, M. P., Heise, L., Russo, N. F. (1994). The global health burden of rape. *Psychology of Women Quarterly, 18,* 509–537.

Kotler, P, & Wingard, D. L. (1989). The effect of occupational, marital and parental roles on mortality: The Alameda County study. *American Journal of Public Health, 79,* 607–612.

Krantz, D. S., & Manuck, S. B. (1984). Acute psychophysiologic reactivity and risk of cardiovascular disease: A review and methodological critique. *Psychological Bulletin, 96,* 435–464.

Krebs, D. (1975). Empathy and altruism. *Journal of Personality and Social Psychology, 32,* 1134–1146.

Kübler-Ross, E. (1969). *On death and dying.* New York: Macmillan.

———. (1975). *Death: The final stage of growth.* Englewood Cliffs, NJ: Prentice-Hall.

Kuebli, J., & Fivush, R. (1992). Gender differences in parent-child conversations about past emotions. *Sex Roles, 27,* 683–698.

Kuhlman, D. M., & Marshello, A. E. J. (1975). Individual differences in game motivation as moderators of pre-programmed strategy effects in prisoner's dilemma. *Journal of Personality and Social Psychology, 32,* 922–931.

Kurtines, W., & Greif, E. B. (1974). The development of moral thought: Review and evaluation of Kohlberg's approach. *Psychological Bulletin, 8,* 453–70.

Lakein, A. (1973). *How to get control of your time and your life.* New York: Signet.

Langer, E. J. (1983). *The psychology of control.* Beverly Hills, CA: Sage.

Langlois, J. H., & Roggman, L. A. (1990). Attractive faces are only average. *Psychological Science, 1,* 115–121.

Larsen, R. J., & Ketelaar, T. (1989). Extraversion, neuroticism and susceptibility to positive and negative mood induction procedures. *Personality and Individual Differences, 10,* 1221–1228.

———. (1991). Personality and susceptibility to positive and negative emotional states. *Journal of Personality and Social Psychology, 61,* 132–140.

Lasch, C. (1995). *The Revolt of the Elites and the Betrayal of Democracy.* New York: W. W. Norton.

Lauer, J., & Lauer, R. (June 1985). Marriages made to last. *Psychology Today,* pp. 22–26.

Laumann, E. O., Gagnon, J. H., Michael, R. T., & Michaels, S. (1994). *The social organization of sexuality: Sexual practices in the United States.* Chicago: University of Chicago Press.

Lavine, L. O., & Lombardo, J. P. (1984). Self-disclosure: Intimate and non-intimate disclosures to parents and best friends as a function of Bem sex-role category. *Sex Roles, 11,* 735–744.

Lawson, K. D. (1975). The relationship of the socialization of anger, separation and warmth to the development of ascendant independence. *Dissertation Abstracts,* University of California, Berkeley. Order No. 77–4506, 95 pages.

Layton, W. L. (1955). Interest measurement: theory and research on the Strong Vocational Interest Blank: A conference report. *Journal of Consulting Psychology, 2,* 10–12.

Lazare, A. (January/February 1995). Go ahead and say you're sorry. *Psychology Today.*

Lazarus, R. S. (1985). The costs and benefits of denial. In A. Monat & R. S. Lazarus (Eds.), *Stress and coping: An anthology* (2nd ed). New York: Columbia University Press.

Lear, M. (December 20, 1987). The pain of loneliness. *The New York Times Magazine,* pp. 47–78.

Leavy, R. L. (1983). Social support and psychological disorder: A review. *Journal of Community Psychology, 11,* 3–21.

Leenaars, A. A. (1995). Suicide. In H. Wass & R. A. Neimeyer (Eds.), *Dying.* Washington, DC: Taylor & Francis.

Lefcourt, H. M. (1982). *Locus of control: Current trends in theory and research.* Hillsdale, NJ: Erlbaum.

Lerner, H. G. (1985). *The dance of anger. A woman's guide to changing the patterns of intimate relationships.* New York: Harper & Row.

LeVay, S. (February 24, 1992). *Newsweek,* pp. 46–53.

Levin, J., & Arluck, A. (1985). An exploratory analysis of sex differences in gossip. *Sex Roles, 12,* 281–285.

Levine, L. W. (1996). *The opening of the American mind.* Boston: Beacon Press.

Levine, M. (1988). *Effective problem solving.* Englewood Cliffs, NJ: Prentice-Hall.

Levine, P. R., & Wallen, R. (1954). Adolescent vocational interests and later occupation. *Journal of Applied Psychology, 38,* 428–431.

Levine, R. V. (1990). The pace of life. *American Scientist, 78,* September–October, 450–458.

Levinson, D. J. (1986). A conception of adult development. *American Psychologist, 41*(1), 3–13.

Levinson, D. J., & Levinson, J. D. (1996). *The seasons of a woman's life.* New York: Knopf.

Libbee, G. (1996). Personal communication.

Liebert, R. M., & Spiegler, M. D. (1994). *Personality* (7th ed.). Pacific Grove, CA: Brooks/Cole.

Lifton, R. J. (1993). *The protean self.* New York: Basic Books.

Lindbergh, A. (1955). *Gift from the sea.* New York: Pantheon.

Livingston, J. D. (April 24, 1998). Personal communication. Workshop on Chemical Dependency: Assessment & Treatment. California School of Professional Psychology.

Loftus, E. F. (1993). The reality of repressed memories. *American Psychologist, 48,* 518–537.

Loftus, E. F., Polonsky, S., & Fullilove, M. T. (1994). Memories of childhood sexual abuse: Remembering and repressing. *Psychology of Women Quarterly, 18,* 67–84.

London, P. (1970). The rescuers: Motivational hypotheses about Christians who saved Jews from the Nazis. In J. R. McCaulay & L. Berkowitz (Eds.), *Altruism and helping behavior.* New York: Academic Press.

Long, P. (October, 1987). "Laugh and be well?" *Psychology Today,* pp. 28–29.

Lore, R. K., & Schultz, L. A. (January 1993). Control of Human Aggression. *American Psychologist,* pp. 16–24.

Luck, P. W., & Heiss, J. (1972). Social determinants of self-esteem in adult males. *Sociology and Social Research, 57,* 69–84.

Luft, J. (1969). *Of Human interaction.* Palo Alto, CA: National Press Books.

——. (1970). *Group processes: An Introduction to Group Dynamics.* Palo Alto: Mayfield Publishing Co.

Lykes, M. B., & Stewart, A. (1982). Studying the effect of early experiences on women's career achievement. Paper presented at the annual meeting of the American Psychological Association, Washington, D.C.

Maccoby, E. (Aug. 15, 1998). *The Great Childcare Debate.* American Psychological Association Annual Convention in San Francisco, CA.

Maccoby, E. E. (1990). Gender and relationships: A developmental account. *American Psychologist, 45,* 513–520.

Maccoby, E. E., & Jacklin, C. N. (1974). *The psychology of sex differences.* Stanford, CA: Stanford University Press.

Maddi, S. R., & Kobasa, S. C. (1984). *The hardy executive: Health under stress.* Homewood, IL: Dow Jones-Irwin.

Maier, S. (1991). *God's love song.* Corvallis, OR: Postal Instant Press.

Major, B. (1981). Gender patterns in touching behavior. In C. Mayo & N. M. Henley (Eds.), *Gender and nonverbal behavior.* New York: Springer-Verlag.

Malamuth, N. M., Sockloskie, R. J., Koss, M. P., & Tanaka, J. S. (1991). Characteristics of aggressors against women: Testing a model using a national sample of college students. *Journal of Consulting and Clinical Psychology, 58,* 704–712.

Marcus, R. F., Telleen, S., and Poke, E. J. (1979). Relation between cooperation and empathy in young children. *Developmental Psychology, 15,* 346–347.

Markus, H. R., & Kitayama, S. (1991). Culture and self: Implications for cognition, emotion, and motivation. *Psychological Review, 98,* 224–253.

Martin G. B., & Clark, R. D., III (1982). Distress crying in neonates: Species and peer specificity. *Developmental Psychology, 18*, 3–11.

Martin, R. A, & Lefcourt, H. M. (1983). Sense of humor as a moderator of the relation between stressors and moods. *Journal of Personality and Social Psychology, 45*, 1313–1324.

Martinez, C. (1988). Mexican-Americans. In L. Comas-Diaz & E. E. H. Griffith (Eds.), *Clinical guidelines in cross-cultural mental health*. New York: John Wiley.

Maslow, A. H. (1962). Lessons from the peak-experiences. *Journal of Humanistic Psychology 2*(1), 9–18.

——. (1966). *The psychology of science: A reconnaissance*. New York: Harper & Row.

——. (1967). Self-actualization and beyond. In J. F. T. Buegenthal (Ed.), *Challenges of humanistic psychology*. New York: McGraw-Hill.

——. (1968). Peak-experiences as acute identity-experiences. In C. Gordan & K. J. Gergen (Eds.), *The Self in Social Interaction*. New York: J. Wiley.

——. (1970). *Motivation and personality* (3rd ed.). New York: HarperCollins.

——. (1971). *The farther reaches of human nature*. New York: Viking.

——. (1976). *The farther reaches of human nature*. New York, NY: Penguin.

——. (1987). *Motivation and personality*, (3rd ed.). New York: Harper.

Massimini, F., & Massimo, C. (1988). The systematic assessment of flow in daily experience. In M. Csikszentmihalyi & I. S. Csikszentmihalyi (Eds.), *Optimal experience: Psychology studies of flow in consciousness*. Cambridge: Cambridge University Press.

Masters, W. H., & Johnson, V. E. (1966). *Human sexual response*. Boston: Little Brown.

——. (1970). *Human sexual inadequacy*. Boston: Little Brown.

Matarazzo, J. D. (1984). Behavioral immunogens and pathogens in health and illness. In B. L. Hammonds & C. J. Scheirer (eds.), *Psychology and health: The master lecture series*, (Vol. 3). Washington, DC: The American Psychological Association.

Matlin, M. W. (1996). *The psychology of women*. (3rd Ed.). New York: Harcourt Brace.

Matthews, C., & Clark, R. D. (1982). Marital satisfaction: A validation approach. *Basic and Applied Social Psychology, 3*, 169–186.

Matthews, K. A., Batson, C. D. Horn, J., & Rosenmann, R. H. (1981). "Principle in his nature which interest him in the fortune of others . . .": The heritability of empathic concern for others. *Journal of Personality, 49*, 237–247.

May, R. (1973). *Man's Search for Himself*. New York: Dell.

——. (1981). *Freedom and destiny*. New York: Norton.

Mayeroof, M. (1990). *On Caring*. New York: Harper.

McCaffrey, M. (1986). Focus on success: How to use the power of self-image psychology. Chicago, IL: Nightingale-Conat. [sound cassettes].

McCarthy, R., & McCarthy, E. (1984). *Sexual awareness: Enhancing sexual pleasure*. New York: Carroll & Graf.

McConnell, J. V. (1983). *Understanding human behavior*. (4th ed.). New York: Holt, Rinehart & Winston.

McCrae, R. R., & Costa, P. T., Jr. (1987). Validation of the five-factor model of personality across instruments and observers. *Journal of Personality and Social Psychology, 52*, 81–90.

McDougall (1920). *The Group Mind*. Cambridge, MA.

McGill, M. E. (1985). *The McGill report of male intimacy*. New York: Harper & Row.

McLynn, F. (1997). *Carl Gustav Jung: A biography*. Boston, MA: St. Martin's Press.

Mead, M. (1935). *Sex and temperament in three primitive societies*. New York: Morrow.

Medawar, P. B. (1984). *The limits of science*. New York: Harper & Row.

Mednick, M. T. (1989). On the politics of psychological constructs: Stop the bandwagon, I want to get off. *American Psychologist, 44*(8), 1118–1123.

Menninger Clinic (1996). Brochure received from the Charles F. Menninger Society. Topeka, KS.

Michael, R. T., Gagnon, J. H., Laumann, E. O., & Kolata, G. (1994) *Sex in America: A definitive survey.* Boston: Little, Brown.

Michelozzi, B. N. *"Coming Alive from Nine to Five. The Career Search Handbook."* Moral, Dale, "Which Career Is Right for You?" *The Black Collegian, Vol. 17,* No. 1.

Midlarsky, E., and Bryan, J. H. (1972). Affect expressions and children's imitative altruism. *Journal of Abnormal and Social Psychology, 63,* 570–574.

Mihschel, W., & Mischell, H. N. (1974). A cognitive social learning approach to morality and self-regulation. In T. Lickona (Ed.), *Men and morality.* New York: Holt, Rinehart & Winston.

Mikulincer, M., & Nachshon, O. (1991). Attachment styles and patterns of self-disclosure. *Journal of Personality & Social Psychology, 61*(2), 321–331.

Miller, C. T. (1984). Self-schemas, gender, and social comparison: A clarification of the related attributes hypothesis. *Journal of Personality and Social Psychology, 46,* 1222–1229.

Miller, P. C., Lefcourt, H. M., Holmes, J. G., Ware, E. E., & Saley, W. E. (1986). Marital locus of control and marital problem solving. *Journal of Personality and Social Psychology, 51,* 161–169.

Miller, R. A., & Eisenberg, N. (1988). The relation of empathy to aggressive and externalizing/antisocial behavior. *Psychological Bulletin, 103,* 324–344.

Miller, W. R. *"The Psychological Viewpoint Questionnaire."*

Minuchin, S. (1974). *Families and family therapy.* Cambridge, MA: Harvard University Press.

Mischel, W. (1966). A social-learning view of sex differences in behavior. In E. Maccoby (Ed.), *The development of sex differences.* Stanford, CA: Stanford University Press.

———. (1970). Sex-typing and socialization. In P. Mussen (Ed.), *Carmicheal's manual of child psychology* (Vol. 2). New York: Wiley.

Mischel, W., Shoda, Y, & Peake, P. K. (1988). The nature of adolescent competencies predicted by preschool delay of gratification. *Journal of Personality and Social Psychology, 54,* 587–694.

Mitford, J. (1963). *The American way of death.* New York: Simon & Schuster.

Money, J. (1988). *Gay, straight and in-between: The Sexology of erotic orientation.* London: Oxford University Press.

Monte, C. F. (1991). *Beneath the mask* (4th ed.). New York: Holt, Rinehart and Winston, Inc.

Moore, C. (1989). Female sexual arousal disorder and inhibited female orgasm. In American Psychiatric Association (Ed.), *Treatments of psychiatric disorders: A task force report of the American Psychiatric Association.* Washington, DC: American Psychiatric Association.

Moore, T. (1994). *Care of the soul: A Guide for cultivating depth and sacredness in everyday life.* New York: Harper Perennial.

Mrela, C. K. (1995). Public Health Services, Office of Health Planning, Evaluation and Statistics, Arizona Center for Health Statistics.

Muehlenhard, C. L., & Linton, M. A. (1987). Date rape and sexual aggression in dating situation: Incidence and risk factors. *Journal of Counseling Psychology, 34,* 186–196.

Multiple Adjective Affect Checklist, Revised (MAACL-R). (1965).

Murname, J. J., & Levy, F. (1996). *Teaching the New Basic Skills.* New York: Martin Kessler Books.

Mussen, P. H., & Eisenberg-Berg, N. (1977). *Roots of caring, sharing, and helping. The development of prosocial behavior in children.* San Francisco: Freeman.

Myers, D. G. (1991). *Searching for joy: Who is happy—and why.* Paper presented at the annual meeting of the American Psychological Association, San Francisco.

———. (1992). *The pursuit of happiness: Who is happy—and why.* New York: Morrow.

Naisbitt, J., & Adurdene, P. (1990). *Megatrends 2000.* New York: Morrow.

Narcisco, J., & Burkett, D. (1975). *Relating redefined.* Upper Saddle River, NJ: Prentice-Hall.

National Gay Task Force (Ed.) (September 30, 1977). *Gay civil right support statements and resolutions packet.*

Neal, R. E. (1971). *The Art of Dying.* New York: Harper & Row.

Nelson , J. D., Gelfand, D. M., & Hartmann, D. P. (1969). Children's aggression following competition and exposure to an aggressive model. *Child Development, 40*(4), 1085–1097.

Neugarten, B. L., Wood, V., Kraines, R. J., & Loomis, B. (1963). Women's attitudes towards the menopause. *Vita Humana, 6,* 140–151.

Nevid, J. S., Rathus, L. F., Rathus, S. A. (1995). *Human sexuality.* Boston: Allyn & Bacon.

Newell, A., & Simon, H. A. (1972). In D. F. Halpern (1989), *Thought and knowledge* (2nd ed.). Hillsdale, NJ: Lawrence Erlbaum Association.

Nisan, M., & Kohlberg, L. (1982). Universality and variation in moral judgment: A longitudinal and cross-sectional study in Turkey. *Child Development, 53,* 865–876.

Noll, R. (1997). *The Aryan Christ: The secret life of Carl Jung.* New York: Random House.

Norwicki, S., & Strickland, B. R. (1973). A locus of control scale for children. *Journal of Consulting and Clinical Psychology, 40,* 148–154.

Novotny, A. (1995). Personal communication.

1991 American family values study: A return to family values. (1991). Springfield, MA: Massachusetts Mutual Life Insurance Company.

O'Bannion, T. (1997). *A learning college for the 21st century.* Phoenix, Arizona: Oryx Press.

O'Brien, P. E., & Gaborit, M. (1992). Codependency: A disorder separate from chemical dependency. *Journal of Clinical Psychology, 48*(1), 219–233.

O'Brien, S. (1989). *American Indian tribal government.* Norman: University of Oklahoma Press.

O'Connor, P. (1985). *Understanding Jung, understanding yourself.* New York: Paulist Press.

O'Connor, Patrick D. (1996). Psychospiritual intervention and employee assistance professionals. CA: *EAPA Exchange. July/August.*

O'Neil, J. M., Helm, B. J., Gable, R. K., David, L., & Wrightsman, L. S. (1986). Gender-role conflict scale: College men's fear of femininity. *Sex Roles, 14,* 335–350.

Offer, D., & Offer, J. B. (1975). *From teenage to young manhood.* New York: Basic Books.

Ogilvie, D. M. (1987). The undesired self: A neglected variable in personality research. *Journal of Personality and Social Psychology, 52,* 379–385.

————. (June 1988). *Dreaded states and desired outcomes.* Paper presented at the meeting of the Society of Personology, Durham, NC.

Oliner, S. P., & Oliner, P. M. (1988). *The altruistic personality: Rescuers of Jews in Nazi Europe.* New York: The Free Press.

Ornstein, R. (1993). *The roots of the self.* San Francisco, CA: HarperCollins Publishers.

Ornstein, R. and Sobel, D. (1993). *Healthy pleasures.* Menlo Park, CA: Addison-Wesley.

Paniagua, F. A. (1994). *Assessing and treating culturally diverse clients.* Thousand Oaks, CA: Sage.

Parke, R. D. (1981). *Fathers.* Cambridge, MA: Harvard University Press.

Parker, K. (July 17, 1997). Forget Day-Care Research—Trust Your Instincts. *USA Today.*

Parkes, K. (1984). Locus of control, cognitive appraisal, and coping in stressful episodes. *Journal of Personality and Social Psychology, 46,* 655–668.

Parkes, K. R. (1984). Coping in stressful episodes: The role of individual differences, environmental factors, and situational characteristics. *Journal of Personality and Social Psychology, 51,* 1277–1292.

Parlee, M. B. (1973). The premenstrual syndrom. *Psychological Bulletin, 80,* 454–465.

Peabody, D. & Goldberg, L. R. (1989). Some determinants of factor structures from personality-trait descriptors. *Journal of Personality and Social Psychology, 57,* 552–567.

Peale, N. V. (1952). *The power of positive thinking.* New York: Prentice-Hall.

Peck, M. S. (1978). *The road less traveled.* New York: Simon & Schuster, Touchstone Books.

Pennebaker, J. (1991). *Opening up: The healing power of confiding in others.* New York: Avon Books.

Pennebaker, J. W., Colder, M., & Sharp, L. K. (1990). Accelerating the coping process. *Journal of Personality and Social Psychology, 58*(3), 528–537.

Perls, F. S. (1970). Four lectures. In J. Fagan & I. L. Shepherd (Eds.), *Gestalt Therapy Now* (pp.14–38). New York: Harper & Row.

Perry, J. D., & Whipple, B. (1981). Pelvic muscle strength of female ejaculators: Evidence in support of a new theory of orgasm. *Journal of Sex Research, 17,* 22–39.

Perry, W. G. (1970). *Forms of intellectual and ethical developing in the college years, a scheme.* New York: Holt, Rinehart, and Winston.

Peterson, C., & Barrett, L. C. (1987). Explanatory style and academic performance among university freshmen. *Journal of Personality and Social Psychology, 53,* 603–607.

Piaget, J. (1928). *Judgment and reasoning in the child.* New York: Harcourt Brace.

———. (1952). *The origins of intelligence in children.* New York: Norton.

Pillard, R. C. (1990). The Kinsey Scale: Is it familial? In D. P. McWhirter, S. A. Sanders, & J. M. Reinish (Eds.), *Homosexuality/Heterosexuality: Concepts of sexual orientation.* New York: Oxford University Press.

Pirsig, R. M. (1974). *Zen and the art of motorcycle maintenance.* New York: William Morrow and Company.

Pleck, J. (1981). *The myth of masculinity.* Cambridge, MA: MIT Press.

Plomin, R., & Rende, R. (1991). Human behavioral genetics. *Annual Review of Psychology, 42,* 161–190.

Plomin, R., Chipeur, H. M., & Loehlin, J. C. (1990). Behavioral genetics and personality. In L. A. Pervin (Ed.), *Handbook of personality theory and research.* New York: Guilford Press.

Polkinghorne, D. (1988). *Narrative knowing and the human sciences.* Albany, NY: State University of New York Press.

Potkay, C. R., & Allen, B. P. (1986). *Personality: Theory, research, and applications.* Monterey, CA: Brooks/Cole.

Powell, C. (1998, April 26). Interview on *Meet the Press.* National Broadcasting Company.

Prentky, R. A., & Knight, R. A. (1991). Identifying critical dimensions for discriminating among rapists. *Journal of Consulting and Clinical Psychology, 59,* 643–661.

Pyszczynski, T., Greenberg, J., & LaPrelle, J. (1985). Social comparison after success and failure: Biased search for information consistent with a self-serving conclusion. *Journal of Experimental Social Psychology, 21,* 195–211.

Radke-Yarrow, M., Zahn-Waxler, C., & Chapman, M. (1983). Children's prosocial disposition and behavior. In P. H. Mussen (Ed.), *Handbook of child* psychology (Volume IV: Socialization, personality, and social development, E. M. Hetherington, Ed.), New York: Wiley.

Reinisch, J. M. (1990). *The Kinsey Institute new report on sex: What you must know to be sexually literate.* New York: St. Martin's.

Rest, J. R. (1983). Moral development. In P.H. Mussen (Ed.), *Handbook of child psychology* (4th ed., Vol. 3, pp. 556–629). New York: Wiley.

Rest, J. R. (1983). Morality, In P.H. Mussen (Ed.) *Handbook of child psychology* Volume III: Cognitive development. J. H. Flavell & E. M. Marchman, Eds.). New York: Wiley.

Reuters, Limited. (April 5, 1997). Archives.

Richard, L. S., Wakefield, J. A., & Lewak, R. (1990). *Personality and Individual Differences, 11,* 39–43.

Richardson, E. H. (1981). Cultural and historical perspectives on counseling American Indians. In D. W. Sue (Ed.), *Counseling the culturally different: Theory and practice.* New York: John Wiley.

Richelle, M. N. (1995). *B. F. Skinner: A reappraisal.* Hillsdale, NJ: Erlbaum.

Riger, S. (1991). Gender dilemmas in sexual harassment policies and procedures. *American Psychologist, 46,* 497–505.

Roderick, R. (1991). *Philosophy and Human Values.* Books on tape. The Teaching Co.

Rodin, J. (1988). Aging and health: Effects of the sense of control. *Science, 233,* 1271–1276.

Rogers, C. R. (1961). *On becoming a person: A therapist's view of psychotherapy.* Boston: Houghton Mifflin.

———. (1951). *Client-centered therapy.* Boston: Houghton Mifflin.

Rook, K. S. (1984). Promoting social bonding: Strategies for helping the lonely and socially isolated. *American Psychologist, 39,* 1389–1407.

Rosenbaum, M. E. (1980). Cooperation and competition. In P. B. Paulus (Ed.), *The psychology of group influence.* Hillsdale, NJ: Erlbaum.

Rosenberg, & Pearlin, (1978).

Rosenhan, D. L., Salovey, P., & Harris, K. (1981). The joys of helping: Focus of attention mediates the impact of positive affect on altruism. *Journal of Personality and Social Psychology, 40,* 899–905.

Rosenheim, E., & Muchnik, B. (1984/1985). Death concerns in differential levels of consciousness as functions of defense strategy and religious beliefs. *Omega, Journal of Death and Dying, 155,* 15–24.

Rosenthal, R. (1991). Teacher expectancy effects: A brief update 25 years after the Pygmalion experiment. *Journal of Reach in Education, 1,* 3–12.

Rosenthal, R., & Jaccobson, L. (1968). *Pygmalion in the classroom: Teacher expectation and pupils' intellectual development.* New York: Holt, Rinehart & Winston.

Rosolack, T. K., & Hampson, S. E. (1991). A new typology of health behaviours for personality-health predictions: The case of locus of control. *European Journal of Personality, 5,* 151–168.

Rotter, J. B. (1966). Generalized expectancies for internal versus external control of reinforcement. *Psychological Monographs, 80,* 1–28.

Rotter, N. G., & Rotter, G. S. (1988). Sex differences in the encoding and decoding of negative facial emotions. *Journal of Nonverbal Behavior, 12,* 139–148.

Rubin, G. (1984). Thinking sex: Notes for a radical theory of the politics of sexuality. In C. S. Vance (Ed.), *Pleasure and anger: Exploring female sexuality.* Boston: Routledge & Kegan Paul.

Rubin, Z. (1982). Child without friends. In L. A. Peplau & D. Perlman (Eds.), *Loneliness: A sourcebook of current theory, research, and therapy.* New York: Wiley.

Rudestam, K. E. (1971). Stockholm and Los Angeles: A cross-cultural study of the communication of suicidal intent. *Journal of Consulting and Clinical Psychology, 36*(1), 82–90.

Ruggiero, V. R. (1995). *Beyond feelings.* (4th ed.) Mountain View, CA: Mayfield Publishing Company.

Ruiz, R. A. (1981). Cultural and historical perspectives in counseling Hispanics. In D. W. Sue (Ed.), *Counseling the culturally different: Theory and practice.* New York: John Wiley.

Rushton , J. P., & Campbell, A. C. (1977). Modeling, vicarious reinforcement and extraversion on blood donating in adults: Immediate and long-term effects. *European Journal of Social Psychology, 7,* 297–306.

Rushton, J. P. (1976). Socialization and the altruistic behavior of children. *Psychological Bulletin, 83,* 898–913.

———. (1982). Altruism in society. A social learning perspective. *Ethics, 92,* 425–447.

———. (1989). Genetic similarity, human altruism, and group selection. *Behavioral and Brain Sciences, 12,* 503–518.

Rushton, J. P., Fulker, D. W., Neale, M. C., Nias, D. K. B., & Eysenck, H. J. (1986). Altruism and aggression: The heritability of individual differences. *Journal of Personality and Social Psychology, 50,* 1192–1198.

Russell, D. (1982). The measurement of loneliness. In L. A. Peplau and D. Perlman

(Eds.), *Loneliness: A sourcebook of current theory, research and therapy.* New York: Wiley.

Russell, D., Peplau, L. A., & Cutrona, C. E. (1980). The revised UCLA loneliness scale: Concurrent and discriminant validity evidence. *Journal of Personality and Social Psychology, 39,* 472–480.

Russell, J. A. (1983). Pancultural aspects of the human conceptual organization of emotions. *Journal of Personality and Social Psychology, 45,* 1281–1288.

Sacks, C. H., & Bugenthal, D. P. (1987). Attributions as moderators of affective and behavioral responses to social failure. *Journal of Personality and Social Psychology, 53,* 939–947.

Sagi, A. (1990). Attachment theory and research from a cross-cultural perspective. *Human Development, 33*(1), 10–22.

Sagi, A., and Hoffman, M. L. (1976). Empathic distress in newborns. *Developmental Psychology, 12,* 175–176.

Salovey, R., & Rodin, J. (1984). Some antecedents and consequences of social-comparison jealousy. *Journal of Personality and Social Psychology, 47,* 780–792.

Sandoval, M. C., & De La Roza, M. C. (1986). A cultural perspective for serving Hispanic clients. In H. P. Lefley & P. B. Pedersen (Eds.), *Cross-cultural training for mental health professions.* Springfield, IL: Charles C. Thomas.

Scanlon, T. J., Luben, R. N., Scanlon, F. L., & Singleton, N. (1993, 18–25 December). Is Friday the 13th bad for your health? *British Medical Journal, 307,* 1584–1586.

Scarr, S. (1990). Mother's proper place: Children's needs and women's rights. *Journal of Social Behavior and Personality, 5,* 507–515.

Schaap, C., & Hansen-Nawas, C. (1987). Marital interaction, affect and conflict resolution. *Sexual and Marital Therapy, 2*(1), 35–51.

Schaef, A. W. (1986). *Codependence misdiagnosed-mistreated.* Minneapolis: Winston Press.

Schafer, R. (1960). The loving and beloved super ego in Freud's structural theory. In O. Fenichel et al. (Eds.), *Psychoanalytic study of the child* (Vol. 15). New York: International Universities Press.

Schafer, W. (1992). *Stress management for wellness* (2nd ed.). Orlando, FL: Harcourt Brace Jovanovich College Publishers.

Scheier, M. F., & Carver, C. S. (1985). Optimism, coping and health: Assessment and implications of generalized outcome expectancies. *Health Psychology, 4*(3), 219–247.

Scheier, M. F., Weintraub, J. K., & Carver, C. S. (1986). Coping with stress: Divergent strategies of optimists and pessimists. *Journal of Personality and Social Psychology, 51*(6), 1208–1217.

Schlessinger, L. (June 15, 1995). KFI radio talk show.

Schmidt, L. A., & Fox, N. A. (1995). Individual differences in young adults' shyness and sociability. *Personality and Individual Differences, 19*(4), 455–462.

Schmidt, L. A., & Sermatt (1983). *Journal of Personality & Social Psychology, 44,* 1038–1047.

Schnitzer, E. (1977). *Looking in.* Idyllwild, CA: Strawberry Valley Press.

Schreyer, R. (1984). *A summary of the recreation benefit specification workshop.* Logan: Utah State University, Department of Forest Resources.

Schultz, D. (1990). *Theories of personality* (4th ed.). Pacific Grove, CA: Brooks/Cole.

Schulz, R. (1978). *The psychology of death, dying and bereavement.* Reading, MA: Addison-Wesley.

Schutte, N. S., Malouff, J. M., Post-Gorden, J. C., & Rodasta, A. L. (April, 1988). Effects of playing videogames on children's aggressive and other behaviors. *Journal of Applied Social Psychology, 18*(5), 454–460.

Sears, R. R., Rau, I., & Alpert, R. (1965). *Identification and child rearing.* Stanford, CA: Stanford University Press.

Segal, J. (1986). *Winning life's toughest battles.* New York: McGraw-Hill.

Seligman, M. E. P. (1988). Boomer blues. *Psychology Today.* October, 1988, p. 50–51.

———. (1988). Why is there so much depression today? The waxing of the individual and the waning of the commons. The G. Stanely Hall Lecture, American Psychological Association convention, Atlanta, GA.

———. (1990). *Learned optimism: How to change your mind and your life.* New York: Pocket Books.

———. (August 14, 1998). Epidemic of depression. American Psychological Association convention, San Francisco.

———. (1990). *Learned optimism: How to change you mind and your life.* New York: Pocket Books.

Selye, H. (1956). *The stress of life.* New York: McGraw-Hill.

Senge, P. M. (1990). *The fifth discipline.* New York: Doubleday.

Serbin, L. A., & O'Leary, K. D. (1975, December). How nursery school teaches girls to shut up. *Psychology Today, 9*(9), 56–58.

Shaver, P. R., & Hazan, C. (1993). Adult romantic attachment: Theory and empirical evidence. In D. Perlman & W. H. Jones (Eds.), *Advances in personal relationships* (Vol. 4). Greenwich, CT: JAI Press.

Shaver, P. R., Hazan, C., & Bradshaw, D. (1988). Love as attachment: The integration of three behavioral systems. In R. J. Sternberg & M. L. Barnes (Eds.), *The psychology of love.* New Haven: Yale University Press.

Sheldrake, R. (1996). *A glorious accident.* Conversations with William Kayser. KCET television program. (June 15, 1994).

Sheppard, H. L., Herrick, W. (1972). *Where have all the robots gone?* New York: Free Press.

Sherrod, D. (1989). The influence of gender on same-sex friendships. In C. Hendrick (Ed.), *Review of personality and social psychology* (Vol. 10: Close relationships). Newbury Park, CA: Sage.

Shields, S. A. (1994). *Practicing social constructionism: Confessions of a feminist empiricist.* Paper presented at the annual meeting of the American Psychological Association, Los Angeles.

———. (1995). The role of emotion beliefs and values in gender development. In N. Eisenberg (Ed.), *Social development.* (pp. 212–232). Thousand Oaks, CA: Sage.

Shneidman, E. S., & Farberow, N. L. (Eds.). (1957). *Clues to suicide.* New York: McGraw-Hill.

Shoda, Y., Mischel, W., & Peake, P. K. (1990). Predicting adolescent cognitive and self-regulatory competencies from the preschool delay of gratification: Identifying diagnostic conditions. *Developmental Psychology 26,* 978–986.

Shultz, T. R., Wright, K., & Schliefer, M. (1986). Assignment of moral responsibility and punishment, *Child Development, 57,* 177–184.

Shure, G. H., Meeker, R. J., & Hansford, E. A. (1965). The effectiveness of pacifist strategies in bargaining games. *Journal of Conflict Resolution, 9,*106–117.

Siegel, B. S. (1989). *Peace, love & healing.* New York: Harper & Row.

Simon, S. B., Howe, L. W. & Kirschenbaum, H. (1972). *Values Clarification.* New York: Hart Publishing Company, Inc.

Simon, B. S., Howe, L. W., & Kirschenbaum, H. (1972). *Values clarification.* New York: Hart Publishing Company, Inc.

Simpson, J. A., Campbell, B., & Berscheid, E. (1986). The association between romantic love and marriage: Kephart (1967) twice revisited. *Personality and Social Psychology Bulletin, 12,* 363–372.

Skinner, B. F. (1953). *Science and human behavior.* New York: Macmillan.

Slaby, A. E., Garfinkel, B. D., & Garfinkel, L. F. (1994). *No one say my pain.* New York: Norton.

Sleek, S. (April, 1997). Job seekers aided by psychology's strategies. *APA Monitor.* Washington, DC: American Psychological Association.

Smith, M. J. (1975). *When I say no, I feel guilty.* New York: Bantam.

Smither, R. D. (1994). *The psychology of work and human performance* (2nd ed.). New York: HarperCollins.

Snarey, J. R. (1985). Cross-cultural universality of social-moral development: A critical review of Kohlergian research. *Psychological Bulletin, 97,* 202–232.

Snarey, J. R., Reimer, J., & Kohlberg, L. (1985a). Development of social-moral reasoning among kibbutz adolescents: A longitudinal cross-cultural study. *Development Psychology, 21,* 3–17.

———. (1985b). The kibbutz as a model for moral education: A longitudinal cross-cultural study. *Journal of Applied Developmental Psychology, 6* 151–172.

Snodgrass, M. A. (1987). The relationships of differential loneliness, intimacy, and characterological attributional style to duration of loneliness. *Journal of Social Behavior and Personality, 2,* 173–186.

Sobel, D. (May, 1993). Outsmarting stress. *Working Woman.*

Solomon, L. (1960). The influence of some types of power relationships and game strategies upon the development of interpersonal trust. *Journal of Abnormal and Social Psychology, 61,* 223–230.

Spiegler, M. D. (1983). *Contemporary behavioral therapy.* Palo Alto, CA: Mayfield.

Spielberger, C. D., Johnson, E. H., Russell, S. F., Crane, R. J., Jacobs, G. A., & Worden, T. J. (1985). The experience and expression of anger. In M. A. Chesney, S. E. Goldston, & R. H. Rosenman (Eds.), *Anger and hostility in behavioral medicine.* New York: McGraw-Hill.

Spitzberg, B. H., & Hurt, H. T. (1987). The relationship of interpersonal competence and skills to reported loneliness across time. *Journal of Social Behavior and Personality, 2,* 157–172.

Staub, E. (1989). *The roots of evil.* Cambridge, MA: Cambridge University Press.

Staub, E. (Ed.). (1978). *Positive social behavior and morality (Vol. 1): Social and personal development.* New York: Academic Press.

Stekel, W. (1949). *Compulsion and doubt.* New York, NY: W. W. Norton.

Sternberg, R. J. (1986). A triangular theory of love. *Psychological Review, 93,* 119–135.

———. (1988). *The triangle of love.* New York: Basic.

———. (1991). *Love the way you want it.* New York: Bantam Books.

———. (1986). *Intelligence Applied.* Orlando, Florida: Harcourt Brace Jovanovich, Inc.

Sterns, C. Z., & Sterns, P. N. (1986). *Anger: The struggle for emotional control in American's history.* Chicago: University of Chicago Press.

Stier, D. S., & Hall, J. A. (1984). Gender differences in touch: An empirical and theoretical review. *Journal of Personality and Social Psychology, 47,* 440–459.

Stine, G. J. (1995). *AIDS update 1994–1995.* Englewood Cliffs, NJ: Prentice Hall.

Stone, A. A. L., Bovbjerg, D. H., Neale, J. M., Napoli, A., Valdimarsdottir, H., Cox, D., Hayden, G., & Gwaltney, J. M., Jr. (1992). Development of the common cold symptoms following experimental rhinovirus infection is related to prior stressful life events. *Behavioral Medicine, 13,* 70–74.

Stotland, E. (1969). Exploratory investigations of empathy. In L. Berkowitz (Ed.), *Advances in experimental social psychology* (Vol. 4, pp. 271–314). New York: Academic Press.

Strumpel, B. (Ed.) (1976). Economic means for human needs: Social indicators of well-being and discontent. Ann Arbor: Survey Research Center, Institute for Social Research, University of Michigan.

Stuart, R. B. (1967). Decentration in the development of children's concepts of moral and causal judgment. *Journal of Genetic Psychology, 111,* 59–68.

Sumerlin, J. R., & Bundrick, C. M. (1996). Brief index of self-actualization: A measure of Maslow's model. *Journal of Social Behavior & Personality. 11*(2), 253–271.

Sundstrom, E., De Meuse, K. P., & Futrell, D. (1990). Work teams: Applications and effectiveness. *American Psychologist, 45,* 120–133.

Super, D. E. (1980). A life-span life-space approach to career development. *Journal of Vocational Behavior, 16,* 282–298.

———. (1990). A life-span Life-space approach to career development. In D. Brown, L. Brooks, & Associates (Eds.), *Career choice and development* (2nd ed., pp. 197–261). San Francisco: Jossey-Bass.

Susman-Stillman, A., Kalkose, M., Egeland, B., & Waldman, I. (1996). Infant temperament and maternal sensitivity as predictors of attachment security. *Infant Behavior & Development, 19*(1), 33–47.

Sweeney, P. D., Anderson, K., & Bailey, S. (1986). Attributional style in depression: A meta-analytic review. *Journal of Personality and Social Psychology, 50,* 947–991.

Swenson, C. H., Eskew, R. W., & Kohlhepp, K. A. (1981). Stage of the family life cycle, ego development, and the marriage relationship. *Journal of Marriage and the Family, 43*(4), 841–853.

Szasz, T. S. (1977). *The manufacture of madness.* New York: Dell.

Tavris, C. (1989). *Anger: The misunderstood emotion.* New York: Touchstone.

———. (March 2, 1996). Personal communication. Presentation at California State University, Long Beach.

Taylor, S. E. (1986). *Health psychology.* New York: Random House.

Taylor, S. E., & Brown, J. D. (1988). Illusion and well-being: A social psychological perspective on mental health. *Psychological Bulletin, 103,* 193–210.

Taylor, S. E., Wood, J. V., & Lichtman, R. R. (1983). It could be worse: Selective evaluation as a response to victimization. *Journal of Social Issues, 39,* 19–40.

Teleki, G. (1973). *The predatory behavior of wild chimpanzees.* Lewisburg, PA: Bucknell University Press.

Terkel, S. (1997). *Working: People talk about what they do all day and how they feel about what they do.* New Press.

Terman, L. M. & Oden, M. H. (1947). *Genetic studies of genius: The gifted child grows up* (Vol. 4). Stanford, CA: Stanford University Press.

———. (1959). *The gifted group in mid-life.* Vol. 5, Genetic studies of genius. Stanford, CA: Stanford University Press.

Terman, L. M., assisted by Baldwin, B. T., Bronson, E., Devoss, J. C., Fuller, F., Goodenough, F. L., Kelley, T. L., Lima, M., Marshall, H., Moore, A. H., Raubenheiner, A. S., Ruch, G. M., Willoughby, R. L., Wyman, J. B., & Yates, H. H. (1925). *Mental and physical traits of a thousand gifted children: Genetic studies of genius* (Vol. 1). Stanford, CA: Stanford University Press.

Tesser, A., & Collins, J. E. (1988). Emotion in social reflection and comparison situations: Intuitive, systematic, and exploratory approaches. *Journal of Personality and Social Psychology, 55,* 695–709.

Tesser, A., Millar, M., & Moore, J. (1988). Some affective consequences of social comparison and reflection processes: The pain and pleasure of being close. *Journal of Personality and Social Psychology, 54,* 49–61.

Tessina, T. (1989). *Gay relationships: How to find them, how to improve them, how to make them last.* New York: Tarcher/Perigree.

Test, D. W., Farebother, C. & Spooner, F. (1989, September). A comparison of the social interactions of workers with and without disabilities. *Journal of Employment Counseling. 25*(3), 122–131.

Tett, R. P., Jackson, D.N., & Rothstein, M. *(1991). Personality measures as predictors of job performance: A meta-analytic review.* Personnel Psychology, 44, 703–742.

Theorell, T. (1974). Life events before and after the onset of a premature myocardial infarction. In B. S. Dohrenwend & B. P. Dohrenwend (Eds.), *Stressful life events: Their nature and effects.* New York: Wiley.

Thibaut, J., & Kelly, H. H. (1959). *The social psychology of groups.* New York: Wiley.

Thompson, W. (1972). *Correlates of the self concept.* Nashville: Counselor Recordings and Tests.

Thorndike, E. L. (1901a, June). Notes on child study [Monograph]. *Columbia University contributions of Philosophy, Psychology, and Education. 8,* (Nos. 3–4). New York: MacMillan.

———. (1901b). *The human nature club: An introduction to the study of mental life.* New York: Longmans, Green.

———. (1906). *The principles of teaching, based on psychology.* New York: A. G. Seiler.

———. (1940). *Human nature and the social order.* New York: MacMillan.

Tinsley, H. E. A., & Eldridge, B. D. (1995). Psychological benefits of leisure participation: A taxonomy of leisure activities based on their need-gratifying properties.

Journal of Counseling Psychology, 42(2), 123–132.

Tinsley, H. E. A. (1984). The psychological benefits of leisure counseling. *Society and Leisure, 7*, 125–140.

Tinsley, H. E. A., Barrett, T. C., & Kass, R. A. (1977). Leisure activities and need satisfaction. *Journal of Leisure Research, 9*, 110–120.

Tinsley, H. E. A., Hinson, J. A., Tinsley, D. J. & Holt, M. S. (1993). Attributes of leisure and work experiences. *Journal of Counseling Psychology, 40*, 447–455.

Tinsley, H.E.A. & Johnson, T. L. (1984). A preliminary taxonomy of leisure activities. *Journal of Leisure Research, 16*, 234–244.

Tinsley, H.E.A. & Kass, R. A. (1978). Leisure activities and need satisfaction: A replication and extension. *Journal of Leisure Research, 10*, 191–202.

———. (1979). The latent structure of the need satisfying properties of leisure activities. *Journal of Leisure Research, 11*, 278–291.

Tinsley, H.E.A., & Tinsely, (1986). A theory of the attributes, benefits, and causes of leisure experience. *Leisure sciences, Vol. 8(1)*, 1–45.

Tofler, G. H., Stone, P. H., Maclure, M., Edelman, E., Davis, V. G., Robertson, T., Antman, E. M., Muller, J. E., & The MILIS Study Group. (1990). Analysis of possible triggers of acute myocardial infarction (the MILIS study). *The American Journal of Cardiology, 66*, 22–27.

Travis, J. W., & Ryan, R. S. (1988). *Wellness workbook* (2nd ed.). Berkeley, CA: Ten Speed Press.

Trickett, P. K., & Putnam, F. W. (1993). Impact of child sexual abuse on females: Toward a developmental, psychobiological integration. *Psychological Science, 4*, 81–87.

Troiden, R. R. (1989). The formation of homosexual identities. *The Journal of Homosexuality, 17*, 43–73.

Turiel, E. (1966). An experimental test of the sequentiality of developmental states in the child's moral judgments. *Journal of Personality and Social Psychology, 3*, 611–618.

Tzeng, M. (1992). The effect of socioeconomic heterogamy and changes on marital dissolution for first marriages. *Journal of Marriage and Family, 54*, 609–619.

Vaillant, G. (1977). *Adaptation to life.* Boston: Little, Brown.

Vance, M. & Deacon, D. (1996, December 5 issue). *Bits & Pieces.* Fairfield, NJ: Economics Press, Inc.

Wade, C, & Tavris, C. (1990). *Psychology.* New York: Harper & Row.

Wahba, M.A., and Bridwell, L. G. (1976). Maslow reconsidered: A review of research on need hierarchy theory. *Organizational Behavior and Human Performance, 15*, 212–240.

Walker, L. J. (1984). Sex differences in the development of word reasoning: A critical review. *Child Development, 55*, 677–691.

Walker, L. J. (1989). A longitudinal study of moral reasoning. *Child Development, 60*, 157–166.

Walster, E., & Walster, G. W. (1978). *A new look at love.* Reading, MA: Addison-Wesley.

Watson, J. B. (1913). Psychology as a behaviorist views it. *Psychological Review, 20*, 158–177.

Weiner, B. (1986). *An attributional theory of emotion and motivation.* New York: Springer-Verlag.

Weiner, B., Kun, A., and Benesh-Weiner, M. (1980). The development of mastery, emotions and morality from an attributional perspective. In W. A. Collins (Ed.), *Minnesota Symposium on Child Development* (Vol. 13). Hillsdale, NJ: Lawrence Erlbaum.

Weiner, R., Graham, S., & Chandler, C. C. (1982). Pity, anger, and guilt: An attributional analysis. *Personality and Social Psychology Bulletin, 8*, 226–232.

Wertheimer, M. (1970). *A brief history of psychology.* New York: Holt, Rinehart & Winston.

Wheeler, L., Koestner, R., & Driver, R. E. (1982). Related attributes in the choice of comparison others. *Journal of Experimental Social Psychology, 18*, 489–500.

Whitcher, S. J., & Fisher, J. D. (1979). Multidimensional reaction to therapeutic touch in a hospital setting. *Journal of Personality and Social Psychology, 37,* 87–96.

White, R. W. (1972). *The enterprise of living: Growth and organization personality.* New York: Holt, Rinehart and Winston.

Whitfield, C. L. (1987). *Healing the child within: Discovery and recovery for adult children of dysfunctional families.* Deerfield Beach, FL: Health Communications.

———. (1991). *Co-dependence: Healing the human condition.* Deerfield Beach, FL: Health Communications.

Whitley, B. E., Jr. (1988). Masculinity, femininity, and self-esteem. A multitrait-multimethod analysis. *Sex Roles, 18,* 419–432.

Whitman, W. (1993). "Song of Myself" In G. McMichael (Ed.). Selected poems of Walt Whitman to Anthology of American Literature. Upper Saddle River: Prentice Hall.

Wiley, J., & Camacho, T. (1980). Life-style and future health: Evidence from the Alameda County study. *Preventive Medicine, 9,* 1–21.

Wilkinson, D. (1995). Central civilizations. In S. K. Sanderson (Ed.), *Civilizations and world systems: Studying world-historical change* (pp. 46–74). London: Altamira Press.

Williams, R. B. (1989). *The trusting heart: Great news about Type A behavior.* New York: Random House.

———. (1995). Coronary prone behaviors, hostility, and cardiovascular health: Implications for behavioral and pharmacological interventions. In K. Orth-Gomer & N. Schneiderman (Eds.), Behavioral medicine approaches to cardiovascular disease prevention. Hillsdale, NJ: Erlbaum.

Williams, R. B., Jr., Barefoot, J. C. (1988). Coronary-prone behavior: The emerging role of the hostility complex. In B. K. Houston & C. R. Snyder (Eds.), Type A behavior pattern: Research, theory, and intervention. New York: Wiley.

Williams, T. M. (Ed.) (1986). *The impact of television: A natural experiment in three communities.* Orlando, FL: Academcia Press.

Wills, T. A. (1981). Downward comparison principles in social psychology. *Psychological Bulletin, 90,* 245–271.

Wilson, D. W. (1981). Is helping a laughing matter? *Psychology, 18,* 6–9.

Wilson, E. O. (1975). *Sociobiology: The new synthesis.* Cambridge, MA: Harvard University Press.

Wilson, F. L. (1995). The effects of age, gender, and ethnic-cultural background on moral reasoning. *Journal of Social Behavior & Personality, 10* (1), 67–78.

Wilson, J. Q. (1993). *The moral sense.* New York: The Free Press.

Wittenberg, M. T., & Reis, H. T. (1986). Loneliness, social skills, and social perception. *Personality and Social Psychology Bulletin, 12,* 121–130.

Wohlfarth, T. (1995). Personal communication.

Wood, J. V., Taylor, S. E., & Lichtman, R. R. (1985). Social comparison in adjustment to breast cancer. *Journal of Personality and Social Psychology, 49,* 1169–1183.

Wright, P. H., & Wright, K. D. (1991). Codependency: Addictive love, adjustive relating, or both? *Contemporary Family Therapy: An International Journal, 13*(5), 435–454.

Wright, R. (1994, August 14). Our cheating hearts. *Time Magazine.*

Yalom, I. D. (1980). *Existential psychotherapy.* New York: Basic Books.

———. (1985). *The theory and practice of group psychotherapy.* New York: Basic Books.

Yankelovich, D. (1978, May). The new psychological contracts at work. *Psychology Today,* 46–47, 49–50.

———. (1981). *New Rules.* New York: Random House.

Yankelovich, D., Clancy, Shulman, G. I. (June 3, 1991). *Time,* p. 51.

Zahn-Waxler, C., and Radke-Yarrow, M. (1982). The development of altruism: Alternative research strategies. In N. Eisenberg-Berg (Ed.), *The development of prosocial behavior.* New York: Academic Press.

Zimbardo, P. G. (1995). *On time: Our perspectives govern our lives.* Paper presented at the Annual Western Psychological Association Convention, April 2, 1995.

———. (1969). The human choice: Individuation, reason, and order versus deindividuation, impulse, and chaos. In *Nebraska symposium on motivation.* Lincoln: University of Nebraska Press.

———. (1972). The Stanford prison experiment. A slide/tape presentation produced by Philip G. Zimbardo, Inc., P. O. Box 4395, Stanford, CA 94305.

———. (1977). *Shyness.* New York: Jove.

Zuckerman, M., & Lubin, B. (1965). Manual for the Multiple Affect Adjective Checklist, Revised. San Diego, CA: Educational and Industrial Testing Service.

INDEX